AHA Hospital Statistics™

2021 Edition

**NOT TO BE TAKEN
FROM THE LIBRARY**

D1604756

AHA Institutional Members $252.00
Nonmembers $325.00
AHA Catalog NUMBER 082021
Telephone ORDERS 1-800-AHA-2626

ISSN 0090-6662
ISBN-13: 978-1-55648-458-2

Copyright © 1999 by Health Forum an American Hospital Association company
Copyright © 2000-2021 by Health Forum LLC, an affiliate of the American Hospital Association

All rights reserved. No portion of Hospital Statistics may be duplicated or reproduced
without prior written consent of Health Forum, LLC.
Printed in the U.S.A.

AUSTIN COMMUNITY COLLEGE
LIBRARY SERVICES

Contents

Acknowledgments
& Advisements

Acknowledgments

The 2021 edition of *AHA Hospital Statistics* is published by Health Forum, an affiliate of the American Hospital Association, Rick Pollack, President and CEO.

Advisements

The data published here should be used with the following advisements: The data are based on replies to an annual survey that seeks a variety of information, not all of which is published in this book. The information gathered by the survey includes specific services, but not all of each hospital's services. Therefore, the data do not reflect an exhaustive list of all services offered by all hospitals. For information on the availability of additional data, please contact Health Forum, (800) 821-2039.

Health Forum does not assume responsibility for the accuracy of information voluntarily reported by the individual institutions surveyed. The purpose of this publication is to provide basic data reflecting the delivery of health care in the United States and associated areas, and is not to serve an official and all-inclusive list of services offered by individual hospitals.

The Impacts of the COVID-19 Pandemic on Hospitals, Health Systems and the Communities They Serve

Hospital Statistics Introduction Chapter

Each year, the American Hospital Association (AHA) releases "AHA Hospital Statistics." These data are widely used by health field observers, researchers and policymakers to help understand trends and key facts about America's hospitals and health systems and the care they provide to patients and communities. The data in this edition include key statistics for the years 2015 to 2019, and therefore do not reflect any impacts from the COVID-19 pandemic in 2020 and thereafter.

The pandemic has resulted in historic challenges for hospitals and health systems and the communities they serve. These challenges vary widely among hospitals, health systems and communities. Although the AHA Annual Survey data does not yet illustrate these effects, there have been a number of studies and datasets that have begun to measure the impact of COVID-19 on hospitals, patients and communities.

Data compiled by the Center for Systems Science and Engineering (CSSE) at Johns Hopkins University show that as of the beginning of January 2021, there were over 20 million confirmed COVID-19 cases and over 350,000 reported deaths from COVID-19 in the United States alone.[1] The U.S. Department of Health & Human Services (HHS) also began releasing national, state and hospital level data on COVID-19 trends in December 2020. According to the HHS Protect Public Data Hub, which draws from hospital and state reporting, in many states most or all intensive care unit beds were being utilized, largely to treat patients with COVID-19, by January 2021.[2] Hospitals have never before experienced such a widespread, national health crisis.

The surging number of cases and hospitalization rates have directly impacted the U.S. health care system and its ability to continue to provide access to care. The pandemic has put severe financial pressure on hospitals, including, but not limited to: the astronomical costs of preparing for a surge of COVID-19 patients; added expenses due to supply chain and labor market disruptions; months of essential hospital revenue being erased due to the combination of a forced shutdown and slowdown of regular operations for non-emergent care; and the high cost of treating COVID-19 cases, which tend to be incredibly resource intensive.

In a pair of reports released in May and June of 2020, the AHA projected that hospital and health system financial losses would amount to at least $323.1 billion through the end of 2020. Importantly, those analyses did not account for the subsequent surges of the pandemic that manifested later in the year. The AHA's estimates also did not include all expenses, such as increased acquisition costs for drugs, increased labor costs and costs associated with acquiring non-personal protective equipment (PPE) supplies and equipment.[3] Losses on that scale have seriously threatened hospitals' and health systems' financial sustainability. In fact, a July 2020 report from Kaufman Hall projected that more than half of all hospitals would have negative margins during the fourth quarter

---

[1] Center for Systems Science and Engineering (CSSE) at Johns Hopkins University. COVID-19 Dashboard. https://coronavirus.jhu.edu/map.html

[2] HHS Protect Public Data Hub. State Representative Estimates for Hospital Utilization. https://protect-public.hhs.gov/

[3] AHA. Hospitals and Health Systems Continue to Face Unprecedented Financial Challenges due to COVID-19. June 2020. https://www.aha.org/press-releases/2020-06-30-new-aha-report-losses-deepen-hospitals-health-systems

of 2020.[4] Even the $175 billion in provider relief funds provided by the Coronavirus Aid, Relief, and Economic Security (CARES) Act falls far short of covering these losses.[5]

These projected losses were driven largely by sustained lower hospital volume. In December 2020, Kaufman Hall reported in its monthly National Hospital Flash Report that compared to the prior year, total hospital discharges in 2020 had dropped 5.1%; adjusted discharges, a blend of inpatient and outpatient utilization, had dropped 10.6%; and emergency department visits had dropped 16.3%. Meanwhile, the high intensity of care required for those hospitalized with COVID-19 drove an increase in the average length of stay of 8.7%.[6] According to data from the Centers for Medicare & Medicaid Services (CMS) in its Preliminary Medicare COVID-19 Data Snapshot, more than half of COVID-19 hospitalizations of Medicare beneficiaries were 8 days or longer, and 20% were 16 days or longer. Those hospitalized with COVID-19 were also more likely to have existing chronic conditions, making their treatment that much more complex. CMS examined the prevalence of chronic conditions among COVID-19 hospitalized Medicare fee-for-service beneficiaries and found that 80% had hypertension, 62% had hyperlipidemia, 51% had chronic kidney disease, and half had diabetes.[7]

The long-term impacts of the COVID-19 pandemic on hospitals, health systems and the communities they serve are difficult to project, but it is already clear they will be severe and, in many cases, catastrophic. In 2020, almost 50 hospitals had already closed or entered bankruptcy through October.[8] These challenges are of particular concern in rural communities, where many hospitals are already under tremendous financial stress. Rural hospitals face a variety of unique circumstances: low patient volume; challenging payer mix; geographic isolation; limited access to essential services; aging infrastructure and access to capital; workforce shortages; and health care coverage inadequacies, among other challenges.[9] Since 2010, over 130 rural hospital have closed according to the Cecil G. Sheps Center for Health Services Research at the University of North Carolina.[10]

The historical data contained in this edition of Hospital Statistics will be critical in establishing a baseline to measure the full impact of the COVID-19 pandemic in 2020 and beyond, and to demonstrate the importance of hospitals and health systems for the communities they serve. In 2019, America's hospitals and health systems treated 143 million people in emergency departments, provided 642 million outpatient visits, performed over 28 million surgeries and delivered over 3.5 million babies. Hospitals and health systems also play important roles in their communities beyond that of health care providers – they are often economic anchors that create jobs and purchase goods and services from others in their community. For example, in 2019

[4] Kaufman Hall. The Effect of COVID-19 on Hospital Financial Health. July 2020. https://www.aha.org/system/files/media/file/2020/07/KH-COVID-Hospital-Financial-Health_FINAL.pdf

[5] HHS. CARES Act Provider Relief Fund. https://www.hhs.gov/coronavirus/cares-act-provider-relief-fund/index.html

[6] Kaufman Hall. National Hospital Flash Report. December 2020. https://www.kaufmanhall.com/ideas-resources/research-report/national-hospital-flash-report-december-2020

[7] CMS. Preliminary Medicare COVID-19 Data Snapshot. November 2020. https://www.cms.gov/files/document/medicare-covid-19-data-snapshot-fact-sheet.pdf

[8] Ellison, A. Becker's Hospital Review. 47 hospitals closed, filed for bankruptcy this year. October 16, 2020. https://www.beckershospitalreview.com/finance/47-hospitals-closed-filed-for-bankruptcy-this-year.html

[9] AHA. Rural Report. April 2019. https://www.aha.org/guidesreports/2019-02-04-rural-report-2019

[10] Cecil G. Sheps Center for Health Services Research at the University of North Carolina Chapel Hill. NC Rural Health Research Program. https://www.shepscenter.unc.edu/programs-projects/rural-health/rural-hospital-closures/

hospitals: employed more than 6 million individuals in full- or part- time positions; purchased more than $1 trillion in goods and services from other businesses; supported almost 18 million, or one out of nine, jobs; and supported roughly $2.30 of additional business activity in the economy for every dollar they spent.[11]

As additional data examining the impacts of the COVID-19 pandemic become available in 2021 and the years ahead, those impacts will already be felt by hospital front-line staff and the people in the communities served by our nation's hospitals and health systems.

---

[11] AHA. 2019 Annual Survey of Hospitals.

How to Use this Book

For more than seven decades, *AHA Hospital Statistics*™ has reported aggregate hospital data derived from the AHA Annual Survey and is the definitive source when doing trend analysis with data by bed size category, U.S. Census Divisions, States, and Metropolitan Areas. As the health care delivery system changes, so have the data tracked by the survey and presented in this report. Recent additions include:

- **Community health indicators** that offer readers a connection to the community for their analysis and planning: the data are broken down into beds, admissions, inpatient days, ER outpatient visits, and other indicators per 1000 population, as well as expense per capita.

- **Utilization, personnel and finance** by all CBSAs in the United States.

- **Five-year trend data** on insurance products, and managed care contracts enable you to identify changes in relationships between hospitals and other health care systems and providers.

- **Tables 3 through 6 have been organized** to show breakdowns between inpatient and outpatient care to better reflect market shifts toward outpatient-centered care. Additional clarity is gained by the breakdown between total facility data (which includes nursing home type units under the control of the hospital) and hospital units (which exclude the nursing home data).

TABLE 6	Sample State

U.S. Community Hospitals
(Nonfederal, short-term general and other special hospitals)

Overview 2015–2019

	2019	2018	2017	2016	2015
Physician Models					
Independent Practice Association	14	17	17	17	14
Group Practice without Walls	4	5	5	8	4
Open Physician-Hospital Organization	20	21	24	23	18
Closed Physician-Hospital Organization	21	17	18	17	11
Management Service Organization	14	18	20	14	9
Integrated Salary Model	35	29	30	26	24
Equity Model	4	3	4	6	3
Foundation	9	8	23	21	19

Example of five-year trend data

- **Facilities and Services information** on more than 100 categories of hospital facilities and services in Table 7. At a glance, you can determine the number and percentage of hospitals offering a specific service such as Oncology, Palliative Care Program, Complementary Medicine, Women's Health Services and Tobacco Cessation.

- **Plus, System and Group Purchasing Organizations** that demonstrate ways in which organizations are linked.

The survey instrument and the glossary

A good place to begin your analysis is the AHA Annual Survey instrument. Found on page 217, it includes the instructions, questions, and terms that were used to gather the data for fiscal year 2019. This can be extremely valuable for a clearer understanding of the data we collect and the tables presented in *AHA Hospital Statistics*.

Please also review the glossary in the back of the book. The glossary contains complete definitions for specific terms used in the tables and text of *AHA Hospital Statistics*. These definitions will clarify how terminology is being used.

As mentioned above, it is important to note that the primary focus of the most detailed data contained in *AHA Hospital Statistics* is community hospitals. As defined, community hospitals are all non-federal, short-term general and special hospitals whose facilities and services are available to the public. If the majority of a hospital's patients are admitted to units where the average length of stay is 30 days or less, a hospital may still be classified as short-term even if it includes a nursing-home-type unit. (For a more complete definition of community hospitals, please see the glossary definition, located on page 203.)

Getting the most out of *AHA Hospital Statistics*

This section of the book provides an introduction for getting the most out of your *AHA Hospital Statistics* 2021 edition. Here, you'll find a guide to the book, with insights into each table.

Equity model: An arrangement that allows established practitioners to become shareholders in a professional corporation in exchange for tangible and intangible assets of their existing practices.

Expenses: Includes all expenses for the reporting period including payroll, non-payroll, and all nonoperating expenses. *Payroll expenses* include all salaries and wages. *Non-payroll expenses* are all professional fees and those salary expenditures excluded from payroll. *Labor related expenses* are defined as payroll expenses plus employee benefits. *Non-labor related expenses* are all other non-payroll expenses. *Bad debt* has been reclassified from a "reduction in revenue" to an expense in accordance with the revised AICPA Audit Guide. However, for purposes of historical consistency, the expense total that appears throughout *AHA Hospital Statistics does not include "bad debt" as an expense item.* Note: Financial data may not add due to rounding.

Extracorporeal shock wave lithotripter (ESWL): A medical device used for treating stones in the kidney or urethra. The device disintegrates kidney stones noninvasively through the transmission of acoustic shock waves directed at the stones.

Fitness center: Provides exercise, testing, or evaluation programs and fitness activities to the community and hospital employees.

Example of Glossary definitions.

Table 1	Historical Trends in Utilization, Personnel, and Finances for Selected Years from 1946 through 2019

CLASSIFICATION	YEAR	HOSPITALS	BEDS (in thousands)	ADMISSIONS (in thousands)	AVERAGE DAILY CENSUS (in thousands)	ADJUSTED AVERAGE DAILY CENSUS (in thousands)
Total United States	1946	6,125	1,436	15,675	1,142	—
	1950	6,788	1,456	18,483	1,253	—
	1955	6,956	1,604	21,073	1,363	—
	1960	6,876	1,658	25,027	1,402	—
	1965	7,123	1,704	28,812	1,403	—
	1970	7,123	1,616	31,759	1,298	—
	1971	7,097	1,556	32,664	1,237	—
	1972	7,061	1,550	33,265	1,209	—
	1973	7,123	1,535	34,352	1,189	—
	1974	7,174	1,513	35,506	1,167	—
	1975	7,156	1,466	36,157	1,125	—
	1976	7,082	1,434	36,776	1,090	—
	1977	7,099	1,407	37,060	1,066	—
	1978	7,015	1,381	37,243	1,042	—
	1979	6,988	1,372	37,802	1,043	—
	1980	6,965	1,365	38,892	1,060	—
	1981	6,933	1,362	39,169	1,061	—
	1982	6,915	1,360	39,095	1,053	—
	1983	6,888	1,350	38,887	1,028	—
	1984	6,872	1,339	37,938	970	—
	1985	6,872	1,318	36,304	910	—
	1986	6,841	1,290	35,219	883	—
	1987	6,821	1,267	34,439	873	—
	1988	6,780	1,248	34,107	863	—
	1989	6,720	1,226	33,742	853	—
	1990	6,649	1,213	33,774	844	—
	1991	6,634	1,202	33,567	827	—
	1992	6,539	1,178	33,536	807	—
	1993	6,467	1,163	33,201	783	—
	1994	6,374	1,128	33,125	745	—
	1995	6,291	1,081	33,282	710	—
	1996	6,201	1,062	33,307	685	—
	1997	6,097	1,035	33,624	673	—
	1998	6,021	1,013	33,766	662	—
	1999	5,890	994	34,181	657	—
	2000	5,810	984	34,891	650	—
	2001	5,801	987	35,644	658	—
	2002	5,794	976	36,326	662	—
	2003	5,764	965	36,611	657	—
	2004	5,759	956	36,942	658	—
	2005	5,756	947	37,006	656	—

Example of Table 1

Table 1 — Historical Trends in Utilization, Personnel and Finances for Selected Years from 1946 through 2019

Table 1 at a Glance

This table is used to evaluate historical data and allows you to examine long-term trends in health care with data dating back more than sixty years. Table 1 reports on all hospitals in the United States. One important note: Hospitals included in this table include AHA-member and non-member hospitals. A hospital does not need to be an AHA member to be included.

This table segments the data into various organizational structure categories. Here's a brief look at these different classifications:

- Total United States Hospitals
- Total Non-Federal Short-term and other special hospitals
- Community hospitals
- Non-government not-for-profit community hospitals
- Investor-owned (for-profit) community hospitals
- State and local government community hospitals

Table 1 also provides input on nationwide utilization, personnel and finance trends. You'll find answers to questions such as: *Over the past 25 years, what trends do I see comparing the average length of stay at government and non-government not-for-profit community hospitals and investor-owned for-profit community hospitals? or What has been the trend in outpatient visits?*

Table 2 — 2019 U.S. Hospitals: Utilization, Personnel and Finances

Table 2 at a Glance

This table takes a closer look at U.S. Hospitals for 2019. It offers a snapshot of utilization, personnel and finance statistics, and breaks down this information for specialty hospitals. In addition, this is the only table that outlines data on federal hospitals. You'll be able to use this table to better understand the number of beds set-up and staffed, how many personnel and trainees are on the payroll, and what the financial implications of these may be.

Total U.S.

TABLE 3

TOTAL UNITED STATES

U.S. Community Hospitals
(Nonfederal, short-term general and other special hospitals)

Utilization, Personnel, Revenue and Expenses, Community Health Indicators 2015–2019

	2019	2018	2017	2016	2015
TOTAL FACILITY (Includes Hospital and Nursing Home Units)					
Utilization - Inpatient					
Beds	798,921	799,444	800,828	802,088	811,154
Admissions	34,305,620	34,031,587	33,817,285	33,516,951	34,062,869
Inpatient Days	186,198,977	186,089,454	185,171,082	183,342,577	185,325,318
Average Length of Stay	5.5	5.5	5.5	5.5	5.4
Inpatient Surgeries	9,146,015	9,163,230	9,090,300	9,156,859	9,279,901
Births	3,656,809	3,769,965	3,792,223	3,766,328	3,728,411
Utilization - Outpatient					
Emergency Outpatient Visits	144,814,804	144,842,743	143,472,685	137,807,901	134,869,015
Other Outpatient Visits	621,261,320	611,955,033	587,316,680	562,424,090	549,358,304
Total Outpatient Visits	766,076,124	756,797,776	730,789,365	700,231,991	684,227,319
Outpatient Surgeries	19,075,759	18,987,342	18,255,921	17,974,397	17,978,474
Personnel					
Full Time RNs	1,286,055	1,243,105	1,209,663	1,170,228	1,137,567
Full Time LPNs	65,258	65,671	65,168	64,001	68,296
Part Time RNs	543,927	530,458	511,318	502,481	500,762
Part Time LPNs	22,550	22,602	22,800	22,805	25,027
Total Full Time	4,536,326	4,428,178	4,316,593	4,211,435	4,183,224
Total Part Time	1,615,066	1,562,816	1,498,135	1,471,483	1,479,747
Revenue - Inpatient					
Gross Inpatient Revenue	$1,828,199,494,787	$1,724,871,915,665	$1,626,668,095,308	$1,514,448,739,994	$1,442,275,606,491
Revenue - Outpatient					
Gross Outpatient Revenue	$1,735,481,161,564	$1,595,298,023,801	$1,449,622,014,476	$1,308,063,724,756	$1,191,794,532,181

Example of Table 3. Helps contrast acute and long-term care

Table 3 — Total United States

Table 3 at a Glance
This table provides a look at all U.S. Community Hospitals, in terms of general overview with utilization by inpatient and outpatient, personnel, revenue, expenses and community health indicators. It provides a snapshot of the past five years, allowing you to track emerging trends.

This national information can be compared to local or regional trends, for benchmarking:

- Both inpatient and outpatient information is included, for better evaluation of data.

- Reporting by total facility *Includes hospital and Nursing Home Units* and hospital unit only *Excludes Separate Nursing Home Units* helps contrast acute and long-term care.

- Community health indicators can help uncover trends and help determine future facility needs.

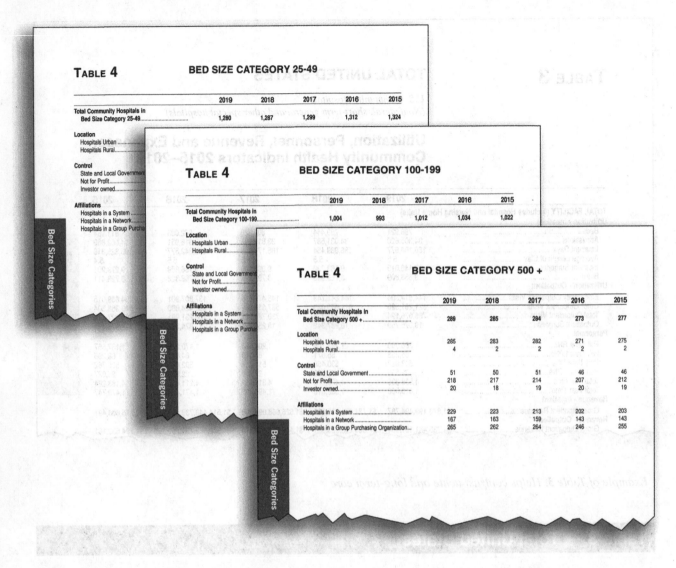

Example of Table 4. Compares facilities with peers.

Table 4 — Bed Size Categories

Table 4 at a Glance

This table provides a look at all U.S. Community Hospitals, broken down by bed size. The table includes general overview, utilization, personnel, and revenue and expense information. These categories of bed sizes were developed by the AHA, and have become an industry standard. By categorizing each facility into a peer group, this table provides a snapshot of the past five years allowing you to compare facilities with their peers.

TABLE 5

U.S. CENSUS DIVISION 2: MIDDLE ATLANTIC

U.S. Community Hospitals
(Nonfederal, short-term general and other special hospitals)

Utilization, Personnel, Revenue and Expenses, Community Health Indicators 2015–2019

	2019	2018	2017	2016	2015
COMMUNITY HEALTH INDICATORS PER 1000 POPULATION					
Total Population (in thousands)...	38,292	38,216	38,184	38,147	38,108
Inpatient					
Beds.........	3.6	3.8	3.9	4.0	4.1
Admissions..................	135.8	136.7	136.2	138.3	137.4
Inpatient Days..............	963.5	988.8	1,019.0	1,093.8	1,145.0
Inpatient Surgeries..............	42.2	41.4	41.2	42.7	43.6
Births.........................	13.0	13.2	13.6	13.7	14.3
Outpatient					
Emergency Outpatient Visits......	367.7	362.0	363.4	379.5	360.1
Other Outpatient Visits..........	1,970.9	1,802.3	1,767.7	1,680.3	1,573.9
Total Outpatient Visits..........	2,338.6	2,164.3	2,131.1	2,059.8	1,934.0
Outpatient Surgeries............	67.8	62.4	59.9	55.4	53.5
Expense per Capita (per person)....	$1,494.9	$1,462.7	$1,428.6	$1,429.8	$1,369.2

Example of Table 5. Uncovers trends to determine future facility needs.

Table 5 — U.S. Census Divisions

Table 5 at a Glance

This table provides a look at all U.S. Community Hospitals, broken down by Census Division. The table includes general overview, utilization, personnel, and expenses, and community health indicator information. It provides a snapshot of the past five years, allowing you to track trends on a regional level. In addition, this allows you to compare this data to other population based health indicators, offering a more comprehensive look than the survey data alone. Community health indicators can help uncover trends and help determine future facility needs.

Table 6 — States

Table 6 at a Glance

This table provides a look at all U.S. Community Hospitals, broken down by State. The table includes general overview, utilization, personnel, revenue and expenses, and community health indicator information. It provides a snapshot of the past five years, allowing you to track trends on a state level.

Note:

You can use the information in tables 3, 4, 5 and 6 to make accurate comparisons across Total U.S., Bed Size Category, Census Division and State.

Table 7 — 2019 Facilities and Services in the U.S. Census Divisions and States

Table 7 at a Glance

This table examines facilities and services by both Census Division and State. A comprehensive alphabetical guide helps make each facility or service easy to find. This table will allow you to better understand what service lines are emerging and how many facilities offer a particular service in a discrete state or region.

This collection of facilities and services information data is unique to *AHA Hospital Statistics* and the list is continually growing. Recent additions include:

- Air ambulance services
- Diabetes prevention program
- Off-campus emergency department
- Employment support services
- Supportive housing services
- Other remote patient monitoring
- Other telehealth

Example of Table 7.

Table 7 (Continued)

CLASSIFICATION	HOSPITALS REPORTING	CHILDREN'S WELLNESS PROGRAM		CHIROPRACTIC SERVICES		COMMUNITY OUTREACH		COMPLEMENTARY AND ALTERNATIVE MEDICINE SERVICES	
		Number	Percent	Number	Percent	Number	Percent	Number	Percent
UNITED STATES	4,580	894	19.5	131	2.9	3,221	70.2	950	20.?
COMMUNITY HOSPITALS	3,865	864	22.4	100	2.6	2,970	76.8	887	22.?
CENSUS DIVISION 1, NEW ENGLAND	172	82	36.0	9	5.2	145	84.3	82	47.7
Connecticut	30	9	30.0	0	0.0	26	86.7	19	63.5
Maine	32	12	37.5	2	6.3	27	84.4	13	40.6
Massachusetts	64	25	39.1	3	4.7	52	81.3	27	42.2
New Hampshire	25	12	48.0	2	8.0	21	84.0	14	56.0
Rhode Island	10	1	10.0	1	10.0	9	90.0	3	30.0
Vermont	11	3	27.3	1	9.1	10	90.9	6	54.5
CENSUS DIVISION 2, MIDDLE ATLANTIC	404	131	32.4	20	5.0	322	79.7	140	34.7
New Jersey	62	33	53.2	2	3.2	53	85.5	31	50.0
New York	142	58	40.8	11	7.7	125	88.5	56	39.?
Pennsylvania	200	40	20.0	7	3.5	144	72.0	53	2?
CENSUS DIVISION 3, SOUTH ATLANTIC	671	115	17.1	10	1.5	499	74.4	131	19.
Delaware	10	6	60.0	0	0.0	6	60.0	3	30.?
District of Columbia	11	5	45.5	0	0.0	9	81.8	6	54.?
Florida	180	21	11.7	4	2.2	125	69.4	31	17.2
Georgia	100	9	9.0	2	2.0	70	70.0	17	17.0
Maryland	44	15	34.1	0	0.0	38	86.4	22	50.0
North Carolina	108	18	16.7	1	0.9	90	83.3	17	15.7
South Carolina	79	14	17.7	0	0.0	57	72.2	5	6.3
Virginia	84	13	15.5	2	2.4	66	78.6	26	31.?
West Virginia	55	14	25.5	1	1.8	38	69.1		
CENSUS DIVISION 4, EAST NORTH CENTRAL	706	184	26.1	31	4.4	560	79.3	226	3?
Illinois	185	55	33.3	8	4.8	137	83.0	46	2?
Indiana	122	25	20.5	5	4.1	100	82.0	29	23.?
Michigan	130	45	34.6	5	3.8	113	86.9	46	35.4
Ohio	144	29	20.1	10	6.9	123	85.4	52	36.?
Wisconsin	145	30	20.7	3	2.1	87	60.0	53	36.?
CENSUS DIVISION 5, EAST SOUTH CENTRAL	357	48	13.4	4	1.1	250	69.7	23	6.3
Alabama	102	9	8.8	2	2.0	55	53.9	0	0.0
Kentucky	88	14	15.9	1	1.1	64	72.7	12	13.6
Mississippi	104	17	16.3	1	1.0	64	61.5	4	?
Tennessee	73	9	12.3	0	0.0	47	64.4	7	?
CENSUS DIVISION 6, WEST NORTH CENTRAL	637	111	17.4	26	4.1	421	66.1	109	17.?
Iowa	124	25	20.2	4	3.2	96	77.4	29	23.?
Kansas	143	10	7.0	1	0.7	64	44.8	8	5.6
Minnesota	105	24	22.9	8	7.6	81	77.1	31	29.5
Missouri	143	28	19.6	6	4.2	95	66.4	24	16.8
Nebraska	54	11	20.4	6	23.1	44	81.5	7	13.0
North Dakota	26	6	23.1	6	23.1	16	61.5	6	23.?
South Dakota	42	7	16.7	1	2.4	25	59.5	4	?
CENSUS DIVISION 7, WEST SOUTH CENTRAL	891	94	10.5	6	0.7	471	52.9	48	?
Arkansas	88	8	9.1	0	0.0	50	56.8	5	?
Louisiana	95	20	21.1	1	1.1	52	54.7	9	?
Oklahoma	116	9	7.8	0	0.0	60	51.7	5	?
Texas	592	57	9.6	5	0.8	309	52.2	90	?
CENSUS DIVISION 8, MOUNTAIN	519	71	22.3	18	4.1	235	73.7	83	25.?
Arizona	48	13	27.1	3	5.8	35	72.9	19	?
Colorado	72	16	22.2	4	5.6	59	60.6	33	?
Idaho	32	9	28.1	2	6.3	26	81.3	6	?
Montana	57	11	19.3	2	3.5	37	64.9	10	?
Nevada	26	4	18.4	2	7.7	16	61.5	3	?
New Mexico	29	9	31.0	0	0.0	22	75.9	3	?
Utah	35	7	20.0	0	0.0	24	68.6	6	?
Wyoming	20	2	10.0	0	0.0	17	85.0	3	?
CENSUS DIVISION 9, PACIFIC	425	77	18.2	12	2.8	338	79.9	108	?
Alaska	15	4	26.7	1	6.7	8	53.3	2	?
California	248	38	15.3	7	2.8	197	79.4	85	?
Hawaii	17	6	35.3	1	5.9	14	82.4	5	?
Oregon	64	12	19.4	2	3.2	58	90.3	16	?
Washington	81	17	21.0	2	2.5	63	77.8	18	?

These new categories reflect the trends as hospitals expand their service lines to mirror the needs of their patients. For example, services such as acupuncture or massage therapy are now accounted for in the Complementary Medicine service item.

This table can answer questions such as: *What percentage of hospitals in the United States offer complementary medicine or wound management? or How are these new services distributed by state?*

Table 8 — Utilization, Personnel and Finances in Community Hospitals by Metropolitan Area for 2019

Table 8 at a Glance

This table provides a look at all U.S. Community Hospitals, broken down by Metropolitan Area. The table includes general overview, utilization, personnel, and finance information. It provides a snapshot of the past year.

Additional Resources

Again, in the back of the book you will find the comprehensive glossary and the 2019 annual survey questionnaire. The survey itself can be a valuable resource to understanding what was asked in order to gather the data in the book. This survey is also used to produce the *AHA Guide®* and AHA Annual Survey Database™.

Hospital Requirements

Hospital Requirements

An institution is considered a hospital by the American Hospital Association if it is licensed as general or specialty hospital by the appropriate state agency, and accredited as a hospital by one of the following organizations: The Joint Commission; Healthcare Facilities Accreditation Program (HFAP); DNV Healthcare accreditation; Center for Improvement in Healthcare Quality accreditation; or Medicare certified as a provider of acute service under Title 18 of the Social Security Act.

Types of Hospitals

Hospitals are categorized as one of four types of hospitals: general, special, rehabilitation and chronic disease, or psychiatric.

General

The primary function of the institution is to provide patient services, diagnostic and therapeutic, for a variety of medical conditions. A general hospital also shall provide:

- diagnostic x-ray services with facilities and staff for a variety of procedures
- clinical laboratory service with facilities and staff for a variety of procedures and with anatomical pathology services regularly and conveniently available
- operating room service with facilities and staff.

Special

The primary function of the institution is to provide diagnostic and treatment services for patients who have specified medical conditions, both surgical and nonsurgical. A special hospital also shall provide:

- such diagnostic and treatment services as may be determined by the Executive Committee of the Board of Trustees of the American Hospital Association to be appropriate for the specified medical conditions for which medical services are provided shall be maintained in the institution with suitable facilities and staff. If such conditions do not normally require diagnostic x-ray service, laboratory service, or operating room service, and if any such services are therefore not maintained in the institution, there shall be written arrangements to make them available to patients requiring them.
- clinical laboratory services capable of providing tissue diagnosis when offering pregnancy termination services.

Rehabilitation and Chronic Disease

The primary function of the institution is to provide diagnostic and treatment services to handicapped or disabled individuals requiring restorative and adjustive services. A rehabilitation and chronic disease hospital also shall provide:

- arrangements for diagnostic x-ray services, as required, on a regular and conveniently available basis
- arrangements for clinical laboratory service, as required on a regular and conveniently available basis
- arrangements for operating room service, as required, on a regular and conveniently available basis
- a physical therapy service with suitable facilities and staff in the institution
- an occupational therapy service with suitable facilities and staff in the institution
- arrangements for psychological and social work services on a regular and conveniently available basis

- arrangements for educational and vocational services on a regular and conveniently available basis
- written arrangements with a general hospital for the transfer of patients who require medical, obstetrical, or surgical services not available in the institution.

Psychiatric
The primary function of the institution is to provide diagnostic and treatment services for patients who have psychiatric-related illnesses. A psychiatric hospital also shall provide:

- arrangements for clinical laboratory service, as required, on a regular and conveniently available basis
- arrangements for diagnostic x-ray services, as required on a regular and conveniently available basis
- psychiatric, psychological, and social work service with facilities and staff in the institution
- arrangements for electroencephalograph services, as required, on a regular and conveniently available basis.
- written arrangements with a general hospital for the transfer of patients who require medical, obstetrical, or surgical services not available in the institution.

Data Comparability

The economic climate, demographic characteristics, personnel issues, and health care financing and payment policies differ by region, state, and city across the country. *Differences in these factors must be taken into account when using the data.* In addition, the profiles of hospitals across comparison groups vary. For example, states will differ in terms of the number and percentage of hospitals by size, ownership, services provided, types of patients treated, and so forth. *Differences in these variables also must be taken into consideration when doing a comparative analysis.*

Notes on the Survey

The 2021 edition of *AHA Hospital Statistics*™ draws its data from the 2019 AHA Annual Survey of Hospitals. It is the statistical complement to the 2021 edition of the *AHA Guide*®, which contains selected data about individual hospitals.

The AHA Survey was mailed to all hospitals, in the U.S. and its associated areas: American Samoa, Guam, the Marshall Islands, Puerto Rico, and the Virgin Islands. U.S. government hospitals located outside the U.S. were not included. Overall, the average response rate over the past five years has been approximately 83 percent.

Reporting Period
In completing the survey, hospitals were requested to report data for a full year, in accord with their fiscal year, ending in 2019. The statistical table present data reported or estimated for a 12-month period, except for data on personnel, which represent situations as they existed at the end of the reporting period.

Respondents
Data for Tables 1 and 2 include 6,090 hospitals in the U.S. Data on community hospitals (nonfederal, short-term general and other special hospitals) only are presented in Tables 3-6, and Table 8.

It is important to note that the hospitals included in *AHA Hospital Statistics* are not necessarily identical to those included in *AHA Guide*. The institutions listed in the 2021 edition of *AHA Guide* include all of those institutions CMS certified, or Joint Commission accredited as of September 2020. Tables 1-6 in *AHA Hospital Statistics* present data for hospitals that were in operation during the 12-month reporting period ending 2019.

Estimates
Estimates were made of data for nonreporting hospitals and for reporting hospitals that submitted incomplete AHA Annual Survey questionnaires. Estimates were not made for beds, bassinets and facilities and services. Data for beds and bassinets of nonreporting hospitals were based on the most recent information from those hospitals. (Note that in all statistical tables, whenever bed-size categories are listed, all eight categories appear, whether or not there are hospitals in every category.)

Missing revenue, expenses, admissions, births, inpatient days, surgical operations, outpatient visits, and full-time-equivalent personnel values are estimates from regression models. For all other variables the estimates were based on ratios such as per bed averages derived from data reported by hospitals similar in size, control, major service provided, length of stay, and geographical characteristics to the hospitals that did not report this information.

Notes on the Survey

The 2021 edition of AHA Hospital Statistics™ draws its data from the 2019 AHA Annual Survey of Hospitals. It is the statistical complement to the 2021 edition of the AHA Guide™, which contains selected data about individual hospitals.

The AHA Survey was mailed to all hospitals in the U.S. and its associated areas: American Samoa, Guam, the Marshall Islands, Puerto Rico, and the Virgin Islands. U.S. government hospitals located outside the U.S. were not included. Overall, the average response rate over the past five years has been approximately 83 percent.

Reporting Period

In completing the survey, hospitals were requested to report data for a full year, in accord with their fiscal year, ending in 2019. The statistical table present data reported or estimated for a 12-month period, except for data on personnel, which represent situations as they existed at the end of the reporting period.

Respondents

Data for Tables 1 and 2 include 6,090 hospitals in the U.S. Data on community hospitals (nonfederal, short-term general and other special hospitals) only are presented in Tables 3–6, and Table 8.

It is important to note that the hospitals included in AHA Hospital Statistics are not necessarily identical to those included in AHA Guide. The institutions listed in the 2021 edition of AHA Guide include all of those institutions CMS-certified or Joint Commission accredited as of September 2020. Tables 1–6 in AHA Hospital Statistics present data for hospitals that were in operation during the 12-month reporting period ending 2019.

Estimates

Estimates were made of data for nonreporting hospitals and for reporting hospitals that submitted incomplete AHA Annual Survey questionnaires. Estimates were not made for beds, bassinets and facilities and services. Data for beds and bassinets of nonreporting hospitals were based on the most recent information from those hospitals. (Note that in all statistical tables, whenever bed-size categories are listed, all eight categories appear, whether or not there are hospitals in every category.)

Missing revenue, expenses, admissions, births, inpatient days, surgical operations, outpatient visits, and full-time-equivalent personnel values are estimates from regression models. For all other variables the estimates were based on ratios, such as per bed averages derived from data reported by hospitals similar in size, control, major service provided, length of stay, and geographical characteristics to the hospitals that did not report this information.

Tables 1–2

Note: These data represent hospital performance in the years 2015 – 2019 and do not reflect any impacts from the COVID-19 pandemic in 2020 and thereafter.

Table 1

Historical Trends in Utilization, Personnel, and Finances for Selected Years from 1946 through 2019

Data are for all hospitals in the United States. Data are estimated for nonreporting hospitals with the exception of newborn and outpatient data before 1972. Personnel data exclude residents, interns, and students from 1952 on; personnel data include full-time personnel and full-time equivalents for part-time personnel from 1954 on. As a result of the AHA Annual Survey validation process, the New York state expense data from 1976 were revised after the 1977 edition was published. The revised figures are included below. In order to provide trend data on a consistent basis, the 1970 and 1971 psychiatric and long-term data have been slightly modified. The 1982 FTE figures have been updated to provide the most accurate data possible.

Classification: Total United States

YEAR	HOSPITALS	BEDS (in thousands)	ADMISSIONS (in thousands)	AVERAGE DAILY CENSUS (in thousands)	ADJUSTED AVERAGE DAILY CENSUS (in thousands)	AVERAGE STAY (days)	OUTPATIENT VISITS (in thousands)	NEWBORNS Bassinets	NEWBORNS Births	FTE PERSONNEL Number (in thousands)	FTE PERSONNEL Per 100 Adjusted Census	TOTAL EXPENSES Amount (In Millions of dollars)	TOTAL EXPENSES Adjusted per Inpatient Stay (dollars)	TOTAL EXPENSES Adjusted per Inpatient Day (dollars)
1946	6,125	1,436	15,675	1,142	—	—	—	85,585	2,135,327	830	—	$1,963	—	—
1950	6,788	1,456	18,483	1,253	—	—	—	90,101	2,742,780	1,058	—	$3,651	—	—
1955	6,956	1,604	21,073	1,363	—	—	—	98,823	3,476,753	1,301	—	$5,594	—	—
1960	6,876	1,658	25,027	1,402	—	—	—	102,764	3,835,735	1,598	—	$8,421	—	—
1965	7,123	1,704	28,812	1,403	—	—	125,793	101,287	3,565,344	1,952	—	$12,948	—	—
1970	7,123	1,616	31,759	1,298	—	—	181,370	97,128	3,537,000	2,537	—	$25,556	—	—
1971	7,097	1,556	32,664	1,237	—	—	199,725	94,344	3,464,513	2,589	—	$28,812	—	—
1972	7,061	1,550	33,265	1,209	—	—	219,182	92,960	3,231,875	2,671	—	$32,667	—	—
1973	7,123	1,535	34,352	1,189	—	—	233,555	90,071	3,087,210	2,769	—	$36,290	—	—
1974	7,174	1,513	35,506	1,167	—	—	250,481	88,269	3,043,386	2,919	—	$41,406	—	—
1975	7,156	1,466	36,157	1,125	—	—	254,844	86,875	3,091,629	3,023	—	$48,706	—	—
1976	7,082	1,434	36,776	1,090	—	—	270,951	85,284	3,067,063	3,108	—	$56,005	—	—
1977	7,099	1,407	37,060	1,066	—	—	263,775	83,193	3,223,699	3,213	—	$63,630	—	—
1978	7,015	1,381	37,243	1,042	—	—	263,606	80,650	3,250,373	3,280	—	$70,927	—	—
1979	6,988	1,372	37,802	1,043	—	—	262,009	79,720	3,376,467	3,382	—	$79,796	—	—
1980	6,965	1,365	38,892	1,060	—	—	262,951	79,842	3,500,043	3,492	—	$91,886	—	—
1981	6,933	1,362	39,169	1,061	—	—	265,332	78,823	3,558,274	3,661	—	$107,146	—	—
1982	6,915	1,360	39,095	1,053	—	—	313,667	77,998	3,615,751	3,746	—	$123,219	—	—
1983	6,888	1,350	38,887	1,028	—	—	273,168	77,837	3,596,146	3,707	—	$136,315	—	—
1984	6,872	1,339	37,938	970	—	—	276,566	77,845	3,563,106	3,630	—	$144,114	—	—
1985	6,872	1,318	36,304	910	—	—	282,140	77,202	3,630,961	3,625	—	$153,327	—	—
1986	6,841	1,290	35,219	883	—	—	294,634	76,002	3,680,178	3,647	—	$165,194	—	—
1987	6,821	1,267	34,439	873	—	—	310,707	74,770	3,698,294	3,742	—	$178,662	—	—
1988	6,780	1,248	34,107	863	—	—	336,208	72,568	3,794,369	3,839	—	$196,704	—	—
1989	6,720	1,226	33,742	853	—	—	352,248	71,491	3,920,384	3,937	—	$214,886	—	—
1990	6,649	1,213	33,774	844	—	—	368,184	70,539	4,046,704	4,063	—	$234,870	—	—
1991	6,634	1,202	33,567	827	—	—	387,675	69,464	4,047,504	4,165	—	$258,508	—	—
1992	6,539	1,178	33,536	807	—	—	417,874	69,052	4,007,179	4,236	—	$282,531	—	—
1993	6,467	1,163	33,201	783	—	—	435,619	67,911	3,949,788	4,289	—	$301,538	—	—
1994	6,374	1,128	33,125	745	—	—	453,584	67,311	3,886,667	4,270	—	$310,834	—	—
1995	6,291	1,081	33,282	710	—	—	483,195	66,256	3,833,132	4,273	—	$320,252	—	—
1996	6,201	1,062	33,307	685	—	—	505,455	65,138	3,790,678	4,276	—	$330,531	—	—
1997	6,097	1,035	33,624	673	—	—	520,600	64,649	3,811,522	4,333	—	$342,334	—	—
1998	6,021	1,013	33,766	662	—	—	545,481	63,485	3,795,212	4,407	—	$355,450	—	—
1999	5,890	994	34,181	657	—	—	573,461	62,714	3,829,881	4,369	—	$372,933	—	—
2000	5,810	984	34,891	650	—	—	592,673	61,915	3,940,017	4,454	—	$395,391	—	—
2001	5,801	987	35,644	658	—	—	612,276	61,527	3,929,733	4,535	—	$426,849	—	—
2002	5,794	976	36,326	662	—	—	640,515	62,151	3,934,421	4,610	—	$462,222	—	—
2003	5,764	965	36,611	657	—	—	648,560	60,699	3,976,886	4,651	—	$498,104	—	—
2004	5,759	956	36,942	658	—	—	662,131	59,660	3,965,906	4,696	—	$533,853	—	—
2005	5,756	947	37,006	656	—	—	673,689	59,073	4,048,442	4,791	—	$570,534	—	—
2006	5,747	947	37,189	653	—	—	690,425	58,670	4,126,598	4,907	—	$607,355	—	—
2007	5,708	945	37,120	645	—	—	693,510	58,429	4,128,796	5,024	—	$641,124	—	—
2008	5,815	951	37,529	649	—	—	709,960	58,133	4,109,081	5,116	—	$690,074	—	—
2009	5,795	944	37,480	641	—	—	741,551	58,078	4,001,748	5,178	—	$726,671	—	—
2010	5,754	942	36,915	627	—	—	750,408	57,396	3,871,751	5,184	—	$750,602	—	—
2011	5,724	924	36,565	615	—	—	754,454	57,022	3,767,697	5,196	—	$773,547	—	—
2012	5,723	921	36,156	600	—	—	777,961	56,693	3,754,085	5,258	—	$829,665	—	—
2013	6,230	940	36,095	607	—	—	795,759	57,539	3,778,696	5,456	—	$873,841	—	—
2014	6,174	928	35,562	600	—	—	811,975	56,951	3,818,308	5,413	—	$907,755	—	—
2015	6,180	930	35,899	608	—	—	844,487	56,606	3,826,138	5,522	—	$955,976	—	—
2016	6,168	928	36,110	610	—	—	877,137	56,449	3,804,132	5,698	—	$1,012,752	—	—
2017	6,210	931	36,510	614	—	—	880,451	55,801	3,693,124	5,841	—	$1,060,933	—	—
2018	6,146	924	36,354	612	—	—	—	55,565	—	—	—	—	—	—

Note: These data represent hospital performance in the years 2015 – 2019 and do not reflect any impacts from the COVID-19 pandemic in 2020 and thereafter.

Table 1 (Continued)

CLASSIFICATION	YEAR	HOSPITALS	BEDS (in thousands)	ADMISSIONS (in thousands)	AVERAGE DAILY CENSUS (in thousands)	ADJUSTED AVERAGE DAILY CENSUS (in thousands)	AVERAGE STAY (days)	OUTPATIENT VISITS (in thousands)	NEWBORNS Bassinets	NEWBORNS Births	FTE PERSONNEL Number (in thousands)	FTE PERSONNEL Per 100 Adjusted Census	TOTAL EXPENSES Amount (In Millions of dollars)	TOTAL EXPENSES Adjusted per Inpatient Stay (dollars)	TOTAL EXPENSES Adjusted per Inpatient Day (dollars)
Total nonfederal short-term general and other special	1946	4,444	473	13,655	341	—	9.1	—	80,987	2,087,503	505	—	$1,169	—	—
	1950	5,031	505	16,663	372	—	8.1	—	86,019	2,660,982	662	—	$2,120	—	—
	1955	5,237	568	19,100	407	—	7.8	—	93,868	3,304,451	826	—	$3,434	—	—
	1960	5,407	639	22,970	477	—	7.6	—	98,127	3,678,051	1,080	—	$5,617	—	—
	1965	5,736	741	26,463	563	620	7.8	92,631	96,782	3,413,370	1,386	224	$9,147	$316.37	$40.56
	1970	5,859	848	29,252	662	727	8.2	133,545	93,079	3,403,064	1,929	265	$19,560	$604.59	$73.73
	1971	5,865	867	30,142	665	736	8.0	148,423	90,444	3,337,605	1,999	272	$22,400	$667.44	$83.43
	1972	5,843	884	30,767	664	739	7.9	166,983	89,315	3,119,446	2,056	278	$25,549	$747.42	$94.61
	1973	5,891	903	31,761	681	768	7.8	178,939	86,851	2,987,089	2,149	280	$28,496	$793.88	$101.78
	1974	5,977	931	32,943	701	793	7.8	194,838	85,208	2,947,342	2,289	289	$32,751	$883.04	$113.21
	1975	5,979	947	33,519	708	806	7.7	196,311	83,834	2,998,590	2,399	298	$39,110	$1,024.72	$133.08
	1976	5,956	961	34,068	715	816	7.7	207,725	82,307	2,962,305	2,483	304	$45,402	$1,172.25	$152.24
	1977	5,973	974	34,353	717	820	7.6	204,238	80,228	3,117,756	2,581	315	$51,832	$1,316.70	$173.25
	1978	5,935	980	34,575	720	841	7.6	204,461	78,090	3,156,570	2,662	323	$58,348	$1,470.13	$193.81
	1979	5,923	988	35,160	729	841	7.6	203,873	77,277	3,287,157	2,762	328	$66,184	$1,631.16	$215.75
	1980	5,904	992	36,198	748	861	7.6	206,752	77,539	3,408,699	2,879	334	$76,970	$1,844.19	$244.44
	1981	5,879	1,007	36,494	764	876	7.6	206,729	76,567	3,465,683	3,039	347	$90,739	$2,167.70	$283.94
	1982	5,863	1,015	36,429	763	882	7.6	250,888	75,739	3,514,761	3,110	353	$105,094	$2,493.09	$326.68
	1983	5,843	1,021	36,201	750	869	7.6	213,995	75,471	3,490,629	3,102	357	$116,632	$2,775.55	$368.01
	1984	5,814	1,020	35,202	703	824	7.3	216,474	75,587	3,456,467	3,023	367	$123,550	$2,984.00	$409.85
	1985	5,784	1,003	33,501	650	780	7.1	222,773	74,899	3,521,296	3,003	385	$130,700	$3,238.94	$459.57
	1986	5,728	982	32,410	631	774	7.1	234,270	73,688	3,584,530	3,032	392	$140,907	$3,529.60	$499.19
	1987	5,659	961	31,633	624	780	7.2	247,704	72,516	3,602,416	3,120	400	$152,909	$3,848.74	$536.96
	1988	5,579	949	31,480	622	795	7.2	271,436	70,361	3,706,748	3,209	404	$168,941	$4,194.39	$581.08
	1989	5,497	936	31,141	619	805	7.3	287,909	69,436	3,831,051	3,307	411	$185,204	$4,572.23	$630.59
	1990	5,420	929	31,203	620	820	7.3	302,691	68,443	3,958,646	3,423	417	$203,927	$4,929.93	$681.52
	1991	5,370	926	31,084	612	828	7.2	323,202	67,440	3,965,489	3,539	427	$225,230	$5,345.63	$745.37
	1992	5,321	923	31,053	606	832	7.1	349,397	67,095	3,925,024	3,624	436	$248,318	$5,788.52	$815.99
	1993	5,289	921	30,770	593	834	7.0	368,358	66,060	3,870,392	3,681	441	$266,382	$6,120.94	$874.98
	1994	5,256	904	30,739	569	814	6.8	384,880	65,728	3,809,367	3,697	454	$276,148	$6,230.33	$929.65
	1995	5,220	874	30,966	549	811	6.5	415,710	64,742	3,764,756	3,718	458	$286,073	$6,220.54	$966.79
	1996	5,160	864	31,116	531	800	6.2	440,845	63,646	3,723,907	3,728	466	$293,920	$6,225.95	$1,005.45
	1997	5,082	855	31,595	529	813	6.1	450,907	63,247	3,742,240	3,794	467	$306,088	$6,266.24	$1,031.68
	1998	5,039	842	31,830	527	821	6.0	474,366	62,162	3,726,234	3,835	467	$319,035	$6,387.53	$1,064.93
	1999	4,977	831	32,377	527	835	5.9	495,850	61,534	3,760,295	3,840	461	$335,405	$6,512.44	$1,101.47
	2000	4,934	825	33,102	534	850	5.8	522,970	60,845	3,880,166	3,916	461	$356,757	$6,650.68	$1,147.99
	2001	4,927	828	33,834	541	866	5.8	539,316	60,454	3,870,191	3,990	459	$383,911	$6,979.29	$1,216.04
	2002	4,949	823	34,501	542	887	5.7	557,336	59,974	3,873,395	4,072	459	$416,791	$7,353.17	$1,288.63
	2003	4,918	815	34,800	540	895	5.7	563,804	59,662	3,915,842	4,112	461	$450,403	$7,798.19	$1,378.78
	2004	4,942	810	35,098	542	910	5.8	573,126	58,710	3,931,508	4,151	456	$481,517	$8,168.06	$1,449.90
	2005	4,956	804	35,265	540	930	5.7	587,296	58,195	3,987,766	4,260	458	$516,172	$8,538.30	$1,521.58
	2006	4,947	805	35,403	535	940	5.6	599,597	57,832	4,075,193	4,347	462	$552,276	$8,972.85	$1,610.76
	2007	4,915	803	35,370	538	944	5.6	603,411	57,546	4,077,962	4,468	473	$583,550	$9,377.82	$1,694.38
	2008	5,026	810	35,776	529	963	5.5	624,185	57,301	4,073,724	4,552	473	$626,823	$9,789.69	$1,780.45
	2009	5,023	807	35,603	520	973	5.5	643,420	57,302	3,960,432	4,594	472	$657,242	$10,042.56	$1,851.44
	2010	4,995	806	35,160	514	974	5.4	651,617	56,610	3,818,399	4,603	473	$678,254	$10,316.07	$1,908.59
	2011	4,983	799	34,852	508	983	5.4	657,071	56,290	3,730,342	4,654	473	$702,822	$10,542.09	$1,959.69
	2012	5,010	802	34,438	509	992	5.4	675,223	55,987	3,715,479	4,732	477	$757,213	$11,222.23	$2,089.07
	2013	5,372	813	34,079	504	977	5.4	684,488	55,824	3,728,411	4,874	477	$794,245	$11,663.39	$2,157.53
	2014	5,330	804	33,545	508	1,018	5.4	700,472	55,181	3,766,328	4,829	499	$821,766	$12,019.23	$2,213.34
	2015	5,293	802	33,861	508	1,046	5.5	731,067	56,844	3,792,223	4,948	474	$867,108	$12,356.58	$2,271.71
	2016	5,278	801	34,052	511	1,077	5.5	757,095	56,294	3,769,965	5,088	473	$920,188	$12,756.07	$2,337.15
	2017	5,274	800	34,351	511	1,093	5.5	766,368	55,953	3,656,809	5,217	473	$966,492	$13,121.85	$2,423.23
	2018	5,210	794	34,268	508	1,101	5.4	766,630	54,943	3,637,593	5,239	477	$1,010,559	$13,543.26	$2,516.35
	2019	5,153	789	34,094	508	1,112	5.4	785,473	54,468	3,567,799	5,316	478	$1,056,785	$14,101.93	$2,605.62

Note: These data represent hospital performance in the years 2015 – 2019 and do not reflect any impacts from the COVID-19 pandemic in 2020 and thereafter.

Table 1 (Continued)

CLASSIFICATION: Total community hospitals

YEAR	HOSPITALS	BEDS (in thousands)	ADMISSIONS (in thousands)	AVERAGE DAILY CENSUS (in thousands)	ADJUSTED AVERAGE DAILY CENSUS (in thousands)	AVERAGE STAY (days)	OUTPATIENT VISITS (in thousands)	NEWBORNS Bassinets	NEWBORNS Births	FTE PERSONNEL Number (in thousands)	FTE PERSONNEL Per 100 Adjusted Census	TOTAL EXPENSES Amount (in Millions of dollars)	TOTAL EXPENSES Adjusted per Inpatient Stay (dollars)	TOTAL EXPENSES Adjusted per Inpatient Day (dollars)
1975	5,875	942	33,435	706	798	7.7	190,672	83,829	2,998,552	2,392	300	$38,962	$1,030.34	$133.81
1976	5,857	956	33,979	713	810	7.7	201,247	82,296	2,962,216	2,475	306	$45,240	$1,176.25	$152.76
1979	5,842	984	35,099	727	833	7.6	198,778	77,266	3,287,012	2,756	331	$66,004	$1,641.67	$217.34
1980	5,830	988	36,143	747	857	7.6	202,310	77,522	3,408,482	2,873	335	$76,851	$1,851.04	$245.12
1981	5,813	1,003	36,438	763	873	7.6	202,768	76,561	3,465,401	3,033	347	$90,572	$2,171.20	$284.33
1982	5,801	1,012	36,379	762	878	7.6	248,124	75,733	3,514,457	3,103	353	$104,876	$2,500.52	$327.37
1983	5,783	1,018	36,152	749	864	7.6	210,044	75,465	3,490,254	3,096	358	$116,438	$2,789.18	$369.49
1984	5,759	1,017	35,155	702	820	7.3	211,961	75,581	3,456,308	3,017	368	$123,336	$2,995.38	$411.10
1985	5,732	1,001	33,449	649	777	7.1	218,716	74,893	3,521,135	2,997	386	$130,499	$3,244.74	$460.19
1986	5,678	978	32,379	629	770	7.1	231,912	73,682	3,584,408	3,025	393	$140,654	$3,532.51	$500.81
1987	5,611	958	31,601	622	776	7.2	245,524	72,510	3,602,296	3,114	401	$152,585	$3,850.16	$538.96
1988	5,533	947	31,453	620	787	7.2	269,129	70,325	3,706,402	3,205	407	$168,722	$4,206.73	$586.33
1989	5,455	933	31,116	618	796	7.2	285,712	69,405	3,830,615	3,303	415	$184,898	$4,587.87	$636.96
1990	5,384	927	31,181	619	813	7.2	301,329	68,412	3,958,263	3,420	421	$203,693	$4,946.68	$686.83
1991	5,342	924	31,064	611	820	7.2	322,048	67,434	3,965,396	3,535	431	$225,023	$5,359.56	$752.10
1992	5,292	921	31,034	604	827	7.1	348,522	67,089	3,924,944	3,620	437	$248,095	$5,794.43	$819.83
1993	5,261	919	30,748	592	828	7.0	366,885	66,054	3,870,376	3,677	444	$266,089	$6,132.06	$880.52
1994	5,229	902	30,718	568	812	6.7	382,924	65,722	3,809,367	3,692	455	$275,779	$6,229.83	$930.71
1995	5,194	873	30,945	548	809	6.5	414,345	64,736	3,764,698	3,714	459	$285,588	$6,215.51	$967.69
1996	5,134	862	31,099	531	799	6.2	439,863	63,640	3,723,871	3,725	466	$293,755	$6,224.94	$1,006.14
1997	5,057	853	31,577	528	811	6.1	450,140	63,241	3,742,191	3,790	467	$305,763	$6,261.93	$1,032.70
1998	5,015	830	31,812	525	819	6.0	474,193	62,156	3,726,233	3,831	468	$318,834	$6,385.99	$1,066.96
1999	4,956	824	32,359	526	833	5.9	495,346	61,528	3,760,295	3,838	461	$335,246	$6,511.72	$1,102.61
2000	4,915		33,089	533	849	5.8	521,404	60,839		3,911	461	$356,564	$6,648.82	$1,149.40
2001	4,908	826	33,814	540	865	5.7	538,480	60,448	3,880,166	3,987	461	$383,735	$6,979.53	$1,217.27
2002	4,927	821	34,478	539	886	5.7	556,404	59,974	3,873,395	4,069	459	$416,591	$7,354.60	$1,289.87
2003	4,895	813	34,783	541	894	5.7	563,186	59,662	3,915,842	4,109	460	$450,124	$7,796.41	$1,379.48
2004	4,919	808	35,086	540	909	5.6	571,569	58,710	3,931,508	4,148	456	$481,247	$8,165.55	$1,450.35
2005	4,936	802	35,239	538	929	5.6	584,429	58,195	3,987,766	4,257	458	$515,740	$8,534.90	$1,522.42
2006	4,927	803	35,378	533	939	5.6	599,553	57,832	4,075,193	4,343	463	$551,835	$8,970.31	$1,612.23
2007	4,897	801	35,346	536	943	5.5	603,300	57,546	4,077,962	4,465	474	$583,252	$9,377.17	$1,696.10
2008	5,010	808	35,761	528	962	5.5	624,098	57,301	4,073,724	4,550	473	$626,577	$9,788.25	$1,782.28
2009	5,008	806	35,527	520	970	5.4	641,953	57,282	3,959,605	4,585	472	$656,156	$10,045.15	$1,852.59
2010	4,985	805	35,149	513	973	5.4	651,424	56,610	3,818,399	4,600	473	$677,968	$10,313.44	$1,909.64
2011	4,973	797	34,843	509	982	5.4	656,079	56,290	3,730,342	4,650	473	$702,091	$10,532.52	$1,959.58
2012	4,999	801	34,422	507	991	5.4	674,971	55,987	3,715,479	4,731	477	$756,917	$11,220.70	$2,090.01
2013	5,359	811	34,063	509	976	5.4	684,227	56,844	3,728,411	4,872	499	$793,919	$11,661.64	$2,158.83
2014	5,308	802	33,517	503	1,017	5.5	700,233	56,294	3,766,328	4,826	475	$821,224	$12,017.28	$2,214.84
2015	5,280	801	33,818	507	1,045	5.5	730,789	55,953	3,792,223	4,947	473	$866,817	$12,360.16	$2,272.58
2016	5,267	799	34,032	510	1,076	5.5	756,798	55,824	3,769,965	5,087	473	$919,821	$12,755.62	$2,338.07
2017	5,262	798	34,306	510	1,092	5.4	766,077	55,181	3,656,809	5,215	478	$966,204	$13,126.02	$2,424.17
2018	5,198	793	34,251	508	1,100	5.4	766,393	54,943	3,637,593	5,239	476	$1,010,271	$13,542.37	$2,517.38
2019	5,141	788	34,078	507	1,111	5.4	785,236	54,468	3,567,799	5,315	478	$1,056,497	$14,101.17	$2,606.70

Note: These data represent hospital performance in the years 2015 – 2019 and do not reflect any impacts from the COVID-19 pandemic in 2020 and thereafter.

Table 1 (Continued)

CLASSIFICATION: Nongovernment not-for-profit community hospitals

YEAR	HOSPITALS	BEDS (in thousands)	ADMISSIONS (in thousands)	AVERAGE DAILY CENSUS (in thousands)	ADJUSTED AVERAGE DAILY CENSUS (in thousands)	AVERAGE STAY (days)	OUTPATIENT VISITS (in thousands)	NEWBORNS Bassinets	NEWBORNS Births	FTE PERSONNEL Number (in thousands)	FTE PERSONNEL Per 100 Adjusted Census	TOTAL EXPENSES Amount (In Millions of dollars)	TOTAL EXPENSES Adjusted per Inpatient Stay (dollars)	TOTAL EXPENSES Adjusted per Inpatient Day (dollars)
1975	3,339	658	23,722	510	574	7.8	131,435	57,496	2,131,057	1,712	298	$27,938	$1,040.21	$133.36
1976	3,345	670	24,082	517	586	7.9	140,914	56,442	2,100,917	1,791	306	$32,764	$1,208.23	$152.94
1979	3,330	690	24,874	528	603	7.7	139,565	52,859	2,308,548	1,999	332	$47,937	$1,684.40	$218.06
1980	3,322	692	25,566	542	621	7.7	142,156	52,659	2,389,478	2,086	336	$55,780	$1,901.64	$245.74
1981	3,340	706	25,945	555	636	7.8	143,380	52,302	2,455,033	2,213	399	$66,267	$2,225.17	$285.64
1982	3,338	712	25,898	553	637	7.8	176,245	51,566	2,483,345	2,265	355	$76,806	$2,572.93	$330.41
1983	3,347	718	25,827	544	629	7.7	150,839	51,649	2,465,604	2,270	362	$85,637	$2,868.80	$373.78
1984	3,351	716	25,236	512	598	7.4	153,281	51,491	2,446,540	2,222	372	$90,814	$3,072.51	$415.04
1985	3,349	707	24,179	476	569	7.2	158,953	51,424	2,507,288	2,216	389	$96,150	$3,307.41	$462.69
1986	3,323	689	23,483	460	563	7.2	167,633	50,885	2,547,170	2,241	398	$103,524	$3,589.64	$503.64
1987	3,274	673	22,937	455	566	7.2	177,413	50,133	2,557,294	2,298	406	$112,325	$3,914.23	$543.67
1988	3,242	668	22,939	456	577	7.3	195,363	48,828	2,653,794	2,373	412	$124,703	$4,272.95	$591.13
1989	3,220	661	22,792	455	584	7.3	209,191	48,305	2,751,426	2,454	420	$136,889	$4,649.22	$642.45
1990	3,191	657	22,878	455	596	7.3	221,073	47,441	2,833,204	2,533	424	$150,673	$5,001.24	$692.36
1991	3,175	656	22,964	451	603	7.2	238,204	47,229	2,845,995	2,624	435	$166,806	$5,393.30	$758.21
1992	3,173	656	23,056	445	606	7.1	257,887	47,185	2,846,386	2,692	443	$183,793	$5,808.80	$828.44
1993	3,154	651	22,749	432	602	6.9	270,138	46,214	2,802,164	2,711	451	$197,187	$6,177.69	$897.70
1994	3,139	637	22,704	413	589	6.6	282,653	46,381	2,792,116	2,719	462	$204,219	$6,256.72	$950.31
1995	3,092	610	22,557	393	578	6.4	303,851	45,198	2,725,641	2,702	468	$209,614	$6,279.17	$994.39
1996	3,045	598	22,542	379	567	6.1	320,746	44,650	2,683,750	2,711	478	$215,950	$6,344.05	$1,042.04
1997	3,000	591	22,905	376	575	6.0	330,215	44,484	2,698,086	2,765	481	$225,287	$6,392.74	$1,074.26
1998	3,026	588	23,282	377	587	5.9	352,114	44,087	2,715,958	2,834	483	$237,978	$6,525.68	$1,110.50
1999	3,012	587	23,871	381	605	5.8	370,784	44,172	2,746,453	2,862	473	$251,534	$6,607.51	$1,139.89
2000	3,003	583	24,452	382	618	5.7	393,168	43,655	2,833,615	2,919	472	$267,051	$6,717.48	$1,182.32
2001	2,998	585	24,983	385	628	5.6	404,901	43,640	2,829,691	2,971	473	$287,250	$7,051.76	$1,255.25
2002	3,025	582	25,425	391	646	5.6	416,910	43,241	2,820,159	3,039	471	$312,726	$7,457.84	$1,328.81
2003	2,984	575	25,668	389	647	5.5	424,215	42,965	2,854,764	3,059	473	$337,696	$7,904.93	$1,429.62
2004	2,967	568	25,757	388	655	5.5	430,262	41,968	2,844,617	3,077	470	$359,414	$8,266.64	$1,501.09
2005	2,958	561	25,881	388	667	5.5	441,653	41,585	2,876,677	3,155	473	$385,993	$8,670.83	$1,585.34
2006	2,919	559	25,798	385	671	5.4	453,501	40,888	2,905,275	3,207	473	$412,868	$9,189.58	$1,685.62
2007	2,913	554	25,752	380	673	5.4	455,825	40,681	2,907,002	3,286	478	$436,319	$9,592.93	$1,776.06
2008	2,923	557	25,899	380	683	5.4	469,804	40,567	2,901,854	3,340	488	$468,080	$10,080.50	$1,875.78
2009	2,918	556	25,783	375	690	5.3	485,935	40,467	2,822,527	3,369	489	$492,853	$10,379.09	$1,956.71
2010	2,904	556	25,532	368	691	5.3	494,178	39,946	2,750,163	3,388	488	$510,744	$10,651.81	$2,025.05
2011	2,903	548	25,185	362	694	5.2	496,643	39,651	2,692,577	3,427	490	$528,303	$10,932.55	$2,088.05
2012	2,894	545	24,751	354	697	5.2	512,237	39,778	2,684,600	3,477	494	$563,960	$11,563.17	$2,214.26
2013	2,975	548	24,470	354	687	5.3	518,438	40,498	2,706,635	3,513	499	$589,184	$12,002.72	$2,288.81
2014	2,943	539	23,895	347	709	5.3	528,258	39,768	2,728,345	3,523	513	$606,297	$12,375.64	$2,344.81
2015	2,932	537	24,115	350	729	5.3	551,762	39,510	2,744,467	3,593	496	$641,799	$12,745.02	$2,412.96
2016	2,943	540	24,356	353	751	5.3	574,044	39,641	2,750,958	3,716	493	$683,326	$13,157.14	$2,486.48
2017	2,968	545	24,789	357	768	5.3	581,848	39,744	2,710,049	3,841	494	$721,391	$13,503.97	$2,573.64
2018	2,937	543	24,730	356	781	5.2	580,598	39,692	2,687,592	3,848	500	$755,788	$13,882.59	$2,652.80
2019	2,946	546	24,728	358	796	5.3	595,360	39,632	2,651,823	3,929	493	$794,697	$14,446.18	$2,737.79

Note: These data represent hospital performance in the years 2015 – 2019 and do not reflect any impacts from the COVID-19 pandemic in 2020 and thereafter.

Table 1 (Continued)

Investor-owned (for-profit) community hospitals

CLASSIFICATION / YEAR	HOSPITALS	BEDS (in thousands)	ADMISSIONS (in thousands)	AVERAGE DAILY CENSUS (in thousands)	ADJUSTED AVERAGE DAILY CENSUS (in thousands)	AVERAGE STAY (days)	OUTPATIENT VISITS (in thousands)	NEWBORNS Bassinets	NEWBORNS Births	FTE PERSONNEL Number (in thousands)	FTE PERSONNEL Per 100 Adjusted Census	TOTAL EXPENSES Amount (In Millions of dollars)	TOTAL EXPENSES Adjusted per Inpatient Stay (dollars)	TOTAL EXPENSES Adjusted per Inpatient Day (dollars)
1975	775	73	2,646	48	53	6.6	7,713	4,062	141,392	139	263	$2,561	$876.48	$132.80
1976	752	76	2,734	50	54	6.6	8,048	4,044	144,751	147	272	$3,085	$1,031.91	$156.35
1979	727	83	2,963	53	59	6.6	9,289	4,110	174,843	174	300	$4,820	$1,476.42	$225.87
1980	730	87	3,165	57	62	6.5	9,696	4,439	199,722	189	304	$5,847	$1,675.85	$257.12
1981	729	88	3,239	58	63	6.5	9,961	4,523	207,405	203	322	$6,856	$1,952.56	$299.02
1982	748	91	3,316	60	66	6.6	13,193	4,736	219,675	212	320	$8,177	$2,224.75	$340.03
1983	757	94	3,299	59	66	6.5	10,389	5,039	228,883	213	323	$9,208	$2,517.53	$385.42
1984	786	100	3,314	57	64	6.3	11,090	5,807	242,088	214	335	$10,251	$2,748.51	$438.30
1985	805	104	3,242	54	63	6.1	12,378	6,117	266,839	221	350	$11,486	$3,033.06	$500.48
1986	834	107	3,231	54	65	6.1	14,896	6,305	291,112	229	354	$12,987	$3,341.79	$552.40
1987	828	106	3,157	54	66	6.2	16,566	6,391	306,492	242	367	$14,067	$3,617.19	$585.01
1988	790	104	3,090	53	66	6.2	17,926	6,254	308,828	249	379	$15,545	$4,022.77	$649.33
1989	769	102	3,071	53	67	6.3	19,341	6,354	325,711	261	390	$17,240	$4,406.20	$707.90
1990	749	101	3,066	54	69	6.4	20,110	6,261	340,555	273	396	$18,822	$4,727.27	$751.55
1991	738	100	3,016	52	69	6.3	21,174	6,358	359,115	281	409	$20,516	$5,133.53	$820.19
1992	723	99	2,969	51	69	6.3	22,900	6,519	357,776	285	412	$22,496	$5,548.24	$888.73
1993	717	99	2,946	51	69	6.2	22,936	6,395	363,358	289	417	$23,077	$5,643.21	$914.39
1994	719	101	3,035	50	70	6.1	26,443	6,329	354,477	302	434	$23,445	$5,528.91	$923.90
1995	752	106	3,428	55	77	5.8	31,940	7,164	408,339	343	443	$26,653	$5,425.20	$946.99
1996	759	109	3,684	56	82	5.6	37,347	7,441	444,697	359	437	$28,385	$5,207.44	$945.49
1997	797	115	3,953	60	89	5.5	40,919	8,026	465,919	385	433	$31,179	$5,218.69	$961.96
1998	771	113	3,971	60	90	5.5	42,072	7,895	466,025	383	425	$31,732	$5,262.44	$968.00
1999	747	107	3,905	58	86	5.5	39,896	7,486	467,585	362	422	$31,179	$5,350.07	$999.03
2000	749	110	4,141	61	90	5.4	43,378	7,792	503,497	378	418	$34,969	$5,642.18	$1,057.32
2001	754	109	4,197	63	92	5.4	44,706	7,413	494,669	379	413	$37,348	$5,971.81	$1,121.31
2002	766	108	4,365	64	93	5.3	45,215	7,467	496,988	380	407	$40,082	$6,161.44	$1,180.83
2003	790	110	4,481	65	95	5.3	44,246	7,491	515,693	391	411	$43,953	$6,589.91	$1,264.50
2004	835	113	4,599	68	100	5.4	44,962	7,763	534,503	406	406	$48,971	$7,139.13	$1,362.42
2005	868	114	4,618	68	101	5.3	46,016	7,714	546,307	421	418	$51,833	$7,351.96	$1,412.74
2006	890	115	4,735	68	103	5.2	44,237	8,012	574,113	423	413	$55,030	$7,422.08	$1,471.53
2007	873	116	4,626	66	101	5.2	43,943	7,760	555,670	432	429	$56,405	$7,823.44	$1,535.98
2008	982	121	4,839	70	109	5.3	44,897	7,791	562,711	450	414	$61,762	$7,984.62	$1,555.55
2009	998	122	4,887	70	112	5.3	47,281	7,965	553,233	464	414	$64,367	$8,037.18	$1,573.64
2010	1,013	125	4,925	71	113	5.3	48,201	7,965	525,427	474	420	$67,168	$8,336.16	$1,628.90
2011	1,025	128	5,060	73	119	5.3	50,013	8,137	508,330	485	409	$70,340	$8,262.74	$1,627.65
2012	1,068	135	5,224	77	124	5.3	53,854	8,192	530,941	515	414	$79,114	$8,860.94	$1,746.85
2013	1,351	145	5,346	81	126	5.3	56,935	8,400	532,235	613	487	$89,444	$9,519.01	$1,839.53
2014	1,341	146	5,407	82	139	5.5	60,277	8,665	547,008	572	411	$93,780	$9,649.97	$1,849.54
2015	1,345	146	5,506	83	143	5.5	62,567	8,863	560,964	588	410	$97,949	$9,758.88	$1,876.67
2016	1,350	146	5,625	84	148	5.5	65,542	8,876	550,448	609	413	$104,138	$9,903.56	$1,929.73
2017	1,322	142	5,433	81	144	5.5	63,203	8,319	487,406	591	412	$104,704	$10,273.14	$1,996.11
2018	1,296	140	5,437	81	142	5.4	62,224	8,173	494,130	594	418	$108,447	$10,683.61	$2,093.10
2019	1,233	132	5,309	78	136	5.4	60,101	7,703	464,258	573	420	$106,859	$10,764.43	$2,149.37

Note: These data represent hospital performance in the years 2015 – 2019 and do not reflect any impacts from the COVID-19 pandemic in 2020 and thereafter.

Table 1 (Continued)

CLASSIFICATION	YEAR	HOSPITALS	BEDS (in thousands)	ADMISSIONS (in thousands)	AVERAGE DAILY CENSUS (in thousands)	ADJUSTED AVERAGE DAILY CENSUS (in thousands)	AVERAGE STAY (days)	OUTPATIENT VISITS (in thousands)	NEWBORNS Bassinets	NEWBORNS Births	FTE PERSONNEL Number (in thousands)	FTE PERSONNEL Per 100 Adjusted Census	TOTAL EXPENSES Amount (In Millions of dollars)	TOTAL EXPENSES Adjusted per Inpatient Stay (dollars)	TOTAL EXPENSES Adjusted per Inpatient Day (dollars)
State and local government community hospitals	1975	1,761	210	7,067	148	171	7.6	51,525	22,271	726,103	540	316	$8,463	$1,030.86	$135.64
	1976	1,760	210	7,163	146	170	7.5	52,286	21,810	716,548	537	315	$9,391	$1,132.50	$151.00
	1979	1,785	211	7,262	146	171	7.4	49,924	20,297	803,621	583	341	$13,247	$1,561.04	$211.89
	1980	1,778	209	7,413	149	174	7.3	50,459	20,424	819,282	598	343	$15,204	$1,750.13	$238.63
	1981	1,744	210	7,255	150	174	7.6	49,427	19,736	802,963	618	354	$17,449	$2,071.57	$274.25
	1982	1,715	210	7,165	149	175	7.6	58,685	19,431	811,437	627	320	$19,893	$2,364.09	$311.56
	1983	1,679	207	7,025	145	170	7.6	48,816	18,777	795,767	613	360	$21,593	$2,621.28	$347.56
	1984	1,622	201	6,606	133	158	7.3	47,590	18,283	767,680	581	368	$22,271	$2,823.13	$385.17
	1985	1,578	189	6,028	119	145	7.2	47,386	17,352	747,008	561	387	$22,863	$3,106.14	$432.84
	1986	1,521	182	5,665	114	142	7.4	49,383	16,492	746,126	555	391	$24,143	$3,404.69	$466.17
	1987	1,509	180	5,507	113	144	7.5	51,544	15,986	738,510	573	399	$26,192	$3,717.77	$499.33
	1988	1,501	175	5,424	112	145	7.6	55,840	15,243	743,780	583	403	$28,474	$4,033.67	$538.63
	1989	1,466	170	5,253	110	145	7.7	57,179	14,746	753,478	589	406	$30,769	$4,430.12	$582.15
	1990	1,444	169	5,236	111	148	7.7	60,146	14,710	784,504	614	415	$34,198	$4,837.76	$634.45
	1991	1,429	168	5,084	108	148	7.8	62,670	13,847	760,286	630	424	$37,701	$5,339.75	$695.89
	1992	1,396	166	5,008	108	152	7.9	67,734	13,385	720,782	643	424	$41,806	$5,870.76	$753.92
	1993	1,390	169	5,054	109	157	7.8	71,811	13,445	704,854	676	430	$45,825	$6,205.52	$799.73
	1994	1,371	164	4,979	104	154	7.6	73,828	13,012	662,774	672	438	$48,115	$6,513.39	$858.62
	1995	1,350	157	4,961	100	154	7.4	78,554	12,374	630,718	670	435	$49,322	$6,445.18	$877.85
	1996	1,330	155	4,873	96	150	7.2	81,770	11,549	595,424	654	437	$49,420	$6,418.65	$903.41
	1997	1,260	148	4,720	92	148	7.1	79,007	10,731	578,186	640	433	$49,298	$6,475.07	$913.62
	1998	1,218	139	4,559	87	142	7.0	80,008	10,174	544,250	614	433	$49,123	$6,612.23	$949.36
	1999	1,197	136	4,583	86	143	6.9	84,667	9,870	546,257	614	430	$52,534	$6,923.35	$1,006.91
	2000	1,163	131	4,496	83	140	6.7	84,858	9,392	543,054	614	438	$54,544	$7,106.05	$1,063.75
	2001	1,156	132	4,634	85	145	6.7	88,873	9,395	549,035	637	438	$59,137	$7,400.01	$1,113.79
	2002	1,136	130	4,688	84	147	6.6	94,280	9,266	553,044	651	442	$63,783	$7,772.93	$1,188.12
	2003	1,121	129	4,634	84	152	6.6	94,725	9,206	545,385	658	434	$68,475	$8,205.10	$1,237.64
	2004	1,117	128	4,730	85	154	6.5	96,345	8,979	552,388	666	431	$72,861	$8,473.18	$1,291.06
	2005	1,110	128	4,740	85	161	6.5	96,760	8,896	564,782	681	424	$77,914	$8,793.26	$1,329.64
	2006	1,119	128	4,848	86	165	6.5	101,845	8,932	595,805	713	433	$83,974	$9,147.40	$1,400.09
	2007	1,111	131	4,967	87	169	6.4	103,532	9,105	615,290	747	443	$90,528	$9,523.22	$1,472.26
	2008	1,105	131	5,023	86	170	6.3	109,398	8,943	609,159	760	446	$96,735	$9,826.94	$1,552.32
	2009	1,092	127	4,857	83	168	6.2	108,738	8,850	583,845	751	447	$98,937	$10,067.96	$1,611.31
	2010	1,068	125	4,693	80	169	6.2	109,045	8,699	542,809	738	437	$100,056	$10,283.35	$1,624.93
	2011	1,045	121	4,598	78	170	6.2	109,423	8,502	529,435	738	434	$103,448	$10,531.65	$1,666.96
	2012	1,037	120	4,447	77	170	6.3	108,880	8,017	499,938	739	435	$113,843	$11,668.15	$1,831.00
	2013	1,033	118	4,247	74	163	6.3	108,854	7,946	489,541	736	451	$115,291	$12,014.95	$1,868.24
	2014	1,024	117	4,215	74	169	6.4	111,698	7,861	490,975	741	440	$121,147	$12,583.26	$1,969.61
	2015	1,003	118	4,197	74	173	6.4	116,460	7,580	486,792	766	442	$127,069	$13,051.3	$2,008.96
	2016	974	113	4,051	73	177	6.5	117,212	7,307	468,559	762	431	$132,357	$13,701.45	$2,047.97
	2017	972	111	4,084	72	180	6.4	121,026	7,118	459,354	783	434	$140,109	$14,014.85	$2,128.78
	2018	965	110	4,084	71	177	6.4	1,23,571	7,078	455,871	797	450	$146,036	$14,591.12	$2,260.47
	2019	962	110	4,041	71	179	6.5	1,29,775	7,133	451,718	813	454	$154,941	$15,517.76	$2,372.24

Note: These data represent hospital performance in the years 2015 – 2019 and do not reflect any impacts from the COVID-19 pandemic in 2020 and thereafter.

Table 2

2019 U.S. Hospitals: Utilization, Personnel, and Finances

Excludes U.S.-Associated Areas and Puerto Rico hospitals.

CLASSIFICATION	HOSPITALS	BEDS	ADMISSIONS	INPATIENT DAYS	ADJUSTED INPATIENT DAYS	AVERAGE DAILY CENSUS	ADJUSTED AVERAGE DAILY CENSUS	AVERAGE STAY (DAYS)	SURGICAL OPERATIONS	OUTPATIENT VISITS Emergency	OUTPATIENT VISITS Total	NEWBORNS Bassinets	NEWBORNS Births
UNITED STATES	6,090	919,559	36,241,815	222,933,235	—	610,761	—	—	29,326,351	147,451,211	900,689,496	55,085	3,608,425
6-24 Beds	842	13,744	381,260	1,794,085	—	4,914	—	—	865,845	3,366,873	23,372,539	665	21,682
25-49	1,396	46,053	1,243,624	7,596,673	—	20,815	—	—	1,844,353	9,900,479	61,678,766	3,137	118,122
50-99	1,160	82,269	2,378,984	17,521,195	—	47,993	—	—	2,206,284	12,466,895	77,693,667	4,630	201,898
100-199	1,195	170,099	6,300,130	38,946,549	—	106,710	—	—	4,883,561	29,607,019	166,713,419	10,897	596,774
200-299	619	150,576	6,203,386	36,344,638	—	99,573	—	—	4,718,569	25,811,973	141,543,079	9,932	646,545
300-399	372	129,264	5,575,564	32,312,176	—	88,524	—	—	3,844,023	20,249,795	108,377,883	8,359	601,184
400-499	179	79,535	3,486,792	20,242,047	—	55,458	—	—	2,570,002	12,576,530	81,656,638	4,539	352,236
500 or more	327	248,019	10,672,075	68,175,872	—	186,774	—	—	8,393,714	33,471,647	239,653,505	12,926	1,069,984
Psychiatric	636	86,724	1,284,234	26,522,437	—	72,664	—	—	6,772	85,579	10,900,979	0	0
Hospitals	630	84,031	1,284,005	25,582,494	—	70,089	—	—	6,772	85,579	10,900,979	0	0
Inst. for Intellectual Disabilities	6	2,693	229	939,943	—	2,575	—	—	0	0	0	0	0
General	4,583	777,549	33,842,210	183,370,636	—	502,376	—	—	28,157,258	146,182,022	865,890,995	54,448	3,551,260
Hospitals	4,568	776,354	33,823,760	183,087,687	—	501,598	—	—	28,153,200	146,154,224	865,115,254	54,448	3,551,260
Hospital units of institutions	15	1,195	18,450	282,949	—	778	—	—	4,058	27,798	775,741	0	0
TB and other respiratory diseases	2	126	139	12,748	—	35	—	—	0	0	112,359	0	0
Obstetrics and gynecology	11	1,571	74,005	343,362	—	940	—	—	56,797	210,831	1,422,917	525	49,305
Eye, ear, nose and throat	2	58	1,645	5,537	—	15	—	—	49,254	21,629	568,609	0	0
Rehabilitation	302	21,026	395,837	5,425,227	—	14,869	—	—	13,931	0	7,909,606	40	302
Orthopedic	42	1,526	78,258	206,652	—	566	—	—	214,023	100,794	1,712,102	0	0
Chronic Disease	3	141	553	35,580	—	97	—	—	0	4,619	62,769	0	0
Surgical	93	2,038	111,782	217,753	—	595	—	—	352,636	195,986	1,495,896	34	4,524
Cancer	17	3,118	126,805	888,630	—	2,434	—	—	151,861	121,780	7,106,592	0	0
Heart	14	952	47,199	193,739	—	532	—	—	42,664	59,578	839,004	40	302
Acute long-term care hospital	361	23,070	239,398	5,287,518	—	14,478	—	—	239,357	345,627	1,874,949	0	0
All other	24	1,660	39,750	423,416	—	1,160	—	—	41,798	122,766	792,719	38	3,034
Federal	208	37,560	848,241	9,466,894	—	25,934	—	—	938,502	3,728,673	106,108,389	612	40,620
Psychiatric	11	2,640	24,185	810,639	—	2,219	—	—	3,567	12,567	3,533,122	0	0
General and other special	197	34,920	824,056	8,656,255	—	23,715	—	—	934,935	3,716,106	102,575,267	612	40,620
Nonfederal	5,882	881,999	35,393,574	213,466,341	—	584,827	—	—	28,387,849	143,722,538	794,581,107	54,473	3,567,805
Psychiatric	625	84,084	1,260,049	25,711,798	—	70,445	—	—	3,205	73,012	7,367,857	0	0
Hospitals	619	81,391	1,259,820	24,771,855	—	67,870	—	—	3,205	73,012	7,367,857	0	0
Inst. for Intellectual Disabilities	6	2,693	229	939,943	—	2,575	—	—	0	0	0	0	0
TB and other respiratory diseases	2	126	139	12,748	17,422	35	47	91.7	0	0	112,359	0	0
Long-term general and other special	102	8,644	38,937	2,313,367	2,861,869	6,335	7,839	59.4	15,947	217,242	1,627,978	5	6
Short-term general and other special	5,153	789,145	34,094,449	185,428,428	405,578,673	508,012	1,111,985	5.4	28,368,697	143,432,284	785,472,913	54,468	3,567,799
Hospital units of institutions	12	1,150	16,349	278,500	278,500	765	765	17	0	0	237,657	0	0
Community Hospitals	5,141	787,995	34,078,100	185,149,928	405,300,173	507,247	1,111,220	5.4	28,368,697	143,432,284	785,235,256	54,468	3,567,799
6-24 Beds	734	11,896	328,106	1,364,348	7,383,616	3,738	20,283	4.2	832,343	3,140,643	18,660,124	603	17,580
25-49	1,257	41,049	1,133,257	6,399,323	23,774,858	17,532	65,287	5.6	1,808,254	9,557,119	58,216,115	2,999	111,185
50-99	897	63,176	1,927,731	12,627,390	37,303,600	34,591	102,476	6.6	2,070,917	11,440,166	60,578,704	4,429	190,015
100-199	952	136,707	5,548,899	29,492,392	72,835,509	80,810	199,625	5.3	4,705,382	28,888,633	140,702,458	10,809	585,757
200-299	515	125,372	5,813,060	28,915,694	61,000,473	79,212	167,123	5	4,422,006	25,049,922	115,557,358	9,804	639,859
300-399	326	113,166	5,412,719	27,379,817	52,949,128	75,011	145,331	5.1	3,720,383	19,952,051	94,835,718	8,359	601,183
400-499	163	72,228	3,394,108	18,087,000	35,050,710	49,556	96,021	5.3	2,498,002	12,204,408	70,951,403	4,539	352,236
500 or more	297	224,401	10,520,220	60,883,964	115,002,279	166,797	315,074	5.8	8,311,410	33,199,342	225,733,376	12,926	1,069,984
Nongovernment not-for-profit	2,946	545,778	24,728,294	130,570,628	290,269,349	357,730	795,831	5.3	20,592,421	102,958,290	595,359,662	39,632	2,651,823
Investor-owned (for profit)	1,233	131,772	5,308,609	28,477,602	49,716,392	78,024	136,397	5.4	4,071,722	21,401,527	60,100,646	7,703	464,258
State and Local Government	962	110,445	4,041,197	26,101,698	65,314,432	71,493	178,992	6.5	3,704,554	19,072,467	129,774,948	7,133	451,718

Note: These data represent hospital performance in the years 2015 – 2019 and do not reflect any impacts from the COVID-19 pandemic in 2020 and thereafter.

 AHA Hospital Statistics © 2021 Health Forum LLC, an affiliate of the American Hospital Association

Table 2 (Continued)

U.S. Hospitals

CLASSIFICATION	FULL-TIME EQUIVALENT PERSONNEL — Physicians and Dentists	Registered Nurses	Licensed Practical Nurses	Other Salaried Personnel	Total Personnel	FULL-TIME EQUIVALENT TRAINEES — Medical and Dental Residents	Other Trainees	Total Trainees	EXPENSES / LABOR — Payroll (in thousands)	Employee Benefits (in thousands)	Total (in thousands)	Percent of Total	Amount (in thousands)	TOTAL — Adjusted Per Admission	Adjusted Per Inpatient Day
UNITED STATES	189,800	1,733,921	104,664	3,960,604	5,988,989	123,127	16,870	139,997	$438,464,420	$116,481,881	$554,946,301	$47.8	$1,161,032,419	—	—
6-24 Beds	3,448	27,516	3,904	83,634	118,502	136	187	323	$7,145,481	$1,783,421	$8,928,902	$46.6	$19,165,815	—	—
25-49	9,706	76,468	12,108	233,636	331,918	433	906	1,339	$20,667,275	$5,196,160	$25,863,434	$48.8	$53,037,711	—	—
50-99	11,950	115,969	13,667	302,921	444,507	1,727	1,121	2,848	$29,674,986	$7,615,507	$37,290,493	$50.2	$74,216,096	—	—
100-199	25,667	268,426	19,742	638,644	952,479	7,990	1,325	9,315	$67,185,029	$17,486,574	$84,671,603	$48.5	$174,603,042	—	—
200-299	29,237	271,768	17,855	611,991	930,851	11,656	2,906	14,562	$68,713,976	$17,808,070	$86,522,047	$48.3	$179,211,306	—	—
300-399	19,983	241,478	10,185	505,540	777,186	11,728	1,317	13,045	$58,531,850	$15,361,239	$73,893,090	$46.9	$157,653,803	—	—
400-499	16,860	163,006	6,828	360,242	546,936	15,869	1,784	17,653	$44,512,630	$12,369,059	$56,881,689	$48.1	$118,152,700	—	—
500 or more	72,949	569,290	20,375	1,223,996	1,886,610	73,588	7,324	80,912	$142,033,192	$38,861,850	$180,895,042	$47.0	$384,991,947	—	—
Psychiatric	4,784	37,028	7,408	184,085	233,305	639	512	1,151	$13,006,508	$4,262,295	$17,268,802	$67.5	$25,589,562	—	—
Hospitals	4,713	36,677	7,105	177,100	225,595	639	512	1,151	$12,754,604	$4,143,856	$16,898,460	$67.2	$25,162,281	—	—
Inst. for Intellectual Disabilities	71	351	303	6,985	7,710	0	0	0	$251,904	$118,439	$370,343	$86.7	$427,281	—	—
General	177,470	1,620,481	90,443	3,570,282	5,458,676	120,716	14,823	135,539	$404,579,167	$107,241,303	$511,820,470	$47.4	$1,079,915,024	—	—
Hospitals	177,156	1,620,112	90,315	3,567,955	5,455,538	120,708	14,805	135,513	$404,390,775	$107,191,648	$511,582,422	$47.4	$1,079,442,565	—	—
Hospital units of institutions	314	369	128	2,327	3,138	8	18	26	$188,392	$49,656	$238,048	$50.4	$472,459	—	—
TB and other respiratory diseases	154	155	28	1,388	1,725	0	25	25	$145,322	$19,233	$164,555	$55.8	$294,867	—	—
Obstetrics and gynecology	97	3,824	55	4,996	8,972	128	4	132	$707,884	$160,696	$868,581	$37.3	$2,330,883	—	—
Eye, ear, nose and throat	174	295	6	1,946	2,421	72	41	113	$141,136	$30,450	$171,586	$39.3	$436,561	—	—
Rehabilitation	1,193	19,524	1,905	62,173	84,795	474	62	536	$4,923,550	$1,141,087	$6,064,637	$54.4	$11,157,634	—	—
Orthopedic	736	3,609	256	10,947	15,548	59	4	63	$1,439,456	$337,394	$1,776,850	$47.8	$3,720,863	—	—
Chronic Disease	11	166	10	651	838	0	0	0	$54,438	$19,068	$73,505	$60.7	$121,188	—	—
Surgical	77	4,896	216	8,851	14,040	1	0	1	$948,168	$214,596	$1,162,765	$32.9	$3,534,536	—	—
Cancer	4,494	16,294	247	53,932	74,967	1,018	1,394	2,412	$6,516,824	$1,766,693	$8,283,517	$42.6	$19,428,069	—	—
Heart	87	2,763	177	5,137	8,164	6	0	6	$530,012	$123,427	$653,439	$38.0	$1,721,160	—	—
Acute long-term care hospital	215	21,774	3,751	48,892	74,632	5	1	6	$4,633,276	$933,925	$5,567,201	$52.4	$10,631,584	—	—
All other	308	3,112	162	7,324	10,906	9	4	13	$838,678	$231,714	$1,070,392	$49.8	$2,150,489	—	—
Federal	33,581	83,195	22,573	286,465	425,814	8,216	6,148	14,364	$31,965,831	$10,437,661	$42,403,492	$54.8	$77,340,550	—	—
Psychiatric	722	2,645	777	11,124	15,268	107	154	261	$1,290,724	$441,710	$1,732,434	$66.1	$2,619,914	—	—
General and other special	32,859	80,550	21,796	275,341	410,546	8,109	5,994	14,103	$30,675,108	$9,995,951	$40,671,058	$54.4	$74,720,636	—	—
Nonfederal	156,219	1,650,726	82,091	3,674,139	5,563,175	114,911	10,722	125,633	$406,498,589	$106,044,220	$512,542,809	$47.3	$1,083,691,869	—	—
Psychiatric	4,062	34,383	6,631	172,961	218,037	532	358	890	$11,715,784	$3,820,585	$15,536,369	$67.6	$22,969,648	—	—
Hospitals	3,991	34,032	6,328	165,976	210,327	532	358	890	$11,463,880	$3,702,146	$15,166,026	$67.3	$22,542,367	—	—
Inst. for Intellectual Disabilities	71	351	303	6,985	7,710	0	0	0	$251,904	$118,439	$370,343	$86.7	$427,281	—	—
TB and other respiratory diseases	154	155	28	1,388	1,725	0	25	25	$145,322	$19,233	$164,555	$55.8	$294,867	$212,287.11	$16,924.97
Long-term general and other special	333	5,923	811	20,423	27,490	5	6	11	$1,725,128	$425,232	$2,150,360	$59.0	$3,642,786	$71,777.62	$1,272.87
Short-term general and other special	151,670	1,610,265	74,621	3,479,367	5,315,923	114,374	10,333	124,707	$392,912,355	$101,779,171	$494,691,525	$46.8	$1,056,784,568	$14,101.93	$2,605.62
Hospital units of institutions	127	115	115	608	965	0	0	0	$95,833	$19,167	$115,000	$40.0	$287,500	$17,585.17	$1,032.32
Community Hospitals	151,543	1,610,150	74,506	3,478,759	5,314,958	114,374	10,333	124,707	$392,816,521	$101,760,004	$494,576,525	$46.8	$1,056,497,068	$14,101.17	$2,606.70
6-24 Beds	1,972	24,647	3,589	67,220	97,428	41	37	78	$6,116,343	$1,466,447	$7,582,790	$44.5	$17,052,065	$9,154.47	$2,309.45
25-49	7,558	69,750	9,802	198,885	285,995	261	830	1,091	$18,206,597	$4,579,191	$22,785,789	$48.2	$47,303,681	$9,672.87	$1,989.65
50-99	7,200	95,709	8,443	236,518	347,870	702	167	869	$22,645,750	$5,581,674	$28,227,425	$47.8	$59,086,738	$10,274.71	$1,583.94
100-199	17,285	236,350	13,466	528,237	795,338	4,957	725	5,682	$56,103,804	$13,931,496	$70,035,301	$47.3	$148,187,316	$11,113.44	$2,034.55
200-299	19,292	245,968	10,482	506,376	782,118	8,722	764	9,486	$58,333,855	$14,682,783	$73,016,638	$46.8	$155,998,257	$12,864.95	$2,557.33
300-399	16,063	228,502	7,019	452,164	703,748	11,124	925	12,049	$53,839,244	$13,567,627	$67,406,871	$46.1	$146,203,334	$13,878.03	$2,761.20
400-499	13,427	154,397	4,559	326,096	498,479	15,411	870	16,281	$40,852,743	$11,164,192	$52,016,934	$47.8	$108,862,646	$16,613.77	$3,105.86
500 or more	68,746	554,827	17,146	1,163,263	1,803,982	73,156	6,015	79,171	$136,718,185	$36,786,593	$173,504,777	$46.4	$373,803,032	$18,810.92	$3,250.40
Nongovernment not-for-profit	125,186	1,183,111	46,557	2,574,345	3,929,199	84,378	7,583	91,961	$294,694,471	$74,840,502	$369,534,973	$46.5	$794,696,564	$14,446.18	$2,737.79
Investor-owned (for profit)	4,507	203,202	11,188	354,036	572,933	4,743	228	4,971	$38,293,134	$8,484,684	$46,777,818	$43.8	$106,859,058	$10,764.43	$2,149.37
State and Local Government	21,850	223,837	16,761	550,378	812,826	25,253	2,522	27,775	$59,828,916	$18,434,818	$78,263,734	$50.5	$154,941,447	$15,517.76	$2,372.24

Note: These data represent hospital performance in the years 2015 – 2019 and do not reflect any impacts from the COVID-19 pandemic in 2020 and thereafter.

Tables 3–6

Total U.S.

Note: These data represent hospital performance in the years 2015 – 2019 and do not reflect any impacts from the COVID-19 pandemic in 2020 and thereafter.

TABLE 3

TOTAL UNITED STATES

U.S. Community Hospitals
(Nonfederal, short-term general and other special hospitals)

Overview 2015–2019

	2019	2018	2017	2016	2015
TOTAL U.S. Community Hospitals	5,141	5,198	5,262	5,267	5,280
Bed Size Category					
6-24	734	709	702	679	661
25-49	1,257	1,273	1,280	1,287	1,299
50-99	897	926	958	984	981
100-199	952	976	1,004	993	1,012
200-299	515	534	525	536	540
300-399	326	316	326	326	326
400-499	163	172	178	177	177
500 +	297	292	289	285	284
Location					
Hospitals Urban	3,336	3,377	3,387	3,385	3,393
Hospitals Rural	1,805	1,821	1,875	1,882	1,887
Control					
State and Local Government	962	965	972	974	1,003
Not for Profit	2,946	2,937	2,968	2,943	2,932
Investor owned	1,233	1,296	1,322	1,350	1,345
Affiliations					
Hospitals in a System	3,453	3,491	3,494	3,467	3,418
Hospitals in a Group Purchasing Organization	3,341	3,491	3,583	3,726	3,753

Note: These data represent hospital performance in the years 2015 – 2019 and do not reflect any impacts from the COVID-19 pandemic in 2020 and thereafter.

Total U.S.

TABLE 3

TOTAL UNITED STATES

U.S. Community Hospitals
(Nonfederal, short-term general and other special hospitals)

Utilization, Personnel, Revenue and Expenses, Community Health Indicators 2015–2019

	2019	2018	2017	2016	2015
TOTAL FACILITY (Includes Hospital and Nursing Home Units)					
Utilization - Inpatient					
Beds	787,995	792,417	798,921	799,444	800,828
Admissions	34,078,100	34,251,159	34,305,620	34,031,587	33,817,285
Inpatient Days	185,149,928	185,307,228	186,198,977	186,089,454	185,171,082
Average Length of Stay	5.4	5.4	5.4	5.5	5.5
Inpatient Surgeries	8,950,559	8,999,976	9,146,015	9,163,230	9,090,300
Births	3,567,799	3,637,593	3,656,809	3,769,965	3,792,223
Utilization - Outpatient					
Emergency Outpatient Visits	143,432,284	143,454,611	144,814,804	144,842,743	143,472,685
Other Outpatient Visits	641,802,972	622,937,901	621,261,320	611,955,033	587,316,680
Total Outpatient Visits	785,235,256	766,392,512	766,076,124	756,797,776	730,789,365
Outpatient Surgeries	19,418,138	19,168,038	19,075,759	18,987,342	18,255,921
Personnel					
Full Time RNs	1,322,217	1,306,941	1,286,055	1,243,105	1,209,663
Full Time LPNs	63,352	63,951	65,258	65,671	65,168
Part Time RNs	575,878	559,832	543,927	530,458	511,318
Part Time LPNs	22,403	22,170	22,550	22,602	22,800
Total Full Time	4,600,213	4,549,056	4,536,326	4,428,178	4,316,593
Total Part Time	1,678,799	1,632,575	1,615,066	1,562,816	1,498,135
Revenue - Inpatient					
Gross Inpatient Revenue	$2,065,300,409,602	$1,954,134,346,431	$1,828,199,494,787	$1,724,871,915,665	$1,626,668,095,308
Revenue - Outpatient					
Gross Outpatient Revenue	$2,046,742,087,953	$1,899,176,649,534	$1,735,481,161,564	$1,595,298,023,801	$1,449,622,014,476
Revenue and Expenses - Totals					
(Includes Inpatient and Outpatient)*					
Total Gross Revenue	$4,112,042,497,555	$3,853,310,995,965	$3,563,680,656,351	$3,320,169,939,466	$3,076,290,109,784
Deductions from Revenue	3,047,888,562,684	2,837,413,915,863	2,593,749,705,025	2,390,464,007,070	2,193,434,642,349
Net Patient Revenue	1,064,153,934,871	1,015,897,080,102	969,930,951,326	929,705,932,396	882,855,467,435
Other Operating Revenue	73,503,463,990	66,870,658,766	62,161,422,278	56,838,224,377	53,572,386,431
Other Nonoperating Revenue	21,220,276,450	10,967,818,652	22,129,124,318	11,530,927,436	5,666,404,837
Total Net Revenue	1,158,877,675,311	1,093,735,557,520	1,054,221,497,922	998,075,084,209	942,094,258,703
Total Expenses	1,056,497,068,465	1,010,271,111,825	966,204,238,616	919,821,623,351	866,817,436,729
HOSPITAL UNIT (Excludes Separate Nursing Home Units)					
Utilization - Inpatient					
Beds	755,167	757,609	762,082	757,845	756,638
Admissions	33,965,386	34,130,471	34,177,056	33,879,304	33,658,444
Inpatient Days	174,701,046	174,295,886	174,595,676	172,927,585	171,607,055
Average Length of Stay	5.1	5.1	5.1	5.1	5.1
Personnel					
Total Full Time	4,576,265	4,524,517	4,510,522	4,401,015	4,288,501
Total Part Time	1,665,851	1,618,824	1,601,249	1,548,166	1,482,541
Revenue and Expenses - Totals					
(Includes Inpatient and Outpatient)					
Total Net Revenue	$1,155,500,329,913	$1,090,294,539,512	$1,050,729,351,406	$994,186,728,374	$937,897,597,460
Total Expenses	1,053,626,260,562	1,007,386,710,365	963,274,967,298	916,791,175,275	863,389,336,253
COMMUNITY HEALTH INDICATORS PER 1000 POPULATION					
Total Population (in thousands)	328,240	327,167	325,719	323,128	321,419
Inpatient					
Beds	2.4	2.4	2.5	2.5	2.5
Admissions	103.8	104.7	105.3	105.3	105.2
Inpatient Days	564.1	566.4	571.7	575.9	576.1
Inpatient Surgeries	27.3	27.5	28.1	28.4	28.3
Births	10.9	11.1	11.2	11.7	11.8
Outpatient					
Emergency Outpatient Visits	437	438.5	444.6	448.3	446.4
Other Outpatient Visits	1,955.3	1,904	1,907.4	1,893.8	1,827.3
Total Outpatient Visits	2,392.3	2,342.5	2,352	2,342.1	2,273.6
Outpatient Surgeries	59.2	58.6	58.6	58.8	56.8
Expense per Capita (per person)	$3,218.7	$3,087.9	$2,966.4	$2,846.6	$2,696.8

*Calculating the total margin using an aggregate average for all U.S. hospitals based on total revenue and expenses can be misleading and should be avoided. Individual hospital margins vary widely and are driven by a range of factors, including facility or system size and type; local payer mix; geographic location; patient demographics; services provided, both clinical and non-medical; and relationships and affiliations with other entities in the community.

Note: These data represent hospital performance in the years 2015 – 2019 and do not reflect any impacts from the COVID-19 pandemic in 2020 and thereafter.

TABLE 3

TABLE 4

BED SIZE CATEGORY 6-24

U.S. Community Hospitals
(Nonfederal, short-term general and other special hospitals)

Overview 2015–2019

	2019	2018	2017	2016	2015
Total Community Hospitals in					
Bed Size Category 6-24..............................	734	709	702	679	661
Location					
Hospitals Urban	308	305	296	280	271
Hospitals Rural	426	404	406	399	390
Control					
State and Local Government	230	218	207	200	189
Not for Profit	324	307	305	290	284
Investor owned...	180	184	190	189	188
Affiliations					
Hospitals in a System	331	323	315	299	288
Hospitals in a Group Purchasing Organization...	445	438	426	438	415

Note: These data represent hospital performance in the years 2015 – 2019 and do not reflect any impacts from the COVID-19 pandemic in 2020 and thereafter.

Bed Size Categories

TABLE 4

BED SIZE CATEGORY 6-24

U.S. Community Hospitals
(Nonfederal, short-term general and other special hospitals)

Utilization, Personnel, Revenue and Expenses, Community Health Indicators 2015–2019

	2019	2018	2017	2016	2015
TOTAL FACILITY (Includes Hospital and Nursing Home Units)					
Utilization - Inpatient					
Beds	11,896	11,520	11,420	11,113	10,774
Admissions	328,106	300,190	286,420	274,695	269,510
Inpatient Days	1,364,348	1,368,699	1,311,383	1,276,782	1,249,593
Average Length of Stay	4.2	4.6	4.6	4.6	4.6
Inpatient Surgeries	90,819	96,125	96,791	93,894	85,293
Births	17,580	17,548	16,930	17,632	16,291
Utilization - Outpatient					
Emergency Outpatient Visits	3,140,643	2,874,014	2,826,451	2,518,497	2,417,585
Other Outpatient Visits	15,519,481	13,476,883	13,905,536	12,632,030	11,522,438
Total Outpatient Visits	18,660,124	16,350,897	16,731,987	15,150,527	13,940,023
Outpatient Surgeries	741,524	742,399	677,532	741,276	717,094
Personnel					
Full Time RNs	18,087	17,602	16,675	15,747	15,235
Full Time LPNs	2,887	2,666	2,742	2,708	2,678
Part Time RNs	13,100	11,798	11,384	10,194	9,731
Part Time LPNs	1,386	1,193	1,283	1,110	1,175
Total Full Time	76,788	73,136	71,027	67,929	64,546
Total Part Time	41,447	36,620	36,550	33,843	31,925
Revenue - Inpatient					
Gross Inpatient Revenue	$11,073,178,942	$10,830,956,036	$9,778,688,709	$9,142,081,581	$9,088,328,423
Revenue - Outpatient					
Gross Outpatient Revenue	$34,793,590,931	$31,775,025,112	$29,547,336,214	$26,198,110,530	$23,331,509,886
Revenue and Expenses - Totals **(Includes Inpatient and Outpatient)**					
Total Gross Revenue	$45,866,769,873	$42,605,981,148	$39,326,024,923	$35,340,192,111	$32,419,838,309
Deductions from Revenue	29,073,900,834	26,901,565,705	24,219,961,379	21,589,046,761	19,509,123,127
Net Patient Revenue	16,792,869,039	15,704,415,443	15,106,063,544	13,751,145,350	12,910,715,182
Other Operating Revenue	1,337,920,877	1,205,409,702	1,173,202,312	1,065,907,619	1,006,317,298
Other Nonoperating Revenue	251,464,148	181,272,094	264,323,188	156,929,101	125,822,443
Total Net Revenue	18,382,254,064	17,091,097,239	16,543,589,044	14,973,982,070	14,042,854,923
Total Expenses	17,052,064,513	16,009,948,476	15,339,422,895	13,691,403,067	12,655,032,137
HOSPITAL UNIT (Excludes Separate Nursing Home Units)					
Utilization - Inpatient					
Beds	11,874	11,502	11,388	11,099	10,736
Admissions	328,085	300,172	286,401	274,656	269,488
Inpatient Days	1,357,228	1,347,775	1,299,954	1,264,707	1,235,131
Average Length of Stay	4.1	4.5	4.5	4.6	4.6
Personnel					
Total Full Time	76,654	73,092	70,900	67,875	64,420
Total Part Time	41,425	36,606	36,502	33,814	31,820
Revenue and Expenses - Totals **(Includes Inpatient and Outpatient)**					
Total Net Revenue	$18,379,175,469	$17,086,982,642	$16,534,305,204	$14,970,628,566	$14,029,507,210
Total Expenses	17,049,897,171	16,008,113,736	15,330,350,410	13,689,670,442	12,647,866,538

Bed Size Categories

Note: These data represent hospital performance in the years 2015 – 2019 and do not reflect any impacts from the COVID-19 pandemic in 2020 and thereafter.

TABLE 4

BED SIZE CATEGORY 25-49

U.S. Community Hospitals
(Nonfederal, short-term general and other special hospitals)

Overview 2015–2019

	2019	2018	2017	2016	2015
Total Community Hospitals in					
Bed Size Category 25-49...............................	1,257	1,273	1,280	1,287	1,299
Location					
Hospitals Urban	539	537	525	534	549
Hospitals Rural..	718	736	755	753	750
Control					
State and Local Government.............................	330	344	345	348	358
Not for Profit...	604	596	599	602	598
Investor owned...	323	333	336	337	343
Affiliations					
Hospitals in a System	755	751	744	735	722
Hospitals in a Group Purchasing Organization...	744	793	825	856	864

Note: These data represent hospital performance in the years 2015 – 2019 and do not reflect any impacts from the COVID-19 pandemic in 2020 and thereafter.

16   AHA Hospital Statistics © 2021 Health Forum LLC, an affiliate of the American Hospital Association

Table **4**

BED SIZE CATEGORY 25-49

U.S. Community Hospitals
(Nonfederal, short-term general and other special hospitals)

Utilization, Personnel, Revenue and Expenses, Community Health Indicators 2015–2019

	2019	2018	2017	2016	2015
TOTAL FACILITY (Includes Hospital and Nursing Home Units)					
Utilization - Inpatient					
Beds	41,049	41,235	41,577	41,873	42,432
Admissions	1,133,257	1,132,000	1,152,958	1,158,573	1,174,221
Inpatient Days	6,399,323	6,387,419	6,524,153	6,664,309	6,843,482
Average Length of Stay	5.6	5.6	5.7	5.8	5.8
Inpatient Surgeries	297,298	286,320	277,388	274,982	265,572
Births	111,185	111,188	111,036	117,092	117,682
Utilization - Outpatient					
Emergency Outpatient Visits	9,557,119	9,306,326	9,597,498	9,627,150	9,588,377
Other Outpatient Visits	48,658,996	48,273,206	48,106,283	45,989,021	43,712,954
Total Outpatient Visits	58,216,115	57,579,532	57,703,781	55,616,171	53,301,331
Outpatient Surgeries	1,510,956	1,431,257	1,431,999	1,438,892	1,315,512
Personnel					
Full Time RNs	52,139	51,921	52,041	51,219	50,240
Full Time LPNs	7,935	7,945	8,226	8,386	8,590
Part Time RNs	35,206	32,476	30,989	29,900	29,568
Part Time LPNs	3,768	3,644	3,615	3,603	3,603
Total Full Time	227,492	225,583	224,884	224,394	220,934
Total Part Time	119,164	109,257	107,614	104,414	101,989
Revenue - Inpatient					
Gross Inpatient Revenue	$44,383,108,147	$41,516,929,635	$42,200,271,489	$40,859,498,214	$36,665,977,457
Revenue - Outpatient					
Gross Outpatient Revenue	$91,522,487,499	$84,350,985,021	$80,927,112,832	$73,479,316,580	$65,092,119,761
Revenue and Expenses - Totals **(Includes Inpatient and Outpatient)**					
Total Gross Revenue	$135,905,595,646	$125,867,914,656	$123,127,384,321	$114,338,814,794	$101,758,097,218
Deductions from Revenue	88,888,144,627	81,300,001,569	79,919,021,230	72,521,186,543	62,405,035,622
Net Patient Revenue	47,017,451,019	44,567,913,087	43,208,363,091	41,817,628,251	39,353,061,596
Other Operating Revenue	3,612,918,068	3,380,029,691	3,437,207,504	3,165,988,389	3,381,277,188
Other Nonoperating Revenue	713,154,514	678,717,959	800,579,184	453,216,555	290,603,836
Total Net Revenue	51,343,523,601	48,626,660,737	47,446,149,779	45,436,833,195	43,024,942,620
Total Expenses	47,303,681,222	45,162,296,596	43,902,826,128	41,990,899,330	39,447,143,677
HOSPITAL UNIT (Excludes Separate Nursing Home Units)					
Utilization - Inpatient					
Beds	40,112	40,232	40,507	40,782	41,006
Admissions	1,131,886	1,130,378	1,151,645	1,156,428	1,170,796
Inpatient Days	6,096,572	6,078,511	6,205,300	6,327,160	6,405,967
Average Length of Stay	5.4	5.4	5.4	5.5	5.5
Personnel					
Total Full Time	226,715	224,796	224,119	223,573	219,983
Total Part Time	118,472	108,699	107,091	103,857	101,417
Revenue and Expenses - Totals **(Includes Inpatient and Outpatient)**					
Total Net Revenue	$51,246,787,231	$48,537,943,978	$47,361,509,525	$45,355,140,097	$42,931,418,685
Total Expenses	47,235,444,449	45,104,946,538	43,844,827,581	41,929,469,606	39,367,348,971

Note: These data represent hospital performance in the years 2015 – 2019 and do not reflect any impacts from the COVID-19 pandemic in 2020 and thereafter.

Bed Size Categories

TABLE 4

BED SIZE CATEGORY 50-99

U.S. Community Hospitals
(Nonfederal, short-term general and other special hospitals)

Overview 2015–2019

	2019	2018	2017	2016	2015
Total Community Hospitals in					
Bed Size Category 50-99..................................	897	926	958	984	981
Location					
Hospitals Urban	538	554	566	579	567
Hospitals Rural...	359	372	392	405	414
Control					
State and Local Government............................	140	140	152	157	170
Not for Profit...	440	456	472	471	474
Investor owned..	317	330	334	356	337
Affiliations					
Hospitals in a System	619	642	649	667	656
Hospitals in a Group Purchasing Organization...	532	558	591	651	656

Bed Size Categories

Note: These data represent hospital performance in the years 2015 – 2019 and do not reflect any impacts from the COVID-19 pandemic in 2020 and thereafter.

TABLE 4

BED SIZE CATEGORY 50-99

U.S. Community Hospitals
(Nonfederal, short-term general and other special hospitals)

Utilization, Personnel, Revenue and Expenses, Community Health Indicators 2015–2019

	2019	2018	2017	2016	2015
TOTAL FACILITY (Includes Hospital and Nursing Home Units)					
Utilization - Inpatient					
Beds	63,176	65,577	67,626	69,353	69,428
Admissions	1,927,731	1,952,262	2,009,164	2,051,600	2,068,108
Inpatient Days	12,627,390	12,870,385	13,205,034	13,757,454	13,944,884
Average Length of Stay	6.6	6.6	6.6	6.7	6.7
Inpatient Surgeries	434,339	440,205	463,475	477,900	475,783
Births	190,015	198,622	206,130	217,012	223,851
Utilization - Outpatient					
Emergency Outpatient Visits	11,440,166	11,795,684	11,821,744	12,325,400	12,300,312
Other Outpatient Visits	49,138,538	48,671,114	50,097,108	49,763,388	50,061,523
Total Outpatient Visits	60,578,704	60,466,798	61,918,852	62,088,788	62,361,835
Outpatient Surgeries	1,636,578	1,631,225	1,693,119	1,677,328	1,627,896
Personnel					
Full Time RNs	74,371	74,287	73,880	73,248	70,989
Full Time LPNs	6,858	7,164	7,493	7,875	7,521
Part Time RNs	42,678	41,920	41,802	40,239	38,553
Part Time LPNs	3,196	3,075	3,130	3,228	3,296
Total Full Time	278,717	279,600	288,891	288,209	282,937
Total Part Time	139,994	138,503	134,689	133,104	129,805
Revenue - Inpatient					
Gross Inpatient Revenue	$84,207,178,410	$79,994,046,508	$75,850,968,886	$78,004,363,998	$72,496,665,325
Revenue - Outpatient					
Gross Outpatient Revenue	$132,359,221,236	$123,999,677,235	$116,294,503,085	$108,608,744,641	$99,303,107,157
Revenue and Expenses - Totals					
(Includes Inpatient and Outpatient)					
Total Gross Revenue	$216,566,399,646	$203,993,723,743	$192,145,471,971	$186,613,108,639	$171,799,772,482
Deductions from Revenue	154,833,482,785	144,623,520,680	133,443,528,400	129,271,400,259	116,619,928,734
Net Patient Revenue	61,732,916,861	59,370,203,063	58,701,943,571	57,341,708,380	55,179,843,748
Other Operating Revenue	2,582,880,857	3,223,851,504	2,841,250,532	2,407,584,609	2,297,948,097
Other Nonoperating Revenue	1,104,851,425	690,716,864	976,628,990	1,010,087,635	474,657,665
Total Net Revenue	65,420,649,143	63,284,771,431	62,519,823,093	60,759,380,624	57,952,449,510
Total Expenses	59,086,738,054	58,260,509,684	57,027,149,040	55,024,483,921	52,625,115,630
HOSPITAL UNIT (Excludes Separate Nursing Home Units)					
Utilization - Inpatient					
Beds	57,123	58,952	60,921	61,412	61,225
Admissions	1,918,858	1,940,103	1,997,189	2,035,369	2,052,732
Inpatient Days	10,706,740	10,830,300	11,110,149	11,301,269	11,443,238
Average Length of Stay	5.6	5.6	5.6	5.6	5.6
Personnel					
Total Full Time	275,188	275,781	284,814	283,403	278,170
Total Part Time	137,459	135,502	131,682	129,831	126,385
Revenue and Expenses - Totals					
(Includes Inpatient and Outpatient)					
Total Net Revenue	$64,961,069,998	$62,644,969,868	$61,992,352,547	$60,176,787,492	$57,370,883,476
Total Expenses	58,695,109,279	57,803,310,461	56,620,413,956	54,587,299,929	52,175,749,266

Bed Size Categories

Note: These data represent hospital performance in the years 2015 – 2019 and do not reflect any impacts from the COVID-19 pandemic in 2020 and thereafter.

TABLE 4

BED SIZE CATEGORY 100-199

U.S. Community Hospitals
(Nonfederal, short-term general and other special hospitals)

Overview 2015–2019

	2019	2018	2017	2016	2015
Total Community Hospitals in					
Bed Size Category 100-199..........................	952	976	1,004	993	1,012
Location					
Hospitals Urban	720	737	754	741	759
Hospitals Rural.......................................	232	239	250	252	253
Control					
State and Local Government.............................	104	108	112	120	128
Not for Profit..	622	618	630	614	615
Investor owned..	226	250	262	259	269
Affiliations					
Hospitals in a System	727	753	769	751	755
Hospitals in a Group Purchasing Organization...	631	663	688	696	722

Note: These data represent hospital performance in the years 2015 – 2019 and do not reflect any impacts from the COVID-19 pandemic in 2020 and thereafter.

TABLE 4

BED SIZE CATEGORY 100-199

U.S. Community Hospitals
(Nonfederal, short-term general and other special hospitals)

Utilization, Personnel, Revenue and Expenses, Community Health Indicators 2015–2019

	2019	2018	2017	2016	2015
TOTAL FACILITY (Includes Hospital and Nursing Home Units)					
Utilization - Inpatient					
Beds	136,707	140,651	144,449	143,276	146,402
Admissions	5,548,899	5,681,848	5,832,423	5,792,440	5,874,950
Inpatient Days	29,492,392	30,172,662	31,065,823	30,839,169	31,197,826
Average Length of Stay	5.3	5.3	5.3	5.3	5.3
Inpatient Surgeries	1,295,666	1,327,988	1,393,776	1,410,645	1,432,005
Births	585,757	613,615	618,215	661,966	685,860
Utilization - Outpatient					
Emergency Outpatient Visits	28,888,633	29,428,234	30,807,241	30,347,648	30,524,600
Other Outpatient Visits	111,813,825	109,134,141	112,650,412	108,921,984	105,452,877
Total Outpatient Visits	140,702,458	138,562,375	143,457,653	139,269,632	135,977,477
Outpatient Surgeries	3,409,716	3,492,140	3,519,122	3,468,590	3,428,174
Personnel					
Full Time RNs	189,072	191,742	195,418	188,253	186,608
Full Time LPNs	11,404	11,833	12,714	12,961	12,986
Part Time RNs	94,581	94,773	91,651	89,108	89,124
Part Time LPNs	4,151	4,317	4,284	4,490	4,785
Total Full Time	658,501	667,890	685,798	664,767	657,239
Total Part Time	285,005	282,551	287,514	272,582	268,823
Revenue - Inpatient					
Gross Inpatient Revenue	$284,945,823,099	$276,093,068,193	$261,616,656,494	$244,638,343,616	$242,773,915,327
Revenue - Outpatient					
Gross Outpatient Revenue	$347,249,197,564	$330,116,908,756	$308,226,085,579	$283,794,182,313	$263,510,107,907
Revenue and Expenses - Totals					
(Includes Inpatient and Outpatient)					
Total Gross Revenue	$632,195,020,663	$606,209,976,949	$569,842,742,073	$528,432,525,929	$506,284,023,234
Deductions from Revenue	477,870,052,587	453,873,247,949	421,195,235,299	385,763,913,509	369,351,494,568
Net Patient Revenue	154,324,968,076	152,336,729,000	148,647,506,774	142,668,612,420	136,932,528,666
Other Operating Revenue	6,060,714,244	6,038,214,375	6,069,573,210	5,538,614,499	5,297,327,380
Other Nonoperating Revenue	2,123,232,564	1,510,436,888	2,384,719,238	1,588,767,597	1,087,873,784
Total Net Revenue	162,508,914,884	159,885,380,263	157,101,799,222	149,795,994,516	143,317,729,830
Total Expenses	148,187,315,995	145,774,705,204	143,208,395,246	137,745,139,413	131,156,836,622
HOSPITAL UNIT (Excludes Separate Nursing Home Units)					
Utilization - Inpatient					
Beds	126,528	130,053	133,173	131,565	133,813
Admissions	5,517,976	5,649,668	5,798,467	5,754,004	5,833,603
Inpatient Days	26,336,252	26,820,362	27,530,031	27,043,414	27,180,189
Average Length of Stay	4.8	4.7	4.7	4.7	4.7
Personnel					
Total Full Time	651,489	661,376	678,751	657,840	649,799
Total Part Time	280,866	278,786	283,425	268,422	264,301
Revenue and Expenses - Totals					
(Includes Inpatient and Outpatient)					
Total Net Revenue	$161,550,975,020	$158,979,606,115	$156,120,327,656	$148,749,917,312	$142,258,138,929
Total Expenses	147,420,009,006	145,072,641,675	142,388,712,781	136,974,942,673	130,325,913,440

Note: These data represent hospital performance in the years 2015 – 2019 and do not reflect any impacts from the COVID-19 pandemic in 2020 and thereafter.

Bed Size Categories

TABLE 4

BED SIZE CATEGORY 200-299

U.S. Community Hospitals
(Nonfederal, short-term general and other special hospitals)

Overview 2015–2019

	2019	2018	2017	2016	2015
Total Community Hospitals in					
Bed Size Category 200-299............................	515	534	525	536	540
Location					
Hospitals Urban	465	485	474	483	480
Hospitals Rural..	50	49	51	53	60
Control					
State and Local Government	56	54	56	47	49
Not for Profit..	356	368	362	376	377
Investor owned...	103	112	107	113	114
Affiliations					
Hospitals in a System	402	415	398	408	401
Hospitals in a Group Purchasing Organization...	351	384	379	410	413

Bed Size Categories

Note: These data represent hospital performance in the years 2015 – 2019 and do not reflect any impacts from the COVID-19 pandemic in 2020 and thereafter.

TABLE 4

BED SIZE CATEGORY 200-299

U.S. Community Hospitals
(Nonfederal, short-term general and other special hospitals)

Utilization, Personnel, Revenue and Expenses, Community Health Indicators 2015–2019

	2019	2018	2017	2016	2015
TOTAL FACILITY (Includes Hospital and Nursing Home Units)					
Utilization - Inpatient					
Beds	125,372	130,039	128,567	130,944	132,511
Admissions	5,813,060	6,059,101	5,901,380	5,899,749	5,961,613
Inpatient Days	28,915,694	29,818,814	29,357,896	29,685,052	30,185,830
Average Length of Stay	5.0	4.9	5.0	5.0	5.1
Inpatient Surgeries	1,459,807	1,507,119	1,477,047	1,543,196	1,556,491
Births	639,859	668,737	641,735	669,548	681,351
Utilization - Outpatient					
Emergency Outpatient Visits	25,049,922	25,763,395	24,991,925	25,357,995	25,394,219
Other Outpatient Visits	90,507,436	91,108,227	90,251,134	92,626,063	88,712,242
Total Outpatient Visits	115,557,358	116,871,622	115,243,059	117,984,058	114,106,461
Outpatient Surgeries	2,962,199	3,028,436	2,984,593	3,037,046	2,973,379
Personnel					
Full Time RNs	199,684	200,697	191,481	188,761	185,992
Full Time LPNs	9,095	9,017	8,848	8,731	8,965
Part Time RNs	92,587	94,255	86,857	87,628	85,457
Part Time LPNs	2,778	2,980	2,781	3,002	3,190
Total Full Time	664,859	672,784	663,746	658,090	646,286
Total Part Time	253,497	261,448	247,905	250,868	247,434
Revenue - Inpatient					
Gross Inpatient Revenue	$335,240,971,129	$328,565,952,560	$293,205,465,736	$288,233,540,105	$275,115,799,389
Revenue - Outpatient					
Gross Outpatient Revenue	$324,229,840,662	$311,758,492,335	$274,681,515,373	$260,731,807,994	$239,981,662,067
Revenue and Expenses - Totals					
(Includes Inpatient and Outpatient)					
Total Gross Revenue	$659,470,811,791	$640,324,444,895	$567,886,981,109	$548,965,348,099	$515,097,461,456
Deductions from Revenue	500,270,435,902	483,904,772,060	422,295,188,737	406,609,958,906	377,088,997,065
Net Patient Revenue	159,200,375,889	156,419,672,835	145,591,792,372	142,355,389,193	138,008,464,391
Other Operating Revenue	10,518,031,727	9,312,684,078	8,558,847,012	7,590,883,742	7,089,406,292
Other Nonoperating Revenue	2,639,070,250	2,067,585,082	2,997,312,305	1,121,754,713	661,460,068
Total Net Revenue	172,357,477,866	167,799,941,995	157,147,951,689	151,068,027,648	145,759,330,751
Total Expenses	155,998,257,292	153,795,250,842	144,573,168,126	139,577,553,074	133,990,565,452
HOSPITAL UNIT (Excludes Separate Nursing Home Units)					
Utilization - Inpatient					
Beds	121,032	125,081	123,225	124,879	125,940
Admissions	5,794,088	6,037,697	5,879,090	5,870,263	5,929,111
Inpatient Days	27,525,745	28,272,785	27,713,594	27,774,329	28,108,010
Average Length of Stay	4.8	4.7	4.7	4.7	4.7
Personnel					
Total Full Time	661,108	668,565	659,895	653,525	641,497
Total Part Time	251,566	259,006	246,062	248,463	244,907
Revenue and Expenses - Totals					
(Includes Inpatient and Outpatient)					
Total Net Revenue	$171,850,602,019	$167,277,236,690	$156,626,396,116	$150,481,613,192	$145,108,108,511
Total Expenses	155,595,065,939	153,369,117,497	144,165,193,240	139,115,462,086	133,426,533,719

Bed Size Categories

Note: These data represent hospital performance in the years 2015 – 2019 and do not reflect any impacts from the COVID-19 pandemic in 2020 and thereafter.

TABLE 4

TABLE 4 — BED SIZE CATEGORY 300-399

U.S. Community Hospitals
(Nonfederal, short-term general and other special hospitals)

Overview 2015–2019

	2019	2018	2017	2016	2015
Total Community Hospitals in					
Bed Size Category 300-399.............	326	316	326	326	326
Location					
Hospitals Urban......................................	312	301	313	311	311
Hospitals Rural.......................................	14	15	13	15	15
Control					
State and Local Government......................	26	27	24	28	31
Not for Profit..	259	244	251	241	239
Investor owned.......................................	41	45	51	57	56
Affiliations					
Hospitals in a System	258	247	257	252	251
Hospitals in a Group Purchasing Organization...	251	252	259	258	267

Note: These data represent hospital performance in the years 2015 – 2019 and do not reflect any impacts from the COVID-19 pandemic in 2020 and thereafter.

Bed Size Categories

TABLE **4**

BED SIZE CATEGORY 300-399

U.S. Community Hospitals
(Nonfederal, short-term general and other special hospitals)

Utilization, Personnel, Revenue and Expenses, Community Health Indicators 2015–2019

	2019	2018	2017	2016	2015
TOTAL FACILITY (Includes Hospital and Nursing Home Units)					
Utilization - Inpatient					
Beds	113,166	109,634	112,745	112,577	112,455
Admissions	5,412,719	5,238,165	5,423,160	5,331,203	5,262,176
Inpatient Days	27,379,817	26,539,470	27,202,964	27,121,803	26,795,261
Average Length of Stay	5.1	5.1	5.0	5.1	5.1
Inpatient Surgeries	1,339,783	1,282,576	1,344,675	1,359,326	1,357,395
Births	601,183	581,720	607,994	613,760	615,418
Utilization - Outpatient					
Emergency Outpatient Visits	19,952,051	19,039,409	20,167,290	20,499,067	20,225,688
Other Outpatient Visits	74,883,667	68,229,543	69,077,082	65,722,792	67,637,921
Total Outpatient Visits	94,835,718	87,268,952	89,244,372	86,221,859	87,863,609
Outpatient Surgeries	2,380,600	2,227,227	2,296,325	2,286,604	2,241,108
Personnel					
Full Time RNs	189,507	179,100	186,324	179,329	172,767
Full Time LPNs	6,205	6,066	6,370	6,889	6,586
Part Time RNs	77,986	70,873	70,363	69,248	67,627
Part Time LPNs	1,642	1,700	1,810	1,890	1,874
Total Full Time	609,571	571,379	583,150	576,077	562,350
Total Part Time	212,430	197,569	196,975	194,564	186,034
Revenue - Inpatient					
Gross Inpatient Revenue	$331,938,543,627	$306,938,841,700	$304,818,908,631	$280,597,556,752	$265,645,362,957
Revenue - Outpatient					
Gross Outpatient Revenue	$280,572,152,552	$250,594,007,283	$244,167,243,699	$222,604,869,777	$207,236,507,753
Revenue and Expenses - Totals					
(Includes Inpatient and Outpatient)					
Total Gross Revenue	$612,510,696,179	$557,532,848,983	$548,986,152,330	$503,202,426,529	$472,881,870,710
Deductions from Revenue	463,477,320,679	421,526,843,881	416,336,037,183	375,800,264,832	350,115,114,752
Net Patient Revenue	149,033,375,500	136,006,005,102	132,650,115,147	127,402,161,697	122,766,755,958
Other Operating Revenue	8,555,174,934	6,815,780,527	6,345,361,823	6,462,417,145	5,932,273,631
Other Nonoperating Revenue	3,167,617,076	1,163,991,719	2,808,947,575	1,440,869,063	579,235,644
Total Net Revenue	160,756,167,510	143,985,777,348	141,804,424,545	135,305,447,905	129,278,265,233
Total Expenses	146,203,333,959	133,643,420,415	130,558,477,866	125,675,146,111	119,036,254,837
HOSPITAL UNIT (Excludes Separate Nursing Home Units)					
Utilization - Inpatient					
Beds	110,530	106,565	109,507	109,709	108,969
Admissions	5,396,430	5,219,274	5,403,146	5,311,011	5,240,771
Inpatient Days	26,553,307	25,593,987	26,229,602	26,253,272	25,845,364
Average Length of Stay	4.9	4.9	4.9	4.9	4.9
Personnel					
Total Full Time	607,659	569,151	580,848	574,021	559,783
Total Part Time	211,718	196,540	195,980	193,655	184,990
Revenue and Expenses - Totals					
(Includes Inpatient and Outpatient)					
Total Net Revenue	$160,379,483,371	$143,588,448,352	$141,392,172,422	$134,954,919,007	$128,804,888,548
Total Expenses	145,902,221,759	133,369,098,772	130,265,500,477	125,428,359,609	118,779,535,305

Bed Size Categories

Note: These data represent hospital performance in the years 2015 – 2019 and do not reflect any impacts from the COVID-19 pandemic in 2020 and thereafter.

TABLE **4**

BED SIZE CATEGORY 400-499

U.S. Community Hospitals
(Nonfederal, short-term general and other special hospitals)

Overview 2015–2019

	2019	2018	2017	2016	2015
Total Community Hospitals in					
Bed Size Category 400-499............................	163	172	178	177	177
Location					
Hospitals Urban	159	168	174	174	174
Hospitals Rural	4	4	4	3	3
Control					
State and Local Government	25	25	25	24	27
Not for Profit...	116	125	131	132	131
Investor owned	22	22	22	21	19
Affiliations					
Hospitals in a System	120	126	133	132	132
Hospitals in a Group Purchasing Organization...	120	141	150	155	152

Note: These data represent hospital performance in the years 2015 – 2019 and do not reflect any impacts from the COVID-19 pandemic in 2020 and thereafter.

TABLE **4**

BED SIZE CATEGORY 400-499

U.S. Community Hospitals
(Nonfederal, short-term general and other special hospitals)

Utilization, Personnel, Revenue and Expenses, Community Health Indicators 2015–2019

	2019	2018	2017	2016	2015
TOTAL FACILITY (Includes Hospital and Nursing Home Units)					
Utilization - Inpatient					
Beds	72,228	76,085	78,819	78,381	78,276
Admissions	3,394,108	3,640,816	3,702,602	3,635,759	3,623,728
Inpatient Days	18,087,000	19,206,768	19,681,221	19,526,076	19,473,188
Average Length of Stay	5.3	5.3	5.3	5.4	5.4
Inpatient Surgeries	927,948	998,127	1,068,403	1,023,758	1,010,724
Births	352,236	391,871	411,062	423,939	411,527
Utilization - Outpatient					
Emergency Outpatient Visits	12,204,408	12,996,637	13,024,540	13,365,313	12,899,493
Other Outpatient Visits	58,746,995	62,225,182	64,043,413	63,490,384	60,672,737
Total Outpatient Visits	70,951,403	75,221,819	77,067,953	76,855,697	73,572,230
Outpatient Surgeries	1,570,054	1,691,233	1,715,438	1,731,964	1,657,487
Personnel					
Full Time RNs	125,093	133,759	133,957	130,381	130,384
Full Time LPNs	3,874	4,552	4,922	4,685	5,331
Part Time RNs	58,605	61,069	63,947	62,368	55,114
Part Time LPNs	1,376	1,329	1,791	1,637	1,672
Total Full Time	432,759	465,042	475,228	459,454	455,341
Total Part Time	164,005	166,852	179,541	168,874	148,821
Revenue - Inpatient					
Gross Inpatient Revenue	$225,285,771,201	$225,740,270,635	$210,182,049,797	$195,381,045,588	$180,553,181,341
Revenue - Outpatient					
Gross Outpatient Revenue	$198,988,155,047	$193,541,835,015	$179,560,208,114	$165,777,551,470	$147,175,644,365
Revenue and Expenses - Totals **(Includes Inpatient and Outpatient)**					
Total Gross Revenue	$424,273,926,248	$419,282,105,650	$389,742,257,911	$361,158,597,058	$327,728,825,706
Deductions from Revenue	316,827,242,612	310,630,131,102	281,916,354,523	259,825,436,261	232,365,473,589
Net Patient Revenue	107,446,683,636	108,651,974,548	107,825,903,388	101,333,160,797	95,363,352,117
Other Operating Revenue	8,315,410,932	9,056,159,360	8,282,744,699	7,037,077,408	6,844,706,592
Other Nonoperating Revenue	2,216,416,640	1,397,558,796	2,974,682,811	1,510,800,476	629,938,259
Total Net Revenue	117,978,511,208	119,105,692,704	119,083,330,898	109,881,038,681	102,837,996,968
Total Expenses	108,862,645,703	111,036,054,693	110,015,554,300	101,971,588,975	95,428,252,524
HOSPITAL UNIT (Excludes Separate Nursing Home Units)					
Utilization - Inpatient					
Beds	70,517	74,451	76,442	75,456	75,634
Admissions	3,387,037	3,632,418	3,692,145	3,623,636	3,612,535
Inpatient Days	17,520,212	18,667,855	18,918,935	18,582,706	18,592,108
Average Length of Stay	5.2	5.1	5.1	5.1	5.1
Personnel					
Total Full Time	431,441	463,521	473,219	456,875	453,504
Total Part Time	163,339	166,075	178,390	167,786	147,860
Revenue and Expenses - Totals **(Includes Inpatient and Outpatient)**					
Total Net Revenue	$117,770,402,499	$118,950,248,786	$118,815,857,506	$109,423,042,300	$102,416,396,046
Total Expenses	108,689,914,266	110,869,485,113	109,780,991,366	101,678,240,509	95,075,355,257

Note: These data represent hospital performance in the years 2015 – 2019 and do not reflect any impacts from the COVID-19 pandemic in 2020 and thereafter.

Bed Size Categories

TABLE **4**

BED SIZE CATEGORY 500 +

U.S. Community Hospitals
(Nonfederal, short-term general and other special hospitals)

Overview 2015–2019

	2019	2018	2017	2016	2015
Total Community Hospitals in					
Bed Size Category 500 +.................................	297	292	289	285	284
Location					
Hospitals Urban	295	290	285	283	282
Hospitals Rural..	2	2	4	2	2
Control					
State and Local Government	51	49	51	50	51
Not for Profit..	225	223	218	217	214
Investor owned..	21	20	20	18	19
Affiliations					
Hospitals in a System	241	234	229	223	213
Hospitals in a Group Purchasing Organization...	267	262	265	262	264

Bed Size Categories

Note: These data represent hospital performance in the years 2015 – 2019 and do not reflect any impacts from the COVID-19 pandemic in 2020 and thereafter.

TABLE 4

BED SIZE CATEGORY 500 +

U.S. Community Hospitals
(Nonfederal, short-term general and other special hospitals)

Utilization, Personnel, Revenue and Expenses, Community Health Indicators 2015–2019

	2019	2018	2017	2016	2015
TOTAL FACILITY (Includes Hospital and Nursing Home Units)					
Utilization - Inpatient					
Beds	224,401	217,676	213,718	211,927	208,550
Admissions	10,520,220	10,246,777	9,997,513	9,887,568	9,582,979
Inpatient Days	60,883,964	58,943,011	57,850,503	57,218,809	55,481,018
Average Length of Stay	5.8	5.8	5.8	5.8	5.8
Inpatient Surgeries	3,104,899	3,061,516	3,024,460	2,979,529	2,907,037
Births	1,069,984	1,054,292	1,043,707	1,049,016	1,040,243
Utilization - Outpatient					
Emergency Outpatient Visits	33,199,342	32,250,912	31,578,115	30,801,673	30,122,411
Other Outpatient Visits	192,534,034	181,819,605	173,130,352	172,809,371	159,543,988
Total Outpatient Visits	225,733,376	214,070,517	204,708,467	203,611,044	189,666,399
Outpatient Surgeries	5,206,511	4,924,121	4,757,631	4,605,642	4,295,271
Personnel					
Full Time RNs	474,264	457,833	436,279	416,167	397,448
Full Time LPNs	15,094	14,708	13,943	13,436	12,511
Part Time RNs	161,135	152,668	146,934	141,773	136,144
Part Time LPNs	4,106	3,932	3,856	3,642	3,205
Total Full Time	1,651,526	1,593,642	1,543,602	1,489,258	1,426,960
Total Part Time	463,257	439,775	424,278	404,567	383,304
Revenue - Inpatient					
Gross Inpatient Revenue	$748,225,835,047	$684,454,281,164	$630,546,485,045	$588,015,485,811	$544,328,865,089
Revenue - Outpatient					
Gross Outpatient Revenue	$637,027,442,462	$573,039,718,777	$502,077,156,668	$454,103,440,496	$403,991,355,580
Revenue and Expenses - Totals					
(Includes Inpatient and Outpatient)					
Total Gross Revenue	$1,385,253,277,509	$1,257,493,999,941	$1,132,623,641,713	$1,042,118,926,307	$948,320,220,669
Deductions from Revenue	1016647982658	914,653,832,917	814,424,378,274	739,082,799,999	665,979,474,892
Net Patient Revenue	368,605,294,851	342,840,167,024	318,199,263,439	303,036,126,308	282,340,745,777
Other Operating Revenue	32,520,412,351	27,838,529,529	25,453,235,186	23,569,750,966	21,723,129,953
Other Nonoperating Revenue	9,004,469,833	3,277,539,250	8,921,931,027	4,248,502,296	1,816,813,138
Total Net Revenue	410,130,177,035	373,956,235,803	352,574,429,652	330,854,379,570	305,880,688,868
Total Expenses	373,803,031,727	346,588,925,915	321,579,245,015	304,145,409,460	282,478,235,850
HOSPITAL UNIT (Excludes Separate Nursing Home Units)					
Utilization - Inpatient					
Beds	217,451	210,773	206,919	202,943	199,315
Admissions	10,491,026	10,220,761	9,968,973	9,853,937	9,549,408
Inpatient Days	58,604,990	56,684,311	55,588,111	54,380,728	52,797,048
Average Length of Stay	5.6	5.5	5.6	5.5	5.5
Personnel					
Total Full Time	1,646,011	1,588,235	1,537,976	1,483,903	1,421,345
Total Part Time	461,006	437,610	422,117	402,338	380,861
Revenue and Expenses - Totals					
(Includes Inpatient and Outpatient)					
Total Net Revenue	$409,361,834,306	$373,229,103,081	$351,886,430,430	$330,074,680,408	$304,978,256,055
Total Expenses	373,038,598,693	345,789,996,573	320,878,977,487	303,387,730,421	281,591,033,757

Note: These data represent hospital performance in the years 2015 – 2019 and do not reflect any impacts from the COVID-19 pandemic in 2020 and thereafter.

Bed Size Categories

Census Divisions

Census Division 1

New England
Connecticut, Maine, Massachusetts, New Hampshire, Rhode Island, Vermont

Census Division 2

Middle Atlantic
New Jersey, New York, Pennsylvania

Census Division 3

South Atlantic
Delaware, District of Columbia, Florida, Georgia, Maryland, North Carolina, South Carolina, Virginia, West Virginia

Census Division 4

East North Central
Illinois, Indiana, Michigan, Ohio, Wisconsin

Census Division 5

East South Central
Alabama, Kentucky, Mississippi, Tennessee

Census Division 6

West North Central
Iowa, Kansas, Minnesota, Missouri, Nebraska, North Dakota, South Dakota

Census Division 7

West South Central
Arkansas, Louisiana, Oklahoma, Texas

Census Division 8

Mountain
Arizona, Colorado, Idaho, Montana, Nevada, New Mexico, Utah, Wyoming

Census Division 9

Pacific
Alaska, California, Hawaii, Oregon, Washington

U.S. Census Divisions

Note: These data represent hospital performance in the years 2015 – 2019 and do not reflect any impacts from the COVID-19 pandemic in 2020 and thereafter.

TABLE 5

U.S. CENSUS DIVISION 1: NEW ENGLAND

U.S. Community Hospitals
(Nonfederal, short-term general and other special hospitals)

Overview 2015–2019

	2019	2018	2017	2016	2015
Total Community Hospitals in Census Division 1, New England	192	194	194	197	198
Bed Size Category					
6-24	10	6	7	8	9
25-49	40	43	45	44	43
50-99	41	46	44	45	46
100-199	52	49	49	50	50
200-299	20	21	20	20	19
300-399	13	13	13	13	13
400-499	7	6	6	6	7
500 +	9	10	10	11	11
Location					
Hospitals Urban	138	140	139	142	143
Hospitals Rural	54	54	55	55	55
Control					
State and Local Government	5	5	6	6	7
Not for Profit	164	165	165	165	165
Investor owned	23	24	23	26	26
Affiliations					
Hospitals in a System	125	124	116	114	111
Hospitals in a Group Purchasing Organization	130	130	136	144	143

Note: These data represent hospital performance in the years 2015 – 2019 and do not reflect any impacts from the COVID-19 pandemic in 2020 and thereafter.

TABLE 5

U.S. CENSUS DIVISION 1: NEW ENGLAND

U.S. Community Hospitals
(Nonfederal, short-term general and other special hospitals)

Utilization, Personnel, Revenue and Expenses, Community Health Indicators 2015–2019

	2019	2018	2017	2016	2015
TOTAL FACILITY (Includes Hospital and Nursing Home Units)					
Utilization - Inpatient					
Beds	32,559	32,518	32,381	32,798	32,982
Admissions	1,567,740	1,568,835	1,575,699	1,572,638	1,564,096
Inpatient Days	8,682,964	8,594,184	8,500,057	8,389,746	8,414,349
Average Length of Stay	5.5	5.5	5.4	5.3	5.4
Inpatient Surgeries	408,843	404,164	409,253	421,285	403,646
Births	140,837	141,919	142,432	145,980	146,737
Utilization - Outpatient					
Emergency Outpatient Visits	7,366,120	7,232,392	7,169,939	7,203,699	7,432,227
Other Outpatient Visits	42,698,043	41,702,724	41,935,936	41,650,761	42,528,908
Total Outpatient Visits	50,064,163	48,935,116	49,105,875	48,854,460	49,961,135
Outpatient Surgeries	962,963	944,218	945,843	955,559	933,953
Personnel					
Full Time RNs	59,673	55,675	52,855	51,635	49,718
Full Time LPNs	1,780	1,751	1,819	1,906	1,876
Part Time RNs	44,256	43,281	42,823	42,561	42,203
Part Time LPNs	927	961	989	1,022	1,065
Total Full Time	257,916	250,096	245,661	241,784	232,406
Total Part Time	134,921	132,766	130,616	129,384	124,979
Revenue - Inpatient					
Gross Inpatient Revenue	$76,933,552,852	$69,320,012,790	$65,351,524,702	$61,830,211,505	$59,894,209,408
Revenue - Outpatient					
Gross Outpatient Revenue	$100,646,085,816	$92,986,888,760	$85,502,734,369	$79,400,285,127	$73,575,255,239
Revenue and Expenses - Totals (Includes Inpatient and Outpatient)					
Total Gross Revenue	$177,579,638,668	$162,306,901,550	$150,854,259,071	$141,230,496,632	$133,469,464,647
Deductions from Revenue	117,799,450,968	105,988,883,876	97,672,640,734	89,734,448,326	84,542,326,724
Net Patient Revenue	59,780,187,700	56,318,017,674	53,181,618,337	51,496,048,306	48,927,137,923
Other Operating Revenue	7,647,887,856	6,956,242,998	6,403,861,165	5,852,308,514	5,443,226,980
Other Nonoperating Revenue	448,909,073	721,832,247	1,349,590,545	435,024,537	1,610,536
Total Net Revenue	67,876,984,629	63,996,092,919	60,935,070,047	57,783,381,357	54,371,975,439
Total Expenses	64,448,761,769	61,818,990,334	58,229,116,358	55,722,351,201	52,320,879,636
HOSPITAL UNIT (Excludes Separate Nursing Home Units)					
Utilization - Inpatient					
Beds	31,709	31,668	31,545	31,971	32,099
Admissions	1,565,910	1,566,971	1,573,483	1,568,033	1,560,023
Inpatient Days	8,418,636	8,331,410	8,229,699	8,111,694	8,190,451
Average Length of Stay	5.4	5.3	5.2	5.2	5.3
Personnel					
Total Full Time	257,053	249,149	244,828	240,793	231,833
Total Part Time	134,266	131,956	129,934	128,662	124,482
Revenue and Expenses - Totals (Includes Inpatient and Outpatient)					
Total Net Revenue	$67,793,133,094	$63,862,618,896	$60,842,803,483	$57,713,090,473	$54,306,839,201
Total Expenses	64,364,350,372	61,737,516,328	58,146,580,760	55,650,107,626	52,258,626,830
COMMUNITY HEALTH INDICATORS PER 1000 POPULATION					
Total Population (in thousands)	14,845	14,853	14,810	14,736	14,728
Inpatient					
Beds	2.2	2.2	2.2	2.2	2.2
Admissions	105.6	105.6	106.4	106.7	106.2
Inpatient Days	584.9	578.6	573.9	569.4	571.3
Inpatient Surgeries	27.5	27.2	27.6	28.6	27.4
Births	9.5	9.6	9.6	9.9	10
Outpatient					
Emergency Outpatient Visits	496.2	486.9	484.1	488.9	504.6
Other Outpatient Visits	2,876.2	2,807.6	2,831.6	2,826.6	2,887.7
Total Outpatient Visits	3,372.4	3,294.6	3,315.7	3,315.4	3,392.4
Outpatient Surgeries	64.9	63.6	63.9	64.8	63.4
Expense per Capita (per person)	$4,341.4	$4,162	$3,931.7	$3,781.5	$3,552.6

Note: These data represent hospital performance in the years 2015 – 2019 and do not reflect any impacts from the COVID-19 pandemic in 2020 and thereafter.

U.S. Census Divisions

TABLE 5

U.S. CENSUS DIVISION 2: MIDDLE ATLANTIC

U.S. Community Hospitals
(Nonfederal, short-term general and other special hospitals)

Overview 2015–2019

	2019	2018	2017	2016	2015
Total Community Hospitals					
in Census Division 2, Middle Atlantic	435	447	451	447	450
Bed Size Category					
6-24	23	20	19	17	17
25-49	46	50	49	45	45
50-99	66	70	71	68	69
100-199	115	115	120	114	110
200-299	62	72	68	79	81
300-399	48	44	46	43	50
400-499	21	24	23	25	21
500 + ...	54	52	55	56	57
Location					
Hospitals Urban	366	375	378	373	376
Hospitals Rural	69	72	73	74	74
Control					
State and Local Government	27	25	24	25	26
Not for Profit	348	355	357	348	349
Investor owned	60	67	70	74	75
Affiliations					
Hospitals in a System	301	312	313	309	297
Hospitals in a Group Purchasing Organization...	292	305	310	320	318

Note: These data represent hospital performance in the years 2015 – 2019 and do not reflect any impacts from the COVID-19 pandemic in 2020 and thereafter.

U.S. Census Divisions

TABLE 5

U.S. CENSUS DIVISION 2: MIDDLE ATLANTIC

U.S. Community Hospitals
(Nonfederal, short-term general and other special hospitals)

Utilization, Personnel, Revenue and Expenses, Community Health Indicators 2015–2019

	2019	2018	2017	2016	2015
TOTAL FACILITY (Includes Hospital and Nursing Home Units)					
Utilization - Inpatient					
Beds	108,395	109,558	110,228	111,576	111,933
Admissions	4,847,024	4,919,808	4,952,686	4,881,134	4,801,155
Inpatient Days	28,091,060	28,429,768	28,747,702	28,914,190	28,945,442
Average Length of Stay	5.8	5.8	5.8	5.9	6.0
Inpatient Surgeries	1,210,079	1,240,226	1,260,590	1,291,183	1,278,886
Births	437,062	449,748	453,226	458,856	456,132
Utilization - Outpatient					
Emergency Outpatient Visits	18,582,130	18,746,561	19,015,614	19,270,939	18,800,932
Other Outpatient Visits	97,478,356	95,944,515	95,492,856	94,082,875	94,685,833
Total Outpatient Visits	116,060,486	114,691,076	114,508,470	113,353,814	113,486,765
Outpatient Surgeries	2,753,593	2,651,080	2,755,513	2,791,357	2,638,686
Personnel					
Full Time RNs	196,433	191,768	187,285	181,017	172,602
Full Time LPNs	7,996	8,418	8,050	7,631	7,756
Part Time RNs	63,586	64,203	62,635	63,572	62,891
Part Time LPNs	2,167	2,387	2,356	2,083	2,345
Total Full Time	731,633	715,362	709,056	686,863	664,024
Total Part Time	204,982	211,260	207,512	204,785	200,419
Revenue - Inpatient					
Gross Inpatient Revenue	$323,661,026,295	$310,286,173,968	$290,627,007,329	$273,728,219,303	$259,514,194,359
Revenue - Outpatient					
Gross Outpatient Revenue	$291,983,315,540	$269,976,112,983	$244,410,827,628	$223,895,470,604	$199,070,271,649
Revenue and Expenses - Totals **(Includes Inpatient and Outpatient)**					
Total Gross Revenue	$615,644,341,835	$580,262,286,951	$535,037,834,957	$497,623,689,907	$458,584,466,008
Deductions from Revenue	458,828,346,638	431,039,813,469	392,884,763,242	360,654,188,619	330,264,595,845
Net Patient Revenue	156,815,995,197	149,222,473,482	142,153,071,715	136,969,501,288	128,319,870,163
Other Operating Revenue	13,618,805,935	11,885,774,926	10,485,737,315	10,075,295,538	8,788,492,843
Other Nonoperating Revenue	3,438,079,363	1,540,333,205	3,092,173,756	1,766,195,709	822,319,089
Total Net Revenue	173,872,880,495	162,648,581,613	155,730,982,786	148,810,992,535	137,930,682,095
Total Expenses	164,736,016,632	155,671,561,838	147,584,661,438	141,061,102,926	132,115,490,562
HOSPITAL UNIT (Excludes Separate Nursing Home Units)					
Utilization - Inpatient					
Beds	102,125	102,862	103,972	105,327	105,383
Admissions	4,821,486	4,895,085	4,927,855	4,855,503	4,773,917
Inpatient Days	25,982,699	26,173,836	26,587,023	26,813,342	26,714,754
Average Length of Stay	5.4	5.3	5.4	5.5	5.6
Personnel					
Total Full Time	726,842	710,333	704,448	682,044	659,101
Total Part Time	202,385	208,325	204,986	202,194	197,710
Revenue and Expenses - Totals **(Includes Inpatient and Outpatient)**					
Total Net Revenue	$173,129,796,966	$161,895,608,899	$155,067,991,642	$148,100,904,512	$137,158,329,913
Total Expenses	164,091,967,282	154,928,089,646	146,977,890,632	140,507,459,911	131,381,363,604
COMMUNITY HEALTH INDICATORS PER 1000 POPULATION					
Total Population (in thousands)	41,138	41,258	41,661	41,474	41,556
Inpatient					
Beds	2.6	2.7	2.6	2.7	2.7
Admissions	117.8	119.2	118.9	117.7	115.5
Inpatient Days	682.9	689.1	690	697.2	696.5
Inpatient Surgeries	29.4	30.1	30.3	31.1	30.8
Births	10.6	10.9	10.9	11.1	11
Outpatient					
Emergency Outpatient Visits	451.7	454.4	456.4	464.7	452.4
Other Outpatient Visits	2,369.6	2,325.5	2,292.2	2,268.5	2,278.5
Total Outpatient Visits	2,821.3	2,779.9	2,748.6	2,733.1	2,730.9
Outpatient Surgeries	66.9	64.3	66.1	67.3	63.5
Expense per Capita (per person)	$4,004.5	$3,773.1	$3,542.5	$3,401.2	$3,179.2

Note: These data represent hospital performance in the years 2015 – 2019 and do not reflect any impacts from the COVID-19 pandemic in 2020 and thereafter.

U.S. Census Divisions

TABLE 5

U.S. CENSUS DIVISION 3: SOUTH ATLANTIC

U.S. Community Hospitals
(Nonfederal, short-term general and other special hospitals)

Overview 2015–2019

	2019	2018	2017	2016	2015
Total Community Hospitals					
in Census Division 3, South Atlantic.............	752	762	772	777	776
Bed Size Category					
6-24	42	38	37	35	33
25-49	127	139	136	141	146
50-99	151	150	155	159	150
100-199	170	170	179	180	185
200-299	102	107	106	97	100
300-399	59	56	57	63	58
400-499	31	34	38	39	43
500 + ...	70	68	64	63	61
Location					
Hospitals Urban	571	575	577	576	575
Hospitals Rural.................................	181	187	195	201	201
Control					
State and Local Government	119	116	117	120	130
Not for Profit....................................	431	422	431	426	416
Investor owned.................................	202	224	224	231	230
Affiliations					
Hospitals in a System	608	609	616	609	603
Hospitals in a Group Purchasing Organization...	425	465	472	518	531

Note: These data represent hospital performance in the years 2015 – 2019 and do not reflect any impacts from the COVID-19 pandemic in 2020 and thereafter.

U.S. Census Divisions

TABLE 5

U.S. CENSUS DIVISION 3: SOUTH ATLANTIC

U.S. Community Hospitals
(Nonfederal, short-term general and other special hospitals)

Utilization, Personnel, Revenue and Expenses, Community Health Indicators 2015–2019

	2019	2018	2017	2016	2015
TOTAL FACILITY (Includes Hospital and Nursing Home Units)					
Utilization - Inpatient					
Beds	155,077	155,252	156,661	156,005	155,048
Admissions	7,091,809	7,048,355	6,984,783	6,964,479	6,928,987
Inpatient Days	38,487,726	38,380,244	38,275,242	38,040,494	37,744,998
Average Length of Stay	5.4	5.4	5.5	5.5	5.4
Inpatient Surgeries	1,837,512	1,818,474	1,853,499	1,858,852	1,848,627
Births	681,302	693,224	692,369	718,961	713,380
Utilization - Outpatient					
Emergency Outpatient Visits	29,444,522	29,421,949	29,427,572	30,111,854	29,291,065
Other Outpatient Visits	96,031,889	91,349,681	89,486,998	89,269,211	81,308,444
Total Outpatient Visits	125,476,411	120,771,630	118,914,570	119,381,065	110,599,509
Outpatient Surgeries	3,531,359	3,534,616	3,549,269	3,571,128	3,461,813
Personnel					
Full Time RNs	265,371	260,893	254,336	248,715	245,634
Full Time LPNs	10,945	11,322	11,281	11,657	11,226
Part Time RNs	86,674	84,678	84,437	80,780	79,807
Part Time LPNs	2,981	3,164	3,180	2,992	3,019
Total Full Time	873,851	853,293	842,087	828,955	819,601
Total Part Time	248,136	240,572	244,142	230,625	230,190
Revenue - Inpatient					
Gross Inpatient Revenue	$395,665,371,754	$377,032,361,778	$337,071,905,359	$323,223,182,426	$303,627,447,165
Revenue - Outpatient					
Gross Outpatient Revenue	$368,229,296,426	$345,879,406,350	$308,366,745,577	$289,502,664,972	$263,543,811,931
Revenue and Expenses - Totals (Includes Inpatient and Outpatient)					
Total Gross Revenue	$763,894,668,180	$722,911,768,128	$645,438,650,936	$612,725,847,398	$567,171,259,096
Deductions from Revenue	575,114,889,132	540,856,878,155	472,523,824,118	446,974,466,650	410,233,958,738
Net Patient Revenue	188,779,779,048	182,054,889,973	172,914,826,818	165,751,380,748	156,937,300,358
Other Operating Revenue	9,043,308,093	7,972,766,763	7,423,653,408	7,222,778,667	7,124,386,646
Other Nonoperating Revenue	4,195,599,149	1,903,883,723	3,641,262,398	1,624,905,284	847,067,335
Total Net Revenue	202,018,686,290	191,931,540,459	183,979,742,624	174,599,064,699	164,908,754,339
Total Expenses	180,686,824,830	171,614,912,124	163,845,481,573	157,287,329,689	149,736,371,726
HOSPITAL UNIT (Excludes Separate Nursing Home Units)					
Utilization - Inpatient					
Beds	148,208	148,197	148,474	147,494	146,512
Admissions	7,065,484	7,022,307	6,954,431	6,930,946	6,895,436
Inpatient Days	36,367,150	36,163,691	35,667,474	35,317,674	34,938,376
Average Length of Stay	5.1	5.1	5.1	5.1	5.1
Personnel					
Total Full Time	868,270	847,710	835,911	822,891	813,376
Total Part Time	246,157	238,701	241,984	228,612	227,914
Revenue and Expenses - Totals (Includes Inpatient and Outpatient)					
Total Net Revenue	$201,423,930,874	$191,375,003,372	$183,305,444,355	$173,929,226,809	$164,194,813,402
Total Expenses	180,106,730,968	171,072,168,619	163,233,180,906	156,691,799,119	149,094,286,196
COMMUNITY HEALTH INDICATORS PER 1000 POPULATION					
Total Population (in thousands)	65,785	65,322	64,706	63,923	63,277
Inpatient					
Beds	2.4	2.4	2.4	2.4	2.5
Admissions	107.8	107.9	107.9	109	109.5
Inpatient Days	585.1	587.6	591.5	595.1	596.5
Inpatient Surgeries	27.9	27.8	28.6	29.1	29.2
Births	10.4	10.6	10.7	11.2	11.3
Outpatient					
Emergency Outpatient Visits	447.6	450.4	454.8	471.1	462.9
Other Outpatient Visits	1,459.8	1,398.4	1383	1,396.5	1285
Total Outpatient Visits	1,907.4	1,848.9	1,837.8	1,867.6	1,747.9
Outpatient Surgeries	53.7	54.1	54.9	55.9	54.7
Expense per Capita (per person)	$2,746.6	$2,627.2	$2,532.2	$2,460.6	$2,366.4

Note: These data represent hospital performance in the years 2015 – 2019 and do not reflect any impacts from the COVID-19 pandemic in 2020 and thereafter.

U.S. Census Divisions

TABLE 5

U.S. CENSUS DIVISION 4: EAST NORTH CENTRAL

U.S. Community Hospitals
(Nonfederal, short-term general and other special hospitals)

Overview 2015–2019

	2019	2018	2017	2016	2015
Total Community Hospitals					
in Census Division 4, East North Central	786	790	798	800	799
Bed Size Category					
6-24	91	94	86	85	82
25-49	214	204	215	209	211
50-99	127	130	130	140	141
100-199	147	153	162	158	160
200-299	93	98	87	93	90
300-399	44	39	48	48	48
400-499	29	30	29	26	25
500 + ...	41	42	41	41	42
Location					
Hospitals Urban	520	523	527	529	525
Hospitals Rural	266	267	271	271	274
Control					
State and Local Government	72	73	74	77	82
Not for Profit	594	592	594	592	589
Investor owned	120	125	130	131	128
Affiliations					
Hospitals in a System	567	563	565	557	548
Hospitals in a Group Purchasing Organization...	575	595	616	614	613

Note: These data represent hospital performance in the years 2015 – 2019 and do not reflect any impacts from the COVID-19 pandemic in 2020 and thereafter.

U.S. Census Divisions

TABLE 5

U.S. CENSUS DIVISION 4: EAST NORTH CENTRAL

U.S. Community Hospitals
(Nonfederal, short-term general and other special hospitals)

Utilization, Personnel, Revenue and Expenses, Community Health Indicators 2015–2019

	2019	2018	2017	2016	2015
TOTAL FACILITY (Includes Hospital and Nursing Home Units)					
Utilization - Inpatient					
Beds	119,505	120,431	120,736	121,229	121,622
Admissions	5,110,267	5,172,215	5,214,548	5,228,579	5,242,877
Inpatient Days	26,249,955	26,044,143	26,260,795	26,365,860	26,505,511
Average Length of Stay	5.1	5.0	5.0	5.0	5.1
Inpatient Surgeries	1,355,515	1,358,165	1,380,263	1,398,408	1,389,830
Births	494,785	509,652	516,804	526,761	529,316
Utilization - Outpatient					
Emergency Outpatient Visits	23,077,533	23,484,742	23,897,233	23,605,718	23,449,181
Other Outpatient Visits	142,254,069	137,450,943	136,706,994	133,694,756	128,207,598
Total Outpatient Visits	165,331,602	160,935,685	160,604,227	157,300,474	151,656,779
Outpatient Surgeries	3,475,789	3,376,611	3,315,630	3,338,721	3,237,099
Personnel					
Full Time RNs	207,972	210,140	203,759	198,727	192,693
Full Time LPNs	7,667	7,375	7,467	7,483	7,320
Part Time RNs	103,444	100,904	100,528	100,456	96,641
Part Time LPNs	3,528	3,300	3,575	3,697	3,888
Total Full Time	741,577	739,498	727,272	720,352	699,819
Total Part Time	330,869	313,164	324,355	311,429	298,257
Revenue - Inpatient					
Gross Inpatient Revenue	$267,766,072,067	$250,746,080,306	$243,538,573,096	$230,746,665,771	$219,502,768,303
Revenue - Outpatient					
Gross Outpatient Revenue	$327,769,163,782	$301,714,760,289	$284,277,236,033	$262,668,327,994	$242,488,289,719
Revenue and Expenses - Totals (Includes Inpatient and Outpatient)					
Total Gross Revenue	$595,535,235,849	$552,460,840,595	$527,815,809,129	$493,414,993,765	$461,991,058,022
Deductions from Revenue	420,520,870,088	386,921,862,869	368,675,734,372	339,703,465,116	314,575,493,329
Net Patient Revenue	175,014,365,761	165,538,977,726	159,140,074,757	153,711,528,649	147,415,564,693
Other Operating Revenue	12,042,647,376	10,753,628,778	10,409,900,979	9,302,273,067	8,952,183,723
Other Nonoperating Revenue	5,216,928,208	959,496,411	4,992,318,253	3,135,831,056	152,534,827
Total Net Revenue	192,273,941,345	177,252,102,915	174,542,293,989	166,149,632,772	156,520,283,243
Total Expenses	172,406,307,769	163,823,031,053	157,010,029,843	150,771,194,405	143,004,245,304
HOSPITAL UNIT (Excludes Separate Nursing Home Units)					
Utilization - Inpatient					
Beds	116,132	116,940	116,999	117,012	116,923
Admissions	5,093,042	5,154,039	5,195,053	5,203,892	5,217,258
Inpatient Days	25,168,834	25,004,277	25,162,892	25,104,084	25,122,980
Average Length of Stay	4.9	4.9	4.8	4.8	4.8
Personnel					
Total Full Time	739,612	737,274	724,883	717,812	697,066
Total Part Time	329,394	311,753	322,818	309,605	296,145
Revenue and Expenses - Totals (Includes Inpatient and Outpatient)					
Total Net Revenue	$191,949,332,422	$176,942,534,983	$174,197,294,404	$165,629,888,462	$156,016,367,637
Total Expenses	172,135,215,314	163,580,923,008	156,743,956,191	150,459,681,796	142,675,288,534
COMMUNITY HEALTH INDICATORS PER 1000 POPULATION					
Total Population (in thousands)	46,902	46,932	46,885	46,756	46,787
Inpatient					
Beds	2.5	2.6	2.6	2.6	2.6
Admissions	109	110.2	111.2	111.8	112.1
Inpatient Days	559.7	554.9	560.1	563.9	566.5
Inpatient Surgeries	28.9	28.9	29.4	29.9	29.7
Births	10.5	10.9	11	11.3	11.3
Outpatient					
Emergency Outpatient Visits	492	500.4	509.7	504.9	501.2
Other Outpatient Visits	3,033	2,928.7	2,915.8	2,859.4	2,740.2
Total Outpatient Visits	3,525	3,429.1	3,425.5	3,364.3	3,241.4
Outpatient Surgeries	74.1	71.9	70.7	71.4	69.2
Expense per Capita (per person)	$3,675.9	$3,490.7	$3,348.8	$3,224.6	$3,056.5

Note: These data represent hospital performance in the years 2015 – 2019 and do not reflect any impacts from the COVID-19 pandemic in 2020 and thereafter.

U.S. Census Divisions

TABLE 5

U.S. CENSUS DIVISION 5: EAST SOUTH CENTRAL

U.S. Community Hospitals
(Nonfederal, short-term general and other special hospitals)

Overview 2015–2019

	2019	2018	2017	2016	2015
Total Community Hospitals					
in Census Division 5, East South Central......	414	420	433	436	438
Bed Size Category					
6-24	26	23	21	22	21
25-49	128	129	134	130	137
50-99	87	92	98	104	93
100-199	86	87	87	89	92
200-299	33	32	35	37	39
300-399	20	23	25	24	26
400-499	12	11	10	10	9
500 + ...	22	23	23	20	21
Location					
Hospitals Urban	206	208	210	213	213
Hospitals Rural..................................	208	212	223	223	225
Control					
State and Local Government	107	106	107	106	109
Not for Profit.....................................	186	187	189	186	183
Investor owned..................................	121	127	137	144	146
Affiliations					
Hospitals in a System	291	296	307	311	310
Hospitals in a Group Purchasing Organization...	219	234	250	255	255

Note: These data represent hospital performance in the years 2015 – 2019 and do not reflect any impacts from the COVID-19 pandemic in 2020 and thereafter.

U.S. Census Divisions

TABLE 5

U.S. CENSUS DIVISION 5: EAST SOUTH CENTRAL

U.S. Community Hospitals
(Nonfederal, short-term general and other special hospitals)

Utilization, Personnel, Revenue and Expenses, Community Health Indicators 2015–2019

	2019	2018	2017	2016	2015
TOTAL FACILITY (Includes Hospital and Nursing Home Units)					
Utilization - Inpatient					
Beds	59,389	61,065	61,933	61,566	61,840
Admissions	2,374,549	2,376,945	2,408,935	2,410,333	2,375,117
Inpatient Days	13,613,204	13,684,891	13,763,525	13,776,156	13,730,078
Average Length of Stay	5.7	5.8	5.7	5.7	5.8
Inpatient Surgeries	679,486	653,249	660,467	674,940	654,679
Births	219,009	206,549	205,116	216,788	218,837
Utilization - Outpatient					
Emergency Outpatient Visits	10,371,715	10,182,201	10,175,145	10,208,107	10,291,598
Other Outpatient Visits	36,956,859	35,982,640	33,910,566	31,805,510	29,436,831
Total Outpatient Visits	47,328,574	46,164,841	44,085,711	42,013,617	39,728,429
Outpatient Surgeries	1,493,309	1,441,870	1,411,863	1,415,800	1,342,713
Personnel					
Full Time RNs	89,609	88,794	89,214	84,698	81,184
Full Time LPNs	5,212	5,312	5,186	5,431	5,756
Part Time RNs	32,322	30,742	28,285	29,775	26,724
Part Time LPNs	1,588	1,478	1,353	1,430	1,384
Total Full Time	294,223	292,690	295,100	277,141	272,012
Total Part Time	89,322	86,272	75,873	81,603	72,314
Revenue - Inpatient					
Gross Inpatient Revenue	$119,690,613,810	$116,414,010,283	$110,850,380,099	$103,537,591,698	$97,423,609,419
Revenue - Outpatient					
Gross Outpatient Revenue	$124,249,099,799	$120,838,680,439	$112,324,249,572	$102,216,851,815	$94,635,629,536
Revenue and Expenses - Totals (Includes Inpatient and Outpatient)					
Total Gross Revenue	$243,939,713,609	$237,252,690,722	$223,174,629,671	$205,754,443,513	$192,059,238,955
Deductions from Revenue	188,154,457,010	183,714,360,562	170,613,750,920	155,562,498,971	143,924,680,071
Net Patient Revenue	55,785,256,599	53,538,330,160	52,560,878,751	50,191,944,542	48,134,558,884
Other Operating Revenue	2,657,325,378	3,376,199,918	2,530,319,162	2,122,408,528	2,026,642,821
Other Nonoperating Revenue	840,445,588	630,632,298	862,457,322	432,014,508	270,564,942
Total Net Revenue	59,283,027,565	57,545,162,376	55,953,655,235	52,746,367,578	50,431,766,647
Total Expenses	54,743,321,912	54,472,166,409	52,142,988,014	48,065,025,107	45,792,700,335
HOSPITAL UNIT (Excludes Separate Nursing Home Units)					
Utilization - Inpatient					
Beds	56,560	57,886	58,702	58,249	57,974
Admissions	2,366,700	2,366,974	2,399,564	2,399,500	2,360,408
Inpatient Days	12,696,422	12,659,569	12,734,582	12,708,944	12,522,541
Average Length of Stay	5.4	5.3	5.3	5.3	5.3
Personnel					
Total Full Time	291,944	290,865	293,169	274,875	269,548
Total Part Time	88,576	85,582	75,224	80,928	71,587
Revenue and Expenses - Totals (Includes Inpatient and Outpatient)					
Total Net Revenue	$59,012,209,075	$57,243,364,763	$55,689,546,150	$52,426,793,648	$50,104,387,026
Total Expenses	54,557,988,039	54,256,477,081	51,949,397,807	47,828,983,049	45,538,459,158
COMMUNITY HEALTH INDICATORS PER 1000 POPULATION					
Total Population (in thousands)	19,176	19,113	19,029	18,940	18,877
Inpatient					
Beds	3.1	3.2	3.3	3.3	3.3
Admissions	123.8	124.4	126.6	127.3	125.8
Inpatient Days	709.9	716	723.3	727.4	727.4
Inpatient Surgeries	35.4	34.2	34.7	35.6	34.7
Births	11.4	10.8	10.8	11.4	11.6
Outpatient					
Emergency Outpatient Visits	540.9	532.7	534.7	539	545.2
Other Outpatient Visits	1,927.2	1,882.6	1782	1,679.3	1,559.4
Total Outpatient Visits	2,468.1	2,415.4	,2316.8	2,218.2	2,104.6
Outpatient Surgeries	77.9	75.4	74.2	74.8	71.1
Expense per Capita (per person)	$2,854.8	$2,850	$2,740.2	$2,537.7	$2,425.9

Note: These data represent hospital performance in the years 2015 – 2019 and do not reflect any impacts from the COVID-19 pandemic in 2020 and thereafter.

U.S. Census Divisions

TABLE 5

U.S. CENSUS DIVISION 6: WEST NORTH CENTRAL

U.S. Community Hospitals
(Nonfederal, short-term general and other special hospitals)

Overview 2015–2019

	2019	2018	2017	2016	2015
Total Community Hospitals					
in Census Division 6, West North Central	690	695	707	707	711
Bed Size Category					
6-24	184	174	175	166	160
25-49	207	217	215	221	224
50-99	131	134	143	144	149
100-199	82	83	84	87	90
200-299	31	29	33	33	34
300-399	23	25	23	22	22
400-499	9	10	13	12	13
500 + ...	23	23	21	22	19
Location					
Hospitals Urban	252	257	255	255	259
Hospitals Rural	438	438	452	452	452
Control					
State and Local Government	252	257	255	255	259
Not for Profit	438	438	452	452	452
Investor owned	70	72	78	77	77
Affiliations					
Hospitals in a System	393	396	387	380	377
Hospitals in a Group Purchasing Organization...	505	530	545	566	559

Note: These data represent hospital performance in the years 2015 – 2019 and do not reflect any impacts from the COVID-19 pandemic in 2020 and thereafter.

U.S. Census Divisions

TABLE 5

U.S. CENSUS DIVISION 6: WEST NORTH CENTRAL

U.S. Community Hospitals
(Nonfederal, short-term general and other special hospitals)

Utilization, Personnel, Revenue and Expenses, Community Health Indicators 2015–2019

	2019	2018	2017	2016	2015
TOTAL FACILITY (Includes Hospital and Nursing Home Units)					
Utilization - Inpatient					
Beds	65,660	65,986	66,538	66,863	67,175
Admissions	2,350,517	2,394,336	2,364,074	2,342,091	2,362,168
Inpatient Days	14,357,163	14,276,160	14,368,825	14,407,021	14,500,523
Average Length of Stay	6.1	6.0	6.1	6.2	6.1
Inpatient Surgeries	637,623	642,326	640,065	640,714	637,649
Births	248,734	254,862	263,309	268,409	269,450
Utilization - Outpatient					
Emergency Outpatient Visits	9,072,506	9,097,043	9,279,951	9,333,691	9,086,629
Other Outpatient Visits	63,541,419	61,459,345	59,949,830	58,815,832	54,821,386
Total Outpatient Visits	72,613,925	70,556,388	69,229,781	68,149,523	63,908,015
Outpatient Surgeries	1,546,701	1,511,307	1,513,858	1,474,098	1,441,415
Personnel					
Full Time RNs	92,304	89,720	90,570	86,845	85,648
Full Time LPNs	7,521	7,478	7,851	7,872	7,295
Part Time RNs	65,646	63,857	62,180	59,993	57,486
Part Time LPNs	3,924	3,932	3,840	4,089	3,998
Total Full Time	362,149	360,002	363,788	350,055	341,426
Total Part Time	188,614	184,236	182,796	178,375	169,794
Revenue - Inpatient					
Gross Inpatient Revenue	$113,408,745,471	$108,010,284,501	$101,222,231,765	$96,350,276,173	$91,076,952,927
Revenue - Outpatient					
Gross Outpatient Revenue	$140,889,870,644	$129,734,978,274	$119,625,573,925	$110,840,488,972	$100,766,113,874
Revenue and Expenses - Totals (Includes Inpatient and Outpatient)					
Total Gross Revenue	$254,298,616,115	$237,745,262,775	$220,847,805,690	$207,190,765,145	$191,843,066,801
Deductions from Revenue	174,487,425,593	160,982,453,970	147,648,643,930	136,875,950,492	125,564,533,862
Net Patient Revenue	79,811,190,522	76,762,808,805	73,199,161,760	70,314,814,653	66,278,532,939
Other Operating Revenue	5,378,701,207	4,591,142,983	4,453,925,579	4,080,125,886	3,945,267,080
Other Nonoperating Revenue	1,568,461,857	924,933,220	1,776,845,712	690,644,022	519,461,226
Total Net Revenue	86,758,353,586	82,278,885,008	79,429,933,051	75,085,584,561	70,743,261,245
Total Expenses	81,141,173,326	77,502,964,153	74,332,887,649	70,756,761,886	65,575,921,394
HOSPITAL UNIT (Excludes Separate Nursing Home Units)					
Utilization - Inpatient					
Beds	59,187	58,686	58,591	58,456	58,629
Admissions	2,338,478	2,380,728	2,349,441	2,326,725	2,345,773
Inpatient Days	12,245,081	11,954,884	11,881,917	11,693,107	11,793,242
Average Length of Stay	5.2	5.0	5.1	5.0	5.0
Personnel					
Total Full Time	358,581	356,186	359,134	345,419	336,821
Total Part Time	185,236	180,414	178,757	174,221	165,607
Revenue and Expenses - Totals (Includes Inpatient and Outpatient)					
Total Net Revenue	$86,265,546,147	$81,743,832,020	$78,851,249,035	$74,484,223,614	$70,145,580,361
Total Expenses	80,683,436,697	77,038,677,926	73,790,388,076	70,244,857,066	65,062,430,876
COMMUNITY HEALTH INDICATORS PER 1000 POPULATION					
Total Population (in thousands)	21,427	21,377	21,294	21,185	21,120
Inpatient					
Beds	3.1	3.1	3.1	3.2	3.2
Admissions	109.7	112	111	110.6	111.8
Inpatient Days	670.1	667.8	674.8	680	686.6
Inpatient Surgeries	29.8	30	30.1	30.2	30.2
Births	11.6	11.9	12.4	12.7	12.8
Outpatient					
Emergency Outpatient Visits	423.4	425.6	435.8	440.6	430.2
Other Outpatient Visits	2,965.5	2875	2,815.3	2,776.2	2,595.7
Total Outpatient Visits	3,389	3,300.6	3,251.1	3,216.8	3,025.9
Outpatient Surgeries	72.2	70.7	71.1	69.6	68.2
Expense per Capita (per person)	$3,786.9	$3,625.6	$3,490.8	$3,339.9	$3,104.9

Note: These data represent hospital performance in the years 2015 – 2019 and do not reflect any impacts from the COVID-19 pandemic in 2020 and thereafter.

U.S. Census Divisions

TABLE 5

U.S. CENSUS DIVISION 7: WEST SOUTH CENTRAL

U.S. Community Hospitals
(Nonfederal, short-term general and other special hospitals)

Overview 2015–2019

	2019	2018	2017	2016	2015
Total Community Hospitals in Census Division 7, West South Central	880	894	908	915	919
Bed Size Category					
6-24	216	215	214	209	203
25-49	273	270	273	282	279
50-99	137	146	153	167	173
100-199	105	113	116	104	113
200-299	58	57	59	61	61
300-399	41	41	41	40	34
400-499	12	14	14	15	18
500 +	38	38	38	37	38
Location					
Hospitals Urban	597	609	612	617	620
Hospitals Rural	283	285	296	298	299
Control					
State and Local Government	192	197	196	195	198
Not for Profit	283	277	289	291	289
Investor owned	405	420	423	429	432
Affiliations					
Hospitals in a System	517	533	542	547	535
Hospitals in a Group Purchasing Organization	680	687	711	735	731

Note: These data represent hospital performance in the years 2015 – 2019 and do not reflect any impacts from the COVID-19 pandemic in 2020 and thereafter.

44 AHA Hospital Statistics © 2021 Health Forum LLC, an affiliate of the American Hospital Association

TABLE 5

U.S. CENSUS DIVISION 7: WEST SOUTH CENTRAL

U.S. Community Hospitals
(Nonfederal, short-term general and other special hospitals)

Utilization, Personnel, Revenue and Expenses, Community Health Indicators 2015–2019

	2019	2018	2017	2016	2015
TOTAL FACILITY (Includes Hospital and Nursing Home Units)					
Utilization - Inpatient					
Beds	100,863	101,604	103,632	104,550	105,504
Admissions	4,159,278	4,111,344	4,140,484	4,083,773	4,061,793
Inpatient Days	21,792,893	21,799,328	22,004,809	22,428,019	22,152,153
Average Length of Stay	5.2	5.3	5.3	5.5	5.5
Inpatient Surgeries	1,121,608	1,147,081	1,160,291	1,141,313	1,143,331
Births	517,514	524,852	526,266	546,527	557,494
Utilization - Outpatient					
Emergency Outpatient Visits	18,544,338	18,555,948	18,272,095	17,776,792	17,407,271
Other Outpatient Visits	56,540,198	54,642,033	53,945,843	52,700,393	51,593,031
Total Outpatient Visits	75,084,536	73,197,981	72,217,938	70,477,185	69,000,302
Outpatient Surgeries	2,296,243	2,258,979	2,238,829	2,233,905	2,167,878
Personnel					
Full Time RNs	163,209	160,967	156,517	147,458	146,482
Full Time LPNs	12,527	12,490	12,803	12,946	13,342
Part Time RNs	46,173	45,531	46,578	42,998	41,328
Part Time LPNs	2,998	2,975	3,169	3,371	3,244
Total Full Time	510,946	506,553	497,635	491,716	483,728
Total Part Time	127,495	128,010	130,105	123,953	120,056
Revenue - Inpatient					
Gross Inpatient Revenue	$267,981,904,955	$250,007,475,401	$234,136,883,451	$219,217,167,814	$203,967,767,145
Revenue - Outpatient					
Gross Outpatient Revenue	$251,277,493,538	$229,798,345,492	$210,883,979,867	$191,661,353,361	$172,325,001,033
Revenue and Expenses - Totals					
(Includes Inpatient and Outpatient)					
Total Gross Revenue	$519,259,398,493	$479,805,820,893	$445,020,863,318	$410,878,521,175	$376,292,768,178
Deductions from Revenue	407,345,064,226	373,182,420,440	342,825,712,608	312,294,718,576	281,570,972,294
Net Patient Revenue	111,914,334,267	106,623,400,453	102,195,150,710	98,583,802,599	94,721,795,884
Other Operating Revenue	8,615,083,612	8,280,006,531	8,076,640,558	7,359,754,157	6,884,471,468
Other Nonoperating Revenue	1,722,593,867	1,388,258,023	1,985,706,768	1,376,270,607	961,453,633
Total Net Revenue	122,252,011,746	116,291,665,007	112,257,498,036	107,319,827,363	102,567,720,985
Total Expenses	108,791,172,633	105,979,025,827	102,290,621,099	97,186,117,632	91,348,374,898
HOSPITAL UNIT (Excludes Separate Nursing Home Units)					
Utilization - Inpatient					
Beds	99,373	100,186	101,976	101,124	102,029
Admissions	4,153,930	4,104,425	4,132,590	4,070,222	4,051,052
Inpatient Days	21,382,592	21,389,647	21,542,774	21,471,621	21,552,026
Average Length of Stay	5.1	5.2	5.2	5.3	5.3
Personnel					
Total Full Time	509,878	505,468	496,385	490,236	482,456
Total Part Time	127,277	127,784	129,850	123,578	119,709
Revenue and Expenses - Totals					
(Includes Inpatient and Outpatient)					
Total Net Revenue	$122,147,563,591	$116,187,074,787	$112,145,199,486	$107,140,343,993	$102,353,166,397
Total Expenses	108,693,032,202	105,891,857,095	102,185,229,938	97,023,654,812	91,159,380,304
COMMUNITY HEALTH INDICATORS PER 1000 POPULATION					
Total Population (in thousands)	40,619	40,319	39,924	39,456	39,029
Inpatient					
Beds	2.5	2.5	2.6	2.6	2.7
Admissions	102.4	102	103.7	103.5	104.1
Inpatient Days	536.5	540.7	551.2	568.4	567.6
Inpatient Surgeries	27.6	28.5	29.1	28.9	29.3
Births	12.7	13	13.2	13.9	14.3
Outpatient					
Emergency Outpatient Visits	456.5	460.2	457.7	450.5	446
Other Outpatient Visits	1,391.9	1,355.3	1,351.2	1,335.7	1,321.9
Total Outpatient Visits	1,848.5	1,815.5	1,808.9	1,786.2	1,767.9
Outpatient Surgeries	56.5	56	56.1	56.6	55.5
Expense per Capita (per person)	$2,678.3	$2,628.5	$2,562.1	$2,463.1	$2,340.5

Note: These data represent hospital performance in the years 2015 – 2019 and do not reflect any impacts from the COVID-19 pandemic in 2020 and thereafter.

U.S. Census Divisions

TABLE 5

U.S. CENSUS DIVISION 8: MOUNTAIN

U.S. Community Hospitals
(Nonfederal, short-term general and other special hospitals)

Overview 2015–2019

	2019	2018	2017	2016	2015
Total Community Hospitals					
in Census Division 8, Mountain	439	441	440	431	431
Bed Size Category					
6-24	95	92	94	87	86
25-49	124	124	117	116	113
50-99	80	79	84	82	87
100-199	60	68	66	66	65
200-299	33	35	34	34	34
300-399	20	18	17	18	19
400-499	11	10	11	11	11
500 + ...	16	15	17	17	16
Location					
Hospitals Urban	240	243	239	232	232
Hospitals Rural	199	198	201	199	199
Control					
State and Local Government	94	95	95	93	94
Not for Profit	215	212	208	203	206
Investor owned	130	134	137	135	131
Affiliations					
Hospitals in a System	275	282	268	264	264
Hospitals in a Group Purchasing Organization...	228	249	243	243	259

Note: These data represent hospital performance in the years 2015 – 2019 and do not reflect any impacts from the COVID-19 pandemic in 2020 and thereafter.

TABLE 5

U.S. CENSUS DIVISION 8: MOUNTAIN

U.S. Community Hospitals
(Nonfederal, short-term general and other special hospitals)

Utilization, Personnel, Revenue and Expenses, Community Health Indicators 2015–2019

	2019	2018	2017	2016	2015
TOTAL FACILITY (Includes Hospital and Nursing Home Units)					
Utilization - Inpatient					
Beds	49,513	49,444	49,910	49,691	49,745
Admissions	2,112,291	2,147,839	2,088,118	2,064,230	2,047,337
Inpatient Days	10,799,364	10,874,737	10,849,687	10,860,416	10,701,261
Average Length of Stay	5.1	5.1	5.2	5.3	5.2
Inpatient Surgeries	563,422	572,138	571,857	545,833	547,910
Births	258,112	263,794	256,103	270,077	276,794
Utilization - Outpatient					
Emergency Outpatient Visits	8,569,341	8,562,516	8,741,450	8,540,234	8,857,912
Other Outpatient Visits	35,478,058	35,421,848	39,392,323	38,753,142	37,101,728
Total Outpatient Visits	44,047,399	43,984,364	48,133,773	47,293,376	45,959,640
Outpatient Surgeries	1,170,024	1,211,911	1,188,246	1,144,071	1,090,393
Personnel					
Full Time RNs	83,816	85,140	81,652	79,537	77,678
Full Time LPNs	2,840	2,869	3,060	3,112	3,148
Part Time RNs	33,533	31,574	30,664	29,098	25,732
Part Time LPNs	1,200	1,083	1,109	1,099	1,042
Total Full Time	277,723	281,487	278,710	274,117	264,643
Total Part Time	97,673	91,042	90,331	86,903	76,673
Revenue - Inpatient					
Gross Inpatient Revenue	$143,160,734,761	$137,224,403,523	$127,065,584,270	$114,320,337,601	$107,570,651,520
Revenue - Outpatient					
Gross Outpatient Revenue	$138,561,364,536	$129,460,066,439	$118,381,642,743	$105,495,701,593	$96,561,960,931
Revenue and Expenses - Totals					
(Includes Inpatient and Outpatient)					
Total Gross Revenue	$281,722,099,297	$266,684,469,962	$245,447,227,013	$219,816,039,194	$204,132,612,451
Deductions from Revenue	211,453,183,115	199,477,161,151	181,193,923,278	160,309,936,042	148,266,285,800
Net Patient Revenue	70,268,916,182	67,207,308,811	64,253,303,735	59,506,103,152	55,866,326,651
Other Operating Revenue	2,811,249,840	2,642,791,209	2,431,647,680	2,249,148,855	2,142,968,711
Other Nonoperating Revenue	1,047,436,742	805,265,924	984,257,937	406,012,596	375,435,111
Total Net Revenue	74,127,602,764	70,655,365,944	67,669,209,352	62,161,264,603	58,384,730,473
Total Expenses	63,435,905,805	61,661,821,730	59,207,230,262	55,285,409,890	52,063,591,337
HOSPITAL UNIT (Excludes Separate Nursing Home Units)					
Utilization - Inpatient					
Beds	47,636	47,538	47,489	46,882	46,678
Admissions	2,109,615	2,143,477	2,082,167	2,057,743	2,039,745
Inpatient Days	10,226,487	10,307,405	10,138,723	10,026,784	9,786,684
Average Length of Stay	4.8	4.8	4.9	4.9	4.8
Personnel					
Total Full Time	276,545	280,127	277,141	272,318	262,908
Total Part Time	97,007	90,271	89,378	85,867	75,665
Revenue and Expenses - Totals					
(Includes Inpatient and Outpatient)					
Total Net Revenue	$73,997,016,166	$70,512,118,218	$67,427,260,242	$61,940,126,738	$58,168,286,532
Total Expenses	63,319,539,818	61,537,623,972	59,022,094,359	55,116,798,098	51,891,279,458
COMMUNITY HEALTH INDICATORS PER 1000 POPULATION					
Total Population (in thousands)	24,855	24,552	24,158	23,855	23,530
Inpatient					
Beds	2	2	2.1	2.1	2.1
Admissions	85	87.5	86.4	86.5	87
Inpatient Days	434.5	442.9	449.1	455.3	454.8
Inpatient Surgeries	22.7	23.3	23.7	22.9	23.3
Births	10.4	10.7	10.6	11.3	11.8
Outpatient					
Emergency Outpatient Visits	344.8	348.7	361.8	358	376.4
Other Outpatient Visits	,1427.4	1,442.7	1,630.6	1,624.5	1,576.8
Total Outpatient Visits	1,772.2	1,791.4	1,992.4	1,982.5	1,953.2
Outpatient Surgeries	47.1	49.4	49.2	48	46.3
Expense per Capita (per person)	$2552.2	2,511.4	2,450.8	2,317.6	2,212.6

Note: These data represent hospital performance in the years 2015 – 2019 and do not reflect any impacts from the COVID-19 pandemic in 2020 and thereafter.

U.S. Census Divisions

TABLE 5

U.S. CENSUS DIVISION 9: PACIFIC

U.S. Community Hospitals
(Nonfederal, short-term general and other special hospitals)

Overview 2015–2019

	2019	2018	2017	2016	2015
Total Community Hospitals					
in Census Division 9, Pacific	553	555	559	557	558
Bed Size Category					
6-24	47	47	49	50	50
25-49	98	97	96	99	101
50-99	77	79	80	75	73
100-199	135	138	141	145	147
200-299	83	83	83	82	82
300-399	58	57	56	55	56
400-499	31	33	34	33	30
500 +	24	21	20	18	19
Location					
Hospitals Urban	446	447	450	448	450
Hospitals Rural	107	108	109	109	108
Control					
State and Local Government	127	127	130	129	132
Not for Profit	324	325	329	325	326
Investor owned	102	103	100	103	100
Affiliations					
Hospitals in a System	376	376	380	376	373
Hospitals in a Group Purchasing Organization	287	296	300	331	344

Note: These data represent hospital performance in the years 2015 – 2019 and do not reflect any impacts from the COVID-19 pandemic in 2020 and thereafter.

U.S. Census Divisions

TABLE 5

U.S. CENSUS DIVISION 9: PACIFIC

U.S. Community Hospitals
(Nonfederal, short-term general and other special hospitals)

Utilization, Personnel, Revenue and Expenses, Community Health Indicators 2015–2019

	2019	2018	2017	2016	2015
TOTAL FACILITY (Includes Hospital and Nursing Home Units)					
Utilization - Inpatient					
Beds	97,034	96,559	96,902	95,166	94,979
Admissions	4,464,625	4,511,482	4,576,293	4,484,330	4,433,755
Inpatient Days	23,075,599	23,223,773	23,428,335	22,907,552	22,476,767
Average Length of Stay	5.2	5.1	5.1	5.1	5.1
Inpatient Surgeries	1,136,471	1,164,153	1,209,730	1,190,702	1,185,742
Births	570,444	592,993	601,184	617,606	624,083
Utilization - Outpatient					
Emergency Outpatient Visits	18,404,079	18,171,259	18,835,805	18,791,709	18,855,870
Other Outpatient Visits	70,824,081	68,984,172	70,439,974	71,182,553	67,632,921
Total Outpatient Visits	89,228,160	87,155,431	89,275,779	89,974,262	86,488,791
Outpatient Surgeries	2,188,157	2,237,446	2,156,708	2,062,703	1,941,971
Personnel					
Full Time RNs	163,830	163,844	169,867	164,473	158,024
Full Time LPNs	6,864	6,936	7,741	7,633	7,449
Part Time RNs	100,244	95,062	85,797	81,225	78,506
Part Time LPNs	3,090	2,890	2,979	2,819	2,815
Total Full Time	550,195	550,075	577,017	557,195	538,934
Total Part Time	256,787	245,253	229,336	215,759	205,453
Revenue - Inpatient					
Gross Inpatient Revenue	$357,032,387,637	$335,093,543,881	$318,335,404,716	$301,918,263,374	$284,090,495,062
Revenue - Outpatient					
Gross Outpatient Revenue	$303,136,397,872	$278,787,410,508	$251,708,171,850	$229,616,879,363	$206,655,680,564
Revenue and Expenses - Totals (Includes Inpatient and Outpatient)					
Total Gross Revenue	$660,168,785,509	$613,880,954,389	$570,043,576,566	$531,535,142,737	$490,746,175,626
Deductions from Revenue	494,184,875,914	455,250,081,371	419,710,711,823	388,354,334,278	354,491,795,686
Net Patient Revenue	165,983,909,595	158,630,873,018	150,332,864,743	143,180,808,459	136,254,379,940
Other Operating Revenue	11,688,454,693	10,412,104,660	9,945,736,432	8,574,131,165	8,264,746,159
Other Nonoperating Revenue	2,741,822,603	2,093,183,601	3,444,511,627	1,664,029,117	1,715,958,138
Total Net Revenue	180,414,186,891	171,136,161,279	163,723,112,802	153,418,968,741	146,235,084,237
Total Expenses	166,107,583,789	157,726,638,357	151,561,222,380	143,686,330,615	134,859,861,537
HOSPITAL UNIT (Excludes Separate Nursing Home Units)					
Utilization - Inpatient					
Beds	94,237	93,646	94,334	91,330	90,411
Admissions	4,450,741	4,496,465	4,562,472	4,466,740	4,414,832
Inpatient Days	22,213,145	22,311,167	22,650,592	21,680,335	20,986,001
Average Length of Stay	5.0	5.0	5.0	4.9	4.8
Personnel					
Total Full Time	547,540	547,405	574,623	554,627	535,392
Total Part Time	255,553	244,038	228,318	214,499	203,722
Revenue and Expenses - Totals (Includes Inpatient and Outpatient)					
Total Net Revenue	$179,781,801,578	$170,532,383,574	$163,202,562,609	$152,822,130,125	$145,449,826,991
Total Expenses	165,673,999,870	157,343,376,690	151,226,248,629	143,267,833,798	134,328,221,293
COMMUNITY HEALTH INDICATORS PER 1000 POPULATION					
Total Population (in thousands)	53,492	53,441	53,253	52,802	52,514
Inpatient					
Beds	1.8	1.8	1.8	1.8	1.8
Admissions	83.5	84.4	85.9	84.9	84.4
Inpatient Days	431.4	434.6	439.9	433.8	428
Inpatient Surgeries	21.2	21.8	22.7	22.6	22.6
Births	10.7	11.1	11.3	11.7	11.9
Outpatient					
Emergency Outpatient Visits	344.1	340	353.7	355.9	359.1
Other Outpatient Visits	1,324	1,290.8	1,322.8	1,348.1	1,287.9
Total Outpatient Visits	1,668.1	1,630.9	1,676.5	1,704	1,647
Outpatient Surgeries	40.9	41.9	40.5	39.1	37
Expense per Capita (per person)	$3,105.3	$2,951.4	$2,846.1	$2,721.2	$2,568.1

Note: These data represent hospital performance in the years 2015 – 2019 and do not reflect any impacts from the COVID-19 pandemic in 2020 and thereafter.

U.S. Census Divisions

TABLE 6

ALABAMA

U.S. Community Hospitals
(Nonfederal, short-term general and other special hospitals)

Overview 2015–2019

	2019	2018	2017	2016	2015
Total Community Hospitals in Alabama	101	101	102	103	103
Bed Size Category					
6-24	5	5	4	5	6
25-49	28	27	30	29	32
50-99	25	26	25	26	20
100-199	21	22	21	21	23
200-299	7	6	8	8	9
300-399	7	7	7	7	6
400-499	2	2	1	2	2
500 + ...	6	6	6	5	5
Location					
Hospitals Urban	63	63	62	62	62
Hospitals Rural	38	38	40	41	41
Control					
State and Local Government	36	37	38	39	38
Not for Profit	32	30	27	26	26
Investor owned	33	34	37	38	39
Affiliations					
Hospitals in a System	70	69	69	68	67
Hospitals in a Group Purchasing Organization...	36	39	35	37	39

Note: These data represent hospital performance in the years 2015 – 2019 and do not reflect any impacts from the COVID-19 pandemic in 2020 and thereafter.

States

TABLE 6

ALABAMA

U.S. Community Hospitals
(Nonfederal, short-term general and other special hospitals)

Utilization, Personnel, Revenue and Expenses, Community Health Indicators 2015–2019

	2019	2018	2017	2016	2015
TOTAL FACILITY (Includes Hospital and Nursing Home Units)					
Utilization - Inpatient					
Beds	15,248	15,278	15,216	15,426	14,946
Admissions	637,490	628,561	628,563	635,617	621,258
Inpatient Days	3,633,143	3,614,731	3,596,377	3,611,737	3,470,865
Average Length of Stay	5.7	5.8	5.7	5.7	5.6
Inpatient Surgeries	206,790	184,009	186,128	188,602	179,423
Births	64,583	54,302	55,178	58,959	59,221
Utilization - Outpatient					
Emergency Outpatient Visits	2,488,864	2,340,055	2,327,525	2,219,724	2,483,878
Other Outpatient Visits	7,547,271	7,671,113	6,932,284	6,578,133	6,254,117
Total Outpatient Visits	10,036,135	10,011,168	9,259,809	8,797,857	8,737,995
Outpatient Surgeries	485,735	416,529	412,077	397,205	369,010
Personnel					
Full Time RNs	24,821	24,371	23,991	22,476	22,006
Full Time LPNs	1,047	1,104	1,055	1,156	1,157
Part Time RNs	8,374	7,433	7,995	8,554	8,115
Part Time LPNs	411	332	343	347	331
Total Full Time	75,955	73,116	71,611	70,463	70,142
Total Part Time	24,837	21,425	21,313	22,352	20,777
Revenue - Inpatient					
Gross Inpatient Revenue	$30,720,815,754	$30,048,454,316	$28,875,634,627	$27,037,976,778	$25,293,057,844
Revenue - Outpatient					
Gross Outpatient Revenue	$28,739,172,739	$28,814,808,567	$26,213,584,324	$24,614,811,000	$23,422,875,009
Revenue and Expenses - Totals					
(Includes Inpatient and Outpatient)					
Total Gross Revenue	$59,459,988,493	$58,863,262,883	$55,089,218,951	$51,652,787,778	$48,715,932,853
Deductions from Revenue	46,555,022,861	46,865,500,932	43,466,133,232	40,225,680,622	37,858,963,918
Net Patient Revenue	12,904,965,632	11,997,761,951	11,623,085,719	11,427,107,156	10,856,968,935
Other Operating Revenue	843,534,627	728,383,843	675,713,884	670,890,505	628,727,907
Other Nonoperating Revenue	222,775,772	111,261,681	268,557,069	170,649,053	34,680,595
Total Net Revenue	13,971,276,031	12,837,407,475	12,567,356,672	12,268,646,714	11,520,377,437
Total Expenses	12,726,511,676	11,942,777,633	11,596,934,569	10,943,795,352	10,424,031,054
HOSPITAL UNIT (Excludes Separate Nursing Home Units)					
Utilization - Inpatient					
Beds	14,779	14,809	14,579	14,793	14,416
Admissions	636,236	627,420	627,790	634,134	619,945
Inpatient Days	3,478,648	3,454,326	3,393,391	3,398,467	3,303,436
Average Length of Stay	5.5	5.5	5.4	5.4	5.3
Personnel					
Total Full Time	75,648	72,874	71,259	69,892	69,711
Total Part Time	24,779	21,374	21,241	22,189	20,642
Revenue and Expenses - Totals					
(Includes Inpatient and Outpatient)					
Total Net Revenue	$13,937,344,763	$12,800,918,344	$12,539,717,204	$12,211,589,964	$11,491,426,915
Total Expenses	12,705,585,139	11,920,491,116	11,582,886,825	10,902,476,926	10,387,274,180
COMMUNITY HEALTH INDICATORS PER 1000 POPULATION					
Total Population (in thousands)	4,903	4,888	4,875	4,863	4,859
Inpatient					
Beds	3.1	3.1	3.1	3.2	3.1
Admissions	130	128.6	128.9	130.7	127.9
Inpatient Days	741	739.5	737.8	742.7	714.3
Inpatient Surgeries	42.2	37.6	38.2	38.8	36.9
Births	13.2	11.1	11.3	12.1	12.2
Outpatient					
Emergency Outpatient Visits	507.6	478.7	477.5	456.4	511.2
Other Outpatient Visits	1,539.3	1,569.4	1,422.1	1,352.6	1,287.1
Total Outpatient Visits	2,046.9	2,048.2	1,899.5	1,809	1,798.3
Outpatient Surgeries	99.1	85.2	84.5	81.7	75.9
Expense per Capita (per person)	$2,595.6	$2,443.3	$2,379	$2,250.3	$2,145.3

Note: These data represent hospital performance in the years 2015 – 2019 and do not reflect any impacts from the COVID-19 pandemic in 2020 and thereafter.

States

TABLE 6

ALASKA

U.S. Community Hospitals
(Nonfederal, short-term general and other special hospitals)

Overview 2015–2019

	2019	2018	2017	2016	2015
Total Community Hospitals in Alaska	20	21	21	21	21
Bed Size Category					
6-24	5	5	5	4	4
25-49	5	6	6	7	7
50-99	5	5	5	5	5
100-199	3	3	3	3	3
200-299	1	1	1	1	1
300-399	0	0	0	0	0
400-499	1	1	1	1	1
500 +	0	0	0	0	0
Location					
Hospitals Urban	6	6	6	6	6
Hospitals Rural	14	15	15	15	15
Control					
State and Local Government	6	7	8	7	6
Not for Profit	11	11	10	11	11
Investor owned	3	3	3	3	3
Affiliations					
Hospitals in a System	7	7	7	7	8
Hospitals in a Group Purchasing Organization	6	6	8	9	10

Note: These data represent hospital performance in the years 2015 – 2019 and do not reflect any impacts from the COVID-19 pandemic in 2020 and thereafter.

States

TABLE 6

ALASKA

U.S. Community Hospitals
(Nonfederal, short-term general and other special hospitals)

Utilization, Personnel, Revenue and Expenses, Community Health Indicators 2015–2019

	2019	2018	2017	2016	2015
TOTAL FACILITY (Includes Hospital and Nursing Home Units)					
Utilization - Inpatient					
Beds...	1,606	1,636	1,630	1,647	1,634
Admissions.................................	49,888	52,846	52,418	51,022	52,637
Inpatient Days.............................	382,686	393,049	381,239	384,938	378,062
Average Length of Stay.................	7.7	7.4	7.3	7.5	7.2
Inpatient Surgeries......................	18,415	17,193	20,079	18,924	13,138
Births...	7,831	8,323	8,465	9,687	9,721
Utilization - Outpatient					
Emergency Outpatient Visits............	329,868	320,990	381,678	342,017	324,973
Other Outpatient Visits....................	1,510,113	1,635,915	1,839,755	1,717,104	1,635,792
Total Outpatient Visits....................	1,839,981	1,956,905	2,221,433	2,059,121	1,960,765
Outpatient Surgeries......................	45,121	48,009	44,729	51,311	33,963
Personnel					
Full Time RNs.............................	2,432	2,470	2,821	2,597	2,338
Full Time LPNs...........................	155	150	133	120	86
Part Time RNs............................	986	1,074	1,088	1,165	822
Part Time LPNs..........................	54	62	34	49	22
Total Full Time............................	8,976	9,422	10,328	10,134	8,453
Total Part Time...........................	3,098	3,310	2,982	3,196	2,251
Revenue - Inpatient					
Gross Inpatient Revenue..................	$4,919,429,664	$4,082,142,790	$4,545,321,364	$3,953,723,400	$3,489,110,219
Revenue - Outpatient					
Gross Outpatient Revenue...............	$4,568,219,099	$5,377,635,278	$5,069,155,066	$4,330,578,373	$3,360,897,973
Revenue and Expenses - Totals					
(Includes Inpatient and Outpatient)					
Total Gross Revenue......................	$9,487,648,763	$9,459,778,068	$9,614,476,430	$8,284,301,773	$6,850,008,192
Deductions from Revenue................	6,811,656,684	6,829,414,363	6,987,397,369	5,740,953,226	4,496,841,752
Net Patient Revenue.......................	2,675,992,079	2,630,363,705	2,627,079,061	2,543,348,547	2,353,166,440
Other Operating Revenue.................	100,041,999	243,891,610	365,717,138	255,918,888	284,505,976
Other Nonoperating Revenue...........	119,926,256	19,993,286	82,054,896	44,074,181	7,386,912
Total Net Revenue.........................	2,895,960,334	2,894,248,601	3,074,851,095	2,843,341,616	2,645,059,328
Total Expenses.............................	2,175,917,980	2,287,357,893	2,642,628,585	2,291,293,712	1,963,422,824
HOSPITAL UNIT (Excludes Separate Nursing Home Units)					
Utilization - Inpatient					
Beds..	1,363	1,451	1,491	1,424	1,379
Admissions.................................	49,587	52,542	52,209	50,600	52,272
Inpatient Days.............................	307,241	335,047	348,206	312,802	296,315
Average Length of Stay.................	6.2	6.4	6.7	6.2	5.7
Personnel					
Total Full Time............................	8,710	9,221	10,142	9,871	8,119
Total Part Time...........................	2,967	3,211	2,917	3,042	2,108
Revenue and Expenses - Totals					
(Includes Inpatient and Outpatient)					
Total Net Revenue.........................	$2,840,991,520	$2,849,059,136	$3,040,547,422	$2,790,416,270	$2,596,163,699
Total Expenses.............................	2,135,416,045	2,257,704,759	2,617,428,807	2,251,240,758	1,923,795,139
COMMUNITY HEALTH INDICATORS PER 1000 POPULATION					
Total Population (in thousands).........	732	737	740	742	738
Inpatient					
Beds..	2.2	2.2	2.2	2.2	2.2
Admissions.................................	68.2	71.7	70.9	68.8	71.3
Inpatient Days.............................	523.1	533	515.3	518.9	512
Inpatient Surgeries......................	25.2	23.3	27.1	25.5	17.8
Births...	10.7	11.3	11.4	13.1	13.2
Outpatient					
Emergency Outpatient Visits............	450.9	435.3	515.9	461	440.1
Other Outpatient Visits....................	2,064.3	2,218.4	2,486.8	2,314.5	2,215.2
Total Outpatient Visits....................	2,515.2	2,653.7	3,002.8	2,775.5	2,655.3
Outpatient Surgeries......................	61.7	65.1	60.5	69.2	46
Expense per Capita (per person).........	$2,974.4	$3,101.8	$3,572.1	$3,088.4	$2,658.9

Note: These data represent hospital performance in the years 2015 – 2019 and do not reflect any impacts from the COVID-19 pandemic in 2020 and thereafter.

States

TABLE 6

ARIZONA

U.S. Community Hospitals
(Nonfederal, short-term general and other special hospitals)

Overview 2015–2019

	2019	2018	2017	2016	2015
Total Community Hospitals in Arizona	80	83	83	84	84
Bed Size Category					
6-24	13	15	15	14	12
25-49	14	14	13	14	15
50-99	14	14	16	15	15
100-199	13	14	11	14	16
200-299	8	9	11	10	9
300-399	5	6	6	6	6
400-499	6	6	6	6	6
500 + ...	7	5	5	5	5
Location					
Hospitals Urban	71	74	74	75	75
Hospitals Rural...	9	9	9	9	9
Control					
State and Local Government	4	4	5	4	5
Not for Profit..	43	43	42	43	46
Investor owned...	33	36	36	37	33
Affiliations					
Hospitals in a System	59	61	59	60	60
Hospitals in a Group Purchasing Organization...	38	47	41	36	44

Note: These data represent hospital performance in the years 2015 – 2019 and do not reflect any impacts from the COVID-19 pandemic in 2020 and thereafter.

States

TABLE 6

ARIZONA

U.S. Community Hospitals
(Nonfederal, short-term general and other special hospitals)

Utilization, Personnel, Revenue and Expenses, Community Health Indicators 2015–2019

	2019	2018	2017	2016	2015
TOTAL FACILITY (Includes Hospital and Nursing Home Units)					
Utilization - Inpatient					
Beds....................................	14,038	13,846	13,918	13,903	14,012
Admissions.............................	655,961	651,618	651,064	638,265	636,419
Inpatient Days........................	3,152,127	3,112,261	3,079,118	3,069,875	3,006,541
Average Length of Stay	4.8	4.8	4.7	4.8	4.7
Inpatient Surgeries.............................	174,655	171,517	172,616	166,231	166,370
Births.....................................	73,933	78,909	73,229	76,051	78,101
Utilization - Outpatient					
Emergency Outpatient Visits..............	2,403,474	2,195,768	2,173,898	2,128,481	2,328,632
Other Outpatient Visits........................	6,834,901	6,235,673	6,385,894	6,351,899	6,631,501
Total Outpatient Visits........................	9,238,375	8,431,441	8,559,792	8,480,380	8,960,133
Outpatient Surgeries.........................	302,106	327,574	316,655	293,483	268,525
Personnel					
Full Time RNs	24,048	24,406	24,648	25,095	23,946
Full Time LPNs	545	401	520	639	569
Part Time RNs	7,069	6,866	7,121	6,693	5,150
Part Time LPNs	158	109	136	145	97
Total Full Time	73,448	72,235	73,874	74,820	71,818
Total Part Time	17,936	16,549	17,375	17,416	13,238
Revenue - Inpatient					
Gross Inpatient Revenue	$42,937,482,521	$42,048,413,647	$38,592,599,767	$35,349,524,715	$32,283,089,602
Revenue - Outpatient					
Gross Outpatient Revenue	$37,623,024,873	$36,339,102,700	$33,132,876,010	$30,494,034,624	$27,543,122,602
Revenue and Expenses - Totals					
(Includes Inpatient and Outpatient)					
Total Gross Revenue	$80,560,507,394	$78,387,516,347	$71,725,475,777	$65,843,559,339	$59,826,212,204
Deductions from Revenue	62,865,533,247	61,709,412,733	55,530,228,554	50,768,979,353	45,392,282,623
Net Patient Revenue.........................	17,694,974,147	16,678,103,614	16,195,247,223	15,074,579,986	14,433,929,581
Other Operating Revenue..................	750,093,635	742,769,994	701,646,183	554,015,620	545,903,135
Other Nonoperating Revenue	171,916,275	111,847,232	215,957,431	77,391,425	51,879,312
Total Net Revenue.........................	18,616,984,057	17,532,720,840	17,112,850,837	15,705,987,031	15,031,712,028
Total Expenses	16,672,228,141	15,971,157,767	15,492,616,879	14,499,241,249	14,098,268,721
HOSPITAL UNIT (Excludes Separate Nursing Home Units)					
Utilization - Inpatient					
Beds...	14,038	13,768	13,840	13,825	13,910
Admissions.................................	655,961	650,017	649,629	636,819	634,650
Inpatient Days.............................	3,152,127	3,094,745	3,058,136	3,049,581	2,983,884
Average Length of Stay	4.8	4.8	4.7	4.8	4.7
Personnel					
Total Full Time	73,448	72,182	73,811	74,762	71,747
Total Part Time	17,936	16,544	17,362	17,404	13,222
Revenue and Expenses - Totals					
(Includes Inpatient and Outpatient)					
Total Net Revenue.............................	$18,616,984,057	$17,525,073,455	$17,066,085,299	$15,670,525,036	$14,997,280,215
Total Expenses	16,672,228,141	15,958,656,247	15,480,970,646	14,487,932,710	14,089,184,781
COMMUNITY HEALTH INDICATORS PER 1000 POPULATION					
Total Population (in thousands)	7,279	7,172	7,016	6,931	6,828
Inpatient					
Beds...	1.9	1.9	2	2	2.1
Admissions.................................	90.1	90.9	92.8	92.1	93.2
Inpatient Days.............................	433.1	434	438.9	442.9	440.3
Inpatient Surgeries.........................	24	23.9	24.6	24	24.4
Births.....................................	10.2	11	10.4	11	11.4
Outpatient					
Emergency Outpatient Visits..............	3,30.2	306.2	309.8	307.1	341
Other Outpatient Visits........................	939	869.5	910.2	916.4	971.2
Total Outpatient Visits........................	1,269.2	1,175.7	1,220	1,223.5	1,312.3
Outpatient Surgeries.........................	41.5	45.7	45.1	42.3	39.3
Expense per Capita (per person).........	$2,290.5	$2,227	$2,208.1	2,091.9	$$2,064.8

Note: These data represent hospital performance in the years 2015 – 2019 and do not reflect any impacts from the COVID-19 pandemic in 2020 and thereafter.

AHA Hospital Statistics © 2021 Health Forum LLC, an affiliate of the American Hospital Association **55**

States

TABLE 6

ARKANSAS

U.S. Community Hospitals
(Nonfederal, short-term general and other special hospitals)

Overview 2015–2019

	2019	2018	2017	2016	2015
Total Community Hospitals in Arkansas	89	88	88	88	87
Bed Size Category					
6-24	11	10	7	7	7
25-49	36	33	37	38	35
50-99	13	14	13	14	15
100-199	15	16	14	11	13
200-299	6	6	7	8	9
300-399	6	7	7	7	5
400-499	0	0	1	1	2
500 + ...	2	2	2	2	1
Location					
Hospitals Urban	42	41	39	39	38
Hospitals Rural..	47	47	49	49	49
Control					
State and Local Government	8	9	10	10	10
Not for Profit..	55	51	48	52	51
Investor owned...	26	28	30	26	26
Affiliations					
Hospitals in a System	49	47	48	48	47
Hospitals in a Group Purchasing Organization...	73	76	73	73	74

Note: These data represent hospital performance in the years 2015 – 2019 and do not reflect any impacts from the COVID-19 pandemic in 2020 and thereafter.

States

TABLE 6

ARKANSAS

U.S. Community Hospitals
(Nonfederal, short-term general and other special hospitals)

Utilization, Personnel, Revenue and Expenses, Community Health Indicators 2015–2019

	2019	2018	2017	2016	2015
TOTAL FACILITY (Includes Hospital and Nursing Home Units)					
Utilization - Inpatient					
Beds	9,145	9,517	9,664	9,634	9,569
Admissions	364,291	358,222	363,070	359,359	357,286
Inpatient Days	1,826,976	1,828,470	1,861,122	1,846,634	1,859,244
Average Length of Stay	5.0	5.1	5.1	5.1	5.2
Inpatient Surgeries	92,357	94,924	95,013	94,627	94,607
Births	34,678	34,821	35,517	35,864	36,206
Utilization - Outpatient					
Emergency Outpatient Visits	1,556,206	1,509,448	1,519,156	1,515,989	1,492,359
Other Outpatient Visits	4,914,195	4,925,120	4,629,383	4,570,177	4,184,351
Total Outpatient Visits	6,470,401	6,434,568	6,148,539	6,086,166	5,676,710
Outpatient Surgeries	226,136	215,656	203,105	200,832	195,650
Personnel					
Full Time RNs	13,347	12,821	12,629	12,661	12,720
Full Time LPNs	1,349	1,504	1,446	1,472	1,474
Part Time RNs	5,410	5,533	5,093	3,699	3,663
Part Time LPNs	352	385	370	380	361
Total Full Time	42,713	42,361	42,385	42,533	41,865
Total Part Time	15,322	16,318	15,207	10,725	10,694
Revenue - Inpatient					
Gross Inpatient Revenue	$14,814,502,613	$13,777,391,679	$13,396,489,708	$12,460,694,916	$11,700,149,701
Revenue - Outpatient					
Gross Outpatient Revenue	$17,025,641,576	$15,450,146,464	$14,212,477,805	$12,952,790,887	$11,967,218,307
Revenue and Expenses - Totals					
(Includes Inpatient and Outpatient)					
Total Gross Revenue	$31,840,144,189	$29,227,538,143	$27,608,967,513	$25,413,485,803	$23,667,368,008
Deductions from Revenue	23,653,997,200	21,507,898,507	20,249,177,829	18,458,098,464	17,048,393,940
Net Patient Revenue	8,186,146,989	7,719,639,636	7,359,789,684	6,955,387,339	6,618,974,068
Other Operating Revenue	433,117,737	395,516,849	381,973,773	307,097,211	250,191,038
Other Nonoperating Revenue	145,788,360	44,821,792	118,736,986	82,544,865	42,144,248
Total Net Revenue	8,765,053,086	8,159,978,277	7,860,500,443	7,345,029,415	6,911,309,354
Total Expenses	8,049,927,966	7,797,448,234	7,372,516,174	6,803,364,553	6,428,954,340
HOSPITAL UNIT (Excludes Separate Nursing Home Units)					
Utilization - Inpatient					
Beds	8,837	9,193	9,311	9,326	9,201
Admissions	364,093	357,700	362,439	358,734	356,680
Inpatient Days	1,739,783	1,732,975	1,762,734	1,756,049	1,758,250
Average Length of Stay	4.8	4.8	4.9	4.9	4.9
Personnel					
Total Full Time	42,523	42,133	42,099	42,354	41,654
Total Part Time	15,277	16,292	15,172	10,699	10,636
Revenue and Expenses - Totals					
(Includes Inpatient and Outpatient)					
Total Net Revenue	$8,748,689,466	$8,140,915,011	$7,841,622,879	$7,325,492,355	$6,890,484,637
Total Expenses	8,036,213,344	7,784,943,299	7,356,700,895	6,789,080,213	6,412,183,234
COMMUNITY HEALTH INDICATORS PER 1000 POPULATION					
Total Population (in thousands)	3,018	3,014	3,004	2,988	2,978
Inpatient					
Beds	3	3.2	3.2	3.2	3.2
Admissions	120.7	118.9	120.9	120.3	120
Inpatient Days	605.4	606.7	619.5	618	624.3
Inpatient Surgeries	30.6	31.5	31.6	31.7	31.8
Births	11.5	11.6	11.8	12	12.2
Outpatient					
Emergency Outpatient Visits	515.7	500.8	505.7	507.3	501.1
Other Outpatient Visits	1,628.4	1,634.2	1,540.9	1,529.4	1405
Total Outpatient Visits	2,144.1	2,135	2,046.6	2,036.7	1,906.1
Outpatient Surgeries	74.9	71.6	67.6	67.2	65.7
Expense per Capita (per person)	$2,667.5	$2,587.2	$2,454	$2,276.7	$2,158.7

Note: These data represent hospital performance in the years 2015 – 2019 and do not reflect any impacts from the COVID-19 pandemic in 2020 and thereafter.

States

TABLE **6**

CALIFORNIA

U.S. Community Hospitals
(Nonfederal, short-term general and other special hospitals)

Overview 2015–2019

	2019	2018	2017	2016	2015
Total Community Hospitals in California...........	359	359	362	360	360
Bed Size Category					
6-24	14	14	15	15	16
25-49	43	41	40	41	42
50-99	48	49	49	45	43
100-199	98	101	103	110	110
200-299	69	68	68	65	66
300-399	46	46	47	46	46
400-499	24	26	26	25	24
500 +	17	14	14	13	13
Location					
Hospitals Urban	329	329	332	330	330
Hospitals Rural	30	30	30	30	30
Control					
State and Local Government	66	64	65	63	64
Not for Profit	204	206	208	208	210
Investor owned	89	89	89	89	86
Affiliations					
Hospitals in a System	259	258	261	258	253
Hospitals in a Group Purchasing Organization...	157	161	170	199	213

Note: These data represent hospital performance in the years 2015 – 2019 and do not reflect any impacts from the COVID-19 pandemic in 2020 and thereafter.

States

TABLE 6

CALIFORNIA

U.S. Community Hospitals
(Nonfederal, short-term general and other special hospitals)

Utilization, Personnel, Revenue and Expenses, Community Health Indicators 2015–2019

	2019	2018	2017	2016	2015
TOTAL FACILITY (Includes Hospital and Nursing Home Units)					
Utilization - Inpatient					
Beds	73,109	72,511	73,195	72,004	71,715
Admissions	3,361,823	3,400,991	3,452,477	3,384,619	3,324,507
Inpatient Days	17,440,927	17,484,281	17,744,125	17,375,662	17,019,301
Average Length of Stay	5.2	5.1	5.1	5.1	5.1
Inpatient Surgeries	799,100	818,787	857,163	841,709	847,174
Births	426,158	444,730	446,852	461,287	469,747
Utilization - Outpatient					
Emergency Outpatient Visits	13,079,880	13,026,736	13,460,106	13,688,436	13,792,047
Other Outpatient Visits	42,786,381	42,624,149	43,696,913	45,898,449	43,798,963
Total Outpatient Visits	55,866,261	55,650,885	57,157,019	59,586,885	57,591,010
Outpatient Surgeries	1,475,806	1,545,410	1,479,725	1,376,228	1,342,559
Personnel					
Full Time RNs	122,686	122,839	128,579	121,266	117,086
Full Time LPNs	5,667	5,771	6,418	6,033	5,974
Part Time RNs	73,095	69,397	62,556	60,798	57,468
Part Time LPNs	2,414	2,261	2,347	2,206	2,186
Total Full Time	402,618	401,556	426,573	399,525	389,414
Total Part Time	182,281	176,220	164,147	156,905	148,916
Revenue - Inpatient					
Gross Inpatient Revenue	$292,076,356,188	$273,084,481,382	$259,909,932,608	$247,487,254,287	$232,570,927,093
Revenue - Outpatient					
Gross Outpatient Revenue	$232,506,529,764	$212,980,344,588	$191,470,747,704	$174,838,843,059	$156,754,034,665
Revenue and Expenses - Totals					
(Includes Inpatient and Outpatient)					
Total Gross Revenue	$524,582,885,952	$486,064,825,970	$451,380,680,312	$422,326,097,346	$389,324,961,758
Deductions from Revenue	401,866,145,823	368,832,652,577	340,809,314,083	317,209,061,450	289,551,701,992
Net Patient Revenue	122,716,740,129	117,232,173,393	110,571,366,229	105,117,035,896	99,773,259,766
Other Operating Revenue	8,805,237,564	7,944,019,278	7,373,673,021	6,237,432,451	5,915,855,092
Other Nonoperating Revenue	2,062,274,315	1,672,128,304	2,678,576,375	1,263,341,664	1,336,798,281
Total Net Revenue	133,584,252,008	126,848,320,975	120,623,615,625	112,617,810,011	107,025,913,139
Total Expenses	122,630,620,283	115,912,149,428	110,902,410,525	105,192,746,282	98,800,359,182
HOSPITAL UNIT (Excludes Separate Nursing Home Units)					
Utilization - Inpatient					
Beds	70,684	70,149	70,915	68,777	68,059
Admissions	3,348,373	3,386,782	3,439,379	3,369,165	3,308,119
Inpatient Days	16,692,108	16,718,712	17,042,357	16,335,596	15,833,308
Average Length of Stay	5.0	4.9	5.0	4.8	4.8
Personnel					
Total Full Time	400,349	399,421	424,523	397,558	386,762
Total Part Time	181,330	175,267	163,260	156,032	147,625
Revenue and Expenses - Totals					
(Includes Inpatient and Outpatient)					
Total Net Revenue	$133,030,278,390	$126,354,259,915	$120,157,794,110	$112,141,226,910	$106,372,486,411
Total Expenses	122,262,644,754	115,598,967,583	110,613,699,579	104,868,183,144	98,382,552,632
COMMUNITY HEALTH INDICATORS PER 1000 POPULATION					
Total Population (in thousands)	39,512	39,557	39,537	39,250	39,145
Inpatient					
Beds	1.9	1.8	1.9	1.8	1.8
Admissions	85.1	86	87.3	86.2	84.9
Inpatient Days	441.4	442	448.8	442.7	434.8
Inpatient Surgeries	20.2	20.7	21.7	21.4	21.6
Births	10.8	11.2	11.3	11.8	12
Outpatient					
Emergency Outpatient Visits	331	329.3	340.4	348.7	352.3
Other Outpatient Visits	1,082.9	1,077.5	1,105.2	1,169.4	1,118.9
Total Outpatient Visits	1,413.9	1,406.9	1,445.7	1,518.1	1,471.2
Outpatient Surgeries	37.4	39.1	37.4	35.1	34.3
Expense per Capita (per person)	$3,103.6	$2,930.3	$2,805.1	$2,680.1	$2,524

Note: These data represent hospital performance in the years 2015 – 2019 and do not reflect any impacts from the COVID-19 pandemic in 2020 and thereafter.

States

TABLE 6

COLORADO

U.S. Community Hospitals
(Nonfederal, short-term general and other special hospitals)

Overview 2015–2019

	2019	2018	2017	2016	2015
Total Community Hospitals in Colorado............	90	89	89	86	88
Bed Size Category					
6-24	18	18	20	16	18
25-49	26	24	22	23	24
50-99	17	17	18	17	17
100-199	10	12	11	10	10
200-299	6	7	6	8	7
300-399	8	6	5	5	5
400-499	4	3	4	4	4
500 + ...	1	2	3	3	3
Location					
Hospitals Urban	50	49	49	46	48
Hospitals Rural..	40	40	40	40	40
Control					
State and Local Government	26	27	26	24	25
Not for Profit..	46	43	43	43	42
Investor owned..	18	19	20	19	21
Affiliations					
Hospitals in a System	59	59	56	52	55
Hospitals in a Group Purchasing Organization...	53	53	56	60	60

Note: These data represent hospital performance in the years 2015 – 2019 and do not reflect any impacts from the COVID-19 pandemic in 2020 and thereafter.

States

TABLE 6

COLORADO

U.S. Community Hospitals
(Nonfederal, short-term general and other special hospitals)

Utilization, Personnel, Revenue and Expenses, Community Health Indicators 2015–2019

	2019	2018	2017	2016	2015
TOTAL FACILITY (Includes Hospital and Nursing Home Units)					
Utilization - Inpatient					
Beds	10,665	10,574	10,793	10,874	10,646
Admissions	446,955	446,553	445,190	429,370	428,378
Inpatient Days	2,290,705	2,251,677	2,225,569	2,222,898	2,189,200
Average Length of Stay	5.1	5.0	5.0	5.2	5.1
Inpatient Surgeries	138,225	142,149	142,249	132,068	127,395
Births	53,923	57,141	59,221	61,795	62,844
Utilization - Outpatient					
Emergency Outpatient Visits	2,105,511	2,037,141	2,000,092	2,038,472	2,084,609
Other Outpatient Visits	8,146,582	7,357,929	7,398,577	7,074,702	6,783,043
Total Outpatient Visits	10,252,093	9,395,070	9,398,669	9,113,174	8,867,652
Outpatient Surgeries	260,588	263,552	251,802	254,491	249,948
Personnel					
Full Time RNs	18,907	18,705	18,007	17,694	17,035
Full Time LPNs	520	525	574	502	554
Part Time RNs	8,301	7,984	7,777	7,595	6,735
Part Time LPNs	250	202	234	226	206
Total Full Time	64,482	61,261	61,837	59,978	57,797
Total Part Time	24,538	23,875	24,313	22,728	19,225
Revenue - Inpatient					
Gross Inpatient Revenue	$38,960,699,836	$36,227,741,798	$33,700,836,075	$30,693,433,843	$28,980,827,929
Revenue - Outpatient					
Gross Outpatient Revenue	$39,252,755,438	$34,598,156,298	$31,433,059,267	$27,169,644,489	$25,845,024,764
Revenue and Expenses - Totals					
(Includes Inpatient and Outpatient)					
Total Gross Revenue	$78,213,455,274	$70,825,898,096	$65,133,895,342	$57,863,078,332	$54,825,852,693
Deductions from Revenue	60,165,420,314	53,957,578,944	49,382,913,078	43,179,452,597	40,732,139,747
Net Patient Revenue	18,048,034,960	16,868,319,152	15,750,982,264	14,683,625,735	14,093,712,946
Other Operating Revenue	717,215,320	743,736,166	660,542,442	624,912,473	555,943,564
Other Nonoperating Revenue	475,798,265	421,522,630	419,008,905	143,935,558	140,814,200
Total Net Revenue	19,241,048,545	18,033,577,948	16,830,533,611	15,452,473,766	14,790,470,710
Total Expenses	15,976,705,181	15,093,334,288	14,271,275,490	13,425,728,556	12,842,090,285
HOSPITAL UNIT (Excludes Separate Nursing Home Units)					
Utilization - Inpatient					
Beds	10,338	10,386	10,290	10,279	10,052
Admissions	446,611	446,412	444,220	428,006	426,663
Inpatient Days	2,194,672	2,192,505	2,090,680	2,043,296	2,012,216
Average Length of Stay	4.9	4.9	4.7	4.8	4.7
Personnel					
Total Full Time	64,287	61,096	61,608	59,594	57,438
Total Part Time	24,447	23,808	24,197	22,578	19,082
Revenue and Expenses - Totals					
(Includes Inpatient and Outpatient)					
Total Net Revenue	$19,225,616,157	$18,020,987,067	$16,801,588,272	$15,407,441,587	$14,748,533,542
Total Expenses	15,959,784,200	15,077,031,477	14,235,109,577	13,384,654,709	12,800,429,586
COMMUNITY HEALTH INDICATORS PER 1000 POPULATION					
Total Population (in thousands)	5,759	5,696	5,607	5,541	5,457
Inpatient					
Beds	1.9	1.9	1.9	2	2
Admissions	77.6	78.4	79.4	77.5	78.5
Inpatient Days	397.8	395.3	396.9	401.2	401.2
Inpatient Surgeries	24	25	25.4	23.8	23.3
Births	9.4	10	10.6	11.2	11.5
Outpatient					
Emergency Outpatient Visits	365.6	357.7	356.7	367.9	382
Other Outpatient Visits	1,414.6	1,291.9	1,319.5	1,276.9	1,243.1
Total Outpatient Visits	1,780.3	1,649.5	1,676.2	1,644.8	1,625.1
Outpatient Surgeries	45.3	46.3	44.9	45.9	45.8
Expense per Capita (per person)	$2,774.3	$2,650	$2,545.2	$2,423.2	$2,353.5

Note: These data represent hospital performance in the years 2015 – 2019 and do not reflect any impacts from the COVID-19 pandemic in 2020 and thereafter.

States

TABLE 6

CONNECTICUT

U.S. Community Hospitals
(Nonfederal, short-term general and other special hospitals)

Overview 2015–2019

	2019	2018	2017	2016	2015
Total Community Hospitals in Connecticut.......	31	32	32	32	32
Bed Size Category					
6-24	0	0	0	0	0
25-49	3	3	3	3	3
50-99	7	8	8	8	8
100-199	12	11	12	12	11
200-299	3	4	3	2	2
300-399	2	3	3	3	3
400-499	2	1	1	1	2
500 + ...	2	2	2	3	3
Location					
Hospitals Urban	29	30	30	30	30
Hospitals Rural...	2	2	2	2	2
Control					
State and Local Government	1	1	1	1	1
Not for Profit..	29	31	31	30	30
Investor owned...	1	0	0	1	1
Affiliations					
Hospitals in a System	21	21	21	20	19
Hospitals in a Group Purchasing Organization...	23	23	24	25	24

Note: These data represent hospital performance in the years 2015 – 2019 and do not reflect any impacts from the COVID-19 pandemic in 2020 and thereafter.

States

TABLE 6

CONNECTICUT

U.S. Community Hospitals
(Nonfederal, short-term general and other special hospitals)

Utilization, Personnel, Revenue and Expenses, Community Health Indicators 2015–2019

	2019	2018	2017	2016	2015
TOTAL FACILITY (Includes Hospital and Nursing Home Units)					
Utilization - Inpatient					
Beds	7,246	7,194	7,086	7,278	7,531
Admissions	372,553	366,087	371,009	375,154	377,150
Inpatient Days	2,049,145	2,005,853	1,993,586	1,951,522	2,008,771
Average Length of Stay	5.5	5.5	5.4	5.2	5.3
Inpatient Surgeries	102,223	106,446	104,658	111,590	102,747
Births	34,843	35,161	35,626	36,478	36,680
Utilization - Outpatient					
Emergency Outpatient Visits	1,701,496	1,755,177	1,698,661	1,671,516	1,663,519
Other Outpatient Visits	6,999,551	7,293,140	7,634,946	7,644,309	7,239,266
Total Outpatient Visits	8,701,047	9,048,317	9,333,607	9,315,825	8,902,785
Outpatient Surgeries	228,193	222,221	216,877	220,046	209,981
Personnel					
Full Time RNs	12,631	12,465	11,858	11,502	11,070
Full Time LPNs	207	235	240	224	225
Part Time RNs	7,722	7,804	7,858	8,256	7,884
Part Time LPNs	111	123	150	142	148
Total Full Time	45,017	45,739	45,784	45,080	43,638
Total Part Time	24,128	23,785	24,670	25,222	22,897
Revenue - Inpatient					
Gross Inpatient Revenue	$18,689,560,520	$17,368,671,033	$16,681,363,756	$16,384,469,099	$16,472,383,493
Revenue - Outpatient					
Gross Outpatient Revenue	$22,106,914,682	$20,393,629,046	$19,187,823,394	$18,392,571,010	$17,231,977,464
Revenue and Expenses - Totals					
(Includes Inpatient and Outpatient)					
Total Gross Revenue	$40,796,475,202	$37,762,300,079	$35,869,187,150	$34,777,040,109	$33,704,360,957
Deductions from Revenue	27,943,555,398	25,637,296,174	24,591,177,189	23,650,482,376	22,907,056,578
Net Patient Revenue	12,852,919,804	12,125,003,905	11,278,009,961	11,126,557,733	10,797,304,379
Other Operating Revenue	770,947,757	740,953,328	681,684,437	620,331,081	507,484,212
Other Nonoperating Revenue	87,579,989	249,508,984	365,707,447	219,500,367	-14,004,628
Total Net Revenue	13,711,447,550	13,115,466,217	12,325,401,845	11,966,389,181	11,290,783,963
Total Expenses	13,054,730,150	12,568,658,113	11,649,294,414	11,386,587,495	10,833,514,095
HOSPITAL UNIT (Excludes Separate Nursing Home Units)					
Utilization - Inpatient					
Beds	7,142	7,090	6,982	7,174	7,427
Admissions	372,205	365,713	370,645	374,812	376,759
Inpatient Days	2,012,482	1,969,438	1,956,827	1,914,811	1,972,229
Average Length of Stay	5.4	5.4	5.3	5.1	5.2
Personnel					
Total Full Time	44,974	45,687	45,734	45,012	43,557
Total Part Time	24,090	23,722	24,618	25,152	22,803
Revenue and Expenses - Totals					
(Includes Inpatient and Outpatient)					
Total Net Revenue	$13,697,829,497	$13,101,970,688	$12,312,136,145	$11,953,471,349	$11,277,901,563
Total Expenses	13,041,899,335	12,556,396,201	11,640,088,731	11,377,360,293	10,824,084,611
COMMUNITY HEALTH INDICATORS PER 1000 POPULATION					
Total Population (in thousands)	3,565	3,573	3,588	3,576	3,591
Inpatient					
Beds	2	2	2	2	2.1
Admissions	104.5	102.5	103.4	104.9	105
Inpatient Days	574.7	561.4	555.6	545.7	559.4
Inpatient Surgeries	28.7	29.8	29.2	31.2	28.6
Births	9.8	9.8	9.9	10.2	10.2
Outpatient					
Emergency Outpatient Visits	477.2	491.3	473.4	467.4	463.3
Other Outpatient Visits	1,963.3	2,041.4	2,127.8	2,137.4	2016
Total Outpatient Visits	2,440.5	2,532.7	2,601.2	2,604.8	2,479.3
Outpatient Surgeries	64	62.2	60.4	61.5	58.5
Expense per Capita (per person)	$3,661.6	$3,518	$3,246.6	$3,183.8	$3,016.9

Note: These data represent hospital performance in the years 2015 – 2019 and do not reflect any impacts from the COVID-19 pandemic in 2020 and thereafter.

States

TABLE **6**   DELAWARE

U.S. Community Hospitals
(Nonfederal, short-term general and other special hospitals)

Overview 2015–2019

	2019	2018	2017	2016	2015
Total Community Hospitals in Delaware............	7	7	8	7	7
Bed Size Category					
6-24	0	0	0	0	0
25-49	1	1	2	1	1
50-99	1	1	1	1	1
100-199	2	2	2	2	2
200-299	1	1	1	1	1
300-399	1	1	1	1	1
400-499	0	0	0	0	0
500 + ...	1	1	1	1	1
Location					
Hospitals Urban	7	7	8	7	7
Hospitals Rural..	0	0	0	0	0
Control					
State and Local Government	0	0	0	0	0
Not for Profit...	6	6	6	6	6
Investor owned..	1	1	2	1	1
Affiliations					
Hospitals in a System	5	4	5	5	4
Hospitals in a Group Purchasing Organization...	6	5	7	6	6

Note: These data represent hospital performance in the years 2015 – 2019 and do not reflect any impacts from the COVID-19 pandemic in 2020 and thereafter.

States

TABLE 6

DELAWARE

U.S. Community Hospitals
(Nonfederal, short-term general and other special hospitals)

Utilization, Personnel, Revenue and Expenses, Community Health Indicators 2015–2019

	2019	2018	2017	2016	2015
TOTAL FACILITY (Includes Hospital and Nursing Home Units)					
Utilization - Inpatient					
Beds	2,112	2,101	2,111	2,059	2,106
Admissions	103,328	102,324	103,162	100,716	106,139
Inpatient Days	569,518	556,545	555,629	519,070	567,289
Average Length of Stay	5.5	5.4	5.4	5.2	5.3
Inpatient Surgeries	29,522	30,357	29,675	29,481	32,640
Births	10,358	10,798	10,972	11,430	11,269
Utilization - Outpatient					
Emergency Outpatient Visits	478,571	460,493	470,429	469,403	463,845
Other Outpatient Visits	1,727,202	1,705,927	1,618,485	1,710,846	1,787,677
Total Outpatient Visits	2,205,773	2,166,420	2,088,914	2,180,249	2,251,522
Outpatient Surgeries	59,934	59,911	62,312	60,646	64,599
Personnel					
Full Time RNs	4,699	4,729	4,535	4,443	4,424
Full Time LPNs	145	163	136	118	119
Part Time RNs	1,972	1,827	2,056	2,118	2,229
Part Time LPNs	90	113	100	38	43
Total Full Time	17,221	16,743	17,127	16,675	16,428
Total Part Time	5,891	5,830	6,257	5,952	6,177
Revenue - Inpatient					
Gross Inpatient Revenue	$4,640,672,785	$4,524,086,491	$4,224,418,870	$3,947,910,339	$3,785,257,174
Revenue - Outpatient					
Gross Outpatient Revenue	$5,054,261,252	$5,032,921,962	$4,140,812,973	$3,856,305,152	$3,578,655,796
Revenue and Expenses - Totals					
(Includes Inpatient and Outpatient)					
Total Gross Revenue	$9,694,934,037	$9,557,008,453	$8,365,231,843	$7,804,215,491	$7,363,912,970
Deductions from Revenue	5,704,825,082	5,832,799,633	4,783,774,142	4,386,738,942	4,088,740,893
Net Patient Revenue	3,990,108,955	3,724,208,820	3,581,457,701	3,417,476,549	3,275,172,077
Other Operating Revenue	105,848,541	132,417,762	113,064,550	121,878,449	112,919,384
Other Nonoperating Revenue	102,071,641	153,396,922	177,838,022	-23,074,370	48,098,253
Total Net Revenue	4,198,029,137	4,010,023,504	3,872,360,273	3,516,280,628	3,436,189,714
Total Expenses	3,757,034,482	3,528,135,912	3,350,000,939	3,246,810,925	3,130,591,165
HOSPITAL UNIT (Excludes Separate Nursing Home Units)					
Utilization - Inpatient					
Beds	2,112	2,101	2,111	2,059	2,106
Admissions	103,328	102,324	103,162	100,716	106,139
Inpatient Days	569,518	556,545	555,629	519,070	567,289
Average Length of Stay	5.5	5.4	5.4	5.2	5.3
Personnel					
Total Full Time	17,221	16,743	17,127	16,675	16,428
Total Part Time	5,891	5,830	6,257	5,952	6,177
Revenue and Expenses - Totals					
(Includes Inpatient and Outpatient)					
Total Net Revenue	$4,198,029,137	$4,010,023,504	$3,872,360,273	$3,516,280,628	$3,436,189,714
Total Expenses	3,757,034,482	3,528,135,912	3,350,000,939	3,246,810,925	3,130,591,165
COMMUNITY HEALTH INDICATORS PER 1000 POPULATION					
Total Population (in thousands)	974	967	962	952	946
Inpatient					
Beds	2.2	2.2	2.2	2.2	2.2
Admissions	106.1	105.8	107.2	105.8	112.2
Inpatient Days	584.9	575.4	577.6	545.2	599.7
Inpatient Surgeries	30.3	31.4	30.8	31	34.5
Births	10.6	11.2	11.4	12	11.9
Outpatient					
Emergency Outpatient Visits	491.5	476.1	489	493	490.4
Other Outpatient Visits	1,773.7	1,763.8	1,682.5	1,797	1,889.9
Total Outpatient Visits	2,265.2	2,240	2,171.6	2,290	2,380.2
Outpatient Surgeries	61.5	61.9	64.8	63.7	68.3
Expense per Capita (per person)	$3,858.3	$3,647.9	$3,482.6	$3,410.3	$3,309.5

Note: These data represent hospital performance in the years 2015 – 2019 and do not reflect any impacts from the COVID-19 pandemic in 2020 and thereafter.

States

TABLE 6

DISTRICT OF COLUMBIA

U.S. Community Hospitals
(Nonfederal, short-term general and other special hospitals)

Overview 2015–2019

	2019	2018	2017	2016	2015
Total Community Hospitals in District of Columbia	10	10	11	11	11
Bed Size Category					
6-24	0	0	0	0	0
25-49	0	0	0	0	0
50-99	0	1	1	1	1
100-199	3	2	2	3	2
200-299	2	2	2	1	2
300-399	3	3	3	3	3
400-499	1	1	2	2	2
500 +	1	1	1	1	1
Location					
Hospitals Urban	10	10	11	11	11
Hospitals Rural	0	0	0	0	0
Control					
State and Local Government	0	0	0	0	0
Not for Profit	7	7	8	8	8
Investor owned	3	3	3	3	3
Affiliations					
Hospitals in a System	8	7	8	8	8
Hospitals in a Group Purchasing Organization	6	6	6	5	6

Note: These data represent hospital performance in the years 2015 – 2019 and do not reflect any impacts from the COVID-19 pandemic in 2020 and thereafter.

States

TABLE 6

DISTRICT OF COLUMBIA

U.S. Community Hospitals
(Nonfederal, short-term general and other special hospitals)

Utilization, Personnel, Revenue and Expenses, Community Health Indicators 2015–2019

	2019	2018	2017	2016	2015
TOTAL FACILITY (Includes Hospital and Nursing Home Units)					
Utilization - Inpatient					
Beds	3,186	3,114	3,542	3,449	3,590
Admissions	124,261	116,149	127,666	126,578	129,047
Inpatient Days	900,757	825,717	938,804	948,524	950,661
Average Length of Stay	7.2	7.1	7.4	7.5	7.4
Inpatient Surgeries	38,447	37,776	39,004	37,194	37,098
Births	12,682	13,399	14,592	14,725	13,139
Utilization - Outpatient					
Emergency Outpatient Visits	418,267	430,067	474,464	476,259	496,827
Other Outpatient Visits	2,370,694	2,166,534	2,087,625	2,129,340	2,251,154
Total Outpatient Visits	2,788,961	2,596,601	2,562,089	2,605,599	2,747,981
Outpatient Surgeries	63,458	63,736	70,512	65,550	63,068
Personnel					
Full Time RNs	6,473	6,417	6,331	6,278	6,294
Full Time LPNs	130	145	178	172	200
Part Time RNs	2,521	2,421	2,303	1,672	1,453
Part Time LPNs	28	35	39	33	36
Total Full Time	22,981	23,385	24,689	23,369	23,215
Total Part Time	6,147	5,975	6,162	4,553	4,481
Revenue - Inpatient					
Gross Inpatient Revenue	$11,080,028,468	$10,660,939,427	$9,758,645,187	$8,407,719,505	$8,076,303,894
Revenue - Outpatient					
Gross Outpatient Revenue	$7,867,551,018	$7,493,619,540	$6,539,182,922	$5,626,000,810	$5,437,986,154
Revenue and Expenses - Totals					
(Includes Inpatient and Outpatient)					
Total Gross Revenue	$18,947,579,486	$18,154,558,967	$16,297,828,109	$14,033,720,315	$13,514,290,048
Deductions from Revenue	13,711,768,217	13,050,137,687	11,568,354,654	9,464,321,731	9,162,113,899
Net Patient Revenue	5,235,811,269	5,104,421,280	4,729,473,455	4,569,398,584	4,352,176,149
Other Operating Revenue	246,145,484	243,501,480	327,835,003	288,482,386	298,773,643
Other Nonoperating Revenue	142,698,714	144,241,555	99,186,000	-1,681,270	30,835,705
Total Net Revenue	5,624,655,467	5,492,164,315	5,156,494,458	4,856,199,700	4,681,785,497
Total Expenses	5,212,331,103	5,016,017,937	4,692,276,685	4,503,224,661	4,252,693,489
HOSPITAL UNIT (Excludes Separate Nursing Home Units)					
Utilization - Inpatient					
Beds	3,079	3,069	3,245	3,161	3,218
Admissions	123,529	115,464	126,215	125,103	128,394
Inpatient Days	867,115	813,225	839,619	846,819	823,863
Average Length of Stay	7.0	7.0	6.7	6.8	6.4
Personnel					
Total Full Time	22,591	23,218	24,620	23,308	23,079
Total Part Time	5,894	5,918	6,123	4,528	4,438
Revenue and Expenses - Totals					
(Includes Inpatient and Outpatient)					
Total Net Revenue	$5,594,851,190	$5,487,215,082	$5,120,843,109	$4,820,039,291	$4,642,415,151
Total Expenses	5,182,815,679	5,011,443,967	4,657,103,082	4,493,486,091	4,220,791,003
COMMUNITY HEALTH INDICATORS PER 1000 POPULATION					
Total Population (in thousands)	706	702	694	681	672
Inpatient					
Beds	4.5	4.4	5.1	5.1	5.3
Admissions	176.1	165.3	184	185.8	192
Inpatient Days	1276.3	1175.5	1352.8	1392.5	1414.2
Inpatient Surgeries	54.5	53.8	56.2	54.6	55.2
Births	18	19.1	21	21.6	19.5
Outpatient					
Emergency Outpatient Visits	592.7	612.2	683.7	699.2	739.1
Other Outpatient Visits	3,359.1	3,084.2	3,008.2	3,126.0	3,348.8
Total Outpatient Visits	3,951.8	3,696.5	3,691.9	3,825.2	4,087.9
Outpatient Surgeries	89.9	90.7	101.6	96.2	93.8
Expense per Capita (per person)	7,385.5	7,140.7	6,761.5	6,611	6,326.3

Note: These data represent hospital performance in the years 2015 – 2019 and do not reflect any impacts from the COVID-19 pandemic in 2020 and thereafter.

States

TABLE **6**

FLORIDA

U.S. Community Hospitals
(Nonfederal, short-term general and other special hospitals)

Overview 2015–2019

	2019	2018	2017	2016	2015
Total Community Hospitals in Florida	212	217	220	222	222
Bed Size Category					
6-24	7	8	7	7	5
25-49	16	20	20	22	27
50-99	44	45	47	48	45
100-199	49	48	51	50	51
200-299	36	39	37	37	38
300-399	23	22	24	25	23
400-499	14	12	12	13	14
500 + ...	23	23	22	20	19
Location					
Hospitals Urban	195	197	200	200	200
Hospitals Rural.......................................	17	20	20	22	22
Control					
State and Local Government	22	22	23	25	24
Not for Profit...	88	82	84	84	85
Investor owned..	102	113	113	113	113
Affiliations					
Hospitals in a System	183	187	188	187	185
Hospitals in a Group Purchasing Organization...	100	100	100	120	119

Note: These data represent hospital performance in the years 2015 – 2019 and do not reflect any impacts from the COVID-19 pandemic in 2020 and thereafter.

TABLE 6

FLORIDA

U.S. Community Hospitals
(Nonfederal, short-term general and other special hospitals)

Utilization, Personnel, Revenue and Expenses, Community Health Indicators 2015–2019

	2019	2018	2017	2016	2015
TOTAL FACILITY (Includes Hospital and Nursing Home Units)					
Utilization - Inpatient					
Beds	55,733	54,744	55,111	54,487	53,712
Admissions	2,645,062	2,629,196	2,569,757	2,571,170	2,538,567
Inpatient Days	12,940,795	13,141,776	13,018,789	12,936,721	12,704,463
Average Length of Stay	4.9	5.0	5.1	5.0	5.0
Inpatient Surgeries	629,691	622,351	616,561	623,555	609,507
Births	205,759	211,751	203,121	217,888	210,929
Utilization - Outpatient					
Emergency Outpatient Visits	10,186,649	9,399,251	9,198,458	9,537,747	9,169,808
Other Outpatient Visits	21,446,444	17,591,262	17,107,814	17,065,686	17,253,783
Total Outpatient Visits	31,633,093	26,990,513	26,306,272	26,603,433	26,423,591
Outpatient Surgeries	890,405	934,752	883,477	893,911	862,005
Personnel					
Full Time RNs	87,526	86,303	83,588	81,690	80,086
Full Time LPNs	2,442	2,535	2,642	2,910	2,875
Part Time RNs	23,805	23,697	24,569	21,953	22,425
Part Time LPNs	654	774	957	828	844
Total Full Time	269,698	260,999	256,360	252,336	248,245
Total Part Time	69,186	68,493	71,582	61,943	64,415
Revenue - Inpatient					
Gross Inpatient Revenue	$180,660,670,298	$173,007,911,300	$146,699,233,586	$146,637,782,412	$135,105,433,289
Revenue - Outpatient					
Gross Outpatient Revenue	$145,667,503,833	$135,278,705,697	$113,576,911,399	$108,684,986,260	$97,418,931,615
Revenue and Expenses - Totals					
(Includes Inpatient and Outpatient)					
Total Gross Revenue	$326,328,174,131	$308,286,616,997	$260,276,144,985	$255,322,768,672	$232,524,364,904
Deductions from Revenue	267,157,483,478	249,757,947,604	206,697,621,079	203,817,838,489	183,886,903,596
Net Patient Revenue	59,170,690,653	58,528,669,393	53,578,523,906	51,504,930,183	48,637,461,308
Other Operating Revenue	2,996,020,855	2,784,686,944	2,331,832,452	2,426,902,454	2,496,569,643
Other Nonoperating Revenue	1,415,718,524	875,249,008	871,232,021	774,706,694	388,322,871
Total Net Revenue	63,582,430,032	62,188,605,345	56,781,588,379	54,706,539,331	51,522,353,822
Total Expenses	56,199,231,597	52,399,260,305	49,114,873,588	47,496,444,148	45,968,770,839
HOSPITAL UNIT (Excludes Separate Nursing Home Units)					
Utilization - Inpatient					
Beds	54,837	53,891	54,258	53,602	52,709
Admissions	2,640,157	2,625,090	2,565,679	2,566,404	2,533,255
Inpatient Days	12,654,992	12,855,377	12,735,121	12,655,416	12,384,395
Average Length of Stay	4.8	4.9	5.0	4.9	4.9
Personnel					
Total Full Time	268,687	259,888	255,378	251,343	247,239
Total Part Time	68,909	68,149	71,274	61,662	64,086
Revenue and Expenses - Totals					
(Includes Inpatient and Outpatient)					
Total Net Revenue	$63,500,505,988	$62,108,581,870	$56,699,990,364	$54,619,316,402	$51,396,606,880
Total Expenses	56,084,764,195	52,315,057,310	49,025,979,384	47,394,790,722	45,837,729,168
COMMUNITY HEALTH INDICATORS PER 1000 POPULATION					
Total Population (in thousands)	21,478	21,299	20,984	20,612	20,271
Inpatient					
Beds	2.6	2.6	2.6	2.6	2.6
Admissions	123.2	123.4	122.5	124.7	125.2
Inpatient Days	602.5	617	620.4	627.6	626.7
Inpatient Surgeries	29.3	29.2	29.4	30.3	30.1
Births	9.6	9.9	9.7	10.6	10.4
Outpatient					
Emergency Outpatient Visits	474.3	441.3	438.3	462.7	452.4
Other Outpatient Visits	998.5	825.9	815.3	827.9	851.1
Total Outpatient Visits	1,472.8	1,267.2	1,253.6	1,290.6	1,303.5
Outpatient Surgeries	41.5	43.9	42.1	43.4	42.5
Expense per Capita (per person)	$2,616.6	$2,460.1	$2,340.5	$2,304.3	$2,267.7

Note: These data represent hospital performance in the years 2015 – 2019 and do not reflect any impacts from the COVID-19 pandemic in 2020 and thereafter.

States

TABLE **6**

GEORGIA

U.S. Community Hospitals
(Nonfederal, short-term general and other special hospitals)

Overview 2015–2019

	2019	2018	2017	2016	2015
Total Community Hospitals in Georgia...............	143	145	147	150	149
Bed Size Category					
6-24	7	6	6	7	7
25-49	35	38	39	40	39
50-99	26	26	25	27	26
100-199	33	34	36	36	37
200-299	14	13	13	12	12
300-399	10	10	10	10	9
400-499	4	4	6	6	7
500 +	14	14	12	12	12
Location					
Hospitals Urban	87	89	91	93	92
Hospitals Rural........................	56	56	56	57	57
Control					
State and Local Government	35	38	37	40	48
Not for Profit.........................	85	80	83	79	70
Investor owned........................	23	27	27	31	31
Affiliations					
Hospitals in a System	96	97	98	95	92
Hospitals in a Group Purchasing Organization...	68	78	80	79	80

Note: These data represent hospital performance in the years 2015 – 2019 and do not reflect any impacts from the COVID-19 pandemic in 2020 and thereafter.

States

TABLE 6

GEORGIA

U.S. Community Hospitals
(Nonfederal, short-term general and other special hospitals)

Utilization, Personnel, Revenue and Expenses, Community Health Indicators 2015–2019

	2019	2018	2017	2016	2015
TOTAL FACILITY (Includes Hospital and Nursing Home Units)					
Utilization - Inpatient					
Beds	24,896	25,114	25,244	25,214	24,913
Admissions	1,035,793	1,016,445	1,003,595	994,538	980,203
Inpatient Days	6,500,916	6,425,502	6,348,851	6,307,933	6,216,226
Average Length of Stay	6.3	6.3	6.3	6.3	6.3
Inpatient Surgeries	258,026	246,657	262,586	260,874	257,763
Births	121,077	121,738	123,813	123,918	125,173
Utilization - Outpatient					
Emergency Outpatient Visits	4,629,550	4,687,842	4,740,490	4,658,874	4,470,800
Other Outpatient Visits	15,841,438	15,265,159	14,678,150	14,470,559	12,497,612
Total Outpatient Visits	20,470,988	19,953,001	19,418,640	19,129,433	16,968,412
Outpatient Surgeries	526,682	503,413	499,283	490,011	474,256
Personnel					
Full Time RNs	39,317	37,550	36,664	35,727	35,635
Full Time LPNs	2,322	2,424	2,430	2,554	2,408
Part Time RNs	13,149	13,138	11,577	11,611	10,979
Part Time LPNs	621	685	597	684	652
Total Full Time	131,533	126,515	125,979	126,754	123,015
Total Part Time	38,350	37,925	34,087	34,153	32,506
Revenue - Inpatient					
Gross Inpatient Revenue	$53,745,183,805	$50,764,910,205	$47,337,447,155	$44,291,642,662	$42,401,157,349
Revenue - Outpatient					
Gross Outpatient Revenue	$52,134,147,541	$49,302,974,163	$45,623,717,681	$41,884,620,409	$39,002,432,686
Revenue and Expenses - Totals					
(Includes Inpatient and Outpatient)					
Total Gross Revenue	$105,879,331,346	$100,067,884,368	$92,961,164,836	$86,176,263,071	$81,403,590,035
Deductions from Revenue	77,949,306,704	73,872,840,191	67,897,462,826	62,179,729,640	58,650,136,866
Net Patient Revenue	27,930,024,642	26,195,044,177	25,063,702,010	23,996,533,431	22,753,453,169
Other Operating Revenue	1,600,600,499	1,401,829,691	1,318,216,089	1,164,429,971	1,048,482,786
Other Nonoperating Revenue	361,713,211	382,909,479	501,200,885	14,527,578	155,650,000
Total Net Revenue	29,892,338,352	27,979,783,347	26,883,118,984	25,175,490,980	23,957,585,955
Total Expenses	27,514,935,427	25,879,332,910	24,699,064,139	23,351,736,425	21,785,219,076
HOSPITAL UNIT (Excludes Separate Nursing Home Units)					
Utilization - Inpatient					
Beds	22,331	22,530	22,196	22,223	21,990
Admissions	1,029,529	1,010,305	996,519	987,575	973,576
Inpatient Days	5,670,304	5,597,786	5,356,502	5,318,927	5,203,277
Average Length of Stay	5.5	5.5	5.4	5.4	5.3
Personnel					
Total Full Time	129,680	124,759	123,958	124,849	120,868
Total Part Time	37,963	37,606	33,703	33,763	31,931
Revenue and Expenses - Totals					
(Includes Inpatient and Outpatient)					
Total Net Revenue	$29,711,834,436	$27,823,499,696	$26,684,779,204	$25,005,658,757	$23,769,377,707
Total Expenses	27,344,714,809	25,732,517,728	24,532,894,862	23,196,248,891	21,618,044,952
COMMUNITY HEALTH INDICATORS PER 1000 POPULATION					
Total Population (in thousands)	10,617	10,519	10,429	10,310	10,215
Inpatient					
Beds	2.3	2.4	2.4	2.4	2.4
Admissions	97.6	96.6	96.2	96.5	96
Inpatient Days	612.3	610.8	608.7	611.8	608.5
Inpatient Surgeries	24.3	23.4	25.2	25.3	25.2
Births	11.4	11.6	11.9	12	12.3
Outpatient					
Emergency Outpatient Visits	436	445.6	454.5	451.9	437.7
Other Outpatient Visits	1,492	1,451.1	1,407.4	1,403.5	1,223.5
Total Outpatient Visits	1,928.1	1,896.8	1,861.9	1,855.4	1,661.1
Outpatient Surgeries	49.6	47.9	47.9	47.5	46.4
Expense per Capita (per person)	2,591.5	2,460.1	2,368.2	2,264.9	2,132.7

Note: These data represent hospital performance in the years 2015 – 2019 and do not reflect any impacts from the COVID-19 pandemic in 2020 and thereafter.

States

TABLE 6

HAWAII

U.S. Community Hospitals
(Nonfederal, short-term general and other special hospitals)

Overview 2015–2019

	2019	2018	2017	2016	2015
Total Community Hospitals in Hawaii	22	22	23	23	24
Bed Size Category					
6-24	5	5	6	6	6
25-49	3	3	3	3	3
50-99	3	3	4	5	5
100-199	8	8	7	6	7
200-299	2	2	2	2	2
300-399	0	0	0	0	0
400-499	0	0	0	0	0
500 + ...	1	1	1	1	1
Location					
Hospitals Urban	15	15	15	15	16
Hospitals Rural...	7	7	8	8	8
Control					
State and Local Government	4	5	5	6	9
Not for Profit..	18	17	18	17	15
Investor owned..	0	0	0	0	0
Affiliations					
Hospitals in a System	18	18	19	19	20
Hospitals in a Group Purchasing Organization...	9	9	8	13	16

Note: These data represent hospital performance in the years 2015 – 2019 and do not reflect any impacts from the COVID-19 pandemic in 2020 and thereafter.

States

TABLE 6

HAWAII

U.S. Community Hospitals
(Nonfederal, short-term general and other special hospitals)

Utilization, Personnel, Revenue and Expenses, Community Health Indicators 2015–2019

	2019	2018	2017	2016	2015
TOTAL FACILITY (Includes Hospital and Nursing Home Units)					
Utilization - Inpatient					
Beds	2,731	2,749	2,594	2,488	2,645
Admissions	113,544	108,634	111,293	110,104	110,061
Inpatient Days	706,387	710,649	706,540	703,010	717,607
Average Length of Stay	6.2	6.5	6.3	6.4	6.5
Inpatient Surgeries	25,595	30,499	25,051	29,232	30,138
Births	15,328	16,298	19,322	18,495	17,140
Utilization - Outpatient					
Emergency Outpatient Visits	497,344	462,713	452,405	468,601	487,500
Other Outpatient Visits	2,279,269	2,244,228	2,215,832	2,107,180	1,962,647
Total Outpatient Visits	2,776,613	2,706,941	2,668,237	2,575,781	2,450,147
Outpatient Surgeries	70,317	63,849	60,366	58,636	56,872
Personnel					
Full Time RNs	4,401	4,217	3,910	4,510	4,331
Full Time LPNs	158	152	170	170	198
Part Time RNs	1,475	1,556	1,296	1,413	1,487
Part Time LPNs	56	50	55	48	43
Total Full Time	14,937	14,523	14,532	15,310	15,195
Total Part Time	4,450	4,626	3,989	3,973	4,007
Revenue - Inpatient					
Gross Inpatient Revenue	$5,964,210,266	$6,226,151,157	$5,064,700,177	$4,781,623,649	$4,577,583,888
Revenue - Outpatient					
Gross Outpatient Revenue	$6,294,636,384	$5,984,315,978	$5,252,961,749	$4,718,970,176	$4,190,277,597
Revenue and Expenses - Totals					
(Includes Inpatient and Outpatient)					
Total Gross Revenue	$12,258,846,650	$12,210,467,135	$10,317,661,926	$9,500,593,825	$8,767,861,485
Deductions from Revenue	8,623,717,179	8,355,388,479	6,795,830,332	6,134,403,356	5,555,573,283
Net Patient Revenue	3,635,129,471	3,855,078,656	3,521,831,594	3,366,190,469	3,212,288,202
Other Operating Revenue	707,916,781	315,745,461	225,694,184	217,984,188	233,450,364
Other Nonoperating Revenue	60,760,083	83,776,460	127,041,497	30,217,539	54,891,387
Total Net Revenue	4,403,806,335	4,254,600,577	3,874,567,275	3,614,392,196	3,500,629,953
Total Expenses	4,106,036,758	3,931,578,561	3,738,396,611	3,556,186,542	3,350,489,890
HOSPITAL UNIT (Excludes Separate Nursing Home Units)					
Utilization - Inpatient					
Beds	2,731	2,644	2,594	2,360	2,320
Admissions	113,544	108,556	111,275	109,558	108,928
Inpatient Days	706,387	678,989	706,319	671,095	610,787
Average Length of Stay	6.2	6.3	6.3	6.1	5.6
Personnel					
Total Full Time	14,937	14,405	14,517	15,265	14,918
Total Part Time	4,450	4,623	3,989	3,953	3,953
Revenue and Expenses - Totals					
(Includes Inpatient and Outpatient)					
Total Net Revenue	$4,403,806,335	$4,243,703,207	$3,874,567,275	$3,596,598,513	$3,450,094,108
Total Expenses	4,106,036,758	3,922,172,191	3,738,396,611	3,543,403,181	3,306,636,383
COMMUNITY HEALTH INDICATORS PER 1000 POPULATION					
Total Population (in thousands)	1,416	1,420	1,428	1,429	1,432
Inpatient					
Beds	1.9	1.9	1.8	1.7	1.8
Admissions	80.2	76.5	78	77.1	76.9
Inpatient Days	498.9	500.3	494.9	492.1	501.3
Inpatient Surgeries	18.1	21.5	17.5	20.5	21.1
Births	10.8	11.5	13.5	12.9	12
Outpatient					
Emergency Outpatient Visits	351.3	325.7	316.9	328	340.5
Other Outpatient Visits	1,609.8	1,579.9	1,552.2	1,475.0	1,370.9
Total Outpatient Visits	1,961.1	1,905.6	1,869.1	1,803.1	1,711.5
Outpatient Surgeries	49.7	44.9	42.3	41	39.7
Expense per Capita (per person)	2,900.0	2,767.8	2,618.8	2,489.4	2,340.4

Note: These data represent hospital performance in the years 2015 – 2019 and do not reflect any impacts from the COVID-19 pandemic in 2020 and thereafter.

States

TABLE 6

IDAHO

U.S. Community Hospitals
(Nonfederal, short-term general and other special hospitals)

Overview 2015–2019

	2019	2018	2017	2016	2015
Total Community Hospitals in Idaho	46	45	46	44	44
Bed Size Category					
6-24	17	17	16	17	15
25-49	13	13	12	11	12
50-99	7	6	9	8	9
100-199	4	4	4	3	3
200-299	2	3	3	3	2
300-399	2	1	1	1	2
400-499	0	0	0	0	0
500 +	1	1	1	1	1
Location					
Hospitals Urban	22	21	19	17	17
Hospitals Rural	24	24	27	27	27
Control					
State and Local Government	17	17	18	18	18
Not for Profit	19	20	18	17	17
Investor owned	10	8	10	9	9
Affiliations					
Hospitals in a System	24	24	24	23	23
Hospitals in a Group Purchasing Organization	22	23	26	27	25

Note: These data represent hospital performance in the years 2015 – 2019 and do not reflect any impacts from the COVID-19 pandemic in 2020 and thereafter.

States

TABLE 6

IDAHO

U.S. Community Hospitals
(Nonfederal, short-term general and other special hospitals)

Utilization, Personnel, Revenue and Expenses, Community Health Indicators 2015–2019

	2019	2018	2017	2016	2015
TOTAL FACILITY (Includes Hospital and Nursing Home Units)					
Utilization - Inpatient					
Beds	3,468	3,396	3,531	3,388	3,425
Admissions	138,405	139,996	142,843	133,215	131,581
Inpatient Days	639,152	630,699	722,719	674,515	643,867
Average Length of Stay	4.6	4.5	5.1	5.1	4.9
Inpatient Surgeries	41,061	40,049	38,797	36,562	36,100
Births	19,277	19,152	19,347	19,484	20,474
Utilization - Outpatient					
Emergency Outpatient Visits	688,976	720,026	697,045	675,761	682,440
Other Outpatient Visits	5,744,940	5,541,913	5,138,377	4,904,213	5,206,241
Total Outpatient Visits	6,433,916	6,261,939	5,835,422	5,579,974	5,888,681
Outpatient Surgeries	100,924	95,034	98,424	94,377	91,487
Personnel					
Full Time RNs	5,953	6,723	6,013	5,599	5,686
Full Time LPNs	413	463	507	491	478
Part Time RNs	2,214	3,180	2,652	2,361	2,520
Part Time LPNs	150	176	175	174	172
Total Full Time	21,795	26,903	25,974	26,608	25,769
Total Part Time	7,473	10,050	8,419	7,961	8,414
Revenue - Inpatient					
Gross Inpatient Revenue	$7,152,774,610	$7,313,625,418	$7,312,478,673	$5,922,043,662	$5,320,925,720
Revenue - Outpatient					
Gross Outpatient Revenue	$8,005,089,997	$8,695,441,207	$7,706,151,712	$6,956,049,447	$6,220,752,093
Revenue and Expenses - Totals					
(Includes Inpatient and Outpatient)					
Total Gross Revenue	$15,157,864,607	$16,009,066,625	$15,018,630,385	$12,878,093,109	$11,541,677,813
Deductions from Revenue	10,250,798,120	10,574,621,793	9,461,988,644	8,051,698,061	7,086,862,605
Net Patient Revenue	4,907,066,487	5,434,444,832	5,556,641,741	4,826,395,048	4,454,815,208
Other Operating Revenue	305,457,357	239,387,790	183,596,412	144,054,151	136,171,360
Other Nonoperating Revenue	42,187,887	46,272,702	64,784,568	29,924,550	15,031,098
Total Net Revenue	5,254,711,731	5,720,105,324	5,805,022,721	5,000,373,749	4,606,017,666
Total Expenses	4,016,492,989	5,173,114,253	5,339,960,660	4,563,697,020	4,195,690,588
HOSPITAL UNIT (Excludes Separate Nursing Home Units)					
Utilization - Inpatient					
Beds	3,331	3,291	3,295	3,183	3,180
Admissions	138,216	139,857	142,393	132,815	131,113
Inpatient Days	598,430	601,076	655,819	615,828	579,403
Average Length of Stay	4.3	4.3	4.6	4.6	4.4
Personnel					
Total Full Time	21,699	26,842	25,789	26,485	25,619
Total Part Time	7,401	9,991	8,305	7,889	8,296
Revenue and Expenses - Totals					
(Includes Inpatient and Outpatient)					
Total Net Revenue	$5,244,137,691	$5,711,272,543	$5,785,009,783	$4,981,847,536	$4,588,407,928
Total Expenses	4,006,933,393	5,166,586,575	5,323,613,091	4,551,852,106	4,183,033,932
COMMUNITY HEALTH INDICATORS PER 1000 POPULATION					
Total Population (in thousands)	1,787	1,754	1,717	1,683	1,655
Inpatient					
Beds	1.9	1.9	2.1	2	2.1
Admissions	77.4	79.8	83.2	79.1	79.5
Inpatient Days	357.7	359.5	420.9	400.7	389.1
Inpatient Surgeries	23	22.8	22.6	21.7	21.8
Births	10.8	10.9	11.3	11.6	12.4
Outpatient					
Emergency Outpatient Visits	385.5	410.5	406	401.5	412.4
Other Outpatient Visits	3,214.7	3,159.2	2,992.7	2,913.7	3,145.9
Total Outpatient Visits	3,600.3	3,569.7	3,398.7	3,315.2	3,558.3
Outpatient Surgeries	56.5	54.2	57.3	56.1	55.3
Expense per Capita (per person)	$2,247.5	$2,949	$3,110.2	$2,711.4	$2,535.3

Note: These data represent hospital performance in the years 2015 – 2019 and do not reflect any impacts from the COVID-19 pandemic in 2020 and thereafter.

States

TABLE **6**

ILLINOIS

U.S. Community Hospitals
(Nonfederal, short-term general and other special hospitals)

Overview 2015–2019

	2019	2018	2017	2016	2015
Total Community Hospitals in Illinois	185	187	189	189	188
Bed Size Category					
6-24	16	16	14	14	16
25-49	38	36	37	35	35
50-99	26	27	28	32	29
100-199	47	47	54	49	49
200-299	26	28	24	29	29
300-399	15	15	17	15	16
400-499	9	10	7	7	6
500 + ...	8	8	8	8	8
Location					
Hospitals Urban	128	130	131	131	130
Hospitals Rural	57	57	58	58	58
Control					
State and Local Government	23	23	23	23	24
Not for Profit	146	146	146	145	143
Investor owned	16	18	20	21	21
Affiliations					
Hospitals in a System	124	123	128	126	125
Hospitals in a Group Purchasing Organization...	138	139	144	144	149

Note: These data represent hospital performance in the years 2015 – 2019 and do not reflect any impacts from the COVID-19 pandemic in 2020 and thereafter.

TABLE 6

ILLINOIS

U.S. Community Hospitals
(Nonfederal, short-term general and other special hospitals)

Utilization, Personnel, Revenue and Expenses, Community Health Indicators 2015–2019

	2019	2018	2017	2016	2015
TOTAL FACILITY (Includes Hospital and Nursing Home Units)					
Utilization - Inpatient					
Beds	31,262	32,066	31,996	31,873	31,823
Admissions	1,326,907	1,357,534	1,364,376	1,377,652	1,385,953
Inpatient Days	6,762,533	6,822,518	6,882,225	6,898,909	6,827,990
Average Length of Stay	5.1	5.0	5.0	5.0	4.9
Inpatient Surgeries	320,080	322,415	330,136	347,888	354,815
Births	132,191	136,669	141,539	147,094	148,744
Utilization - Outpatient					
Emergency Outpatient Visits	5,631,309	5,488,964	5,630,049	5,533,962	5,556,422
Other Outpatient Visits	33,589,589	32,139,739	31,945,388	32,555,203	32,014,417
Total Outpatient Visits	39,220,898	37,628,703	37,575,437	38,089,165	37,570,839
Outpatient Surgeries	721,407	734,668	717,855	740,446	755,329
Personnel					
Full Time RNs	54,321	53,339	51,577	50,475	49,064
Full Time LPNs	1,642	1,351	1,458	1,432	1,448
Part Time RNs	24,433	22,996	24,693	21,840	23,064
Part Time LPNs	680	482	597	512	529
Total Full Time	188,286	184,073	176,871	176,838	173,895
Total Part Time	88,987	77,898	91,256	70,056	72,077
Revenue - Inpatient					
Gross Inpatient Revenue	$74,487,092,614	$70,557,018,710	$68,234,158,866	$65,264,725,254	$61,802,651,499
Revenue - Outpatient					
Gross Outpatient Revenue	$88,637,200,421	$83,981,627,892	$79,158,726,167	$72,424,068,382	$67,143,188,040
Revenue and Expenses - Totals					
(Includes Inpatient and Outpatient)					
Total Gross Revenue	$163,124,293,035	$154,538,646,602	$147,392,885,033	$137,688,793,636	$128,945,839,539
Deductions from Revenue	120,404,938,657	113,323,802,464	107,849,899,103	99,650,575,691	92,652,197,929
Net Patient Revenue	42,719,354,378	41,214,844,138	39,542,985,930	38,038,217,945	36,293,641,610
Other Operating Revenue	3,100,791,214	2,568,321,367	2,270,985,342	1,830,045,808	2,137,345,481
Other Nonoperating Revenue	982,109,079	649,014,328	1,357,513,730	1,723,122,194	163,550,113
Total Net Revenue	46,802,254,671	44,432,179,833	43,171,485,002	41,591,385,947	38,594,537,204
Total Expenses	42,851,312,470	41,193,864,321	39,236,137,639	37,077,167,759	35,872,183,416
HOSPITAL UNIT (Excludes Separate Nursing Home Units)					
Utilization - Inpatient					
Beds	30,661	31,370	31,227	30,868	30,729
Admissions	1,321,111	1,351,510	1,358,521	1,369,118	1,377,209
Inpatient Days	6,588,816	6,632,896	6,697,835	6,628,569	6,549,361
Average Length of Stay	5.0	4.9	4.9	4.8	4.8
Personnel					
Total Full Time	187,884	183,575	176,460	176,384	173,327
Total Part Time	88,658	77,592	90,959	69,741	71,658
Revenue and Expenses - Totals					
(Includes Inpatient and Outpatient)					
Total Net Revenue	$46,739,260,552	$44,355,591,100	$43,111,397,814	$41,380,305,019	$38,393,201,864
Total Expenses	42,805,437,610	41,139,612,120	39,187,355,431	36,982,904,648	35,779,914,464
COMMUNITY HEALTH INDICATORS PER 1000 POPULATION					
Total Population (in thousands)	12,672	12,741	12,802	12,802	12,860
Inpatient					
Beds	2.5	2.5	2.5	2.5	2.5
Admissions	104.7	106.5	106.6	107.6	107.8
Inpatient Days	533.7	535.5	537.6	538.9	530.9
Inpatient Surgeries	25.3	25.3	25.8	27.2	27.6
Births	10.4	10.7	11.1	11.5	11.6
Outpatient					
Emergency Outpatient Visits	444.4	430.8	439.8	432.3	432.1
Other Outpatient Visits	2,650.7	2,522.5	2,495.3	2,543.1	2,489.5
Total Outpatient Visits	3,095.1	2,953.3	2,935.1	2,975.4	2,921.5
Outpatient Surgeries	56.9	57.7	56.1	57.8	58.7
Expense per Capita (per person)	$3,381.6	$3,233.2	$3,064.8	$2,896.3	$2,789.4

Note: These data represent hospital performance in the years 2015 – 2019 and do not reflect any impacts from the COVID-19 pandemic in 2020 and thereafter.

States

TABLE 6

INDIANA

U.S. Community Hospitals
(Nonfederal, short-term general and other special hospitals)

Overview 2015–2019

	2019	2018	2017	2016	2015
Total Community Hospitals in Indiana...............	129	132	132	134	136
Bed Size Category					
6-24	14	15	14	14	14
25-49	42	42	43	45	47
50-99	22	23	23	22	22
100-199	21	22	24	25	25
200-299	12	13	12	13	12
300-399	6	6	5	5	5
400-499	7	5	6	5	5
500 + ...	5	6	5	5	6
Location					
Hospitals Urban	87	89	91	93	93
Hospitals Rural....................................	42	43	41	41	43
Control					
State and Local Government	26	25	26	26	27
Not for Profit	72	73	72	72	72
Investor owned....................................	31	34	34	36	37
Affiliations					
Hospitals in a System	94	94	93	95	97
Hospitals in a Group Purchasing Organization...	86	97	99	102	96

Note: These data represent hospital performance in the years 2015 – 2019 and do not reflect any impacts from the COVID-19 pandemic in 2020 and thereafter.

States

TABLE 6

INDIANA

U.S. Community Hospitals
(Nonfederal, short-term general and other special hospitals)

Utilization, Personnel, Revenue and Expenses, Community Health Indicators 2015–2019

	2019	2018	2017	2016	2015
TOTAL FACILITY (Includes Hospital and Nursing Home Units)					
Utilization - Inpatient					
Beds	18,237	18,156	17,821	17,936	18,306
Admissions	735,348	728,676	715,442	715,146	715,653
Inpatient Days	3,864,788	3,707,730	3,686,520	3,713,338	3,789,207
Average Length of Stay	5.3	5.1	5.2	5.2	5.3
Inpatient Surgeries	206,319	196,696	190,373	199,452	188,854
Births	78,181	80,843	77,809	79,396	78,764
Utilization - Outpatient					
Emergency Outpatient Visits	3,379,414	3,700,024	3,526,829	3,480,695	3,546,717
Other Outpatient Visits	18,475,586	17,783,847	17,385,991	17,861,240	16,829,211
Total Outpatient Visits	21,855,000	21,483,871	20,912,820	21,341,935	20,375,928
Outpatient Surgeries	490,657	475,903	455,449	502,004	446,076
Personnel					
Full Time RNs	25,149	26,712	25,221	24,338	23,989
Full Time LPNs	1,194	1,255	1,246	1,158	1,261
Part Time RNs	15,693	15,140	15,419	16,000	14,442
Part Time LPNs	580	574	613	592	613
Total Full Time	92,244	96,556	92,299	92,372	91,030
Total Part Time	46,924	45,487	46,153	44,992	41,644
Revenue - Inpatient					
Gross Inpatient Revenue	$43,214,920,213	$38,878,433,396	$36,994,949,495	$34,460,007,043	$32,553,063,266
Revenue - Outpatient					
Gross Outpatient Revenue	$51,227,014,541	$44,823,289,471	$41,931,420,629	$38,998,210,596	$35,372,605,251
Revenue and Expenses - Totals					
(Includes Inpatient and Outpatient)					
Total Gross Revenue	$94,441,934,754	$83,701,722,867	$78,926,370,124	$73,458,217,639	$67,925,668,517
Deductions from Revenue	67,634,266,772	59,340,348,381	55,420,080,141	50,940,632,393	46,270,658,365
Net Patient Revenue	26,807,667,982	24,361,374,486	23,506,289,983	22,517,585,246	21,655,010,152
Other Operating Revenue	1,850,076,248	1,806,176,001	1,674,318,897	1,824,366,987	1,535,969,523
Other Nonoperating Revenue	1,214,132,443	-96,848,963	996,835,885	449,845,276	-68,660,470
Total Net Revenue	29,871,876,673	26,070,701,524	26,177,444,765	24,791,797,509	23,122,319,205
Total Expenses	25,028,910,868	23,492,018,667	22,215,113,382	21,662,042,795	19,780,623,659
HOSPITAL UNIT (Excludes Separate Nursing Home Units)					
Utilization - Inpatient					
Beds	17,600	17,467	17,126	17,186	17,267
Admissions	734,134	726,794	713,575	712,265	712,566
Inpatient Days	3,637,267	3,532,634	3,507,737	3,514,723	3,514,053
Average Length of Stay	5.0	4.9	4.9	4.9	4.9
Personnel					
Total Full Time	92,053	96,100	91,885	92,015	90,323
Total Part Time	46,680	45,145	45,845	44,634	41,167
Revenue and Expenses - Totals					
(Includes Inpatient and Outpatient)					
Total Net Revenue	$29,822,016,992	$26,019,731,224	$26,125,262,164	$24,729,147,061	$23,033,995,206
Total Expenses	24,983,202,197	23,462,198,170	22,176,512,621	21,622,019,579	19,713,185,720
COMMUNITY HEALTH INDICATORS PER 1000 POPULATION					
Total Population (in thousands)	6,732	6,692	6,667	6,633	6,620
Inpatient					
Beds	2.7	2.7	2.7	2.7	2.8
Admissions	109.2	108.9	107.3	107.8	108.1
Inpatient Days	574.1	554.1	553	559.8	572.4
Inpatient Surgeries	30.6	29.4	28.6	30.1	28.5
Births	11.6	12.1	11.7	12	11.9
Outpatient					
Emergency Outpatient Visits	502	552.9	529	524.8	535.8
Other Outpatient Visits	2,744.4	2,657.5	2,607.8	2,692.8	2,542.3
Total Outpatient Visits	3,246.3	3,210.4	3,136.9	3,217.5	3,078.1
Outpatient Surgeries	72.9	71.1	68.3	75.7	67.4
Expense per Capita (per person)	$3,717.8	$3,510.5	$3,332.2	$3,265.8	$2,988.2

Note: These data represent hospital performance in the years 2015 – 2019 and do not reflect any impacts from the COVID-19 pandemic in 2020 and thereafter.

States

TABLE **6**

IOWA

U.S. Community Hospitals
(Nonfederal, short-term general and other special hospitals)

Overview 2015–2019

	2019	2018	2017	2016	2015
Total Community Hospitals in Iowa	117	118	117	118	119
Bed Size Category					
6-24	28	25	25	25	22
25-49	47	49	48	48	51
50-99	20	20	20	20	22
100-199	10	11	10	11	10
200-299	6	6	7	7	7
300-399	3	4	4	4	4
400-499	0	0	0	0	0
500 + ...	3	3	3	3	3
Location					
Hospitals Urban	36	37	34	35	36
Hospitals Rural...	81	81	83	83	83
Control					
State and Local Government	59	59	58	58	59
Not for Profit..	55	56	57	58	58
Investor owned..	3	3	2	2	2
Affiliations					
Hospitals in a System	88	89	78	77	74
Hospitals in a Group Purchasing Organization...	116	116	113	117	119

Note: These data represent hospital performance in the years 2015 – 2019 and do not reflect any impacts from the COVID-19 pandemic in 2020 and thereafter.

TABLE 6

IOWA

U.S. Community Hospitals
(Nonfederal, short-term general and other special hospitals)

Utilization, Personnel, Revenue and Expenses, Community Health Indicators 2015–2019

	2019	2018	2017	2016	2015
TOTAL FACILITY (Includes Hospital and Nursing Home Units)					
Utilization - Inpatient					
Beds	9,459	9,423	9,365	9,552	9,608
Admissions	308,139	315,047	315,667	315,146	325,123
Inpatient Days	1,879,720	1,913,280	1,937,198	1,930,469	1,977,340
Average Length of Stay	6.1	6.1	6.1	6.1	6.1
Inpatient Surgeries	78,137	82,348	81,261	82,456	79,852
Births	37,417	37,441	38,237	39,034	39,100
Utilization - Outpatient					
Emergency Outpatient Visits	1,317,142	1,359,801	1,348,809	1,369,607	1,363,799
Other Outpatient Visits	10,902,397	10,134,622	10,222,405	10,066,760	9,692,797
Total Outpatient Visits	12,219,539	11,494,423	11,571,214	11,436,367	11,056,596
Outpatient Surgeries	260,513	248,337	253,467	254,174	255,548
Personnel					
Full Time RNs	13,120	13,490	12,716	12,860	12,402
Full Time LPNs	791	801	814	759	742
Part Time RNs	7,017	7,047	6,892	6,777	6,449
Part Time LPNs	420	467	403	518	519
Total Full Time	49,024	50,371	48,393	47,907	46,747
Total Part Time	22,987	23,162	23,108	22,932	21,640
Revenue - Inpatient					
Gross Inpatient Revenue	$11,618,007,443	$11,188,108,879	$10,516,870,326	$10,204,775,701	$9,783,286,716
Revenue - Outpatient					
Gross Outpatient Revenue	$17,988,734,852	$16,431,436,558	$14,972,359,965	$14,161,466,846	$12,979,201,679
Revenue and Expenses - Totals					
(Includes Inpatient and Outpatient)					
Total Gross Revenue	$29,606,742,295	$27,619,545,437	$25,489,230,291	$24,366,242,547	$22,762,488,395
Deductions from Revenue	19,943,105,369	18,326,761,481	16,656,693,131	15,643,117,079	14,413,539,150
Net Patient Revenue	9,663,636,926	9,292,783,956	8,832,537,160	8,723,125,468	8,348,949,245
Other Operating Revenue	848,044,781	780,952,347	739,484,280	712,536,434	667,629,369
Other Nonoperating Revenue	354,012,720	112,755,305	327,631,324	146,959,168	140,063,075
Total Net Revenue	10,865,694,427	10,186,491,608	9,899,652,764	9,582,621,070	9,156,641,689
Total Expenses	10,143,103,866	9,859,076,269	9,376,783,236	8,998,959,972	8,472,369,408
HOSPITAL UNIT (Excludes Separate Nursing Home Units)					
Utilization - Inpatient					
Beds	8,152	8,045	7,824	7,986	8,030
Admissions	306,666	312,710	313,180	312,326	322,071
Inpatient Days	1,457,375	1,441,340	1,449,722	1,436,856	1,478,571
Average Length of Stay	4.8	4.6	4.6	4.6	4.6
Personnel					
Total Full Time	48,392	49,691	47,656	47,185	46,025
Total Part Time	22,344	22,429	22,288	22,151	20,871
Revenue and Expenses - Totals					
(Includes Inpatient and Outpatient)					
Total Net Revenue	$10,781,545,259	$10,088,769,947	$9,800,591,168	$9,492,100,853	$9,070,795,149
Total Expenses	10,069,629,764	9,781,507,405	9,295,878,507	8,924,734,007	8,399,843,682
COMMUNITY HEALTH INDICATORS PER 1000 POPULATION					
Total Population (in thousands)	3,155	3,156	3,146	3,135	3,124
Inpatient					
Beds	3	3	3	3	3.1
Admissions	97.7	99.8	100.3	100.5	104.1
Inpatient Days	595.8	606.2	615.8	615.8	633
Inpatient Surgeries	24.8	26.1	25.8	26.3	25.6
Births	11.9	11.9	12.2	12.5	12.5
Outpatient					
Emergency Outpatient Visits	417.5	430.8	428.8	436.9	436.6
Other Outpatient Visits	3,455.5	3,211.1	3,249.6	3,211.4	3,102.8
Total Outpatient Visits	3,873	3,641.9	3,678.4	3,648.3	3,539.4
Outpatient Surgeries	82.6	78.7	80.6	81.1	81.8
Expense per Capita (per person)	$3,214.9	$3,123.8	$2,980.8	$2,870.8	$2,712.1

Note: These data represent hospital performance in the years 2015 – 2019 and do not reflect any impacts from the COVID-19 pandemic in 2020 and thereafter.

States

TABLE **6**

KANSAS

U.S. Community Hospitals
(Nonfederal, short-term general and other special hospitals)

Overview 2015–2019

	2019	2018	2017	2016	2015
Total Community Hospitals in Kansas...............	138	139	144	143	143
Bed Size Category					
6-24	38	31	33	33	31
25-49	55	60	59	57	57
50-99	23	26	30	30	31
100-199	12	12	12	13	14
200-299	5	5	5	5	5
300-399	2	2	2	1	2
400-499	0	0	0	1	0
500 +	3	3	3	3	3
Location					
Hospitals Urban	44	45	45	44	44
Hospitals Rural.......................................	94	94	99	99	99
Control					
State and Local Government	61	62	62	62	65
Not for Profit..	50	50	52	52	51
Investor owned......................................	27	27	30	29	27
Affiliations					
Hospitals in a System	54	55	58	54	53
Hospitals in a Group Purchasing Organization...	110	111	115	131	137

Note: These data represent hospital performance in the years 2015 – 2019 and do not reflect any impacts from the COVID-19 pandemic in 2020 and thereafter.

TABLE 6

KANSAS

U.S. Community Hospitals
(Nonfederal, short-term general and other special hospitals)

Utilization, Personnel, Revenue and Expenses, Community Health Indicators 2015–2019

	2019	2018	2017	2016	2015
TOTAL FACILITY (Includes Hospital and Nursing Home Units)					
Utilization - Inpatient					
Beds..	9,544	9,659	9,899	9,913	10,079
Admissions.....................................	316,464	318,566	316,472	312,254	308,536
Inpatient Days................................	1,936,123	1,870,624	1,910,634	1,952,068	1,939,567
Average Length of Stay	6.1	5.9	6.0	6.3	6.3
Inpatient Surgeries..........................	78,814	78,271	75,280	77,376	76,009
Births...	32,477	32,642	36,477	38,049	38,418
Utilization - Outpatient					
Emergency Outpatient Visits..............	1,196,829	1,196,146	1,195,636	1,233,808	1,237,301
Other Outpatient Visits.....................	7,734,885	7,612,888	7,088,959	6,647,463	6,244,996
Total Outpatient Visits......................	8,931,714	8,809,034	8,284,595	7,881,271	7,482,297
Outpatient Surgeries........................	205,955	199,316	194,337	195,575	191,715
Personnel					
Full Time RNs.................................	13,552	13,310	13,293	13,410	12,432
Full Time LPNs...............................	1,238	1,196	1,241	1,207	1,030
Part Time RNs................................	5,798	5,407	5,447	5,387	5,226
Part Time LPNs...............................	405	404	373	355	392
Total Full Time................................	47,489	45,894	46,833	45,167	42,298
Total Part Time...............................	19,033	17,782	17,645	17,419	15,564
Revenue - Inpatient					
Gross Inpatient Revenue	$16,842,622,097	$16,231,862,372	$14,825,538,265	$13,754,805,803	$12,829,556,393
Revenue - Outpatient					
Gross Outpatient Revenue	$20,966,910,808	$18,906,048,147	$17,380,326,815	$15,547,913,194	$13,858,975,826
Revenue and Expenses - Totals					
(Includes Inpatient and Outpatient)					
Total Gross Revenue	$37,809,532,905	$35,137,910,519	$32,205,865,080	$29,302,718,997	$26,688,532,219
Deductions from Revenue	27,977,196,372	25,720,173,567	23,420,655,882	20,983,340,008	18,936,223,597
Net Patient Revenue........................	9,832,336,533	9,417,736,952	8,785,209,198	8,319,378,989	7,752,308,622
Other Operating Revenue.................	618,087,085	535,629,621	404,599,928	420,295,497	415,203,315
Other Nonoperating Revenue............	147,350,696	125,964,542	203,067,179	71,735,083	2,201,599
Total Net Revenue...........................	10,597,774,314	10,079,331,115	9,392,876,305	8,811,409,569	8,169,713,536
Total Expenses...............................	9,810,088,922	9,141,985,246	8,717,686,849	8,089,610,415	7,543,430,309
HOSPITAL UNIT (Excludes Separate Nursing Home Units)					
Utilization - Inpatient					
Beds...	8,510	8,586	8,766	8,625	8,678
Admissions.....................................	314,931	316,835	314,640	310,634	306,569
Inpatient Days................................	1,541,312	1,542,998	1,569,660	1,501,114	1,516,264
Average Length of Stay	4.9	4.9	5.0	4.8	4.9
Personnel					
Total Full Time................................	46,755	45,129	46,060	44,242	41,368
Total Part Time...............................	18,636	17,362	17,236	16,943	15,055
Revenue and Expenses - Totals					
(Includes Inpatient and Outpatient)					
Total Net Revenue...........................	$10,531,283,952	$10,010,469,469	$9,313,318,330	$8,738,217,315	$8,090,610,426
Total Expenses	9,752,650,081	9,077,879,655	8,634,099,185	8,030,136,721	7,476,082,228
COMMUNITY HEALTH INDICATORS PER 1000 POPULATION					
Total Population (in thousands)..........	2,913	2,912	2,913	2,907	2,912
Inpatient					
Beds...	3.3	3.3	3.4	3.4	3.5
Admissions.....................................	108.6	109.4	108.6	107.4	106
Inpatient Days................................	664.6	642.5	655.9	671.4	666.1
Inpatient Surgeries..........................	27.1	26.9	25.8	26.6	26.1
Births...	11.1	11.2	12.5	13.1	13.2
Outpatient					
Emergency Outpatient Visits..............	410.8	410.8	410.4	424.4	424.9
Other Outpatient Visits.....................	2,655	2,614.8	2,433.5	2,286.5	2,144.8
Total Outpatient Visits......................	3,065.8	3,025.6	2,843.9	2,710.9	2,569.8
Outpatient Surgeries	70.7	68.5	66.7	67.3	65.8
Expense per Capita (per person)........	$3,367.3	$3,140	$2,992.6	$2,782.5	$2,590.8

Note: These data represent hospital performance in the years 2015 – 2019 and do not reflect any impacts from the COVID-19 pandemic in 2020 and thereafter.

States

TABLE 6

KENTUCKY

U.S. Community Hospitals
(Nonfederal, short-term general and other special hospitals)

Overview 2015–2019

	2019	2018	2017	2016	2015
Total Community Hospitals in Kentucky	104	105	109	110	108
Bed Size Category					
6-24	5	5	5	4	3
25-49	41	40	40	38	37
50-99	14	15	16	20	20
100-199	23	23	24	24	24
200-299	8	9	11	11	9
300-399	6	7	9	9	11
400-499	4	2	1	1	1
500 + ...	3	4	3	3	3
Location					
Hospitals Urban	38	39	43	44	44
Hospitals Rural	66	66	66	66	64
Control					
State and Local Government	11	11	11	10	12
Not for Profit	72	72	76	77	76
Investor owned	21	22	22	23	20
Affiliations					
Hospitals in a System	81	82	87	88	87
Hospitals in a Group Purchasing Organization...	39	50	67	73	75

Note: These data represent hospital performance in the years 2015 – 2019 and do not reflect any impacts from the COVID-19 pandemic in 2020 and thereafter.

TABLE 6

KENTUCKY

U.S. Community Hospitals
(Nonfederal, short-term general and other special hospitals)

Utilization, Personnel, Revenue and Expenses, Community Health Indicators 2015–2019

	2019	2018	2017	2016	2015
TOTAL FACILITY (Includes Hospital and Nursing Home Units)					
Utilization - Inpatient					
Beds................................	14,151	14,329	14,115	14,314	14,372
Admissions........................	557,552	560,981	560,311	563,240	558,979
Inpatient Days...................	3,097,160	3,157,874	3,109,708	3,131,068	3,124,169
Average Length of Stay.....	5.6	5.6	5.5	5.6	5.6
Inpatient Surgeries............	152,306	154,042	157,202	161,015	149,677
Births...............................	54,340	53,245	51,034	55,003	53,551
Utilization - Outpatient					
Emergency Outpatient Visits..........	2,693,016	2,679,937	2,551,891	2,607,126	2,512,293
Other Outpatient Visits...............	12,781,236	12,219,136	11,861,846	11,277,451	10,530,286
Total Outpatient Visits...............	15,474,252	14,899,073	14,413,737	13,884,577	13,042,579
Outpatient Surgeries..............	362,945	378,009	375,896	381,540	371,144
Personnel					
Full Time RNs....................	22,230	22,063	21,673	20,687	19,312
Full Time LPNs..................	873	993	932	1,114	1,423
Part Time RNs...................	8,299	7,890	7,077	7,117	7,018
Part Time LPNs..................	247	249	248	239	289
Total Full Time...................	70,264	69,590	68,966	67,323	66,318
Total Part Time..................	22,126	20,882	18,818	19,595	19,962
Revenue - Inpatient					
Gross Inpatient Revenue..................	$29,349,674,753	$27,922,583,363	$25,439,271,058	$23,957,337,034	$21,689,736,794
Revenue - Outpatient					
Gross Outpatient Revenue..............	$32,196,995,062	$31,327,377,737	$28,181,172,622	$26,219,689,105	$24,030,691,691
Revenue and Expenses - Totals					
(Includes Inpatient and Outpatient)					
Total Gross Revenue..............	$61,546,669,815	$59,249,961,100	$53,620,443,680	$50,177,026,139	$45,720,428,485
Deductions from Revenue...............	46,253,534,126	44,882,047,761	39,974,240,869	36,989,058,278	33,221,412,847
Net Patient Revenue..........	15,293,135,689	14,367,913,339	13,646,202,811	13,187,967,861	12,499,015,638
Other Operating Revenue..............	639,385,637	587,998,145	460,278,980	527,907,529	493,337,445
Other Nonoperating Revenue............	287,220,827	125,708,599	262,751,428	73,557,949	29,244,430
Total Net Revenue.............	16,219,742,153	15,081,620,083	14,369,233,219	13,789,433,339	13,021,597,513
Total Expenses.................	14,575,498,231	14,077,164,334	13,526,306,127	12,870,942,144	11,871,401,511
HOSPITAL UNIT (Excludes Separate Nursing Home Units)					
Utilization - Inpatient					
Beds...............................	13,924	13,849	13,623	13,779	13,651
Admissions.......................	555,623	557,438	556,142	558,270	552,288
Inpatient Days...................	3,028,089	3,022,680	2,964,296	2,978,210	2,911,955
Average Length of Stay.....	5.4	5.4	5.3	5.3	5.3
Personnel					
Total Full Time...................	70,016	69,268	68,623	66,896	65,683
Total Part Time..................	21,987	20,680	18,657	19,475	19,797
Revenue and Expenses - Totals					
(Includes Inpatient and Outpatient)					
Total Net Revenue.............	$16,165,460,345	$15,002,160,142	$14,300,441,899	$13,704,097,399	$12,926,276,245
Total Expenses.................	14,546,257,965	14,031,846,494	13,480,070,188	12,812,542,345	11,806,227,301
COMMUNITY HEALTH INDICATORS PER 1000 POPULATION					
Total Population (in thousands).........	4,468	4,468	4,454	4,437	4,425
Inpatient					
Beds...............................	3.2	3.2	3.2	3.2	3.2
Admissions.......................	124.8	125.5	125.8	126.9	126.3
Inpatient Days...................	693.2	706.7	698.2	705.7	706
Inpatient Surgeries............	34.1	34.5	35.3	36.3	33.8
Births...............................	12.2	11.9	11.5	12.4	12.1
Outpatient					
Emergency Outpatient Visits..........	602.8	599.8	572.9	587.6	567.7
Other Outpatient Visits..............	2,860.8	2,734.6	2,663.1	2,541.7	2,379.7
Total Outpatient Visits..............	3,463.6	3,334.3	3,236	3,129.3	2,947.4
Outpatient Surgeries.............	81.2	84.6	84.4	86	83.9
Expense per Capita (per person).........	$3,262.4	$3,150.4	$3,036.8	$2,900.8	$2,682.7

Note: These data represent hospital performance in the years 2015 – 2019 and do not reflect any impacts from the COVID-19 pandemic in 2020 and thereafter.

States

Overview 2015–2019

	2019	2018	2017	2016	2015
Total Community Hospitals in Louisiana............	155	158	163	164	168
Bed Size Category					
6-24	41	43	46	46	46
25-49	56	57	53	51	53
50-99	21	19	23	25	26
100-199	16	18	20	20	21
200-299	9	9	10	12	12
300-399	6	6	5	5	4
400-499	2	2	2	2	2
500 + ...	4	4	4	3	4
Location					
Hospitals Urban	113	116	118	119	123
Hospitals Rural...	42	42	45	45	45
Control					
State and Local Government	46	47	44	45	47
Not for Profit..	45	45	47	48	46
Investor owned	64	66	72	71	75
Affiliations					
Hospitals in a System....................................	81	84	82	84	86
Hospitals in a Group Purchasing Organization...	55	52	65	67	70

Note: These data represent hospital performance in the years 2015 – 2019 and do not reflect any impacts from the COVID-19 pandemic in 2020 and thereafter.

States

TABLE 6

LOUISIANA

U.S. Community Hospitals
(Nonfederal, short-term general and other special hospitals)

Utilization, Personnel, Revenue and Expenses, Community Health Indicators 2015–2019

	2019	2018	2017	2016	2015
TOTAL FACILITY (Includes Hospital and Nursing Home Units)					
Utilization - Inpatient					
Beds	15,226	15,272	15,649	15,484	15,730
Admissions	566,912	551,844	582,708	580,466	587,438
Inpatient Days	3,138,996	3,143,237	3,269,781	3,280,472	3,348,738
Average Length of Stay	5.5	5.7	5.6	5.7	5.7
Inpatient Surgeries	147,189	155,113	161,723	164,445	156,035
Births	60,330	64,371	61,233	64,144	69,229
Utilization - Outpatient					
Emergency Outpatient Visits	2,806,279	2,938,738	2,884,237	2,924,310	2,757,044
Other Outpatient Visits	10,716,632	9,986,720	10,147,792	8,999,058	9,743,346
Total Outpatient Visits	13,522,911	12,925,458	13,032,029	11,923,368	12,500,390
Outpatient Surgeries	347,556	351,952	328,365	342,743	322,376
Personnel					
Full Time RNs	22,376	21,447	21,328	21,346	21,647
Full Time LPNs	3,232	2,941	3,009	2,877	3,021
Part Time RNs	8,137	7,928	9,009	8,612	8,593
Part Time LPNs	879	808	912	831	861
Total Full Time	80,381	77,809	73,574	76,674	76,359
Total Part Time	23,693	23,037	25,330	24,820	25,037
Revenue - Inpatient					
Gross Inpatient Revenue	$27,595,322,815	$26,364,349,061	$26,353,243,868	$25,367,115,795	$23,636,202,281
Revenue - Outpatient					
Gross Outpatient Revenue	$31,795,842,778	$30,038,801,334	$27,895,243,945	$25,105,248,635	$23,069,411,270
Revenue and Expenses - Totals					
(Includes Inpatient and Outpatient)					
Total Gross Revenue	$59,391,165,593	$56,403,150,395	$54,248,487,813	$50,472,364,430	$46,705,613,551
Deductions from Revenue	44,578,381,239	41,855,453,971	40,544,198,814	37,258,510,377	33,788,626,465
Net Patient Revenue	14,812,784,354	14,547,696,424	13,704,288,999	13,213,854,053	12,916,987,086
Other Operating Revenue	1,179,587,455	1,032,123,112	1,159,947,074	1,042,706,509	815,860,125
Other Nonoperating Revenue	280,550,018	157,135,654	160,894,753	83,899,016	45,037,057
Total Net Revenue	16,272,921,827	15,736,955,190	15,025,130,826	14,340,459,578	13,777,884,268
Total Expenses	15,069,875,085	14,718,473,226	14,288,866,792	13,455,133,714	12,672,224,525
HOSPITAL UNIT (Excludes Separate Nursing Home Units)					
Utilization - Inpatient					
Beds	14,579	14,624	14,996	14,957	15,217
Admissions	565,132	549,898	580,815	578,071	585,053
Inpatient Days	2,968,018	2,970,547	3,081,441	3,087,996	3,203,314
Average Length of Stay	5.3	5.4	5.3	5.3	5.5
Personnel					
Total Full Time	79,897	77,393	73,117	76,399	75,960
Total Part Time	23,579	22,909	25,165	24,693	24,908
Revenue and Expenses - Totals					
(Includes Inpatient and Outpatient)					
Total Net Revenue	$16,231,016,753	$15,697,302,969	$14,992,270,856	$14,306,399,774	$13,746,355,871
Total Expenses	15,025,755,229	14,678,748,888	14,255,029,380	13,426,836,407	12,645,746,776
COMMUNITY HEALTH INDICATORS PER 1000 POPULATION					
Total Population (in thousands)	4,649	4,660	4,684	4,682	4,671
Inpatient					
Beds	3.3	3.3	3.3	3.3	3.4
Admissions	121.9	118.4	124.4	124	125.8
Inpatient Days	675.2	674.5	698	700.7	717
Inpatient Surgeries	31.7	33.3	34.5	35.1	33.4
Births	13	13.8	13.1	13.7	14.8
Outpatient					
Emergency Outpatient Visits	603.7	630.6	615.7	624.6	590.3
Other Outpatient Visits	2,305.2	2,143.1	2,166.3	1,922.2	2,086
Total Outpatient Visits	2,908.9	2,773.7	2,782	2,546.8	2,676.3
Outpatient Surgeries	74.8	75.5	70.1	73.2	69
Expense per Capita (per person)	$3,241.7	$3,158.5	$3,050.4	$2,874	$2,713.1

Note: These data represent hospital performance in the years 2015 – 2019 and do not reflect any impacts from the COVID-19 pandemic in 2020 and thereafter.

States

TABLE 6

MAINE

U.S. Community Hospitals
(Nonfederal, short-term general and other special hospitals)

Overview 2015–2019

	2019	2018	2017	2016	2015
Total Community Hospitals in Maine	34	34	34	34	34
Bed Size Category					
6-24	3	2	3	3	3
25-49	15	15	14	14	15
50-99	7	8	8	8	7
100-199	6	6	6	5	5
200-299	0	0	0	1	1
300-399	2	2	2	2	2
400-499	0	0	0	0	0
500 + ...	1	1	1	1	1
Location					
Hospitals Urban	13	13	13	13	13
Hospitals Rural.......................................	21	21	21	21	21
Control					
State and Local Government	2	2	2	2	3
Not for Profit..	31	31	31	31	30
Investor owned.......................................	1	1	1	1	1
Affiliations					
Hospitals in a System	21	20	21	22	22
Hospitals in a Group Purchasing Organization...	27	26	26	28	29

Note: These data represent hospital performance in the years 2015 – 2019 and do not reflect any impacts from the COVID-19 pandemic in 2020 and thereafter.

States

TABLE 6   MAINE

U.S. Community Hospitals
(Nonfederal, short-term general and other special hospitals)

Utilization, Personnel, Revenue and Expenses, Community Health Indicators 2015–2019

	2019	2018	2017	2016	2015
TOTAL FACILITY (Includes Hospital and Nursing Home Units)					
Utilization - Inpatient					
Beds	3,482	3,400	3,410	3,397	3,478
Admissions	128,560	131,750	132,963	135,281	137,950
Inpatient Days	892,731	873,078	860,280	851,357	816,880
Average Length of Stay	6.9	6.6	6.5	6.3	5.9
Inpatient Surgeries	39,044	37,817	40,716	40,697	39,339
Births	11,594	11,899	12,260	12,524	11,798
Utilization - Outpatient					
Emergency Outpatient Visits	721,184	681,465	682,348	678,948	964,240
Other Outpatient Visits	6,025,317	5,262,248	5,648,238	5,271,196	6,239,268
Total Outpatient Visits	6,746,501	5,943,713	6,330,586	5,950,144	7,203,508
Outpatient Surgeries	106,759	105,073	107,700	108,801	105,713
Personnel					
Full Time RNs	6,426	6,295	6,083	5,762	6,119
Full Time LPNs	181	220	280	269	335
Part Time RNs	3,461	3,379	3,317	2,945	3,511
Part Time LPNs	77	94	107	106	141
Total Full Time	29,945	29,223	28,471	27,178	26,456
Total Part Time	11,449	11,671	11,996	10,927	11,607
Revenue - Inpatient					
Gross Inpatient Revenue	$5,729,935,081	$5,445,597,920	$5,049,483,409	$4,429,901,617	$4,571,897,264
Revenue - Outpatient					
Gross Outpatient Revenue	$8,350,486,386	$7,684,175,315	$7,228,971,325	$6,500,678,123	$6,083,795,956
Revenue and Expenses - Totals					
(Includes Inpatient and Outpatient)					
Total Gross Revenue	$14,080,421,467	$13,129,773,235	$12,278,454,734	$10,930,579,740	$10,655,693,220
Deductions from Revenue	8,158,171,514	7,525,377,446	7,023,784,148	5,972,381,386	5,991,204,223
Net Patient Revenue	5,922,249,953	5,604,395,789	5,254,670,586	4,958,198,354	4,664,488,997
Other Operating Revenue	461,271,134	482,534,665	444,432,749	409,506,843	344,974,562
Other Nonoperating Revenue	25,836,472	80,422,219	106,196,522	39,795,272	16,792,277
Total Net Revenue	6,409,357,559	6,167,352,673	5,805,299,857	5,407,500,469	5,026,255,836
Total Expenses	6,242,766,922	6,001,324,758	5,561,474,952	5,281,349,738	4,912,530,828
HOSPITAL UNIT (Excludes Separate Nursing Home Units)					
Utilization - Inpatient					
Beds	2,995	2,913	2,876	2,901	2,984
Admissions	127,506	130,627	131,517	131,949	135,289
Inpatient Days	745,071	725,327	687,357	677,182	714,550
Average Length of Stay	5.8	5.6	5.2	5.1	5.3
Personnel					
Total Full Time	29,360	28,475	27,832	26,427	26,139
Total Part Time	11,055	11,156	11,479	10,396	11,351
Revenue and Expenses - Totals					
(Includes Inpatient and Outpatient)					
Total Net Revenue	$6,366,263,560	$6,127,225,984	$5,746,316,576	$5,372,226,471	$4,998,768,917
Total Expenses	6,200,914,852	5,960,626,073	5,509,149,337	5,243,064,736	4,886,600,125
COMMUNITY HEALTH INDICATORS PER 1000 POPULATION					
Total Population (in thousands)	1,344	1,338	1,336	1,331	1,329
Inpatient					
Beds	2.6	2.5	2.6	2.6	2.6
Admissions	95.6	98.4	99.5	101.6	103.8
Inpatient Days	664.1	652.3	644	639.4	614.5
Inpatient Surgeries	29	28.3	30.5	30.6	29.6
Births	8.6	8.9	9.2	9.4	8.9
Outpatient					
Emergency Outpatient Visits	536.5	509.2	510.8	509.9	725.4
Other Outpatient Visits	4,482.4	3,931.7	4,228	3,958.9	4,693.6
Total Outpatient Visits	5,018.9	4,440.9	4,738.8	4,468.8	5,418.9
Outpatient Surgeries	79.4	78.5	80.6	81.7	79.5
Expense per Capita (per person)	$4,644.2	$4,483.9	$4,163.1	$3,966.5	$3,695.5

Note: These data represent hospital performance in the years 2015 – 2019 and do not reflect any impacts from the COVID-19 pandemic in 2020 and thereafter.

States

TABLE **6**

MARYLAND

U.S. Community Hospitals
(Nonfederal, short-term general and other special hospitals)

Overview 2015–2019

	2019	2018	2017	2016	2015
Total Community Hospitals in Maryland............	48	50	51	51	51
Bed Size Category					
6-24	0	0	0	0	0
25-49	3	3	3	4	4
50-99	10	9	9	8	7
100-199	13	12	14	15	15
200-299	11	14	12	9	10
300-399	5	4	6	8	7
400-499	4	5	5	5	6
500 + ...	2	3	2	2	2
Location					
Hospitals Urban	44	46	47	47	47
Hospitals Rural..	4	4	4	4	4
Control					
State and Local Government	0	0	0	0	0
Not for Profit..	47	49	50	50	50
Investor owned..	1	1	1	1	1
Affiliations					
Hospitals in a System	36	36	37	37	36
Hospitals in a Group Purchasing Organization...	38	36	38	37	43

Note: These data represent hospital performance in the years 2015 – 2019 and do not reflect any impacts from the COVID-19 pandemic in 2020 and thereafter.

TABLE 6

MARYLAND

U.S. Community Hospitals
(Nonfederal, short-term general and other special hospitals)

Utilization, Personnel, Revenue and Expenses, Community Health Indicators 2015–2019

	2019	2018	2017	2016	2015
TOTAL FACILITY (Includes Hospital and Nursing Home Units)					
Utilization - Inpatient					
Beds	10,894	11,577	11,607	11,648	11,879
Admissions	543,185	566,730	581,640	589,392	596,516
Inpatient Days	2,923,810	2,974,120	2,991,695	3,027,850	3,052,607
Average Length of Stay	5.4	5.2	5.1	5.1	5.1
Inpatient Surgeries	150,382	155,910	165,197	168,882	171,451
Births	62,147	64,499	64,273	67,010	67,711
Utilization - Outpatient					
Emergency Outpatient Visits	2,206,790	2,222,930	2,403,879	2,517,321	2,488,461
Other Outpatient Visits	7,245,106	7,608,996	6,900,993	10,323,775	6,940,745
Total Outpatient Visits	9,451,896	9,831,926	9,304,872	12,841,096	9,429,206
Outpatient Surgeries	308,729	333,618	348,568	363,303	350,235
Personnel					
Full Time RNs	22,751	21,349	21,875	21,287	20,865
Full Time LPNs	362	372	354	389	414
Part Time RNs	9,360	9,418	9,985	9,087	8,309
Part Time LPNs	136	172	133	155	157
Total Full Time	78,454	74,694	75,552	75,818	74,949
Total Part Time	28,069	28,344	29,554	28,763	27,279
Revenue - Inpatient					
Gross Inpatient Revenue	$12,361,067,681	$13,115,504,195	$12,811,275,178	$12,263,125,916	$12,932,959,279
Revenue - Outpatient					
Gross Outpatient Revenue	$9,581,832,539	$11,335,487,431	$11,259,051,688	$10,786,754,638	$11,342,366,816
Revenue and Expenses - Totals					
(Includes Inpatient and Outpatient)					
Total Gross Revenue	$21,942,900,220	$24,450,991,626	$24,070,326,866	$23,049,880,554	$24,275,326,095
Deductions from Revenue	6,191,300,900	8,448,899,144	8,369,790,182	7,827,604,972	9,592,824,701
Net Patient Revenue	15,751,599,320	16,002,092,482	15,700,536,684	15,222,275,582	14,682,501,394
Other Operating Revenue	1,129,783,229	971,258,153	956,698,682	892,444,891	790,914,902
Other Nonoperating Revenue	197,271,933	219,216,162	319,979,452	-114,814,750	-19,539,599
Total Net Revenue	17,078,654,482	17,192,566,797	16,977,214,818	15,999,905,723	15,453,876,697
Total Expenses	16,270,674,599	16,206,265,902	15,928,893,444	15,670,406,755	14,840,392,246
HOSPITAL UNIT (Excludes Separate Nursing Home Units)					
Utilization - Inpatient					
Beds	10,729	11,412	11,394	11,417	11,554
Admissions	541,045	564,878	579,880	586,857	593,348
Inpatient Days	2,876,278	2,923,945	2,942,114	2,966,565	2,957,249
Average Length of Stay	5.3	5.2	5.1	5.1	5.0
Personnel					
Total Full Time	78,344	74,590	75,379	75,658	74,679
Total Part Time	27,956	28,221	29,388	28,629	27,132
Revenue and Expenses - Totals					
(Includes Inpatient and Outpatient)					
Total Net Revenue	$17,060,908,765	$17,174,701,758	$16,958,186,929	$15,974,822,998	$15,418,373,557
Total Expenses	16,251,946,750	16,186,002,613	15,907,000,858	15,646,829,355	14,805,360,651
COMMUNITY HEALTH INDICATORS PER 1000 POPULATION					
Total Population (in thousands)	6,046	6,043	6,052	6,016	6,006
Inpatient					
Beds	1.8	1.9	1.9	1.9	2
Admissions	89.8	93.8	96.1	98	99.3
Inpatient Days	483.6	492.2	494.3	503.3	508.2
Inpatient Surgeries	24.9	25.8	27.3	28.1	28.5
Births	10.3	10.7	10.6	11.1	11.3
Outpatient					
Emergency Outpatient Visits	365	367.9	397.2	418.4	414.3
Other Outpatient Visits	1,198.4	1,259.2	1,140.2	1,715.9	1,155.6
Total Outpatient Visits	1,563.4	1,627.1	1,537.4	2,134.3	1,569.9
Outpatient Surgeries	51.1	55.2	57.6	60.4	58.3
Expense per Capita (per person)	$2,691.3	$2,681.9	$2,631.9	$2,604.6	$2,470.8

Note: These data represent hospital performance in the years 2015 – 2019 and do not reflect any impacts from the COVID-19 pandemic in 2020 and thereafter.

States

TABLE 6

MASSACHUSETTS

U.S. Community Hospitals
(Nonfederal, short-term general and other special hospitals)

Overview 2015–2019

	2019	2018	2017	2016	2015
Total Community Hospitals in Massachusetts...	74	75	75	77	78
Bed Size Category					
6-24	4	3	3	3	4
25-49	4	6	8	8	8
50-99	14	16	15	17	18
100-199	25	23	22	22	22
200-299	11	11	11	11	10
300-399	8	7	7	7	7
400-499	3	4	3	3	3
500 +	5	5	6	6	6
Location					
Hospitals Urban	72	73	72	74	75
Hospitals Rural	2	2	3	3	3
Control					
State and Local Government	2	2	3	3	3
Not for Profit	56	56	56	56	57
Investor owned	16	17	16	18	18
Affiliations					
Hospitals in a System	57	58	51	52	51
Hospitals in a Group Purchasing Organization...	47	48	47	52	51

Note: These data represent hospital performance in the years 2015 – 2019 and do not reflect any impacts from the COVID-19 pandemic in 2020 and thereafter.

TABLE **6**

MASSACHUSETTS

U.S. Community Hospitals
(Nonfederal, short-term general and other special hospitals)

Utilization, Personnel, Revenue and Expenses, Community Health Indicators 2015–2019

	2019	2018	2017	2016	2015
TOTAL FACILITY (Includes Hospital and Nursing Home Units)					
Utilization - Inpatient					
Beds	15,561	15,649	15,650	15,783	15,609
Admissions	777,310	780,198	780,695	769,189	764,216
Inpatient Days	4,222,166	4,205,986	4,139,660	4,070,997	4,066,706
Average Length of Stay	5.4	5.4	5.3	5.3	5.3
Inpatient Surgeries	191,744	183,251	186,558	192,700	188,021
Births	65,577	66,086	65,673	67,394	67,950
Utilization - Outpatient					
Emergency Outpatient Visits	3,385,519	3,306,597	3,323,247	3,333,951	3,259,551
Other Outpatient Visits	20,075,088	20,059,097	19,552,119	19,725,735	19,708,626
Total Outpatient Visits	23,460,607	23,365,694	22,875,366	23,059,686	22,968,177
Outpatient Surgeries	429,341	420,141	430,006	435,484	430,891
Personnel					
Full Time RNs	28,648	25,517	24,399	23,987	22,258
Full Time LPNs	852	752	763	848	798
Part Time RNs	24,790	23,799	23,829	23,611	23,415
Part Time LPNs	517	490	487	533	520
Total Full Time	130,455	124,637	121,875	120,773	114,981
Total Part Time	72,454	70,628	69,931	69,656	67,367
Revenue - Inpatient					
Gross Inpatient Revenue	$39,623,134,770	$34,227,455,608	$32,419,915,790	$30,265,082,301	$28,369,343,026
Revenue - Outpatient					
Gross Outpatient Revenue	$48,301,762,132	$44,148,215,230	$40,032,642,495	$36,706,063,615	$33,805,120,905
Revenue and Expenses - Totals					
(Includes Inpatient and Outpatient)					
Total Gross Revenue	$87,924,896,902	$78,375,670,838	$72,452,558,285	$66,971,145,916	$62,174,463,931
Deductions from Revenue	58,658,472,367	51,145,263,278	46,657,933,670	42,104,612,780	38,645,096,775
Net Patient Revenue	29,266,424,535	27,230,407,560	25,794,624,615	24,866,533,136	23,529,367,156
Other Operating Revenue	5,421,740,973	4,928,632,177	4,512,682,152	4,149,885,652	3,950,093,994
Other Nonoperating Revenue	247,396,432	264,677,778	638,968,323	151,858,972	13,933,523
Total Net Revenue	34,935,561,940	32,423,717,515	30,946,275,090	29,168,277,760	27,493,394,673
Total Expenses	32,932,794,064	31,599,573,131	29,941,210,139	28,367,505,871	26,502,594,673
HOSPITAL UNIT (Excludes Separate Nursing Home Units)					
Utilization - Inpatient					
Beds	15,500	15,588	15,650	15,754	15,580
Admissions	777,301	780,182	780,695	768,592	763,589
Inpatient Days	4,203,114	4,184,868	4,139,660	4,062,940	4,058,460
Average Length of Stay	5.4	5.4	5.3	5.3	5.3
Personnel					
Total Full Time	130,441	124,602	121,875	120,764	114,974
Total Part Time	72,439	70,585	69,931	69,642	67,350
Revenue and Expenses - Totals					
(Includes Inpatient and Outpatient)					
Total Net Revenue	$34,929,645,569	$32,363,718,667	$30,946,275,090	$29,164,160,915	$27,489,025,820
Total Expenses	32,925,000,316	31,591,770,550	29,941,210,139	28,362,196,974	26,497,267,680
COMMUNITY HEALTH INDICATORS PER 1000 POPULATION					
Total Population (in thousands)	6,893	6,902	6,860	6,812	6,794
Inpatient					
Beds	2.3	2.3	2.3	2.3	2.3
Admissions	112.8	113	113.8	112.9	112.5
Inpatient Days	612.6	609.4	603.5	597.6	598.5
Inpatient Surgeries	27.8	26.5	27.2	28.3	27.7
Births	9.5	9.6	9.6	9.9	10
Outpatient					
Emergency Outpatient Visits	491.2	479.1	484.5	489.4	479.7
Other Outpatient Visits	2,912.6	2,906.2	2,850.2	2,895.8	2,900.7
Total Outpatient Visits	3,403.8	3,385.3	3,334.7	3,385.3	3,380.4
Outpatient Surgeries	62.3	60.9	62.7	63.9	63.4
Expense per Capita (per person)	$4,778.1	$4,578.2	$4,364.7	$4,164.5	$3,900.6

Note: These data represent hospital performance in the years 2015 – 2019 and do not reflect any impacts from the COVID-19 pandemic in 2020 and thereafter.

States

TABLE 6

U.S. Community Hospitals
(Nonfederal, short-term general and other special hospitals)

Overview 2015–2019

	2019	2018	2017	2016	2015
Total Community Hospitals in Michigan.............	145	144	145	147	148
Bed Size Category					
6-24	14	15	14	14	13
25-49	46	43	46	43	44
50-99	23	23	22	27	30
100-199	20	21	21	21	19
200-299	13	14	10	10	12
300-399	11	9	11	13	12
400-499	6	8	10	8	8
500 + ...	12	11	11	11	10
Location					
Hospitals Urban	93	92	91	93	93
Hospitals Rural...	52	52	54	54	55
Control					
State and Local Government	6	6	7	10	12
Not for Profit..	113	113	112	110	111
Investor owned...	26	25	26	27	25
Affiliations					
Hospitals in a System	113	111	114	111	110
Hospitals in a Group Purchasing Organization...	113	113	116	112	108

Note: These data represent hospital performance in the years 2015 – 2019 and do not reflect any impacts from the COVID-19 pandemic in 2020 and thereafter.

States

TABLE 6

MICHIGAN

U.S. Community Hospitals
(Nonfederal, short-term general and other special hospitals)

Utilization, Personnel, Revenue and Expenses, Community Health Indicators 2015–2019

	2019	2018	2017	2016	2015
TOTAL FACILITY (Includes Hospital and Nursing Home Units)					
Utilization - Inpatient					
Beds	24,809	24,949	24,987	25,144	24,943
Admissions	1,115,500	1,134,295	1,148,126	1,160,797	1,168,830
Inpatient Days	5,744,466	5,717,822	5,774,074	5,824,152	5,889,759
Average Length of Stay	5.1	5.0	5.0	5.0	5.0
Inpatient Surgeries	291,580	299,602	310,832	309,796	306,288
Births	101,496	104,990	106,026	106,510	107,136
Utilization - Outpatient					
Emergency Outpatient Visits	4,903,345	5,008,903	5,088,160	5,157,734	5,007,114
Other Outpatient Visits	32,495,099	34,017,938	33,130,754	32,275,038	30,689,235
Total Outpatient Visits	37,398,444	39,026,841	38,218,914	37,432,772	35,696,349
Outpatient Surgeries	700,069	681,400	666,907	681,704	658,070
Personnel					
Full Time RNs	45,682	45,984	45,037	43,621	42,217
Full Time LPNs	1,079	1,148	1,310	1,534	1,321
Part Time RNs	19,195	19,538	17,927	18,824	18,513
Part Time LPNs	481	560	503	719	690
Total Full Time	152,788	156,339	158,816	160,077	153,910
Total Part Time	62,221	61,971	59,077	62,924	59,354
Revenue - Inpatient					
Gross Inpatient Revenue	$48,169,001,071	$45,201,003,334	$43,389,473,979	$41,494,261,701	$39,351,728,038
Revenue - Outpatient					
Gross Outpatient Revenue	$55,160,238,061	$51,946,828,351	$48,760,756,193	$45,930,141,227	$42,357,655,090
Revenue and Expenses - Totals					
(Includes Inpatient and Outpatient)					
Total Gross Revenue	$103,329,239,132	$97,147,831,685	$92,150,230,172	$87,424,402,928	$81,709,383,128
Deductions from Revenue	68,558,254,676	64,167,181,688	60,241,364,080	56,422,123,195	52,481,922,913
Net Patient Revenue	34,770,984,456	32,980,649,997	31,908,866,092	31,002,279,733	29,227,460,215
Other Operating Revenue	1,636,722,759	1,614,727,971	1,497,587,151	1,418,608,721	1,345,964,491
Other Nonoperating Revenue	543,303,485	311,332,622	668,174,494	228,345,738	55,142,541
Total Net Revenue	36,951,010,700	34,906,710,590	34,074,627,737	32,649,234,192	30,628,567,247
Total Expenses	34,685,804,350	33,084,724,457	31,762,862,798	30,678,766,927	29,000,739,583
HOSPITAL UNIT (Excludes Separate Nursing Home Units)					
Utilization - Inpatient					
Beds	23,943	24,079	24,116	24,252	24,050
Admissions	1,111,702	1,130,879	1,144,691	1,157,039	1,164,723
Inpatient Days	5,459,489	5,437,171	5,490,437	5,536,643	5,590,264
Average Length of Stay	4.9	4.8	4.8	4.8	4.8
Personnel					
Total Full Time	152,244	155,719	158,107	159,297	153,145
Total Part Time	61,824	61,589	58,582	62,531	58,780
Revenue and Expenses - Totals					
(Includes Inpatient and Outpatient)					
Total Net Revenue	$36,865,996,080	$34,825,062,888	$33,987,039,192	$32,556,335,061	$30,535,532,440
Total Expenses	34,620,512,048	33,022,842,713	31,702,143,480	30,619,374,769	28,933,640,822
COMMUNITY HEALTH INDICATORS PER 1000 POPULATION					
Total Population (in thousands)	9,987	9,996	9,962	9,928	9,923
Inpatient					
Beds	2.5	2.5	2.5	2.5	2.5
Admissions	111.7	113.5	115.2	116.9	117.8
Inpatient Days	575.2	572	579.6	586.6	593.6
Inpatient Surgeries	29.2	30	31.2	31.2	30.9
Births	10.2	10.5	10.6	10.7	10.8
Outpatient					
Emergency Outpatient Visits	491	501.1	510.7	519.5	504.6
Other Outpatient Visits	3,253.8	3,403.2	3,325.6	3,250.8	3,092.9
Total Outpatient Visits	3,744.8	3,904.3	3,836.4	3,770.3	3,597.5
Outpatient Surgeries	70.1	68.2	66.9	68.7	66.3
Expense per Capita (per person)	$3,473.1	$3,309.8	$3,188.3	$3,090	$2,922.7

Note: These data represent hospital performance in the years 2015 – 2019 and do not reflect any impacts from the COVID-19 pandemic in 2020 and thereafter.

States

TABLE 6

MINNESOTA

U.S. Community Hospitals
(Nonfederal, short-term general and other special hospitals)

Overview 2015–2019

	2019	2018	2017	2016	2015
Total Community Hospitals in Minnesota...........	125	127	129	129	130
Bed Size Category					
6-24	30	31	32	27	24
25-49	30	31	31	33	33
50-99	28	29	29	30	33
100-199	22	21	22	24	25
200-299	2	2	2	2	3
300-399	5	5	4	4	4
400-499	5	5	6	6	5
500 +	3	3	3	3	3
Location					
Hospitals Urban	52	53	53	53	54
Hospitals Rural	73	74	76	76	76
Control					
State and Local Government	30	29	32	32	31
Not for Profit	95	98	97	97	99
Investor owned	0	0	0	0	0
Affiliations					
Hospitals in a System	86	86	85	83	84
Hospitals in a Group Purchasing Organization...	78	92	90	92	91

Note: These data represent hospital performance in the years 2015 – 2019 and do not reflect any impacts from the COVID-19 pandemic in 2020 and thereafter.

TABLE 6

MINNESOTA

U.S. Community Hospitals
(Nonfederal, short-term general and other special hospitals)

Utilization, Personnel, Revenue and Expenses, Community Health Indicators 2015–2019

	2019	2018	2017	2016	2015
TOTAL FACILITY (Includes Hospital and Nursing Home Units)					
Utilization - Inpatient					
Beds	13,901	13,895	13,992	14,277	14,393
Admissions	551,113	572,213	557,820	546,613	547,399
Inpatient Days	3,331,744	3,337,371	3,310,521	3,319,384	3,357,517
Average Length of Stay	6.0	5.8	5.9	6.1	6.1
Inpatient Surgeries	174,668	174,122	177,900	174,253	173,157
Births	62,602	65,245	66,404	67,449	67,081
Utilization - Outpatient					
Emergency Outpatient Visits	2,028,615	2,051,970	2,092,544	2,019,387	1,961,075
Other Outpatient Visits	11,568,410	11,326,938	11,751,668	11,499,803	10,278,747
Total Outpatient Visits	13,597,025	13,378,908	13,844,212	13,519,190	12,239,822
Outpatient Surgeries	398,574	379,490	381,553	335,648	335,562
Personnel					
Full Time RNs	13,148	12,213	13,762	12,678	13,120
Full Time LPNs	1,162	1,261	1,465	1,579	1,554
Part Time RNs	30,040	29,707	27,944	27,073	25,092
Part Time LPNs	1,494	1,446	1,619	1,679	1,615
Total Full Time	82,823	81,418	86,026	83,523	83,073
Total Part Time	74,440	73,637	72,011	71,017	66,846
Revenue - Inpatient					
Gross Inpatient Revenue	$26,890,745,766	$26,345,458,420	$24,252,197,440	$23,766,111,231	$22,441,151,417
Revenue - Outpatient					
Gross Outpatient Revenue	$29,798,199,410	$27,965,021,764	$25,746,965,622	$24,607,182,442	$22,431,972,337
Revenue and Expenses - Totals					
(Includes Inpatient and Outpatient)					
Total Gross Revenue	$56,688,945,176	$54,310,480,184	$49,999,163,062	$48,373,293,673	$44,873,123,754
Deductions from Revenue	36,178,086,135	34,193,594,354	30,772,082,886	29,987,533,574	27,385,010,912
Net Patient Revenue	20,510,859,041	20,116,885,830	19,227,080,176	18,385,760,099	17,488,112,842
Other Operating Revenue	1,152,686,006	991,936,977	1,119,105,564	974,290,684	879,946,693
Other Nonoperating Revenue	332,960,321	213,177,521	479,293,091	60,420,818	85,927,538
Total Net Revenue	21,996,505,368	21,322,000,328	20,825,478,831	19,420,471,601	18,453,987,073
Total Expenses	20,867,096,579	20,054,257,322	19,400,142,385	18,651,840,870	17,156,049,679
HOSPITAL UNIT (Excludes Separate Nursing Home Units)					
Utilization - Inpatient					
Beds	12,461	11,831	12,017	12,144	12,098
Admissions	548,106	568,980	554,420	542,848	543,432
Inpatient Days	2,874,105	2,691,360	2,677,440	2,622,349	2,602,118
Average Length of Stay	5.2	4.7	4.8	4.8	4.8
Personnel					
Total Full Time	82,283	80,617	85,179	82,582	82,103
Total Part Time	73,108	72,119	70,607	69,419	65,186
Revenue and Expenses - Totals					
(Includes Inpatient and Outpatient)					
Total Net Revenue	$21,855,074,822	$21,154,646,565	$20,664,678,838	$19,238,547,023	$18,281,872,718
Total Expenses	20,742,224,181	19,910,800,819	19,244,214,744	18,485,511,994	16,999,260,248
COMMUNITY HEALTH INDICATORS PER 1000 POPULATION					
Total Population (in thousands)	5,640	5,611	5,577	5,520	5,490
Inpatient					
Beds	2.5	2.5	2.5	2.6	2.6
Admissions	97.7	102	100	99	99.7
Inpatient Days	590.8	594.8	593.6	601.3	611.6
Inpatient Surgeries	31	31	31.9	31.6	31.5
Births	11.1	11.6	11.9	12.2	12.2
Outpatient					
Emergency Outpatient Visits	359.7	365.7	375.2	365.8	357.2
Other Outpatient Visits	2,051.3	2,018.6	2,107.3	2,083.3	1,872.4
Total Outpatient Visits	2,411	2,384.3	2,482.6	2,449.1	2,229.6
Outpatient Surgeries	70.7	67.6	68.4	60.8	61.1
Expense per Capita (per person)	3,700.1	3,574	3,478.8	3,379	3,125.2

Note: These data represent hospital performance in the years 2015 – 2019 and do not reflect any impacts from the COVID-19 pandemic in 2020 and thereafter.

States

TABLE 6

MISSISSIPPI

U.S. Community Hospitals
(Nonfederal, short-term general and other special hospitals)

Overview 2015–2019

	2019	2018	2017	2016	2015
Total Community Hospitals in Mississippi........	97	99	100	99	101
Bed Size Category					
6-24	6	6	5	6	5
25-49	34	35	36	33	35
50-99	21	21	22	24	23
100-199	18	20	20	20	20
200-299	10	8	6	6	8
300-399	2	3	4	3	3
400-499	2	2	3	3	3
500 + ...	4	4	4	4	4
Location					
Hospitals Urban	32	32	29	28	28
Hospitals Rural................................	65	67	71	71	73
Control					
State and Local Government	39	38	39	39	40
Not for Profit....................................	33	35	35	32	30
Investor owned................................	25	26	26	28	31
Affiliations					
Hospitals in a System.......................	48	50	51	52	54
Hospitals in a Group Purchasing Organization...	87	93	91	91	86

Note: These data represent hospital performance in the years 2015 – 2019 and do not reflect any impacts from the COVID-19 pandemic in 2020 and thereafter.

States

TABLE 6

MISSISSIPPI

U.S. Community Hospitals
(Nonfederal, short-term general and other special hospitals)

Utilization, Personnel, Revenue and Expenses, Community Health Indicators 2015–2019

	2019	2018	2017	2016	2015
TOTAL FACILITY (Includes Hospital and Nursing Home Units)					
Utilization - Inpatient					
Beds	11,624	12,071	12,328	12,243	12,451
Admissions	370,790	369,559	378,375	381,882	361,998
Inpatient Days	2,525,724	2,453,579	2,481,030	2,477,062	2,516,647
Average Length of Stay	6.8	6.6	6.6	6.5	7.0
Inpatient Surgeries	93,644	86,467	87,969	94,477	96,762
Births	34,622	33,643	35,445	36,114	37,441
Utilization - Outpatient					
Emergency Outpatient Visits	1,793,977	1,749,095	1,805,514	1,834,612	1,790,278
Other Outpatient Visits	5,367,757	5,430,498	4,942,015	4,326,306	3,820,752
Total Outpatient Visits	7,161,734	7,179,593	6,747,529	6,160,918	5,611,030
Outpatient Surgeries	193,380	195,664	188,279	186,674	176,609
Personnel					
Full Time RNs	13,246	13,432	13,274	12,968	13,049
Full Time LPNs	1,281	1,248	1,217	1,232	1,284
Part Time RNs	5,047	4,780	4,839	4,855	4,408
Part Time LPNs	359	307	339	290	321
Total Full Time	47,030	46,842	46,427	47,296	47,977
Total Part Time	14,039	13,265	12,963	13,233	12,361
Revenue - Inpatient					
Gross Inpatient Revenue	$16,848,057,614	$16,258,892,712	$15,641,056,256	$15,123,310,237	$14,372,764,006
Revenue - Outpatient					
Gross Outpatient Revenue	$19,489,794,966	$18,163,950,537	$16,875,769,849	$16,009,248,352	$14,145,489,387
Revenue and Expenses - Totals (Includes Inpatient and Outpatient)					
Total Gross Revenue	$36,337,852,580	$34,422,843,249	$32,516,826,105	$31,132,558,589	$28,518,253,393
Deductions from Revenue	28,118,389,497	26,529,019,775	24,746,105,041	23,391,369,766	21,015,239,533
Net Patient Revenue	8,219,463,083	7,893,823,474	7,770,721,064	7,741,188,823	7,503,013,860
Other Operating Revenue	259,694,972	315,613,223	270,227,976	319,121,912	301,727,802
Other Nonoperating Revenue	97,459,379	86,644,467	84,966,831	72,583,587	82,928,542
Total Net Revenue	8,576,617,434	8,296,081,164	8,125,915,871	8,132,894,322	7,887,670,204
Total Expenses	8,148,566,981	7,994,945,019	7,806,529,535	7,291,741,978	7,313,556,349
HOSPITAL UNIT (Excludes Separate Nursing Home Units)					
Utilization - Inpatient					
Beds	9,997	10,439	10,709	10,658	10,925
Admissions	369,466	368,179	377,360	380,987	361,013
Inpatient Days	1,976,787	1,903,088	1,949,699	1,932,996	1,992,552
Average Length of Stay	5.4	5.2	5.2	5.1	5.5
Personnel					
Total Full Time	45,666	45,984	45,600	46,522	47,284
Total Part Time	13,553	12,879	12,599	12,899	12,057
Revenue and Expenses - Totals (Includes Inpatient and Outpatient)					
Total Net Revenue	$8,439,464,978	$8,163,843,428	$8,002,112,719	$8,003,374,011	$7,764,801,938
Total Expenses	8,052,546,301	7,898,213,667	7,713,801,855	7,198,296,105	7,234,720,309
COMMUNITY HEALTH INDICATORS PER 1000 POPULATION					
Total Population (in thousands)	2,976	2,987	2,984	2,989	2,992
Inpatient					
Beds	3.9	4	4.1	4.1	4.2
Admissions	124.6	123.7	126.8	127.8	121
Inpatient Days	848.7	821.5	831.4	828.8	841
Inpatient Surgeries	31.5	29	29.5	31.6	32.3
Births	11.6	11.3	11.9	12.1	12.5
Outpatient					
Emergency Outpatient Visits	602.8	585.7	605	613.8	598.3
Other Outpatient Visits	1,803.6	1,818.3	1,656.1	1,447.5	1,276.8
Total Outpatient Visits	2,406.4	2,404	2,261.2	2,061.4	1,875.1
Outpatient Surgeries	65	65.5	63.1	62.5	59
Expense per Capita (per person)	$2,738	$2,677	$2,616	$2,439.7	$2,444.1

Note: These data represent hospital performance in the years 2015 – 2019 and do not reflect any impacts from the COVID-19 pandemic in 2020 and thereafter.

TABLE **6**

MISSOURI

U.S. Community Hospitals
(Nonfederal, short-term general and other special hospitals)

Overview 2015–2019

	2019	2018	2017	2016	2015
Total Community Hospitals in Missouri..............	120	122	126	126	128
Bed Size Category					
6-24	14	13	16	15	15
25-49	34	36	35	37	38
50-99	22	22	21	22	22
100-199	20	21	22	21	24
200-299	10	9	12	12	10
300-399	8	9	8	7	7
400-499	4	4	4	3	5
500 +	8	8	8	9	7
Location					
Hospitals Urban	71	73	73	73	75
Hospitals Rural..	49	49	53	53	53
Control					
State and Local Government	30	31	31	31	31
Not for Profit...	67	66	66	66	66
Investor owned...	23	25	29	29	31
Affiliations					
Hospitals in a System	75	76	79	79	79
Hospitals in a Group Purchasing Organization...	117	118	122	125	121

Note: These data represent hospital performance in the years 2015 – 2019 and do not reflect any impacts from the COVID-19 pandemic in 2020 and thereafter.

States

TABLE 6

MISSOURI

U.S. Community Hospitals
(Nonfederal, short-term general and other special hospitals)

Utilization, Personnel, Revenue and Expenses, Community Health Indicators 2015–2019

	2019	2018	2017	2016	2015
TOTAL FACILITY (Includes Hospital and Nursing Home Units)					
Utilization - Inpatient					
Beds	18,455	18,749	18,930	18,771	18,810
Admissions	769,249	780,377	773,308	774,128	787,250
Inpatient Days	4,184,603	4,143,162	4,141,096	4,134,271	4,153,017
Average Length of Stay	5.4	5.3	5.4	5.3	5.3
Inpatient Surgeries	192,947	190,425	190,597	192,909	194,981
Births	70,183	71,561	71,671	73,188	73,498
Utilization - Outpatient					
Emergency Outpatient Visits	2,927,912	2,979,022	3,090,141	3,151,743	3,124,931
Other Outpatient Visits	22,775,037	22,201,008	21,759,933	21,272,728	20,059,461
Total Outpatient Visits	25,702,949	25,180,030	24,850,074	24,424,471	23,184,392
Outpatient Surgeries	397,796	397,218	396,669	398,758	388,076
Personnel					
Full Time RNs	33,376	31,859	31,537	30,877	30,507
Full Time LPNs	2,458	2,341	2,375	2,463	2,425
Part Time RNs	12,073	11,458	11,536	11,034	11,454
Part Time LPNs	587	543	523	549	552
Total Full Time	114,494	113,185	112,366	110,257	107,121
Total Part Time	37,410	35,430	35,268	34,155	34,443
Revenue - Inpatient					
Gross Inpatient Revenue	$38,674,909,179	$36,185,168,903	$34,196,874,205	$32,682,788,508	$31,179,811,756
Revenue - Outpatient					
Gross Outpatient Revenue	$45,581,918,339	$42,158,690,520	$39,777,826,054	$36,651,885,244	$33,124,620,409
Revenue and Expenses - Totals					
(Includes Inpatient and Outpatient)					
Total Gross Revenue	$84,256,827,518	$78,343,859,423	$73,974,700,259	$69,334,673,752	$64,304,432,165
Deductions from Revenue	60,326,122,841	55,506,948,840	51,954,522,721	48,294,313,912	44,364,341,627
Net Patient Revenue	23,930,704,677	22,836,910,583	22,020,177,538	21,040,359,840	19,940,090,538
Other Operating Revenue	1,571,948,238	1,323,740,658	1,375,671,345	1,236,609,926	1,252,755,683
Other Nonoperating Revenue	472,574,787	343,375,075	518,082,536	292,279,236	237,769,792
Total Net Revenue	25,975,227,702	24,504,026,316	23,913,931,419	22,569,249,002	21,430,616,013
Total Expenses	24,264,933,681	23,401,894,939	22,608,623,983	21,452,674,937	20,253,175,567
HOSPITAL UNIT (Excludes Separate Nursing Home Units)					
Utilization - Inpatient					
Beds	17,667	17,979	18,029	17,841	17,841
Admissions	765,769	776,718	769,280	769,871	782,515
Inpatient Days	3,958,285	3,921,677	3,901,459	3,890,237	3,891,041
Average Length of Stay	5.2	5.0	5.1	5.1	5.0
Personnel					
Total Full Time	114,085	112,882	111,686	109,568	106,342
Total Part Time	37,203	35,270	34,957	33,836	34,114
Revenue and Expenses - Totals					
(Includes Inpatient and Outpatient)					
Total Net Revenue	$25,932,932,728	$24,452,480,509	$23,852,254,053	$22,500,329,976	$21,346,760,255
Total Expenses	24,209,988,863	23,347,532,146	22,550,816,214	21,391,192,093	20,178,157,068
COMMUNITY HEALTH INDICATORS PER 1000 POPULATION					
Total Population (in thousands)	6,137	6,126	6,114	6,093	6,084
Inpatient					
Beds	3	3.1	3.1	3.1	3.1
Admissions	125.3	127.4	126.5	127.1	129.4
Inpatient Days	681.8	676.3	677.4	678.5	682.6
Inpatient Surgeries	31.4	31.1	31.2	31.7	32
Births	11.4	11.7	11.7	12	12.1
Outpatient					
Emergency Outpatient Visits	477.1	486.3	505.5	517.3	513.7
Other Outpatient Visits	3,710.8	3,623.8	3,559.3	3,491.3	3,297.3
Total Outpatient Visits	4,187.9	4,110.1	4,064.8	4,008.6	3,810.9
Outpatient Surgeries	64.8	64.8	64.9	65.4	63.8
Expense per Capita (per person)	$3,953.6	$3,819.8	$3,698.1	$3,520.9	$3,329.1

Note: These data represent hospital performance in the years 2015 – 2019 and do not reflect any impacts from the COVID-19 pandemic in 2020 and thereafter.

States

TABLE 6

MONTANA

U.S. Community Hospitals
(Nonfederal, short-term general and other special hospitals)

Overview 2015–2019

	2019	2018	2017	2016	2015
Total Community Hospitals in Montana.............	57	56	55	54	54
Bed Size Category					
6-24	14	12	13	12	12
25-49	23	24	22	20	17
50-99	11	11	11	13	16
100-199	5	6	6	5	5
200-299	3	2	1	2	2
300-399	0	0	0	0	1
400-499	0	0	1	1	0
500 + ...	1	1	1	1	1
Location					
Hospitals Urban	9	9	8	8	8
Hospitals Rural..	48	47	47	46	46
Control					
State and Local Government	6	7	7	8	9
Not for Profit...	46	44	43	40	40
Investor owned..	5	5	5	6	5
Affiliations					
Hospitals in a System	17	19	12	13	13
Hospitals in a Group Purchasing Organization...	41	45	41	43	43

Note: These data represent hospital performance in the years 2015 – 2019 and do not reflect any impacts from the COVID-19 pandemic in 2020 and thereafter.

States

TABLE 6

MONTANA

U.S. Community Hospitals
(Nonfederal, short-term general and other special hospitals)

Utilization, Personnel, Revenue and Expenses, Community Health Indicators 2015–2019

	2019	2018	2017	2016	2015
TOTAL FACILITY (Includes Hospital and Nursing Home Units)					
Utilization - Inpatient					
Beds	3,614	3,542	3,622	3,757	3,914
Admissions	100,441	98,467	98,752	94,522	94,844
Inpatient Days	758,902	752,407	772,654	807,341	863,320
Average Length of Stay	7.6	7.6	7.8	8.5	9.1
Inpatient Surgeries	27,217	31,005	30,154	28,054	27,672
Births	10,378	10,965	11,091	10,933	11,561
Utilization - Outpatient					
Emergency Outpatient Visits	452,994	423,628	496,531	427,836	414,058
Other Outpatient Visits	4,145,710	4,024,075	3,887,431	3,619,140	3,249,436
Total Outpatient Visits	4,598,704	4,447,703	4,383,962	4,046,976	3,663,494
Outpatient Surgeries	76,293	81,268	75,718	63,216	58,591
Personnel					
Full Time RNs	4,810	3,972	4,084	3,642	3,646
Full Time LPNs	349	377	329	348	420
Part Time RNs	2,970	2,807	2,828	2,721	2,242
Part Time LPNs	170	200	198	218	216
Total Full Time	19,294	19,182	18,955	17,770	17,014
Total Part Time	9,315	10,164	10,173	9,914	7,993
Revenue - Inpatient					
Gross Inpatient Revenue	$3,988,610,910	$3,437,334,556	$3,501,728,307	$3,366,743,226	$3,022,578,540
Revenue - Outpatient					
Gross Outpatient Revenue	$6,217,366,019	$5,329,471,258	$4,998,732,851	$4,385,747,039	$3,937,326,560
Revenue and Expenses - Totals					
(Includes Inpatient and Outpatient)					
Total Gross Revenue	$10,205,976,929	$8,766,805,814	$8,500,461,158	$7,752,490,265	$6,959,905,100
Deductions from Revenue	5,682,477,882	4,785,212,567	4,690,985,631	4,317,474,812	3,705,665,159
Net Patient Revenue	4,523,499,047	3,981,593,247	3,809,475,527	3,435,015,453	3,254,239,941
Other Operating Revenue	246,581,589	216,386,411	204,620,060	177,120,640	136,136,733
Other Nonoperating Revenue	133,365,625	51,066,895	88,317,593	43,682,886	51,831,904
Total Net Revenue	4,903,446,261	4,249,046,553	4,102,413,180	3,655,818,979	3,442,208,578
Total Expenses	4,258,260,987	3,841,363,151	3,574,679,836	3,363,175,798	3,091,174,733
HOSPITAL UNIT (Excludes Separate Nursing Home Units)					
Utilization - Inpatient					
Beds	2,909	2,770	2,747	2,633	2,683
Admissions	99,350	97,336	97,211	92,823	93,137
Inpatient Days	542,941	523,978	515,745	491,147	491,442
Average Length of Stay	5.5	5.4	5.3	5.3	5.3
Personnel					
Total Full Time	18,830	18,592	18,362	17,041	16,331
Total Part Time	9,026	9,771	9,724	9,284	7,469
Revenue and Expenses - Totals					
(Includes Inpatient and Outpatient)					
Total Net Revenue	$4,856,952,428	$4,201,806,543	$4,028,828,782	$3,590,657,886	$3,371,448,104
Total Expenses	4,211,672,529	3,795,345,858	3,519,469,009	3,301,831,163	3,027,941,902
COMMUNITY HEALTH INDICATORS PER 1000 POPULATION					
Total Population (in thousands)	1,069	1,062	1,050	1,043	1,033
Inpatient					
Beds	3.4	3.3	3.4	3.6	3.8
Admissions	94	92.7	94	90.7	91.8
Inpatient Days	710.1	708.3	735.5	774.4	835.8
Inpatient Surgeries	25.5	29.2	28.7	26.9	26.8
Births	9.7	10.3	10.6	10.5	11.2
Outpatient					
Emergency Outpatient Visits	423.8	398.8	472.7	410.4	400.9
Other Outpatient Visits	3,878.9	3,788.1	3,700.6	3,471.5	3,145.8
Total Outpatient Visits	4,302.8	4,186.8	4,173.2	3,881.9	3,546.6
Outpatient Surgeries	71.4	76.5	72.1	60.6	56.7
Expense per Capita (per person)	$3,984.2	$3,616.1	$3,402.9	$3,226	$2,992.6

Note: These data represent hospital performance in the years 2015 – 2019 and do not reflect any impacts from the COVID-19 pandemic in 2020 and thereafter.

States

TABLE 6

NEBRASKA

U.S. Community Hospitals
(Nonfederal, short-term general and other special hospitals)

Overview 2015–2019

	2019	2018	2017	2016	2015
Total Community Hospitals in Nebraska	93	93	94	94	94
Bed Size Category					
6-24	44	41	36	33	32
25-49	16	18	20	24	24
50-99	14	15	19	18	19
100-199	10	10	10	10	9
200-299	3	3	3	3	4
300-399	4	3	3	4	4
400-499	0	1	1	0	0
500 + ...	2	2	2	2	2
Location					
Hospitals Urban	27	27	28	28	28
Hospitals Rural	66	66	66	66	66
Control					
State and Local Government	35	36	36	36	35
Not for Profit..	51	50	51	51	52
Investor owned......................................	7	7	7	7	7
Affiliations					
Hospitals in a System	31	31	29	29	29
Hospitals in a Group Purchasing Organization...	38	47	49	48	45

Note: These data represent hospital performance in the years 2015 – 2019 and do not reflect any impacts from the COVID-19 pandemic in 2020 and thereafter.

States

TABLE 6

NEBRASKA

U.S. Community Hospitals
(Nonfederal, short-term general and other special hospitals)

Utilization, Personnel, Revenue and Expenses, Community Health Indicators 2015–2019

	2019	2018	2017	2016	2015
TOTAL FACILITY (Includes Hospital and Nursing Home Units)					
Utilization - Inpatient					
Beds	6,756	6,842	6,975	6,946	7,031
Admissions	203,201	209,821	204,819	199,599	199,725
Inpatient Days	1,405,254	1,400,332	1,427,631	1,366,767	1,383,745
Average Length of Stay	6.9	6.7	7.0	6.8	6.9
Inpatient Surgeries	61,182	61,889	61,973	62,320	63,598
Births	22,793	23,814	24,334	25,223	26,263
Utilization - Outpatient					
Emergency Outpatient Visits	923,344	817,775	816,532	847,018	736,871
Other Outpatient Visits	5,137,276	4,876,424	4,804,344	4,505,795	4,114,418
Total Outpatient Visits	6,060,620	5,694,199	5,620,876	5,352,813	4,851,289
Outpatient Surgeries	138,482	143,948	144,538	148,823	133,347
Personnel					
Full Time RNs	9,641	9,444	9,367	8,369	8,611
Full Time LPNs	719	760	772	697	655
Part Time RNs	5,055	4,441	4,575	4,548	4,052
Part Time LPNs	328	295	304	350	285
Total Full Time	33,042	32,680	32,783	30,555	30,531
Total Part Time	16,243	14,888	15,107	15,576	13,951
Revenue - Inpatient					
Gross Inpatient Revenue	$10,513,388,787	$9,824,403,592	$8,882,408,899	$8,135,440,019	$7,825,388,016
Revenue - Outpatient					
Gross Outpatient Revenue	$11,974,300,696	$10,892,595,571	$9,851,318,080	$9,066,638,392	$8,139,489,940
Revenue and Expenses - Totals					
(Includes Inpatient and Outpatient)					
Total Gross Revenue	$22,487,689,483	$20,716,999,163	$18,733,726,979	$17,202,078,411	$15,964,877,956
Deductions from Revenue	14,918,560,932	13,525,014,596	11,922,150,052	10,718,822,128	10,052,446,972
Net Patient Revenue	7,569,128,551	7,191,984,567	6,811,576,927	6,483,256,283	5,912,430,984
Other Operating Revenue	420,422,770	389,233,702	382,243,135	333,314,914	339,525,035
Other Nonoperating Revenue	200,535,929	75,123,939	87,068,433	84,764,683	18,939,078
Total Net Revenue	8,190,087,250	7,656,342,208	7,280,888,495	6,901,335,880	6,270,895,097
Total Expenses	7,413,795,158	7,004,650,806	6,656,754,805	6,214,549,605	5,511,683,885
HOSPITAL UNIT (Excludes Separate Nursing Home Units)					
Utilization - Inpatient					
Beds	6,360	6,317	6,282	6,198	6,392
Admissions	202,578	209,097	203,913	198,698	198,978
Inpatient Days	1,274,442	1,236,103	1,216,341	1,139,416	1,185,617
Average Length of Stay	6.3	5.9	6.0	5.7	6.0
Personnel					
Total Full Time	32,796	32,341	32,331	30,126	30,141
Total Part Time	16,089	14,715	14,870	15,296	13,728
Revenue and Expenses - Totals					
(Includes Inpatient and Outpatient)					
Total Net Revenue	$8,160,683,865	$7,620,927,644	$7,239,685,510	$6,858,425,960	$6,233,927,758
Total Expenses	7,387,164,655	6,972,051,693	6,620,503,865	6,180,817,671	5,480,873,779
COMMUNITY HEALTH INDICATORS PER 1000 POPULATION					
Total Population (in thousands)	1,934	1,929	1,920	1,907	1,896
Inpatient					
Beds	3.5	3.5	3.6	3.6	3.7
Admissions	105	108.8	106.7	104.7	105.3
Inpatient Days	726.5	725.8	743.5	716.7	729.8
Inpatient Surgeries	31.6	32.1	32.3	32.7	33.5
Births	11.8	12.3	12.7	13.2	13.9
Outpatient					
Emergency Outpatient Visits	477.3	423.9	425.3	444.1	388.6
Other Outpatient Visits	2,655.7	2,527.6	2,502.2	2,362.6	2,169.8
Total Outpatient Visits	3,133.1	2,951.5	2,927.4	2,806.8	2,558.4
Outpatient Surgeries	71.6	74.6	75.3	78	70.3
Expense per Capita (per person)	$3,832.6	$3,630.7	$3,466.9	$3,258.6	$2,906.7

Note: These data represent hospital performance in the years 2015 – 2019 and do not reflect any impacts from the COVID-19 pandemic in 2020 and thereafter.

States

TABLE 6

NEVADA

U.S. Community Hospitals
(Nonfederal, short-term general and other special hospitals)

Overview 2015–2019

	2019	2018	2017	2016	2015
Total Community Hospitals in Nevada................	43	44	44	42	41
Bed Size Category					
6-24	7	5	5	7	8
25-49	7	7	7	6	5
50-99	9	11	11	10	9
100-199	10	11	11	9	9
200-299	3	4	4	3	4
300-399	4	3	3	4	3
400-499	1	1	0	0	0
500 + ...	2	2	3	3	3
Location					
Hospitals Urban	32	33	33	31	30
Hospitals Rural	11	11	11	11	11
Control					
State and Local Government	6	6	7	6	5
Not for Profit.....................................	14	15	14	14	14
Investor owned..................................	23	23	23	22	22
Affiliations					
Hospitals in a System	31	32	31	30	30
Hospitals in a Group Purchasing Organization...	12	13	16	14	17

Note: These data represent hospital performance in the years 2015 – 2019 and do not reflect any impacts from the COVID-19 pandemic in 2020 and thereafter.

States

TABLE 6

NEVADA

U.S. Community Hospitals
(Nonfederal, short-term general and other special hospitals)

Utilization, Personnel, Revenue and Expenses, Community Health Indicators 2015–2019

	2019	2018	2017	2016	2015
TOTAL FACILITY (Includes Hospital and Nursing Home Units)					
Utilization - Inpatient					
Beds	6,309	6,493	6,475	6,187	6,028
Admissions	282,453	305,935	287,029	297,845	289,024
Inpatient Days	1,539,908	1,693,329	1,622,253	1,684,508	1,632,124
Average Length of Stay	5.5	5.5	5.7	5.7	5.6
Inpatient Surgeries	55,423	59,540	58,219	52,272	60,831
Births	29,049	26,694	22,228	25,666	26,424
Utilization - Outpatient					
Emergency Outpatient Visits	956,217	1,063,257	987,106	950,434	1,003,568
Other Outpatient Visits	2,386,454	2,597,573	2,286,818	2,497,214	2,172,449
Total Outpatient Visits	3,342,671	3,660,830	3,273,924	3,447,648	3,176,017
Outpatient Surgeries	85,267	95,625	99,109	101,909	101,016
Personnel					
Full Time RNs	9,864	9,901	9,202	8,393	8,675
Full Time LPNs	344	360	355	338	299
Part Time RNs	2,239	2,346	2,226	2,020	2,191
Part Time LPNs	75	94	69	64	76
Total Full Time	29,422	29,871	28,401	25,520	25,688
Total Part Time	6,365	6,651	6,421	5,774	6,418
Revenue - Inpatient					
Gross Inpatient Revenue	$22,026,167,081	$21,725,263,156	$19,013,184,691	$16,359,057,382	$16,806,038,705
Revenue - Outpatient					
Gross Outpatient Revenue	$16,038,079,174	$15,753,024,346	$14,249,772,510	$12,492,666,320	$11,440,956,313
Revenue and Expenses - Totals					
(Includes Inpatient and Outpatient)					
Total Gross Revenue	$38,064,246,255	$37,478,287,502	$33,262,957,201	$28,851,723,702	$28,246,995,018
Deductions from Revenue	31,311,176,068	30,813,100,349	26,902,721,416	23,020,302,981	22,719,000,011
Net Patient Revenue	6,753,070,187	6,665,187,153	6,360,235,785	5,831,420,721	5,527,995,007
Other Operating Revenue	135,859,971	104,887,217	110,436,759	180,827,619	176,174,838
Other Nonoperating Revenue	81,719,081	72,812,833	49,781,829	36,685,552	35,548,963
Total Net Revenue	6,970,649,239	6,842,887,203	6,520,454,373	6,048,933,892	5,739,718,808
Total Expenses	6,270,609,688	6,172,520,507	5,832,395,986	5,649,355,966	5,232,106,601
HOSPITAL UNIT (Excludes Separate Nursing Home Units)					
Utilization - Inpatient					
Beds	6,309	6,493	6,404	6,071	5,965
Admissions	282,453	305,935	286,936	297,744	289,004
Inpatient Days	1,539,908	1,693,329	1,601,399	1,652,758	1,612,344
Average Length of Stay	5.5	5.5	5.6	5.6	5.6
Personnel					
Total Full Time	29,422	29,871	28,375	25,461	25,665
Total Part Time	6,365	6,651	6,395	5,747	6,406
Revenue and Expenses - Totals					
(Includes Inpatient and Outpatient)					
Total Net Revenue	$6,970,649,239	$6,842,887,203	$6,515,344,842	$6,041,928,217	$5,737,786,585
Total Expenses	6,270,609,688	6,172,520,507	5,828,112,631	5,644,534,936	5,230,109,375
COMMUNITY HEALTH INDICATORS PER 1000 POPULATION					
Total Population (in thousands)	3,080	3,034	2,998	2,940	2,891
Inpatient					
Beds	2	2.1	2.2	2.1	2.1
Admissions	91.7	100.8	95.7	101.3	100
Inpatient Days	499.9	558	541.1	573	564.6
Inpatient Surgeries	18	19.6	19.4	17.8	21
Births	9.4	8.8	7.4	8.7	9.1
Outpatient					
Emergency Outpatient Visits	310.4	350.4	329.3	323.3	347.2
Other Outpatient Visits	774.8	856	762.8	849.4	751.5
Total Outpatient Visits	1,085.2	1,206.4	1,092	1,172.6	1,098.6
Outpatient Surgeries	27.7	31.5	33.1	34.7	34.9
Expense per Capita (per person)	$2,035.8	$2,034.2	$1,945.4	$1,921.5	$1,809.9

Note: These data represent hospital performance in the years 2015 – 2019 and do not reflect any impacts from the COVID-19 pandemic in 2020 and thereafter.

States

TABLE **6**

NEW HAMPSHIRE

U.S. Community Hospitals
(Nonfederal, short-term general and other special hospitals)

Overview 2015–2019

	2019	2018	2017	2016	2015
Total Community Hospitals in New Hampshire...	28	28	28	28	28
Bed Size Category					
6-24	2	1	1	1	1
25-49	10	11	11	11	10
50-99	7	7	7	6	7
100-199	5	5	5	6	6
200-299	3	3	3	3	3
300-399	0	0	0	0	0
400-499	1	1	1	1	1
500 +	0	0	0	0	0
Location					
Hospitals Urban	11	11	11	11	11
Hospitals Rural	17	17	17	17	17
Control					
State and Local Government	0	0	0	0	0
Not for Profit	23	24	24	24	24
Investor owned	5	4	4	4	4
Affiliations					
Hospitals in a System	15	14	12	8	7
Hospitals in a Group Purchasing Organization...	20	22	24	24	23

Note: These data represent hospital performance in the years 2015 – 2019 and do not reflect any impacts from the COVID-19 pandemic in 2020 and thereafter.

States

TABLE 6

NEW HAMPSHIRE

U.S. Community Hospitals
(Nonfederal, short-term general and other special hospitals)

Utilization, Personnel, Revenue and Expenses, Community Health Indicators 2015–2019

	2019	2018	2017	2016	2015
TOTAL FACILITY (Includes Hospital and Nursing Home Units)					
Utilization - Inpatient					
Beds	2,804	2,783	2,784	2,792	2,819
Admissions	121,800	124,365	125,925	124,840	120,080
Inpatient Days	648,227	656,919	650,448	654,451	651,556
Average Length of Stay	5.3	5.3	5.2	5.2	5.4
Inpatient Surgeries	34,925	33,927	35,712	34,031	33,616
Births	11,541	12,365	12,671	13,017	13,485
Utilization - Outpatient					
Emergency Outpatient Visits	712,254	618,367	653,750	653,672	670,738
Other Outpatient Visits	5,113,669	4,765,795	4,733,688	4,589,175	4,732,025
Total Outpatient Visits	5,825,923	5,384,162	5,387,438	5,242,847	5,402,763
Outpatient Surgeries	89,419	90,592	88,265	86,929	85,009
Personnel					
Full Time RNs	5,987	5,643	5,318	5,247	5,164
Full Time LPNs	262	283	295	310	265
Part Time RNs	3,518	3,487	3,129	2,747	2,666
Part Time LPNs	84	78	98	79	81
Total Full Time	26,168	24,835	24,837	24,027	23,186
Total Part Time	12,150	11,890	10,159	9,049	9,131
Revenue - Inpatient					
Gross Inpatient Revenue	$6,405,651,607	$5,743,423,655	$5,198,315,247	$4,868,308,563	$4,681,725,519
Revenue - Outpatient					
Gross Outpatient Revenue	$11,245,573,154	$10,572,222,987	$9,575,854,906	$8,756,510,168	$7,960,187,285
Revenue and Expenses - Totals					
(Includes Inpatient and Outpatient)					
Total Gross Revenue	$17,651,224,761	$16,315,646,642	$14,774,170,153	$13,624,818,731	$12,641,912,804
Deductions from Revenue	11,961,225,149	10,851,727,364	9,538,315,281	8,668,511,254	8,085,622,586
Net Patient Revenue	5,689,999,612	5,463,919,278	5,235,854,872	4,956,307,477	4,556,290,218
Other Operating Revenue	398,314,319	339,674,061	276,634,876	240,104,568	210,402,508
Other Nonoperating Revenue	28,636,784	61,121,860	112,456,780	6,673,937	3,370,504
Total Net Revenue	6,116,950,715	5,864,715,199	5,624,946,528	5,203,085,982	4,770,063,230
Total Expenses	5,625,095,753	5,408,006,148	5,127,353,481	4,814,609,303	4,465,458,316
HOSPITAL UNIT (Excludes Separate Nursing Home Units)					
Utilization - Inpatient					
Beds	2,759	2,738	2,739	2,747	2,716
Admissions	121,765	124,331	125,898	124,825	119,988
Inpatient Days	633,607	642,472	634,407	638,304	618,237
Average Length of Stay	5.2	5.2	5.0	5.1	5.2
Personnel					
Total Full Time	26,144	24,818	24,822	24,003	23,135
Total Part Time	12,106	11,876	10,150	9,034	9,104
Revenue and Expenses - Totals					
(Includes Inpatient and Outpatient)					
Total Net Revenue	$6,114,165,729	$5,861,753,805	$5,621,471,313	$5,199,781,022	$4,763,300,694
Total Expenses	5,622,109,290	5,405,736,986	5,125,234,911	4,812,487,558	4,459,583,467
COMMUNITY HEALTH INDICATORS PER 1000 POPULATION					
Total Population (in thousands)	1,360	1,356	1,343	1,335	1,331
Inpatient					
Beds	2.1	2.1	2.1	2.1	2.1
Admissions	89.6	91.7	93.8	93.5	90.2
Inpatient Days	476.7	484.3	484.4	490.3	489.7
Inpatient Surgeries	25.7	25	26.6	25.5	25.3
Births	8.5	9.1	9.4	9.8	10.1
Outpatient					
Emergency Outpatient Visits	523.8	455.9	486.9	489.7	504.1
Other Outpatient Visits	3,760.8	3,513.4	3,525.2	3,438.1	3,556.3
Total Outpatient Visits	4,284.7	3,969.3	4,012.1	3,927.8	4,060.4
Outpatient Surgeries	65.8	66.8	65.7	65.1	63.9
Expense per Capita (per person)	$4,137	$3,986.9	$3,818.4	$3,607	$3,356

Note: These data represent hospital performance in the years 2015 – 2019 and do not reflect any impacts from the COVID-19 pandemic in 2020 and thereafter.

States

TABLE 6

NEW JERSEY

U.S. Community Hospitals
(Nonfederal, short-term general and other special hospitals)

Overview 2015–2019

	2019	2018	2017	2016	2015
Total Community Hospitals in New Jersey	81	82	82	81	81
Bed Size Category					
6-24	1	1	1	1	1
25-49	5	6	6	5	4
50-99	13	12	11	11	11
100-199	23	23	23	21	21
200-299	8	10	11	12	13
300-399	17	16	16	16	17
400-499	5	5	4	5	4
500 + ...	9	9	10	10	10
Location					
Hospitals Urban	81	82	82	81	81
Hospitals Rural	0	0	0	0	0
Control					
State and Local Government	2	0	0	1	1
Not for Profit	62	62	62	60	61
Investor owned	17	20	20	20	19
Affiliations					
Hospitals in a System	60	60	61	59	58
Hospitals in a Group Purchasing Organization...	61	62	58	53	56

Note: These data represent hospital performance in the years 2015 – 2019 and do not reflect any impacts from the COVID-19 pandemic in 2020 and thereafter.

States

TABLE 6

NEW JERSEY

U.S. Community Hospitals
(Nonfederal, short-term general and other special hospitals)

Utilization, Personnel, Revenue and Expenses, Community Health Indicators 2015–2019

	2019	2018	2017	2016	2015
TOTAL FACILITY (Includes Hospital and Nursing Home Units)					
Utilization - Inpatient					
Beds	20,863	20,901	21,201	21,201	21,045
Admissions	1,073,799	1,066,632	1,076,863	1,007,338	980,822
Inpatient Days	5,068,308	5,075,543	5,085,634	4,962,663	5,075,803
Average Length of Stay	4.7	4.8	4.7	4.9	5.2
Inpatient Surgeries	210,766	217,639	221,055	230,250	235,740
Births	94,782	97,196	97,326	97,658	99,344
Utilization - Outpatient					
Emergency Outpatient Visits	3,633,427	3,752,248	3,785,951	3,751,369	3,543,837
Other Outpatient Visits	11,073,241	10,201,572	11,641,301	10,896,969	12,700,484
Total Outpatient Visits	14,706,668	13,953,820	15,427,252	14,648,338	16,244,321
Outpatient Surgeries	365,248	353,431	352,422	357,762	370,753
Personnel					
Full Time RNs	32,827	32,323	31,376	31,573	29,758
Full Time LPNs	592	611	646	721	666
Part Time RNs	13,464	13,657	13,700	13,627	13,996
Part Time LPNs	197	222	251	256	242
Total Full Time	112,000	109,986	108,578	108,882	104,655
Total Part Time	43,486	44,038	45,793	44,695	43,019
Revenue - Inpatient					
Gross Inpatient Revenue	$70,999,654,893	$69,531,776,176	$65,967,060,435	$62,344,355,839	$60,854,355,384
Revenue - Outpatient					
Gross Outpatient Revenue	$54,444,275,673	$50,578,890,459	$46,792,506,732	$42,302,262,480	$39,698,016,898
Revenue and Expenses - Totals					
(Includes Inpatient and Outpatient)					
Total Gross Revenue	$125,443,930,566	$120,110,666,635	$112,759,567,167	$104,646,618,319	$100,552,372,282
Deductions from Revenue	99,313,843,878	95,592,183,353	89,304,707,257	81,712,559,502	78,676,009,040
Net Patient Revenue	26,130,086,688	24,518,483,282	23,454,859,910	22,934,058,817	21,876,363,242
Other Operating Revenue	1,488,883,243	1,439,509,521	1,413,452,650	1,561,631,361	1,438,561,075
Other Nonoperating Revenue	651,509,531	154,891,494	518,351,086	434,767,553	-10,775,588
Total Net Revenue	28,270,479,462	26,112,884,297	25,386,663,646	24,930,457,731	23,304,148,729
Total Expenses	26,389,783,113	24,869,827,038	23,641,356,793	22,900,963,558	21,902,851,599
HOSPITAL UNIT (Excludes Separate Nursing Home Units)					
Utilization - Inpatient					
Beds	20,342	20,350	20,620	20,810	20,801
Admissions	1,070,945	1,063,167	1,072,428	1,004,285	977,681
Inpatient Days	4,896,405	4,895,405	4,897,361	4,833,242	4,995,981
Average Length of Stay	4.6	4.6	4.6	4.8	5.1
Personnel					
Total Full Time	111,588	109,668	108,255	108,414	104,456
Total Part Time	43,367	43,894	45,602	44,474	42,925
Revenue and Expenses - Totals					
(Includes Inpatient and Outpatient)					
Total Net Revenue	$28,214,432,362	$26,054,039,525	$25,314,988,333	$24,877,478,184	$23,265,863,043
Total Expenses	26,349,621,967	24,812,674,345	23,585,081,884	22,863,182,639	21,878,470,259
COMMUNITY HEALTH INDICATORS PER 1000 POPULATION					
Total Population (in thousands)	8,882	8,909	9,006	8,944	8,958
Inpatient					
Beds	2.3	2.3	2.4	2.4	2.3
Admissions	120.9	119.7	119.6	112.6	109.5
Inpatient Days	570.6	569.7	564.7	554.8	566.6
Inpatient Surgeries	23.7	24.4	24.5	25.7	26.3
Births	10.7	10.9	10.8	10.9	11.1
Outpatient					
Emergency Outpatient Visits	409.1	421.2	420.4	419.4	395.6
Other Outpatient Visits	1,246.7	1,145.1	1,292.7	1,218.3	1,417.8
Total Outpatient Visits	1,655.7	1,566.3	1,713.1	1,637.7	1,813.4
Outpatient Surgeries	41.1	39.7	39.1	40	41.4
Expense per Capita (per person)	$2,971.1	$2,791.7	$2,625.2	$2,560.3	$2,445.1

Note: These data represent hospital performance in the years 2015 – 2019 and do not reflect any impacts from the COVID-19 pandemic in 2020 and thereafter.

States

TABLE 6

NEW MEXICO

U.S. Community Hospitals
(Nonfederal, short-term general and other special hospitals)

Overview 2015–2019

	2019	2018	2017	2016	2015
Total Community Hospitals in New Mexico.......	42	41	41	41	41
Bed Size Category					
6-24	8	7	7	6	7
25-49	14	14	14	14	12
50-99	12	10	10	10	12
100-199	4	6	6	7	5
200-299	2	2	2	2	3
300-399	0	0	0	0	0
400-499	0	0	0	0	0
500 + ...	2	2	2	2	2
Location					
Hospitals Urban	17	16	16	16	16
Hospitals Rural	25	25	25	25	25
Control					
State and Local Government	9	8	8	8	8
Not for Profit	15	15	15	15	16
Investor owned	18	18	18	18	18
Affiliations					
Hospitals in a System	32	31	31	30	28
Hospitals in a Group Purchasing Organization...	21	18	17	19	22

Note: These data represent hospital performance in the years 2015 – 2019 and do not reflect any impacts from the COVID-19 pandemic in 2020 and thereafter.

States

TABLE 6

NEW MEXICO

U.S. Community Hospitals
(Nonfederal, short-term general and other special hospitals)

Utilization, Personnel, Revenue and Expenses, Community Health Indicators 2015–2019

	2019	2018	2017	2016	2015
TOTAL FACILITY (Includes Hospital and Nursing Home Units)					
Utilization - Inpatient					
Beds.................................	3,765	3,811	3,876	3,966	4,106
Admissions..........................	198,127	189,362	179,750	183,887	182,030
Inpatient Days......................	888,056	854,720	903,657	884,294	887,182
Average Length of Stay	4.5	4.5	5.0	4.8	4.9
Inpatient Surgeries....................	42,943	45,914	47,063	46,533	45,804
Births..................................	19,279	19,047	18,730	20,200	22,899
Utilization - Outpatient					
Emergency Outpatient Visits..............	876,730	1,055,906	1,035,170	1,068,994	1,055,068
Other Outpatient Visits......................	3,124,219	4,746,854	5,333,029	5,756,551	5,126,614
Total Outpatient Visits......................	4,000,949	5,802,760	6,368,199	6,825,545	6,181,682
Outpatient Surgeries.....................	117,576	124,064	125,413	111,577	107,261
Personnel					
Full Time RNs........................	6,567	7,724	6,926	7,265	7,241
Full Time LPNs.......................	245	340	372	309	345
Part Time RNs........................	4,624	2,909	2,583	2,561	2,310
Part Time LPNs.......................	234	134	133	122	111
Total Full Time	23,305	26,441	25,320	25,300	25,753
Total Part Time	14,768	7,746	7,530	7,591	7,106
Revenue - Inpatient					
Gross Inpatient Revenue	$9,673,773,912	$9,532,660,452	$9,443,175,880	$8,425,914,812	$8,197,233,564
Revenue - Outpatient					
Gross Outpatient Revenue	$12,523,268,203	$11,528,880,387	$11,548,841,298	$10,143,015,763	$9,099,714,998
Revenue and Expenses - Totals					
(Includes Inpatient and Outpatient)					
Total Gross Revenue	$22,197,042,115	$21,061,540,839	$20,992,017,178	$18,568,930,575	$17,296,948,562
Deductions from Revenue	15,705,599,780	14,761,185,396	14,828,970,155	12,673,373,255	12,016,779,875
Net Patient Revenue.......................	6,491,442,335	6,300,355,443	6,163,047,023	5,895,557,320	5,280,168,687
Other Operating Revenue.................	299,623,653	281,330,833	275,482,731	261,439,767	272,553,422
Other Nonoperating Revenue	54,301,235	51,182,179	78,147,688	38,114,532	49,880,430
Total Net Revenue........................	6,845,367,223	6,632,868,455	6,516,677,442	6,195,111,619	5,602,602,539
Total Expenses	6,190,447,652	5,852,188,093	5,744,621,613	5,467,066,379	4,914,551,926
HOSPITAL UNIT (Excludes Separate Nursing Home Units)					
Utilization - Inpatient					
Beds.................................	3,765	3,796	3,861	3,966	4,106
Admissions..........................	198,127	189,246	179,611	183,887	182,030
Inpatient Days......................	888,056	852,656	901,360	884,294	887,182
Average Length of Stay	4.5	4.5	5.0	4.8	4.9
Personnel					
Total Full Time	23,305	26,430	25,301	25,300	25,753
Total Part Time	14,768	7,742	7,529	7,591	7,106
Revenue and Expenses - Totals					
(Includes Inpatient and Outpatient)					
Total Net Revenue............................	$6,845,367,223	$6,624,653,127	$6,505,219,925	$6,195,111,619	$5,602,602,539
Total Expenses	6,190,447,652	5,847,731,120	5,740,295,527	5,467,066,379	4,914,551,926
COMMUNITY HEALTH INDICATORS PER 1000 POPULATION					
Total Population (in thousands)	2,097	2,095	2,088	2,081	2,085
Inpatient					
Beds.................................	1.8	1.8	1.9	1.9	2
Admissions..........................	94.5	90.4	86.1	88.4	87.3
Inpatient Days......................	423.5	407.9	432.8	424.9	425.5
Inpatient Surgeries....................	20.5	21.9	22.5	22.4	22
Births..................................	9.2	9.1	9	9.7	11
Outpatient					
Emergency Outpatient Visits..............	418.1	503.9	495.8	513.7	506
Other Outpatient Visits......................	1,490	2,265.3	2554	2,766.2	2,458.7
Total Outpatient Visits......................	1,908.1	2,769.2	3,049.8	3,279.9	2,964.7
Outpatient Surgeries.....................	56.1	59.2	60.1	53.6	51.4
Expense per Capita (per person)........	$2,952.3	$2,792.8	$2,751.2	$2,627.1	$2,357

Note: These data represent hospital performance in the years 2015 – 2019 and do not reflect any impacts from the COVID-19 pandemic in 2020 and thereafter.

States

TABLE 6

NEW YORK

U.S. Community Hospitals
(Nonfederal, short-term general and other special hospitals)

Overview 2015–2019

	2019	2018	2017	2016	2015
Total Community Hospitals in New York............	163	166	168	170	171
Bed Size Category					
6-24	10	9	9	8	8
25-49	11	10	11	11	11
50-99	12	15	16	17	17
100-199	44	45	45	42	40
200-299	29	31	29	36	38
300-399	15	14	15	12	13
400-499	13	14	14	14	12
500 + ...	29	28	29	30	32
Location					
Hospitals Urban	128	131	133	134	135
Hospitals Rural	35	35	35	36	36
Control					
State and Local Government	24	24	23	23	24
Not for Profit	139	142	145	147	147
Investor owned	0	0	0	0	0
Affiliations					
Hospitals in a System	100	104	105	105	97
Hospitals in a Group Purchasing Organization...	121	123	126	126	129

Note: These data represent hospital performance in the years 2015 – 2019 and do not reflect any impacts from the COVID-19 pandemic in 2020 and thereafter.

States

TABLE 6

NEW YORK

U.S. Community Hospitals
(Nonfederal, short-term general and other special hospitals)

Utilization, Personnel, Revenue and Expenses, Community Health Indicators 2015–2019

	2019	2018	2017	2016	2015
TOTAL FACILITY (Includes Hospital and Nursing Home Units)					
Utilization - Inpatient					
Beds	52,084	51,927	51,808	52,575	52,854
Admissions	2,236,457	2,268,877	2,272,583	2,275,661	2,215,822
Inpatient Days	14,681,148	14,740,138	14,972,556	15,243,808	15,084,390
Average Length of Stay	6.6	6.5	6.6	6.7	6.8
Inpatient Surgeries	571,170	568,405	580,655	586,743	569,541
Births	214,850	217,662	221,466	226,884	225,215
Utilization - Outpatient					
Emergency Outpatient Visits	8,766,573	8,729,833	8,632,643	9,056,617	8,631,910
Other Outpatient Visits	51,469,089	50,303,781	48,967,490	48,626,937	48,846,990
Total Outpatient Visits	60,235,662	59,033,614	57,600,133	57,683,554	57,478,900
Outpatient Surgeries	1,463,590	1,356,429	1,460,200	1,465,369	1,314,186
Personnel					
Full Time RNs	100,575	96,994	93,135	90,016	84,767
Full Time LPNs	5,158	5,201	5,021	4,602	4,859
Part Time RNs	26,787	25,934	24,994	25,457	23,789
Part Time LPNs	1,232	1,377	1,296	1,043	1,240
Total Full Time	398,754	386,206	378,431	365,018	348,489
Total Part Time	89,101	93,756	90,199	89,026	85,558
Revenue - Inpatient					
Gross Inpatient Revenue	$146,822,947,833	$134,417,416,125	$124,932,631,504	$116,374,216,764	$106,728,200,045
Revenue - Outpatient					
Gross Outpatient Revenue	$123,694,336,089	$111,104,260,887	$98,626,535,779	$90,435,926,427	$78,090,536,716
Revenue and Expenses - Totals					
(Includes Inpatient and Outpatient)					
Total Gross Revenue	$270,517,283,922	$245,521,677,012	$223,559,167,283	$206,810,143,191	$184,818,736,761
Deductions from Revenue	189,124,328,880	168,761,181,285	150,611,189,817	136,436,439,702	120,123,763,642
Net Patient Revenue	81,392,955,042	76,760,495,727	72,947,977,466	70,373,703,489	64,694,973,119
Other Operating Revenue	9,110,956,304	7,675,142,147	6,472,538,104	6,253,412,226	5,122,999,466
Other Nonoperating Revenue	2,286,649,779	657,051,422	1,867,219,220	1,239,270,779	506,419,429
Total Net Revenue	92,790,561,125	85,092,689,296	81,287,734,790	77,866,386,494	70,324,392,014
Total Expenses	89,518,161,594	83,388,233,327	78,606,242,354	75,137,848,371	68,887,871,710
HOSPITAL UNIT (Excludes Separate Nursing Home Units)					
Utilization - Inpatient					
Beds	47,424	46,972	47,306	48,027	47,650
Admissions	2,221,564	2,255,980	2,261,181	2,264,800	2,203,015
Inpatient Days	13,085,402	13,022,211	13,374,285	13,680,222	13,278,628
Average Length of Stay	5.9	5.8	5.9	6.0	6.0
Personnel					
Total Full Time	395,272	382,299	374,813	361,427	344,453
Total Part Time	87,064	91,370	88,197	87,075	83,320
Revenue and Expenses - Totals					
(Includes Inpatient and Outpatient)					
Total Net Revenue	$92,217,109,900	$84,507,253,497	$80,821,129,744	$77,339,027,537	$69,717,914,289
Total Expenses	89,010,728,441	82,789,925,455	78,156,794,479	74,714,804,194	68,311,960,203
COMMUNITY HEALTH INDICATORS PER 1000 POPULATION					
Total Population (in thousands)	19,454	19,542	19,849	19,745	19,796
Inpatient					
Beds	2.7	2.7	2.6	2.7	2.7
Admissions	115	116.1	114.5	115.3	111.9
Inpatient Days	754.7	754.3	754.3	772	762
Inpatient Surgeries	29.4	29.1	29.3	29.7	28.8
Births	11	11.1	11.2	11.5	11.4
Outpatient					
Emergency Outpatient Visits	450.6	446.7	434.9	458.7	436
Other Outpatient Visits	2,645.7	2,574.1	2,467	2,462.7	2,467.5
Total Outpatient Visits	3,096.4	3,020.8	2,901.9	2,921.4	2,903.6
Outpatient Surgeries	75.2	69.4	73.6	74.2	66.4
Expense per Capita (per person)	$4,601.6	$4,267.1	$3,960.1	$3,805.4	$3,479.9

Note: These data represent hospital performance in the years 2015 – 2019 and do not reflect any impacts from the COVID-19 pandemic in 2020 and thereafter.

States

TABLE 6

NORTH CAROLINA

U.S. Community Hospitals
(Nonfederal, short-term general and other special hospitals)

Overview 2015–2019

	2019	2018	2017	2016	2015
Total Community Hospitals in North Carolina	111	112	114	115	115
Bed Size Category					
6-24	9	8	7	6	6
25-49	24	24	24	24	24
50-99	18	21	23	27	26
100-199	31	32	32	29	30
200-299	10	9	11	10	10
300-399	4	3	2	4	4
400-499	3	3	3	3	3
500 +	12	12	12	12	12
Location					
Hospitals Urban	70	70	67	66	66
Hospitals Rural	41	42	47	49	49
Control					
State and Local Government	31	29	30	28	27
Not for Profit	65	68	69	67	68
Investor owned	15	15	15	20	20
Affiliations					
Hospitals in a System	97	99	101	101	104
Hospitals in a Group Purchasing Organization	59	76	76	91	95

Note: These data represent hospital performance in the years 2015 – 2019 and do not reflect any impacts from the COVID-19 pandemic in 2020 and thereafter.

States

TABLE 6

NORTH CAROLINA

U.S. Community Hospitals
(Nonfederal, short-term general and other special hospitals)

Utilization, Personnel, Revenue and Expenses, Community Health Indicators 2015–2019

	2019	2018	2017	2016	2015
TOTAL FACILITY (Includes Hospital and Nursing Home Units)					
Utilization - Inpatient					
Beds	21,673	21,549	21,841	21,878	21,632
Admissions	1,032,683	1,024,837	1,018,888	1,009,284	1,007,043
Inpatient Days	5,596,083	5,502,157	5,545,924	5,485,726	5,467,511
Average Length of Stay	5.4	5.4	5.4	5.4	5.4
Inpatient Surgeries	283,748	285,426	294,024	281,805	281,589
Births	108,667	110,479	113,203	115,681	116,273
Utilization - Outpatient					
Emergency Outpatient Visits	4,445,970	4,793,370	4,960,946	4,952,316	4,817,883
Other Outpatient Visits	18,568,986	18,469,802	18,613,003	15,815,321	15,082,446
Total Outpatient Visits	23,014,956	23,263,172	23,573,949	20,767,637	19,900,329
Outpatient Surgeries	596,249	587,633	586,833	595,644	569,849
Personnel					
Full Time RNs	43,114	42,771	41,514	41,297	40,565
Full Time LPNs	1,766	1,769	1,588	1,382	1,371
Part Time RNs	15,109	14,519	13,413	13,171	14,362
Part Time LPNs	501	428	372	313	329
Total Full Time	148,535	146,313	142,583	138,790	140,686
Total Part Time	40,362	38,005	36,444	36,178	37,615
Revenue - Inpatient					
Gross Inpatient Revenue	$49,471,116,149	$46,973,061,631	$43,354,278,672	$40,033,087,884	$38,149,057,513
Revenue - Outpatient					
Gross Outpatient Revenue	$60,386,223,259	$55,509,253,316	$51,441,079,747	$47,263,405,140	$42,434,511,142
Revenue and Expenses - Totals					
(Includes Inpatient and Outpatient)					
Total Gross Revenue	$109,857,339,408	$102,482,314,947	$94,795,358,419	$87,296,493,024	$80,583,568,655
Deductions from Revenue	78,488,629,118	72,346,884,696	65,614,306,443	59,671,446,299	54,619,685,081
Net Patient Revenue	31,368,710,290	30,135,430,251	29,181,051,976	27,625,046,725	25,963,883,574
Other Operating Revenue	1,365,731,656	1,145,745,764	1,055,549,303	909,206,892	875,711,323
Other Nonoperating Revenue	1,262,846,178	-125,378,021	568,086,844	489,754,286	70,175,039
Total Net Revenue	33,997,288,124	31,155,797,994	30,804,688,123	29,024,007,903	26,909,769,936
Total Expenses	29,063,167,196	28,206,407,402	27,043,562,604	25,578,336,019	24,472,546,863
HOSPITAL UNIT (Excludes Separate Nursing Home Units)					
Utilization - Inpatient					
Beds	20,760	20,572	20,877	20,592	20,570
Admissions	1,027,961	1,020,171	1,013,765	1,003,299	1,001,513
Inpatient Days	5,326,712	5,204,818	5,243,844	5,093,710	5,132,545
Average Length of Stay	5.2	5.1	5.2	5.1	5.1
Personnel					
Total Full Time	147,948	145,712	142,003	138,040	139,894
Total Part Time	40,042	37,702	36,235	35,830	37,225
Revenue and Expenses - Totals					
(Includes Inpatient and Outpatient)					
Total Net Revenue	$33,924,942,103	$31,080,132,190	$30,728,667,407	$28,939,245,077	$26,830,202,110
Total Expenses	28,994,918,740	28,112,191,832	26,975,139,476	25,495,396,508	24,405,142,483
COMMUNITY HEALTH INDICATORS PER 1000 POPULATION					
Total Population (in thousands)	10,488	10,384	10,273	10,147	10,043
Inpatient					
Beds	2.1	2.1	2.1	2.2	2.2
Admissions	98.5	98.7	99.2	99.5	100.3
Inpatient Days	533.6	529.9	539.8	540.6	544.4
Inpatient Surgeries	27.1	27.5	28.6	27.8	28
Births	10.4	10.6	11	11.4	11.6
Outpatient					
Emergency Outpatient Visits	423.9	461.6	482.9	488.1	479.7
Other Outpatient Visits	1,770.5	1,778.7	1,811.8	1,558.7	1,501.8
Total Outpatient Visits	2,194.4	2,240.4	2,294.7	2,046.7	1,981.6
Outpatient Surgeries	56.9	56.6	57.1	58.7	56.7
Expense per Capita (per person)	$2,771.1	$2,716.4	$2,632.4	$2,520.8	$2,436.8

Note: These data represent hospital performance in the years 2015 – 2019 and do not reflect any impacts from the COVID-19 pandemic in 2020 and thereafter.

States

TABLE 6

NORTH DAKOTA

U.S. Community Hospitals
(Nonfederal, short-term general and other special hospitals)

Overview 2015–2019

	2019	2018	2017	2016	2015
Total Community Hospitals in North Dakota......	40	39	40	40	40
Bed Size Category					
6-24	10	11	12	12	14
25-49	13	12	10	10	10
50-99	10	9	11	11	9
100-199	2	2	2	2	2
200-299	3	2	2	2	3
300-399	0	1	1	1	0
400-499	0	0	1	1	1
500 + ...	2	2	1	1	1
Location					
Hospitals Urban	8	8	8	8	8
Hospitals Rural...	32	31	32	32	32
Control					
State and Local Government	0	0	0	0	0
Not for Profit...	38	37	38	38	38
Investor owned...	2	2	2	2	2
Affiliations					
Hospitals in a System	19	19	19	19	19
Hospitals in a Group Purchasing Organization...	15	15	18	19	17

Note: These data represent hospital performance in the years 2015 – 2019 and do not reflect any impacts from the COVID-19 pandemic in 2020 and thereafter.

TABLE 6

NORTH DAKOTA

U.S. Community Hospitals
(Nonfederal, short-term general and other special hospitals)

Utilization, Personnel, Revenue and Expenses, Community Health Indicators 2015–2019

	2019	2018	2017	2016	2015
TOTAL FACILITY (Includes Hospital and Nursing Home Units)					
Utilization - Inpatient					
Beds	3,323	3,235	3,210	3,260	3,183
Admissions	93,282	90,838	88,600	90,877	92,352
Inpatient Days	692,274	671,636	683,497	701,386	666,539
Average Length of Stay	7.4	7.4	7.7	7.7	7.2
Inpatient Surgeries	25,027	25,363	25,922	25,612	26,043
Births	10,910	11,037	13,254	13,137	13,109
Utilization - Outpatient					
Emergency Outpatient Visits	318,834	313,632	408,172	371,089	385,322
Other Outpatient Visits	2,649,479	2,500,361	1,866,620	2,273,123	2,267,225
Total Outpatient Visits	2,968,313	2,813,993	2,274,792	2,644,212	2,652,547
Outpatient Surgeries	79,926	78,829	74,643	78,048	76,448
Personnel					
Full Time RNs	4,295	3,689	4,603	4,100	3,715
Full Time LPNs	619	540	629	795	540
Part Time RNs	2,714	2,986	2,889	2,634	2,736
Part Time LPNs	432	534	367	444	456
Total Full Time	15,966	15,895	17,219	15,967	14,792
Total Part Time	8,895	9,394	9,446	8,946	8,934
Revenue - Inpatient					
Gross Inpatient Revenue	$3,559,133,372	$3,287,002,131	$3,782,933,634	$3,533,156,153	$2,756,294,460
Revenue - Outpatient					
Gross Outpatient Revenue	$6,986,064,188	$6,455,979,211	$5,655,386,851	$5,218,580,430	$4,961,154,801
Revenue and Expenses - Totals (Includes Inpatient and Outpatient)					
Total Gross Revenue	$10,545,197,560	$9,742,981,342	$9,438,320,485	$8,751,736,583	$7,717,449,261
Deductions from Revenue	6,420,093,710	5,838,183,735	5,747,888,702	5,001,324,621	4,281,622,247
Net Patient Revenue	4,125,103,850	3,904,797,607	3,690,431,783	3,750,411,962	3,435,827,014
Other Operating Revenue	378,459,014	274,851,321	188,898,228	184,634,957	195,835,576
Other Nonoperating Revenue	31,003,092	6,177,540	39,963,723	22,168,901	16,523,124
Total Net Revenue	4,534,565,956	4,185,826,468	3,919,293,734	3,957,215,820	3,648,185,714
Total Expenses	4,358,748,826	4,076,971,712	3,747,438,919	3,764,650,593	3,394,209,261
HOSPITAL UNIT (Excludes Separate Nursing Home Units)					
Utilization - Inpatient					
Beds	2,882	2,813	2,696	2,755	2,682
Admissions	92,584	90,090	87,732	90,062	91,487
Inpatient Days	545,409	533,761	512,269	531,621	504,193
Average Length of Stay	5.9	5.9	5.8	5.9	5.5
Personnel					
Total Full Time	15,542	15,583	16,762	15,722	14,550
Total Part Time	8,727	9,228	9,235	8,821	8,729
Revenue and Expenses - Totals (Includes Inpatient and Outpatient)					
Total Net Revenue	$4,484,884,493	$4,145,108,555	$3,869,365,865	$3,904,906,417	$3,595,128,392
Total Expenses	4,318,719,659	4,047,335,954	3,700,930,403	3,726,681,439	3,355,476,243
COMMUNITY HEALTH INDICATORS PER 1000 POPULATION					
Total Population (in thousands)	762	760	755	758	757
Inpatient					
Beds	4.4	4.3	4.2	4.3	4.2
Admissions	122.4	119.5	117.3	119.9	122
Inpatient Days	908.4	883.6	904.8	925.4	880.6
Inpatient Surgeries	32.8	33.4	34.3	33.8	34.4
Births	14.3	14.5	17.5	17.3	17.3
Outpatient					
Emergency Outpatient Visits	418.4	412.6	540.3	489.6	509.1
Other Outpatient Visits	3,476.7	3,289.6	2,471.1	2,999	2,995.3
Total Outpatient Visits	3,895.1	3,702.2	3,011.4	3,488.6	3,504.4
Outpatient Surgeries	104.9	103.7	98.8	103	101
Expense per Capita (per person)	$5,719.7	$5,363.9	$4,960.9	$4,966.9	$4,484.2

Note: These data represent hospital performance in the years 2015 – 2019 and do not reflect any impacts from the COVID-19 pandemic in 2020 and thereafter.

States

TABLE 6

OHIO

U.S. Community Hospitals
(Nonfederal, short-term general and other special hospitals)

Overview 2015–2019

	2019	2018	2017	2016	2015
Total Community Hospitals in Ohio	195	194	198	196	194
Bed Size Category					
6-24	15	15	14	12	12
25-49	52	50	53	54	51
50-99	31	30	30	29	29
100-199	38	40	39	40	44
200-299	30	31	30	30	25
300-399	9	7	12	11	12
400-499	7	7	6	6	6
500 + ...	13	14	14	14	15
Location					
Hospitals Urban	137	136	139	137	135
Hospitals Rural..	58	58	59	59	59
Control					
State and Local Government	16	17	16	16	17
Not for Profit..	141	139	142	143	141
Investor owned..	38	38	40	37	36
Affiliations					
Hospitals in a System	137	136	137	136	132
Hospitals in a Group Purchasing Organization...	106	116	128	127	130

Note: These data represent hospital performance in the years 2015 – 2019 and do not reflect any impacts from the COVID-19 pandemic in 2020 and thereafter.

TABLE 6

OHIO

U.S. Community Hospitals
(Nonfederal, short-term general and other special hospitals)

Utilization, Personnel, Revenue and Expenses, Community Health Indicators 2015–2019

	2019	2018	2017	2016	2015
TOTAL FACILITY (Includes Hospital and Nursing Home Units)					
Utilization - Inpatient					
Beds	33,303	33,157	33,621	33,876	33,954
Admissions	1,424,277	1,430,126	1,452,329	1,439,585	1,430,892
Inpatient Days	7,276,750	7,177,655	7,266,478	7,248,654	7,240,349
Average Length of Stay	5.1	5.0	5.0	5.0	5.1
Inpatient Surgeries	372,142	373,607	377,028	366,543	368,376
Births	121,829	124,524	128,419	129,375	129,950
Utilization - Outpatient					
Emergency Outpatient Visits	6,889,120	6,788,537	7,152,080	7,040,720	6,884,267
Other Outpatient Visits	39,185,868	36,539,086	37,061,651	34,565,927	33,209,434
Total Outpatient Visits	46,074,988	43,327,623	44,213,731	41,606,647	40,093,701
Outpatient Surgeries	991,010	959,629	958,009	911,579	887,852
Personnel					
Full Time RNs	63,050	64,854	61,993	61,290	60,411
Full Time LPNs	3,065	3,009	2,781	2,721	2,631
Part Time RNs	26,745	26,037	26,666	27,646	25,262
Part Time LPNs	1,141	1,083	1,225	1,278	1,409
Total Full Time	229,332	229,304	222,143	218,967	212,919
Total Part Time	80,071	77,532	79,065	83,407	78,358
Revenue - Inpatient					
Gross Inpatient Revenue	$78,581,052,387	$73,390,571,731	$72,689,711,162	$68,662,538,596	$65,574,002,406
Revenue - Outpatient					
Gross Outpatient Revenue	$92,832,885,618	$84,750,964,349	$81,246,806,136	$74,452,340,262	$69,352,958,894
Revenue and Expenses - Totals					
(Includes Inpatient and Outpatient)					
Total Gross Revenue	$171,413,938,005	$158,141,536,080	$153,936,517,298	$143,114,878,858	$134,926,961,300
Deductions from Revenue	122,710,177,385	112,218,752,622	109,458,420,234	100,414,765,582	93,603,143,993
Net Patient Revenue	48,703,760,620	45,922,783,458	44,478,097,064	42,700,113,276	41,323,817,307
Other Operating Revenue	4,142,644,167	3,649,249,843	3,538,489,750	3,181,814,697	3,083,802,721
Other Nonoperating Revenue	2,002,223,646	-127,550,361	1,540,654,457	571,420,327	-128,364,418
Total Net Revenue	54,848,628,433	49,444,482,940	49,557,241,271	46,453,348,300	44,279,255,610
Total Expenses	48,553,908,441	45,768,512,363	44,155,244,109	42,637,034,035	40,491,640,251
HOSPITAL UNIT (Excludes Separate Nursing Home Units)					
Utilization - Inpatient					
Beds	32,813	32,653	33,079	33,238	33,303
Admissions	1,419,408	1,424,751	1,445,941	1,432,175	1,423,344
Inpatient Days	7,118,253	7,014,378	7,079,649	7,037,483	7,026,457
Average Length of Stay	5.0	4.9	4.9	4.9	4.9
Personnel					
Total Full Time	228,882	228,844	221,672	218,436	212,481
Total Part Time	79,874	77,317	78,825	83,025	78,077
Revenue and Expenses - Totals					
(Includes Inpatient and Outpatient)					
Total Net Revenue	$54,798,528,918	$49,392,959,058	$49,491,045,840	$46,380,721,370	$44,217,058,327
Total Expenses	48,502,572,563	45,715,381,356	44,100,481,881	42,577,842,814	40,434,174,525
COMMUNITY HEALTH INDICATORS PER 1000 POPULATION					
Total Population (in thousands)	11,689	11,689	11,659	11,614	11,613
Inpatient					
Beds	2.8	2.8	2.9	2.9	2.9
Admissions	121.8	122.3	124.6	123.9	123.2
Inpatient Days	622.5	614	623.3	624.1	623.4
Inpatient Surgeries	31.8	32	32.3	31.6	31.7
Births	10.4	10.7	11	11.1	11.2
Outpatient					
Emergency Outpatient Visits	589.4	580.7	613.5	606.2	592.8
Other Outpatient Visits	3,352.3	3,125.8	3,178.9	2,976.1	2,859.6
Total Outpatient Visits	3,941.7	3,706.6	3,792.4	3,582.3	3,452.4
Outpatient Surgeries	84.8	82.1	82.2	78.5	76.5
Expense per Capita (per person)	$4,153.8	$3,915.4	$3,787.4	$3,671.1	$3,486.6

Note: These data represent hospital performance in the years 2015 – 2019 and do not reflect any impacts from the COVID-19 pandemic in 2020 and thereafter.

States

TABLE 6

OKLAHOMA

U.S. Community Hospitals
(Nonfederal, short-term general and other special hospitals)

Overview 2015–2019

	2019	2018	2017	2016	2015
Total Community Hospitals in Oklahoma	124	125	129	128	128
Bed Size Category					
6-24	35	35	36	34	34
25-49	46	44	44	47	47
50-99	17	20	23	22	22
100-199	14	14	14	13	12
200-299	3	3	3	2	3
300-399	3	3	3	4	4
400-499	0	0	0	0	0
500 + ...	6	6	6	6	6
Location					
Hospitals Urban	63	64	65	65	65
Hospitals Rural	61	61	64	63	63
Control					
State and Local Government	38	38	39	39	40
Not for Profit..	37	39	41	37	36
Investor owned..	49	48	49	52	52
Affiliations					
Hospitals in a System	66	68	70	72	68
Hospitals in a Group Purchasing Organization...	83	77	87	89	90

Note: These data represent hospital performance in the years 2015 – 2019 and do not reflect any impacts from the COVID-19 pandemic in 2020 and thereafter.

TABLE 6

OKLAHOMA

U.S. Community Hospitals
(Nonfederal, short-term general and other special hospitals)

Utilization, Personnel, Revenue and Expenses, Community Health Indicators 2015–2019

	2019	2018	2017	2016	2015
TOTAL FACILITY (Includes Hospital and Nursing Home Units)					
Utilization - Inpatient					
Beds	11,305	11,144	11,475	11,733	11,681
Admissions	427,388	422,246	420,377	423,192	417,874
Inpatient Days	2,308,688	2,296,383	2,278,209	2,322,517	2,274,841
Average Length of Stay	5.4	5.4	5.4	5.5	5.4
Inpatient Surgeries	112,531	113,241	111,298	114,257	110,626
Births	49,839	48,998	48,385	52,663	48,485
Utilization - Outpatient					
Emergency Outpatient Visits	1,945,709	1,825,825	1,915,881	1,872,023	1,918,470
Other Outpatient Visits	6,087,737	5,781,804	5,931,786	5,400,094	4,877,209
Total Outpatient Visits	8,033,446	7,607,629	7,847,667	7,272,117	6,795,679
Outpatient Surgeries	297,269	299,912	298,062	308,705	286,478
Personnel					
Full Time RNs	14,765	14,366	14,367	14,320	13,911
Full Time LPNs	1,461	1,374	1,418	1,520	1,571
Part Time RNs	5,145	4,541	4,772	4,537	4,406
Part Time LPNs	354	325	344	395	378
Total Full Time	50,181	48,660	48,031	48,944	48,288
Total Part Time	14,632	12,413	14,185	13,754	13,670
Revenue - Inpatient					
Gross Inpatient Revenue	$23,788,252,971	$22,430,638,837	$20,802,461,884	$20,644,933,881	$18,297,261,931
Revenue - Outpatient					
Gross Outpatient Revenue	$25,626,164,125	$23,334,739,018	$21,114,422,128	$19,789,096,790	$17,705,595,827
Revenue and Expenses - Totals					
(Includes Inpatient and Outpatient)					
Total Gross Revenue	$49,414,417,096	$45,765,377,855	$41,916,884,012	$40,434,030,671	$36,002,857,758
Deductions from Revenue	38,119,486,791	35,120,625,862	31,692,210,283	30,536,433,222	26,410,602,517
Net Patient Revenue	11,294,930,305	10,644,751,993	10,224,673,729	9,897,597,449	9,592,255,241
Other Operating Revenue	347,257,456	322,347,396	343,746,238	313,647,471	308,129,033
Other Nonoperating Revenue	108,214,528	127,331,220	221,877,932	38,443,530	83,638,733
Total Net Revenue	11,750,402,289	11,094,430,609	10,790,297,899	10,249,688,450	9,984,023,007
Total Expenses	10,758,963,822	10,060,788,649	9,667,546,273	9,370,788,599	9,066,246,642
HOSPITAL UNIT (Excludes Separate Nursing Home Units)					
Utilization - Inpatient					
Beds	11,099	10,938	11,254	11,442	11,468
Admissions	426,834	421,720	419,826	422,324	417,402
Inpatient Days	2,244,046	2,232,707	2,209,530	2,231,521	2,212,654
Average Length of Stay	5.3	5.3	5.3	5.3	5.3
Personnel					
Total Full Time	50,049	48,503	47,882	48,692	48,059
Total Part Time	14,622	12,383	14,163	13,710	13,612
Revenue and Expenses - Totals					
(Includes Inpatient and Outpatient)					
Total Net Revenue	$11,736,927,461	$11,083,264,819	$10,778,365,699	$10,234,060,884	$9,973,680,613
Total Expenses	10,749,961,247	10,052,953,053	9,653,400,032	9,354,497,305	9,057,450,178
COMMUNITY HEALTH INDICATORS PER 1000 POPULATION					
Total Population (in thousands)	3,957	3,943	3,931	3,924	3,911
Inpatient					
Beds	2.9	2.8	2.9	3	3
Admissions	108	107.1	106.9	107.9	106.8
Inpatient Days	583.4	582.4	579.6	591.9	581.6
Inpatient Surgeries	28.4	28.7	28.3	29.1	28.3
Births	12.6	12.4	12.3	13.4	12.4
Outpatient					
Emergency Outpatient Visits	491.7	463	487.4	477.1	490.5
Other Outpatient Visits	1,538.5	1,466.3	1,509	1,376.3	1,246.9
Total Outpatient Visits	2,030.2	1,929.4	1,996.4	1,853.4	1,737.4
Outpatient Surgeries	75.1	76.1	75.8	78.7	73.2
Expense per Capita (per person)	$2,719	$2,551.5	$2,459.4	$2,388.3	$2,317.9

Note: These data represent hospital performance in the years 2015 – 2019 and do not reflect any impacts from the COVID-19 pandemic in 2020 and thereafter.

States

TABLE 6

OREGON

U.S. Community Hospitals
(Nonfederal, short-term general and other special hospitals)

Overview 2015–2019

	2019	2018	2017	2016	2015
Total Community Hospitals in Oregon...............	61	61	61	61	61
Bed Size Category					
6-24...	12	12	12	13	12
25-49...	20	20	20	20	21
50-99...	7	7	6	5	5
100-199...	12	12	13	12	12
200-299...	1	2	2	3	3
300-399...	4	3	3	3	3
400-499...	2	2	3	4	3
500 +...	3	3	2	1	2
Location					
Hospitals Urban	35	35	35	35	35
Hospitals Rural...	26	26	26	26	26
Control					
State and Local Government	11	11	11	11	11
Not for Profit...	47	47	47	47	47
Investor owned...	3	3	3	3	3
Affiliations					
Hospitals in a System................................	44	44	44	44	43
Hospitals in a Group Purchasing Organization...	59	59	59	59	59

Note: These data represent hospital performance in the years 2015 – 2019 and do not reflect any impacts from the COVID-19 pandemic in 2020 and thereafter.

States

Table 6

OREGON

U.S. Community Hospitals
(Nonfederal, short-term general and other special hospitals)

Utilization, Personnel, Revenue and Expenses, Community Health Indicators 2015–2019

	2019	2018	2017	2016	2015
TOTAL FACILITY (Includes Hospital and Nursing Home Units)					
Utilization - Inpatient					
Beds	6,975	6,889	6,906	6,863	6,950
Admissions	348,059	347,802	348,059	346,517	352,347
Inpatient Days	1,602,392	1,589,931	1,572,311	1,543,944	1,541,696
Average Length of Stay	4.6	4.6	4.5	4.5	4.4
Inpatient Surgeries	120,185	119,793	124,481	125,700	123,098
Births	41,043	41,999	43,286	44,145	44,304
Utilization - Outpatient					
Emergency Outpatient Visits	1,571,368	1,581,113	1,584,195	1,597,435	1,569,323
Other Outpatient Visits	11,245,103	10,697,576	10,447,396	9,899,003	9,324,868
Total Outpatient Visits	12,816,471	12,278,689	12,031,591	11,496,438	10,894,191
Outpatient Surgeries	241,546	223,416	210,270	209,719	202,767
Personnel					
Full Time RNs	13,954	13,893	13,350	12,904	12,229
Full Time LPNs	156	166	156	154	155
Part Time RNs	8,592	7,815	8,219	7,921	7,274
Part Time LPNs	76	73	76	89	78
Total Full Time	48,459	48,106	45,821	45,134	43,567
Total Part Time	22,740	21,266	22,300	21,149	18,971
Revenue - Inpatient					
Gross Inpatient Revenue	$15,251,945,731	$14,421,176,343	$13,743,363,797	$12,943,793,855	$12,109,866,304
Revenue - Outpatient					
Gross Outpatient Revenue	$17,878,375,353	$16,207,608,813	$14,719,541,782	$13,597,783,846	$12,189,067,679
Revenue and Expenses - Totals					
(Includes Inpatient and Outpatient)					
Total Gross Revenue	$33,130,321,084	$30,628,785,156	$28,462,905,579	$26,541,577,701	$24,298,933,983
Deductions from Revenue	20,022,350,216	18,355,192,163	16,481,954,247	15,139,777,925	13,504,391,340
Net Patient Revenue	13,107,970,868	12,273,592,993	11,980,951,332	11,401,799,776	10,794,542,643
Other Operating Revenue	738,552,055	746,630,531	698,321,177	714,136,123	691,731,339
Other Nonoperating Revenue	212,798,885	151,126,374	266,061,673	102,198,075	253,652,658
Total Net Revenue	14,059,321,808	13,171,349,898	12,945,334,182	12,218,133,974	11,739,926,640
Total Expenses	13,363,786,551	12,591,357,442	12,089,476,807	11,595,877,741	10,848,340,732
HOSPITAL UNIT (Excludes Separate Nursing Home Units)					
Utilization - Inpatient					
Beds	6,935	6,849	6,866	6,834	6,899
Admissions	348,049	347,782	348,040	346,504	352,317
Inpatient Days	1,595,469	1,582,906	1,565,993	1,536,570	1,526,203
Average Length of Stay	4.6	4.6	4.5	4.4	4.3
Personnel					
Total Full Time	48,428	48,076	45,793	45,110	43,530
Total Part Time	22,733	21,260	22,295	21,137	18,937
Revenue and Expenses - Totals					
(Includes Inpatient and Outpatient)					
Total Net Revenue	$14,057,241,730	$13,169,264,786	$12,943,459,087	$12,216,694,195	$11,737,220,370
Total Expenses	13,361,154,125	12,588,748,152	12,087,627,674	11,593,720,376	10,845,467,436
COMMUNITY HEALTH INDICATORS PER 1000 POPULATION					
Total Population (in thousands)	4,218	4,191	4,143	4,093	4,029
Inpatient					
Beds	1.7	1.6	1.7	1.7	1.7
Admissions	82.5	83	84	84.7	87.5
Inpatient Days	379.9	379.4	379.5	377.2	382.7
Inpatient Surgeries	28.5	28.6	30	30.7	30.6
Births	9.7	10	10.4	10.8	11
Outpatient					
Emergency Outpatient Visits	372.6	377.3	382.4	390.2	389.5
Other Outpatient Visits	2,666.1	2,552.7	2,521.8	2,418.2	2,314.5
Total Outpatient Visits	3,038.7	2,930	2,904.2	2,808.5	2,704
Outpatient Surgeries	57.3	53.3	50.8	51.2	50.3
Expense per Capita (per person)	$3,168.5	$3,004.6	$2,918.2	$2,832.8	$2,692.6

Note: These data represent hospital performance in the years 2015 – 2019 and do not reflect any impacts from the COVID-19 pandemic in 2020 and thereafter.

States

TABLE **6**

PENNSYLVANIA

U.S. Community Hospitals
(Nonfederal, short-term general and other special hospitals)

Overview 2015–2019

	2019	2018	2017	2016	2015
Total Community Hospitals in Pennsylvania	191	199	201	196	198
Bed Size Category					
6-24...	12	10	9	8	8
25-49...	30	34	32	29	30
50-99...	41	43	44	40	41
100-199...	48	47	52	51	49
200-299...	25	31	28	31	30
300-399...	16	14	15	15	20
400-499...	3	5	5	6	5
500 +...	16	15	16	16	15
Location					
Hospitals Urban	157	162	163	158	160
Hospitals Rural..	34	37	38	38	38
Control					
State and Local Government	1	1	1	1	1
Not for Profit..	147	151	150	141	141
Investor owned..	43	47	50	54	56
Affiliations					
Hospitals in a System.............................	141	148	147	145	142
Hospitals in a Group Purchasing Organization...	110	120	126	141	133

Note: These data represent hospital performance in the years 2015 – 2019 and do not reflect any impacts from the COVID-19 pandemic in 2020 and thereafter.

States

TABLE 6

PENNSYLVANIA

U.S. Community Hospitals
(Nonfederal, short-term general and other special hospitals)

Utilization, Personnel, Revenue and Expenses, Community Health Indicators 2015–2019

	2019	2018	2017	2016	2015
TOTAL FACILITY (Includes Hospital and Nursing Home Units)					
Utilization - Inpatient					
Beds	35,448	36,730	37,219	37,800	38,034
Admissions	1,536,768	1,584,299	1,603,240	1,598,135	1,604,511
Inpatient Days	8,341,604	8,614,087	8,689,512	8,707,719	8,785,249
Average Length of Stay	5.4	5.4	5.4	5.4	5.5
Inpatient Surgeries	428,143	454,182	458,880	474,190	473,605
Births	127,430	134,890	134,434	134,314	131,573
Utilization - Outpatient					
Emergency Outpatient Visits	6,182,130	6,264,480	6,597,020	6,462,953	6,625,185
Other Outpatient Visits	34,936,026	35,439,162	34,884,065	34,558,969	33,138,359
Total Outpatient Visits	41,118,156	41,703,642	41,481,085	41,021,922	39,763,544
Outpatient Surgeries	924,755	941,220	942,891	968,226	953,747
Personnel					
Full Time RNs	63,031	62,451	62,774	59,428	58,077
Full Time LPNs	2,246	2,606	2,383	2,308	2,231
Part Time RNs	23,335	24,612	23,941	24,488	25,106
Part Time LPNs	738	788	809	784	863
Total Full Time	220,879	219,170	222,047	212,963	210,880
Total Part Time	72,395	73,466	71,520	71,064	71,842
Revenue - Inpatient					
Gross Inpatient Revenue	$105,838,423,569	$106,336,981,667	$99,727,315,390	$95,009,646,700	$91,931,638,930
Revenue - Outpatient					
Gross Outpatient Revenue	$113,844,703,778	$108,292,961,637	$98,991,785,117	$91,157,281,697	$81,281,718,035
Revenue and Expenses - Totals					
(Includes Inpatient and Outpatient)					
Total Gross Revenue	$219,683,127,347	$214,629,943,304	$198,719,100,507	$186,166,928,397	$173,213,356,965
Deductions from Revenue	170,390,173,880	166,686,448,831	152,968,866,168	142,505,189,415	131,464,823,163
Net Patient Revenue	49,292,953,467	47,943,494,473	45,750,234,339	43,661,738,982	41,748,533,802
Other Operating Revenue	3,018,966,388	2,771,123,258	2,599,746,561	2,260,251,951	2,226,932,302
Other Nonoperating Revenue	499,920,053	728,390,289	706,603,450	92,157,377	326,675,248
Total Net Revenue	52,811,839,908	51,443,008,020	49,056,584,350	46,014,148,310	44,302,141,352
Total Expenses	48,828,071,925	47,413,501,473	45,337,062,291	43,022,290,997	41,324,767,253
HOSPITAL UNIT (Excludes Separate Nursing Home Units)					
Utilization - Inpatient					
Beds	34,359	35,540	36,046	36,490	36,932
Admissions	1,528,977	1,575,938	1,594,246	1,586,418	1,593,221
Inpatient Days	8,000,892	8,256,220	8,315,377	8,299,878	8,440,145
Average Length of Stay	5.2	5.2	5.2	5.2	5.3
Personnel					
Total Full Time	219,982	218,366	221,380	212,203	210,192
Total Part Time	71,954	73,061	71,187	70,645	71,465
Revenue and Expenses - Totals					
(Includes Inpatient and Outpatient)					
Total Net Revenue	$52,698,254,704	$51,334,315,877	$48,931,873,565	$45,884,398,791	$44,174,552,581
Total Expenses	48,731,616,874	47,325,489,846	45,236,014,269	42,929,473,078	41,190,933,142
COMMUNITY HEALTH INDICATORS PER 1000 POPULATION					
Total Population (in thousands)	12,802	12,807	12,806	12,784	12,803
Inpatient					
Beds	2.8	2.9	2.9	3	3
Admissions	120	123.7	125.2	125	125.3
Inpatient Days	651.6	672.6	678.6	681.1	686.2
Inpatient Surgeries	33.4	35.5	35.8	37.1	37
Births	10	10.5	10.5	10.5	10.3
Outpatient					
Emergency Outpatient Visits	482.9	489.1	515.2	505.5	517.5
Other Outpatient Visits	2,729	2,767.2	2,724.1	2,703.3	2,588.4
Total Outpatient Visits	3,211.9	3,256.3	3,239.3	3,208.8	3,105.9
Outpatient Surgeries	72.2	73.5	73.6	75.7	74.5
Expense per Capita (per person)	$3,814.1	$3,702.1	$3,540.4	$3,365.3	$3,227.9

Note: These data represent hospital performance in the years 2015 – 2019 and do not reflect any impacts from the COVID-19 pandemic in 2020 and thereafter.

States

TABLE 6

RHODE ISLAND

U.S. Community Hospitals
(Nonfederal, short-term general and other special hospitals)

Overview 2015–2019

	2019	2018	2017	2016	2015
Total Community Hospitals in Rhode Island......	11	11	11	12	12
Bed Size Category					
6-24	0	0	0	0	0
25-49	0	0	1	1	0
50-99	4	4	3	3	3
100-199	3	3	3	4	5
200-299	2	2	2	2	2
300-399	1	1	1	1	1
400-499	0	0	0	0	0
500 +	1	1	1	1	1
Location					
Hospitals Urban	11	11	11	12	12
Hospitals Rural	0	0	0	0	0
Control					
State and Local Government	0	0	0	0	0
Not for Profit	11	9	9	10	10
Investor owned	0	2	2	2	2
Affiliations					
Hospitals in a System	10	10	10	11	11
Hospitals in a Group Purchasing Organization...	6	6	7	7	7

Note: These data represent hospital performance in the years 2015 – 2019 and do not reflect any impacts from the COVID-19 pandemic in 2020 and thereafter.

States

TABLE 6

RHODE ISLAND

U.S. Community Hospitals
(Nonfederal, short-term general and other special hospitals)

Utilization, Personnel, Revenue and Expenses, Community Health Indicators 2015–2019

	2019	2018	2017	2016	2015
TOTAL FACILITY (Includes Hospital and Nursing Home Units)					
Utilization - Inpatient					
Beds	2,191	2,187	2,156	2,307	2,339
Admissions	116,276	115,483	115,669	118,327	117,005
Inpatient Days	554,916	549,531	554,246	564,857	577,681
Average Length of Stay	4.8	4.8	4.8	4.8	4.9
Inpatient Surgeries	28,588	28,498	27,405	29,475	27,987
Births	12,002	11,401	10,853	11,283	11,349
Utilization - Outpatient					
Emergency Outpatient Visits	528,353	546,514	500,399	547,657	546,113
Other Outpatient Visits	1,770,347	1,627,424	1,589,171	1,835,025	1,776,845
Total Outpatient Visits	2,298,700	2,173,938	2,089,570	2,382,682	2,322,958
Outpatient Surgeries	66,690	66,889	62,985	65,860	64,721
Personnel					
Full Time RNs	3,363	3,281	2,907	2,906	2,911
Full Time LPNs	77	75	57	71	66
Part Time RNs	2,950	2,835	2,895	3,258	2,946
Part Time LPNs	47	48	37	52	51
Total Full Time	13,562	13,401	12,645	12,794	12,792
Total Part Time	9,179	8,786	8,533	9,440	8,628
Revenue - Inpatient					
Gross Inpatient Revenue	$4,632,784,730	$4,714,227,205	$4,297,561,050	$4,311,146,280	$4,289,888,054
Revenue - Outpatient					
Gross Outpatient Revenue	$6,336,625,183	$5,996,687,189	$5,527,295,528	$5,266,236,508	$4,864,838,086
Revenue and Expenses - Totals					
(Includes Inpatient and Outpatient)					
Total Gross Revenue	$10,969,409,913	$10,710,914,394	$9,824,856,578	$9,577,382,788	$9,154,726,140
Deductions from Revenue	7,471,995,289	7,339,662,373	6,587,087,008	6,287,937,110	5,991,680,759
Net Patient Revenue	3,497,414,624	3,371,252,021	3,237,769,570	3,289,445,678	3,163,045,381
Other Operating Revenue	278,274,949	246,861,588	299,961,004	271,331,562	268,801,154
Other Nonoperating Revenue	8,762,738	21,378,805	24,652,681	-16,102,465	-1,554,971
Total Net Revenue	3,784,452,311	3,639,492,414	3,562,383,255	3,544,674,775	3,430,291,564
Total Expenses	3,791,359,950	3,570,713,915	3,510,873,781	3,557,534,952	3,404,037,616
HOSPITAL UNIT (Excludes Separate Nursing Home Units)					
Utilization - Inpatient					
Beds	2,191	2,187	2,156	2,307	2,339
Admissions	116,276	115,483	115,669	118,327	117,005
Inpatient Days	554,916	549,531	554,246	564,857	577,681
Average Length of Stay	4.8	4.8	4.8	4.8	4.9
Personnel					
Total Full Time	13,562	13,401	12,645	12,794	12,792
Total Part Time	9,179	8,786	8,533	9,440	8,628
Revenue and Expenses - Totals					
(Includes Inpatient and Outpatient)					
Total Net Revenue	$3,784,452,311	$3,639,492,414	$3,562,383,255	$3,544,674,775	$3,430,291,564
Total Expenses	3,791,359,950	3,570,713,915	3,510,873,781	3,557,534,952	3,404,037,616
COMMUNITY HEALTH INDICATORS PER 1000 POPULATION					
Total Population (in thousands)	1,059	1,057	1,060	1,056	1,056
Inpatient					
Beds	2.1	2.1	2	2.2	2.2
Admissions	109.8	109.2	109.2	112	110.8
Inpatient Days	523.8	519.7	523.1	534.7	546.9
Inpatient Surgeries	27	27	25.9	27.9	26.5
Births	11.3	10.8	10.2	10.7	10.7
Outpatient					
Emergency Outpatient Visits	498.7	516.9	472.2	518.4	517
Other Outpatient Visits	1,671.1	1,539.2	1,499.7	1737	1,682.1
Total Outpatient Visits	2,169.9	2,056.1	1,972	2,255.4	2,199.2
Outpatient Surgeries	63	63.3	59.4	62.3	61.3
Expense per Capita (per person)	$3,578.9	$3,377.2	$3,313.3	$3,367.5	$3,222.6

Note: These data represent hospital performance in the years 2015 – 2019 and do not reflect any impacts from the COVID-19 pandemic in 2020 and thereafter.

States

TABLE 6

SOUTH CAROLINA

U.S. Community Hospitals
(Nonfederal, short-term general and other special hospitals)

Overview 2015–2019

	2019	2018	2017	2016	2015
Total Community Hospitals in South Carolina...	72	69	70	70	70
Bed Size Category					
6-24	3	1	2	1	2
25-49	18	19	16	17	17
50-99	18	15	17	17	16
100-199	11	11	12	13	13
200-299	9	9	10	8	9
300-399	6	6	4	4	3
400-499	2	4	5	5	6
500 +	5	4	4	5	4
Location					
Hospitals Urban	56	54	55	55	55
Hospitals Rural	16	15	15	15	15
Control					
State and Local Government	20	14	15	15	19
Not for Profit	32	30	31	30	28
Investor owned	20	25	24	25	23
Affiliations					
Hospitals in a System	61	58	58	58	58
Hospitals in a Group Purchasing Organization...	59	64	62	65	63

Note: These data represent hospital performance in the years 2015 – 2019 and do not reflect any impacts from the COVID-19 pandemic in 2020 and thereafter.

States

TABLE 6

SOUTH CAROLINA

U.S. Community Hospitals
(Nonfederal, short-term general and other special hospitals)

Utilization, Personnel, Revenue and Expenses, Community Health Indicators 2015–2019

	2019	2018	2017	2016	2015
TOTAL FACILITY (Includes Hospital and Nursing Home Units)					
Utilization - Inpatient					
Beds..........	12,055	12,120	12,357	12,388	12,347
Admissions..........	542,122	533,023	525,641	525,029	523,730
Inpatient Days..........	2,902,583	2,856,120	2,822,503	2,820,750	2,829,685
Average Length of Stay..........	5.4	5.4	5.4	5.4	5.4
Inpatient Surgeries..........	166,740	166,063	169,712	179,421	183,355
Births..........	52,331	51,006	52,509	53,735	54,587
Utilization - Outpatient					
Emergency Outpatient Visits..........	2,408,169	2,509,535	2,471,755	2,543,747	2,470,621
Other Outpatient Visits..........	7,046,024	7,065,878	6,958,171	6,887,043	5,790,738
Total Outpatient Visits..........	9,454,193	9,575,413	9,429,926	9,430,790	8,261,359
Outpatient Surgeries..........	357,747	336,386	338,299	327,895	314,828
Personnel					
Full Time RNs..........	19,467	20,302	20,582	20,504	20,365
Full Time LPNs..........	644	634	684	725	593
Part Time RNs..........	7,292	6,142	5,960	5,878	5,190
Part Time LPNs..........	207	197	184	197	142
Total Full Time..........	60,610	63,150	65,350	66,130	64,131
Total Part Time..........	19,064	16,482	17,085	15,767	14,551
Revenue - Inpatient					
Gross Inpatient Revenue..........	$27,996,687,056	$27,201,177,908	$25,527,354,490	$24,390,196,272	$23,100,092,850
Revenue - Outpatient					
Gross Outpatient Revenue..........	$29,071,467,837	$28,406,047,786	$25,206,112,553	$24,185,225,044	$21,189,443,623
Revenue and Expenses - Totals					
(Includes Inpatient and Outpatient)					
Total Gross Revenue..........	$57,068,154,893	$55,607,225,694	$50,733,467,043	$48,575,421,316	$44,289,536,473
Deductions from Revenue..........	43,308,470,698	42,493,865,972	38,012,804,829	36,235,963,574	32,878,860,388
Net Patient Revenue..........	13,759,684,195	13,113,359,722	12,720,662,214	12,339,457,742	11,410,676,085
Other Operating Revenue..........	413,241,221	368,591,245	372,224,361	333,129,054	491,319,749
Other Nonoperating Revenue..........	227,163,627	10,145,853	297,293,199	225,878,085	122,029,853
Total Net Revenue..........	14,400,089,043	13,492,096,820	13,390,179,774	12,898,464,881	12,024,025,687
Total Expenses..........	12,963,240,601	12,391,540,003	12,103,968,251	11,514,797,706	10,634,789,126
HOSPITAL UNIT (Excludes Separate Nursing Home Units)					
Utilization - Inpatient					
Beds..........	11,792	11,711	11,907	11,968	11,935
Admissions..........	540,927	531,084	523,105	521,968	520,952
Inpatient Days..........	2,820,660	2,727,563	2,686,062	2,694,138	2,697,309
Average Length of Stay..........	5.2	5.1	5.1	5.2	5.2
Personnel					
Total Full Time..........	60,290	62,790	64,759	65,647	63,793
Total Part Time..........	18,936	16,285	16,807	15,603	14,419
Revenue and Expenses - Totals					
(Includes Inpatient and Outpatient)					
Total Net Revenue..........	$14,359,377,408	$13,444,893,922	$13,323,998,593	$12,831,443,432	$11,985,271,771
Total Expenses..........	12,933,493,254	12,348,558,643	12,043,658,997	11,458,089,086	10,591,085,495
COMMUNITY HEALTH INDICATORS PER 1000 POPULATION					
Total Population (in thousands)..........	5,149	5,084	5,024	4,961	4,896
Inpatient					
Beds..........	2.3	2.4	2.5	2.5	2.5
Admissions..........	105.3	104.8	104.6	105.8	107
Inpatient Days..........	563.7	561.8	561.8	568.6	577.9
Inpatient Surgeries..........	32.4	32.7	33.8	36.2	37.4
Births..........	10.2	10	10.5	10.8	11.1
Outpatient					
Emergency Outpatient Visits..........	467.7	493.6	492	512.7	504.6
Other Outpatient Visits..........	1,368.5	1,389.8	1,384.9	1,388.2	1,182.7
Total Outpatient Visits..........	1,836.2	1,883.4	1,876.8	1,900.9	1,687.3
Outpatient Surgeries..........	69.5	66.2	67.3	66.1	64.3
Expense per Capita (per person).........	$2,517.8	$2,437.3	$2,409.1	$2,321	$2,172.1

Note: These data represent hospital performance in the years 2015 – 2019 and do not reflect any impacts from the COVID-19 pandemic in 2020 and thereafter.

States

TABLE **6**

SOUTH DAKOTA

U.S. Community Hospitals
(Nonfederal, short-term general and other special hospitals)

Overview 2015–2019

	2019	2018	2017	2016	2015
Total Community Hospitals in South Dakota	57	57	57	57	57
Bed Size Category					
6-24	20	22	21	21	22
25-49	12	11	12	12	11
50-99	14	13	13	13	13
100-199	6	6	6	6	6
200-299	2	2	2	2	2
300-399	1	1	1	1	1
400-499	0	0	1	1	2
500 + ...	2	2	1	1	0
Location					
Hospitals Urban	14	14	14	14	14
Hospitals Rural	43	43	43	43	43
Control					
State and Local Government	4	4	4	4	4
Not for Profit	45	45	45	45	45
Investor owned	8	8	8	8	8
Affiliations					
Hospitals in a System	40	40	39	39	39
Hospitals in a Group Purchasing Organization...	31	31	38	34	29

Note: These data represent hospital performance in the years 2015 – 2019 and do not reflect any impacts from the COVID-19 pandemic in 2020 and thereafter.

States

TABLE 6

SOUTH DAKOTA

U.S. Community Hospitals
(Nonfederal, short-term general and other special hospitals)

Utilization, Personnel, Revenue and Expenses, Community Health Indicators 2015–2019

	2019	2018	2017	2016	2015
TOTAL FACILITY (Includes Hospital and Nursing Home Units)					
Utilization - Inpatient					
Beds	4,222	4,183	4,167	4,144	4,071
Admissions	109,069	107,474	107,388	103,474	101,783
Inpatient Days	927,445	939,755	958,248	1,002,676	1,022,798
Average Length of Stay	8.5	8.7	8.9	9.7	10.0
Inpatient Surgeries	26,848	29,908	27,132	25,788	24,009
Births	12,352	13,122	12,932	12,329	11,981
Utilization - Outpatient					
Emergency Outpatient Visits	359,830	378,697	328,117	341,039	277,330
Other Outpatient Visits	2,773,935	2,807,104	2,455,901	2,550,160	2,163,742
Total Outpatient Visits	3,133,765	3,185,801	2,784,018	2,891,199	2,441,072
Outpatient Surgeries	65,455	64,169	68,651	63,072	60,719
Personnel					
Full Time RNs	5,172	5,715	5,292	4,551	4,861
Full Time LPNs	534	579	555	372	349
Part Time RNs	2,949	2,811	2,897	2,540	2,477
Part Time LPNs	258	243	251	194	179
Total Full Time	19,311	20,559	20,168	16,679	16,864
Total Part Time	9,606	9,943	10,211	8,330	8,416
Revenue - Inpatient					
Gross Inpatient Revenue	$5,309,938,827	$4,948,280,204	$4,765,408,996	$4,273,198,758	$4,261,464,169
Revenue - Outpatient					
Gross Outpatient Revenue	$7,593,742,351	$6,925,206,503	$6,241,390,538	$5,586,822,424	$5,270,698,882
Revenue and Expenses - Totals	$12,903,681,178	$11,873,486,707	$11,006,799,534	$9,860,021,182	$9,532,163,051
(Includes Inpatient and Outpatient)					
Total Gross Revenue	$12,903,681,178	$11,873,486,707	$11,006,799,534	$9,860,021,182	$9,532,163,051
Deductions from Revenue	8,724,260,234	7,871,777,397	7,174,650,556	6,247,499,170	6,131,349,357
Net Patient Revenue	4,179,420,944	4,001,709,310	3,832,148,978	3,612,522,012	3,400,813,694
Other Operating Revenue	389,053,313	294,798,357	243,923,099	218,443,474	194,371,409
Other Nonoperating Revenue	30,024,312	48,359,298	121,739,426	12,316,133	18,037,020
Total Net Revenue	4,598,498,569	4,344,866,965	4,197,811,503	3,843,281,619	3,613,222,123
Total Expenses	4,283,406,294	3,964,127,859	3,825,457,472	3,584,475,494	3,245,003,285
HOSPITAL UNIT (Excludes Separate Nursing Home Units)					
Utilization - Inpatient					
Beds	3,155	3,115	2,977	2,907	2,908
Admissions	107,844	106,298	106,276	102,286	100,721
Inpatient Days	594,153	587,645	555,026	571,514	615,438
Average Length of Stay	5.5	5.5	5.2	5.6	6.1
Personnel					
Total Full Time	18,728	19,943	19,460	15,994	16,292
Total Part Time	9,129	9,291	9,564	7,755	7,924
Revenue and Expenses - Totals					
(Includes Inpatient and Outpatient)					
Total Net Revenue	$4,519,141,028	$4,271,429,331	$4,111,355,271	$3,751,696,070	$3,526,485,663
Total Expenses	4,203,059,494	3,901,570,254	3,743,945,158	3,505,783,141	3,172,737,628
COMMUNITY HEALTH INDICATORS PER 1000 POPULATION					
Total Population (in thousands)	885	882	870	865	858
Inpatient					
Beds	4.8	4.7	4.8	4.8	4.7
Admissions	123.3	121.8	123.5	119.6	118.6
Inpatient Days	1,048.4	1,065.2	1,101.9	1,158.6	1,191.4
Inpatient Surgeries	30.3	33.9	31.2	29.8	28
Births	14	14.9	14.9	14.2	14
Outpatient					
Emergency Outpatient Visits	406.7	429.2	377.3	394.1	323.1
Other Outpatient Visits	3,135.6	3,181.8	2,824	2,946.6	2,520.5
Total Outpatient Visits	3,542.3	3,611.1	3,201.2	3,40.7	2,843.5
Outpatient Surgeries	74	72.7	78.9	72.9	70.7
Expense per Capita (per person)	$4,841.9	$4,493.3	$4,398.8	$4,141.7	$3,780

Note: These data represent hospital performance in the years 2015 – 2019 and do not reflect any impacts from the COVID-19 pandemic in 2020 and thereafter.

States

TABLE **6**

TENNESSEE

U.S. Community Hospitals
(Nonfederal, short-term general and other special hospitals)

Overview 2015–2019

	2019	2018	2017	2016	2015
Total Community Hospitals in Tennessee.........	112	115	122	124	126
Bed Size Category					
6-24	10	7	7	7	7
25-49	25	27	28	30	33
50-99	27	30	35	34	30
100-199	24	22	22	24	25
200-299	8	9	10	12	13
300-399	5	6	5	5	6
400-499	4	5	5	4	3
500 + ...	9	9	10	8	9
Location					
Hospitals Urban	73	74	76	79	79
Hospitals Rural	39	41	46	45	47
Control					
State and Local Government	21	20	19	18	19
Not for Profit	49	50	51	51	51
Investor owned	42	45	52	55	56
Affiliations					
Hospitals in a System	92	95	100	103	102
Hospitals in a Group Purchasing Organization...	57	52	57	54	55

Note: These data represent hospital performance in the years 2015 – 2019 and do not reflect any impacts from the COVID-19 pandemic in 2020 and thereafter.

States

TABLE 6

TENNESSEE

U.S. Community Hospitals
(Nonfederal, short-term general and other special hospitals)

Utilization, Personnel, Revenue and Expenses, Community Health Indicators 2015–2019

	2019	2018	2017	2016	2015
TOTAL FACILITY (Includes Hospital and Nursing Home Units)					
Utilization - Inpatient					
Beds	18,366	19,387	20,274	19,583	20,071
Admissions	808,717	817,844	841,686	829,594	832,882
Inpatient Days	4,357,177	4,458,707	4,576,410	4,556,289	4,618,397
Average Length of Stay	5.4	5.5	5.4	5.5	5.5
Inpatient Surgeries	226,746	228,731	229,168	230,846	228,817
Births	65,464	65,359	63,459	66,712	68,624
Utilization - Outpatient					
Emergency Outpatient Visits	3,395,858	3,413,114	3,490,215	3,546,645	3,505,149
Other Outpatient Visits	11,260,595	10,661,893	10,174,421	9,623,620	8,831,676
Total Outpatient Visits	14,656,453	14,075,007	13,664,636	13,170,265	12,336,825
Outpatient Surgeries	451,249	451,668	435,611	450,381	425,950
Personnel					
Full Time RNs	29,312	28,928	30,276	28,567	26,817
Full Time LPNs	2,011	1,967	1,982	1,929	1,892
Part Time RNs	10,602	10,639	8,374	9,249	7,183
Part Time LPNs	571	590	423	554	443
Total Full Time	100,974	103,142	108,096	92,059	87,575
Total Part Time	28,320	30,700	22,779	26,423	19,214
Revenue - Inpatient					
Gross Inpatient Revenue	$42,772,065,689	$42,184,079,892	$40,894,418,158	$37,418,967,649	$36,068,050,775
Revenue - Outpatient					
Gross Outpatient Revenue	$43,823,137,032	$42,532,543,598	$41,053,722,777	$35,373,103,358	$33,036,573,449
Revenue and Expenses - Totals (Includes Inpatient and Outpatient)					
Total Gross Revenue	$86,595,202,721	$84,716,623,490	$81,948,140,935	$72,792,071,007	$69,104,624,224
Deductions from Revenue	67,227,510,526	65,437,792,094	62,427,271,778	54,956,390,305	51,829,063,773
Net Patient Revenue	19,367,692,195	19,278,831,396	19,520,869,157	17,835,680,702	17,275,560,451
Other Operating Revenue	914,710,142	1,744,204,707	1,124,098,322	604,488,582	602,849,667
Other Nonoperating Revenue	232,989,610	307,017,551	246,181,994	115,223,919	123,711,375
Total Net Revenue	20,515,391,947	21,330,053,654	20,891,149,473	18,555,393,203	18,002,121,493
Total Expenses	19,292,745,024	20,457,279,423	19,213,217,783	16,958,545,633	16,183,711,421
HOSPITAL UNIT (Excludes Separate Nursing Home Units)					
Utilization - Inpatient					
Beds	17,860	18,789	19,791	19,019	18,982
Admissions	805,375	813,937	838,272	826,109	827,162
Inpatient Days	4,212,898	4,279,475	4,427,196	4,399,271	4,314,598
Average Length of Stay	5.2	5.3	5.3	5.3	5.2
Personnel					
Total Full Time	100,614	102,739	107,687	91,565	86,870
Total Part Time	28,257	30,649	22,727	26,365	19,091
Revenue and Expenses - Totals (Includes Inpatient and Outpatient)					
Total Net Revenue	$20,469,938,989	$21,276,442,849	$20,847,274,328	$18,507,732,274	$17,921,881,928
Total Expenses	19,253,598,634	20,405,925,804	19,172,638,939	16,915,667,673	16,110,237,368
COMMUNITY HEALTH INDICATORS PER 1000 POPULATION					
Total Population (in thousands)	6,829	6,770	6,716	6,651	6,600
Inpatient					
Beds	2.7	2.9	3	2.9	3
Admissions	118.4	120.8	125.3	124.7	126.2
Inpatient Days	638	658.6	681.4	685	699.7
Inpatient Surgeries	33.2	33.8	34.1	34.7	34.7
Births	9.6	9.7	9.4	10	10.4
Outpatient					
Emergency Outpatient Visits	497.3	504.2	519.7	533.2	531.1
Other Outpatient Visits	1,648.9	1,574.9	1,515	1,446.9	1,338.1
Total Outpatient Visits	2,146.2	2,079	2,034.6	1,980.1	1,869.1
Outpatient Surgeries	66.1	66.7	64.9	67.7	64.5
Expense per Capita (per person)	$2,825	$3021.8	$2,860.8	$2,549.7	$2,452

Note: These data represent hospital performance in the years 2015 – 2019 and do not reflect any impacts from the COVID-19 pandemic in 2020 and thereafter.

TABLE 6

TEXAS

U.S. Community Hospitals
(Nonfederal, short-term general and other special hospitals)

Overview 2015–2019

	2019	2018	2017	2016	2015
Total Community Hospitals in Texas	512	523	528	535	536
Bed Size Category					
6-24	129	127	125	122	116
25-49	135	136	139	146	144
50-99	86	93	94	106	110
100-199	60	65	68	60	67
200-299	40	39	39	39	37
300-399	26	25	26	24	21
400-499	10	12	11	12	14
500 +	26	26	26	26	27
Location					
Hospitals Urban	379	388	390	394	394
Hospitals Rural	133	135	138	141	142
Control					
State and Local Government	100	103	103	101	101
Not for Profit	146	142	153	154	156
Investor owned	266	278	272	280	279
Affiliations					
Hospitals in a System	321	334	342	343	334
Hospitals in a Group Purchasing Organization	469	482	486	506	497

Note: These data represent hospital performance in the years 2015 – 2019 and do not reflect any impacts from the COVID-19 pandemic in 2020 and thereafter.

TABLE **6**

TEXAS

U.S. Community Hospitals
(Nonfederal, short-term general and other special hospitals)

Utilization, Personnel, Revenue and Expenses, Community Health Indicators 2015–2019

	2019	2018	2017	2016	2015
TOTAL FACILITY (Includes Hospital and Nursing Home Units)					
Utilization - Inpatient					
Beds	65,187	65,671	66,844	67,699	68,524
Admissions	2,800,687	2,779,032	2,774,329	2,720,756	2,699,195
Inpatient Days	14,518,233	14,531,238	14,595,697	14,978,396	14,669,330
Average Length of Stay	5.2	5.2	5.3	5.5	5.4
Inpatient Surgeries	769,531	783,803	792,257	767,984	782,063
Births	372,667	376,662	381,131	393,856	403,574
Utilization - Outpatient					
Emergency Outpatient Visits	12,236,144	12,281,937	11,952,821	11,464,470	11,239,398
Other Outpatient Visits	34,821,634	33,948,389	33,236,882	33,731,064	32,788,125
Total Outpatient Visits	47,057,778	46,230,326	45,189,703	45,195,534	44,027,523
Outpatient Surgeries	1,425,282	1,391,459	1,409,297	1,381,625	1,363,374
Personnel					
Full Time RNs	112,721	112,333	108,193	99,131	98,204
Full Time LPNs	6,485	6,671	6,930	7,077	7,276
Part Time RNs	27,481	27,529	27,704	26,150	24,666
Part Time LPNs	1,413	1,457	1,543	1,765	1,644
Total Full Time	337,671	337,723	333,645	323,565	317,216
Total Part Time	73,848	76,242	75,383	74,654	70,655
Revenue - Inpatient					
Gross Inpatient Revenue	$201,783,826,556	$187,435,095,824	$173,584,687,991	$160,744,423,222	$150,334,153,232
Revenue - Outpatient					
Gross Outpatient Revenue	$176,829,845,059	$160,974,658,676	$147,661,835,989	$133,814,217,049	$119,582,775,629
Revenue and Expenses - Totals					
(Includes Inpatient and Outpatient)					
Total Gross Revenue	$378,613,671,615	$348,409,754,500	$321,246,523,980	$294,558,640,271	$269,916,928,861
Deductions from Revenue	300,993,198,996	274,698,442,100	250,340,125,682	226,041,676,513	204,323,349,372
Net Patient Revenue	77,620,472,619	73,711,312,400	70,906,398,298	68,516,963,758	65,593,579,489
Other Operating Revenue	6,655,120,964	6,530,019,174	6,190,973,473	5,696,302,966	5,510,291,272
Other Nonoperating Revenue	1,188,040,961	1,058,969,357	1,484,197,097	1,171,383,196	790,633,595
Total Net Revenue	85,463,634,544	81,300,300,931	78,581,568,868	75,384,649,920	71,894,504,356
Total Expenses	74,912,405,760	73,402,315,718	70,961,691,860	67,556,830,766	63,180,949,391
HOSPITAL UNIT (Excludes Separate Nursing Home Units)					
Utilization - Inpatient					
Beds	64,858	65,431	66,415	65,399	66,143
Admissions	2,797,871	2,775,107	2,769,510	2,711,093	2,691,917
Inpatient Days	14,430,745	14,453,418	14,489,069	14,396,055	14,377,808
Average Length of Stay	5.2	5.2	5.2	5.3	5.3
Personnel					
Total Full Time	337,409	337,439	333,287	322,791	316,783
Total Part Time	73,799	76,200	75,350	74,476	70,553
Revenue and Expenses - Totals					
(Includes Inpatient and Outpatient)					
Total Net Revenue	$85,430,929,911	$81,265,591,988	$78,532,940,052	$75,274,390,980	$71,742,645,276
Total Expenses	74,881,102,382	73,375,211,855	70,920,099,631	67,453,240,887	63,044,000,116
COMMUNITY HEALTH INDICATORS PER 1000 POPULATION					
Total Population (in thousands)	28,996	28,702	28,305	27,863	27,469
Inpatient					
Beds	2.2	2.3	2.4	2.4	2.5
Admissions	96.6	96.8	98	97.6	98.3
Inpatient Days	500.7	506.3	515.7	537.6	534
Inpatient Surgeries	26.5	27.3	28	27.6	28.5
Births	12.9	13.1	13.5	14.1	14.7
Outpatient					
Emergency Outpatient Visits	422	427.9	422.3	411.5	409.2
Other Outpatient Visits	1,200.9	1,182.8	1,174.3	1,210.6	1,193.6
Total Outpatient Visits	1,622.9	1,610.7	1,596.6	1,622.1	1,602.8
Outpatient Surgeries	49.2	48.5	49.8	49.6	49.6
Expense per Capita (per person)	$2,583.6	$2,557.4	$2,507.1	$2,424.6	$2,300.1

Note: These data represent hospital performance in the years 2015 – 2019 and do not reflect any impacts from the COVID-19 pandemic in 2020 and thereafter.

States

TABLE 6

UTAH

U.S. Community Hospitals
(Nonfederal, short-term general and other special hospitals)

Overview 2015–2019

	2019	2018	2017	2016	2015
Total Community Hospitals in Utah	53	54	53	53	52
Bed Size Category					
6-24	12	11	11	10	9
25-49	18	19	18	19	19
50-99	3	3	3	3	3
100-199	11	12	12	12	12
200-299	6	5	5	5	5
300-399	1	2	2	2	2
400-499	0	0	0	0	1
500 + ...	2	2	2	2	1
Location					
Hospitals Urban	35	36	35	35	34
Hospitals Rural..	18	18	18	18	18
Control					
State and Local Government	7	7	7	6	6
Not for Profit..	28	28	27	27	27
Investor owned..	18	19	19	20	19
Affiliations					
Hospitals in a System	43	44	43	43	42
Hospitals in a Group Purchasing Organization...	29	30	28	27	28

Note: These data represent hospital performance in the years 2015 – 2019 and do not reflect any impacts from the COVID-19 pandemic in 2020 and thereafter.

States

TABLE 6

UTAH

U.S. Community Hospitals
(Nonfederal, short-term general and other special hospitals)

Utilization, Personnel, Revenue and Expenses, Community Health Indicators 2015–2019

	2019	2018	2017	2016	2015
TOTAL FACILITY (Includes Hospital and Nursing Home Units)					
Utilization - Inpatient					
Beds	5,664	5,767	5,712	5,770	5,650
Admissions	248,428	274,083	240,934	243,709	240,052
Inpatient Days	1,151,548	1,194,433	1,139,575	1,129,420	1,103,164
Average Length of Stay	4.6	4.4	4.7	4.6	4.6
Inpatient Surgeries	73,686	71,535	70,404	72,448	72,696
Births	46,849	46,147	46,271	49,503	47,766
Utilization - Outpatient					
Emergency Outpatient Visits	862,136	849,372	1,112,859	1,007,531	1,041,543
Other Outpatient Visits	4,027,335	3,856,761	7,871,063	7,533,256	6,834,890
Total Outpatient Visits	4,889,471	4,706,133	8,983,922	8,540,787	7,876,433
Outpatient Surgeries	196,250	193,340	186,746	195,998	188,361
Personnel					
Full Time RNs	11,510	11,407	10,572	9,789	9,430
Full Time LPNs	264	240	276	333	359
Part Time RNs	5,473	4,824	4,850	4,632	4,025
Part Time LPNs	122	122	117	114	126
Total Full Time	36,919	35,801	35,302	34,989	32,298
Total Part Time	15,265	13,939	14,147	13,745	12,371
Revenue - Inpatient					
Gross Inpatient Revenue	$16,821,048,877	$15,464,723,405	$13,982,831,428	$12,735,004,491	$11,611,854,744
Revenue - Outpatient					
Gross Outpatient Revenue	$16,116,996,130	$14,716,885,149	$12,871,647,711	$11,723,900,325	$10,589,950,273
Revenue and Expenses - Totals (Includes Inpatient and Outpatient)					
Total Gross Revenue	$32,938,045,007	$30,181,608,554	$26,854,479,139	$24,458,904,816	$22,201,805,017
Deductions from Revenue	22,834,530,473	20,612,036,728	18,149,378,070	16,273,841,433	14,878,061,933
Net Patient Revenue	10,103,514,534	9,569,571,826	8,705,101,069	8,185,063,383	7,323,743,084
Other Operating Revenue	261,685,360	232,173,862	213,917,239	211,784,431	224,656,811
Other Nonoperating Revenue	43,683,462	22,288,114	8,770,044	15,002,583	16,639,658
Total Net Revenue	10,408,883,356	9,824,033,802	8,927,788,352	8,411,850,397	7,565,039,553
Total Expenses	8,333,125,424	7,862,119,399	7,255,419,720	6,744,726,492	6,217,782,791
HOSPITAL UNIT (Excludes Separate Nursing Home Units)					
Utilization - Inpatient					
Beds	5,561	5,648	5,525	5,564	5,438
Admissions	247,986	273,596	240,232	242,718	239,116
Inpatient Days	1,125,123	1,167,887	1,075,150	1,067,385	1,036,992
Average Length of Stay	4.5	4.3	4.5	4.4	4.3
Personnel					
Total Full Time	36,814	35,690	35,179	34,903	32,234
Total Part Time	15,175	13,845	14,039	13,708	12,325
Revenue and Expenses - Totals (Includes Inpatient and Outpatient)					
Total Net Revenue	$10,397,823,415	$9,812,486,508	$8,910,560,200	$8,396,910,741	$7,551,752,171
Total Expenses	8,327,585,058	7,856,269,775	7,239,413,429	6,731,514,820	6,207,466,257
COMMUNITY HEALTH INDICATORS PER 1000 POPULATION					
Total Population (in thousands)	3,206	3,161	3,102	3,051	2,996
Inpatient					
Beds	1.8	1.8	1.8	1.9	1.9
Admissions	77.5	86.7	77.7	79.9	80.1
Inpatient Days	359.2	377.9	367.4	370.2	368.2
Inpatient Surgeries	23	22.6	22.7	23.7	24.3
Births	14.6	14.6	14.9	16.2	15.9
Outpatient					
Emergency Outpatient Visits	268.9	268.7	358.8	330.2	347.7
Other Outpatient Visits	1,256.2	1,220.1	2,537.6	2,468.9	2,281.4
Total Outpatient Visits	1,525.1	1,488.8	2,896.3	2,799.1	2,629.1
Outpatient Surgeries	61.2	61.2	60.2	64.2	62.9
Expense per Capita (per person)	$2,599.3	$2,487.1	$2,339.1	$2,210.5	$2,075.4

Note: These data represent hospital performance in the years 2015 – 2019 and do not reflect any impacts from the COVID-19 pandemic in 2020 and thereafter.

States

TABLE 6

VERMONT

U.S. Community Hospitals
(Nonfederal, short-term general and other special hospitals)

Overview 2015–2019

	2019	2018	2017	2016	2015
Total Community Hospitals in Vermont............	14	14	14	14	14
Bed Size Category					
6-24	1	0	0	1	1
25-49	8	8	8	7	7
50-99	2	3	3	3	3
100-199	1	1	1	1	1
200-299	1	1	1	1	1
300-399	0	0	0	0	0
400-499	1	0	1	1	1
500 + ...	0	1	0	0	0
Location					
Hospitals Urban	2	2	2	2	2
Hospitals Rural.......................................	12	12	12	12	12
Control					
State and Local Government	0	0	0	0	0
Not for Profit..	14	14	14	14	14
Investor owned.......................................	0	0	0	0	0
Affiliations					
Hospitals in a System	1	1	1	1	1
Hospitals in a Group Purchasing Organization...	7	5	8	8	9

Note: These data represent hospital performance in the years 2015 – 2019 and do not reflect any impacts from the COVID-19 pandemic in 2020 and thereafter.

States

TABLE 6

VERMONT

U.S. Community Hospitals
(Nonfederal, short-term general and other special hospitals)

Utilization, Personnel, Revenue and Expenses, Community Health Indicators 2015–2019

	2019	2018	2017	2016	2015
TOTAL FACILITY (Includes Hospital and Nursing Home Units)					
Utilization - Inpatient					
Beds	1,275	1,305	1,295	1,241	1,206
Admissions	51,241	50,952	49,438	49,847	47,695
Inpatient Days	315,779	302,817	301,837	296,562	292,755
Average Length of Stay	6.2	5.9	6.1	5.9	6.1
Inpatient Surgeries	12,319	14,225	14,204	12,792	11,936
Births	5,280	5,007	5,349	5,284	5,475
Utilization - Outpatient					
Emergency Outpatient Visits	317,314	324,272	311,534	317,955	328,066
Other Outpatient Visits	2,714,071	2,695,020	2,777,774	2,585,321	2,832,878
Total Outpatient Visits	3,031,385	3,019,292	3,089,308	2,903,276	3,160,944
Outpatient Surgeries	42,561	39,302	40,010	38,439	37,638
Personnel					
Full Time RNs	2,618	2,474	2,290	2,231	2,196
Full Time LPNs	201	186	184	184	187
Part Time RNs	1,815	1,977	1,795	1,744	1,781
Part Time LPNs	91	128	110	110	124
Total Full Time	12,769	12,261	12,049	11,932	11,353
Total Part Time	5,561	6,006	5,327	5,090	5,349
Revenue - Inpatient					
Gross Inpatient Revenue	$1,852,486,144	$1,820,637,369	$1,704,885,450	$1,571,303,645	$1,508,972,052
Revenue - Outpatient					
Gross Outpatient Revenue	$4,304,724,279	$4,191,958,993	$3,950,146,721	$3,778,225,703	$3,629,335,543
Revenue and Expenses - Totals					
(Includes Inpatient and Outpatient)					
Total Gross Revenue	$6,157,210,423	$6,012,596,362	$5,655,032,171	$5,349,529,348	$5,138,307,595
Deductions from Revenue	3,606,031,251	3,489,557,241	3,274,343,438	3,050,523,420	2,921,665,803
Net Patient Revenue	2,551,179,172	2,523,039,121	2,380,688,733	2,299,005,928	2,216,641,792
Other Operating Revenue	317,338,724	217,587,179	188,465,947	161,148,808	161,470,550
Other Nonoperating Revenue	50,696,658	44,722,601	101,608,792	33,298,454	-16,926,169
Total Net Revenue	2,919,214,554	2,785,348,901	2,670,763,472	2,493,453,190	2,361,186,173
Total Expenses	2,802,014,930	2,670,714,269	2,438,909,591	2,314,763,842	2,202,744,108
HOSPITAL UNIT (Excludes Separate Nursing Home Units)					
Utilization - Inpatient					
Beds	1,122	1,152	1,142	1,088	1,053
Admissions	50,857	50,635	49,059	49,528	47,393
Inpatient Days	269,446	259,774	257,202	253,600	249,294
Average Length of Stay	5.3	5.1	5.2	5.1	5.3
Personnel					
Total Full Time	12,572	12,166	11,920	11,793	11,236
Total Part Time	5,397	5,831	5,223	4,998	5,246
Revenue and Expenses - Totals					
(Includes Inpatient and Outpatient)					
Total Net Revenue	$2,900,776,428	$2,768,457,338	$2,654,221,104	$2,478,775,941	$2,347,550,643
Total Expenses	2,783,066,629	2,652,272,603	2,420,023,861	2,297,463,113	2,187,053,331
COMMUNITY HEALTH INDICATORS PER 1000 POPULATION					
Total Population (in thousands)	624	626	624	625	626
Inpatient					
Beds	2	2.1	2.1	2	1.9
Admissions	82.1	81.4	79.3	79.8	76.2
Inpatient Days	506.1	483.5	484	474.8	467.6
Inpatient Surgeries	19.7	22.7	22.8	20.5	19.1
Births	8.5	8	8.6	8.5	8.7
Outpatient					
Emergency Outpatient Visits	508.5	517.8	499.5	509.1	524
Other Outpatient Visits	4,349.5	4,303.1	4454	4,139.2	4,525.1
Total Outpatient Visits	4,858.1	4,820.8	4,953.5	4,648.3	5,049.1
Outpatient Surgeries	68.2	62.8	64.2	61.5	60.1
Expense per Capita (per person)	$4,490.5	$4,264.3	$3,910.7	$3,706	$3,518.5

Note: These data represent hospital performance in the years 2015 – 2019 and do not reflect any impacts from the COVID-19 pandemic in 2020 and thereafter.

States

TABLE 6

VIRGINIA

U.S. Community Hospitals
(Nonfederal, short-term general and other special hospitals)

Overview 2015–2019

	2019	2018	2017	2016	2015
Total Community Hospitals in Virginia	97	96	95	95	95
Bed Size Category					
6-24	12	11	11	10	9
25-49	13	15	15	16	17
50-99	22	21	20	18	17
100-199	18	17	18	20	22
200-299	14	14	13	12	11
300-399	5	5	5	6	6
400-499	3	5	5	5	5
500 + ...	10	8	8	8	8
Location					
Hospitals Urban	72	71	69	68	68
Hospitals Rural	25	25	26	27	27
Control					
State and Local Government	4	4	4	4	4
Not for Profit	68	67	67	68	68
Investor owned	25	25	24	23	23
Affiliations					
Hospitals in a System	87	86	86	85	85
Hospitals in a Group Purchasing Organization...	50	58	59	67	66

Note: These data represent hospital performance in the years 2015 – 2019 and do not reflect any impacts from the COVID-19 pandemic in 2020 and thereafter.

TABLE 6

VIRGINIA

U.S. Community Hospitals
(Nonfederal, short-term general and other special hospitals)

Utilization, Personnel, Revenue and Expenses, Community Health Indicators 2015–2019

	2019	2018	2017	2016	2015
TOTAL FACILITY (Includes Hospital and Nursing Home Units)					
Utilization - Inpatient					
Beds	18,143	18,065	17,840	17,943	17,875
Admissions	824,998	801,397	797,032	794,741	791,388
Inpatient Days	4,653,339	4,553,821	4,513,293	4,494,671	4,423,932
Average Length of Stay	5.6	5.7	5.7	5.7	5.6
Inpatient Surgeries	210,051	199,518	205,163	204,056	200,330
Births	90,519	90,839	90,720	94,912	94,088
Utilization - Outpatient					
Emergency Outpatient Visits	3,627,232	3,686,696	3,522,286	3,776,039	3,718,523
Other Outpatient Visits	15,079,644	14,646,870	14,636,600	14,112,837	13,400,261
Total Outpatient Visits	18,706,876	18,333,566	18,158,886	17,888,876	17,118,784
Outpatient Surgeries	515,142	485,832	519,546	531,196	524,703
Personnel					
Full Time RNs	31,741	31,019	29,209	27,849	27,984
Full Time LPNs	1,933	2,078	2,096	2,235	2,038
Part Time RNs	10,220	10,643	11,516	12,212	11,792
Part Time LPNs	494	499	525	514	550
Total Full Time	105,671	101,666	96,042	92,350	92,784
Total Part Time	30,937	30,033	33,370	33,763	33,544
Revenue - Inpatient					
Gross Inpatient Revenue	$45,529,832,708	$40,744,448,522	$38,199,699,602	$35,433,087,260	$32,821,698,062
Revenue - Outpatient					
Gross Outpatient Revenue	$46,622,890,565	$42,344,065,034	$40,329,089,798	$37,920,140,697	$34,648,770,316
Revenue and Expenses - Totals					
(Includes Inpatient and Outpatient)					
Total Gross Revenue	$92,152,723,273	$83,088,513,556	$78,528,789,400	$73,353,227,957	$67,470,468,378
Deductions from Revenue	67,683,796,508	60,663,284,867	56,729,574,563	52,498,341,552	47,457,989,273
Net Patient Revenue	24,468,926,765	22,425,228,689	21,799,214,837	20,854,886,405	20,012,479,105
Other Operating Revenue	772,340,850	628,391,278	663,717,319	793,231,378	764,225,275
Other Nonoperating Revenue	322,494,321	197,655,203	604,010,698	206,319,395	70,943,172
Total Net Revenue	25,563,761,936	23,251,275,170	23,066,942,854	21,854,437,178	20,847,647,552
Total Expenses	22,533,768,775	21,052,814,535	20,280,704,720	19,705,571,358	18,796,506,872
HOSPITAL UNIT (Excludes Separate Nursing Home Units)					
Utilization - Inpatient					
Beds	16,702	16,534	16,176	16,259	16,234
Admissions	820,384	796,467	791,150	788,569	785,192
Inpatient Days	4,230,499	4,083,446	3,980,725	3,948,133	3,886,540
Average Length of Stay	5.2	5.1	5.0	5.0	4.9
Personnel					
Total Full Time	104,790	100,583	94,731	91,149	91,801
Total Part Time	30,501	29,596	32,752	33,240	33,074
Revenue and Expenses - Totals					
(Includes Inpatient and Outpatient)					
Total Net Revenue	$25,435,926,197	$23,115,583,602	$22,924,881,746	$21,712,032,835	$20,705,402,558
Total Expenses	22,410,923,047	20,927,106,165	20,140,841,542	19,572,253,756	18,667,568,401
COMMUNITY HEALTH INDICATORS PER 1000 POPULATION					
Total Population (in thousands)	8,536	8,518	8,470	8,412	8,383
Inpatient					
Beds	2.1	2.1	2.1	2.1	2.1
Admissions	96.7	94.1	94.1	94.5	94.4
Inpatient Days	545.2	534.6	532.9	534.3	527.7
Inpatient Surgeries	24.6	23.4	24.2	24.3	23.9
Births	10.6	10.7	10.7	11.3	11.2
Outpatient					
Emergency Outpatient Visits	425	432.8	415.9	448.9	443.6
Other Outpatient Visits	1,766.7	1,719.6	1,728	1,677.7	1,598.5
Total Outpatient Visits	2,191.7	2,152.4	2,143.9	2,126.6	2,042.1
Outpatient Surgeries	60.4	57	61.3	63.1	62.6
Expense per Capita (per person)	$2,640	$2,471.7	$2,394.4	$2,342.6	$2,242.2

Note: These data represent hospital performance in the years 2015 – 2019 and do not reflect any impacts from the COVID-19 pandemic in 2020 and thereafter.

States

TABLE 6

WASHINGTON

U.S. Community Hospitals
(Nonfederal, short-term general and other special hospitals)

Overview 2015–2019

	2019	2018	2017	2016	2015
Total Community Hospitals in Washington.......	91	92	92	92	92
Bed Size Category					
6-24	11	11	11	12	12
25-49	27	27	27	28	28
50-99	14	15	16	15	15
100-199	14	14	15	14	15
200-299	10	10	10	11	10
300-399	8	8	6	6	7
400-499	4	4	4	3	2
500 + ...	3	3	3	3	3
Location					
Hospitals Urban	61	62	62	62	63
Hospitals Rural......................................	30	30	30	30	29
Control					
State and Local Government	40	40	41	42	41
Not for Profit..	44	44	46	42	43
Investor owned......................................	7	8	5	8	8
Affiliations					
Hospitals in a System	48	49	49	48	49
Hospitals in a Group Purchasing Organization...	56	61	55	51	46

Note: These data represent hospital performance in the years 2015 – 2019 and do not reflect any impacts from the COVID-19 pandemic in 2020 and thereafter.

TABLE 6

WASHINGTON

U.S. Community Hospitals
(Nonfederal, short-term general and other special hospitals)

Utilization, Personnel, Revenue and Expenses, Community Health Indicators 2015–2019

	2019	2018	2017	2016	2015
TOTAL FACILITY (Includes Hospital and Nursing Home Units)					
Utilization - Inpatient					
Beds	12,613	12,774	12,577	12,164	12,035
Admissions	591,311	601,209	612,046	592,068	594,203
Inpatient Days	2,943,207	3,045,863	3,024,120	2,899,998	2,820,101
Average Length of Stay	5.0	5.1	4.9	4.9	4.7
Inpatient Surgeries	173,176	177,881	182,956	175,137	172,194
Births	80,084	81,643	83,259	83,992	83,171
Utilization - Outpatient					
Emergency Outpatient Visits	2,925,619	2,779,707	2,957,421	2,695,220	2,682,027
Other Outpatient Visits	13,003,215	11,782,304	12,240,078	11,560,817	10,910,651
Total Outpatient Visits	15,928,834	14,562,011	15,197,499	14,256,037	13,592,678
Outpatient Surgeries	355,367	356,762	361,618	366,809	305,810
Personnel					
Full Time RNs	20,357	20,425	21,207	23,196	22,040
Full Time LPNs	728	697	864	1,156	1,036
Part Time RNs	16,096	15,220	12,638	9,928	11,455
Part Time LPNs	490	444	467	427	486
Total Full Time	75,205	76,468	79,763	87,092	82,305
Total Part Time	44,218	39,831	35,918	30,536	31,308
Revenue - Inpatient					
Gross Inpatient Revenue	$38,820,445,788	$37,279,592,209	$35,072,086,770	$32,751,868,183	$31,343,007,558
Revenue - Outpatient					
Gross Outpatient Revenue	$41,888,637,272	$38,237,505,851	$35,195,765,549	$32,130,703,909	$30,161,402,650
Revenue and Expenses - Totals					
(Includes Inpatient and Outpatient)					
Total Gross Revenue	$80,709,083,060	$75,517,098,060	$70,267,852,319	$64,882,572,092	$61,504,410,208
Deductions from Revenue	56,861,006,012	52,877,433,789	48,636,215,792	44,130,138,321	41,383,287,319
Net Patient Revenue	23,848,077,048	22,639,664,271	21,631,636,527	20,752,433,771	20,121,122,889
Other Operating Revenue	1,336,706,294	1,161,817,780	1,282,330,912	1,148,659,515	1,139,203,388
Other Nonoperating Revenue	286,063,064	166,159,177	290,777,186	224,197,658	63,228,900
Total Net Revenue	25,470,846,406	23,967,641,228	23,204,744,625	22,125,290,944	21,323,555,177
Total Expenses	23,831,222,217	23,004,195,033	22,188,309,852	21,050,226,338	19,897,248,909
HOSPITAL UNIT (Excludes Separate Nursing Home Units)					
Utilization - Inpatient					
Beds	12,524	12,553	12,468	11,935	11,754
Admissions	591,188	600,803	611,569	590,913	593,196
Inpatient Days	2,911,940	2,995,513	2,987,717	2,824,272	2,719,388
Average Length of Stay	4.9	5.0	4.9	4.8	4.6
Personnel					
Total Full Time	75,116	76,282	79,648	86,823	82,063
Total Part Time	44,073	39,677	35,857	30,335	31,099
Revenue and Expenses - Totals					
(Includes Inpatient and Outpatient)					
Total Net Revenue	$25,449,483,603	$23,916,096,530	$23,186,194,715	$22,077,194,237	$21,293,862,403
Total Expenses	23,808,748,188	22,975,784,005	22,169,095,958	21,011,286,339	19,869,769,703
COMMUNITY HEALTH INDICATORS PER 1000 POPULATION					
Total Population (in thousands)	7,615	7,536	7,406	7,288	7,170
Inpatient					
Beds	1.7	1.7	1.7	1.7	1.7
Admissions	77.7	79.8	82.6	81.2	82.9
Inpatient Days	386.5	404.2	408.3	397.9	393.3
Inpatient Surgeries	22.7	23.6	24.7	24	24
Births	10.5	10.8	11.2	11.5	11.6
Outpatient					
Emergency Outpatient Visits	384.2	368.9	399.3	369.8	374
Other Outpatient Visits	1,707.6	1,563.6	1,652.8	1,586.3	1,521.6
Total Outpatient Visits	2,091.8	1,932.4	2,052.1	1,956.1	1,895.7
Outpatient Surgeries	46.7	47.3	48.8	50.3	42.6
Expense per Capita (per person)	$3,129.6	$3,052.7	$2,996.1	$2,888.3	$2,774.9

Note: These data represent hospital performance in the years 2015 – 2019 and do not reflect any impacts from the COVID-19 pandemic in 2020 and thereafter.

States

TABLE 6

WEST VIRGINIA

U.S. Community Hospitals
(Nonfederal, short-term general and other special hospitals)

Overview 2015–2019

	2019	2018	2017	2016	2015
Total Community Hospitals in West Virginia	52	56	56	56	56
Bed Size Category					
6-24	4	4	4	4	4
25-49	17	19	17	17	17
50-99	12	11	12	12	11
100-199	10	12	12	12	13
200-299	5	6	7	7	7
300-399	2	2	2	2	2
400-499	0	0	0	0	0
500 + ...	2	2	2	2	2
Location					
Hospitals Urban	30	31	29	29	29
Hospitals Rural......................................	22	25	27	27	27
Control					
State and Local Government	7	9	8	8	8
Not for Profit...	33	33	33	34	33
Investor owned.....................................	12	14	15	14	15
Affiliations					
Hospitals in a System	35	35	35	34	31
Hospitals in a Group Purchasing Organization...	39	42	44	48	53

Note: These data represent hospital performance in the years 2015 – 2019 and do not reflect any impacts from the COVID-19 pandemic in 2020 and thereafter.

States

TABLE 6

WEST VIRGINIA

U.S. Community Hospitals
(Nonfederal, short-term general and other special hospitals)

Utilization, Personnel, Revenue and Expenses, Community Health Indicators 2015–2019

	2019	2018	2017	2016	2015
TOTAL FACILITY (Includes Hospital and Nursing Home Units)					
Utilization - Inpatient					
Beds	6,385	6,868	7,008	6,939	6,994
Admissions	240,377	258,254	257,402	253,031	256,354
Inpatient Days	1,499,925	1,544,486	1,539,754	1,499,249	1,532,624
Average Length of Stay	6.2	6.0	6.0	5.9	6.0
Inpatient Surgeries	70,905	74,416	71,577	73,584	74,894
Births	17,762	18,715	19,166	19,662	20,211
Utilization - Outpatient					
Emergency Outpatient Visits	1,043,324	1,231,765	1,184,865	1,180,148	1,194,297
Other Outpatient Visits	6,706,351	6,829,253	6,886,157	6,753,804	6,304,028
Total Outpatient Visits	7,749,675	8,061,018	8,071,022	7,933,952	7,498,325
Outpatient Surgeries	213,013	229,335	240,439	242,972	238,270
Personnel					
Full Time RNs	10,283	10,453	10,038	9,640	9,416
Full Time LPNs	1,201	1,202	1,173	1,172	1,208
Part Time RNs	3,246	2,873	3,058	3,078	3,068
Part Time LPNs	250	261	273	230	266
Total Full Time	39,148	39,828	38,405	36,733	36,148
Total Part Time	10,130	9,485	9,601	9,553	9,622
Revenue - Inpatient					
Gross Inpatient Revenue	$10,180,112,804	$10,040,322,099	$9,159,552,619	$7,818,630,176	$7,255,487,755
Revenue - Outpatient					
Gross Outpatient Revenue	$11,843,418,582	$11,176,331,421	$10,250,786,816	$9,295,226,822	$8,490,713,783
Revenue and Expenses - Totals					
(Includes Inpatient and Outpatient)					
Total Gross Revenue	$22,023,531,386	$21,216,653,520	$19,410,339,435	$17,113,856,998	$15,746,201,538
Deductions from Revenue	14,919,308,427	14,390,218,361	12,850,135,400	10,892,481,451	9,896,704,041
Net Patient Revenue	7,104,222,959	6,826,435,159	6,560,204,035	6,221,375,547	5,849,497,497
Other Operating Revenue	413,595,758	296,344,446	284,515,649	293,073,192	245,469,941
Other Nonoperating Revenue	163,621,000	46,447,562	202,435,277	53,289,636	-19,447,959
Total Net Revenue	7,681,439,717	7,169,227,167	7,047,154,961	6,567,738,375	6,075,519,479
Total Expenses	7,172,441,050	6,935,137,218	6,632,137,203	6,220,001,692	5,854,862,050
HOSPITAL UNIT (Excludes Separate Nursing Home Units)					
Utilization - Inpatient					
Beds	5,866	6,377	6,310	6,213	6,196
Admissions	238,624	256,524	254,956	250,455	253,067
Inpatient Days	1,351,072	1,400,986	1,327,858	1,274,896	1,285,909
Average Length of Stay	5.7	5.5	5.2	5.1	5.1
Personnel					
Total Full Time	38,719	39,427	37,956	36,222	35,595
Total Part Time	10,065	9,394	9,445	9,405	9,432
Revenue and Expenses - Totals					
(Includes Inpatient and Outpatient)					
Total Net Revenue	$7,637,555,650	$7,130,371,748	$6,991,736,730	$6,510,387,389	$6,010,973,954
Total Expenses	7,146,120,012	6,911,154,449	6,600,561,766	6,187,893,785	5,817,972,878
COMMUNITY HEALTH INDICATORS PER 1000 POPULATION					
Total Population (in thousands)	1,792	1,806	1,816	1,831	1,844
Inpatient					
Beds	3.6	3.8	3.9	3.8	3.8
Admissions	134.1	143	141.8	138.2	139
Inpatient Days	836.9	855.3	847.9	818.8	831.1
Inpatient Surgeries	39.6	41.2	39.4	40.2	40.6
Births	9.9	10.4	10.6	10.7	11
Outpatient					
Emergency Outpatient Visits	582.2	682.1	652.5	644.5	647.6
Other Outpatient Visits	3,742.1	3,781.8	3,792.2	3,688.4	3,418.4
Total Outpatient Visits	4,324.2	4,463.9	4,444.7	4,332.9	4,066.1
Outpatient Surgeries	118.9	127	132.4	132.7	129.2
Expense per Capita (per person)	$4,002.1	$3,840.4	$3,652.3	$3,396.9	$3,174.9

Note: These data represent hospital performance in the years 2015 – 2019 and do not reflect any impacts from the COVID-19 pandemic in 2020 and thereafter.

States

TABLE **6**

WISCONSIN

U.S. Community Hospitals
(Nonfederal, short-term general and other special hospitals)

Overview 2015–2019

	2019	2018	2017	2016	2015
Total Community Hospitals in Wisconsin	132	133	134	134	133
Bed Size Category					
6-24	32	33	30	31	27
25-49	36	33	36	32	34
50-99	25	27	27	30	31
100-199	21	23	24	23	23
200-299	12	12	11	11	12
300-399	3	2	3	4	3
400-499	0	0	0	0	0
500 + ...	3	3	3	3	3
Location					
Hospitals Urban	75	76	75	75	74
Hospitals Rural	57	57	59	59	59
Control					
State and Local Government	1	2	2	2	2
Not for Profit	122	121	122	122	122
Investor owned	9	10	10	10	9
Affiliations					
Hospitals in a System	99	99	93	89	84
Hospitals in a Group Purchasing Organization...	132	130	129	129	130

Note: These data represent hospital performance in the years 2015 – 2019 and do not reflect any impacts from the COVID-19 pandemic in 2020 and thereafter.

TABLE 6

WISCONSIN

U.S. Community Hospitals
(Nonfederal, short-term general and other special hospitals)

Utilization, Personnel, Revenue and Expenses, Community Health Indicators 2015–2019

	2019	2018	2017	2016	2015
TOTAL FACILITY (Includes Hospital and Nursing Home Units)					
Utilization - Inpatient					
Beds	11,894	12,103	12,311	12,400	12,596
Admissions	508,235	521,584	534,275	535,399	541,549
Inpatient Days	2,601,418	2,618,418	2,651,498	2,680,807	2,758,206
Average Length of Stay	5.1	5.0	5.0	5.0	5.1
Inpatient Surgeries	165,394	165,845	171,894	174,729	171,497
Births	61,088	62,626	63,011	64,386	64,722
Utilization - Outpatient					
Emergency Outpatient Visits	2,274,345	2,498,314	2,500,115	2,392,607	2,454,661
Other Outpatient Visits	18,507,927	16,970,333	17,183,210	16,437,348	15,465,301
Total Outpatient Visits	20,782,272	19,468,647	19,683,325	18,829,955	17,919,962
Outpatient Surgeries	572,646	525,011	517,410	502,988	489,772
Personnel					
Full Time RNs	19,770	19,251	19,931	19,003	17,012
Full Time LPNs	687	612	672	638	659
Part Time RNs	17,378	17,193	15,823	16,146	15,360
Part Time LPNs	646	601	637	596	647
Total Full Time	78,927	73,226	77,143	72,098	68,065
Total Part Time	52,666	50,276	48,804	50,050	46,824
Revenue - Inpatient					
Gross Inpatient Revenue	$23,314,005,782	$22,719,053,135	$22,230,279,594	$20,865,133,177	$20,221,323,094
Revenue - Outpatient					
Gross Outpatient Revenue	$39,911,825,141	$36,212,050,226	$33,179,526,908	$30,863,567,527	$28,261,882,444
Revenue and Expenses - Totals					
(Includes Inpatient and Outpatient)					
Total Gross Revenue	$63,225,830,923	$58,931,103,361	$55,409,806,502	$51,728,700,704	$48,483,205,538
Deductions from Revenue	41,213,232,598	37,871,777,714	35,705,970,814	32,275,368,255	29,567,570,129
Net Patient Revenue	22,012,598,325	21,059,325,647	19,703,835,688	19,453,332,449	18,915,635,409
Other Operating Revenue	1,312,412,988	1,115,153,596	1,428,519,839	1,047,436,854	849,101,507
Other Nonoperating Revenue	475,159,555	223,548,785	429,139,687	163,097,521	130,867,061
Total Net Revenue	23,800,170,868	22,398,028,028	21,561,495,214	20,663,866,824	19,895,603,977
Total Expenses	21,286,371,640	20,283,911,245	19,640,671,915	18,716,182,889	17,859,058,395
HOSPITAL UNIT (Excludes Separate Nursing Home Units)					
Utilization - Inpatient					
Beds	11,115	11,371	11,451	11,468	11,574
Admissions	506,687	520,105	532,325	533,295	539,416
Inpatient Days	2,365,009	2,387,198	2,387,234	2,386,666	2,442,845
Average Length of Stay	4.7	4.6	4.5	4.5	4.5
Personnel					
Total Full Time	78,549	73,036	76,759	71,680	67,790
Total Part Time	52,358	50,110	48,607	49,674	46,463
Revenue and Expenses - Totals					
(Includes Inpatient and Outpatient)					
Total Net Revenue	$23,723,529,880	$22,349,190,713	$21,482,549,394	$20,583,379,951	$19,836,579,800
Total Expenses	21,223,490,896	20,240,888,649	19,577,462,778	18,657,539,986	17,814,373,003
COMMUNITY HEALTH INDICATORS PER 1000 POPULATION					
Total Population (in thousands)	5,822	5,814	5,795	5,779	5,771
Inpatient					
Beds	2	2.1	2.1	2.1	2.2
Admissions	87.3	89.7	92.2	92.7	93.8
Inpatient Days	446.8	450.4	457.5	463.9	477.9
Inpatient Surgeries	28.4	28.5	29.7	30.2	29.7
Births	10.5	10.8	10.9	11.1	11.2
Outpatient					
Emergency Outpatient Visits	390.6	429.7	431.4	414	425.3
Other Outpatient Visits	3,178.7	2,919.1	2,964.9	2,844.5	2,679.7
Total Outpatient Visits	3,569.3	3,348.8	3,396.3	3,258.5	3105
Outpatient Surgeries	98.4	90.3	89.3	87	84.9
Expense per Capita (per person)	$3,655.9	$3,489.1	$3,389	$3,238.8	$3,094.4

Note: These data represent hospital performance in the years 2015 – 2019 and do not reflect any impacts from the COVID-19 pandemic in 2020 and thereafter.

States

TABLE 6

WYOMING

U.S. Community Hospitals
(Nonfederal, short-term general and other special hospitals)

Overview 2015–2019

	2019	2018	2017	2016	2015
Total Community Hospitals in Wyoming	28	29	29	27	27
Bed Size Category					
6-24	6	7	7	5	5
25-49	9	9	9	9	9
50-99	7	7	6	6	6
100-199	3	3	5	6	5
200-299	3	3	2	1	2
300-399	0	0	0	0	0
400-499	0	0	0	0	0
500 + ...	0	0	0	0	0
Location					
Hospitals Urban	4	5	5	4	4
Hospitals Rural	24	24	24	23	23
Control					
State and Local Government	19	19	17	19	18
Not for Profit	4	4	6	4	5
Investor owned	5	6	6	4	4
Affiliations					
Hospitals in a System	10	12	12	13	13
Hospitals in a Group Purchasing Organization...	12	20	18	17	20

Note: These data represent hospital performance in the years 2015 – 2019 and do not reflect any impacts from the COVID-19 pandemic in 2020 and thereafter.

TABLE 6

WYOMING

U.S. Community Hospitals
(Nonfederal, short-term general and other special hospitals)

Utilization, Personnel, Revenue and Expenses, Community Health Indicators 2015–2019

	2019	2018	2017	2016	2015
TOTAL FACILITY (Includes Hospital and Nursing Home Units)					
Utilization - Inpatient					
Beds	1,990	2,015	1,983	1,846	1,964
Admissions	41,521	41,825	42,556	43,417	45,009
Inpatient Days	378,966	385,211	384,142	387,565	375,863
Average Length of Stay	9.1	9.2	9.0	8.9	8.4
Inpatient Surgeries	10,212	10,429	12,355	11,665	11,042
Births	5,424	5,739	5,986	6,445	6,725
Utilization - Outpatient					
Emergency Outpatient Visits	223,303	217,418	238,749	242,725	247,994
Other Outpatient Visits	1,067,917	1,061,070	1,091,134	1,016,167	1,097,554
Total Outpatient Visits	1,291,220	1,278,488	1,329,883	1,258,892	1,345,548
Outpatient Surgeries	31,020	31,454	34,379	29,020	25,204
Personnel					
Full Time RNs	2,157	2,302	2,200	2,060	2,019
Full Time LPNs	160	163	127	152	124
Part Time RNs	643	658	627	515	559
Part Time LPNs	41	46	47	36	38
Total Full Time	9,058	9,793	9,047	9,132	8,506
Total Part Time	2,013	2,068	1,953	1,774	1,908
Revenue - Inpatient					
Gross Inpatient Revenue	$1,600,177,014	$1,474,641,091	$1,518,749,449	$1,468,615,470	$1,348,102,716
Revenue - Outpatient					
Gross Outpatient Revenue	$2,784,784,702	$2,499,105,094	$2,440,561,384	$2,130,643,586	$1,885,113,328
Revenue and Expenses - Totals (Includes Inpatient and Outpatient)					
Total Gross Revenue	$4,384,961,716	$3,973,746,185	$3,959,310,833	$3,599,259,056	$3,233,216,044
Deductions from Revenue	2,637,647,231	2,264,012,641	2,246,737,730	2,024,813,550	1,735,493,847
Net Patient Revenue	1,747,314,485	1,709,733,544	1,712,573,103	1,574,445,506	1,497,722,197
Other Operating Revenue	94,732,955	82,118,936	81,405,854	94,994,154	95,428,848
Other Nonoperating Revenue	44,464,912	28,273,339	59,489,879	21,275,510	13,809,546
Total Net Revenue	1,886,512,352	1,820,125,819	1,853,468,836	1,690,715,170	1,606,960,591
Total Expenses	1,718,035,743	1,696,024,272	1,696,260,078	1,572,418,430	1,471,925,692
HOSPITAL UNIT (Excludes Separate Nursing Home Units)					
Utilization - Inpatient					
Beds	1,385	1,386	1,527	1,361	1,344
Admissions	40,911	41,078	41,935	42,931	44,032
Inpatient Days	185,230	181,229	240,434	222,495	183,221
Average Length of Stay	4.5	4.4	5.7	5.2	4.2
Personnel					
Total Full Time	8,740	9,424	8,716	8,772	8,121
Total Part Time	1,889	1,919	1,827	1,666	1,759
Revenue and Expenses - Totals (Includes Inpatient and Outpatient)					
Total Net Revenue	$1,839,485,956	$1,772,951,772	$1,814,623,139	$1,655,704,116	$1,570,475,448
Total Expenses	1,680,279,157	1,663,482,413	1,655,110,449	1,547,411,275	1,438,561,699
COMMUNITY HEALTH INDICATORS PER 1000 POPULATION					
Total Population (in thousands)	579	578	579	586	586
Inpatient					
Beds	3.4	3.5	3.4	3.2	3.4
Admissions	71.7	72.4	73.5	74.2	76.8
Inpatient Days	654.8	666.8	663.1	661.9	641.3
Inpatient Surgeries	17.6	18.1	21.3	19.9	18.8
Births	9.4	9.9	10.3	11	11.5
Outpatient					
Emergency Outpatient Visits	385.8	376.3	412.1	414.6	423.1
Other Outpatient Visits	1,845.2	1,836.6	1,883.5	1,735.6	1,872.6
Total Outpatient Visits	2231	2,212.9	2,295.6	2,150.1	2,295.7
Outpatient Surgeries	53.6	54.4	59.3	49.6	43
Expense per Capita (per person)	$2,968.5	$2,935.6	2,928	$2,685.6	$2,511.4

Note: These data represent hospital performance in the years 2015 – 2019 and do not reflect any impacts from the COVID-19 pandemic in 2020 and thereafter.

States

Table 7

Facilities and Services

Table		Page

7   Facilities and Services in the U. S. Census   155
Divisions and States for 2019

The facilities and services presented in Table 7 are listed below in alphabetical order by major heading (where applicable).

Note: These data represent hospital performance in the years 2015 – 2019 and do not reflect any impacts from the COVID-19 pandemic in 2020 and thereafter.

Note: These data represent hospital performance in the years 2015 – 2019 and do not reflect any impacts from the COVID-19 pandemic in 2020 and thereafter.

Table
7

2019 Facilities and Services in the U.S. Census Divisions and States

These data include only hospital-based facilities and services as reported by responding hospitals in Section C of the 2019 AHA Annual Survey, beginning on page 215. Census divisions represent all U.S. hospitals. Community hospitals are listed separately under United States. No estimates have been made for nonresponding hospitals. Definitions of facilities and services are listed in the Glossary, page 203.

Classification	Hospitals Reporting	Adult Day Care Program — No.	Adult Day Care Program — %	Air Ambulance Services — No.	Air Ambulance Services — %	Airborne Infection Isolation Room — No.	Airborne Infection Isolation Room — %	Alcohol/Drug Abuse or Dependency Inpatient Care Units — No.	Alcohol/Drug Abuse or Dependency Inpatient Care Units — %	Alcohol/Drug Abuse or Dependency Outpatient Services — No.	Alcohol/Drug Abuse or Dependency Outpatient Services — %	Alcoholism-Chemical Dependency Pediatric Services — No.	Alcoholism-Chemical Dependency Pediatric Services — %	Alcoholism-Chemical Dependency Partial Hospitalization Services — No.	Alcoholism-Chemical Dependency Partial Hospitalization Services — %	Alzheimer Center — No.	Alzheimer Center — %	Ambulance Service — No.	Ambulance Service — %	Ambulatory Surgery Center — No.	Ambulatory Surgery Center — %	Arthritis Treatment Center — No.	Arthritis Treatment Center — %
UNITED STATES	4,167	129	3.1	197	4.7	3,407	81.8	392	9.4	602	14.4	103	2.5	300	7.2	202	4.8	633	15.2	1,014	24.3	311	7.5
COMMUNITY HOSPITALS	3,782	113	3	195	5.2	3,296	87.1	269	7.1	466	12.3	67	1.8	205	5.4	188	5	620	16.4	993	26.3	300	7.9
CENSUS DIVISION 1, NEW ENGLAND	156	6	3.8	4	2.6	133	85.3	14	9	50	32.1	8	5.1	19	12.2	17	10.9	22	14.1	53	34	20	12.8
Connecticut	26	4	15.4	1	3.8	24	92.3	2	7.7	12	46.2	2	7.7	7	26.9	4	15.4	4	15.4	12	46.2	5	19.2
Maine	30	0	0	1	3.3	26	86.7	2	6.7	9	30	2	6.7	2	6.7	3	10	8	26.7	10	33.3	0	0
Massachusetts	57	1	1.8	0	0	47	82.5	8	14	16	28.1	2	3.5	7	12.3	7	12.3	6	10.5	17	29.8	9	15.8
New Hampshire	25	1	4	1	4	23	92	0	0	7	28	0	0	1	4	1	4	2	8	8	32	3	12
Rhode Island	7	0	0	0	0	6	85.7	1	14.3	1	14.3	1	14.3	0	0	1	14.3	1	14.3	4	57.1	2	28.6
Vermont	11	0	0	1	9.1	7	63.6	1	9.1	5	45.5	1	9.1	2	18.2	1	9.1	1	9.1	2	18.2	1	9.1
CENSUS DIVISION 2, MIDDLE ATLANTIC	362	23	6.4	24	6.6	316	87.3	61	16.9	98	27.1	14	3.9	31	8.6	36	9.9	80	22.1	154	42.5	51	14.1
New Jersey	70	4	5.7	6	8.6	58	82.9	8	11.4	21	30	2	2.9	8	11.4	7	10	20	28.6	23	32.9	12	17.1
New York	135	15	11.1	3	2.2	122	90.4	41	30.4	62	45.9	8	5.9	20	14.8	15	11.1	26	19.3	81	60	23	17
Pennsylvania	157	4	2.5	15	9.6	136	86.6	12	7.6	15	9.6	4	2.5	3	1.9	14	8.9	34	21.7	50	31.8	16	10.2
CENSUS DIVISION 3, SOUTH ATLANTIC	574	16	2.8	38	6.6	484	84.3	66	11.5	80	13.9	11	1.9	41	7.1	31	5.4	63	11	136	23.7	44	7.7
Delaware	8	1	12.5	1	12.5	5	62.5	0	0	2	25	0	0	0	0	1	12.5	2	25	2	25	0	0
District of Columbia	10	0	0	1	10	7	70	0	0	2	20	0	0	0	0	0	0	2	25	3	30	2	20
Florida	165	4	2.4	11	6.7	143	86.7	18	10.9	17	10.3	2	1.2	13	7.9	11	6.7	11	6.7	39	23.6	9	5.5
Georgia	96	3	3.1	1	1	72	75	6	6.3	10	10.4	2	2.1	6	6.3	4	4.2	12	12.5	16	16.7	3	3.1
Maryland	45	3	6.7	4	8.9	38	84.4	7	15.6	15	33.3	1	2.2	7	15.6	6	13.3	4	8.9	15	33.3	11	24.4
North Carolina	74	1	1.4	5	6.8	68	91.9	9	12.2	10	13.5	3	4.1	2	2.7	4	5.4	11	14.9	21	28.4	5	6.8
South Carolina	68	0	0	2	2.9	54	79.4	15	22.1	4	5.9	0	0	4	5.9	1	1.5	11	16.2	11	16.2	3	4.4
Virginia	63	3	4.8	8	12.7	60	95.2	8	12.7	16	25.4	2	3.2	8	12.7	1	1.6	6	9.5	21	33.3	7	11.1
West Virginia	45	1	2.2	5	11.1	37	82.2	3	6.7	4	8.9	1	2.2	1	2.2	1	2.2	4	8.9	8	17.8	4	8.9
CENSUS DIVISION 4, EAST NORTH CENTRAL	672	17	2.5	25	3.7	549	81.7	84	12.5	130	19.3	19	2.8	69	10.1	52	7.7	84	12.5	176	26.2	70	10.4
Illinois	155	9	5.8	2	1.3	135	87.1	16	10.3	31	20	7	4.5	19	12.3	8	5.2	16	10.3	31	20	17	11
Indiana	117	0	0	5	4.3	97	82.9	11	9.4	23	19.7	8	6.8	10	8.5	2	1.7	29	24.8	31	26.5	4	3.4
Michigan	127	4	3.1	2	1.6	112	88.2	13	10.2	19	15	1	0.8	4	3.1	8	6.3	14	11	40	31.5	13	10.2
Ohio	127	0	0	16	12.6	111	87.4	12	9.4	25	19.7	1	0.8	20	15.7	7	5.5	17	13.4	45	35.4	15	11.8
Wisconsin	146	4	2.7	0	0	94	64.4	32	21.9	32	21.9	2	1.4	15	10.3	27	18.5	8	5.5	29	19.9	21	14.4
CENSUS DIVISION 5, EAST SOUTH CENTRAL	269	6	2.2	10	3.7	210	78.1	21	7.8	19	7.1	6	2.2	12	4.5	10	3.7	41	15.2	46	17.1	16	5.9
Alabama	47	1	2.1	3	6.4	37	78.7	4	8.5	3	6.4	0	0	1	2.1	1	2.1	12	25.5	10	21.3	5	10.6
Kentucky	53	1	1.9	3	5.7	47	88.7	0	0	5	9.4	2	3.8	2	3.8	2	3.8	5	9.4	9	17	3	5.7
Mississippi	102	3	2.9	1	1	68	66.7	12	11.8	6	5.9	4	3.9	7	6.9	4	3.9	11	10.8	12	11.8	4	3.9
Tennessee	67	1	1.5	3	4.5	58	86.6	5	7.5	5	7.5	0	0	2	3	4	6	13	19.4	15	22.4	4	6
CENSUS DIVISION 6, WEST NORTH CENTRAL	562	18	3.2	30	5.3	442	78.6	40	7.1	64	11.4	8	1.4	26	4.6	22	3.9	136	24.2	105	18.7	29	5.2
Iowa	122	2	1.6	4	3.3	93	76.2	7	5.7	18	14.8	1	0.8	1	0.8	5	4.1	51	41.8	27	22.1	3	2.5
Kansas	125	7	5.6	6	4.8	95	76	1	0.8	4	3.2	3	2.4	7	5.8	3	2.4	18	14.4	16	12.8	3	2.4
Minnesota	86	4	4.7	5	5.8	71	82.6	8	9.3	14	16.3	2	2.3	4	4.4	4	4.7	24	27.9	20	23.3	5	5.8
Missouri	137	1	0.7	9	6.6	112	81.8	20	14.6	19	13.9	0	0	9	6.6	5	3.6	22	16.1	20	14.6	4	2.9
Nebraska	40	1	2.5	2	5	31	77.5	2	5	5	12.5	1	2.5	2	5	1	2.5	6	15	10	25	1	2.5
North Dakota	16	0	0	1	6.3	12	75	2	12.5	3	18.8	0	0	2	12.5	0	0	7	43.8	5	31.3	2	12.5
South Dakota	36	3	8.3	3	8.3	28	77.8	0	0	1	2.8	1	2.8	1	2.8	4	11.1	8	22.2	7	19.4	11	31.3
CENSUS DIVISION 7, WEST SOUTH CENTRAL	838	5	0.6	24	2.9	665	79.4	58	6.9	65	7.8	23	2.7	56	6.7	7	0.8	103	12.3	127	15.2	13	1.6
Arkansas	89	2	2.2	3	3.4	79	88.8	7	7.9	7	7.9	4	4.5	8	9	0	0	15	16.9	14	15.7	0	0
Louisiana	89	3	3.4	3	3.4	58	65.2	9	10.1	9	10.1	4	4.5	7	7.9	2	2.2	11	12.4	20	22.5	2	2.2
Oklahoma	106	1	0.9	2	1.9	81	76.4	6	5.7	8	7.5	2	1.9	5	4.7	2	1.9	15	14.2	18	17	1	0.9
Texas	554	2	0.4	16	2.9	447	80.7	36	6.5	41	7.4	13	2.3	36	6.5	3	0.5	62	11.2	75	13.5	10	1.8
CENSUS DIVISION 8, MOUNTAIN	337	17	5	26	7.7	257	76.3	24	7.1	45	13.4	9	2.7	23	6.8	10	3	67	19.9	77	22.8	35	10.4
Arizona	72	1	1.4	2	2.8	50	69.4	5	6.9	12	16.7	1	1.4	6	8.3	3	4.2	14	19.4	14	19.4	6	8.3
Colorado	71	2	2.8	2	2.8	63	88.7	6	8.5	13	18.3	3	4.2	5	7	3	4.2	19	26.8	19	26.8	10	14.1
Idaho	26	2	7.7	3	11.5	22	84.6	3	11.5	5	19.2	1	3.9	3	11.5	1	3.9	9	34.6	5	19.2	3	11.5
Montana	51	12	23.5	4	7.8	37	72.5	2	3.9	3	5.9	0	0	2	3.9	0	0	7	13.7	8	15.7	4	7.8
Nevada	23	0	0	2	8.7	12	52.2	2	8.7	3	13	1	4.3	2	8.7	1	4.3	3	13	5	21.7	0	0
New Mexico	31	0	0	2	6.5	24	77.4	1	3.2	1	3.2	0	0	1	3.2	0	0	5	16.1	13	41.9	2	6.5
Utah	38	0	0	4	10.5	30	78.9	3	7.9	4	10.5	1	2.6	2	5.3	2	5.3	5	13.2	9	23.7	10	26.3
Wyoming	25	0	0	7	28	19	76	4	16	4	16	2	8	2	8	0	0	5	20	4	16	0	0
CENSUS DIVISION 9, PACIFIC	397	21	5.3	16	4	351	88.4	24	6	51	12.8	5	1.3	24	6	17	4.3	37	9.3	140	35.3	33	8.3
Alaska	8	0	0	1	12.5	7	87.5	2	25	2	25	0	0	2	25	0	0	0	0	0	0	0	0
California	242	18	7.4	12	5	214	88.4	16	6.6	34	14	2	0.8	17	7	15	6.2	21	8.7	100	41.3	24	9.9
Hawaii	13	0	0	1	7.7	12	92.3	2	15.4	2	15.4	1	7.7	1	7.7	0	0	1	7.7	4	30.8	1	7.7
Oregon	61	1	1.6	1	1.6	59	96.7	4	6.6	4	6.6	0	0	4	6.6	1	1.6	8	13.1	9	14.8	3	4.9
Washington	73	2	2.7	1	1.4	59	80.8	4	5.5	9	12.3	2	2.7	4	5.5	1	1.4	7	9.6	27	37	5	6.8

Note: These data represent hospital performance in the years 2015–2019 and do not reflect any impacts from the COVID-19 pandemic in 2020 and thereafter.

Table 7 (Continued)

These data include only hospital-based facilities and services as reported by responding hospitals in Section C of the 2019 AHA Annual Survey, beginning on page 215. Census divisions represent all U.S. hospitals. Community hospitals are listed separately under United States. No estimates have been made for nonresponding hospitals. Definitions of facilities and services are listed in the Glossary, page 203.

CLASSIFICATION	HOSPITALS REPORTING	AUXILIARY Number	AUXILIARY Percent	BARIATRIC/WEIGHT CONTROL SERVICES Number	BARIATRIC/WEIGHT CONTROL SERVICES Percent	BIRTHING/LDR/LDRP ROOM Number	BIRTHING/LDR/LDRP ROOM Percent	BLOOD DONOR CENTER Number	BLOOD DONOR CENTER Percent	BREAST CANCER SCREENING Number	BREAST CANCER SCREENING Percent	BURN CARE UNITS Number	BURN CARE UNITS Percent	CASE MANAGEMENT Number	CASE MANAGEMENT Percent	CHAPLAINCY/PASTORAL CARE SERVICES Number	CHAPLAINCY/PASTORAL CARE SERVICES Percent	CHEMOTHERAPY Number	CHEMOTHERAPY Percent
UNITED STATES	4,167	2,283	54.8	1,176	28.2	2,164	51.9	229	5.5	2,881	69.1	137	3.3	3,707	89	2,726	65.6	2,089	50.1
COMMUNITY HOSPITALS	3,782	2,250	59.5	1,145	30.3	2,158	57.1	222	5.9	2,854	75.5	136	3.6	3,489	92.3	2,587	68.4	2,052	54.3
CENSUS DIVISION 1, NEW ENGLAND	156	82	52.6	61	39.1	100	64.1	25	16	123	79.8	7	4.5	151	96.8	122	78.2	106	67.9
Connecticut	26	16	61.5	18	69.2	21	80.8	5	19.2	23	80.8	1	3.8	26	100	25	96.2	23	88.5
Maine	30	21	70	7	23.3	21	76.7	0	0	26	86.7	1	3.3	29	96.7	21	70	20	66.7
Massachusetts	57	22	38.6	27	47.4	33	57.9	16	28.1	41	71.9	4	7	55	96.5	47	82.5	35	61.4
New Hampshire	25	12	48	6	24	14	56	4	16	21	84	0	0	25	100	15	60	17	68
Rhode Island	7	4	57.1	2	28.6	3	42.9	0	0	6	85.7	1	14.3	6	85.7	6	85.7	6	85.7
Vermont	11	7	63.6	1	9.1	6	54.5	0	0	8	72.7	0	0	10	90.9	8	72.7	5	45.5
CENSUS DIVISION 2, MIDDLE ATLANTIC	362	230	63.5	178	49.2	209	57.7	46	12.7	293	80.9	16	4.4	342	94.5	299	82.6	239	66
New Jersey	70	45	64.3	48	68.6	40	57.1	6	8.6	51	72.9	2	2.9	63	90	60	85.7	48	68.6
New York	135	93	68.9	69	51.1	91	67.4	22	16.3	117	86.7	8	5.9	131	97	115	85.2	94	69.6
Pennsylvania	157	92	58.6	61	38.9	78	49.7	18	11.5	125	79.6	6	3.8	148	94.3	124	79	97	61.8
CENSUS DIVISION 3, SOUTH ATLANTIC	574	345	60.1	182	31.7	307	53.5	38	6.6	420	73.2	25	4.4	531	92.5	455	79.3	323	56.3
Delaware	8	4	50	6	62.5	4	50	1	10	4	50	0	0	7	87.5	5	62.5	5	62.5
District of Columbia	10	4	40	6	60	4	50	1	10	5	50	1	10	9	90	6	60	6	60
Florida	165	94	57	59	35.8	77	46.7	8	4.8	112	67.9	9	5.5	154	93.3	129	78.2	93	56.4
Georgia	96	63	65.6	28	29.2	49	51	5	5.2	73	76	3	3.1	88	91.7	74	77.1	48	50
Maryland	45	34	75.6	21	46.7	30	66.7	8	17.8	34	75.6	2	4.4	43	95.6	45	100	35	77.8
North Carolina	74	42	56.8	23	31.1	53	71.6	5	6.8	59	79.7	2	2.7	68	91.9	64	86.5	50	67.6
South Carolina	68	36	52.9	14	20.6	36	52.9	4	5.9	49	72.1	3	4.4	60	88.2	43	63.2	30	44.1
Virginia	63	39	61.9	17	27	35	55.6	8	12.7	49	77.8	4	6.3	61	96.8	54	85.7	39	61.9
West Virginia	45	29	64.4	9	20	18	40	0	0	35	77.8	1	2.2	41	91.1	33	73.3	17	37.8
CENSUS DIVISION 4, EAST NORTH CENTRAL	672	399	59.4	202	30.1	394	58.6	24	3.6	537	79.9	25	3.7	617	91.8	486	72.3	390	58
Illinois	155	107	69	50	32.3	91	58.7	9	5.8	131	84.5	5	3.2	146	94.2	126	81.3	98	63.2
Indiana	117	48	41	23	19.7	68	58.1	2	1.7	83	70.9	2	1.7	104	88.9	83	70.9	61	52.1
Michigan	127	87	68.5	55	43.3	69	54.3	6	4.7	108	85	7	5.5	114	89.8	93	73.2	86	67.7
Ohio	127	77	60.6	43	33.9	75	59.1	7	5.5	101	79.5	6	4.7	122	96.1	106	83.5	87	68.5
Wisconsin	146	80	54.8	31	21.2	91	62.3	0	0	114	78.1	1	3.4	131	89.7	78	53.4	58	39.7
CENSUS DIVISION 5, EAST SOUTH CENTRAL	269	132	49.1	61	22.7	122	45.4	4	1.5	187	69.5	10	3.7	223	86.6	164	61.7	88	32.7
Alabama	47	31	66	14	29.8	27	57.4	1	2.1	36	76.6	4	8.5	43	91.5	29	61.7	22	46.8
Kentucky	53	33	62.3	21	32.1	23	43.4	1	1.9	43	81.1	3	5.7	50	94.3	45	84.9	25	47.2
Mississippi	102	32	31.4	13	12.7	37	36.3	3	3	57	55.9	1	1	76	74.5	37	36.3	17	16.7
Tennessee	67	36	53.7	17	25.4	35	52.2	2	3	51	76.1	2	3	64	95.5	53	79.1	24	35.8
CENSUS DIVISION 6, WEST NORTH CENTRAL	562	347	61.7	125	22.2	285	50.7	17	3	419	74.6	16	2.8	458	81.5	301	53.6	300	53.4
Iowa	122	100	82	25	20.5	62	50.8	2	1.6	114	93.4	2	1.6	110	90.2	56	45.9	76	62.3
Kansas	125	66	52.8	20	16	55	44	6	4.7	69	55.2	2	1.6	90	72	51	40.8	35	28
Minnesota	86	48	55.8	23	26.7	60	69.8	4	4.7	73	84.9	8	5.8	71	82.6	53	61.6	55	63.9
Missouri	137	92	67.2	36	26.3	58	42.3	9	6.6	94	68.6	8	5.8	117	85.4	96	70.1	71	51.8
Nebraska	40	19	47.5	10	25	28	70	0	0	37	92.5	0	5	34	85	23	57.5	32	80
North Dakota	16	13	81.3	6	31.3	8	50	0	0	12	75	0	0	12	75	10	62.5	8	50
South Dakota	36	9	25	6	16.7	14	38.9	1	2.8	20	55.6	0	0	24	66.7	12	33.3	18	50
CENSUS DIVISION 7, WEST SOUTH CENTRAL	838	357	42.6	181	21.6	308	36.8	28	3.3	388	46.3	17	2.2	720	85.9	402	48	214	25.5
Arkansas	89	50	56.2	15	16.9	33	37.1	2	2.2	53	59.6	2	2.2	78	87.6	43	48.3	28	31.5
Louisiana	89	35	39.3	22	24.7	33	36	6	6.7	53	59.6	6	3.4	77	86.5	43	48.3	38	42.7
Oklahoma	106	48	45.3	16	15.1	39	36.8	4	3.8	55	51.9	2	1.9	94	88.7	54	50.9	21	19.8
Texas	554	224	40.4	128	23.1	204	36.8	16	2.9	227	41	10	1.8	471	85	262	47.3	127	22.9
CENSUS DIVISION 8, MOUNTAIN	337	163	49.4	71	21.1	185	54.9	18	5.3	222	65.9	17	2.7	293	86.9	193	57.3	173	51.3
Arizona	71	29	40.3	18	25	29	40.3	2	2.8	38	52.8	2	2.8	69	95.8	50	69.4	37	51.4
Colorado	71	41	57.7	19	26.8	47	66.2	12	16.9	57	80.3	3	4.2	66	93	53	74.6	47	66.2
Idaho	26	18	69.2	7	26.9	16	61.5	2	7.7	18	69.2	0	0	21	80.8	15	57.7	14	53.8
Montana	51	25	49	5	9.8	25	49	1	2	33	64.7	0	0	35	68.6	21	41.2	24	47.1
Nevada	23	4	17.4	4	17.4	8	34.8	0	0	11	47.8	1	4.3	20	87	9	39.1	10	43.5
New Mexico	31	17	54.8	5	16.1	19	61.3	0	0	19	61.3	2	6.5	26	83.9	20	64.5	11	35.5
Utah	38	15	39.5	10	26.3	24	63.2	0	0	28	73.7	1	2.6	35	92.1	13	34.2	18	47.4
Wyoming	25	14	56	3	12	17	68	1	4	18	72	0	3	21	84	13	48	12	48
CENSUS DIVISION 9, PACIFIC	397	228	57.4	115	29	254	64	28	7.3	292	73.6	12	3	362	91.2	313	78.8	256	64.5
Alaska	4	4	50	1	12.5	6	75	0	0	4	50	0	0	7	87.5	6	75	5	62.5
California	242	141	58.3	74	30.6	147	60.7	26	10.7	170	70.2	8	3.3	216	89.3	190	78.5	155	64
Hawaii	13	3	23.1	6	46.2	6	46.2	1	7.7	10	76.9	1	7.7	11	84.6	6	46.2	10	76.9
Oregon	61	42	68.9	13	21.3	47	77	2	3.3	55	90.2	1	3.3	58	95.1	50	82	41	67.2
Washington	73	38	52.1	21	28.8	48	65.8	2	2.7	53	72.6	1	1.4	70	95.9	61	83.6	45	61.6

Note: These data represent hospital performance in the years 2015 – 2019 and do not reflect any impacts from the COVID-19 pandemic in 2020 and thereafter.

Table 7 (Continued)

These data include only hospital-based facilities and services as reported by responding hospitals in Section C of the 2019 AHA Annual Survey, beginning on page 215. Census divisions represent all U.S. hospitals. Community hospitals are listed separately under United States. No estimates have been made for nonresponding hospitals. Definitions of facilities and services are listed in the Glossary, page 203.

CLASSIFICATION	HOSPITALS REPORTING	CHILDREN'S WELLNESS PROGRAM		CHIROPRACTIC SERVICES		COMMUNITY OUTREACH		COMPLEMENTARY AND ALTERNATIVE MEDICINE SERVICES		COMPUTER ASSISTED ORTHOPEDIC SURGERY (CAOS)		CRISIS PREVENTION		DIABETES PREVENTION PROGRAM		DENTAL SERVICES		EMPLOYMENT SUPPORT SERVICES		ENABLING SERVICES		ENROLLMENT ASSISTANCE SERVICES		EXTRACORPOREAL SHOCK WAVE LITHOTRIPTER (ESWL)	
		Number	Percent	Number	Percent	Number	Percent	Number	Percent	Number	Percent	Number	Percent	Number	Percent	Number	Percent	Number	Percent	Number	Percent	Number	Percent	Number	Percent
UNITED STATES	4,167	832	20	144	3.5	2,951	70.8	921	22.1	833	20	1,072	25.7	1,645	39.5	845	20.3	820	19.7	1,372	32.9	2,591	62.2	1,245	29.9
COMMUNITY HOSPITALS	3,782	813	21.5	117	3.1	2,828	74.8	873	23.1	825	21.8	962	25.4	1,582	41.8	755	20	757	20	1,309	34.6	2,484	65.7	1,234	32.6
CENSUS DIVISION 1, NEW ENGLAND	156	54	34.6	8	5.1	136	87.2	77	49.4	46	29.5	59	37.8	76	48.7	36	23.1	59	37.8	83	53.2	134	85.9	74	47.4
Connecticut	26	9	34.6	1	3.8	24	92.3	20	76.9	13	50	19	73.1	9	34.6	13	50	13	50	18	69.2	26	100	18	69.2
Maine	30	12	40	1	3.3	23	76.7	10	33.3	1	3.3	4	13.3	17	56.7	3	10	3	10	13	43.3	22	73.3	10	33.3
Massachusetts	57	18	31.6	4	7	51	89.5	30	52.6	19	33.3	24	42.1	21	36.8	9	15.8	27	47.4	26	45.6	49	86	29	50.9
New Hampshire	25	11	44	2	8	22	88	12	48	7	28	11	44	19	76	7	28	7	28	16	64	22	88	8	32
Rhode Island	7	1	14.3	0	0	7	100	2	28.6	3	42.9	1	14.3	5	71.4	3	42.9	4	57.1	5	71.4	5	71.4	6	85.7
Vermont	11	3	27.3	0	0	9	81.8	3	27.3	3	27.3	0	0	5	45.5	1	9.1	5	45.5	5	45.5	10	90.9	3	27.3
CENSUS DIVISION 2, MIDDLE ATLANTIC	362	119	32.9	19	5.2	302	83.4	141	39	110	30.4	170	47	186	51.4	147	40.6	119	32.9	189	52.2	279	77.1	164	45.3
New Jersey	70	30	42.9	3	4.3	54	77.1	33	47.1	27	38.6	42	60	38	54.3	28	40	30	42.9	43	61.4	51	72.9	30	42.9
New York	135	52	38.5	11	8.1	122	90.4	60	44.4	49	36.3	80	59.3	85	63	71	52.6	47	34.8	66	48.9	116	85.9	71	52.6
Pennsylvania	157	37	23.6	5	3.2	126	80.3	48	30.6	34	21.7	48	30.6	63	40.1	48	30.6	42	26.8	80	51	112	71.3	63	40.1
CENSUS DIVISION 3, SOUTH ATLANTIC	574	108	18.8	14	2.4	441	76.8	126	22	137	23.9	155	27	242	42.2	138	24	113	19.7	229	39.9	381	66.4	204	35.5
Delaware	8	3	37.5	0	0	5	62.5	2	25	3	37.5	2	25	4	50	2	25	3	37.5	3	37.5	4	50	2	25
District of Columbia	10	4	40	0	0	8	80	5	50	4	40	6	60	5	50	5	50	4	40	8	80	7	70	4	40
Florida	165	26	15.8	3	1.8	117	70.9	32	19.4	52	31.5	34	20.6	65	39.4	29	17.6	38	23	58	35.2	108	65.5	73	44.2
Georgia	96	10	10.4	3	3.1	70	72.9	20	20.8	16	16.7	26	27.1	42	43.8	15	15.6	10	10.4	38	39.6	63	65.6	30	31.3
Maryland	45	15	33.3	1	2.2	39	86.7	19	42.2	15	33.3	26	57.8	30	66.7	19	42.2	17	37.8	33	73.3	39	86.7	28	62.2
North Carolina	74	15	20.3	1	1.4	63	85.1	18	24.3	16	21.6	18	24.3	35	47.3	26	35.1	11	14.9	27	36.5	46	62.2	10	13.5
South Carolina	68	12	17.6	0	0	49	72.1	4	5.9	11	16.2	10	14.7	9	13.2	14	20.6	6	8.8	14	20.6	35	51.5	20	29.4
Virginia	63	11	17.5	4	6.3	54	85.7	23	36.5	17	27	26	41.3	31	49.2	24	38.1	12	19	36	57.1	49	77.8	24	38.1
West Virginia	45	12	26.7	2	4.4	36	80	3	6.7	3	6.7	7	15.6	21	46.7	4	8.9	12	26.7	12	26.7	30	66.7	13	28.9
CENSUS DIVISION 4, EAST NORTH CENTRAL	672	168	25	35	5.2	517	76.9	224	33.3	140	20.8	226	33.6	326	48.5	122	18.2	158	23.5	282	42	452	67.3	223	33.2
Illinois	155	40	25.8	9	5.8	127	81.9	41	26.5	40	25.8	68	43.9	75	48.4	41	26.5	39	25.2	70	45.2	108	69.7	52	33.5
Indiana	117	27	23.1	3	2.6	94	80.3	28	23.9	18	15.4	27	23.1	55	47	18	15.4	23	19.7	39	33.3	79	67.5	30	25.6
Michigan	127	40	31.5	6	4.7	115	90.6	53	41.7	28	22	50	39.4	79	62.2	36	28.3	41	32.3	65	51.2	107	84.3	43	33.9
Ohio	127	30	23.6	10	7.9	106	83.5	51	40.2	33	26	40	31.5	73	57.5	27	21.3	34	26.8	59	46.5	93	73.2	53	41.7
Wisconsin	146	31	21.2	7	4.8	75	51.4	51	34.9	21	14.4	41	28.1	44	30.1	0	0	21	14.4	49	33.6	65	44.5	45	30.8
CENSUS DIVISION 5, EAST SOUTH CENTRAL	269	38	14.1	4	1.5	189	70.3	24	8.9	43	16	47	17.5	73	27.1	63	23.4	38	14.1	68	25.3	145	53.9	63	23.4
Alabama	47	4	8.5	3	6.4	34	72.3	3	6.4	12	25.5	7	14.9	14	29.8	4	8.5	12	25.5	12	25.5	33	70.2	12	25.5
Kentucky	53	12	22.6	0	0	44	83	13	24.5	10	18.9	11	20.8	20	37.7	14	26.4	8	15.1	16	30.2	39	73.6	14	26.4
Mississippi	102	15	14.7	1	1	60	58.8	2	2	7	6.9	13	12.7	14	13.7	26	25.5	6	5.9	11	10.8	32	31.4	13	12.7
Tennessee	67	7	10.4	0	0	51	76.1	6	9	14	20.9	16	23.9	25	37.3	19	28.4	12	17.9	29	43.3	41	61.2	24	35.8
CENSUS DIVISION 6, WEST NORTH CENTRAL	562	114	20.3	28	5	374	66.5	100	17.8	59	10.5	108	19.2	267	47.5	71	12.6	89	15.8	140	24.9	334	59.4	112	19.9
Iowa	122	29	23.8	4	3.3	96	78.7	30	24.6	18	14.8	26	21.3	80	65.6	13	10.7	23	18.9	37	30.3	94	77	16	13.1
Kansas	125	13	10.4	1	0.8	57	45.6	9	7.2	7	5.6	9	7.2	55	44	8	6.4	12	9.6	17	13.6	58	46.4	17	13.6
Minnesota	86	26	30.2	11	12.8	70	81.4	24	27.9	10	11.6	22	25.6	42	48.8	9	10.5	18	20.9	22	25.6	53	61.6	17	19.8
Missouri	137	24	17.5	7	5.1	91	66.4	22	16.1	10	7.3	34	24.8	39	28.5	34	24.8	18	13.1	46	33.6	80	58.4	43	31.4
Nebraska	40	6	15	1	2.5	31	77.5	7	17.5	9	22.5	6	15	22	55	3	7.5	9	22.5	9	22.5	30	75	12	30
North Dakota	16	8	50	4	25	10	62.5	5	31.3	3	18.8	6	37.5	12	75	2	12.5	5	31.3	6	37.5	8	50	3	18.8
South Dakota	36	8	22.2	0	0	19	52.8	3	8.3	2	5.6	5	13.9	17	47.2	2	5.6	4	11.1	3	8.3	11	30.6	4	11.1
CENSUS DIVISION 7, WEST SOUTH CENTRAL	838	85	10.1	9	1.1	447	53.3	50	6	118	14.1	101	12.1	187	22.3	121	14.4	108	12.9	133	15.9	352	42	175	20.9
Arkansas	89	8	9	1	1.1	53	59.6	5	5.6	6	6.7	15	16.9	31	34.8	11	12.4	15	16.9	21	23.6	39	43.8	12	13.5
Louisiana	89	19	21.3	3	3.4	49	55.1	8	9	17	19.1	23	25.8	24	27	16	18	14	15.7	22	24.7	47	52.8	21	23.6
Oklahoma	106	9	8.5	0	0	59	55.7	5	4.7	12	11.3	11	10.4	23	21.7	17	16	10	9.4	8	7.5	42	39.6	25	23.6
Texas	554	49	8.8	5	0.9	286	51.6	32	5.8	83	15	52	9.4	109	19.7	77	13.9	69	12.5	82	14.8	224	40.4	117	21.1
CENSUS DIVISION 8, MOUNTAIN	337	69	20.5	13	3.9	245	72.7	75	22.3	75	22.3	103	30.6	127	37.7	50	14.8	67	19.9	102	30.3	228	67.7	85	25.2
Arizona	72	14	19.4	2	2.8	51	70.8	18	25	19	26.4	23	31.9	21	29.2	7	9.7	15	20.8	24	33.3	48	66.7	28	38.9
Colorado	71	16	22.5	3	4.2	61	85.9	29	40.8	19	26.8	23	32.4	32	45.1	11	15.5	19	26.8	24	33.8	55	77.5	14	19.7
Idaho	26	10	38.5	2	7.7	20	76.9	6	23.1	11	42.3	9	34.6	13	50	9	34.6	4	15.4	7	26.9	18	69.2	5	19.2
Montana	51	11	21.6	4	7.8	33	64.7	9	17.6	5	9.8	9	17.6	25	49	1	2	5	9.8	7	13.7	28	54.9	10	19.6
Nevada	23	3	13	0	0	9	39.1	1	4.3	4	17.4	5	21.7	3	13	1	4.3	2	8.7	6	26.1	11	47.8	3	13
New Mexico	31	7	22.6	0	0	23	74.2	2	6.5	3	9.7	5	16.1	4	12.9	6	19.4	3	9.7	5	16.1	21	67.7	10	32.3
Utah	38	3	7.9	1	2.6	29	76.3	6	15.8	9	23.7	26	68.4	20	52.6	11	28.9	13	34.2	25	65.8	33	86.8	11	28.9
Wyoming	25	5	20	1	4	19	76	4	16	5	20	3	12	9	36	4	16	6	24	4	16	14	56	4	16
CENSUS DIVISION 9, PACIFIC	397	77	19.4	14	3.5	300	75.6	104	26.2	105	26.4	103	25.9	161	40.6	97	24.4	70	17.6	146	36.8	286	72	145	36.5
Alaska	8	2	25	0	0	4	50	2	25	1	12.5	3	37.5	4	50	1	12.5	1	12.5	0	0	4	50	3	37.5
California	242	43	17.8	8	3.3	174	71.9	59	24.4	67	27.7	52	21.5	94	38.8	75	31	50	20.7	90	37.2	175	72.3	96	39.7
Hawaii	13	4	30.8	1	7.7	10	76.9	6	46.2	3	23.1	3	23.1	7	53.8	4	30.8	2	15.4	6	46.2	8	61.5	4	30.8
Oregon	61	12	19.7	3	4.9	54	88.5	18	29.5	19	31.1	14	23	26	42.6	6	9.8	6	9.8	22	36.1	44	72.1	19	31.1
Washington	73	16	21.9	2	2.7	58	79.5	19	26	15	20.5	31	42.5	30	41.1	11	15.1	11	15.1	28	38.4	55	75.3	23	31.5

Note: These data represent hospital performance in the years 2015 – 2019 and do not reflect any impacts from the COVID-19 pandemic in 2020 and thereafter.

Table 7 (Continued)

These data include only hospital-based facilities and services as reported by responding hospitals in Section C of the 2019 AHA Annual Survey, beginning on page 215. Census divisions represent all U.S. hospitals. Community hospitals are listed separately under United States. No estimates have been made for nonresponding hospitals. Definitions of facilities and services are listed in the Glossary, page 203.

CLASSIFICATION	HOSPITALS REPORTING	FERTILITY CLINIC		FITNESS CENTER		FREESTANDING OUTPATIENT CARE CENTER		GENETIC TESTING/ COUNSELING		GERIATRIC SERVICES		HEALTH FAIR		COMMUNITY HEALTH EDUCATION		HEALTH RESEARCH		HEALTH SCREENINGS		HEMODIALYSIS	
		Number	Percent	Number	Percent	Number	Percent	Number	Percent	Number	Percent	Number	Percent	Number	Percent	Number	Percent	Number	Percent	Number	Percent
UNITED STATES	4,167	217	5.2	1,250	30	1,451	34.8	845	20.3	1,652	39.6	2,952	70.8	3,282	78.8	1,164	27.9	3,140	75.4	1,339	32.1
COMMUNITY HOSPITALS	3,782	210	5.6	1,185	31.3	1,387	36.7	826	21.8	1,553	41.1	2,853	75.4	3,169	83.8	1,105	29.2	3,033	80.2	1,299	34.3
CENSUS DIVISION 1, NEW ENGLAND	156	25	16	54	34.6	90	57.7	61	39.1	79	50.6	124	79.5	141	90.4	73	46.8	134	85.9	50	32.1
Connecticut	26	6	23.1	15	57.7	22	84.6	16	61.5	18	69.2	25	96.2	26	100	18	69.2	25	96.2	11	42.3
Maine	30	2	6.7	8	26.7	15	50	7	23.3	16	53.3	22	73.3	27	90	7	23.3	27	90	2	6.7
Massachusetts	57	11	19.3	14	24.6	31	54.4	22	38.6	26	45.6	46	80.7	50	87.7	36	63.2	45	78.9	28	49.1
New Hampshire	25	5	20	10	40	14	56	8	32	12	48	20	80	22	88	7	28	23	92	2	8
Rhode Island	7	0	0	3	42.9	4	57.1	4	57.1	5	71.4	6	85.7	6	85.7	3	42.9	6	85.7	5	71.4
Vermont	11	1	9.1	4	36.4	4	36.4	4	36.4	2	18.2	5	45.5	10	90.9	2	18.2	8	72.7	2	18.2
CENSUS DIVISION 2, MIDDLE ATLANTIC	362	50	13.8	110	30.4	206	56.9	144	39.8	205	56.6	304	84	312	86.2	166	45.9	314	86.7	177	48.9
New Jersey	70	10	14.3	23	32.9	34	48.6	34	48.6	43	61.4	53	75.7	56	80	40	57.1	51	72.9	43	61.4
New York	135	26	19.3	46	34.1	90	66.7	61	45.2	83	61.5	123	91.1	127	94.1	71	52.6	127	94.1	81	60
Pennsylvania	157	14	8.9	41	26.1	82	52.2	49	31.2	79	50.3	128	81.5	129	82.2	55	35	136	86.6	53	33.8
CENSUS DIVISION 3, SOUTH ATLANTIC	574	23	4	188	32.8	230	40.1	146	25.4	230	40.1	438	76.3	462	80.5	218	38	457	79.6	259	45.1
Delaware	8	0	0	3	37.5	5	62.5	3	37.5	3	37.5	5	62.5	5	62.5	3	37.5	5	62.5	3	37.5
District of Columbia	10	3	30	4	40	7	70	6	60	6	60	7	70	8	80	7	70	8	80	6	60
Florida	165	3	1.8	50	30.3	62	37.6	40	24.2	64	38.8	120	72.7	136	82.4	66	40	123	74.5	87	52.7
Georgia	96	3	3.1	26	27.1	35	36.5	24	25	28	29.2	72	75	72	75	31	32.3	76	79.2	42	43.8
Maryland	45	5	11.1	18	40	23	51.1	20	44.4	30	66.7	39	86.7	37	82.2	32	71.1	40	88.9	31	68.9
North Carolina	74	3	4.1	27	36.5	32	43.2	15	20.3	31	41.9	62	83.8	66	89.2	26	35.1	66	89.2	28	37.8
South Carolina	68	2	2.9	21	30.9	19	27.9	4	5.9	24	35.3	46	67.6	50	73.5	16	23.5	49	72.1	30	44.1
Virginia	63	4	6.3	25	39.7	32	50.8	26	41.3	31	49.2	52	82.5	53	84.1	30	47.6	55	87.3	30	47.6
West Virginia	45	3	6.7	14	31.1	15	33.3	8	17.8	13	28.9	35	77.8	35	77.8	7	15.6	35	77.8	10	22.2
CENSUS DIVISION 4, EAST NORTH CENTRAL	672	30	4.5	259	38.5	290	43.2	140	20.8	316	47	499	74.3	592	88.1	196	29.2	531	79	212	31.5
Illinois	155	11	7.1	51	32.9	65	41.9	35	22.6	72	46.5	132	85.2	138	89	50	32.3	139	89.7	55	35.5
Indiana	117	1	0.9	41	35	39	33.3	21	17.9	45	38.5	85	72.6	91	77.8	23	19.7	88	75.2	23	19.7
Michigan	127	5	3.9	52	40.9	64	50.4	29	22.8	59	46.5	98	77.2	116	91.3	55	43.3	113	89	42	33.1
Ohio	127	9	7.1	50	39.4	66	52	34	26.8	50	39.4	107	84.3	114	89.8	46	36.2	109	85.8	57	44.9
Wisconsin	146	4	2.7	65	44.5	56	38.4	21	14.4	90	61.6	77	52.7	133	91.1	22	15.1	82	56.2	35	24
CENSUS DIVISION 5, EAST SOUTH CENTRAL	269	10	3.7	63	23.4	71	26.4	37	13.8	74	27.5	184	68.4	190	70.6	63	23.4	189	70.3	75	27.9
Alabama	47	2	4.3	18	38.3	18	38.3	5	10.6	15	31.9	37	78.7	34	72.3	12	25.5	40	85.1	23	48.9
Kentucky	53	2	3.8	6	11.3	16	30.2	10	18.9	17	32.1	38	71.7	43	81.1	14	26.4	41	77.4	15	28.3
Mississippi	102	2	2	23	22.5	15	14.7	9	8.8	15	14.7	55	53.9	60	58.8	12	11.8	55	53.9	14	13.7
Tennessee	67	4	6	16	23.9	22	32.8	13	19.4	27	40.3	54	80.6	53	79.1	25	37.3	53	79.1	23	34.3
CENSUS DIVISION 6, WEST NORTH CENTRAL	562	23	4.1	199	35.4	113	20.1	79	14.1	233	41.5	412	73.3	463	82.4	100	17.8	464	82.6	114	20.3
Iowa	122	5	4.1	45	36.9	15	12.3	15	12.3	56	45.9	106	86.9	112	91.8	15	12.3	114	93.4	25	20.5
Kansas	125	2	1.6	37	29.6	17	13.6	13	10.4	42	33.6	73	58.4	85	68	11	8.8	89	71.2	13	10.4
Minnesota	86	4	4.7	29	33.7	13	15.1	13	15.1	37	43	64	74.4	75	87.2	19	22.1	73	84.9	16	18.6
Missouri	137	11	8	47	34.3	37	27	20	14.6	58	42.3	99	72.3	107	78.1	32	23.4	104	75.9	48	35
Nebraska	40	1	2.5	20	50	7	17.5	10	25	14	35	31	77.5	38	95	12	30	37	92.5	6	15
North Dakota	16	2	12.5	7	43.8	5	31.3	5	31.3	10	62.5	12	75	14	87.5	5	31.3	12	75	0	0
South Dakota	36	1	2.8	14	38.9	3	8.3	3	8.3	16	44.4	27	75	32	88.9	6	16.7	35	97.2	6	16.7
CENSUS DIVISION 7, WEST SOUTH CENTRAL	838	16	1.9	191	22.8	178	21.2	79	9.4	220	26.3	489	58.4	526	62.8	122	14.6	501	59.8	186	22.2
Arkansas	89	3	3.4	22	24.7	14	15.7	6	6.7	27	30.3	62	69.7	64	71.9	11	12.4	62	69.7	16	18
Louisiana	89	1	1.1	21	23.6	27	30.3	18	20.2	30	33.7	50	56.2	64	71.9	24	27	54	60.7	25	28.1
Oklahoma	106	2	1.9	19	17.9	20	18.9	7	6.6	23	21.7	58	54.7	68	64.2	16	15.1	66	62.3	16	15.1
Texas	554	10	1.8	129	23.3	117	21.1	48	8.7	140	25.3	319	57.6	330	59.6	71	12.8	319	57.6	129	23.3
CENSUS DIVISION 8, MOUNTAIN	337	14	4.2	84	24.9	112	33.2	60	17.8	130	38.6	231	68.5	273	81	78	23.1	258	76.6	94	27.9
Arizona	72	1	1.4	16	22.2	28	38.9	10	13.9	19	26.4	50	69.4	58	80.6	29	40.3	49	68.1	33	45.8
Colorado	71	6	8.5	26	36.6	32	45.1	23	32.4	30	42.3	46	64.8	62	87.3	21	29.6	62	87.3	22	31
Idaho	26	0	0	6	23.1	9	34.6	4	15.4	12	46.2	21	80.8	22	84.6	5	19.2	22	84.6	5	19.2
Montana	51	3	5.9	11	21.6	12	23.5	4	7.8	30	58.8	38	74.5	45	88.2	10	19.6	46	90.2	3	5.9
Nevada	23	0	0	0	0	5	21.7	1	4.3	5	21.7	10	43.5	10	43.5	3	13	11	47.8	3	13
New Mexico	40	0	0	6	15	9	22.5	7	17.5	13	32.3	30	75	31	77.5	3	7.5	24	60	6	15
Utah	38	4	10.5	15	39.5	13	34.2	7	18.4	13	34.2	25	65.8	33	86.8	8	21.1	33	86.8	16	42.1
Wyoming	16	0	0	4	25	4	25	4	25	7	44	11	68	12	76	2	12.5	12	76	6	37.5
CENSUS DIVISION 9, PACIFIC	397	26	6.5	102	25.7	161	40.6	99	24.9	166	41.6	271	68.3	323	81.4	148	37.3	292	73.6	172	43.3
Alaska	8	0	0	1	12.5	2	25	0	0	1	12.5	4	50	5	62.5	1	12.5	3	37.5	3	37.5
California	242	19	7.9	59	24.4	105	43.4	70	28.9	109	45	162	66.9	190	78.5	95	39.3	164	67.8	124	51.2
Hawaii	13	1	7.7	4	30.8	8	61.5	3	23.1	6	46.2	10	76.9	11	84.6	8	61.5	10	76.9	5	38.5
Oregon	61	1	1.6	22	36.1	23	37.7	6	9.8	21	34.4	48	78.7	54	88.5	14	23	56	91.8	16	26.2
Washington	73	5	6.8	16	21.9	23	31.5	19	26	28	38.4	47	64.4	63	86.3	30	41.1	57	78.1	24	32.9

Note: These data represent hospital performance in the years 2015 – 2019 and do not reflect any impacts from the COVID-19 pandemic in 2020 and thereafter.

Table 7 (Continued)

These data include only hospital-based facilities and services as reported by responding hospitals in Section C of the 2019 AHA Annual Survey, beginning on page 215. Census divisions represent all U.S. hospitals. Community hospitals are listed separately under United States. No estimates have been made for nonresponding hospitals. Definitions of facilities and services are listed in the Glossary, page 203.

CLASSIFICATION	HOSPITALS REPORTING	HIV/AIDS SERVICES Number	Percent	HOME HEALTH SERVICES Number	Percent	HOSPICE Number	Percent	HOSPITAL-BASED OUTPATIENT CARE CENTER SERVICES Number	Percent	IMMUNIZATION PROGRAM Number	Percent	INDIGENT CARE CLINIC Number	Percent	LINGUISTIC/TRANSLATION SERVICES Number	Percent	MEAL DELIVERY SERVICES Number	Percent	MOBILE HEALTH SERVICES Number	Percent	NEONATAL INTERMEDIATE CARE UNITS Number	Percent
UNITED STATES	4,167	962	23.1	819	19.7	851	20.4	3,113	74.7	1,853	44.5	714	17.1	2,362	56.7	293	7	521	12.5	654	15.7
COMMUNITY HOSPITALS	3,782	912	24.1	788	20.8	814	21.5	3,015	79.7	1,769	46.8	690	18.2	2,258	59.7	282	7.5	493	13	654	17.3
CENSUS DIVISION 1, NEW ENGLAND	156	66	42.3	20	12.8	26	16.7	135	86.5	99	63.5	34	21.8	116	74.4	5	3.2	23	14.7	29	18.6
Connecticut	26	17	65.4	4	15.4	7	26.9	23	88.5	19	73.1	13	50	21	80.8	0	0	4	15.4	5	19.2
Maine	30	11	36.7	4	13.3	1	3.3	25	83.3	20	66.7	4	13.3	17	56.7	1	3.3	3	10	4	13.3
Massachusetts	57	23	40.4	10	17.5	12	21.1	51	89.5	33	57.9	12	21.1	48	84.2	3	5.3	11	19.3	15	26.3
New Hampshire	25	8	32	2	8	2	8	23	92	16	64	3	12	16	64	1	4	5	20	3	12
Rhode Island	7	4	57.1	0	0	1	14.3	6	85.7	5	71.4	0	0	6	85.7	0	0	0	0	1	14.3
Vermont	11	3	27.3	0	0	3	27.3	7	63.6	6	54.5	2	18.2	8	72.7	0	0	0	0	1	9.1
CENSUS DIVISION 2, MIDDLE ATLANTIC	362	153	42.3	75	20.7	99	27.3	296	81.8	214	59.1	150	41.4	237	65.5	24	6.6	84	23.2	109	30.1
New Jersey	70	38	54.3	9	12.9	24	34.3	55	78.6	41	58.6	40	57.1	48	68.6	9	12.9	20	28.6	36	51.4
New York	135	70	51.9	29	21.5	36	26.7	119	88.1	88	65.2	70	51.9	105	77.8	8	5.9	42	31.1	50	37
Pennsylvania	157	45	28.7	37	23.6	39	24.8	122	77.7	85	54.1	40	25.5	84	53.5	7	4.5	22	14	23	14.6
CENSUS DIVISION 3, SOUTH ATLANTIC	574	178	31	107	18.6	117	20.4	424	73.9	208	36.2	111	19.3	337	58.7	15	2.6	90	15.7	123	21.4
Delaware	8	3	37.5	2	25	0	0	5	62.5	3	37.5	2	25	4	50	0	0	0	0	1	12.5
District of Columbia	10	5	50	1	10	2	20	8	80	7	70	4	40	8	80	0	0	5	50	5	50
Florida	165	43	26.1	29	17.6	31	18.8	116	70.3	49	29.7	27	16.4	92	55.8	5	3	21	12.7	24	14.5
Georgia	96	32	33.3	14	14.6	19	19.8	61	63.5	23	24	16	16.7	63	65.6	1	1	15	15.6	30	31.3
Maryland	45	29	64.4	5	11.1	16	35.6	42	93.3	27	60	21	46.7	36	80	3	6.7	12	26.7	7	15.6
North Carolina	74	18	24.3	15	20.3	9	12.2	63	85.1	25	33.8	15	20.3	46	62.2	1	1.4	9	12.2	25	33.8
South Carolina	68	17	25	11	16.2	10	14.7	45	66.2	16	23.5	9	13.2	25	36.8	2	2.9	9	13.2	23	33.8
Virginia	63	24	38.1	19	30.2	27	42.9	50	79.4	36	57.1	12	19	41	65.1	2	3.2	14	22.2	9	14.3
West Virginia	45	7	15.6	11	24.4	3	6.7	34	75.6	22	48.9	5	11.1	22	48.9	1	2	5	11.1	2	4.4
CENSUS DIVISION 4, EAST NORTH CENTRAL	672	159	23.7	138	20.5	152	22.6	547	81.4	323	48.1	134	19.9	368	54.8	85	12.6	87	12.9	86	12.8
Illinois	155	45	29	33	21.3	37	23.9	134	86.5	72	46.5	30	19.4	89	57.4	20	12.9	23	14.8	32	20.6
Indiana	117	21	17.9	21	17.9	22	18.8	83	70.9	48	41	15	12.8	59	50.4	22	18.8	11	9.4	17	14.5
Michigan	127	49	38.6	27	21.3	37	29.1	111	87.4	87	68.5	41	32.3	80	63	9	7.1	18	14.2	16	12.6
Ohio	127	36	28.3	36	28.3	40	31.5	106	83.5	58	45.7	29	22.8	86	67.7	12	9.4	27	21.3	16	16.5
Wisconsin	146	8	5.5	21	14.4	16	11	113	77.4	58	39.7	19	13	54	37	22	15.1	8	5.5	0	0
CENSUS DIVISION 5, EAST SOUTH CENTRAL	269	47	17.5	39	14.5	36	13.4	172	63.9	90	33.5	24	8.9	139	51.7	6	2.2	25	9.3	46	17.1
Alabama	47	8	17	7	14.9	7	14.9	34	72.3	12	25.5	5	10.6	31	66	1	2.1	4	8.5	8	17
Kentucky	53	12	22.6	13	24.5	8	15.1	38	71.7	17	32.1	6	11.3	26	49.1	3	5.7	6	11.3	8	15.1
Mississippi	102	9	8.8	9	8.8	9	8.8	56	54.9	41	40.2	9	8.8	37	36.3			7	6.9	24	23.5
Tennessee	67	18	26.9	10	14.9	12	17.9	44	65.7	20	29.9	4	6	45	67.2	2		8	11.9	6	9
CENSUS DIVISION 6, WEST NORTH CENTRAL	562	99	17.6	172	30.6	142	25.3	463	82.4	288	51.2	54	9.6	292	52	91	16.2	56	10	72	12.8
Iowa	122	22	18	44	36.1	46	37.7	109	89.3	72	59	14	11.5	69	56.6	25	20.5	13	10.7	9	7.4
Kansas	125	11	8.8	29	23.2	15	12	97	77.6	42	33.6	8	6.4	57	45.6	25	20	7	5.6	10	8
Minnesota	86	17	19.8	29	33.7	29	33.7	76	88.4	58	67.4	7	8.1	44	51.2	13	15.1	8	9.3	7	8.1
Missouri	137	32	23.4	36	26.3	27	19.7	103	75.2	62	45.3	17	12.4	74	54	15	10.9	13	9.5	36	26.3
Nebraska	40	6	15	19	47.5	13	32.5	33	82.5	21	52.5	3	7.5	26	65	5	12.5	5	12.5	4	10
North Dakota	16	4	25	5	31.3	6	37.5	14	87.5	10	62.5	2	12.5	9	56.3	2	12.5	3	18.8	2	
South Dakota	36	7	19.4	10	27.8	6	16.7	31	86.1	23	63.9	3	8.3	13	36.1	6	16.7	6	16.7	2	5.6
CENSUS DIVISION 7, WEST SOUTH CENTRAL	838	86	10.3	109	13	89	10.6	525	62.6	271	32.3	89	10.6	375	44.7	31	3.7	66	7.9	79	9.4
Arkansas	89	8	9	28	31.5	10	11.2	54	60.7	22	24.7	4	4.5	40	44.9	5	5.6	9	10.1	7	7.9
Louisiana	89	21	23.6	11	12.4	10	11.2	54	60.7	30	33.7	16	18	39	43.8	3	3.4	9	10.1	8	9
Oklahoma	106	7	6.6	14	13.2	13	12.3	74	69.8	31	29.2	9	8.5	56	52.8	10	9.4	7	6.6	11	10.3
Texas	554	50	9	56	10.1	56	10.1	343	61.9	188	33.9	60	10.8	240	43.3	13	2.3	41	7.4	57	
CENSUS DIVISION 8, MOUNTAIN	337	64	19	64	19	80	23.7	238	70.6	159	47.2	49	14.5	210	62.3	22	6.5	46	13.6	35	10.4
Arizona	72	19	26.4	13	9.7	17	23.6	46	63.9	26	36.3	9	12.5	44	61.1	6	8.3	13	18.1	10	13.9
Colorado	71	20	28.2	13	18.3	17	23.9	59	83.1	40	56.3	14	19.7	52	73.2	5	7	10	14.1	8	11.3
Idaho	26	2	7.7	7	26.9	10	38.5	17	76.9	18	69.2	6	23.1	20	76.9	1	3.8	7	26.9	0	0
Montana	51	7	13.7	15	29.4	16	31.4	42	82.4	30	58.8	7	13.7	20	39.2	7	13.7	8	15.7	1	2
Nevada	23	6	26.1	2	8.7	2	8.7	8	34.8	8	34.8	2	8.7	11	47.8	0	0	0	0	2	8.7
New Mexico	31	4	12.9	8	25.8	5	16.1	24	77.4	16	51.6	6	19.4	20	64.5	2	6.5	2	6.5	0	0
Utah	38	3	7.9	5	13.2	7	18.4	26	68.4	9	23.7	4	10.5	30	78.9	1		6	15.8	5	16.1
Wyoming	25	3	12	7	28	7	28	13	52	13	52	1	4	13	52	1	4			2	8
CENSUS DIVISION 9, PACIFIC	397	110	27.7	95	23.9	110	27.7	313	78.8	201	50.6	69	17.4	288	72.5	14	3.5	44	11.1	75	18.9
Alaska	8	0	0	4	50	4	50	3	37.5	3	37.5	0	0	4	50	0	0	0	0	0	0
California	242	74	30.6	62	25.6	76	31.4	190	78.5	125	51.7	54	22.3	182	75.2	10	4.1	31	12.8	44	18.2
Hawaii	13	6	46.2	3	23.1	4	30.8	11	84.6	5	38.5	1	7.7	10	76.9	1	7.7			2	15.4
Oregon	61	12	19.7	14	23	16	26.2	52	85.2	30	49.2	7	11.5	42	68.9	1	1.6	6	9.8	6	9.8
Washington	73	18	24.7	12	16.4	12	16.4	57	78.1	38	52.1	7	9.6	50	68.5	2	2.7	7	9.6	23	31.5

Note: These data represent hospital performance in the years 2015 – 2019 and do not reflect any impacts from the COVID-19 pandemic in 2020 and thereafter.

Table 7 (Continued)

These data include only hospital-based facilities and services as reported by responding hospitals in Section C of the 2019 AHA Annual Survey, beginning on page 215. Census divisions represent all U.S. hospitals. Community hospitals are listed separately under United States. No estimates have been made for nonresponding hospitals. Definitions of facilities and services are listed in the Glossary, page 203.

CLASSIFICATION	HOSPITALS REPORTING	NEUROLOGICAL SERVICES Number	Percent	NUTRITION PROGRAMS CENTER Number	Percent	OBSTETRICS INPATIENT CARE UNITS Number	Percent	OCCUPATIONAL HEALTH SERVICES Number	Percent	ONCOLOGY SERVICES Number	Percent	ORTHOPEDIC SERVICES Number	Percent	OTHER SPECIAL CARE UNITS Number	Percent	OUTPATIENT SURGERY Number	Percent	PAIN MANAGEMENT PROGRAM Number	Percent	PALLIATIVE CARE PROGRAM Number	Percent
UNITED STATES	4,167	2,098	50.3	3,115	74.8	2,218	53.2	2,743	65.8	2,150	51.6	2,902	69.6	761	18.3	3,316	79.6	2,244	53.9	1,694	40.7
COMMUNITY HOSPITALS	3,782	2,032	53.7	2,949	78	2,211	58.5	2,642	69.9	2,115	55.9	2,851	75.4	742	19.6	3,274	86.6	2,179	57.6	1,641	43.4
CENSUS DIVISION 1, NEW ENGLAND	156	107	68.6	146	99.6	102	65.4	124	79.5	105	67.3	131	84	28	17.9	190	83.3	114	73.1	92	59
Connecticut	26	24	92.3	26	93.6	21	80.8	19	73.1	22	84.6	24	92.3	9	34.6	23	88.5	23	88.5	24	92.3
Maine	30	13	43.3	28	93.3	23	76.7	23	76.7	21	70	24	80	7	23.3	26	86.7	19	63.3	16	53.3
Massachusetts	57	42	73.7	53	93	33	57.9	50	87.7	35	61.4	47	82.5	6	10.5	46	90.7	47	82.5	26	45.6
New Hampshire	25	17	68	24	96	15	60	21	84	16	64	23	92	5	20	21	84	14	56	16	64
Rhode Island	7	5	71.4	6	85.7	3	42.9	6	85.7	6	85.7	6	85.7	1	14.3	6	85.7	4	57.1	3	42.9
Vermont	11	6	54.5	6	81.8	7	63.6	6	54.5	5	45.5	7	63.6	0	0	8	72.7	7	63.6	7	63.6
CENSUS DIVISION 2, MIDDLE ATLANTIC	362	272	75.1	316	87.3	215	59.4	288	79.6	257	71	302	83.4	74	20.4	311	85.9	248	68.5	227	62.7
New Jersey	70	55	78.6	60	85.7	43	61.4	49	70	54	77.1	56	77.1	7	10	56	80	51	72.9	46	65.7
New York	135	107	79.3	121	89.6	92	68.1	118	87.4	99	73.3	117	86.7	30	22.2	121	89.6	93	68.9	98	72.6
Pennsylvania	157	110	70.1	135	86	80	51	121	77.1	104	66.2	129	82.2	37	23.6	134	85.4	104	66.2	83	52.9
CENSUS DIVISION 3, SOUTH ATLANTIC	574	363	63.2	458	79.8	313	54.5	434	75.6	336	58.5	444	77.4	142	24.7	463	80.7	319	55.6	274	47.7
Delaware	8	6	75	5	62.5	4	50	5	62.5	5	62.5	6	75	2	25	6	62.5	6	50	5	62.5
District of Columbia	10	8	80	9	90	5	50	8	80	7	70	8	80	4	40	6	60	7	70	6	60
Florida	165	127	77	134	81.2	80	48.5	121	73.3	102	61.8	135	81.8	57	34.5	136	82.4	97	58.8	82	49.7
Georgia	96	96	53.1	69	71.9	48	50	70	72.9	39	51	66	68.8	15	15.6	74	77.1	50	52.1	41	42.7
Maryland	45	38	84.4	42	93.3	31	68.9	43	95.6	47	86.7	40	88.9	10	22.2	40	88.9	38	84.4	39	86.7
North Carolina	74	46	62.2	61	82.4	53	71.6	61	82.4	30	63.5	61	76.5	22	20.3	66	89.2	46	62.2	31	41.9
South Carolina	68	31	45.6	49	72.1	37	54.4	44	64.7	39	44.1	52	79.4	14	32.4	49	72.1	21	30.9	21	30.9
Virginia	63	39	61.9	56	88.9	35	55.6	57	90.5	39	61.9	50	79.4	14	22.2	52	82.5	37	58.7	37	58.7
West Virginia	45	17	37.8	33	73.3	20	44.4	25	55.6	18	40	26	57.8	3	6.7	35	77.8	19	42.2	12	26.7
CENSUS DIVISION 4, EAST NORTH CENTRAL	672	347	51.6	539	80.2	400	60	464	69	424	63.1	513	76.3	187	27.8	585	87.1	443	65.9	285	42.4
Illinois	155	92	59.4	118	76.1	91	58.7	100	64.5	100	64.5	123	79.4	11	7.1	141	91	107	69	75	48.4
Indiana	117	49	41.9	87	74.4	71	60.7	79	67.5	62	53	85	72.6	15	12.8	94	80.3	83	49.6	37	31.6
Michigan	127	74	58.3	112	88.2	74	58.3	106	83.5	90	70.9	108	85	28	22	113	89	83	65.4	58	45.7
Ohio	127	83	65.4	107	84.3	76	59.8	100	78.7	90	70.9	114	89.8	23	18.1	112	88.2	98	77.2	65	51.2
Wisconsin	146	49	33.6	115	78.8	91	62.3	79	54.1	82	56.2	83	56.8	110	75.3	125	85.6	97	66.4	50	34.2
CENSUS DIVISION 5, EAST SOUTH CENTRAL	269	114	42.4	154	57.2	119	44.2	133	49.4	94	34.9	144	53.5	46	17.1	193	71.7	117	43.5	74	27.5
Alabama	47	27	57.4	32	68.1	26	55.3	30	63.8	19	40.4	36	76.6	9	19.1	40	85.1	26	55.3	19	40.4
Kentucky	53	28	52.8	38	71.7	23	43.4	31	58.5	26	49.1	34	64.2	7	13.2	42	79.2	31	58.5	19	35.8
Mississippi	102	27	26.5	30	29.4	37	36.3	30	29.4	17	16.7	29	28.4	13	12.7	60	58.8	28	27.5	14	13.7
Tennessee	67	32	47.8	41	80.6	33	49.3	42	62.7	32	47.8	45	67.2	17	25.4	51	76.1	32	47.8	22	32.8
CENSUS DIVISION 6, WEST NORTH CENTRAL	562	204	36.3	421	74.9	280	49.8	385	68.5	269	47.9	269	62.1	67	11.9	489	87	303	53.9	193	34.3
Iowa	122	32	26.2	108	88.5	60	49.2	90	73.8	66	66	81	66.4	7	5.7	115	94.3	74	60.7	36	29.5
Kansas	125	30	24	70	56	52	41.6	71	56.8	31	24.8	57	45.6	9	7.2	101	80.8	59	47.2	28	22.4
Minnesota	86	35	40.7	67	77.9	60	69.8	69	80.2	51	59.3	62	72.1	13	15.1	84	97.7	50	58.1	35	40.7
Missouri	137	75	54.7	108	78.8	60	43.8	94	68.6	75	54.7	93	67.9	30	21.9	104	75.9	69	50.4	56	40.9
Nebraska	40	20	50	31	77.5	26	65	28	70	29	72.5	31	77.5	6	15	40	100	27	67.5	20	50
North Dakota	16	6	37.5	13	81.3	8	50	11	68.8	7	43.8	8	50	0	0	16	100	10	62.5	9	56.3
South Dakota	36	6	16.7	24	66.7	14	38.9	22	61.1	10	27.8	12	33.3	2	5.6	29	80.6	14	38.9	9	25
CENSUS DIVISION 7, WEST SOUTH CENTRAL	838	309	36.9	510	60.9	317	37.8	410	48.9	252	30.1	458	54.7	95	11.3	530	63.2	306	36.5	180	21.5
Arkansas	89	26	29.2	45	50.6	34	38.2	40	44.9	28	31.5	46	51.7	6	10.1	62	69.7	29	28.1	14	15.7
Louisiana	89	33	37.1	55	61.8	35	39.3	42	47.2	38	42.7	48	53.9	6	6.7	60	67.4	33	37.1	25	28.1
Oklahoma	106	33	31.1	57	63.7	41	38.7	48	45.3	22	20.8	57	53.8	13	12.3	70	66	39	36.8	19	17.9
Texas	554	217	39.2	363	63.7	207	37.4	280	50.5	164	29.6	307	55.4	67	12.1	338	61	209	37.7	122	22
CENSUS DIVISION 8, MOUNTAIN	337	140	41.5	247	73.3	198	58.8	225	66.8	157	46.6	233	69.1	41	12.2	264	73.3	158	46.9	131	38.9
Arizona	71	35	48.6	57	79.2	33	45.8	55	69.4	35	48.6	58	81.7	11	15.3	64	75	29	44.4	29	40.3
Colorado	71	43	60.6	55	77.5	49	69	55	77.5	45	63.4	58	81.7	12	16.9	64	90.1	38	53.5	38	53.5
Idaho	26	9	34.6	20	76.9	16	61.5	20	76.9	12	46.2	18	69.2	1	3.8	23	88.5	13	50	13	30.8
Montana	51	10	19.6	32	62.7	25	49	29	56.9	19	37.3	26	51	2	3.9	33	64.7	24	47.1	24	47.1
Nevada	23	12	43.5	13	56.5	8	34.8	8	34.8	7	30.4	13	64.5	5	21.7	12	52.2	7	30.4	6	26.1
New Mexico	31	13	38.7	19	61.3	20	64.5	16	51.6	13	41.9	30	64.5	4	12.9	25	80.6	12	50	6	19.4
Utah	38	13	34.2	18	86.8	30	78.9	6	84.2	16	42.1	17	72	6	15.8	33	86.8	19	86.8	14	36.8
Wyoming	25	8	32	18	72	17	68	15	60	10	40	18	72			20	80	13	52	6	24
CENSUS DIVISION 9, PACIFIC	397	242	61	324	81.6	271	68.3	280	70.5	256	64.5	333	83.9	81	20.4	351	88.4	238	59.4	238	59.9
Alaska	8	2	25	8	100	6	75	7	87.5	2	25	5	62.5	0	0	6	75	4	50	3	37.5
California	242	166	68.6	188	77.7	160	66.1	168	69.4	161	66.5	206	85.1	46	19	212	87.6	150	62	158	65.3
Hawaii	13	9	69.2	11	84.6	7	53.8	10	76.9	10	76.9	11	84.6	5	38.5	10	76.9	6	46.2	6	69.2
Oregon	61	25	41	53	86.9	48	78.7	42	68.9	38	62.3	52	85.2	5	11.5	58	95.1	32	52.5	27	44.3
Washington	73	40	54.8	64	87.7	50	68.5	53	72.6	45	61.6	59	80.8	23	31.5	65	89	44	60.3	41	56.2

Note: These data represent hospital performance in the years 2015 – 2019 and do not reflect any impacts from the COVID-19 pandemic in 2020 and thereafter.

Table 7 (Continued)

These data include only hospital-based facilities and services as reported by responding hospitals in Section C of the 2019 AHA Annual Survey, beginning on page 215. Census divisions represent all U.S. hospitals. Community hospitals are listed separately under United States. No estimates have been made for nonresponding hospitals. Definitions of facilities and services are listed in the Glossary, page 203.

CLASSIFICATION	HOSPITALS REPORTING	PALLIATIVE CARE INPATIENT UNIT		PATIENT CONTROLLED ANALGESIA (PCA)		PATIENT EDUCATION CENTER		PATIENT REPRESENTATIVE SERVICES		PHYSICAL REHABILITATION INPATIENT CARE UNITS		PRIMARY CARE DEPARTMENT		PSYCHIATRIC INPATIENT CARE UNITS		PSYCHIATRIC INTENSIVE OUTPATIENT SERVICES		ROBOTIC SURGERY	
		Number	Percent	Number	Percent	Number	Percent	Number	Percent	Number	Percent	Number	Percent	Number	Percent	Number	Percent	Number	Percent
UNITED STATES	4,167	417	10	2,925	70.2	2,264	54.3	2,986	71.7	1,205	28.9	1,855	44.5	1,390	33.4	638	15.3	1,524	36.6
COMMUNITY HOSPITALS	3,782	380	10	2,874	76	2,145	56.7	2,823	74.6	1,176	31.1	1,784	47.2	1,068	28.2	463	12.2	1,504	39.8
CENSUS DIVISION 1, NEW ENGLAND	156	25	16	127	81.4	100	64.1	134	85.9	37	23.7	101	64.7	82	52.6	40	25.6	62	39.7
Connecticut	26	5	19.2	24	92.3	22	84.6	26	100	7	26.9	20	76.9	22	84.6	17	65.4	21	80.8
Maine	30	5	16.7	24	80	13	43.3	24	80	9	30	26	86.7	9	30	5	16.7	3	10
Massachusetts	57	7	12.3	45	78.9	41	71.9	49	86	9	15.8	26	45.6	32	56.1	12	21.1	24	42.1
New Hampshire	25	6	24	21	84	16	64	21	84	7	28	18	72	9	36	3	12	9	36
Rhode Island	7	0	0	6	85.7	5	71.4	6	85.7	3	42.9	4	57.1	5	71.4	1	14.3	4	57.1
Vermont	11	2	18.2	7	63.6	3	27.3	8	72.7	2	18.2	7	63.6	5	45.5	2	18.2	1	9.1
CENSUS DIVISION 2, MIDDLE ATLANTIC	362	46	12.7	295	81.5	240	66.3	308	85.1	131	36.2	217	59.9	194	53.6	76	21	188	51.9
New Jersey	70	9	12.9	53	75.7	50	71.4	60	85.7	15	21.4	44	62.9	39	55.7	27	38.6	43	61.4
New York	135	26	19.3	115	85.2	83	61.5	125	92.6	49	36.3	106	78.5	82	60.7	32	23.7	71	52.6
Pennsylvania	157	11	7	127	80.9	107	68.2	123	78.3	67	42.7	67	42.7	73	46.5	17	10.8	74	47.1
CENSUS DIVISION 3, SOUTH ATLANTIC	574	55	9.6	439	76.5	350	61	444	77.4	182	31.7	217	37.8	220	38.3	84	14.6	258	44.9
Delaware	8	0	0	5	62.5	3	37.5	5	62.5	4	50	3	37.5	3	37.5	0	0	4	50
District of Columbia	10	1	10	6	60	9	90	7	70	3	30	5	50	7	70	1	10	5	50
Florida	165	16	9.7	129	78.2	93	56.4	129	78.2	50	30.3	47	28.5	55	33.3	20	12.1	99	60
Georgia	96	9	9.4	70	72.9	59	61.5	71	74	22	22.9	28	29.2	27	28.1	11	11.5	38	39.6
Maryland	45	10	22.2	40	88.9	34	75.6	43	95.6	8	17.8	27	60	32	71.1	21	46.7	26	57.8
North Carolina	74	5	6.8	63	85.1	49	66.2	60	81.1	19	25.7	31	41.9	33	44.6	9	12.2	31	41.9
South Carolina	68	3	4.4	48	70.6	37	54.4	45	66.2	45	66.2	20	29.4	24	35.3	6	8.8	20	29.4
Virginia	63	8	12.7	51	81	42	66.7	54	85.7	22	34.9	29	46	25	39.7	13	20.6	23	36.5
West Virginia	45	3	6.7	27	60	24	53.3	30	66.7	9	20	27	60	14	31.1	3	6.7	12	26.7
CENSUS DIVISION 4, EAST NORTH CENTRAL	672	73	10.9	500	74.4	453	67.4	534	79.5	223	33.2	352	52.4	245	36.5	111	16.5	262	39
Illinois	155	13	8.4	122	78.7	98	63.2	129	83.2	41	26.5	90	58.1	64	41.3	36	23.2	65	41.9
Indiana	117	14	12	87	74.4	59	50.4	80	68.4	38	32.5	45	38.5	41	35	20	17.1	35	29.9
Michigan	127	16	12.6	100	78.7	84	66.1	110	86.6	43	33.9	92	72.4	49	38.6	13	10.2	62	48.8
Ohio	127	17	13.4	109	85.8	82	64.6	105	82.7	36	28.3	67	52.8	50	39.4	27	21.3	57	44.9
Wisconsin	146	13	8.9	82	56.2	130	89	110	75.3	65	44.5	58	39.7	41	28.1	15	10.3	43	29.5
CENSUS DIVISION 5, EAST SOUTH CENTRAL	289	22	8.2	156	58	130	48.3	179	66.5	70	26	81	30.1	95	35.3	39	14.5	83	30.9
Alabama	47	9	19.1	34	72.3	30	63.8	36	76.6	13	27.7	14	29.8	18	38.3	4	8.5	21	44.7
Kentucky	53	6	11.3	38	71.7	33	62.3	40	75.5	8	15.1	24	43.4	16	30.2	6	11.3	18	34
Mississippi	102	4	3.9	36	35.3	35	34.3	57	55.9	37	36.3	23	23.5	40	39.2	20	19.6	22	21.6
Tennessee	67	3	4.5	48	71.6	32	47.8	46	68.7	12	17.9	20	29.9	21	31.3	9	13.4	22	32.8
CENSUS DIVISION 6, WEST NORTH CENTRAL	562	58	10.3	398	70.8	293	52.1	366	65.1	171	30.4	311	55.3	150	26.7	53	9.4	134	23.8
Iowa	122	7	5.7	97	79.5	61	50	72	59	25	20.5	75	61.5	31	25.4	14	11.5	30	24.6
Kansas	125	13	10.4	71	56.8	55	44	74	59.2	22	17.6	55	44	16	12.8	6	4.8	24	19.2
Minnesota	86	11	12.8	69	80.2	53	61.6	66	76.7	14	16.3	60	69.8	27	31.4	12	14	24	27.9
Missouri	137	13	9.5	102	74.5	83	60.6	98	71.5	88	64.2	57	41.6	60	43.8	14	10.2	35	25.5
Nebraska	40	3	7.5	30	75	19	47.5	28	70	8	20	27	67.5	9	22.5	3	7.5	11	27.5
North Dakota	16	5	31.3	9	56.3	8	50	13	81.3	4	25	13	81.3	5	31.3	2	12.5	6	37.5
South Dakota	36	6	16.7	20	55.6	14	38.9	15	41.7	10	27.8	24	66.7	2	5.6	2	5.6	4	11.1
CENSUS DIVISION 7, WEST SOUTH CENTRAL	838	46	5.5	472	56.3	326	38.9	483	57.6	215	25.7	218	26	217	25.9	132	15.8	235	28
Arkansas	89	5	5.6	52	58.4	31	34.8	54	60.7	25	28.1	27	30.3	33	37.1	14	15.7	15	16.9
Louisiana	89	9	10.1	50	56.2	43	48.3	51	57.3	33	37.1	34	38.2	41	46.1	27	30.3	29	32.6
Oklahoma	106	8	7.5	58	54.7	33	31.1	62	58.5	23	21.7	30	28.3	29	27.4	8	7.5	23	21.7
Texas	554	24	4.3	312	56.3	219	39.5	316	57	134	24.2	127	22.9	114	20.6	83	15	168	30.3
CENSUS DIVISION 8, MOUNTAIN	337	36	10.7	223	66.2	146	43.3	235	69.7	83	24.6	181	53.7	76	22.6	42	12.5	118	35
Arizona	72	9	12.5	43	59.7	31	43.1	49	68.1	21	29.2	24	33.3	21	29.2	12	16.7	33	45.8
Colorado	71	7	9.9	55	77.5	33	46.5	60	84.5	23	32.4	46	64.8	12	16.9	11	15.5	32	45.1
Idaho	26	3	11.5	21	80.8	12	46.2	21	80.8	7	26.9	20	76.9	6	23.1	0	0	11	42.3
Montana	51	9	17.6	25	49	20	39.2	32	62.7	10	19.6	39	76.5	6	11.8	3	5.9	12	23.5
Nevada	23	1	4.3	13	56.5	8	34.8	11	47.8	2	8.7	4	17.4	8	34.8	6	26.1	6	26.1
New Mexico	31	3	9.7	19	61.3	9	29	17	54.8	8	25.8	15	48.4	7	22.6	2	6.5	6	19.4
Utah	38	2	5.3	30	78.9	26	68.4	33	86.8	8	21.1	16	42.1	12	31.6	3	7.9	11	28.9
Wyoming	25	2	8	17	68	7	28	12	48	4	16	17	68	4	16	5	20	7	28
CENSUS DIVISION 9, PACIFIC	397	56	14.1	315	79.3	226	56.9	303	76.3	93	23.4	177	44.6	111	28	61	15.4	184	46.3
Alaska	8	1	12.5	4	50	5	62.5	4	50	1	12.5	3	37.5	3	37.5	2	25	2	25
California	242	35	14.5	187	77.3	137	56.6	181	74.8	63	26	85	35.1	66	27.3	42	17.4	119	49.2
Hawaii	13	1	7.7	10	76.9	9	69.2	10	76.9	1	7.7	6	46.2	4	30.8	2	15.4	6	46.2
Oregon	61	6	9.8	55	90.2	32	52.5	49	80.3	14	23	45	73.8	15	24.6	7	11.5	22	36.1
Washington	73	13	17.8	59	80.8	43	58.9	59	80.8	14	19.2	38	52.1	23	31.5	8	11	35	47.9

Note: These data represent hospital performance in the years 2015 – 2019 and do not reflect any impacts from the COVID-19 pandemic in 2020 and thereafter.

Table 7 (Continued)

These data include only hospital-based facilities and services as reported by responding hospitals in Section C of the 2019 AHA Annual Survey; beginning on page 215. Census divisions represent all U.S. hospitals. Community hospitals are listed separately under United States. No estimates have been made for nonresponding hospitals. Definitions of facilities and services are listed in the Glossary, page 203.

CLASSIFICATION	HOSPITALS REPORTING	RURAL HEALTH CLINIC		SLEEP CENTER		SOCIAL WORK SERVICES		SPORTS MEDICINE		SUPPORT GROUPS		SWING BED SERVICES		TEEN OUTREACH SERVICES		TELEHEALTH		TOBACCO TREATMENT/CESSATION PROGRAM		TRANSPORTATION TO HEALTH FACILITIES	
		Number	Percent	Number	Percent	Number	Percent	Number	Percent	Number	Percent	Number	Percent	Number	Percent	Number	Percent	Number	Percent	Number	Percent
UNITED STATES	4,167	1027	24.6	1,878	45.1	3,544	85	1,869	44.9	2,643	63.4	1,204	28.9	531	12.7	2,554	61.3	2,202	52.8	902	21.6
COMMUNITY HOSPITALS	3,782	994	26.3	1,841	48.7	3,267	86.4	1,851	48.9	2,484	65.7	1,183	31.3	503	13.3	2,362	62.5	2,039	53.9	793	21
CENSUS DIVISION 1, NEW ENGLAND	156	25	16	80	51.3	149	95.5	98	62.8	133	85.3	44	28.2	41	26.3	104	66.7	107	68.6	45	28.8
Connecticut	26	0	0	19	73.1	26	100	21	80.8	26	100	—	—	10	38.5	23	88.5	21	80.8	6	23.1
Maine	30	13	43.3	13	43.3	29	96.7	16	53.3	25	83.3	15	50	6	20	16	53.3	21	70	8	26.7
Massachusetts	57	3	5.3	28	49.1	56	98.2	35	61.4	49	86	6	10.5	19	33.3	35	61.4	33	57.9	20	35.1
New Hampshire	25	7	28	12	48	24	96	17	68	20	80	15	60	5	20	18	72	16	64	6	24
Rhode Island	7	0	0	4	57.1	7	100	4	57.1	6	85.7	1	14.3	1	14.3	4	57.1	5	71.4	1	14.3
Vermont	11	2	18.2	4	36.4	7	63.6	5	45.5	7	63.6	6	54.5	0	0	8	72.7	11	100	4	36.4
CENSUS DIVISION 2, MIDDLE ATLANTIC	362	31	8.6	208	57.5	347	95.9	198	54.7	302	83.4	47	13	98	27.1	257	71	245	67.7	113	31.2
New Jersey	70	0	0	41	58.6	67	95.7	38	54.3	62	88.6	4	5.7	29	41.4	51	72.9	45	64.3	39	55.7
New York	135	20	14.8	73	54.1	128	94.8	79	58.5	113	83.7	19	14.1	36	26.7	94	69.6	96	71.1	39	28.9
Pennsylvania	157	11	7	94	59.9	152	96.8	81	51.6	127	80.9	24	15.3	33	21	112	71.3	104	66.2	35	22.3
CENSUS DIVISION 3, SOUTH ATLANTIC	574	83	14.5	269	46.9	483	84.1	263	45.8	405	70.6	88	15.3	79	13.8	335	58.4	347	60.5	126	22
Delaware	8	1	12.5	4	50	6	75	3	37.5	4	50	0	0	3	37.5	5	62.5	5	62.5	2	25
District of Columbia	10	0	0	6	60	9	90	5	50	8	80	0	0	6	60	5	50	5	50	1	10
Florida	165	17	10.3	60	36.4	131	79.4	77	46.7	115	69.7	15	9.1	18	10.9	97	58.8	93	56.4	19	11.5
Georgia	96	15	15.6	48	50	75	78.1	42	43.8	62	64.6	23	24	10	10.4	50	52.1	63	65.6	19	19.8
Maryland	45	2	4.4	24	54.1	44	97.8	23	51.1	42	93.3	0	0	19	42.2	36	80	36	80	19	42.2
North Carolina	74	14	18.9	38	51.1	67	90.5	40	54.1	57	77	10	13.5	6	8.1	56	75.7	46	62.2	21	28.4
South Carolina	68	13	19.1	26	38.2	55	80.9	22	32.4	40	58.8	8	11.8	7	10.3	18	26.5	27	39.7	14	20.6
Virginia	63	7	11.1	39	61.9	57	90.5	35	55.6	49	77.8	12	19	8	12.7	45	71.4	45	71.4	14	22.2
West Virginia	45	14	31.1	23	51.1	39	86.7	16	35.6	28	62.2	20	44.4	2	4.4	23	51.1	29	64.4	17	37.8
CENSUS DIVISION 4, EAST NORTH CENTRAL	672	148	22	396	58.9	610	90.8	399	59.4	491	73.1	171	25.4	98	14.6	481	71.6	419	62.4	162	24.1
Illinois	155	41	26.5	102	65.8	144	92.9	92	59.4	126	81.3	46	29.7	23	14.8	120	77.4	89	57.4	51	32.9
Indiana	117	21	17.9	71	60.7	90	76.9	51	43.6	82	70.1	32	27.4	14	12	76	65	77	65.8	21	17.9
Michigan	127	50	39.4	86	67.7	121	95.3	82	64.6	108	85	27	21.3	25	19.7	102	80.3	89	70.1	33	26
Ohio	127	15	11.8	75	59.1	117	92.1	94	74	102	80.3	28	22	23	18.1	93	73.2	98	77.2	38	29.9
Wisconsin	146	21	14.4	62	42.5	138	94.5	80	54.8	73	50	38	26	13	8.9	90	61.6	66	45.2	19	13
CENSUS DIVISION 5, EAST SOUTH CENTRAL	269	91	33.8	119	44.2	225	83.6	80	29.7	136	50.6	103	38.3	25	9.3	148	55	124	46.1	46	17.1
Alabama	47	12	25.5	28	59.6	42	89.4	21	44.7	29	61.7	14	29.8	4	8.5	28	59.6	27	57.4	10	21.3
Kentucky	53	21	39.6	30	56.6	45	84.9	17	32.1	34	64.2	19	35.8	7	13.2	33	62.3	31	58.5	6	11.3
Mississippi	102	49	48	26	25.5	83	81.4	18	17.6	32	31.4	52	51	8	7.8	39	38.2	22	21.6	17	16.7
Tennessee	67	9	13.4	35	52.2	55	82.1	24	35.8	41	61.2	18	26.9	6	9	48	71.6	44	65.7	13	19.4
CENSUS DIVISION 6, WEST NORTH CENTRAL	562	264	47	274	48.8	470	83.6	287	51.1	346	61.6	331	58.9	49	8.7	351	62.5	276	49.1	123	21.9
Iowa	122	66	54.1	68	55.7	103	84.4	70	57.4	92	75.4	88	72.1	12	9.8	69	56.6	71	58.2	21	17.2
Kansas	125	70	56	37	29.6	98	78.4	52	41.6	48	38.4	87	69.6	3	2.4	66	52.8	42	33.6	27	21.6
Minnesota	86	29	33.7	42	48.8	78	90.7	46	53.5	67	77.9	44	51.2	11	12.8	66	76.7	52	60.5	10	11.6
Missouri	137	54	39.4	79	57.7	119	86.9	67	48.9	81	59.1	48	35	13	9.5	78	56.9	69	50.4	44	32.1
Nebraska	40	21	52.5	27	67.5	37	92.5	27	67.5	27	67.5	24	60	4	10	33	82.5	23	57.5	13	32.5
North Dakota	16	6	37.5	7	43.8	12	75	10	62.5	12	75	10	62.5	1	6.3	11	68.8	7	43.8	5	31.3
South Dakota	36	18	50	14	38.9	23	63.9	15	41.7	19	52.8	30	83.3	5	13.9	28	77.8	12	33.3	3	8.3
CENSUS DIVISION 7, WEST SOUTH CENTRAL	838	208	24.8	258	30.8	621	74.1	225	26.8	365	43.6	219	26.1	49	5.8	393	46.9	295	35.2	121	14.4
Arkansas	89	25	28.1	44	49.4	65	73	21	23.6	38	42.7	35	39.3	7	7.9	55	61.8	41	46.1	18	20.2
Louisiana	89	25	28.1	28	31.5	72	80.9	29	32.6	46	51.7	21	23.6	12	13.5	58	65.2	41	46.1	20	22.5
Oklahoma	106	37	34.9	45	42.5	72	67.9	37	34.9	37	34.9	46	43.4	4	3.8	62	58.5	44	41.5	18	17
Texas	554	121	21.8	141	25.5	412	74.4	138	24.9	244	44	117	21.1	26	4.7	218	39.4	169	30.5	65	11.7
CENSUS DIVISION 8, MOUNTAIN	337	101	30	143	42.4	271	80.4	151	44.8	187	55.5	130	38.6	32	9.5	225	66.8	173	51.3	67	19.9
Arizona	72	12	16.7	21	29.2	57	79.2	27	37.5	45	62.5	15	20.8	9	12.5	41	56.9	38	52.8	10	13.9
Colorado	71	19	26.8	43	60.6	59	83.1	40	56.3	48	67.6	26	36.6	6	8.5	48	67.6	42	59.2	14	19.7
Idaho	26	16	61.5	14	53.8	22	84.6	14	53.8	13	50	14	53.8	7	26.9	20	76.9	15	57.7	9	34.6
Montana	51	30	58.8	18	35.3	37	72.5	21	41.2	22	43.1	39	76.5	4	7.8	41	80.4	27	52.9	15	29.4
Nevada	23	3	13	3	13	16	69.6	6	26.1	11	47.8	2	8.7	1	4.3	12	52.2	8	34.8	3	13
New Mexico	31	5	16.1	12	38.7	26	83.9	7	22.6	13	41.9	10	32.3	1	3.2	14	45.2	14	45.2	5	16.1
Utah	38	6	15.8	20	52.6	36	94.7	24	63.2	25	65.8	10	26.3	3	7.9	34	89.5	16	42.1	4	10.5
Wyoming	25	10	40	12	48	18	72	12	48	10	40	14	56	1	4	15	60	13	52	7	28
CENSUS DIVISION 9, PACIFIC	397	76	19.1	131	33	368	92.7	168	42.3	278	70	71	17.9	60	15.1	260	65.5	216	54.4	99	24.9
Alaska	8	0	0	5	62.5	7	87.5	2	25	3	37.5	3	37.5	1	12.5	6	75	3	37.5	0	0
California	242	30	12.4	55	22.7	226	93.4	88	36.4	153	63.2	19	7.9	37	15.3	157	64.9	116	47.9	65	26.9
Hawaii	13	2	15.4	6	46.2	12	92.3	8	61.5	10	76.9	3	23.1	3	23.1	8	61.5	10	76.9	4	30.8
Oregon	61	24	39.3	28	45.9	55	90.2	30	49.2	51	83.6	29	47.5	11	18	39	63.9	46	75.4	18	29.5
Washington	73	20	27.4	37	50.7	68	93.2	40	54.8	61	83.6	17	23.3	8	11	50	68.5	41	56.2	12	16.4

Note: These data represent hospital performance in the years 2015 – 2019 and do not reflect any impacts from the COVID-19 pandemic in 2020 and thereafter.

Table 7 (Continued)

These data include only hospital-based facilities and services as reported by responding hospitals in Section C of the 2019 AHA Annual Survey, beginning on page 215. Census divisions represent all U.S. hospitals. Community hospitals are listed separately under United States. No estimates have been made for nonresponding hospitals. Definitions of facilities and services are listed in the Glossary, page 203.

CLASSIFICATION	HOSPITALS REPORTING	URGENT CARE CENTER Number	URGENT CARE CENTER Percent	VIOLENCE PREVENTION PROGRAM-COMMUNITY Number	VIOLENCE PREVENTION PROGRAM-COMMUNITY Percent	VIOLENCE PREVENTION PROGRAM-WORKPLACE Number	VIOLENCE PREVENTION PROGRAM-WORKPLACE Percent	VIRTUAL COLONOSCOPY Number	VIRTUAL COLONOSCOPY Percent	VOLUNTEER SERVICES DEPARTMENT Number	VOLUNTEER SERVICES DEPARTMENT Percent	WOMEN'S HEALTH SERVICES Number	WOMEN'S HEALTH SERVICES Percent	WOUND MANAGEMENT SERVICES Number	WOUND MANAGEMENT SERVICES Percent
UNITED STATES	4,167	1,000	24	500	12	2,418	58	718	17.2	3,079	73.9	2,164	51.9	2,899	69.6
COMMUNITY HOSPITALS	3,782	968	25.6	474	12.5	2,261	59.8	704	18.6	2,946	77.9	2,106	55.7	2,812	74.4
CENSUS DIVISION 1, NEW ENGLAND	156	57	36.5	29	18.6	116	74.4	45	28.8	142	91	114	73.1	121	77.6
Connecticut	26	11	42.3	5	19.2	25	96.2	13	50	25	96.2	20	76.9	24	92.3
Maine	30	11	36.7	5	16.7	17	56.7	5	16.7	26	86.7	21	70	25	83.3
Massachusetts	57	23	40.4	17	29.8	41	71.9	19	33.3	52	91.2	39	68.4	39	68.4
New Hampshire	25	8	32	4	16	19	76	5	20	23	92	23	92	21	84
Rhode Island	7	0	0	0	0	5	71.4	2	28.6	6	85.7	4	57.1	4	57.1
Vermont	11	4	36.4	0	0	9	81.8	1	9.1	10	90.9	7	63.6	8	72.7
CENSUS DIVISION 2, MIDDLE ATLANTIC	362	95	26.2	83	22.9	266	73.5	98	27.1	325	89.8	248	68.5	275	76
New Jersey	70	20	28.6	21	30	59	84.3	19	27.1	56	80	47	67.1	54	77.1
New York	135	46	34.1	37	27.4	106	78.5	38	28.1	130	96.3	108	80	104	77
Pennsylvania	157	29	18.5	25	15.9	101	64.3	41	26.1	139	88.5	93	59.2	117	74.5
CENSUS DIVISION 3, SOUTH ATLANTIC	574	112	19.5	72	12.5	347	60.5	124	21.6	471	82.1	346	60.3	419	73
Delaware	10	4	50	2	25	5	50	1	10	9	90	5	50	7	87.5
District of Columbia	10	0	0	3	30	5	50	1	10	9	90	5	50	9	90
Florida	165	24	14.5	23	13.9	103	62.4	38	23	131	79.4	98	59.4	123	74.5
Georgia	96	21	21.9	6	6.3	60	62.5	13	13.5	73	76	55	57.3	63	65.6
Maryland	45	10	22.2	15	33.3	38	84.4	13	28.9	43	95.6	30	66.7	37	82.2
North Carolina	74	24	32.4	11	14.9	43	58.1	23	31.1	67	90.5	50	67.6	60	81.1
South Carolina	68	6	8.8	2	2.9	31	45.6	9	13.2	51	75	35	51.5	38	55.9
Virginia	63	11	17.5	6	9.5	44	69.8	18	28.6	58	92.1	43	68.3	55	87.3
West Virginia	45	12	26.7	4	8.9	19	42.2	8	17.8	33	73.3	26	57.8	27	60
CENSUS DIVISION 4, EAST NORTH CENTRAL	672	268	39.9	108	16.1	430	64	136	20.2	540	80.4	396	58.9	463	68.9
Illinois	155	55	35.5	29	18.7	112	72.3	42	27.1	135	87.1	91	58.7	106	68.4
Indiana	117	34	29.1	14	12	53	45.3	19	16.2	85	72.6	57	48.7	78	66.7
Michigan	127	55	43.3	22	17.3	97	76.4	23	18.1	116	91.3	88	69.3	96	75.6
Ohio	127	49	38.6	16	12.6	91	71.7	25	19.7	114	89.8	88	69.3	102	80.3
Wisconsin	146	75	51.4	27	18.5	77	52.7	27	18.5	90	61.6	72	49.3	81	55.5
CENSUS DIVISION 5, EAST SOUTH CENTRAL	269	31	11.5	24	8.9	120	44.6	30	11.2	188	69.9	110	40.9	159	59.1
Alabama	47	8	17	2	4.3	28	59.6	6	12.8	39	83	30	63.8	30	63.8
Kentucky	53	8	15.1	11	20.8	27	50.9	8	15.1	43	81.1	28	52.8	34	64.2
Mississippi	102	5	4.9	3	2.9	31	30.4	9	8.8	57	55.9	25	24.5	50	49
Tennessee	67	10	14.9	8	11.9	34	50.7	7	10.4	49	73.1	32	47.8	45	67.2
CENSUS DIVISION 6, WEST NORTH CENTRAL	562	157	27.9	56	10	308	54.8	84	14.9	379	67.4	237	42.2	395	70.3
Iowa	122	31	25.4	14	11.5	57	46.7	14	11.5	97	79.5	62	50.8	91	74.6
Kansas	125	22	17.6	5	4	59	47.2	19	15.2	67	53.6	40	32	82	65.6
Minnesota	86	39	45.3	8	9.3	72	83.7	18	20.9	69	80.2	37	43	62	72.1
Missouri	137	37	27	15	10.9	80	58.4	22	16.1	92	67.2	63	46	98	71.5
Nebraska	40	9	22.5	5	12.5	17	42.5	8	20	27	67.5	16	40	26	65
North Dakota	16	6	37.5	5	31.3	10	62.5	2	12.5	12	75	8	50	11	68.8
South Dakota	36	13	36.1	4	11.1	13	36.1	1	2.8	15	41.7	11	30.6	25	69.4
CENSUS DIVISION 7, WEST SOUTH CENTRAL	838	96	11.5	49	5.8	364	43.4	85	10.1	445	53.1	298	35.6	509	60.7
Arkansas	89	13	14.6	7	7.9	40	44.9	8	9	49	55.1	32	36	55	61.8
Louisiana	89	16	18	5	5.6	40	44.9	6	6.7	48	53.9	40	44.9	54	60.7
Oklahoma	106	15	14.2	1	0.9	47	44.3	10	9.4	66	62.3	43	40.6	63	59.4
Texas	554	52	9.4	36	6.5	237	42.8	61	11	282	50.9	183	33	337	60.8
CENSUS DIVISION 8, MOUNTAIN	337	81	24	27	8	178	52.8	48	14.2	250	74.2	184	54.6	246	73
Arizona	72	13	18.1	6	8.3	37	51.4	17	23.6	54	75	37	51.4	53	73.6
Colorado	71	16	22.5	8	11.3	39	54.9	9	12.7	60	84.5	50	70.4	59	83.1
Idaho	26	7	26.9	2	7.7	12	46.2	3	11.5	19	73.1	15	57.7	19	73.1
Montana	51	16	31.4	1	2	22	43.1	9	17.6	31	60.8	23	45.1	33	64.7
Nevada	23	3	13	1	4.3	13	56.5	0	0	11	47.8	4	17.4	15	65.2
New Mexico	31	9	29	2	6.5	12	38.7	2	6.5	23	74.2	16	51.6	20	64.5
Utah	38	11	28.9	4	10.5	29	76.3	4	10.5	31	81.6	25	65.8	28	73.7
Wyoming	25	6	24	4	16	14	56	4	16	21	84	14	56	19	76
CENSUS DIVISION 9, PACIFIC	397	103	25.9	52	13.1	289	72.8	68	17.1	339	85.4	231	58.2	312	78.6
Alaska	8	0	0	2	25	4	50	1	12.5	3	37.5	3	37.5	6	75
California	242	58	24	40	16.5	183	75.6	42	17.4	207	85.5	130	53.7	182	75.2
Hawaii	13	2	15.4	1	7.7	10	76.9	4	30.8	11	84.6	8	61.5	12	92.3
Oregon	61	21	34.4	1	1.6	41	67.2	13	21.3	55	90.2	44	72.1	55	90.2
Washington	73	22	30.1	8	11	51	69.9	8	11	63	86.3	46	63	57	78.1

Note: These data represent hospital performance in the years 2015 – 2019 and do not reflect any impacts from the COVID-19 pandemic in 2020 and thereafter.

Table 7 (Continued)

These data include only hospital-based facilities and services as reported by responding hospitals in Section C of the 2019 AHA Annual Survey, beginning on page 215. Census divisions represent all U.S. hospitals. Community hospitals are listed separately under United States. No estimates have been made for nonresponding hospitals. Definitions of facilities and services are listed in the Glossary, page 203.

CLASSIFICATION	HOSPITALS REPORTING	GENERAL MEDICAL SURGICAL CARE UNITS				HOUSING SERVICES						INTENSIVE CARE UNITS										ACUTE LONG-TERM CARE UNITS		LONG-TERM CARE UNITS					
		ADULT UNITS		PEDIATRIC UNITS		ASSISTED LIVING		RETIREMENT HOUSING		SUPPORTIVE HOUSING SERVICES		CARDIAC UNITS		MEDICAL SURGICAL UNITS		NEONATAL UNITS		OTHER UNITS		PEDIATRIC UNITS				SKILLED NURSING CARE		INTERMEDIATE NURSING CARE		OTHER LONG-TERM CARE UNITS	
		Number	Percent	Number	Percent	Number	Percent	Number	Percent	Number	Percent	Number	Percent	Number	Percent	Number	Percent	Number	Percent	Number	Percent	Number	Percent	Number	Percent	Number	Percent	Number	Percent
UNITED STATES	4,167	3,488	83.7	1,569	37.7	132	3.2	99	2.4	93	2.2	1,016	24.4	2,520	60.5	921	22.1	438	10.5	370	8.9	208	5	744	17.9	285	6.8	139	3.3
COMMUNITY HOSPITALS	3,782	3,429	90.7	1,558	41.2	123	3.3	97	2.6	64	1.7	1,006	26.6	2,479	65.5	918	24.3	429	11.3	367	9.7	170	4.5	693	18.3	269	7.1	119	3.1
CENSUS DIVISION 1, NEW ENGLAND	156	128	82.1	67	42.9	7	4.5	6	3.8	4	2.6	34	21.8	108	69.2	30	19.2	13	8.3	14	9	8	5.1	22	14.1	19	12.2	5	3.2
Connecticut	26	22	84.6	10	38.5	1	3.8	1	3.8	1	3.8	8	30.8	21	80.8	14	53.8	5	19.2	2	7.7	1	3.8	2	7.7	2	7.7	0	0
Maine	30	27	90	14	46.7	3	10	6	10	0	0	3	10	18	60	2	6.7	2	6.7	2	6.7	2	6.7	9	30	9	30	3	10
Massachusetts	57	42	73.7	26	45.6	2	3.5	1	1.8	3	5.3	17	29.8	38	66.7	10	17.5	2	3.5	7	12.3	5	8.8	4	7	3	5.3	2	3.5
New Hampshire	25	22	88	12	48	2	8	1	4	0	0	4	16	18	72	3	12	3	12	1	4	0	0	6	24	3	12	0	0
Rhode Island	7	6	85.7	3	42.9	0	0	0	0	0	0	1	14.3	6	85.7	0	0	1	14.3	1	14.3	0	0	0	0	2	28.6	0	0
Vermont	11	9	81.8	2	18.2	0	0	0	0	0	0	0	0	7	63.6	1	9.1	0	0	1	9.1	0	0	1	9.1	1	9.1	0	0
CENSUS DIVISION 2, MIDDLE ATLANTIC	362	317	87.6	166	45.9	6	1.7	3	0.8	16	4.4	142	39.2	294	78.5	114	31.5	52	14.4	41	11.3	11	3	78	21.5	18	5	12	3.3
New Jersey	70	56	80	35	50	1	1.4	0	0	4	5.7	24	34.3	56	80	23	32.9	12	17.1	13	18.6	2	2.9	7	10	7	10	3	4.3
New York	135	126	93.3	76	56.3	2	1.5	2	1.5	9	6.7	64	47.4	113	83.7	49	36.3	20	14.8	23	17	5	3.7	42	31.1	7	5.2	6	4.4
Pennsylvania	157	135	86	55	35	3	1.9	1	0.6	3	1.9	54	34.4	115	73.2	42	26.8	20	12.7	5	3.2	4	2.5	29	18.5	8	5.1	3	1.9
CENSUS DIVISION 3, SOUTH ATLANTIC	574	478	83.3	218	38	8	1.4	4	0.7	11	1.9	176	30.7	422	73.5	146	25.4	81	14.1	67	11.7	35	6.1	99	17.2	40	7	21	3.7
Delaware	8	4	50	5	62.5	0	0	0	0	0	0	4	50	5	62.5	3	37.5	1	12.5	2	25	1	12.5	2	30	1	12.5	1	12.5
District of Columbia	10	6	60	2	20	0	0	0	0	0	0	5	50	5	50	5	50	1	10	2	20	1	10	3	30	1	10	0	0
Florida	165	140	84.8	49	29.7	5	3	4	2.1	5	3	67	40.6	128	77.6	50	30.3	27	16.4	30	18.2	12	7.3	20	12.1	8	4.8	5	3
Georgia	96	81	84.4	26	27.1	2	2.1	2	2.1	5	5.2	20	20.8	60	62.5	23	24	9	9.4	4	4.2	4	4.2	19	19.8	4	4.2	5	5.2
Maryland	45	40	88.9	34	75.6	2	4.4	0	0	3	6.7	15	33.3	40	88.9	16	35.6	5	11.1	5	11.1	4	8.9	5	11.1	3	6.7	1	2.2
North Carolina	74	65	87.8	34	45.9	2	2.7	1	1.4	1	1.4	18	24.3	60	81.1	15	20.3	14	18.9	9	12.2	4	5.4	13	17.6	4	5.4	2	2.7
South Carolina	68	52	76.5	31	45.6	1	1.6	0	0	0	0	20	29.4	47	69.1	11	16.2	12	17.6	6	8.8	4	5.9	14	20.6	8	11.8	4	5.9
Virginia	63	53	84.1	20	31.7	0	0	1	1.6	0	0	14	22.2	49	77.8	17	16.2	8	12.7	6	9.5	1	1.6	6	9.5	6	9.5	3	4.8
West Virginia	45	37	82.2	19	42.2	0	0	0	0	3	6.7	14	31.1	26	57.8	6	13.3	4	8.9	3	6.7	3	6.7	13	28.9	6	13.3	1	2.2
CENSUS DIVISION 4, EAST NORTH CENTRAL	672	583	86.8	311	46.3	21	3.1	19	2.8	18	2.7	175	26	432	64.3	123	18.3	119	17.7	61	9.1	19	2.8	91	13.5	25	3.7	25	3.7
Illinois	155	139	89.7	76	49	4	2.6	8	5.2	5	3.2	32	20.6	111	71.6	27	17.4	12	7.7	13	8.4	4	2.6	24	15.5	14	9	5	3.4
Indiana	117	93	79.5	50	42.7	4	3.4	1	0.9	4	3.4	22	18.8	68	58.1	22	18.8	9	7.7	10	8.5	4	3.4	14	15.5	5	6	5	4.7
Michigan	115	115	90.6	45	32.3	3	2.4	2	2.4	4	3.1	28	22	90	70.9	23	18.1	18	14.2	11	8.7	2	1.6	24	18.9	5	3.9	6	4.7
Ohio	127	112	88.2	41	32.3	3	2.4	2	1.6	3	2.4	39	30.7	97	76.4	23	18.1	12	9.4	8	6.3	2	1.6	16	12.6	7	5.5	2	1.6
Wisconsin	146	124	84.9	99	67.8	8	5.5	5	3.4	3	2.1	54	37	66	45.2	29	19.9	68	46.6	19	13	7	4.8	13	8.9	1	0.7	5	3.4
CENSUS DIVISION 5, EAST SOUTH CENTRAL	269	229	85.1	104	38.7	3	1.1	3	1.1	3	1.1	69	25.7	148	55	51	19	29	10.8	22	8.2	18	6.7	48	17.8	12	4.5	5	1.9
Alabama	47	40	85.1	20	42.6	1	2.1	2	4.3	2	4.3	17	36.2	34	72.3	12	25.5	6	12.8	4	8.5	1	2.1	6	12.8	2	4.3	1	2.1
Kentucky	53	44	83	14	26.4	2	3.8	2	3.8	0	0	15	28.3	31	58.5	13	24.5	6	11.3	2	3.8	5	9.4	9	17	3	5.7	0	0
Mississippi	102	89	87.3	52	51	0	0	0	0	0	0	24	23.5	59	58.2	13	12.7	3	2.9	9	8.8	7	6.9	24	23.5	6	5.9	6	5.9
Tennessee	67	56	83.6	18	26.9	0	0	1	1.5	1	1.5	13	19.4	44	65.7	13	19.4	12	17.9	7	10.4	5	7.5	9	13.4	7	10.4	1	1.5
CENSUS DIVISION 6, WEST NORTH CENTRAL	562	515	91.6	251	44.7	43	7.7	49	8.7	15	2.7	103	18.3	259	46.1	75	13.3	39	6.9	37	6.6	14	2.5	220	39.1	100	17.8	36	6.4
Iowa	122	117	95.9	55	45.1	8	6.6	13	10.7	2	1.6	16	13.1	53	43.4	16	13.1	7	5.7	5	4	4	3.3	56	45.9	27	22.1	8	6.6
Kansas	125	115	92	38	30.4	6	4.8	13	10.4	2	1.6	9	7.2	53	35.2	9	7.2	7	5.7	5	4	0	0	52	41.6	37	29.6	8	6.4
Minnesota	86	83	96.5	42	48.8	10	11.6	9	10.4	4	4.7	18	20.9	46	53.5	10	11.6	6	7	9	10.5	1	1.2	32	37.2	4	4.7	4	4.7
Missouri	137	111	81	73	53.3	11	8	1	0.7	4	2.9	39	28.5	77	56.2	21	15.3	15	10.9	8	5.8	8	5.8	31	22.6	12	8.8	4	2.9
Nebraska	40	38	95	16	40	4	10	1	2.5	1	2.5	11	27.5	18	45	10	25	6	15	3	7.5	1	2.5	18	45	9	22.5	5	12.5
North Dakota	16	16	100	6	37.5	2	12.5	2	12.5	1	6.3	4	25	8	50	3	18.8	1	6.3	3	18.8	0	0	9	56.3	9	56.3	2	12.5
South Dakota	36	35	97.2	21	58.3	11	30.6	8	22.2	2	5.6	4	11.1	13	36.1	3	8.3	1	2.8	2	5.6	0	0	22	61.1	9	25	7	19.4
CENSUS DIVISION 7, WEST SOUTH CENTRAL	838	592	70.6	205	24.5	9	1.1	9	1.1	9	1.1	131	15.6	365	43.6	169	20.2	57	6.8	54	6.4	80	9.5	67	8	29	3.5	13	1.6
Arkansas	89	67	75.3	24	26.9	4	4.5	4	4.5	2	2.2	20	22.5	42	47.2	11	12.4	4	8.5	5	5.6	9	10.1	11	12.4	3	3.4	3	3.4
Louisiana	89	59	66.3	29	32.6	4	4.5	4	4.5	2	2.2	19	21.3	50	56.2	24	27	4	4.5	10	11.2	9	10.1	15	16.9	1	1.1	1	1.1
Oklahoma	106	89	84	32	30.2	3	2.8	1	0.9	2	1.9	15	14.2	37	34.9	11	10.4	5	4.7	5	4.7	5	4.7	16	15.1	5	4.7	2	2.2
Texas	554	377	68.1	120	21.7	10	1.8	3	0.5	3	0.5	77	13.9	236	42.6	123	22.2	40	7.2	37	6.7	57	10.3	25	4.5	20	3.6	7	1.3
CENSUS DIVISION 8, MOUNTAIN	337	292	86.6	111	32.9	7	2.1	4	1.2	7	2.1	63	18.7	197	58.5	77	22.8	19	5.6	28	8.3	11	3.3	53	15.7	23	6.8	15	4.5
Arizona	72	56	77.8	15	20.8	3	4.2	3	4.2	3	4.2	20	27.8	45	62.5	19	26.4	7	9.7	8	11.1	3	4.2	11	15.3	6	8.5	4	5.6
Colorado	71	67	94.4	24	33.8	4	5.6	1	1.4	2	2.8	14	19.7	49	69	25	35.2	6	8.5	4	5.6	1	1.4	8	11.3	6	8.5	2	2.8
Idaho	26	24	92.3	10	38.5	1	3.8	3	11.5	1	3.8	5	19.2	13	50	8	30.8	2	7.7	2	7.7	1	3.8	5	19.2	2	7.7	2	7.7
Montana	51	50	98	22	43.1	7	13.7	7	13.7	1	2	5	9.8	22	43.1	7	13.7	1	2	4	7.8	2	3.9	19	37.3	7	13.7	6	11.8
Nevada	23	13	56.5	6	26.1	1	4.3	0	0	0	0	5	21.7	12	52.2	5	21.7	1	4.3	3	13	0	0	1	4.3	1	4.3	0	0
New Mexico	31	28	90.3	13	41.9	0	0	0	0	0	0	6	19.4	20	64.5	4	12.9	2	6.5	4	12.9	0	0	2	6.5	1	3.2	0	0
Utah	38	32	84.2	12	31.6	1	2.6	1	2.6	0	0	8	21.1	19	50	9	23.7	2	5.3	3	7.9	1	4	6	6.5	1	2.6	1	2.6
Wyoming	25	22	88	9	36	3	12	3	12	1	12	0	0	17	17.8	0	0	0	0	0	0	1	4	9	36	3	12	4	16
CENSUS DIVISION 9, PACIFIC	397	354	89.2	136	34.3	9	2.3	10	2.5	10	2.5	123	31	305	76.8	136	34.3	29	7.3	46	11.6	12	3	66	16.6	29	7.3	7	1.8
Alaska	8	7	87.5	4	50	0	0	0	0	0	0	2	25	6	75	1	12.5	1	12.5	1	12.5	1	12.5	1	12.5	1	12.5	1	12.5
California	242	210	86.8	89	36.8	8	3.3	8	3.3	8	3.3	92	38	194	80.2	103	42.6	17	15.4	33	13.6	8	3.3	48	19.8	6	2.5	3	1.2
Hawaii	13	12	92.3	4	30.8	0	0	0	0	0	0	4	30.8	10	76.9	4	30.8	2	15.4	2	15.4	1	7.7	2	15.4	2	15.4	1	7.7
Oregon	61	60	98.4	19	31.1	2	4.9	2	3.3	1	1.6	12	19.7	47	77	10	16.4	4	6.6	4	6.6	0	0	5	8.2	5	8.2	2	7.7
Washington	73	65	89	22	30.1	1	1.4	1	1.4	1	1.4	13	17.8	48	65.8	19	26	6	8.2	6	8.2	2	2.7	8	11	5	2.7	2	2.7

Note: These data represent hospital performance in the years 2015 – 2019 and do not reflect any impacts from the COVID-19 pandemic in 2020 and thereafter.

Table 7 (Continued)

These data include only hospital-based facilities and services as reported by responding hospitals in Section C of the 2019 AHA Annual Survey, beginning on page 215. Census divisions represent all U.S. hospitals. Community hospitals are listed separately under United States. No estimates have been made for nonresponding hospitals. Definitions of facilities and services are listed in the Glossary, page 203.

CARDIOLOGY AND CARDIAC SERVICES

CLASSIFICATION	HOSPITALS REPORTING	ADULT CARDIOLOGY SERVICES		PEDIATRIC CARDIOLOGY SERVICES		ADULT DIAGNOSTIC CATHETERIZATION		PEDIATRIC DIAGNOSTIC CATHETERIZATION		ADULT INTERVENTIONAL CARDIAC CATHETERIZATION		PEDIATRIC INTERVENTIONAL CARDIAC CATHETERIZATION		ADULT CARDIAC SURGERY		PEDIATRIC CARDIAC SURGERY		ADULT CARDIAC ELECTRO PHYSIOLOGY		PEDIATRIC CARDIAC ELECTRO PHYSIOLOGY		CARDIAC REHABILITATION	
		Number	Percent	Number	Percent	Number	Percent	Number	Percent	Number	Percent	Number	Percent	Number	Percent	Number	Percent	Number	Percent	Number	Percent	Number	Percent
UNITED STATES	4,167	2,245	53.9	388	9.3	1,674	40.2	171	4.1	1,513	36.3	158	3.8	1,025	24.6	152	3.6	1,375	33	196	4.7	2,344	56.3
COMMUNITY HOSPITALS	3,782	2,201	58.2	384	10.2	1,648	43.6	171	4.5	1,490	39.4	158	4.2	1,006	26.6	152	4	1,353	35.8	194	5.1	2,317	61.3
CENSUS DIVISION 1, NEW ENGLAND	156	102	65.4	18	11.5	63	40.4	9	5.8	50	32.1	9	5.8	33	21.2	8	5.1	61	39.1	10	6.4	111	71.2
Connecticut	26	22	84.6	4	15.4	17	65.4	2	7.7	15	57.7	2	7.7	11	42.3	2	7.7	18	69.2	3	11.5	21	80.8
Maine	30	16	53.3	3	10	8	26.7	1	3.3	4	13.3	1	3.3	3	10	1	3.3	5	16.7	3	10	20	66.7
Massachusetts	57	41	71.9	7	12.3	23	40.4	3	5.3	19	33.3	3	5.3	14	24.6	3	5.3	24	42.1	3	5.3	38	66.7
New Hampshire	25	12	48	1	4	8	32	1	4	8	32	1	4	3	12	1	4	8	32	0	0	21	84
Rhode Island	7	6	85.7	1	14.3	6	85.7	1	14.3	3	42.9	1	14.3	1	14.3	0	0	5	71.4	0	0	3	42.9
Vermont	11	5	45.5	1	9.1	1	9.1	1	9.1	1	9.1	1	9.1	1	9.1	1	9.1	1	9.1	0	0	8	72.7
CENSUS DIVISION 2, MIDDLE ATLANTIC	362	274	75.7	60	16.6	196	54.1	19	5.2	172	47.5	17	4.7	106	29.3	15	4.1	159	43.9	27	7.5	236	65.2
New Jersey	70	53	75.7	16	22.9	47	67.1	2	2.9	38	54.3	2	2.9	17	24.3	2	2.9	24	34.3	3	4.3	45	64.3
New York	135	107	79.3	36	26.7	59	43.7	12	8.9	50	37	11	8.1	31	23	9	6.7	58	43	14	10.4	82	60.7
Pennsylvania	157	114	72.6	8	5.1	90	57.3	5	3.2	84	53.5	4	2.5	58	36.9	4	2.5	77	49	10	6.4	109	69.4
CENSUS DIVISION 3, SOUTH ATLANTIC	574	382	66.6	61	10.6	304	53	29	5.1	268	46.7	26	4.5	158	27.5	26	4.5	248	43.2	32	5.6	333	58
Delaware	8	6	75	1	12.5	4	50	1	12.5	4	50	1	12.5	3	37.5	1	12.5	3	37.5	2	25	5	62.5
District of Columbia	10	5	50	1	10	4	40	1	10	2	20	1	10	3	30	1	10	4	40	2	20	3	30
Florida	165	122	73.9	28	17	106	64.2	13	7.9	99	60	10	6.1	64	38.8	11	6.7	89	53.9	11	6.7	87	52.7
Georgia	96	54	56.3	6	6.3	47	49	2	2.1	41	42.7	2	2.1	17	17.7	2	2.1	38	39.6	2	2.1	44	45.8
Maryland	45	36	80	6	13.3	31	68.9	2	4.4	24	53.3	2	4.4	10	22.2	2	4.4	30	66.7	3	6.7	31	68.9
North Carolina	74	53	71.6	9	12.2	39	52.7	4	5.4	34	45.9	4	5.4	19	25.7	4	5.4	29	39.2	6	8.1	51	68.9
South Carolina	68	39	57.4	5	7.4	28	41.2	1	1.5	18	26.5	1	1.5	18	26.5	1	1.5	17	25	1	1.5	38	55.9
Virginia	63	43	68.3	7	11.1	31	49.2	4	6.3	32	50.8	4	6.3	16	25.4	4	6.3	29	46	5	7.9	50	79.4
West Virginia	45	24	53.3	3	6.7	14	31.1	1	2.2	14	31.1	1	2.2	8	17.8	1	2.2	10	22.2	1	2.2	24	53.3
CENSUS DIVISION 4, EAST NORTH CENTRAL	672	397	59.1	70	10.4	289	43	20	3	257	38.2	20	3	183	27.2	22	3.3	250	37.2	25	3.7	488	72.6
Illinois	155	112	72.3	26	16.8	86	55.5	7	4.5	80	51.6	8	5.2	56	36.1	9	5.8	73	47.1	10	6.5	114	73.5
Indiana	117	60	51.3	10	8.5	40	34.2	2	1.7	35	29.9	3	2.6	23	19.7	2	1.7	34	29.1	3	2.6	78	66.7
Michigan	127	79	62.2	15	11.8	55	43.3	4	3.1	46	36.2	3	2.4	33	26	5	3.9	51	40.2	4	3.1	93	73.2
Ohio	127	94	74	12	9.4	65	51.2	6	4.7	54	42.5	5	3.9	41	32.3	5	3.9	57	44.9	7	5.5	89	70.1
Wisconsin	146	52	35.6	7	4.8	43	29.5	1	0.7	42	28.8	1	0.7	30	20.5	1	0.7	35	24	1	0.7	114	78.1
CENSUS DIVISION 5, EAST SOUTH CENTRAL	269	133	49.4	18	6.7	98	36.4	11	4.1	80	29.7	9	3.3	58	21.6	11	4.1	68	25.3	11	4.1	120	44.6
Alabama	47	31	66	2	4.3	23	48.9	2	4.3	19	40.4	2	4.3	14	29.8	2	4.3	18	38.3	3	6.4	26	55.3
Kentucky	53	31	58.5	4	7.5	24	45.3	2	3.8	19	35.8	2	3.8	16	30.2	3	5.7	19	35.8	3	5.7	34	64.2
Mississippi	102	32	31.4	4	3.9	21	20.6	1	1	18	17.6	1	1	14	13.7	1	1	13	12.7	2	2	23	22.5
Tennessee	67	42	62.7	8	11.9	30	44.8	6	9	24	35.8	4	6	14	20.9	5	7.5	18	26.9	4	6	37	55.2
CENSUS DIVISION 6, WEST NORTH CENTRAL	562	228	40.6	39	6.9	146	26	15	2.7	143	25.4	16	2.8	91	16.2	13	2.3	117	20.8	18	3.2	422	75.1
Iowa	122	44	36.1	5	4.1	24	19.7	2	1.6	24	19.7	2	1.6	13	10.7	2	1.6	21	17.2	2	1.6	109	89.3
Kansas	125	33	26.4	7	5.6	23	18.4	1	0.8	24	19.2	1	0.8	15	12	2	1.6	15	12	2	1.6	70	56
Minnesota	86	41	47.7	7	8.1	19	22.1	3	3.5	19	22.1	3	3.5	14	16.3	3	3.5	20	23.3	5	5.8	75	87.2
Missouri	137	75	54.7	10	7.3	54	39.4	3	2.2	51	37.2	3	2.2	32	23.4	4	2.9	41	29.9	5	3.6	87	63.5
Nebraska	40	20	50	3	7.5	13	32.5	1	2.5	13	32.5	1	2.5	7	17.5	1	2.5	11	27.5	2	5	35	87.5
North Dakota	16	6	37.5	3	18.8	6	37.5	2	12.5	6	37.5	2	12.5	6	37.5	2	12.5	5	31.3	1	6.3	13	81.3
South Dakota	36	9	25	4	11.1	7	19.4	3	8.3	6	16.7	3	8.3	4	11.1	1	2.8	4	11.1	1	2.8	13	36.1
CENSUS DIVISION 7, WEST SOUTH CENTRAL	838	324	38.7	47	5.6	265	31.6	28	3.3	252	30.1	29	3.5	189	22.6	25	3	207	24.7	26	3.1	295	35.2
Arkansas	89	32	36	9	10.1	26	29.2	2	2.2	26	29.2	5	5.6	17	19.1	5	5.6	19	21.3	2	2.2	29	32.6
Louisiana	89	43	48.3	9	10.1	35	39.3	5	5.6	32	36	5	5.6	26	29.2	5	5.6	30	33.7	4	4.5	34	38.2
Oklahoma	106	46	43.4	5	4.7	27	25.5	2	1.9	27	25.5	2	1.9	15	14.2	2	1.9	18	17	2	1.9	30	28.3
Texas	554	203	36.6	31	5.6	177	31.9	20	3.6	167	30.1	21	3.8	131	23.6	17	3.1	140	25.3	18	3.2	202	36.5
CENSUS DIVISION 8, MOUNTAIN	337	157	46.6	26	7.7	121	35.9	11	3.3	119	35.3	11	3.3	74	22	11	3.3	93	27.6	17	5	159	47.2
Arizona	72	45	62.5	5	6.9	39	54.2	3	4.2	38	52.8	3	4.2	24	33.3	2	2.8	25	34.7	4	5.6	30	41.7
Colorado	71	44	62	5	7	37	52.1	2	2.8	35	49.3	3	4.2	20	28.2	2	2.8	29	40.8	4	5.6	42	59.2
Idaho	26	9	34.6	2	7.7	7	26.9	1	3.8	8	30.8	1	3.8	4	15.4	0	0	5	19.2	1	3.8	11	42.3
Montana	51	14	27.5	3	5.9	8	15.7	0	0	9	17.6	1	2	6	11.8	1	2	11	21.6	1	2	28	54.9
Nevada	23	8	34.8	2	8.7	8	34.8	0	0	7	30.4	1	4.3	6	26.1	1	4.3	7	30.4	1	4.3	7	30.4
New Mexico	31	17	54.8	4	12.9	9	29	3	9.7	9	29	3	9.7	5	16.1	2	6.5	7	22.6	2	6.5	14	45.2
Utah	38	12	31.6	2	5.3	9	23.7	1	2.6	9	23.7	1	2.6	7	18.4	1	2.6	8	21.1	1	2.6	11	28.9
Wyoming	25	8	32	3	12	4	16	0	0	4	16	0	0	2	8	0	0	3	12	0	0	16	64
CENSUS DIVISION 9, PACIFIC	397	248	62.5	49	12.3	192	48.4	27	6.8	172	43.3	22	5.5	133	33.5	21	5.3	172	43.3	30	7.6	180	45.3
Alaska	8	3	37.5	2	25	2	25	2	25	2	25	2	25	1	12.5	1	12.5	1	12.5	0	0	5	62.5
California	242	162	66.9	33	13.6	126	52.1	14	5.8	112	46.3	14	5.8	92	38	14	5.8	115	47.5	20	8.3	102	42.1
Hawaii	13	9	69.2	2	15.4	8	61.5	2	15.4	8	61.5	1	7.7	7	53.8	0	0	9	69.2	1	7.7	7	53.8
Oregon	61	33	54.1	6	9.8	23	37.7	5	8.2	20	32.8	2	3.3	16	26.2	2	3.3	23	37.7	3	4.9	30	49.2
Washington	73	41	56.2	7	9.6	33	45.2	5	6.8	30	41.1	5	6.8	17	23.3	4	5.5	24	32.9	5	6.8	36	49.3

Note: These data represent hospital performance in the years 2015 – 2019 and do not reflect any impacts from the COVID-19 pandemic in 2020 and thereafter.

Table 7 (Continued)

These data include only hospital-based facilities and services as reported by responding hospitals in Section C of the 2019 AHA Annual Survey, beginning on page 215. Census divisions represent all U.S. hospitals. Community hospitals are listed separately under United States. No estimates have been made for nonresponding hospitals. Definitions of facilities and services are listed in the Glossary, page 203.

Classification	Hospitals Reporting	Off-Campus Emergency Dept. No.	Off-Campus Emergency Dept. %	On-Campus Emergency Dept. No.	On-Campus Emergency Dept. %	Pediatric Emergency Dept. No.	Pediatric Emergency Dept. %	Trauma Center (Certified) No.	Trauma Center (Certified) %	Endoscopic Ultrasound No.	Endoscopic Ultrasound %	Ablation of Barrett's Esophagus No.	Ablation of Barrett's Esophagus %	Esophageal Impedance Study No.	Esophageal Impedance Study %	ERCP No.	ERCP %	Optical Colonoscopy No.	Optical Colonoscopy %
UNITED STATES	4,167	314	7.5	3,440	82.6	895	21.5	1,681	40.3	1,606	38.5	1,189	28.5	1,122	26.9	1,784	42.8	2,828	67.9
COMMUNITY HOSPITALS	3,782	313	8.3	3,386	89.5	887	23.5	1,671	44.2	1,575	41.6	1,166	30.8	1,101	29.1	1,758	46.5	2,782	73.6
CENSUS DIVISION 1, NEW ENGLAND	156	13	8.3	128	82.1	40	25.6	49	31.4	74	47.4	58	37.2	55	35.3	82	52.6	119	76.3
Connecticut	26	6	23.1	23	88.5	10	38.5	13	50	18	69.2	16	61.5	17	65.4	22	84.6	22	84.6
Maine	30	3	10	27	90	4	13.3	9	30	12	40	7	23.3	7	23.3	8	26.7	25	83.3
Massachusetts	57	4	7	42	73.7	16	28.1	14	24.6	28	49.1	21	36.8	20	35.1	32	56.1	39	68.4
New Hampshire	25	0	0	21	84	9	36	10	40	10	40	10	40	6	24	11	44	20	80
Rhode Island	7	0	0	6	85.7	1	14.3	1	14.3	4	57.1	3	42.9	2	28.6	5	71.4	5	71.4
Vermont	11	0	0	9	81.8	0	0	2	18.2	2	18.2	1	9.1	3	27.3	4	36.4	8	72.7
CENSUS DIVISION 2, MIDDLE ATLANTIC	362	24	6.6	307	84.8	109	30.1	99	27.3	210	58	151	41.7	133	36.7	242	66.9	283	78.2
New Jersey	70	9	12.9	54	77.1	34	48.6	13	18.6	45	64.3	39	55.7	31	44.3	51	72.9	48	68.6
New York	135	13	9.6	120	88.9	58	43	45	33.3	80	59.3	66	48.9	53	39.3	93	68.9	113	83.7
Pennsylvania	157	2	1.3	133	84.7	17	10.8	41	26.1	85	54.1	46	29.3	49	31.2	98	62.4	122	77.7
CENSUS DIVISION 3, SOUTH ATLANTIC	574	64	11.1	470	81.9	133	23.2	136	23.7	261	45.5	201	35	204	35.5	327	57	424	73.9
Delaware	8	2	25	5	62.5	3	37.5	4	50	2	25	3	37.5	5	62.5	5	62.5	5	62.5
District of Columbia	10	1	10	5	50	3	30	4	40	6	60	4	40	5	50	5	50	6	60
Florida	165	32	19.4	139	84.2	53	32.1	29	17.6	89	53.9	64	38.8	62	37.6	117	70.9	127	77
Georgia	96	1	1	78	81.3	12	12.5	17	17.7	35	36.5	32	33.3	32	33.3	50	52.1	66	68.8
Maryland	45	1	2.2	39	86.7	20	44.4	13	28.9	31	68.9	17	37.8	18	40	33	73.3	33	73.3
North Carolina	74	9	12.2	65	87.8	11	14.9	15	20.3	32	43.2	26	35.1	26	35.1	42	56.8	64	86.5
South Carolina	68	4	5.9	49	72.1	5	7.4	14	20.6	24	35.3	17	25	15	22.1	28	41.2	42	61.8
Virginia	63	13	20.6	54	85.7	22	34.9	15	23.8	29	46	25	39.7	28	44.4	31	49.2	48	76.2
West Virginia	45	1	2.2	36	80	4	8.9	24	53.3	13	28.9	13	28.9	15	33.3	17	37.8	33	73.3
CENSUS DIVISION 4, EAST NORTH CENTRAL	672	60	8.9	575	85.6	154	22.9	301	44.8	271	40.3	228	33.9	213	31.7	293	43.6	472	70.2
Illinois	155	9	5.8	139	89.7	49	31.6	56	36.1	82	52.9	65	41.9	54	34.8	90	58.1	130	83.9
Indiana	117	6	5.1	90	76.9	19	16.2	26	22.2	43	36.8	35	29.9	31	26.5	44	37.6	81	69.2
Michigan	127	13	10.2	112	88.2	29	22.8	71	55.9	58	45.7	43	33.9	39	30.7	58	45.7	100	78.7
Ohio	127	32	25.2	110	86.6	31	24.4	41	32.3	51	40.2	47	37	53	41.7	58	45.7	89	70.1
Wisconsin	146	0	0	124	84.9	26	17.8	107	73.3	37	25.3	38	26	36	24.7	43	29.5	72	49.3
CENSUS DIVISION 5, EAST SOUTH CENTRAL	269	9	3.3	221	82.2	43	16	111	41.3	87	32.3	67	24.9	66	24.5	92	34.2	143	53.2
Alabama	47	2	4.3	41	87.2	6	12.8	23	48.9	21	44.7	13	27.7	14	29.8	23	48.9	34	72.3
Kentucky	53	2	3.8	46	86.8	6	11.3	12	22.6	19	35.8	18	34	17	32.1	26	49.1	31	58.5
Mississippi	102	0	0	79	77.5	11	10.8	67	65.7	19	18.6	17	16.7	15	14.7	17	16.7	35	34.3
Tennessee	67	5	7.5	55	82.1	20	29.9	9	13.4	28	41.8	19	28.4	20	29.9	26	38.8	43	64.2
CENSUS DIVISION 6, WEST NORTH CENTRAL	562	18	3.2	502	89.3	105	18.7	284	50.5	144	25.6	106	18.9	98	17.4	137	24.4	402	71.5
Iowa	122	1	0.8	117	95.9	19	15.6	93	76.2	31	25.4	18	14.8	17	13.9	18	14.8	99	81.1
Kansas	125	6	4.8	111	88.8	17	13.6	33	26.4	16	12.8	16	12.8	15	12	20	16	82	65.6
Minnesota	86	5	5.8	83	96.5	22	25.6	67	77.9	28	32.6	14	16.3	13	15.1	24	27.9	66	76.7
Missouri	137	4	2.9	100	73	23	16.8	32	23.4	42	30.7	36	26.3	31	22.6	53	38.7	88	64.2
Nebraska	40	1	2.5	39	97.5	14	35	25	62.5	15	37.5	16	40	13	32.5	13	32.5	31	77.5
North Dakota	16	0	0	16	100	1	6.3	10	62.5	6	37.5	2	12.5	2	12.5	5	31.3	15	93.8
South Dakota	36	1	2.8	36	100	9	25	24	66.7	6	16.7	4	11.1	6	16.7	4	11.1	21	58.3
CENSUS DIVISION 7, WEST SOUTH CENTRAL	838	81	9.7	606	72.3	116	13.8	358	42.7	221	26.4	153	18.3	136	16.2	253	30.2	439	52.4
Arkansas	89	4	4.5	69	77.5	6	6.7	51	57.3	24	27	12	13.5	16	18	20	22.5	57	64
Louisiana	89	8	9	55	61.8	14	15.7	14	15.7	33	37.1	17	19.1	18	20.2	29	32.6	50	56.2
Oklahoma	106	3	2.8	91	85.8	14	13.2	50	47.2	17	16	17	16	14	13.2	24	22.6	61	57.5
Texas	554	66	11.9	391	70.6	82	14.8	243	43.9	147	26.5	107	19.3	88	15.9	180	32.5	271	48.9
CENSUS DIVISION 8, MOUNTAIN	337	36	10.7	285	84.6	83	24.6	181	53.7	125	37.1	86	25.5	87	25.8	118	35	230	68.2
Arizona	72	20	27.8	54	75	19	26.4	30	41.7	33	45.8	24	33.3	21	29.2	34	47.2	47	65.3
Colorado	71	2	2.8	67	94.4	18	25.4	59	83.1	33	46.5	21	29.6	26	36.6	33	46.5	58	81.7
Idaho	26	0	0	23	88.5	9	34.6	13	50	9	34.6	6	23.1	6	23.1	8	30.8	19	73.1
Montana	51	2	3.9	49	96.1	15	29.4	33	64.7	11	21.6	8	15.7	7	13.7	7	13.7	29	56.9
Nevada	23	2	8.7	12	52.2	6	26.1	6	26.1	7	30.4	5	21.7	3	13	6	26.1	10	43.5
New Mexico	31	1	3.2	27	87.1	4	12.9	8	25.8	13	41.9	7	22.6	7	22.6	11	35.5	22	71
Utah	38	9	23.7	32	84.2	6	15.8	20	52.6	10	26.3	9	23.7	9	23.7	13	34.2	26	68.4
Wyoming	25	0	0	21	84	6	24	12	48	9	36	6	24	8	32	6	24	19	76
CENSUS DIVISION 9, PACIFIC	397	9	2.3	346	87.2	112	28.2	162	40.8	213	53.7	139	35	130	32.7	240	60.5	316	79.6
Alaska	8	0	0	7	87.5	2	25	4	50	2	25	2	25	2	25	2	25	4	50
California	242	4	1.7	202	83.5	80	33.1	60	24.8	140	57.9	89	36.8	85	35.1	171	70.7	193	79.8
Hawaii	13	0	0	12	92.3	4	30.8	7	53.8	9	69.2	5	38.5	5	38.5	10	76.9	9	69.2
Oregon	61	0	0	59	96.7	8	13.1	40	65.6	32	52.5	20	32.8	15	24.6	21	34.4	52	85.2
Washington	73	5	6.8	66	90.4	18	24.7	51	69.9	29	39.7	23	31.5	23	31.5	36	49.3	58	79.5

Note: These data represent hospital performance in the years 2015–2019 and do not reflect any impacts from the COVID-19 pandemic in 2020 and thereafter.

Table 7 (Continued)

These data include only hospital-based facilities and services as reported by responding hospitals in Section C of the 2019 AHA Annual Survey, beginning on page 215. Census divisions represent all U.S. hospitals. Community hospitals are listed separately under United States. No estimates have been made for nonresponding hospitals. Definitions of facilities and services are listed in the Glossary, page 203.

CLASSIFICATION	HOSPITALS REPORTING	ASSISTIVE TECHNOLOGY CENTER No.	%	ELECTRODIAGNOSTIC SERVICES No.	%	PHYSICAL REHAB. OUTPATIENT SERVICES No.	%	PROSTHETIC ORTHOTIC SERVICES No.	%	ROBOT ASSISTED WALKING THERAPY No.	%	SIMULATED REHAB. ENVIRONMENT No.	%	PEDIATRIC CARE No.	%	CONSULTATION/LIAISON SERVICES No.	%	EDUCATION SERVICES No.	%	EMERGENCY SERVICES No.	%
UNITED STATES	4,167	978	23.5	1,204	28.9	2,960	71	814	19.5	233	5.6	1,324	31.8	470	11.3	1,604	38.5	1,064	25.5	1,498	35.9
COMMUNITY HOSPITALS	3,782	929	24.6	1,170	30.9	2,890	76.4	768	20.3	224	5.9	1,282	33.9	329	8.7	1,406	37.2	841	22.2	1,357	35.9
CENSUS DIVISION 1, NEW ENGLAND	156	48	30.8	63	40.4	132	84.6	40	25.6	12	7.7	70	44.9	29	18.6	97	62.2	69	44.2	83	53.2
Connecticut	26	13	50	12	46.2	21	80.8	9	34.6	4	15.4	16	61.5	7	26.9	23	88.5	20	76.9	22	84.6
Maine	30	9	30	10	33.3	27	90	6	20	1	3.3	14	46.7	5	16.7	11	36.7	7	23.3	11	36.7
Massachusetts	57	12	21.1	23	40.4	48	84.2	11	19.3	5	8.8	20	35.1	9	15.8	42	73.7	28	49.1	27	47.4
New Hampshire	25	8	32	10	40	23	92	7	28	1	4	12	48	3	12	13	52	8	32	14	56
Rhode Island	7	3	42.9	3	42.9	5	71.4	4	57.1	0	0	3	42.9	2	28.6	4	57.1	3	42.9	3	42.9
Vermont	11	3	27.3	5	45.5	8	72.7	3	27.3	1	9.1	5	45.5	3	27.3	4	36.4	3	27.3	6	54.5
CENSUS DIVISION 2, MIDDLE ATLANTIC	382	111	30.7	188	51.9	289	75.7	109	30.1	34	9.4	175	48.3	60	16.6	249	68.8	160	44.2	198	54.7
New Jersey	70	27	38.6	40	57.1	53	75.7	31	44.3	7	10	35	50	14	20	51	72.9	45	64.3	43	61.4
New York	135	42	31.1	73	54.1	120	88.9	50	37	15	11.1	57	42.2	29	21.5	102	75.6	68	50.4	83	61.5
Pennsylvania	157	42	26.8	75	47.8	116	73.9	28	17.8	12	7.6	83	52.9	17	10.8	96	61.1	47	29.9	72	45.9
CENSUS DIVISION 3, SOUTH ATLANTIC	574	155	27	190	33.1	409	71.3	164	28.6	40	7	201	35	69	12	249	43.4	156	27.2	239	41.6
Delaware	8	0	0	2	25	5	62.5	3	37.5	1	12.5	4	50	3	37.5	3	37.5	3	37.5	3	37.5
District of Columbia	10	7	70	6	60	7	70	4	40	1	10	5	50	1	10	7	70	4	40	6	60
Florida	165	52	31.5	50	30.3	128	77.6	37	22.4	16	9.7	61	37	19	11.5	71	43	40	24.2	67	40.6
Georgia	96	12	12.5	20	20.8	68	70.8	21	21.9	3	3.1	24	25	4	4.2	36	37.5	17	17.7	29	30.2
Maryland	45	13	28.9	24	53.3	36	80	17	37.8	4	8.9	21	46.7	13	28.9	36	80	28	62.2	35	77.8
North Carolina	74	28	37.8	30	40.5	61	82.4	16	21.6	3	4.1	33	44.6	6	8.1	32	43.2	25	33.8	34	45.9
South Carolina	68	8	11.8	9	13.2	23	33.8	43	63.2	5	7.4	15	22.1	11	16.2	19	27.9	14	20.6	28	41.2
Virginia	63	31	49.2	36	57.1	54	85.7	19	30.2	6	9.5	30	47.6	8	12.7	31	49.2	18	28.6	29	46
West Virginia	45	4	8.9	13	28.9	27	60	4	8.9	1	2.2	8	17.8	4	8.9	14	31.1	7	15.6	8	17.8
CENSUS DIVISION 4, EAST NORTH CENTRAL	672	159	23.7	249	37.1	532	79.2	153	22.8	35	5.2	273	40.6	100	14.9	300	44.6	213	31.7	261	38.8
Illinois	155	38	24.5	70	45.2	127	81.9	41	26.5	6	3.9	64	41.3	27	17.4	76	49	64	41.3	72	46.5
Indiana	117	27	23.1	35	29.9	86	73.5	27	23.1	7	6	40	34.2	13	11.1	32	27.4	29	24.8	34	29.1
Michigan	127	35	27.6	58	45.7	107	84.3	23	18.1	8	6.3	61	48	13	10.2	71	55.9	47	37	54	42.5
Ohio	127	42	33.1	54	42.5	99	78	31	24.4	9	7.1	57	44.9	12	9.4	62	48.8	35	27.6	52	40.9
Wisconsin	146	17	11.6	32	21.9	113	77.4	31	21.2	5	3.4	51	34.9	35	24	59	40.4	38	26	49	33.6
CENSUS DIVISION 5, EAST SOUTH CENTRAL	289	45	16.7	55	20.4	171	59.6	41	15.2	14	5.2	62	23	23	8.6	63	23.4	55	20.4	71	26.4
Alabama	47	8	17	8	17	33	70.2	11	23.4	7	14.9	9	19.1	4	8.5	15	31.9	9	19.1	13	27.7
Kentucky	53	13	24.5	16	30.2	39	73.6	6	11.3	4	7.5	12	22.6	5	9.4	13	24.5	14	26.4	15	28.3
Mississippi	102	10	9.8	15	14.7	52	51	10	9.8	2	2	22	21.6	9	8.8	17	16.7	17	16.7	14	13.7
Tennessee	67	14	20.9	16	23.9	47	70.1	14	20.9	1	1.5	19	28.4	5	7.5	18	26.9	15	22.4	29	43.3
CENSUS DIVISION 6, WEST NORTH CENTRAL	562	105	18.7	128	22.8	455	81	96	17.1	17	3	155	27.6	67	11.9	160	28.5	118	21	180	32
Iowa	122	29	23.8	23	18.9	103	84.4	14	11.5	3	2.5	39	32	17	13.9	39	32	36	29.5	48	39.3
Kansas	125	17	13.6	20	16	104	83.2	12	9.6	7	5.6	25	20	4	3.2	21	16.8	9	7.2	26	20.8
Minnesota	86	22	25.6	23	26.7	74	86	13	15.1	3	3.5	26	30.2	8	9.3	34	39.5	24	27.9	24	27.9
Missouri	137	17	12.4	34	24.8	95	69.3	29	21.2	3	2.2	45	32.8	28	20.4	40	29.2	31	22.6	50	36.5
Nebraska	40	10	25	14	35	33	82.5	12	30	1	2.5	9	22.5	4	10	15	37.5	8	20	9	22.5
North Dakota	16	5	31.3	8	50	15	93.8	6	37.5	0	0	5	31.3	2	12.5	5	31.3	5	31.3	4	25
South Dakota	36	5	13.9	6	16.7	31	86.1	10	27.8	0	0	6	16.7	4	11.1	6	16.7	5	13.9	9	25
CENSUS DIVISION 7, WEST SOUTH CENTRAL	838	182	21.7	107	12.8	470	56.1	77	9.2	42	5	196	23.4	66	7.9	184	22	135	16.1	191	22.8
Arkansas	89	21	23.6	9	10.1	50	56.2	10	11.2	6	6.7	22	24.7	8	9	20	22.5	12	13.5	30	33.7
Louisiana	89	22	24.7	12	13.5	50	56.2	11	12.4	3	3.4	28	31.5	6	6.7	26	29.2	17	19.1	33	37.1
Oklahoma	106	25	23.6	16	15.1	71	67	10	9.4	2	1.9	18	17	8	7.5	31	29.2	18	17	23	21.7
Texas	554	114	20.6	70	12.6	299	54	46	8.3	31	5.6	128	23.1	44	7.9	107	19.3	88	15.9	105	19
CENSUS DIVISION 8, MOUNTAIN	337	81	24	89	26.4	237	70.3	51	15.1	15	4.5	87	25.8	29	8.6	124	36.8	66	19.6	129	38.3
Arizona	72	16	22.2	22	30.6	40	55.6	13	18.1	3	4.2	25	34.7	4	5.6	34	47.2	17	23.6	26	36.1
Colorado	71	19	26.8	22	31	58	81.7	13	18.3	4	5.6	27	38	7	9.9	22	31	15	21.1	26	36.6
Idaho	26	8	30.8	7	26.9	18	69.2	3	11.5	1	3.8	6	23.1	2	7.7	8	30.8	4	15.4	9	34.6
Montana	51	13	25.5	11	21.6	45	88.2	5	9.8	2	3.9	7	13.7	6	11.8	13	25.5	10	19.6	15	29.4
Nevada	23	2	8.7	2	8.7	11	47.8	0	0	2	8.7	5	21.7	3	13	5	21.7	3	13	8	34.8
New Mexico	31	11	35.5	8	25.8	22	71	3	9.7	2	6.5	5	16.1	3	9.7	11	35.5	4	12.9	10	32.3
Utah	38	8	21.1	14	36.8	26	68.4	9	23.7	1	2.6	8	21.1	3	7.9	26	68.4	9	23.7	28	73.7
Wyoming	25	4	16	3	12	17	68	5	20	0	0	4	16	1	4	5	20	4	16	7	28
CENSUS DIVISION 9, PACIFIC	397	92	23.2	135	34	265	66.8	83	20.9	24	6	105	26.4	27	6.8	178	44.8	92	23.2	146	36.8
Alaska	8	1	12.5	1	12.5	6	75	2	25	0	0	0	0	0	0	3	37.5	2	25	3	37.5
California	242	48	19.8	79	32.6	143	59.1	52	21.5	17	7	67	27.7	19	7.9	117	48.3	57	23.6	87	36
Hawaii	13	2	15.4	5	38.5	10	76.9	4	30.8	0	0	2	15.4	1	7.7	4	30.8	3	23.1	6	46.2
Oregon	61	19	31.1	21	34.4	49	80.3	9	14.8	2	3.3	10	16.4	1	1.6	22	36.1	11	18	20	32.8
Washington	73	22	30.1	29	39.7	57	78.1	16	21.9	5	6.8	26	35.6	6	8.2	32	43.8	19	26	30	41.1

Note: These data represent hospital performance in the years 2015 – 2019 and do not reflect any impacts from the COVID-19 pandemic in 2020 and thereafter.

Table 7 (Continued)

These data include only hospital-based facilities and services as reported by responding hospitals in Section C of the 2019 AHA Annual Survey, beginning on page 215. Census divisions represent all U.S. hospitals. Community hospitals are listed separately under United States. No estimates have been made for nonresponding hospitals. Definitions of facilities and services are listed in the Glossary; page 203.

Columns are grouped under **PSYCHIATRIC SERVICES** (Geriatric Services, Outpatient Services, Partial Hospitalization Program, Residential Treatment) and **RADIOLOGY, DIAGNOSTIC** (CT Scanner, Diagnostic Radioisotope Facility, Electron Beam Computed Tomography (EBCT), Full-Field Digital Mammography (FFDM), Magnetic Resonance Imaging (MRI), Intraoperative Magnetic Imaging).

Classification	Hospitals Reporting	Geriatric Svc No.	Geriatric Svc %	Outpatient Svc No.	Outpatient Svc %	Partial Hosp. Pgm No.	Partial Hosp. Pgm %	Residential Trtmt No.	Residential Trtmt %	CT Scanner No.	CT Scanner %	Diag. Radioisotope Fac. No.	Diag. Radioisotope Fac. %	EBCT No.	EBCT %	FFDM No.	FFDM %	MRI No.	MRI %	Intraop. Magnetic Imaging No.	Intraop. Magnetic Imaging %
UNITED STATES	4,167	873	21	1,225	29.4	532	12.8	199	4.8	3,512	84.3	2,400	57.6	340	8.2	2,543	61	2,854	68.5	243	5.8
COMMUNITY HOSPITALS	3,782	686	18.1	1,040	27.5	387	10.2	99	2.6	3,444	91.1	2,363	62.5	334	8.8	2,519	66.6	2,805	74.2	236	6.2
CENSUS DIVISION 1, NEW ENGLAND	156	42	26.9	87	55.8	44	28.2	12	7.7	132	84.6	106	67.9	9	5.8	119	76.3	102	65.4	9	5.8
Connecticut	26	7	26.9	20	76.9	14	53.8	5	19.2	24	92.3	21	80.8	1	3.8	21	80.8	22	84.6	2	7.7
Maine	30	5	16.7	15	50	4	13.3	0	0	27	90	21	70	1	3.3	24	80	19	63.3	0	0
Massachusetts	57	19	33.3	32	56.1	18	31.6	5	8.8	44	77.2	39	68.4	4	7	40	70.2	34	59.6	5	8.8
New Hampshire	25	6	24	11	44	3	12	0	0	22	88	12	48	1	4	21	84	14	56	2	8
Rhode Island	7	2	28.6	3	42.9	3	42.9	1	14.3	6	85.7	6	85.7	0	0	6	85.7	6	85.7	0	0
Vermont	11	3	27.3	6	54.5	2	18.2	1	9.1	9	81.8	6	54.5	2	18.2	8	72.7	7	63.6	0	0
CENSUS DIVISION 2, MIDDLE ATLANTIC	362	114	31.5	160	44.2	62	17.1	24	6.6	317	87.6	289	79.8	49	13.5	277	76.5	291	80.4	26	7.2
New Jersey	70	22	31.4	39	55.7	21	30	6	8.6	54	77.1	53	75.7	12	17.1	49	70	52	74.3	4	5.7
New York	135	45	33.3	80	59.3	24	17.8	11	8.1	126	93.3	109	80.7	19	14.1	111	82.2	109	80.7	13	9.6
Pennsylvania	157	47	29.9	41	26.1	17	10.8	7	4.5	137	87.3	127	80.9	18	11.5	117	74.5	130	82.8	9	5.7
CENSUS DIVISION 3, SOUTH ATLANTIC	574	133	23.2	147	25.6	79	13.8	30	5.2	487	84.8	395	68.8	51	8.9	390	67.9	431	75.1	31	5.4
Delaware	10	3	30	6	60	2	20	1	10	6	60	5	50	1	10	5	50	6	60	0	0
District of Columbia	8	2	25	4	50	1	12.5	0	0	5	62.5	4	50	1	10	3	37.5	5	62.5	0	0
Florida	165	35	21.2	33	20	20	12.1	8	4.8	147	89.1	123	74.5	27	16.4	109	66.1	130	78.8	17	10.3
Georgia	96	19	19.8	18	18.8	10	10.4	5	5.2	82	85.4	60	62.5	4	4.2	64	66.7	68	70.8	2	2.1
Maryland	45	14	31.1	29	64.4	18	40	8	17.8	40	88.9	40	88.9	5	11.1	29	64.4	37	82.2	5	11.1
North Carolina	74	17	23	15	20.3	6	8.1	2	2.7	66	89.2	50	67.6	4	5.4	57	77	60	81.1	2	2.7
South Carolina	68	19	27.9	11	16.2	11	16.2	1	1.5	50	73.5	41	60.3	2	2.9	43	63.2	48	70.6	1	1.5
Virginia	63	14	22.2	23	36.5	11	17.5	3	4.8	54	85.7	45	71.4	5	7.9	47	74.6	51	81	3	4.8
West Virginia	45	10	22.2	8	17.8	4	8.9	2	4.4	37	82.2	27	60	3	6.7	33	73.3	26	57.8	0	0
CENSUS DIVISION 4, EAST NORTH CENTRAL	672	169	25.1	237	35.3	106	15.8	34	5.1	588	87.5	442	65.8	66	9.8	461	68.6	511	76.8	48	7.1
Illinois	155	44	28.4	76	49	35	22.6	3	1.9	141	91	105	67.7	7	4.5	120	77.4	119	76.8	11	7.1
Indiana	117	20	17.1	33	28.2	15	12.8	14	12	94	80.3	69	59	11	9.4	77	65.8	90	76.9	6	5.1
Michigan	127	29	22.8	40	31.5	18	14.2	6	4.7	114	89.8	91	71.7	11	8.7	96	75.6	92	72.4	5	3.9
Ohio	127	29	22.8	41	32.3	24	18.9	8	6.3	115	90.6	96	75.6	22	17.3	92	72.4	105	82.7	14	11
Wisconsin	146	47	32.2	47	32.2	14	9.6	3	2.1	124	84.9	81	55.5	15	10.3	76	52.1	105	71.9	12	8.2
CENSUS DIVISION 5, EAST SOUTH CENTRAL	269	70	26	60	22.3	21	7.8	11	4.1	221	82.2	148	55	29	10.8	140	52	174	64.7	17	6.3
Alabama	47	9	19.1	7	14.9	2	4.3	3	6.4	41	87.2	31	66	4	8.5	30	63.8	38	80.9	1	2.1
Kentucky	53	10	18.9	11	20.8	3	5.7	3	5.7	44	83	31	58.5	4	7.5	31	58.5	39	73.6	3	5.7
Mississippi	102	34	33.3	31	30.4	12	11.8	2	2	82	80.4	43	42.2	10	9.8	35	34.3	48	47.1	10	9.8
Tennessee	67	17	25.4	11	16.4	4	6	3	4.5	54	80.6	43	64.2	11	16.4	44	65.7	49	73.1	3	4.5
CENSUS DIVISION 6, WEST NORTH CENTRAL	562	110	19.6	172	30.6	41	7.3	22	3.9	507	90.2	234	41.6	26	4.6	353	62.8	341	60.7	21	3.7
Iowa	122	19	15.6	45	36.9	9	7.4	3	2.5	115	94.3	41	33.6	5	4.1	104	85.2	71	58.2	2	1.6
Kansas	125	16	12.8	17	13.6	6	4.8	5	4	111	88.8	44	35.2	7	5.6	53	42.4	56	44.8	5	4
Minnesota	86	13	15.1	38	44.2	12	14	6	7	84	97.7	42	48.8	2	2.3	59	68.6	61	70.9	4	4.7
Missouri	137	49	35.8	45	32.8	7	5.1	4	2.9	109	79.6	70	51.1	8	5.8	80	58.4	101	73.7	4	2.9
Nebraska	40	5	12.5	15	37.5	2	5	2	5	39	97.5	19	47.5	2	5	31	77.5	27	67.5	5	12.5
North Dakota	16	5	31.3	6	37.5	3	18.8	0	0	14	87.5	9	56.3	1	6.3	11	68.8	10	62.5	0	0
South Dakota	36	3	8.3	8	22.2	2	5.6	1	2.8	35	97.2	9	25	1	2.8	15	41.7	15	41.7	1	2.8
CENSUS DIVISION 7, WEST SOUTH CENTRAL	838	144	17.2	161	19.2	96	11.5	32	3.8	613	73.2	340	40.6	45	5.4	353	42.1	455	54.3	44	5.3
Arkansas	89	22	24.7	18	20.2	9	10.1	8	9	69	77.5	36	40.4	5	5.6	45	50.6	58	65.2	2	2.2
Louisiana	89	26	29.2	29	32.6	19	21.3	2	2.2	61	68.5	43	48.3	8	9	52	58.4	52	58.4	10	11.2
Oklahoma	106	17	16	19	17.9	7	6.6	9	8.5	91	85.8	40	37.7	6	5.7	52	49.1	62	58.5	0	0
Texas	554	79	14.3	95	17.1	61	11	13	2.3	392	70.8	221	39.9	26	4.7	204	36.8	283	51.1	32	5.8
CENSUS DIVISION 8, MOUNTAIN	337	36	10.7	87	25.8	26	7.7	16	4.7	290	86.1	177	52.5	25	7.4	195	57.9	235	69.7	23	6.8
Arizona	72	12	16.7	19	26.4	6	8.3	9	12.5	55	76.4	45	62.5	5	6.9	33	45.8	51	70.8	9	12.5
Colorado	71	9	12.7	16	22.5	8	11.3	3	4.2	68	95.8	43	60.6	8	11.3	47	66.2	58	81.7	4	5.6
Idaho	26	1	3.8	8	30.8	1	3.8	1	3.8	24	92.3	14	53.8	2	7.7	14	53.8	20	76.9	1	3.8
Montana	51	5	9.8	16	31.4	4	7.8	2	3.9	46	90.2	17	33.3	0	0	30	58.8	26	51	0	0
Nevada	23	4	17.4	4	17.4	2	8.7	0	0	14	60.9	8	34.8	0	0	8	34.8	12	52.2	0	0
New Mexico	31	1	3.2	8	25.8	3	9.7	0	0	27	87.1	18	58.1	3	9.7	21	67.7	20	64.5	5	16.1
Utah	38	3	7.9	10	26.3	2	5.3	1	2.6	34	89.5	21	55.3	4	10.5	28	73.7	32	84.2	2	5.3
Wyoming	25	1	4	6	24	0	0	0	0	22	88	11	44	3	12	14	56	16	64	2	8
CENSUS DIVISION 9, PACIFIC	397	55	13.9	114	28.7	57	14.4	16	4	357	89.9	269	67.8	40	10.1	255	64.2	314	79.1	24	6
Alaska	8	0	0	3	37.5	3	37.5	1	12.5	8	100	4	50	0	0	4	50	6	75	0	0
California	242	42	17.4	69	28.5	40	16.5	9	3.7	213	88	165	68.2	27	11.2	151	62.4	188	77.7	19	7.9
Hawaii	13	0	0	5	38.5	3	23.1	1	7.7	10	76.9	10	76.9	0	0	10	76.9	10	76.9	0	0
Oregon	61	5	8.2	14	23	4	6.6	4	6.6	60	98.4	41	67.2	4	6.6	47	77	51	83.6	4	6.6
Washington	73	8	11	23	31.5	7	9.6	1	1.4	66	90.4	49	67.1	9	12.3	43	58.9	59	80.8	1	1.4

Note: These data represent hospital performance in the years 2015 – 2019 and do not reflect any impacts from the COVID-19 pandemic in 2020 and thereafter.

Table 7 (Continued)

These data include only hospital-based facilities and services as reported by responding hospitals in Section C of the 2019 AHA Annual Survey, beginning on page 215. Census divisions represent all U.S. hospitals. Community hospitals are listed separately under United States. No estimates have been made for nonresponding hospitals. Definitions of facilities and services are listed in the Glossary, page 203.

CLASSIFICATION	HOSPITALS REPORTING	MAGNETO-ENCEPHALOGRAPHY		MULTI-SLICE SPIRAL COMPUTED TOMOGRAPHY (<64 SLICE CT)		MULTI-SLICE SPIRAL COMPUTED TOMOGRAPHY (64+ SLICE CT)		POSITRON EMISSION TOMOGRAPHY (PET)		POSITRON EMISSION TOMOGRAPHY/CT (PET/CT)		SINGLE PHOTON EMISSION COMPUTERIZED TOMOGRAPHY (SPECT)		ULTRASOUND		IMAGE-GUIDED RADIATION THERAPY (IGRT)		INTENSITY-MODULATED RADIATION THERAPY (IMRT)		PROTON BEAM THERAPY	
		Number	Percent	Number	Percent	Number	Percent	Number	Percent	Number	Percent	Number	Percent	Number	Percent	Number	Percent	Number	Percent	Number	Percent
UNITED STATES	4,167	132	3.2	2,157	51.8	2,523	60.5	754	18.1	981	23.5	1,626	39	3,411	81.9	1,098	26.3	1,106	26.5	118	2.8
COMMUNITY HOSPITALS	3,782	127	3.4	2,116	55.9	2,483	65.7	732	19.4	956	25.3	1,596	42.2	3,347	88.5	1,079	28.5	1,092	28.9	115	3
CENSUS DIVISION 1, NEW ENGLAND	156	5	3.2	80	51.3	109	69.9	32	20.5	47	30.1	84	53.8	141	90.4	57	36.5	56	35.9	5	3.2
Connecticut	26	0	0	17	65.4	23	88.5	12	46.2	18	69.2	20	76.9	25	96.2	19	73.1	17	65.4	1	3.8
Maine	30	0	0	11	36.7	20	66.7	4	13.3	7	23.3	12	40	27	90	5	16.7	6	20	0	0
Massachusetts	57	4	7	30	52.6	40	70.2	11	19.3	15	26.3	29	50.9	52	91.2	23	40.4	23	40.4	3	5.3
New Hampshire	25	1	4	13	52	16	64	2	8	3	12	13	52	22	88	6	24	6	24	0	0
Rhode Island	7	0	0	5	71.4	4	57.1	2	28.6	2	28.6	5	71.4	6	85.7	1	14.3	1	14.3	1	14.3
Vermont	11	0	0	4	36.4	6	54.5	1	9.1	2	18.2	5	45.5	9	81.8	3	27.3	3	27.3	0	0
CENSUS DIVISION 2, MIDDLE ATLANTIC	362	13	3.6	221	61	269	74.3	87	24	125	34.5	209	57.7	317	87.6	156	43.1	166	45.9	13	3.6
New Jersey	70	4	5.7	47	67.1	47	67.1	23	32.9	30	42.9	40	57.1	56	80	32	45.7	38	54.3	2	2.9
New York	135	4	3	85	63	107	79.3	31	23	41	30.4	73	54.1	125	92.6	54	40	57	42.2	7	5.2
Pennsylvania	157	5	3.2	89	56.7	115	73.2	33	21	54	34.4	96	61.1	136	86.6	70	44.6	71	45.2	4	2.5
CENSUS DIVISION 3, SOUTH ATLANTIC	574	17	3	360	62.7	372	64.8	121	21.1	159	27.7	275	47.9	486	84.7	197	34.3	199	34.7	15	2.6
Delaware	8	1	12.5	5	62.5	6	62.5	1	12.5	3	37.5	4	50	5	62.5	4	50	4	50	0	0
District of Columbia	10	1	10	5	50	6	60	5	50	5	50	6	60	7	70	5	50	5	50	2	20
Florida	165	7	4.2	110	66.7	111	67.3	45	27.3	56	33.9	73	44.2	142	86.1	49	29.7	47	28.5	4	2.4
Georgia	96	2	2.1	56	58.3	59	61.5	21	21.9	29	30.2	34	35.4	81	84.4	31	32.3	32	33.3	0	0
Maryland	45	2	4.4	34	75.6	37	82.2	14	31.1	16	35.6	32	71.1	40	88.9	23	51.1	23	51.1	3	6.7
North Carolina	74	1	1.4	53	71.6	48	64.9	8	10.8	18	24.3	45	60.8	69	93.2	34	45.9	35	47.3	5	6.8
South Carolina	68	0	0	33	48.5	41	60.3	4	5.9	10	14.7	23	33.8	52	76.5	14	20.6	15	22.1	0	0
Virginia	63	3	4.8	37	58.7	43	68.3	14	22.2	14	22.2	41	65.1	53	84.1	27	42.9	28	44.4	1	1.6
West Virginia	45	0	0	27	60	22	48.9	9	20	8	17.8	17	37.8	37	82.2	10	22.2	10	22.2	0	0
CENSUS DIVISION 4, EAST NORTH CENTRAL	672	26	3.9	337	50.1	457	68	155	23.1	190	28.3	323	48.1	575	85.6	213	31.7	216	32.1	23	3.4
Illinois	155	3	1.9	89	57.4	120	77.4	31	20	47	30.3	71	45.8	137	88.4	54	34.8	56	36.1	6	3.9
Indiana	117	5	4.3	54	46.2	70	59.8	18	15.4	24	20.5	41	35	92	78.6	34	29.1	38	32.5	4	3.4
Michigan	127	3	2.4	65	51.2	102	80.3	19	15	34	26.8	67	52.8	117	92.1	39	30.7	42	33.1	3	2.4
Ohio	127	11	8.7	83	65.4	92	72.4	45	35.4	49	38.6	73	57.5	115	90.6	48	37.8	42	33.1	5	3.9
Wisconsin	146	4	2.7	46	31.5	73	50	42	28.8	36	24.7	71	48.6	114	78.1	38	26	38	26	5	3.4
CENSUS DIVISION 5, EAST SOUTH CENTRAL	289	6	2.2	126	46.8	143	53.2	56	20.8	56	20.8	96	35.7	218	81	57	21.2	57	21.2	5	1.9
Alabama	47	2	4.3	26	55.3	32	68.1	12	25.5	15	31.9	18	38.3	40	85.1	10	21.3	10	21.3	0	0
Kentucky	53	2	3.8	26	49.1	33	62.3	11	20.8	13	24.5	25	47.2	45	84.9	15	28.3	15	28.3	2	3.8
Mississippi	102	1	1	43	42.2	36	35.3	16	15.7	11	10.8	28	27.5	78	76.5	11	10.8	11	10.8	2	2
Tennessee	67	1	1.5	31	46.3	42	62.7	17	25.4	17	25.4	25	37.3	55	82.1	21	31.3	21	31.3	1	1.5
CENSUS DIVISION 6, WEST NORTH CENTRAL	562	15	2.7	257	45.7	315	56	70	12.5	115	20.5	162	28.8	460	81.9	111	19.8	113	20.1	13	2.3
Iowa	122	1	0.8	62	50.8	69	56.6	12	9.8	22	18	34	27.9	115	94.3	18	14.8	17	13.9	3	2.5
Kansas	125	3	2.4	57	45.6	63	41.6	8	6.4	18	12	22	17.6	87	69.6	18	14.4	18	14.4	4	3.2
Minnesota	86	3	3.5	35	40.7	63	73.3	13	15.1	18	20.9	31	36	73	84.9	19	22.1	21	24.4	1	1.2
Missouri	137	4	2.9	54	39.4	81	59.1	21	15.3	41	29.9	51	37.2	108	78.8	36	26.3	38	27.7	3	2.2
Nebraska	40	2	5	24	60	25	62.5	9	22.5	12	30	10	25	37	92.5	11	27.5	10	25	1	2.5
North Dakota	16	2	12.5	9	56.3	9	56.3	4	25	4	25	6	37.5	13	81.3	4	25	4	25	1	6.3
South Dakota	36	0	0	16	44.4	16	44.4	3	8.3	3	8.3	8	22.2	27	75	5	13.9	6	16.7	0	0
CENSUS DIVISION 7, WEST SOUTH CENTRAL	838	24	2.9	374	44.6	364	43.4	83	9.9	101	12.1	184	22	575	68.6	97	11.6	102	12.2	13	1.6
Arkansas	89	3	3.4	37	41.6	43	48.3	9	10.1	9	10.1	17	19.1	68	76.4	9	10.1	8	11.1	1	1.1
Louisiana	89	3	3.4	40	44.9	41	46.1	18	20.2	20	22.5	23	25.8	62	69.7	19	21.3	19	21.3	2	2.2
Oklahoma	106	0	0	51	48.1	56	52.8	11	10.4	19	17.9	25	23.6	80	75.5	19	17.9	19	17.9	1	0.9
Texas	554	18	3.2	246	44.4	224	40.4	45	8.1	53	9.6	119	21.5	365	65.9	50	9	56	10.1	9	1.6
CENSUS DIVISION 8, MOUNTAIN	337	8	2.4	155	46	217	64.4	54	16	68	20.2	102	30.3	279	82.8	85	25.2	81	24	17	5
Arizona	72	3	4.2	41	56.9	41	56.9	11	15.3	14	19.4	29	40.3	55	76.4	15	20.8	15	20.8	6	8.3
Colorado	71	0	0	42	59.2	56	78.9	19	26.8	23	32.4	24	33.8	67	94.4	23	32.4	23	32.4	4	5.6
Idaho	26	0	0	12	46.2	16	61.5	3	11.5	3	11.5	8	30.8	24	92.3	5	19.2	6	23.1	1	3.8
Montana	51	0	0	23	45.1	27	52.9	5	9.8	8	15.7	10	19.6	38	74.5	13	25.5	11	21.6	2	3.9
Nevada	23	2	6.5	4	17.4	10	43.5	2	8.7	3	13	3	13	14	60.9	3	13	2	8.7	2	8.7
New Mexico	31	0	0	15	48.4	21	67.7	4	12.9	6	19.4	5	16.1	26	83.9	8	25.8	9	29	2	6.5
Utah	38	1	2.6	9	23.7	29	76.3	7	18.4	8	21.1	18	47.4	34	89.5	11	28.9	11	28.9	0	0
Wyoming	25	0	0	9	36	17	68	3	12	3	12	5	20	21	84	4	16	4	16	0	0
CENSUS DIVISION 9, PACIFIC	397	18	4.5	247	62.2	277	69.8	96	24.2	120	30.2	191	48.1	360	90.7	125	31.5	116	29.2	14	3.5
Alaska	8	0	0	5	62.5	5	62.5	0	0	0	0	2	25	8	100	2	25	2	25	0	0
California	242	18	7.4	155	64	170	70.2	69	28.5	86	35.5	123	50.8	218	90.1	82	33.9	75	31	10	4.1
Hawaii	13	0	0	4	30.8	9	69.2	1	7.7	3	23.1	4	30.8	10	76.9	4	30.8	4	30.8	0	0
Oregon	61	0	0	38	62.3	41	67.2	12	19.7	13	21.3	30	49.2	58	95.1	16	26.2	15	24.6	2	3.3
Washington	73	0	0	47	64.4	52	71.2	14	19.2	18	24.7	32	43.8	66	90.4	21	28.8	21	28.8	2	2.7

Note: These data represent hospital performance in the years 2015 – 2019 and do not reflect any impacts from the COVID-19 pandemic in 2020 and thereafter.

Table 7 (Continued)

These data include only hospital-based facilities and services as reported by responding hospitals in Section C of the 2019 AHA Annual Survey, beginning on page 215. Census divisions represent all U.S. hospitals. Community hospitals are listed separately under United States. No estimates have been made for nonresponding hospitals. Definitions of facilities and services are listed in the Glossary, page 203.

Columns under **RADIOLOGY, THERAPEUTIC**: Shaped Beam Radiation System, Stereotactic Radiosurgery. Columns under **TRANSPLANT**: Heart, Kidney, Liver, Lung, Tissue.

CLASSIFICATION	HOSPITALS REPORTING	Shaped Beam Radiation System No.	%	Stereotactic Radiosurgery No.	%	Bone Marrow No.	%	Heart No.	%	Kidney No.	%	Liver No.	%	Lung No.	%	Tissue No.	%	Other No.	%
UNITED STATES	4,167	924	22.2	884	21.2	200	4.8	136	3.3	222	5.3	138	3.3	81	1.9	469	11.3	220	5.3
COMMUNITY HOSPITALS	3,782	912	24.1	875	23.1	196	5.2	134	3.5	216	5.7	135	3.6	78	2.1	460	12.2	216	5.7
CENSUS DIVISION 1, NEW ENGLAND	156	53	34	49	31.4	12	7.7	6	3.8	15	9.6	8	5.1	3	1.9	17	10.9	9	5.8
Connecticut	26	16	61.5	15	57.7	2	7.7	2	7.7	2	7.7	2	7.7	0	0	2	7.7	1	3.8
Maine	30	5	16.7	4	13.3	0	0	0	0	1	3.3	0	0	0	0	1	3.3	0	0
Massachusetts	57	22	38.6	21	36.8	9	15.8	4	7	9	15.8	6	10.5	3	5.3	10	17.5	6	10.5
New Hampshire	25	6	24	6	24	1	4	0	0	1	4	0	0	0	0	1	4	1	4
Rhode Island	7	1	14.3	1	14.3	1	14.3	0	0	1	14.3	0	0	0	0	1	14.3	0	0
Vermont	11	3	27.3	2	18.2	1	9.1	0	0	1	9.1	0	0	0	0	2	18.2	1	9.1
CENSUS DIVISION 2, MIDDLE ATLANTIC	362	138	38.1	127	35.1	28	7.7	17	4.7	34	9.4	20	5.5	9	2.5	96	26.5	40	11
New Jersey	70	35	50	30	42.9	2	2.9	2	2.9	4	5.7	1	1.4	1	1.4	24	34.3	4	5.7
New York	135	47	34.8	44	32.6	13	9.6	7	5.2	13	9.6	7	5.2	3	2.2	39	28.9	15	11.1
Pennsylvania	157	56	35.7	53	33.8	13	8.3	8	5.1	17	10.8	12	7.6	5	3.2	33	21	21	13.4
CENSUS DIVISION 3, SOUTH ATLANTIC	574	170	29.6	154	26.8	42	7.3	25	4.4	32	5.6	19	3.3	13	2.3	81	14.1	38	6.6
Delaware	8	4	50	3	37.5	2	25	1	12.5	2	25	1	12.5	0	0	0	0	0	0
District of Columbia	10	5	50	4	40	3	30	0	0	3	30	1	10	0	0	3	30	2	20
Florida	165	38	23	50	30.3	13	7.9	8	4.8	9	5.5	7	4.2	5	3	26	15.8	7	4.2
Georgia	96	29	30.2	28	29.2	3	3.1	2	2.1	3	3.1	2	2.1	1	1	10	10.4	3	3.1
Maryland	45	20	44.4	19	42.2	5	11.1	2	4.4	3	6.7	2	4.4	2	4.4	12	26.7	5	11.1
North Carolina	74	32	43.2	15	20.3	4	5.4	4	5.4	4	5.4	3	4.1	2	2.7	7	9.5	10	13.5
South Carolina	68	12	17.6	10	14.7	4	5.9	1	1.5	1	1.5	1	1.5	1	1.5	5	7.4	3	4.4
Virginia	63	21	33.3	18	28.6	5	7.9	4	6.3	5	7.9	2	3.2	2	3.2	16	25.4	7	11.1
West Virginia	45	9	20	7	15.6	2	4.4	1	2.2	2	4.4	0	0	0	0	2	4.4	1	2.2
CENSUS DIVISION 4, EAST NORTH CENTRAL	672	172	25.6	165	24.6	29	4.3	24	3.6	36	5.4	23	3.4	20	3	80	11.9	27	4
Illinois	155	44	28.4	45	29	8	5.2	9	5.8	9	5.8	6	3.9	4	2.6	18	11.6	7	4.5
Indiana	117	25	21.4	24	20.5	1	0.9	3	2.6	3	2.6	1	0.9	1	0.9	7	6	3	2.6
Michigan	127	35	27.6	34	26.8	7	5.5	6	4.7	10	7.9	6	4.7	5	3.9	22	17.3	7	5.5
Ohio	127	35	27.6	38	29.9	8	6.3	6	4.7	10	7.9	7	5.5	6	4.7	27	21.3	7	5.5
Wisconsin	146	33	22.6	24	16.4	5	3.4	4	2.7	4	2.7	3	2.1	4	2.7	6	4.1	3	2.1
CENSUS DIVISION 5, EAST SOUTH CENTRAL	269	45	16.7	49	18.2	12	4.5	9	3.3	11	4.1	8	3	5	1.9	21	7.8	12	4.5
Alabama	47	8	17	9	19.1	2	4.3	2	4.3	3	6.4	2	4.3	1	2.1	3	6.4	3	6.4
Kentucky	53	11	20.8	12	22.6	3	5.7	3	5.7	3	5.7	2	3.8	2	3.8	8	15.1	3	5.7
Mississippi	102	10	9.8	13	12.7	1	1	1	1	1	1	1	1	1	1	1	1	1	1
Tennessee	67	16	23.9	15	22.4	6	9	3	4.5	4	6	2	3	2	3	9	13.4	5	7.5
CENSUS DIVISION 6, WEST NORTH CENTRAL	562	91	16.2	77	13.7	16	2.8	14	2.5	23	4.1	14	2.5	8	1.4	39	6.9	26	4.6
Iowa	122	17	13.9	12	9.8	1	0.8	1	0.8	5	4.1	2	1.6	2	1.6	4	3.3	5	4.1
Kansas	125	16	12.8	11	8.8	2	1.6	1	0.8	1	0.8	1	0.8	2	1.6	4	3.2	3	2.4
Minnesota	86	13	15.1	13	15.1	4	4.7	4	4.7	4	4.7	3	3.5	3	3.5	7	8.1	2	2.3
Missouri	137	28	20.4	24	17.5	6	4.4	5	3.6	8	5.8	6	4.4	2	1.5	15	10.9	9	6.6
Nebraska	40	10	25	10	25	2	5	2	5	1	2.5	1	2.5	1	2.5	5	12.5	3	7.5
North Dakota	16	3	18.8	4	25	0	0	0	0	2	12.5	0	0	0	0	2	12.5	2	12.5
South Dakota	36	4	11.1	3	8.3	1	2.8	0	0	2	5.6	1	2.8	0	0	2	5.6	2	5.6
CENSUS DIVISION 7, WEST SOUTH CENTRAL	838	82	9.8	100	11.9	19	2.3	16	1.9	33	3.9	21	2.5	10	1.2	45	5.4	27	3.2
Arkansas	89	7	7.9	12	13.5	2	2.2	2	2.2	4	4.5	4	4.5	0	0	5	5.6	1	1.1
Louisiana	89	14	15.7	19	21.3	3	3.4	2	2.2	4	4.5	4	4.5	2	2.2	6	6.7	6	6.7
Oklahoma	106	15	14.2	14	13.2	2	1.9	1	0.9	4	3.8	2	1.9	1	0.9	6	5.7	3	2.8
Texas	554	46	8.3	55	9.9	12	2.2	11	2	23	4.2	14	2.5	7	1.3	28	5.1	17	3.1
CENSUS DIVISION 8, MOUNTAIN	337	66	19.6	59	17.5	14	4.2	9	2.7	14	4.2	10	3	4	1.2	41	12.2	12	3.6
Arizona	71	11	15.3	13	18.1	4	5.6	4	5.6	5	6.9	4	5.6	2	2.8	9	12.7	4	5.6
Colorado	72	19	26.8	13	18.3	3	4.2	2	2.8	3	4.2	4	5.6	1	1.4	9	12.5	4	5.6
Idaho	26	3	11.5	5	19.2	1	3.8	0	0	0	0	0	0	0	0	2	7.7	0	0
Montana	51	10	19.6	11	21.6	1	2	0	0	0	0	0	0	0	0	2	3.9	0	0
Nevada	23	2	8.7	2	8.7	1	4.3	0	0	1	4.3	0	0	0	0	1	4.3	1	4.3
New Mexico	31	6	19.4	6	19.4	1	3.2	0	0	2	6.5	0	0	0	0	2	6.5	0	0
Utah	38	11	28.9	10	26.3	3	7.9	3	7.9	3	7.9	3	7.9	1	2.6	19	50	2	5.3
Wyoming	25	4	16	3	12	0	0	0	0	0	0	0	0	0	0	1	4	0	0
CENSUS DIVISION 9, PACIFIC	397	107	27	104	26.2	28	7.1	16	4	24	6	15	3.8	9	2.3	49	12.3	29	7.3
Alaska	8	2	25	1	12.5	0	0	0	0	0	0	0	0	0	0	0	0	0	0
California	242	71	29.3	70	28.9	19	7.9	12	5	16	6.6	10	4.1	8	3.3	36	14.9	18	7.4
Hawaii	13	1	7.7	3	23.1	1	7.7	0	0	1	7.7	1	7.7	0	0	2	15.4	2	15.4
Oregon	61	14	23	10	16.4	2	3.3	1	1.6	2	3.3	1	1.6	0	0	4	6.6	3	4.9
Washington	73	19	26	20	27.4	7	9.6	3	4.1	5	6.8	3	4.1	1	1.4	7	9.6	6	8.2

Note: These data represent hospital performance in the years 2015 – 2019 and do not reflect any impacts from the COVID-19 pandemic in 2020 and thereafter.

Table 8

Table		Page
8	**Utilization, Personnel, and Finances in Community Hospitals By Metropolitan Area for 2019**	171

CBSAs

Core-Based Statistical Areas

A core-based statistical area is a U.S. geographic area defined by the Office of Management and Budget (OMB) that consists of one or more counties (or equivalents) anchored by an urban center of at least 10,000 people plus adjacent counties that are socioeconomically tied to the urban center by commuting. Areas defined on the basis of these standards applied to Census 2000 data were announced by OMB in June 2003.

When a CBSA encompasses two or more central cities, up to three cities may be specified in the CBSA title. They will be listed in order of population size. When a single central city exists, the CBSA is named for that particular city. A CBSA may extend beyond a single state.

A CBSA containing a single core with a population of 2.5 million or more may be subdivided to form smaller groupings of counties referred to as Metropolitan Divisions. Where they exist, Metropolitan Divisions are shown in this table rather than the entire CBSA.

Note: These data represent hospital performance in the years 2015 – 2019 and do not reflect any impacts from the COVID-19 pandemic in 2020 and thereafter.

TABLE 8

U.S. CENSUS DIVISION 1, NEW ENGLAND

U.S. Community Hospitals
(Nonfederal, short-term general and other special hospitals)

2019 Utilization, Personnel and Finances

CLASSIFICATION	Hospitals	Beds	Admissions	Inpatient Days	Adjusted Inpatient Days	Average Daily Census	Adjusted Average Daily Census	Average Stay (days)	Surgical Operations	NEWBORNS Bassinets	NEWBORNS Births	OUTPATIENT VISITS Emergency	OUTPATIENT VISITS Total
UNITED STATES	5,141	787,995	34,078,100	185,149,928	405,300,173	507,247	1,111,220	5.4	28,368,697	54,468	3,567,799	143,432,284	785,235,256
Nonmetropolitan	1,805	105,939	2,943,396	19,504,162	68,565,291	53,445	188,011	6.6	3,601,239	8,490	332,782	21,679,837	131,209,175
Metropolitan	3,336	682,056	31,134,704	165,645,766	336,734,882	453,802	923,209	5.3	24,767,458	45,978	3,235,017	121,752,447	654,026,081
CENSUS DIVISION 1, NEW ENGLAND.	192	32,559	1,567,740	8,682,964	21,644,014	23,789	59,377	5.5	1,371,806	2,220	140,837	7,366,120	50,064,163
Nonmetropolitan	54	3,289	124,472	789,263	2,980,120	2,164	8,179	6.3	151,691	288	10,896	909,020	8,243,660
Metropolitan	138	29,270	1,443,268	7,893,701	18,663,894	21,625	51,198	5.5	1,220,115	1,932	129,941	6,457,100	41,820,503
Connecticut	31	7,246	372,553	2,049,145	4,526,208	5,615	12,416	5.5	330,416	456	34,843	1,701,496	8,701,047
Nonmetropolitan	2	132	6,677	32,443	86,395	89	253	4.9	6,041	9	512	45,217	341,690
Metropolitan	29	7,114	365,876	2,016,702	4,439,813	5,526	12,163	5.5	324,375	447	34,331	1,656,279	8,359,357
Bridgeport-Stamford-Norwalk	6	1,696	89,665	448,482	1,035,738	1,229	2,837	5	82,511	125	11,223	394,124	1,933,913
Hartford-East Hartford-Middletown..	11	2,615	132,011	727,888	1,516,388	1,996	4,155	5.5	121,673	146	11,631	598,551	3,186,434
New Haven-Milford	8	2,265	114,685	695,690	1,449,674	1,905	3,971	6.1	94,451	102	8,718	438,438	2,451,749
Norwich-New London	2	434	22,995	119,263	348,868	327	955	5.2	20,137	42	2,191	155,216	519,495
Worcester	2	104	6,520	25,379	89,145	69	245	3.9	5,603	32	568	69,950	267,766
Maine	34	3,482	128,560	892,731	2,418,283	2,444	6,625	6.9	145,803	255	11,594	721,184	6,746,501
Nonmetropolitan	21	1,095	35,645	262,098	1,042,674	718	2,855	7.4	44,270	121	3,602	326,372	2,712,312
Metropolitan	13	2,387	92,915	630,633	1,375,609	1,726	3,770	6.8	101,533	134	7,992	394,812	4,034,189
Bangor	4	526	25,521	140,968	324,162	385	888	5.5	26,285	28	1,882	77,877	1,020,632
Lewiston-Auburn	2	540	15,124	147,296	289,443	404	793	9.7	13,192	35	1,083	105,559	683,769
Portland-South Portland	7	1,321	52,270	342,369	762,004	937	2,089	6.6	62,056	71	5,027	211,376	2,329,788
Massachusetts	74	15,561	777,310	4,222,166	10,303,090	11,567	28,223	5.4	621,085	1,029	65,577	3,385,519	23,460,607
Nonmetropolitan	2	100	1,472	24,001	187,466	66	514	16.3	2,994	10	283	24,231	229,403
Metropolitan	72	15,461	775,838	4,198,165	10,115,624	11,501	27,709	5.4	618,091	1,019	65,294	3,361,288	23,231,204
Barnstable Town	3	414	23,337	108,803	284,863	298	781	4.7	13,921	18	1,081	110,194	640,433
Boston	26	6,594	324,114	1,902,267	4,376,748	5,211	11,990	5.9	283,412	322	26,026	1,028,916	9,518,133
Cambridge-Newton-Framingham	19	3,905	193,626	1,003,118	2,524,615	2,748	6,916	5.2	136,651	330	18,733	915,655	5,867,625
Pittsfield	2	300	15,042	70,481	233,071	193	638	4.7	14,513	24	790	77,399	570,263
Providence-Warwick	4	942	55,606	259,303	623,994	710	1,709	4.7	37,630	64	4,307	372,911	1,561,101
Springfield	9	1,632	79,716	417,734	1,045,919	1,145	2,864	5.2	57,861	113	6,505	362,040	2,477,502
Worcester	9	1,674	84,397	436,459	1,026,414	1,196	2,811	5.2	74,103	148	7,852	494,173	2,596,147
New Hampshire	28	2,804	121,800	648,227	2,001,554	1,777	5,552	5.3	124,344	247	11,541	712,254	5,825,923
Nonmetropolitan	17	1,233	52,869	291,252	1,047,596	799	2,870	5.5	64,262	74	3,853	272,793	3,167,019
Metropolitan	11	1,571	68,931	356,975	953,958	978	2,682	5.2	60,082	173	7,688	439,461	2,658,904
Manchester-Nashua	5	852	38,595	194,276	543,395	533	1,556	5	28,947	102	4,384	161,910	1,462,739
Rockingham County-Strafford County	6	719	30,336	162,699	410,563	445	1,126	5.4	31,135	71	3,304	277,551	1,196,165
Rhode Island	11	2,191	116,276	554,916	1,338,058	1,521	3,666	4.8	95,278	115	12,002	528,353	2,298,700
Metropolitan	11	2,191	116,276	554,916	1,338,058	1,521	3,666	4.8	95,278	115	12,002	528,353	2,298,700
Providence-Warwick	11	2,191	116,276	554,916	1,338,058	1,521	3,666	4.8	95,278	115	12,002	528,353	2,298,700
Vermont	14	1,275	51,241	315,779	1,056,821	865	2,895	6.2	54,880	118	5,280	317,314	3,031,385
Nonmetropolitan	12	729	27,809	179,469	615,989	492	1,687	6.5	34,124	74	2,646	240,407	1,793,236
Metropolitan	2	546	23,432	136,310	440,832	373	1,208	5.8	20,756	44	2,634	76,907	1,238,149
Burlington-South Burlington	2	546	23,432	136,310	440,832	373	1,208	5.8	20,756	44	2,634	76,907	1,238,149

CBSAs

Note: These data represent hospital performance in the years 2015 – 2019 and do not reflect any impacts from the COVID-19 pandemic in 2020 and thereafter.

CBSAs

FULL-TIME EQUIVALENT PERSONNEL					FULL-TIME EQUIV. TRAINEES			EXPENSES						
								LABOR				TOTAL		
Physicians and Dentists	Registered Nurses	Licensed Practical Nurses	Other Salaried Personnel	Total Personnel	Medical and Dental Residents	Other Trainees	Total Trainees	Payroll (in thousands)	Employee Benefits (in thousands)	Total (in thousands)	Percent of Total	Amount (in thousands)	Adjusted per Admission	Adjusted per Inpatient Day
151,543	1,610,150	74,506	3,478,759	5,314,958	114,374	10,333	124,707	392,816,521	101,760,004	494,576,525	46.8	1,056,497,068	14,101.17	2,606.7
17,078	158,021	19,998	433,466	628,563	2,057	445	2,502	39,406,654	10,178,727	49,585,381	49.7	99,721,479	9,592.76	1,454.4
134,465	1,452,129	54,508	3,045,293	4,686,395	112,317	9,888	122,205	353,409,867	91,581,277	444,991,145	46.5	956,775,589	14,827.48	2,841.33
14,592	81,799	2,240	216,273	314,904	9,531	943	10,474	23,905,984	5,831,806	29,737,790	46.1	64,448,762	16,071.69	2,977.67
1,869	8,772	441	26,425	37,507	456	44	500	2,981,400	733,656	3,715,056	54.9	6,769,388	14,215.64	2,271.52
12,723	73,027	1,799	189,848	277,397	9,075	899	9,974	20,924,584	5,098,150	26,022,734	45.1	57,679,374	16,321.79	3,090.43
1,536	16,491	264	36,588	54,879	2,108	95	2,203	4,525,722	995,130	5,520,852	42.3	13,054,730	15,489.73	2,884.25
18	319	18	748	1,103	2	0	2	88,159	17,854	106,013	57.5	184,458	10,376.19	2,135.05
1,518	16,172	246	35,840	53,776	2,106	95	2,201	4,437,563	977,276	5,414,839	42.1	12,870,273	15,599.91	2,898.83
372	3,298	39	8,088	11,797	453	13	466	1,071,077	228,699	1,299,776	42.7	3,044,914	14,587.11	2,939.85
811	5,635	106	13,525	20,077	100	60	160	1,609,991	402,590	2,012,581	43.8	4,597,145	16,401.21	3,031.64
246	6,211	87	11,622	18,166	1,552	10	1,562	1,411,593	277,738	1,689,330	39.3	4,297,755	17,481.78	2,964.64
68	746	0	1,859	2,673	0	12	12	264,628	50,968	315,596	44.5	709,285	10,556.57	2,033.11
21	282	14	746	1,063	1	0	1	80,274	17,282	97,556	44.1	221,173	9,633.8	2,481.04
1,820	8,159	220	25,120	35,319	338	14	352	2,595,042	649,702	3,244,744	52	6,242,767	17,060.75	2,581.49
582	2,611	85	9,154	12,432	2	8	10	839,661	217,167	1,056,828	53.6	1,970,697	13,015.89	1,890.04
1,238	5,548	135	15,966	22,887	336	6	342	1,755,381	432,535	2,187,916	51.2	4,272,070	19,915.76	3,105.58
344	1,445	44	3,328	5,161	31	2	33	438,106	106,322	544,428	49.3	1,104,499	18,439.97	3,407.24
191	998	16	2,144	3,349	24	2	26	225,801	46,688	272,490	43.6	624,591	19,899.02	2,157.91
703	3,105	75	10,494	14,377	281	2	283	1,091,473	279,524	1,370,998	53.9	2,542,980	20,637.39	3,337.23
8,257	41,038	1,104	110,124	160,523	5,469	689	6,158	11,600,690	2,911,079	14,511,769	44.1	32,932,794	16,916.65	3,196.4
33	147	5	446	631	0	1	1	71,025	14,662	85,687	56	153,132	12,719.62	816.85
8,224	40,891	1,099	109,678	159,892	5,469	688	6,157	11,529,665	2,896,417	14,426,083	44	32,779,663	16,942.77	3,240.5
149	721	9	2,268	3,147	0	0	0	318,585	81,287	399,872	52.4	763,099	12,209.59	2,678.83
5,512	21,085	351	59,442	86,390	4,691	606	5,297	6,239,744	1,514,056	7,753,800	41.2	18,839,636	24,784.27	4,304.48
672	8,840	353	20,776	30,641	335	18	353	2,253,554	616,299	2,869,852	48.9	5,869,707	11,321.19	2,324.99
83	686	83	2,313	3,165	0	1	1	241,437	65,036	306,473	55.4	553,637	10,978.97	2,375.4
40	1,910	47	4,530	6,527	12	2	14	584,718	148,658	733,376	52.3	1,401,146	10,368.26	2,245.45
806	3,822	80	10,456	15,164	407	44	451	867,224	184,106	1,051,331	46.3	2,272,424	11,167.58	2,172.66
962	3,827	176	9,893	14,858	24	17	41	1,024,404	286,975	1,311,379	42.6	3,080,014	15,056.48	3,000.75
1,538	7,749	305	22,157	31,749	464	29	493	2,432,655	605,666	3,038,320	54	5,625,096	14,385.37	2,810.36
969	3,988	168	10,951	16,076	446	28	474	1,420,720	345,608	1,766,328	55.7	3,173,448	16,425.46	3,029.27
569	3,761	137	11,206	15,673	18	1	19	1,011,934	260,058	1,271,992	51.9	2,451,647	12,392.95	2,569.97
396	2,105	64	6,136	8,701	0	0	0	552,031	149,710	701,741	54.1	1,298,145	11,639.74	2,388.95
173	1,656	73	5,070	6,972	18	1	19	459,903	110,348	570,251	49.4	1,153,502	13,366.34	2,809.56
465	4,838	100	11,885	17,288	800	66	866	1,495,808	363,066	1,858,874	49	3,791,360	13,349.91	2,833.48
465	4,838	100	11,885	17,288	800	66	866	1,495,808	363,066	1,858,874	49	3,791,360	13,349.91	2,833.48
465	4,838	100	11,885	17,288	800	66	866	1,495,808	363,066	1,858,874	49	3,791,360	13,349.91	2,833.48
976	3,524	247	10,399	15,146	352	50	402	1,256,067	307,163	1,563,230	55.8	2,802,015	15,603.94	2,651.36
267	1,707	165	5,126	7,265	6	7	13	561,835	138,365	700,200	54.4	1,287,654	12,652.96	2,090.38
709	1,817	82	5,273	7,881	346	43	389	694,233	168,798	863,031	57	1,514,361	19,463.8	3,435.23
709	1,817	82	5,273	7,881	346	43	389	694,233	168,798	863,031	57	1,514,361	19,463.8	3,435.23

Note: These data represent hospital performance in the years 2015 – 2019 and do not reflect any impacts from the COVID-19 pandemic in 2020 and thereafter.

AHA Hospital Statistics © 2021 Health Forum LLC, an affiliate of the American Hospital Association   **173**

TABLE 8 U.S. CENSUS DIVISION 2, MIDDLE ATLANTIC

U.S. Community Hospitals
(Nonfederal, short-term general and other special hospitals)

2019 Utilization, Personnel and Finances

CLASSIFICATION	Hospitals	Beds	Admissions	Inpatient Days	Adjusted Inpatient Days	Average Daily Census	Adjusted Average Daily Census	Average Stay (days)	Surgical Operations	NEWBORNS Bassinets	NEWBORNS Births	OUTPATIENT VISITS Emergency	OUTPATIENT VISITS Total
UNITED STATES	5,198	792,417	34,251,159	185,307,228	401,318,395	507,697	1,100,206	5.4	28,168,014	54,943	3,637,593	143,454,611	766,392,512
Nonmetropolitan	1,821	108,166	3,008,734	19,667,770	67,543,319	53,878	185,275	6.5	3,542,053	8,752	345,082	21,571,345	129,292,741
Metropolitan	3,377	684,251	31,242,425	165,639,458	333,775,076	453,819	914,931	5.3	24,625,961	46,191	3,292,511	121,883,266	637,099,771
CENSUS DIVISION 2, MIDDLE ATLANTIC	435	108,395	4,847,024	28,091,060	57,197,177	76,958	156,880	5.8	3,963,672	5,947	437,062	18,582,130	116,060,486
Nonmetropolitan	69	7,273	201,032	1,622,681	5,890,973	4,445	16,138	8.1	278,958	422	17,006	1,524,265	11,070,563
Metropolitan	366	101,122	4,645,992	26,468,379	51,306,204	72,513	140,742	5.7	3,684,714	5,525	420,056	17,057,865	104,989,923
New Jersey	81	20,863	1,073,799	5,068,308	9,117,583	13,885	24,988	4.7	576,014	1,291	94,782	3,633,427	14,706,668
Metropolitan	81	20,863	1,073,799	5,068,308	9,117,583	13,885	24,988	4.7	576,014	1,291	94,782	3,633,427	14,706,668
Allentown-Bethlehem-Easton	2	153	7,678	33,592	80,947	92	222	4.4	6,205	0	0	47,844	160,440
Atlantic City-Hammonton	4	848	41,491	202,001	403,654	554	1,105	4.9	17,404	58	1,583	149,981	552,483
Camden	12	3,278	134,957	748,186	1,314,362	2,050	3,611	5.5	90,813	115	11,628	523,371	1,716,857
New Brunswick-Lakewood	20	5,108	353,695	1,297,418	2,189,798	3,553	5,998	3.7	138,942	339	27,563	915,485	3,219,151
New York-Jersey City-White Plains	15	4,710	240,946	1,081,724	1,976,638	2,963	5,416	4.5	129,713	353	23,804	769,490	3,910,662
Newark	18	5,218	229,591	1,350,664	2,430,023	3,702	6,658	5.9	138,881	340	24,289	885,359	3,949,220
Ocean City	1	178	5,827	27,580	88,837	76	243	4.7	3,241	16	314	41,746	216,555
Trenton-Princeton	5	761	35,117	201,206	417,040	551	1,143	5.7	29,551	36	3,398	182,539	604,633
Vineland-Bridgeton	2	386	18,939	104,171	168,231	285	461	5.5	15,515	24	1,891	78,818	282,199
Wilmington	2	223	5,558	21,766	48,053	59	131	3.9	5,749	10	312	38,794	94,468
New York	163	52,084	2,236,457	14,681,148	29,158,734	40,221	80,054	6.6	2,034,760	3,022	214,850	8,766,573	60,235,662
Nonmetropolitan	35	4,093	101,042	977,594	3,443,474	2,681	9,432	9.7	147,176	255	9,835	888,730	6,350,615
Metropolitan	128	47,991	2,135,415	13,703,554	25,715,260	37,540	70,622	6.4	1,887,584	2,767	205,015	7,877,843	53,885,047
Albany-Schenectady-Troy	8	2,301	109,499	629,956	1,308,274	1,727	3,586	5.8	92,474	87	7,945	336,788	2,858,644
Binghamton	2	618	28,258	153,634	400,340	421	1,097	5.4	33,492	52	2,260	236,439	2,873,422
Buffalo-Cheektowaga	10	4,202	133,681	1,154,928	2,123,954	3,165	5,819	8.6	154,408	235	12,867	487,767	2,753,183
Elmira	1	266	11,780	47,943	99,711	131	273	4.1	7,054	20	978	76,777	371,363
Glens Falls	1	334	10,692	46,598	138,700	128	380	4.4	10,932	22	1,202	45,335	737,577
Ithaca	1	159	6,582	30,631	71,731	84	197	4.7	7,685	21	834	54,262	279,783
Kingston	3	280	9,844	54,951	141,740	151	388	5.6	5,612	20	387	33,619	137,316
Nassau County-Suffolk County	18	7,368	388,299	2,310,877	4,042,768	6,330	11,075	6	299,949	398	34,239	1,131,117	5,343,449
New York-Jersey City-White Plains	55	25,370	1,124,683	7,332,733	12,756,401	20,086	34,945	6.5	1,014,796	1,438	115,927	4,267,077	26,922,346
Poughkeepsie-Newburgh-Middletown	6	1,120	58,173	280,923	531,048	768	1,627	4.8	41,880	83	5,939	224,416	1,051,533
Rochester	10	3,112	127,977	943,625	2,443,846	2,586	6,696	7.4	117,781	178	10,591	512,898	6,613,231
Syracuse	6	1,943	88,380	501,096	1,034,885	1,372	2,835	5.7	70,611	133	7,752	289,871	2,458,771
Utica-Rome	4	687	27,694	164,883	423,867	452	1,161	6	17,684	48	2,264	112,126	984,807
Watertown-Fort Drum	3	231	9,873	50,776	197,995	139	543	5.1	13,226	32	1,830	69,351	499,622
Pennsylvania	191	35,448	1,536,768	8,341,604	18,920,860	22,852	51,838	5.4	1,352,898	1,634	127,430	6,182,130	41,118,156
Nonmetropolitan	34	3,180	99,990	645,087	2,447,499	1,764	6,706	6.5	131,782	167	7,171	635,535	4,719,948
Metropolitan	157	32,268	1,436,778	7,696,517	16,473,361	21,088	45,132	5.4	1,221,116	1,467	120,259	5,546,595	36,398,208
Allentown-Bethlehem-Easton	10	2,515	111,254	626,553	1,336,464	1,717	3,661	5.6	92,420	87	9,905	416,167	2,283,479
Altoona	4	496	22,884	116,860	286,704	319	785	5.1	20,195	20	1,513	83,076	491,205
Bloomsburg-Berwick	5	776	33,674	192,200	527,902	527	1,447	5.7	32,528	34	2,948	126,089	1,371,365
Chambersburg-Waynesboro	2	342	13,708	54,806	161,715	150	443	4	12,185	31	1,726	74,986	523,998
East Stroudsburg	2	329	15,649	65,825	140,714	181	386	4.2	7,650	20	981	98,845	348,172
Erie	6	976	40,785	219,380	446,236	601	1,223	5.4	36,692	64	4,026	145,629	481,350
Gettysburg	1	76	5,062	16,325	61,919	45	170	3.2	4,453	16	461	28,898	247,161
Harrisburg-Carlisle	8	1,975	83,340	485,967	1,019,760	1,332	2,795	5.8	73,304	83	7,262	277,937	2,347,246
Johnstown	3	573	19,220	101,905	213,419	279	585	5.3	15,266	14	1,769	62,343	516,862
Lancaster	4	844	42,941	194,712	424,039	534	1,161	4.5	40,486	74	5,983	160,676	2,077,619
Lebanon	1	159	7,187	32,565	91,523	89	251	4.5	7,878	19	720	49,976	294,263
Montgomery County-Bucks County-Chester County	22	3,892	186,199	821,444	1,678,434	2,251	4,596	4.4	126,549	277	21,013	686,427	3,473,049
Philadelphia	25	7,287	331,767	1,911,435	3,663,628	5,239	10,040	5.8	279,372	253	21,395	1,190,372	7,843,806
Pittsburgh	34	7,260	322,795	1,801,086	3,799,442	4,934	10,408	5.6	323,708	279	23,297	1,148,463	7,853,941
Reading	5	1,064	47,452	224,342	489,875	615	1,341	4.7	21,323	56	3,655	177,468	1,369,798
Scranton-Wilkes-Barre	10	1,651	66,766	328,012	841,663	897	2,306	4.9	59,169	55	5,486	287,152	2,090,583
State College	2	333	14,340	62,586	148,245	172	406	4.4	13,989	5	1,283	54,388	331,630
Williamsport	3	433	13,151	108,505	375,620	297	1,029	8.3	14,343	15	1,153	71,190	475,929
York-Hanover	6	958	43,822	261,631	574,911	717	1,575	6	25,727	38	3,803	180,775	1,235,793
Youngstown-Warren-Boardman	4	329	14,782	70,378	191,148	192	524	4.8	13,879	27	1,880	225,738	740,959

Note: These data represent hospital performance in the years 2015 – 2019 and do not reflect any impacts from the COVID-19 pandemic in 2020 and thereafter.

TABLE 8

U.S. CENSUS DIVISION 2, MIDDLE ATLANTIC

U.S. Community Hospitals
(Nonfederal, short-term general and other special hospitals)

2019 Utilization, Personnel and Finances

CBSAs

Physicians and Dentists	Registered Nurses	Licensed Practical Nurses	Other Salaried Personnel	Total Personnel	Medical and Dental Residents	Other Trainees	Total Trainees	Payroll (in thousands)	Employee Benefits (in thousands)	Total (in thousands)	Percent of Total	Amount (in thousands)	Adjusted per Admission	Adjusted per Inpatient Day
144,792	1,586,860	75,060	3,431,822	5,238,534	117,619	9,172	126,791	$377,640,231	$97,798,365	$475,438,596	47.1	$1,010,271,112	$13,542.37	$2,517.38
16,857	155,492	20,586	431,056	623,991	2,007	425	2,432	37,990,709	9,848,267	47,838,976	50.0	95,730,556	9,130.95	1,417.32
127,935	1,431,368	54,474	3,000,766	4,614,543	115,612	8,747	124,359	339,649,522	87,950,099	427,599,621	46.8	914,540,556	14,263.72	2,739.99
30,747	228,222	9,082	531,337	799,388	33,486	1,256	34,742	64,341,310	17,602,629	81,943,939	49.7	164,736,017	16,825.7	2,880.14
896	10,053	1,430	28,915	41,294	203	24	227	2,537,806	673,636	3,211,442	49.7	6,456,197	9,512.54	1,095.95
29,851	218,169	7,652	502,422	758,094	33,283	1,232	34,515	61,803,505	16,928,993	78,732,497	49.7	158,279,820	17,370.42	3085
3,773	39,556	691	86,585	130,605	3,047	90	3,137	10,296,317	2,307,431	12,603,748	47.8	26,389,783	13,562.96	2,894.38
3,773	39,556	691	86,585	130,605	3,047	90	3,137	10,296,317	2,307,431	12,603,748	47.8	26,389,783	13,562.96	2,894.38
44	319	4	735	1,102	26	0	26	96,471	19,044	115,515	51.5	224,162	12,182.03	2,769.24
42	1,478	37	3,314	4,871	64	1	65	388,852	98,366	487,217	46.3	1,053,202	13,228.68	2,609.17
885	5,193	169	12,991	19,238	399	3	402	1,265,099	313,593	1,578,692	42.3	3,730,375	15,576.2	2,838.16
416	10,822	111	20,817	32,166	549	13	562	2,598,631	528,664	3,127,295	49	6,382,716	10,616.03	2,914.75
957	8,816	96	20,583	30,452	637	37	674	2,314,761	512,477	2,827,238	46.2	6,124,713	13,634.07	3,098.55
1,303	10,212	183	22,598	34,296	1,148	27	1,175	2,960,931	655,281	3,616,212	50.3	7,188,278	17,174.85	2,958.11
0	199	0	775	974	0	9	9	53,646	16,454	70,101	56.7	123,566	6,583.51	1,390.93
111	1,739	33	3,308	5,191	67	0	67	390,328	92,969	483,297	47.2	1,023,373	1,337.	2,453.9
3	589	43	1,048	1,683	157	0	157	177,349	55,711	233,060	56.8	410,568	12,984.43	2,440.5
12	189	15	416	632	0	0	0	50,249	14,871	65,120	50.5	128,832	10,434.31	2,681.05
17,121	113,974	5,781	285,331	422,207	20,552	543	21,095	37,446,240	11,033,352	48,479,592	54.2	89,518,162	20,455.8	3,070.03
442	5,438	878	16,428	23,186	65	10	75	1,511,134	404,360	1,915,493	52.5	3,646,463	10,700.81	1,058.95
16,679	108,536	4,903	268,903	399,021	20,487	533	21,020	35,935,106	10,628,993	46,564,099	54.2	85,871,699	21,279.55	3,339.33
400	4,816	267	12,305	17,788	527	4	531	1,164,781	217,355	1,382,136	46.9	2,945,892	12,812.46	2,251.74
202	1,724	141	4,487	6,554	150	7	157	436,584	105,238	541,822	48.1	1,127,207	14,154.85	2,815.62
456	7,040	463	14,165	22,124	225	90	315	1,740,841	549,588	2,290,429	52.2	4,391,286	17,590.19	2,067.51
95	946	41	2,085	3,167	35	2	37	157,336	39,653	196,989	46.7	421,836	17,217.79	4,230.59
78	451	30	1,428	1,987	0	0	0	153,379	26,101	179,480	51.1	351,173	11,034.5	2,531.89
34	434	23	982	1,473	8	2	10	92,547	23,453	116,000	47.7	243,226	15,780.58	3,390.81
34	441	27	1,089	1,591	8	0	8	88,236	22,099	110,335	49	225,222	9,298.23	1,588.98
4,308	17,580	363	42,112	64,363	4,137	13	4,150	6,507,643	1,796,381	8,304,024	58.9	14,090,978	20,645.31	3,485.48
9,078	59,310	1,890	152,290	222,568	13,687	342	14,029	21,564,941	6,735,864	28,300,805	54.1	52,309,312	26,319.55	4,100.63
51	2,367	39	4,793	7,250	162	1	163	556,777	178,429	735,206	49.2	1,494,235	13,518.08	2,813.75
1,543	8,059	917	18,944	29,463	807	67	874	2,033,760	530,663	2,564,423	54.6	4,699,096	14,562.49	1,922.83
206	3,553	433	8,995	13,187	694	1	695	964,165	307,962	1,272,128	49.9	2,547,304	15,039.08	2,461.44
109	1,240	120	3,528	4,997	32	4	36	327,003	58,944	385,948	56.2	686,764	9,976.53	1,620.24
85	575	149	1,700	2,509	15	0	15	147,112	37,261	184,374	54.5	338,167	8,712.73	1,707.96
9,853	74,692	2,610	159,421	246,576	9,887	623	10,510	16,598,753	4,261,846	20,860,599	42.7	48,828,072	14,076.21	2,580.65
454	4,615	552	12,487	18,108	138	14	152	1,026,672	269,277	1,295,948	46.1	2,809,734	8,314.32	1148
9,399	70,077	2,058	146,934	228,468	9,749	609	10,358	15,572,082	3,992,569	19,564,651	42.5	46,018,338	14,698.13	2,793.5
794	4,986	86	12,598	18,464	594	4	598	1,145,811	243,500	1,389,311	41.4	3,353,486	13,947.58	2,509.22
68	901	37	1,641	2,647	1	14	15	181,327	44,028	225,355	38.9	578,626	9,971.15	2,018.2
599	2,078	174	4,968	7,819	713	0	713	425,639	127,661	553,300	39.8	1,390,116	14,379.71	2,633.28
2	524	11	1,607	2,144	0	2	2	156,042	51,869	207,910	57	364,640	8,816.68	2,254.83
34	523	16	1,137	1,710	12	1	13	124,427	29,870	154,296	45	342,552	10,204.41	2,434.38
29	1,917	72	3,015	5,033	100	11	111	266,981	63,117	330,098	37	892,589	10,730.68	2,000.26
0	221	4	491	716	0	0	0	45,200	17,068	62,268	32.7	190,172	9,904.77	3,071.3
1,443	4,313	414	10,330	16,500	937	2	939	974,508	292,612	1,267,120	41.1	3,083,218	17,360.36	3,023.47
0	632	39	1,901	2,572	89	0	89	142,783	33,685	176,468	46.8	377,031	9027	1,766.62
147	1,718	64	5,086	7,015	85	20	105	473,407	141,704	615,111	46	1,338,189	14,212.77	3,155.82
0	265	2	621	888	19	0	19	59,240	21,742	80,982	36.1	224,516	11,115.19	2,453.11
787	7,629	144	14,860	23,420	350	14	364	1,717,593	393,434	2,111,028	47	4,495,838	11,640.01	2,678.59
3,309	19,508	310	41,024	64,151	4,230	332	4,562	5,288,054	1,342,760	6,630,813	46.6	14,244,205	22,517.49	3,888.01
1,460	15,889	283	28,946	46,578	2,087	193	2,280	2,644,030	631,848	3,275,879	35.2	9,319,659	13,067.26	2,452.9
235	2,229	72	5,191	7,727	263	14	277	522,956	140,118	663,074	50.3	1,318,337	12,844.28	2,691.17
376	2,875	146	5,300	8,697	91	0	91	508,135	145,931	654,066	38	1,722,509	9,860.83	2,046.55
16	432	7	1,366	1,821	1	0	1	194,863	57,906	252,768	57.6	438,462	12,757.13	2,957.69
8	657	94	1,177	1,936	0	1	1	156,604	44,037	200,641	42.6	471,531	11,957.77	1,255.34
82	1,990	62	4,215	6,349	162	1	163	415,205	138,994	554,199	37.8	1,467,259	15,316.18	2,552.15
10	790	21	1,460	2,281	15	0	15	129,279	30,684	159,963	39.5	405,404	8,856.07	2,120.89

Note: These data represent hospital performance in the years 2015 – 2019 and do not reflect any impacts from the COVID-19 pandemic in 2020 and thereafter.

TABLE 8

U.S. CENSUS DIVISION 3, SOUTH ATLANTIC

U.S. Community Hospitals
(Nonfederal, short-term general and other special hospitals)

2019 Utilization, Personnel and Finances

CLASSIFICATION	Hospitals	Beds	Admissions	Inpatient Days	Adjusted Inpatient Days	Average Daily Census	Adjusted Average Daily Census	Average Stay (days)	Surgical Operations	NEWBORNS Bassinets	NEWBORNS Births	OUTPATIENT VISITS Emergency	OUTPATIENT VISITS Total
UNITED STATES	5,198	792,417	34,251,159	185,307,228	401,318,395	507,697	1,100,206	5.4	28,168,014	54,943	3,637,593	143,454,611	766,392,512
Nonmetropolitan	1,821	108,166	3,008,734	19,667,770	67,543,319	53,878	185,275	6.5	3,542,053	8,752	345,082	21,571,345	129,292,741
Metropolitan	3,377	684,251	31,242,425	165,639,458	333,775,076	453,819	914,931	5.3	24,625,961	46,191	3,292,511	121,883,266	637,099,771
CENSUS DIVISION 3, SOUTH ATLANTIC	752	155,077	7,091,809	38,487,726	79,524,467	105,433	218,007	5.4	5,368,871	10,014	681,302	29,444,522	125,476,411
Nonmetropolitan	181	15,868	488,199	3,352,297	9,863,014	9,187	27,022	6.9	478,595	1,093	43,821	3,392,696	13,998,204
Metropolitan	571	139,209	6,603,610	35,135,429	69,661,453	96,246	190,985	5.3	4,890,276	8,921	637,481	26,051,826	111,478,207
Delaware	7	2,112	103,328	569,518	1,196,191	1,560	3,277	5.5	89,456	116	10,358	478,571	2,205,773
Metropolitan	7	2,112	103,328	569,518	1,196,191	1,560	3,277	5.5	89,456	116	10,358	478,571	2,205,773
Dover	1	385	20,203	103,200	253,378	283	694	5.1	16,153	10	2,193	105,181	616,156
Salisbury	2	254	16,193	65,057	171,429	178	470	4	18,617	25	1,539	83,009	592,776
Wilmington	4	1,473	66,932	401,261	771,384	1,099	2,113	6	54,686	81	6,626	290,381	996,841
District of Columbia	10	3,186	124,261	900,757	1,571,795	2,468	4,305	7.2	101,905	165	12,682	418,267	2,788,961
Metropolitan	10	3,186	124,261	900,757	1,571,795	2,468	4,305	7.2	101,905	165	12,682	418,267	2,788,961
Washington-Arlington-Alexandria	10	3,186	124,261	900,757	1,571,795	2,468	4,305	7.2	101,905	165	12,682	418,267	2,788,961
Florida	212	55,733	2,645,062	12,940,795	23,752,915	35,456	65,129	4.9	1,520,096	2,741	205,759	10,186,649	31,633,093
Nonmetropolitan	17	746	26,716	114,615	361,228	316	991	4.3	26,208	25	947	238,163	697,525
Metropolitan	195	54,987	2,618,346	12,826,180	23,391,687	35,140	64,138	4.9	1,493,888	2,716	204,812	9,948,486	30,935,568
Cape Coral-Fort Myers	4	1,649	80,199	376,695	726,627	1,031	1,991	4.7	41,871	124	6,032	255,708	524,910
Crestview-Fort Walton Beach-Destin	5	558	26,746	104,655	231,407	287	634	3.9	22,718	51	2,848	135,360	408,132
Deltona-Daytona Beach-Ormond Beach	6	1,582	74,804	364,444	748,673	998	2,052	4.9	45,002	64	3,714	383,706	1,086,256
Fort Lauderdale-Pompano Beach-Sunrise	17	5,103	222,634	1,189,907	2,120,422	3,259	5,808	5.3	118,859	268	22,556	867,944	2,095,139
Gainesville	4	1,551	83,349	464,172	747,137	1,272	2,047	5.6	58,008	40	5,973	193,701	1,298,423
Homosassa Springs	2	332	18,592	72,145	129,373	198	354	3.9	11,483	20	975	104,701	262,644
Jacksonville	15	4,227	196,807	1,005,905	1,890,763	2,756	5,182	5.1	150,092	272	18,095	879,247	2,508,657
Lakeland-Winter Haven	5	1,617	83,988	367,674	728,083	1,008	1,995	4.4	41,715	62	6,106	408,554	669,739
Miami-Miami Beach-Kendall	23	7,547	316,849	1,741,234	3,188,656	4,772	8,735	5.5	164,696	356	23,957	1,157,402	6,982,404
Naples-Marco Island	3	919	41,748	186,380	340,706	511	933	4.5	26,041	35	3,430	239,488	663,350
North Port-Sarasota-Bradenton	8	2,182	101,630	476,657	795,796	1,306	2,181	4.7	60,798	63	5,681	336,334	1,091,417
Ocala	4	718	36,819	177,369	285,905	485	783	4.8	19,839	30	2,444	149,273	267,177
Orlando-Kissimmee-Sanford	15	7,822	358,727	1,761,373	3,164,651	4,825	8,670	4.9	199,461	346	32,156	1,428,760	3,067,046
Palm Bay-Melbourne-Titusville	8	1,496	70,775	320,990	564,259	879	1,545	4.5	41,721	70	4,909	308,460	816,702
Panama City	5	367	24,948	126,415	228,008	347	680	5.1	11,378	37	2,423	123,617	284,634
Pensacola-Ferry Pass-Brent	7	1,373	79,676	358,209	761,994	982	2,088	4.5	47,210	72	6,661	328,047	1,122,344
Port St. Lucie	4	1,086	59,204	251,476	457,640	689	1,254	4.2	30,106	64	3,735	197,766	355,155
Punta Gorda	3	681	27,705	136,831	214,471	375	588	4.9	18,825	22	852	85,677	216,255
Sebastian-Vero Beach	3	454	23,609	105,313	216,924	289	594	4.5	15,330	22	1,015	79,600	148,001
Sebring-Avon Park	2	260	14,323	56,677	128,876	155	353	4	11,798	29	1,338	79,277	238,190
Tallahassee	4	798	45,295	220,097	412,736	602	1,130	4.9	24,486	62	4,529	158,057	986,648
Tampa-St. Petersburg-Clearwater	34	8,952	437,469	2,074,482	3,751,605	5,683	10,277	4.7	235,919	388	29,672	1,453,849	4,199,799
The Villages	1	40	360	10,115	10,351	28	28	28.1	478	0	0	0	13,239
West Palm Beach-Boca Raton-Boynton Beach	13	3,673	192,090	876,965	1,546,624	2,403	4,236	4.6	96,054	219	15,711	593,958	1,629,307
Georgia	143	24,896	1,035,793	6,500,916	14,187,631	17,811	38,872	6.3	784,708	1,848	121,077	4,629,550	20,470,988
Nonmetropolitan	56	5,561	133,338	1,281,500	3,571,666	3,510	9,784	9.6	139,680	307	14,888	918,114	3,596,593
Metropolitan	87	19,335	902,455	5,219,416	10,615,965	14,301	29,088	5.8	645,028	1,541	106,189	3,711,436	16,874,395
Albany	2	460	18,957	112,008	297,901	307	817	5.9	14,159	29	2,142	80,430	1,208,510
Athens-Clarke County	3	560	30,114	154,752	287,859	424	789	5.1	23,540	54	3,762	130,526	515,998
Atlanta-Sandy Springs-Alpharetta	44	10,646	516,374	2,964,636	5,759,636	8,124	15,781	5.7	340,790	879	66,671	2,157,231	9,844,025
Augusta-Richmond County	7	1,522	66,737	381,517	742,442	1,045	2,036	5.7	75,416	96	6,912	275,009	1,339,219
Brunswick	1	532	13,155	156,224	365,430	428	1,001	11.9	10,846	8	1,221	54,175	253,064
Chattanooga	1	35	439	1,415	37,209	4	102	3.2	72	0	0	22,161	30,768
Columbus	4	974	34,265	174,729	326,678	478	895	5.1	22,646	76	3,929	161,939	498,350
Dalton	2	239	10,491	45,055	107,432	123	295	4.3	5,511	40	1,539	69,805	320,365
Gainesville	1	887	38,088	262,410	481,610	719	1,319	6.9	24,474	54	4,708	155,025	430,285
Hinesville	1	25	1,495	4,713	21,302	13	58	3.2	1,936	6	341	5,743	39,160
Macon-Bibb County	5	999	49,783	303,436	541,062	831	1,481	6.1	36,836	114	3,499	136,789	611,306
Rome	2	557	29,229	136,988	307,201	375	842	4.7	17,048	30	2,192	124,537	427,033
Savannah	7	1,288	62,359	365,178	964,510	1,000	2,643	5.9	45,087	71	5,182	170,402	727,324
Valdosta	3	253	14,015	74,522	161,240	205	442	5.3	10,021	40	1,751	55,163	220,973
Warner Robins	4	358	16,954	81,833	214,453	225	587	4.8	16,646	44	2,340	112,501	408,015

Note: These data represent hospital performance in the years 2015 – 2019 and do not reflect any impacts from the COVID-19 pandemic in 2020 and thereafter.

CBSAs

TABLE 8

U.S. CENSUS DIVISION 3, SOUTH ATLANTIC

U.S. Community Hospitals
(Nonfederal, short-term general and other special hospitals)

2019 Utilization, Personnel and Finances

FULL-TIME EQUIVALENT PERSONNEL					FULL-TIME EQUIV. TRAINEES			EXPENSES						
								LABOR				TOTAL		
Physicians and Dentists	Registered Nurses	Licensed Practical Nurses	Other Salaried Personnel	Total Personnel	Medical and Dental Residents	Other Trainees	Total Trainees	Payroll (in thousands)	Employee Benefits (in thousands)	Total (in thousands)	Percent of Total	Amount (in thousands)	Adjusted per Admission	Adjusted per Inpatient Day
144,792	1,586,860	75,060	3,431,822	5,238,534	117,619	9,172	126,791	$377,640,231	$97,798,365	$475,438,596	47.1	$1,010,271,112	$13,542.37	$2,517.38
16,857	155,492	20,586	431,056	623,991	2,007	425	2,432	37,990,709	9,848,267	47,838,976	50.0	95,730,556	9,130.95	1,417.32
127,935	1,431,368	54,474	3,000,766	4,614,543	115,612	8,747	124,359	339,649,522	87,950,099	427,599,621	46.8	914,540,556	14,263.72	2,739.99
20,471	308,713	12,433	635,865	977,482	18,849	1,576	20,425	65,756,358	16,034,543	81,790,902	45.3	180,686,825	12,296.48	2,272.09
1,744	22,473	2,804	57,821	84,842	335	49	384	4,696,243	1,196,518	5,892,762	48.1	12,260,951	8,326.16	1,243.12
18,727	286,240	9,629	578,044	892,640	18,514	1,527	20,041	61,060,115	14,838,025	75,898,140	45.1	168,425,874	12,738.68	2,417.78
811	5,687	191	13,181	19,870	296	1	297	1,673,833	466,960	2,140,793	57	3,757,034	16,910.78	3,140.83
811	5,687	191	13,181	19,870	296	1	297	1,673,833	466,960	2,140,793	57	3,757,034	16,910.78	3,140.83
100	735	33	2,113	2,981	0	0	0	298,284	76,824	375,108	59.2	633,770	12,776.84	2,501.28
127	885	61	2,176	3,249	0	0	0	182,926	51,933	234,859	46	510,887	11,913.78	2,980.16
584	4,067	97	8,892	13,640	296	1	297	1,192,623	338,202	1,530,825	58.6	2,612,378	20,144.34	3,386.61
1,417	7,735	144	15,418	24,714	1,252	89	1,341	2,335,094	431,019	2,766,114	53.1	5,212,331	23,472.1	3,316.16
1,417	7,735	144	15,418	24,714	1,252	89	1,341	2,335,094	431,019	2,766,114	53.1	5,212,331	23,472.1	3,316.16
1,417	7,735	144	15,418	24,714	1,252	89	1,341	2,335,094	431,019	2,766,114	53.1	5,212,331	23,472.1	3,316.16
5,415	99,426	2,767	189,904	297,512	6,438	338	6,776	20,180,004	4,788,317	24,968,321	44.4	56,199,232	11,433.09	2,365.99
78	1,199	147	2,983	4,407	11	1	12	242,283	54,011	296,294	47	630,442	7,216.35	1,745.27
5,337	98,227	2,620	186,921	293,105	6,427	337	6,764	19,937,721	4,734,306	24,672,027	44.4	55,568,790	11,509.39	2,375.58
255	3,311	160	7,630	11,356	629	32	661	901,951	154,313	1,056,264	54.8	1,927,366	12,462.2	2,652.48
11	817	28	1,293	2,149	11	0	11	136,560	27,674	164,234	38.3	429,033	7,076.95	1,854.02
153	2,336	60	5,880	8,429	8	47	55	614,638	164,594	779,233	50.7	1,536,452	9,908.89	2,052.23
872	9,034	270	14,590	24,766	359	9	368	1,639,768	339,426	1,979,194	45.7	4,332,593	10,864.73	2,043.27
16	3,799	60	6,589	10,464	972	16	988	688,872	182,373	871,245	43.3	2,012,061	15,046.03	2,693.03
13	641	22	1,016	1,692	19	1	20	82,816	19,265	102,081	38.7	263,688	7,863.76	2,038.2
612	7,912	129	13,338	21,991	780	26	806	1,456,446	399,869	1,856,315	40.3	4,611,747	12,256.55	2,439.09
0	2,696	19	5,288	8,003	0	0	0	482,509	122,212	604,720	46.4	1,302,239	7,808.08	1,788.59
706	13,022	382	25,578	39,688	1,955	24	1,979	3,102,690	731,792	3,834,482	43.6	8,801,293	14,920.91	2,760.19
167	1,697	50	2,524	4,438	49	4	53	291,034	53,171	344,205	46.5	740,873	9,567.19	2,174.52
170	3,486	206	7,065	10,927	86	8	94	626,996	131,860	758,856	43.8	1,731,662	10,237.56	2,176.01
13	1,318	38	2,050	3,419	18	0	18	232,713	61,752	294,465	44	668,819	10,911.66	2,339.31
769	14,714	268	29,557	45,308	823	118	941	2,837,987	847,068	3,685,055	46.7	7,898,923	12,238.95	2,495.99
37	2,512	47	3,990	6,586	33	1	34	491,763	100,045	591,808	45.7	1,295,571	10,021.12	2,296.06
8	637	36	1,023	1,704	7	1	8	146,436	28,480	174,916	37.9	461,536	9,549.69	2,024.21
19	2,476	76	3,679	6,250	18	0	18	401,908	79,138	481,045	37.1	1,297,152	7185	1,702.31
180	1,887	84	4,252	6,403	24	0	24	376,666	85,220	461,886	48.6	949,408	8,860.88	2,074.57
17	885	30	1,389	2,321	25	1	26	132,188	26,258	158,446	40	396,550	9,104.99	1,848.97
101	743	17	1,530	2,391	19	1	20	139,582	30,983	170,565	47	362,717	7,492.92	1,672.09
38	531	34	1,248	1,851	10	1	11	106,575	29,506	136,081	49.6	274,157	8,441.33	2,127.3
178	1,554	146	4,310	6,188	101	0	101	398,644	65,159	463,803	47	985,892	11,805.82	2,388.67
833	16,442	331	33,053	50,659	315	37	352	3,460,737	810,258	4,270,995	43	9,937,953	12,591.12	2,648.99
0	50	10	97	157	0	0	0	9,555	1,698	11,253	49.1	22,920	62,283.45	2,214.31
169	5,727	117	9,952	15,965	166	10	176	1,178,687	242,192	1,420,878	42.7	3,328,182	9,712.47	2,151.9
2,519	45,889	2,631	97,344	148,383	1,822	501	2,323	10,015,554	2,447,971	12,463,526	45.3	27,514,935	12,463.85	1,939.36
472	6,188	973	17,287	24,920	77	16	93	1,407,624	351,022	1,758,646	48.9	3,594,162	9,393.04	1,006.3
2,047	39,701	1,658	80,057	123,463	1,745	485	2,230	8,607,930	2,096,949	10,704,879	44.8	23,920,774	13,107.72	2,253.28
6	777	44	1,875	2,702	24	6	30	160,562	49,523	210,085	35.6	589,314	11,878.22	1,978.22
9	1,380	47	2,386	3,822	70	12	82	249,218	66,149	315,367	46.3	681,110	11,862.31	2,366.12
1,151	24,247	847	48,533	74,778	1,017	272	1,289	5,293,201	1,278,464	6,571,666	44.7	14,687,653	14,433.37	2,550.1
8	2,953	140	4,849	7,950	1	9	10	581,298	124,605	705,904	40.1	1,760,682	13,592.64	2,371.47
98	384	93	1,667	2,242	0	0	0	168,836	39,656	208,492	57.2	364,663	11,850.87	997.9
0	49	4	113	166	0	0	0	8,113	1,966	10,079	47	21,461	1,859.07	576.77
123	1,223	45	2,555	3,946	104	5	109	238,680	53,455	292,135	43.3	674,556	10,381.15	2,064.9
44	395	20	978	1,437	13	1	14	128,268	32,563	160,831	47	342,475	13,061.09	3,187.83
80	1,851	30	3,085	5,046	65	155	220	348,012	90,401	438,412	46.5	942,607	13,484.3	1,957.2
8	61	14	197	280	0	0	0	23,114	6,481	29,595	53.1	55,738	8,248.93	2,616.56
188	1,790	62	3,630	5,670	204	8	212	369,644	88,591	458,235	44.2	1,037,854	12,076.49	1,918.18
15	996	54	2,161	3,226	39	0	39	274,971	80,972	355,944	51.5	690,516	10,649.87	2,247.77
226	2,080	114	4,609	7,029	163	12	175	479,014	111,387	590,401	44.6	1,325,050	9,666.82	1,373.81
77	797	46	1,770	2,690	26	3	29	159,857	40,615	200,472	47.3	423,846	14,282.46	2,628.67
14	718	98	1,649	2,479	19	2	21	125,143	32,120	157,263	48.7	323,248	7,507.78	1,507.31

Table continues

CBSAs

Note: These data represent hospital performance in the years 2015 – 2019 and do not reflect any impacts from the COVID-19 pandemic in 2020 and thereafter.

TABLE 8

U.S. CENSUS DIVISION 3, SOUTH ATLANTIC CONTINUED

U.S. Community Hospitals
(Nonfederal, short-term general and other special hospitals)

2019 Utilization, Personnel and Finances

CLASSIFICATION	Hospitals	Beds	Admissions	Inpatient Days	Adjusted Inpatient Days	Average Daily Census	Adjusted Average Daily Census	Average Stay (days)	Surgical Operations	NEWBORNS Bassinets	NEWBORNS Births	OUTPATIENT VISITS Emergency	OUTPATIENT VISITS Total
Maryland	48	10,894	543,185	2,923,810	5,427,514	8,007	14,870	5.4	459,111	900	62,147	2,206,790	9,451,896
Nonmetropolitan	4	362	14,641	84,862	230,450	232	632	5.8	14,653	30	981	84,687	429,246
Metropolitan	44	10,532	528,544	2,838,948	5,197,064	7,775	14,238	5.4	444,458	870	61,166	2,122,103	9,022,650
Baltimore-Columbia-Towson	24	6,967	333,626	1,909,557	3,433,449	5,230	9,408	5.7	317,953	441	33,717	1,246,211	5,709,826
California-Lexington Park	1	96	6,354	24,722	62,596	68	171	3.9	7,990	16	1,096	48,962	164,994
Cumberland	1	321	11,094	78,381	178,998	215	490	7.1	7,066	20	932	44,289	528,839
Frederick-Gaithersburg-Rockville	7	1,583	92,532	432,753	723,032	1,185	1,980	4.7	47,856	224	17,383	331,653	1,092,172
Hagerstown-Martinsburg	1	278	15,784	66,782	124,070	183	340	4.2	7,468	41	1,815	66,618	180,084
Salisbury	3	397	19,919	89,413	233,590	245	640	4.5	21,511	28	1,871	104,176	718,014
Washington-Arlington-Alexandria	6	786	44,298	217,503	389,477	595	1,067	4.9	29,502	88	3,803	243,604	492,045
Wilmington	1	104	4,937	19,837	51,852	54	142	4	5,112	12	549	36,590	136,676
North Carolina	111	21,673	1,032,683	5,596,083	12,995,339	15,330	35,633	5.4	879,997	1,548	108,667	4,445,970	23,014,956
Nonmetropolitan	41	3,657	157,922	752,607	2,067,755	2,062	5,664	4.8	139,758	389	15,837	1,025,302	4,272,992
Metropolitan	70	18,016	874,761	4,843,476	10,927,584	13,268	29,969	5.5	740,239	1,159	92,830	3,420,668	18,741,964
Asheville	6	1,267	62,407	318,647	727,755	873	1,993	5.1	61,456	59	5,414	199,854	1,871,162
Burlington	1	329	12,291	65,853	192,383	180	527	5.4	9,741	20	1,253	65,071	317,772
Charlotte-Concord-Gastonia	19	4,349	220,616	1,183,827	2,506,771	3,244	6,869	5.4	172,160	341	24,673	909,981	3,850,336
Durham-Chapel Hill	8	2,444	109,185	747,719	1,774,159	2,049	4,861	6.8	111,001	69	10,279	283,410	3,088,444
Fayetteville	3	754	41,689	190,628	387,038	522	1,061	4.6	17,066	56	5,211	171,476	422,769
Goldsboro	1	274	10,392	47,235	118,648	129	325	4.5	9,222	16	1,323	66,370	234,322
Greensboro-High Point	6	1,616	71,233	362,397	783,938	992	2,147	5.1	43,228	109	8,359	319,057	1,075,508
Greenville	1	974	39,551	270,968	497,317	742	1,363	6.9	20,090	47	3,485	40,296	269,170
Hickory-Lenoir-Morganton	4	757	32,402	156,387	431,536	428	1,182	4.8	35,034	59	3,626	194,578	933,765
Jacksonville	1	149	6,525	28,992	96,884	79	265	4.4	6,620	23	1,351	58,822	130,901
Myrtle Beach-Conway-North Myrtle Beach	2	66	4,839	15,476	56,492	43	155	3.2	6,850	5	494	36,814	200,026
New Bern	1	215	13,995	68,383	146,376	187	401	4.9	15,313	9	980	67,275	163,946
Raleigh-Cary	5	1,873	99,305	524,665	1,289,051	1,437	3,532	5.3	102,930	171	14,891	488,469	3,703,951
Rocky Mount	3	350	15,667	76,204	187,933	209	544	4.9	10,235	34	1,393	85,594	185,182
Wilmington	2	784	38,175	232,173	532,327	636	1,459	6.1	44,441	43	4,123	166,847	504,083
Winston-Salem	7	1,815	96,489	553,922	1,198,976	1,518	3,285	5.7	74,852	98	5,975	266,754	1,790,627
South Carolina	72	12,055	542,122	2,902,583	6,141,493	7,952	16,873	5.4	524,487	894	52,331	2,408,169	9,454,193
Nonmetropolitan	16	1,685	50,591	317,113	881,484	870	2,417	6.3	45,923	116	3,811	387,889	1,275,078
Metropolitan	56	10,370	491,531	2,585,470	5,260,009	7,082	14,456	5.3	478,564	778	48,520	2,020,280	8,179,115
Augusta-Richmond County	2	324	12,584	59,404	111,096	162	305	4.7	8,955	18	1,068	60,981	141,592
Charleston-North Charleston	9	2,048	94,965	534,528	1,006,705	1,464	2,803	5.6	104,311	136	10,079	372,446	1,986,538
Charlotte-Concord-Gastonia	4	466	23,778	132,561	258,011	363	707	5.6	13,912	23	2,065	118,680	252,249
Columbia	8	2,047	103,694	549,267	1,040,781	1,505	2,851	5.3	75,300	200	10,116	355,174	1,295,305
Florence	7	1,147	48,317	259,689	502,653	712	1,378	5.4	52,839	60	3,574	144,171	461,780
Greenville-Anderson	14	2,039	97,632	493,921	1,169,090	1,354	3,202	5.1	114,254	144	11,035	444,145	2,446,318
Hilton Head Island-Bluffton	3	331	17,554	69,627	154,531	190	423	4	20,417	52	1,924	92,498	309,425
Myrtle Beach-Conway-North Myrtle Beach	4	895	49,218	235,462	448,351	645	1,228	4.8	41,664	65	3,253	184,048	579,117
Spartanburg	3	807	32,478	194,687	410,282	533	1,124	6	36,412	44	3,799	132,525	512,005
Sumter	2	266	11,311	56,324	158,509	154	435	5	10,500	36	1,607	115,612	194,786
Virginia	97	18,143	824,998	4,653,339	10,334,221	12,739	28,315	5.6	725,193	1,431	90,519	3,627,232	18,706,876
Nonmetropolitan	25	2,204	61,293	469,641	1,494,602	1,286	4,094	7.7	57,082	126	4,112	412,607	1,666,235
Metropolitan	72	15,939	763,705	4,183,698	8,839,619	11,453	24,221	5.5	668,111	1,305	86,407	3,214,625	17,040,641
Blacksburg-Christiansburg	4	250	16,971	75,206	187,710	206	515	4.4	18,303	32	1,676	100,972	285,075
Charlottesville	3	806	39,800	231,833	524,682	635	1,438	5.8	124,409	41	3,301	117,071	2,640,699
Harrisonburg	1	244	13,240	50,571	150,263	139	412	3.8	16,189	16	1,829	67,002	715,244
Kingsport-Bristol	2	141	7,677	31,083	87,696	85	240	4	10,721	16	581	34,190	223,661
Lynchburg	3	1,208	34,752	323,760	689,383	886	1,889	9.3	15,759	39	2,670	123,428	252,760
Richmond	16	3,603	167,230	956,638	1,843,660	2,618	5,051	5.7	104,314	274	14,655	485,059	2,216,821
Roanoke	3	1,179	64,374	360,722	628,317	988	1,722	5.6	52,284	67	4,752	312,711	825,153
Staunton	1	209	11,472	46,421	154,632	127	424	4	15,497	21	1,021	55,975	904,362
Virginia Beach-Norfolk-Newport News	18	3,519	175,666	932,486	2,090,439	2,553	5,727	5.3	147,391	299	19,602	933,605	5,641,889
Washington-Arlington-Alexandria	20	4,239	209,332	1,049,375	2,228,544	2,872	6,106	5	148,236	479	34,101	909,428	2,966,826
Winchester	1	541	23,191	125,603	254,293	344	697	5.4	15,008	21	2,219	75,184	368,151

CBSAs

Note: These data represent hospital performance in the years 2015 – 2019 and do not reflect any impacts from the COVID-19 pandemic in 2020 and thereafter.

U.S. Community Hospitals
(Nonfederal, short-term general and other special hospitals)

2019 Utilization, Personnel and Finances

FULL-TIME EQUIVALENT PERSONNEL					FULL-TIME EQUIV. TRAINEES			EXPENSES						
								LABOR				TOTAL		
Physicians and Dentists	Registered Nurses	Licensed Practical Nurses	Other Salaried Personnel	Total Personnel	Medical and Dental Residents	Other Trainees	Total Trainees	Payroll (in thousands)	Employee Benefits (in thousands)	Total (in thousands)	Percent of Total	Amount (in thousands)	Adjusted per Admission	Adjusted per Inpatient Day
1,975	27,428	426	59,923	89,752	2,495	243	2,738	6,129,471	1,372,293	7,501,764	46.1	16,270,675	15,677.92	2,997.81
55	688	44	1,666	2,453	9	3	12	144,695	39,121	183,816	49.2	373,521	9,072.87	1,620.83
1,920	26,740	382	58,257	87,299	2,486	240	2,726	5,984,776	1,333,172	7,317,948	46	15,897,154	15,950.76	3,058.87
1,647	18,834	214	40,624	61,319	2,418	217	2,635	4,194,797	945,548	5,140,345	44.7	11,493,720	18,503.7	3,347.57
5	313	0	618	936	0	13	13	62,251	10,804	73,056	48.1	151,738	9,431.75	2,424.08
34	559	57	1,306	1,956	0	0	0	126,698	38,538	165,236	50	330,368	1,304.	1,845.65
18	3,245	17	6,967	10,247	5	4	9	741,632	153,113	894,745	49	1,824,937	11,743.41	2,524.01
6	664	10	1,305	1,985	6	0	6	123,429	29,607	153,035	46.1	331,754	11,313.41	2,673.93
88	1,075	51	2,370	3,584	2	3	5	241,282	59,210	300,492	50.5	594,454	11,130.84	2,544.86
88	1,819	30	4,382	6,319	55	3	58	421,737	81,690	503,427	50	1,007,734	12,138.15	2,587.4
34	231	3	685	953	0	0	0	72,951	14,661	87,612	53.9	162,448	1,258.	3,132.92
3,408	50,672	2,022	108,787	164,889	3,733	92	3,825	10,541,736	2,618,749	13,160,487	45.3	29,063,167	11,816.66	2,236.43
505	7,136	524	16,642	24,807	121	14	135	1,365,439	338,911	1,704,350	47.4	3,594,254	7,913.27	1,738.24
2,903	43,536	1,498	92,145	140,082	3,612	78	3,690	9,176,299	2,279,838	11,456,137	45	25,468,913	12,700.79	2,330.7
373	2,546	111	6,000	9,030	237	17	254	670,362	172,169	842,531	46.7	1,803,118	12,086.53	2,477.64
1	362	1	814	1,178	0	0	0	81,786	30,183	111,969	37.5	298,784	8,321.04	1,553.07
337	10,160	341	18,312	29,150	229	14	243	1,831,732	444,057	2,275,789	41.5	5,489,498	11,399.03	2,189.87
126	7,805	146	16,311	24,388	1,548	3	1,551	1,521,801	360,986	1,882,788	39.6	4,757,957	18,889.48	2,681.81
231	1,352	164	4,203	5,950	108	0	108	428,424	94,350	522,773	59.5	878,623	10,142.36	2,270.12
0	467	18	1,027	1,512	0	0	0	101,898	29,796	131,694	52.4	251,341	9,628.81	2,118.37
552	3,295	263	9,249	13,359	64	0	64	648,987	214,795	863,782	49.2	1,754,299	11,049.87	2,237.8
295	2,165	64	4,616	7,140	310	18	328	412,785	107,227	520,012	46.5	1,118,050	15,402.47	2,248.16
208	1,711	54	3,416	5,389	43	1	44	363,329	91,697	455,026	49.1	926,681	10,210.12	2,147.4
0	259	13	576	848	0	0	0	49,783	13,166	62,948	44.1	142,581	6,538.91	1,471.67
20	177	16	482	695	1	0	1	54,269	12,984	67,253	47.3	142,253	7,841.97	2,518.12
1	569	2	1,150	1,722	0	0	0	106,706	27,466	134,172	45.8	293,140	9,785.36	2,002.65
558	5,808	86	10,781	17,233	9	5	14	1,363,815	273,421	1,637,236	51.4	3,188,027	13,012.19	2,473.16
4	601	43	1,545	2,193	0	0	0	135,032	28,630	163,661	49.5	330,607	8,474.48	1,759.17
6	2,009	38	3,815	5,868	94	0	94	387,990	113,747	501,737	45.7	1,096,827	13,118.22	2,060.44
191	4,250	138	9,848	14,427	969	20	989	1,017,600	265,165	1,282,765	42.8	2,997,129	13,980.52	2,499.74
945	23,113	748	44,553	69,359	768	12	780	4,414,449	1,284,354	5,698,803	44	12,963,241	11,035.26	2,110.76
171	2,021	136	5,753	8,081	52	5	57	495,083	139,202	634,286	48.6	1,305,681	9,224.3	1,481.23
774	21,092	612	38,800	61,278	716	7	723	3,919,366	1,145,151	5,064,517	43.4	11,657,559	11,283.37	2,216.26
7	320	8	547	882	0	0	0	68,714	16,942	85,656	44.5	192,328	8,516.89	1,731.19
53	5,059	150	8,195	13,457	25	1	26	908,808	304,200	1,213,008	43.3	2,801,519	15,161.87	2,782.86
0	881	38	1,742	2,661	0	0	0	134,640	31,002	165,643	41.4	400,355	8,732.22	1,551.7
20	4,380	136	8,799	13,335	286	0	286	793,446	280,472	1,073,919	45.5	2,362,538	11,554.16	2,269.97
101	1,858	66	3,206	5,231	30	0	30	360,883	88,151	449,034	44.7	1,003,971	10,498.82	1,997.34
369	4,408	111	8,326	13,214	126	3	129	860,516	214,012	1,074,528	49.4	2,620,351	10,852.96	2,241.36
34	539	41	1,350	1,964	20	1	21	136,943	36,653	173,595	49.1	353,262	8,996.4	2,286.02
46	1,486	40	2,181	3,753	167	2	169	233,214	55,451	288,666	40.6	710,704	7,445.05	1,585.15
131	1,610	11	3,294	5,046	58	0	58	330,777	94,921	425,698	43	989,502	13,912.54	2,411.76
13	551	11	1,160	1,735	4	0	4	91,424	23,347	114,771	51.5	223,030	6,848.56	1,407.05
3,053	36,853	2,177	77,431	119,514	1,372	252	1,624	7,960,153	1,871,442	9,831,595	43.6	22,533,769	12,181.73	2,180.5
204	2,962	478	7,250	10,894	32	6	38	548,013	137,598	685,611	46.3	1,482,247	6,769.21	991.73
2,849	33,891	1,699	70,181	108,620	1,340	246	1,586	7,412,139	1,733,845	9,145,984	43.4	21,051,522	12,908.46	2,381.5
21	753	53	1,361	2,188	9	0	9	147,353	32,228	179,581	43.9	409,012	9,538.76	2,178.96
111	2,846	156	5,885	8,998	790	43	833	675,545	171,831	847,377	44	1,926,461	20,376.13	3,671.67
93	662	105	1,147	2,007	1	10	11	120,583	34,001	154,584	43.3	357,409	9,085.13	2,378.56
44	551	33	1,294	1,922	11	2	13	51,151	11,373	62,524	40.8	153,138	7,042.12	1,746.24
21	1,128	179	4,875	6,203	24	18	42	325,939	81,880	407,820	45.1	903,390	12,449.21	1,310.43
256	7,416	208	15,587	23,467	141	73	214	1,562,826	398,991	1,961,817	43.1	4,546,542	14,368.24	2,466.04
565	3,066	151	5,753	9,535	29	1	30	774,219	158,455	932,674	49.6	1,879,338	16,557.46	2,991.07
98	468	78	1,430	2,074	0	0	0	155,361	34,557	189,918	52.8	360,018	9,421.11	2,328.23
737	7,635	450	16,121	24,943	145	58	203	1,654,061	415,640	2,069,701	43.5	4,753,281	11,815.5	2,273.82
882	8,406	267	15,337	24,892	190	39	229	1,763,757	356,889	2,120,646	41.3	5,140,376	11,620.24	2,306.61
21	960	19	1,391	2,391	0	2	2	181,342	38,001	219,342	35.2	622,556	13,259.41	2,448.18

Table continues

CBSAs

Note: These data represent hospital performance in the years 2015 – 2019 and do not reflect any impacts from the COVID-19 pandemic in 2020 and thereafter.

TABLE 8

U.S. CENSUS DIVISION 3, SOUTH ATLANTIC CONTINUED

U.S. Community Hospitals
(Nonfederal, short-term general and other special hospitals)

2019 Utilization, Personnel and Finances

CBSAs

CLASSIFICATION	Hospitals	Beds	Admissions	Inpatient Days	Adjusted Inpatient Days	Average Daily Census	Adjusted Average Daily Census	Average Stay (days)	Surgical Operations	NEWBORNS Bassinets	NEWBORNS Births	OUTPATIENT VISITS Emergency	OUTPATIENT VISITS Total
West Virginia	52	6,385	240,377	1,499,925	3,917,368	4,110	10,733	6.2	283,918	371	17,762	1,043,324	7,749,675
Nonmetropolitan	22	1,653	43,698	331,959	1,255,829	911	3,440	7.6	55,291	100	3,245	325,934	2,060,535
Metropolitan	30	4,732	196,679	1,167,966	2,661,539	3,199	7,293	5.9	228,627	271	14,517	717,390	5,689,140
Beckley	4	490	18,861	107,992	263,123	295	721	5.7	19,818	29	890	80,998	276,414
Charleston	7	1,213	47,656	274,670	667,233	753	1,827	5.8	79,472	68	3,570	182,078	1,155,746
Cumberland	1	25	1,738	4,850	24,024	13	66	2.8	524	0	0	12,243	35,905
Hagerstown-Martinsburg	2	236	9,247	48,709	144,730	133	397	5.3	11,719	21	1,047	65,546	337,304
Huntington-Ashland	4	800	34,193	218,877	410,979	600	1,126	6.4	33,101	55	3,000	105,057	933,836
Morgantown	4	963	43,794	270,692	495,057	741	1,357	6.2	45,730	10	2,832	87,141	1,421,357
Parkersburg-Vienna	2	324	18,741	80,627	150,581	221	412	4.3	9,456	20	1,209	51,919	93,048
Washington-Arlington-Alexandria	1	25	1,393	4,071	21,442	11	59	2.9	3,064	4	225	23,525	71,055
Weirton-Steubenville	1	167	6,593	32,489	106,785	89	293	4.9	6,298	21	456	38,038	508,912
Wheeling	3	445	13,709	111,639	299,120	306	820	8.1	18,973	43	1,288	61,590	803,295
Winchester	1	44	754	13,350	78,465	37	215	17.7	472	0	0	9,255	52,268

Note: These data represent hospital performance in the years 2015 – 2019 and do not reflect any impacts from the COVID-19 pandemic in 2020 and thereafter.

TABLE 8

U.S. CENSUS DIVISION 3, SOUTH ATLANTIC CONTINUED

U.S. Community Hospitals
(Nonfederal, short-term general and other special hospitals)

2019 Utilization, Personnel and Finances

FULL-TIME EQUIVALENT PERSONNEL					FULL-TIME EQUIV. TRAINEES			EXPENSES						
								LABOR				TOTAL		
Physicians and Dentists	Registered Nurses	Licensed Practical Nurses	Other Salaried Personnel	Total Personnel	Medical and Dental Residents	Other Trainees	Total Trainees	Payroll (in thousands)	Employee Benefits (in thousands)	Total (in thousands)	Percent of Total	Amount (in thousands)	Adjusted per Admission	Adjusted per Inpatient Day
928	11,910	1,327	29,324	43,489	673	48	721	2,506,062	753,438	3,259,500	45.4	7,172,441	11,853.96	1,830.93
259	2,279	502	6,240	9,280	33	4	37	493,105	136,653	629,758	49.2	1,280,644	8,730.51	1,019.76
669	9,631	825	23,084	34,209	640	44	684	2,012,957	616,785	2,629,741	44.6	5,891,797	12,853.49	2,213.68
49	456	109	1,150	1,764	0	1	1	92,607	26,333	118,941	37	321,032	7,490.77	1,220.08
227	2,584	303	6,274	9,388	172	0	172	596,433	168,708	765,142	49.8	1,535,757	13,130.17	2,301.68
6	60	12	156	234	0	0	0	13,968	4,422	18,391	57.1	32,223	3,742.92	1,341.27
5	470	18	1,150	1,643	0	7	7	79,030	21,785	100,815	39.1	258,058	10,394.66	1,783.03
100	1,751	128	3,789	5,768	0	2	2	344,160	136,479	480,639	44.1	1,090,588	16,266.99	2,653.63
74	2,547	110	5,444	8,175	424	34	458	490,845	149,270	640,115	38.6	1,658,802	20,073.6	3,350.73
64	587	60	1,625	2,336	18	0	18	83,656	27,228	110,884	46.1	240,506	6,495.6	1,597.19
0	81	1	210	292	0	0	0	16,618	5,915	22,532	44.4	50,786	6,921.85	2,368.51
47	290	16	848	1,201	0	0	0	87,175	21,050	108,225	55.2	196,096	9,049.17	1,836.36
93	772	58	2,329	3,252	26	0	26	198,317	53,293	251,611	52.3	480,706	10,686.88	1,607.07
4	33	10	109	156	0	0	0	10,147	2,301	12,448	45.7	27,243	6,146.94	347.2

CBSAs

Note: These data represent hospital performance in the years 2015 – 2019 and do not reflect any impacts from the COVID-19 pandemic in 2020 and thereafter.

TABLE 8

U.S. CENSUS DIVISION 4, EAST NORTH CENTRAL

U.S. Community Hospitals
(Nonfederal, short-term general and other special hospitals)

2019 Utilization, Personnel and Finances

CBSAs

CLASSIFICATION	Hospitals	Beds	Admissions	Inpatient Days	Adjusted Inpatient Days	Average Daily Census	Adjusted Average Daily Census	Average Stay (days)	Surgical Operations	NEWBORNS Bassinets	NEWBORNS Births	OUTPATIENT VISITS Emergency	OUTPATIENT VISITS Total
UNITED STATES	5,198	792,417	34,251,159	185,307,228	401,318,395	507,697	1,100,206	5.4	28,168,014	54,943	3,637,593	143,454,611	766,392,512
Nonmetropolitan	1,821	108,166	3,008,734	19,667,770	67,543,319	53,878	185,275	6.5	3,542,053	8,752	345,082	21,571,345	129,292,741
Metropolitan	3,377	684,251	31,242,425	165,639,458	333,775,076	453,819	914,931	5.3	24,625,961	46,191	3,292,511	121,883,266	637,099,771
CENSUS DIVISION 4, EAST NORTH CENTRAL	786	119,505	5,110,267	26,249,955	63,551,924	71,923	174,161	5.1	4,831,304	9,097	494,785	23,077,533	165,331,602
Nonmetropolitan	266	16,017	518,790	2,785,949	11,530,691	7,636	31,594	5.4	735,869	1,567	55,372	4,246,957	30,144,755
Metropolitan	520	103,488	4,591,477	23,464,006	52,021,233	64,287	142,567	5.1	4,095,435	7,530	439,413	18,830,576	135,186,847
Illinois	185	31,262	1,326,907	6,762,533	15,560,894	18,528	42,634	5.1	1,041,487	2,360	132,191	5,631,309	39,220,898
Nonmetropolitan	57	3,017	96,918	482,732	1,932,926	1,322	5,295	5	125,204	248	8,828	661,983	5,211,140
Metropolitan	128	28,245	1,229,989	6,279,801	13,627,968	17,206	37,339	5.1	916,283	2,112	123,363	4,969,326	34,009,758
Bloomington	3	377	16,268	64,250	134,383	176	368	3.9	13,326	52	2,197	61,935	309,895
Carbondale-Marion	4	398	23,151	85,616	288,789	234	792	3.7	15,923	45	2,498	134,681	558,280
Champaign-Urbana	4	720	33,564	167,542	449,674	458	1,231	5	21,900	49	3,238	121,528	1,792,344
Chicago-Naperville-Evanston	66	18,723	815,680	4,335,547	8,829,372	11,880	24,190	5.3	558,421	1,319	82,819	3,165,350	22,046,989
Danville	2	128	5,333	18,897	69,473	52	190	3.5	2,392	26	453	45,132	78,636
Davenport-Moline-Rock Island	5	560	17,277	82,383	293,457	226	804	4.8	17,362	42	1,432	112,148	795,519
Decatur	2	534	14,745	65,779	193,340	180	530	4.5	17,374	40	1,389	73,104	400,257
Elgin	7	1,098	42,598	184,445	430,511	506	1,181	4.3	30,381	75	4,811	201,089	1,536,542
Kankakee	2	482	17,378	79,448	238,155	217	653	4.6	13,566	35	1,415	74,323	690,799
Lake County-Kenosha County	5	841	46,470	187,878	431,006	515	1,181	4	38,120	114	5,047	211,714	1,314,712
Peoria	8	1,357	58,117	328,620	733,274	900	2,009	5.7	67,967	83	4,656	196,326	1,582,504
Rockford	4	859	40,213	194,820	400,231	534	1,097	4.8	30,978	92	4,408	158,146	859,820
Springfield	2	878	41,922	215,141	412,959	589	1,131	5.1	33,826	38	3,461	123,264	647,868
St. Louis	14	1,290	57,273	269,435	723,344	739	1,982	4.7	54,747	102	5,539	290,586	1,395,593
Indiana	129	18,237	735,348	3,864,788	9,175,381	10,594	25,140	5.3	696,976	1,584	78,181	3,379,414	21,855,000
Nonmetropolitan	42	2,596	75,214	502,621	1,768,651	1,379	4,848	6.7	96,066	266	9,607	649,261	5,156,938
Metropolitan	87	15,641	660,134	3,362,167	7,406,730	9,215	20,292	5.1	600,910	1,318	68,574	2,730,153	16,698,062
Bloomington	1	290	12,439	59,102	145,901	162	400	4.8	8,049	44	1,737	52,378	304,882
Cincinnati	1	60	2,933	8,992	27,078	25	74	3.1	3,973	11	353	19,890	129,217
Columbus	1	235	8,855	32,432	90,620	89	248	3.7	10,987	20	1,212	44,374	252,407
Elkhart-Goshen	2	369	16,276	69,565	148,215	191	406	4.3	19,280	54	2,469	84,034	294,145
Evansville	6	1,245	55,239	289,707	606,352	794	1,661	5.2	43,406	62	4,509	163,972	1,067,355
Fort Wayne	9	1,658	79,807	378,026	788,187	1,037	2,159	4.7	97,628	156	8,194	418,174	1,495,825
Gary	14	3,129	108,259	619,173	1,198,689	1,697	3,283	5.7	82,913	224	6,684	394,322	2,410,959
Indianapolis-Carmel-Anderson	28	5,428	228,856	1,219,034	2,747,347	3,341	7,526	5.3	173,974	482	27,237	953,562	7,739,607
Kokomo	3	343	10,427	43,037	124,343	117	341	4.1	15,269	31	1,177	53,935	334,306
Lafayette-West Lafayette	4	451	23,649	108,516	288,951	298	792	4.6	17,406	50	3,297	135,030	574,445
Louisville-Jefferson County	6	550	26,667	110,139	317,953	301	872	4.1	51,275	49	2,728	96,451	585,185
Michigan City-La Porte	2	262	11,499	49,876	119,635	136	328	4.3	10,762	35	1,203	58,766	286,750
Muncie	2	364	16,156	93,645	184,285	257	505	5.8	6,508	20	1,215	55,246	196,969
South Bend-Mishawaka	3	745	34,982	175,891	318,242	482	872	5	30,432	45	4,039	103,542	383,663
Terre Haute	5	512	24,090	104,692	300,932	288	825	4.3	29,048	35	2,520	96,477	642,347
Michigan	145	24,809	1,115,500	5,744,466	13,990,436	15,739	38,325	5.1	991,649	1,611	101,496	4,903,345	37,398,444
Nonmetropolitan	52	3,335	104,053	608,386	3,117,249	1,668	8,539	5.8	159,296	268	10,692	796,811	5,882,634
Metropolitan	93	21,474	1,011,447	5,136,080	10,873,187	14,071	29,786	5.1	832,353	1,343	90,804	4,106,534	31,515,810
Ann Arbor	5	1,669	88,756	490,307	1,149,417	1,342	3,150	5.5	104,139	70	8,819	215,124	4,857,550
Battle Creek	3	301	11,293	49,814	141,603	136	387	4.4	10,474	26	963	86,269	668,391
Bay City	2	364	16,335	82,912	150,897	227	414	5.1	9,648	14	719	43,807	340,966
Detroit-Dearborn-Livonia	19	5,233	243,410	1,265,357	2,477,564	3,467	6,789	5.2	169,655	284	19,409	1,092,953	6,763,053
Flint	4	1,250	58,980	311,058	538,369	852	1,475	5.3	36,967	89	4,641	216,012	1,020,042
Grand Rapids-Kentwood	13	2,497	107,746	559,212	1,274,145	1,532	3,491	5.2	101,774	184	13,318	564,343	4,828,155
Jackson	2	448	18,221	90,281	197,797	248	542	5	17,669	18	1,459	76,116	885,993
Kalamazoo-Portage	4	807	41,822	188,848	422,942	518	1,158	4.5	39,534	93	4,726	181,606	1,753,304
Lansing-East Lansing	7	1,203	50,841	271,724	655,484	743	1,795	5.3	36,096	55	4,879	278,391	2,253,780
Midland	1	270	14,548	59,166	147,837	162	405	4.1	27,685	23	1,295	29,633	280,933
Monroe	1	100	6,151	25,382	71,877	70	197	4.1	3,757	7	625	38,880	156,656
Muskegon	2	397	19,464	82,991	210,162	228	576	4.3	19,998	28	1,049	104,993	1,037,415
Niles	2	344	12,307	57,114	120,085	157	329	4.6	5,332	35	912	91,711	553,658
Saginaw	3	745	36,756	197,508	410,224	541	1,123	5.4	20,744	27	2,976	136,698	790,399
South Bend-Mishawaka	1	25	218	715	8,041	2	22	3.3	587	0	0	8,902	60,319
Warren-Troy-Farmington Hills	24	5,821	284,599	1,403,691	2,896,743	3,846	7,933	4.9	228,294	390	25,014	941,096	5,265,196

Note: These data represent hospital performance in the years 2015 – 2019 and do not reflect any impacts from the COVID-19 pandemic in 2020 and thereafter.

TABLE 8

U.S. CENSUS DIVISION 4, EAST NORTH CENTRAL

U.S. Community Hospitals
(Nonfederal, short-term general and other special hospitals)

2019 Utilization, Personnel and Finances

FULL-TIME EQUIVALENT PERSONNEL					FULL-TIME EQUIV. TRAINEES			EXPENSES						
								LABOR				TOTAL		
Physicians and Dentists	Registered Nurses	Licensed Practical Nurses	Other Salaried Personnel	Total Personnel	Medical and Dental Residents	Other Trainees	Total Trainees	Payroll (in thousands)	Employee Benefits (in thousands)	Total (in thousands)	Percent of Total	Amount (in thousands)	Adjusted per Admission	Adjusted per Inpatient Day
144,792	1,586,860	75,060	3,431,822	5,238,534	117,619	9,172	126,791	$377,640,351	$97,798,365	$475,438,596	47.1	$1,010,271,112	$13,542.37	$2,517.38
16,857	155,492	20,586	431,056	623,991	2,007	425	2,432	37,990,709	9,848,267	47,838,976	50.0	95,730,556	9,130.95	1,417.32
127,935	1,431,368	54,474	3,000,766	4,614,543	115,612	8,747	124,359	339,649,522	87,950,099	427,599,621	46.8	914,540,556	14,263.72	2,739.99
30,533	259,687	9,426	584,012	883,658	21,065	2,295	23,360	63,677,116	16,126,834	79,803,950	46.3	172,406,308	13,827.72	2,712.84
3,471	29,232	2,902	83,713	119,318	359	110	469	7,774,361	2,162,795	9,937,156	49.4	20,120,685	9,689.6	1,744.97
27,062	230,455	6,524	500,299	764,340	20,706	2,185	22,891	55,902,755	13,964,039	69,866,794	45.9	152,285,623	14,654.63	2,927.37
9,418	66,540	1,982	147,691	225,631	6,854	293	7,147	15,709,065	3,882,172	19,591,238	45.7	42,851,312	13,803.95	2,753.78
538	5,854	672	15,847	22,911	38	4	42	1,435,485	427,095	1,862,580	51.5	3,618,339	9,435.34	1,871.95
8,880	60,686	1,310	131,844	202,720	6,816	289	7,105	14,273,581	3,455,077	17,728,658	45.2	39,232,973	14,419.7	2,878.86
9	701	21	1,415	2,146	21	5	26	120,629	34,317	154,945	44.5	347,823	10,326.97	2,588.29
7	976	44	1,868	2,895	20	0	20	179,464	54,794	234,258	35.5	660,503	9,818.84	2,287.15
28	1,863	75	3,292	5,258	91	0	91	339,187	87,023	426,211	36	1,183,358	13,841.9	2,631.59
7,699	41,474	699	88,508	138,380	6,014	214	6,228	10,193,210	2,456,674	12,649,884	46.1	27,464,069	16,141.54	3,110.53
0	211	17	444	672	0	0	0	48,309	13,973	62,282	37.3	166,979	8,568.29	2,403.51
56	709	21	2,223	3,009	0	0	0	189,308	41,563	230,871	45.7	505,033	8,728.08	1,720.98
79	671	107	2,005	2,862	0	0	0	181,810	45,540	227,350	44.2	514,731	11,789.79	2,662.31
215	2,223	35	4,465	6,938	10	6	16	436,624	94,573	531,197	41.2	1,288,786	12,241.51	2,993.62
91	763	37	2,084	2,975	25	0	25	202,724	43,269	245,993	51.8	474,575	9,273.76	1,992.72
260	2,336	43	4,513	7,152	13	18	31	496,540	112,298	608,837	43.2	1,407,769	12,813.98	3,266.24
199	2,922	82	6,144	9,347	298	16	314	630,105	157,154	787,259	47.8	1,648,471	13,205.31	2,248.1
135	1,934	15	4,030	6,114	20	4	24	388,569	100,626	489,195	49.8	981,417	11,835.99	2,452.13
0	1,684	15	4,644	6,343	303	4	307	386,884	93,885	480,769	38.4	1,251,416	15,535.89	3,030.36
102	2,219	99	6,209	8,629	1	22	23	480,217	119,389	599,606	44.8	1,338,044	8,508.05	1,849.8
2,317	32,995	1,483	77,571	114,366	1,186	154	1,340	8,529,959	2,166,066	10,696,025	42.7	25,028,911	13,576.04	2,727.83
736	4,334	553	13,990	19,613	39	25	64	1,248,287	323,722	1,572,010	49.9	3,149,383	9,402.63	1,780.67
1,581	28,661	930	63,581	94,753	1,147	129	1,276	7,281,672	1,842,343	9,124,015	41.7	21,879,528	14,502.6	2,954.01
8	573	25	1,136	1,742	0	2	2	112,642	27,803	140,445	39.9	352,408	11,476.46	2,415.39
0	117	9	387	513	0	0	0	34,185	7,289	41,474	52.4	79,221	8,969.78	2,925.66
3	334	15	1,261	1,613	0	0	0	86,431	26,678	113,109	40	283,092	11,441.77	3,123.95
34	839	21	1,991	2,885	8	2	10	190,165	48,965	239,130	44.8	533,797	15,336.36	3,601.51
145	2,328	44	4,399	6,916	25	39	64	466,556	130,490	597,045	39	1,532,065	12,627.46	2,526.69
29	3,073	77	5,576	8,755	28	2	30	609,881	170,678	780,559	36.1	2,162,317	12,861.82	2,743.41
355	4,491	165	9,114	14,125	215	19	234	1,139,219	280,234	1,419,453	46.9	3,027,201	14,419.71	2,525.43
576	11,073	332	26,765	38,746	686	40	726	3,232,818	811,496	4,044,313	41.2	9,810,510	17,949.39	3,570.9
13	303	3	632	951	0	2	2	88,494	21,955	110,449	36.6	301,789	9,726.97	2,427.07
227	1,031	54	2,342	3,654	25	3	28	326,387	73,064	399,450	48.4	826,087	13,146.08	2,858.92
55	1,075	103	2,607	3,840	9	1	10	211,378	50,260	261,638	45	581,487	7,777.74	1,828.85
50	444	16	1,192	1,702	4	1	5	133,617	32,998	166,615	43.7	381,053	13,802.27	3,185.13
0	611	20	1,250	1,881	63	16	79	119,042	30,798	149,840	35.9	417,394	12,693.31	2,264.94
47	1,405	18	2,976	4,446	55	2	57	337,008	83,908	420,916	44.6	943,841	14,811.63	2,965.8
39	964	28	1,953	2,984	29	0	29	193,851	45,727	239,578	37	647,266	9,143.98	2,150.87
5,173	55,271	1,316	116,884	178,644	4,989	267	5,256	13,175,337	3,164,798	16,340,135	47.1	34,685,804	1,332.	2,479.25
583	5,389	458	16,158	22,588	46	54	100	1,480,192	389,229	1,869,421	46.9	3,984,774	9,005.99	1,278.3
4,590	49,882	858	100,726	156,056	4,943	213	5,156	11,695,145	2,775,570	14,470,715	47.1	30,701,030	14,208.18	2,823.55
74	7,312	133	14,303	21,822	112	0	112	1,644,834	515,223	2,160,057	46.7	4,623,647	22,004.48	4,022.6
103	678	30	1,678	2,489	2	0	2	192,438	43,821	236,259	56.7	416,337	12,533.46	2,940.17
20	551	17	1,590	2,178	18	0	18	135,185	27,002	162,187	50.1	323,938	10,666.72	2,146.75
1,580	11,999	48	21,184	34,811	1,981	77	2,058	2,883,629	579,330	3,462,958	48.4	7,153,594	15,073.78	2,887.35
48	2,584	25	3,639	6,296	384	16	400	519,058	156,161	675,220	52.1	1,296,549	12,652.72	2,408.29
599	5,291	316	14,352	20,558	195	1	196	1,292,671	328,047	1,620,718	40.1	4,036,859	15,977.69	3,168.29
124	1,007	53	2,623	3,807	113	0	113	286,534	63,123	349,657	52.1	671,476	16,150.18	3,394.77
508	1,863	14	3,723	6,108	6	0	6	598,500	127,547	726,047	52.3	1,387,369	14,581.63	3,280.28
336	2,409	29	6,395	9,169	245	19	264	738,768	166,631	905,400	54	1,676,163	13,408.23	2,557.14
8	683	27	1,306	2,024	23	0	23	123,507	29,579	153,086	36.4	420,190	11,559.23	2,842.25
0	233	1	528	762	50	0	50	48,871	10,685	59,556	42.7	139,373	8,001.65	1,939.04
8	867	11	2,620	3,506	76	0	76	278,494	56,799	335,293	52.4	639,578	12,758.13	3,043.26
67	887	31	1,840	2,825	40	2	42	169,215	41,400	210,616	47.7	441,796	18,164.46	3,679.03
190	1,453	32	3,955	5,630	0	0	0	413,947	97,852	511,799	54.3	942,689	12,256.72	2,297.99
6	24	0	96	126	0	0	0	7,613	1,239	8,852	40.2	22,041	8,989.02	2,741.09
919	12,041	91	20,894	33,945	1,698	98	1,796	2,361,881	531,131	2,893,011	44.4	6,509,431	11,069.11	2,247.16

Table continues

CBSAs

Note: These data represent hospital performance in the years 2015 – 2019 and do not reflect any impacts from the COVID-19 pandemic in 2020 and thereafter.

TABLE 8

U.S. CENSUS DIVISION 4, EAST NORTH CENTRAL CONTINUED

U.S. Community Hospitals
(Nonfederal, short-term general and other special hospitals)

2019 Utilization, Personnel and Finances

CLASSIFICATION	Hospitals	Beds	Admissions	Inpatient Days	Adjusted Inpatient Days	Average Daily Census	Adjusted Average Daily Census	Average Stay (days)	Surgical Operations	NEWBORNS Bassinets	NEWBORNS Births	OUTPATIENT VISITS Emergency	OUTPATIENT VISITS Total
Ohio	195	33,303	1,424,277	7,276,750	16,504,668	19,940	45,265	5.1	1,363,152	2,435	121,829	6,889,120	46,074,988
Nonmetropolitan	58	4,646	163,906	718,593	2,185,342	1,971	5,989	4.4	235,380	538	16,617	1,611,283	8,697,731
Metropolitan	137	28,657	1,260,371	6,558,157	14,319,326	17,969	39,276	5.2	1,127,772	1,897	105,212	5,277,837	37,377,257
Akron	8	2,033	82,276	422,257	1,002,789	1,157	2,747	5.1	75,451	102	7,396	430,723	2,636,890
Canton-Massillon	5	1,118	46,481	229,256	560,459	629	1,536	4.9	34,088	97	4,276	188,683	1,374,264
Cincinnati	21	4,658	204,763	1,111,876	2,189,896	3,045	5,998	5.4	193,430	342	20,153	781,374	5,010,662
Cleveland-Elyria	31	7,853	329,753	1,793,677	4,262,327	4,913	11,678	5.4	352,177	355	21,992	1,274,576	13,825,823
Columbus	23	5,617	248,304	1,342,550	2,643,135	3,678	7,241	5.4	207,076	415	25,421	1,057,329	6,802,684
Dayton-Kettering	12	2,275	112,863	525,674	1,178,739	1,441	3,273	4.7	93,917	115	10,978	628,520	2,676,155
Huntington-Ashland	1	8	205	473	1,568	1	4	2.3	1,670	0	0	1,078	4,911
Lima	5	484	25,308	109,915	245,724	302	674	4.3	18,813	78	1,930	92,841	503,962
Mansfield	3	300	12,744	62,133	155,219	170	425	4.9	9,356	42	1,028	79,093	403,014
Springfield	2	283	14,678	68,911	146,677	188	402	4.7	9,036	25	399	78,392	377,330
Toledo	13	2,369	109,472	531,107	1,213,370	1,456	3,326	4.9	87,432	184	7,694	377,006	2,397,653
Weirton-Steubenville	3	359	9,430	64,901	167,026	178	458	6.9	7,002	18	502	38,209	383,499
Wheeling	1	65	655	2,453	7,644	7	21	3.7	2,275	0	0	7,573	38,634
Youngstown-Warren-Boardman	9	1,235	63,439	292,974	544,753	804	1,493	4.6	36,049	124	3,443	242,440	941,776
Wisconsin	132	11,894	508,235	2,601,418	8,320,545	7,122	22,797	5.1	738,040	1,107	61,088	2,274,345	20,782,272
Nonmetropolitan	57	2,423	78,699	473,617	2,526,523	1,296	6,923	6	119,923	247	9,628	527,619	5,196,312
Metropolitan	75	9,471	429,536	2,127,801	5,794,022	5,826	15,874	5	618,117	860	51,460	1,746,726	15,585,960
Appleton	3	362	17,000	67,695	204,949	185	561	4	36,458	43	2,170	68,078	515,297
Duluth	1	25	651	2,751	53,127	8	146	4.2	1,673	0	0	13,316	55,671
Eau Claire	7	611	25,160	114,403	326,734	313	894	4.5	37,235	60	2,246	76,266	807,614
Fond du Lac	2	162	7,077	27,554	82,810	76	227	3.9	14,806	15	751	41,463	336,673
Green Bay	6	702	32,590	136,562	491,033	373	1,345	4.2	54,600	95	4,568	122,566	1,985,180
Janesville-Beloit	3	243	11,900	49,826	184,735	136	507	4.2	13,075	15	1,165	66,334	1,447,938
La Crosse-Onalaska	2	393	17,612	86,921	417,752	238	1,144	4.9	26,415	29	2,340	79,440	997,990
Lake County-Kenosha County	2	285	13,439	55,978	189,965	153	521	4.2	14,565	67	1,872	92,867	571,240
Madison	11	1,667	79,517	448,219	1,147,968	1,228	3,144	5.6	200,861	91	8,347	233,568	2,198,124
Milwaukee-Waukesha	22	3,699	163,207	885,102	1,974,292	2,424	5,411	5.4	147,234	291	19,866	692,130	4,965,811
Minneapolis-St. Paul-Bloomington	4	82	3,625	9,367	58,580	25	160	2.6	5,754	18	943	29,554	237,595
Oshkosh-Neenah	4	384	16,613	71,934	196,260	197	538	4.3	27,211	54	2,621	61,919	429,280
Racine	2	316	14,037	65,465	189,524	180	519	4.7	11,981	31	1,507	76,218	647,872
Sheboygan	2	173	7,105	23,864	88,084	65	241	3.4	11,281	23	1,150	36,589	184,642
Wausau-Weston	4	367	20,003	82,160	188,209	225	516	4.1	14,968	28	1,914	56,418	205,033

Note: These data represent hospital performance in the years 2015 – 2019 and do not reflect any impacts from the COVID-19 pandemic in 2020 and thereafter.

CBSAs

TABLE 8

U.S. CENSUS DIVISION 4, EAST NORTH CENTRAL CONTINUED

U.S. Community Hospitals
(Nonfederal, short-term general and other special hospitals)

2019 Utilization, Personnel and Finances

CBSAs

FULL-TIME EQUIVALENT PERSONNEL					FULL-TIME EQUIV. TRAINEES			EXPENSES						
								LABOR				TOTAL		
Physicians and Dentists	Registered Nurses	Licensed Practical Nurses	Other Salaried Personnel	Total Personnel	Medical and Dental Residents	Other Trainees	Total Trainees	Payroll (in thousands)	Employee Benefits (in thousands)	Total (in thousands)	Percent of Total	Amount (in thousands)	Adjusted per Admission	Adjusted per Inpatient Day
10,881	76,421	3,639	170,322	261,263	6,972	1,134	8,106	18,792,707	4,786,509	23,579,216	48.6	48,553,908	14,540.89	2,941.83
974	9,357	961	23,064	34,356	154	21	175	2,089,806	606,686	2,696,492	48.9	5,509,343	10,371.8	2,521.04
9,907	67,064	2,678	147,258	226,907	6,818	1,113	7,931	16,702,901	4,179,823	20,882,723	48.5	43,044,565	15,329.56	3,006.05
901	4,965	269	12,066	18,201	535	86	621	1,072,584	265,986	1,338,570	49.7	2,695,738	13,731.21	2,688.24
225	2,143	254	6,398	9,020	124	4	128	361,749	100,036	461,784	49.7	930,008	8,930.45	1,659.37
960	11,188	243	25,476	37,867	1,490	128	1,618	2,899,238	769,934	3,669,172	49.1	7,469,726	17,463.53	3411
3,573	19,685	1,022	42,685	66,965	2,854	718	3,572	5,695,993	1,378,397	7,074,390	53.2	13,309,168	16,827.43	3,122.51
3,633	13,664	337	30,000	47,634	1,209	146	1,355	3,073,136	788,813	3,861,949	44	8,768,694	17,168.27	3,317.54
158	6,317	83	11,809	18,367	437	18	455	1,402,585	318,778	1,721,364	45.5	3,783,189	14,449.03	3,209.52
0	29	2	48	79	0	0	0	4,582	913	5,494	32.5	16,920	24,881.76	10,790.56
62	895	64	1,950	2,971	27	1	28	237,095	61,125	298,220	47.3	630,336	10,635.35	2,565.22
57	554	29	1,259	1,899	15	3	18	126,693	36,062	162,754	48.6	335,107	10,560.21	2,158.93
44	516	22	1,086	1,668	15	1	16	111,009	27,242	138,251	44.4	311,716	9,859.13	2,125.19
138	4,528	170	8,974	13,810	47	4	51	1,128,397	289,930	1,418,327	44	3,224,627	13,389.42	2,657.58
45	463	72	1,422	2,002	0	0	0	115,686	30,809	146,495	51.9	282,047	9,797.73	1,688.64
6	68	5	165	244	0	0	0	10,072	2,540	12,611	47.1	26,748	13,105.28	3,499.2
105	2,049	106	3,920	6,180	65	4	69	464,082	109,259	573,341	45.5	1,260,541	10,392.79	2,313.97
2,744	28,460	1,006	71,544	103,754	1,064	447	1,511	7,470,047	2,127,289	9,597,336	45.1	21,286,372	13,490.41	2,558.29
640	4,298	258	14,654	19,850	82	6	88	1,520,591	416,063	1,936,654	50.2	3,858,845	10,037.42	1,527.33
2,104	24,162	748	56,890	83,904	982	441	1,423	5,949,457	1,711,226	7,660,683	44	17,427,526	14,602.73	3,007.85
2	728	31	1,272	2,033	0	1	1	133,792	34,331	168,123	36.5	460,080	8913	2,244.85
0	53	41	233	327	0	0	0	29,974	6,995	36,969	64.2	57,605	4,581.98	1,084.28
343	1,467	75	3,268	5,153	15	1	16	463,922	147,875	611,797	52.6	1,163,081	15,918.88	3,559.72
0	335	19	1,101	1,455	0	0	0	122,521	34,129	156,651	55.9	280,102	13,142.3	3,382.46
207	1,955	232	5,013	7,407	0	14	14	561,795	137,112	698,908	48.2	1,449,291	12,025.41	2,951.51
0	725	18	1,991	2,734	0	0	0	266,896	82,174	349,070	49.2	709,739	16,057.43	3,841.93
589	1,271	79	2,997	4,936	105	10	115	588,933	175,783	764,716	57.2	1,336,148	15,888.56	3,198.42
85	813	16	2,310	3,224	0	5	5	189,088	49,773	238,861	51.8	461,397	10,037.12	2,428.85
8	3,907	42	11,495	15,452	682	107	789	1,152,191	369,335	1,521,526	47	3,236,342	17,761.9	2,819.19
727	9,939	94	20,828	31,588	162	280	442	1,846,505	507,619	2,354,124	36.8	6,388,551	17,130.38	3,235.87
26	184	7	703	920	0	0	0	77,336	20,050	97,386	47.9	203,115	9,074.53	3,467.31
78	817	43	1,684	2,622	0	2	2	144,430	37,553	181,983	41.4	439,675	9,213.05	2,240.27
19	663	27	1,472	2,181	0	16	16	119,651	34,014	153,665	38.6	398,221	9,606.79	2,101.16
20	322	3	698	1,043	0	5	5	64,584	23,425	88,009	40.4	217,692	8,303.13	2,471.41
0	983	21	1,825	2,829	18	0	18	187,838	51,056	238,894	38.1	626,489	13,280.68	3,328.69

Note: These data represent hospital performance in the years 2015 – 2019 and do not reflect any impacts from the COVID-19 pandemic in 2020 and thereafter.

TABLE 8

U.S. CENSUS DIVISION 5, EAST SOUTH CENTRAL

U.S. Community Hospitals
(Nonfederal, short-term general and other special hospitals)

2019 Utilization, Personnel and Finances

CLASSIFICATION	Hospitals	Beds	Admissions	Inpatient Days	Adjusted Inpatient Days	Average Daily Census	Adjusted Average Daily Census	Average Stay (days)	Surgical Operations	NEWBORNS Bassinets	Births	OUTPATIENT VISITS Emergency	Total
UNITED STATES	5,198	792,417	34,251,159	185,307,228	401,318,395	507,697	1,100,206	5.4	28,168,014	54,943	3,637,593	143,454,611	766,392,512
Nonmetropolitan	1,821	108,166	3,008,734	19,667,770	67,543,319	53,878	185,275	6.5	3,542,053	8,752	345,082	21,571,345	129,292,741
Metropolitan	3,377	684,251	31,242,425	165,639,458	333,775,076	453,819	914,931	5.3	24,625,961	46,191	3,292,511	121,883,266	637,099,771
CENSUS DIVISION 5, EAST SOUTH CENTRAL	414	59,389	2,374,549	13,613,204	30,125,325	37,298	82,581	5.7	2,172,795	3,788	219,009	10,371,715	47,328,574
Nonmetropolitan	208	17,770	497,145	3,269,331	9,277,072	8,952	25,463	6.6	552,245	1,274	50,991	3,260,600	13,634,989
Metropolitan	206	41,619	1,877,404	10,343,873	20,848,253	28,346	57,118	5.5	1,620,550	2,514	168,018	7,111,115	33,693,585
Alabama	101	15,248	637,490	3,633,143	7,678,763	9,956	21,081	5.7	692,525	1,099	64,583	2,488,864	10,036,135
Nonmetropolitan	38	2,639	77,075	406,221	1,256,308	1,112	3,488	5.3	130,747	210	8,275	446,945	1,814,204
Metropolitan	63	12,609	560,415	3,226,922	6,422,455	8,844	17,593	5.8	561,778	889	56,308	2,041,919	8,221,931
Anniston-Oxford	3	244	15,251	74,209	163,363	204	447	4.9	14,945	20	2,056	60,445	697,089
Auburn-Opelika	1	532	16,939	151,648	393,385	415	1,078	9	18,021	31	2,086	55,315	202,126
Birmingham-Hoover	18	4,634	192,941	1,213,237	2,202,242	3,325	6,033	6.3	205,243	340	17,776	666,804	2,820,007
Columbus	2	93	4,864	26,745	30,723	73	84	5.5	6,156	0	0	15,355	21,936
Daphne-Fairhope-Foley	3	298	17,394	67,477	168,796	185	462	3.9	23,160	37	1,773	71,202	297,487
Decatur	2	153	6,571	32,477	93,485	89	256	4.9	8,574	20	673	42,121	228,325
Dothan	5	770	34,841	214,159	450,823	587	1,234	6.1	37,218	57	3,269	106,594	357,512
Florence-Muscle Shoals	3	601	25,506	115,152	268,451	315	736	4.5	17,086	50	2,142	93,174	242,497
Gadsden	3	603	22,959	119,340	209,248	328	573	5.2	21,969	26	1,708	66,245	162,821
Huntsville	4	1,270	65,825	314,902	663,476	862	1,818	4.8	61,920	98	7,131	256,789	1,128,604
Mobile	7	1,511	74,272	423,876	770,239	1,163	2,111	5.7	51,275	89	8,835	232,859	738,379
Montgomery	8	1,069	50,103	273,400	560,135	749	1,533	5.5	71,221	68	5,495	238,487	747,976
Tuscaloosa	4	831	32,949	200,300	448,089	549	1,228	6.1	24,990	53	3,364	136,529	577,172
Kentucky	104	14,151	557,552	3,097,160	6,942,445	8,486	19,022	5.6	515,251	858	54,340	2,693,016	15,474,252
Nonmetropolitan	66	5,632	185,258	1,006,832	2,686,061	2,759	7,359	5.4	204,650	435	18,461	1,225,838	5,579,752
Metropolitan	38	8,519	372,294	2,090,328	4,256,384	5,727	11,663	5.6	310,601	423	35,879	1,467,178	9,894,500
Bowling Green	4	680	24,926	170,770	338,356	468	927	6.9	17,228	19	2,713	88,792	247,325
Cincinnati	7	911	47,203	222,314	468,335	609	1,285	4.7	36,128	38	4,255	189,556	1,761,968
Clarksville	2	157	6,640	36,169	111,474	99	305	5.4	3,674	18	631	44,667	245,196
Elizabethtown-Fort Knox	2	308	14,136	65,253	142,571	179	390	4.6	15,102	26	1,661	72,206	463,271
Evansville	1	123	3,365	18,227	60,498	50	166	5.4	2,824	12	625	24,605	235,521
Huntington-Ashland	1	448	17,585	145,376	284,987	398	781	8.3	11,794	18	2,034	185,089	1,137,622
Lexington-Fayette	11	2,342	97,475	586,345	1,206,713	1,606	3,306	6	77,791	125	8,696	282,368	3,001,217
Louisville-Jefferson County	9	3,190	144,890	771,480	1,441,706	2,114	3,950	5.3	125,516	137	13,184	511,828	1,760,116
Owensboro	1	360	16,074	74,394	201,744	204	553	4.6	20,544	30	2,080	68,067	1,042,264
Mississippi	97	11,624	370,790	2,525,724	6,226,694	6,917	17,058	6.8	287,024	700	34,622	1,793,977	7,161,734
Nonmetropolitan	65	6,733	156,310	1,348,038	3,819,569	3,689	10,463	8.6	132,171	403	16,227	962,486	3,848,991
Metropolitan	32	4,891	214,480	1,177,686	2,407,125	3,228	6,595	5.5	154,853	297	18,395	831,491	3,312,743
Gulfport-Biloxi	8	1,032	44,254	209,002	420,326	574	1,151	4.7	50,853	84	4,334	219,003	1,229,732
Hattiesburg	4	873	37,313	212,242	396,752	582	1,087	5.7	17,670	25	3,605	127,776	264,725
Jackson	16	2,623	111,245	651,573	1,350,971	1,784	3,702	5.9	80,197	146	8,501	387,948	1,586,697
Memphis	4	363	21,668	104,869	239,076	288	655	4.8	6,133	42	1,955	96,764	231,589
Tennessee	112	18,366	808,717	4,357,177	9,277,423	11,939	25,420	5.4	677,995	1,131	65,464	3,395,858	14,656,453
Nonmetropolitan	39	2,766	78,502	508,240	1,515,134	1,392	4,153	6.5	84,677	226	8,028	625,331	2,392,042
Metropolitan	73	15,600	730,215	3,848,937	7,762,289	10,547	21,267	5.3	593,318	905	57,436	2,770,527	12,264,411
Chattanooga	5	1,822	90,340	520,781	982,667	1,428	2,692	5.8	93,102	113	6,331	302,218	1,529,179
Clarksville	1	172	10,900	42,041	90,083	115	247	3.9	8,699	30	2,090	85,451	140,754
Cleveland	1	183	9,140	39,492	89,696	108	246	4.3	6,534	19	949	50,876	97,590
Jackson	2	660	31,944	159,803	366,791	438	1,005	5	33,153	33	3,201	132,156	213,844
Johnson City	5	842	38,299	201,552	414,014	552	1,134	5.3	19,115	43	2,494	112,628	417,904
Kingsport-Bristol	6	848	42,551	185,074	390,995	507	1,071	4.3	26,451	74	2,633	150,504	888,841
Knoxville	11	2,454	113,147	582,789	1,275,977	1,596	3,497	5.2	91,740	141	11,109	371,967	1,778,065
Memphis	13	3,419	147,647	853,370	1,520,490	2,338	4,167	5.8	85,478	182	15,140	650,912	1,977,968
Morristown	2	173	9,687	40,377	111,593	111	305	4.2	13,067	12	837	66,004	181,238
Nashville-Davidson-Murfreesboro-Franklin	27	5,027	236,560	1,223,658	2,519,983	3,354	6,903	5.2	215,979	258	12,652	847,811	5,039,028

Note: These data represent hospital performance in the years 2015 – 2019 and do not reflect any impacts from the COVID-19 pandemic in 2020 and thereafter.

CBSAs

TABLE 8

U.S. CENSUS DIVISION 5, EAST SOUTH CENTRAL

U.S. Community Hospitals
(Nonfederal, short-term general and other special hospitals)

2019 Utilization, Personnel and Finances

FULL-TIME EQUIVALENT PERSONNEL					FULL-TIME EQUIV. TRAINEES			EXPENSES						
								LABOR				TOTAL		
Physicians and Dentists	Registered Nurses	Licensed Practical Nurses	Other Salaried Personnel	Total Personnel	Medical and Dental Residents	Other Trainees	Total Trainees	Payroll (in thousands)	Employee Benefits (in thousands)	Total (in thousands)	Percent of Total	Amount (in thousands)	Adjusted per Admission	Adjusted per inpatient Day
144,792	1,586,860	75,060	3,431,822	5,238,534	117,619	9,172	126,791	$377,640,231	$97,798,365	$475,438,596	47.1	$1,010,271,112	$13,542.37	$2,517.38
16,857	155,492	20,586	431,056	623,991	2,007	425	2,432	37,990,709	9,848,267	47,838,976	50.0	95,730,556	9,130.95	1,417.32
127,935	1,431,368	54,474	3,000,766	4,614,543	115,612	8,747	124,359	339,649,522	87,950,099	427,599,621	46.8	914,540,556	14,263.72	2,739.99
8,058	105,770	6,000	213,240	333,068	5,127	699	5,826	19,930,083	4,894,317	24,824,400	45.3	54,743,322	10,362.54	1,817.19
1,697	22,319	2,355	54,502	80,873	310	55	365	4,383,033	1,108,168	5,491,201	48.1	11,411,478	7,949.3	1,230.07
6,361	83,451	3,645	158,738	252,195	4,817	644	5,461	15,547,050	3,786,149	19,333,199	44.6	43,331,844	11,262.99	2,078.44
1,473	29,011	1,256	54,535	86,275	1,569	527	2,096	4,646,975	1,158,302	5,805,277	45.6	12,726,512	9,309.33	1,657.36
246	3,310	318	8,315	12,189	26	4	30	542,365	132,587	674,953	48.5	1,391,184	5,857.32	1,107.36
1,227	25,701	938	46,220	74,086	1,543	523	2,066	4,104,609	1,025,714	5,130,324	45.3	11,335,328	10,035.18	1,764.95
40	487	53	1,256	1,836	11	2	13	93,164	20,172	113,336	48.8	232,482	6,657.56	1,423.1
52	925	51	2,270	3,298	0	0	0	160,971	44,446	205,417	50.7	404,839	9,213.24	1,029.12
239	10,143	258	15,385	26,025	930	485	1,415	1,673,275	396,285	2,069,560	43.3	4,776,730	13,183.22	2,169.03
0	141	2	319	462	15	0	15	27,276	5,144	32,420	39.7	81,757	12,160.83	2,661.11
31	826	24	1,059	1,940	7	1	8	104,272	25,246	129,518	46.7	277,495	6,400.83	1,643.97
36	317	42	907	1,302	9	0	9	59,134	17,509	76,644	51.2	149,730	7,932.74	1,601.65
140	1,421	85	3,147	4,793	94	4	98	254,480	70,078	324,558	50.1	648,193	9,256.47	1,437.8
63	832	33	1,679	2,607	3	1	4	116,171	28,590	144,760	45.9	315,233	5,337.15	1,174.27
15	821	26	1,283	2,145	21	0	21	111,467	24,691	136,158	43	316,852	8,131.29	1,514.24
284	3,353	141	6,527	10,305	1	0	1	498,698	175,017	673,715	49.6	1,358,498	9,680.12	2,047.55
243	3,034	82	5,624	8,983	431	8	439	452,308	113,517	565,825	45.2	1,251,578	9,248.54	1,624.92
73	2,032	80	3,916	6,101	21	3	24	333,456	58,453	391,909	40.1	978,313	9,253.11	1,746.57
11	1,369	61	2,848	4,289	0	19	19	219,936	46,567	266,503	49	543,627	7,770.32	1,213.21
1,181	26,378	992	51,313	79,864	1,421	48	1,469	5,100,757	1,355,110	6,455,867	44.3	14,575,498	11,342.65	2,099.48
703	8,439	562	20,353	30,057	165	29	194	1,719,172	467,195	2,186,367	46.5	4,697,969	9,147.24	1,749.02
478	17,939	430	30,960	49,807	1,256	19	1,275	3,381,585	887,915	4,269,500	43.2	9,877,530	12,804.3	2,320.64
60	990	36	1,906	2,992	36	2	38	275,585	66,179	341,764	45.5	750,337	16,280.53	2,217.6
53	2,326	42	2,802	5,223	26	0	26	466,358	132,790	599,148	48.5	1,234,279	12,431.68	2,635.46
25	320	20	796	1,161	7	1	8	64,439	15,622	80,061	47.3	169,153	9,044.62	1,517.42
51	703	50	1,791	2,595	37	4	41	152,359	45,869	198,227	52.1	380,593	12,528.99	2,669.5
20	219	8	584	831	5	7	12	32,299	10,562	42,861	45.8	93,578	8,378.35	1,546.79
80	983	29	2,185	3,277	101	5	106	225,756	57,585	283,341	46.6	608,119	17,640.44	2,133.85
36	4,830	103	9,532	14,501	1,040	0	1,040	922,519	240,664	1,163,183	41.8	2,781,244	13,390.36	2,304.81
153	6,920	132	9,740	16,945	4	0	4	1,082,135	264,906	1,347,041	39.7	3,388,893	12,101.72	2,350.61
0	648	10	1,624	2,282	0	0	0	160,135	53,737	213,872	45.4	471,334	10,812.89	2,336.3
1,012	15,768	1,462	35,215	53,457	556	38	594	3,231,008	744,276	3,975,284	48.8	8,148,567	9,170.25	1,308.65
506	7,060	967	17,253	25,786	50	14	64	1,459,102	344,516	1,803,618	49.8	3,619,949	8171	947.74
506	8,708	495	17,962	27,671	506	24	530	1,771,906	399,760	2,171,666	48	4,528,618	10,163.81	1,881.34
257	2,325	187	4,504	7,273	65	2	67	482,062	99,075	581,137	49	1,186,003	12,761.09	2,821.63
30	1,207	63	3,002	4,302	84	0	84	249,450	54,536	303,986	46.5	654,370	10,014.24	1,649.32
218	4,337	228	9,114	13,897	357	22	379	915,314	216,739	1,132,053	48	2,356,510	9,899.47	1,744.31
1	839	17	1,342	2,199	0	0	0	125,080	29,411	154,491	46.6	331,735	6,737.64	1,387.57
4,392	34,613	2,290	72,177	113,472	1,581	86	1,667	6,951,344	1,636,629	8,587,973	44.5	19,292,745	11,074.2	2,079.54
242	3,510	508	8,581	12,841	69	8	77	662,394	163,870	826,263	48.5	1,702,376	7,052.04	1,123.58
4,150	31,103	1,782	63,596	100,631	1,512	78	1,590	6,288,950	1,472,759	7,761,709	44.1	17,590,369	11,721.19	2,266.13
273	3,739	223	6,853	11,088	25	0	25	735,987	197,728	933,716	48.2	1,938,592	11,402.74	1,972.79
0	449	10	607	1,066	0	0	0	54,908	10,241	65,148	43	151,335	6,479.49	1,679.95
0	380	8	515	903	0	0	0	48,252	10,127	58,379	45.1	129,318	6,229.51	1,441.74
5	1,184	111	3,043	4,343	0	0	0	252,280	64,264	316,545	45.5	695,061	9,449.67	1,894.98
0	1,455	116	2,998	4,569	0	0	0	174,320	38,055	212,375	40.6	523,301	6,859.55	1,263.97
51	1,696	93	4,190	6,030	31	3	34	228,176	51,642	279,818	38.4	728,079	7,999.11	1,862.12
280	4,451	276	8,985	13,992	15	44	59	929,116	202,868	1,131,984	45.2	2,506,969	10,141.21	1,964.74
422	5,850	130	11,241	17,643	50	17	67	1,178,069	259,377	1,437,446	41.1	3,497,505	12,601.76	2,300.25
0	344	12	527	883	0	4	4	49,437	10,115	59,551	44.4	134,020	4,998.68	1,200.97
3,119	11,555	803	24,637	40,114	1,391	10	1,401	2,638,405	628,343	3,266,748	44.8	7,286,189	14,743.82	2,891.36

CBSAs

Note: These data represent hospital performance in the years 2015 – 2019 and do not reflect any impacts from the COVID-19 pandemic in 2020 and thereafter.

TABLE 8 U.S. CENSUS DIVISION 6, WEST NORTH CENTRAL

U.S. Community Hospitals
(Nonfederal, short-term general and other special hospitals)

2019 Utilization, Personnel and Finances

CLASSIFICATION	Hospitals	Beds	Admissions	Inpatient Days	Adjusted Inpatient Days	Average Daily Census	Adjusted Average Daily Census	Average Stay (days)	Surgical Operations	NEWBORNS Bassinets	NEWBORNS Births	OUTPATIENT VISITS Emergency	OUTPATIENT VISITS Total
UNITED STATES	5,198	792,417	34,251,159	185,307,228	401,318,395	507,697	1,100,206	5.4	28,168,014	54,943	3,637,593	143,454,611	766,392,512
Nonmetropolitan	1,821	108,166	3,008,734	19,667,770	67,543,319	53,878	185,275	6.5	3,542,053	8,752	345,082	21,571,345	129,292,741
Metropolitan	3,377	684,251	31,242,425	165,639,458	333,775,076	453,819	914,931	5.3	24,625,961	46,191	3,292,511	121,883,266	637,099,771
CENSUS DIVISION 6, WEST NORTH CENTRAL	690	65,660	2,350,517	14,357,163	38,667,959	39,322	106,016	6.1	2,184,324	4,533	248,734	9,072,506	72,613,925
Nonmetropolitan	438	20,454	409,832	3,801,293	14,906,192	10,410	40,896	9.3	557,187	1,500	51,559	2,762,555	24,526,142
Metropolitan	252	45,206	1,940,685	10,555,870	23,761,767	28,912	65,120	5.4	1,627,137	3,033	197,175	6,309,951	48,087,783
Iowa	117	9,459	308,139	1,879,720	6,315,007	5,149	17,307	6.1	338,650	706	37,417	1,317,142	12,219,539
Nonmetropolitan	81	3,537	69,198	622,539	3,105,926	1,704	8,515	9	127,045	263	8,815	488,699	5,257,178
Metropolitan	36	5,922	238,941	1,257,181	3,209,081	3,445	8,792	5.3	211,605	443	28,602	828,443	6,962,361
Ames	3	297	9,172	64,527	209,891	177	575	7	11,609	26	1,341	38,288	338,307
Cedar Rapids	4	738	26,826	147,643	548,834	405	1,504	5.5	28,820	54	3,168	114,841	1,328,274
Davenport-Moline-Rock Island	3	513	22,874	86,395	184,262	237	505	3.8	12,680	33	2,894	97,657	300,951
Des Moines-West Des Moines	8	1,717	75,271	393,019	826,102	1,076	2,263	5.2	53,583	143	10,226	237,388	1,096,953
Dubuque	3	366	12,838	69,708	155,708	191	427	5.4	13,668	38	1,459	50,363	191,012
Iowa City	3	1,064	41,786	276,974	650,274	759	1,781	6.6	39,907	49	3,543	91,949	1,712,154
Omaha-Council Bluffs	3	278	12,143	47,835	125,085	132	342	3.9	11,100	25	809	52,947	177,712
Sioux City	3	389	18,697	93,802	182,897	257	501	5	11,417	33	2,332	66,492	346,832
Waterloo-Cedar Falls	6	560	19,334	77,278	326,028	211	894	4	28,821	42	2,830	78,518	1,470,166
Kansas	138	9,544	316,464	1,936,123	5,234,300	5,305	14,340	6.1	284,769	636	32,477	1,196,829	8,931,714
Nonmetropolitan	94	3,696	71,278	706,080	2,567,983	1,936	7,033	9.9	88,102	267	8,954	370,839	3,383,365
Metropolitan	44	5,848	245,186	1,230,043	2,666,317	3,369	7,307	5	196,667	369	23,523	825,990	5,548,349
Kansas City	18	2,861	121,066	624,274	1,384,833	1,710	3,793	5.2	99,219	181	12,629	377,546	3,517,566
Lawrence	1	142	6,727	24,097	115,646	66	317	3.6	5,769	14	992	38,054	253,668
Manhattan	5	318	6,929	46,540	162,083	127	444	6.7	11,257	34	1,324	39,300	291,953
Topeka	4	723	33,084	141,983	324,398	388	888	4.3	22,523	36	2,634	99,363	390,079
Wichita	16	1,804	77,380	393,149	679,357	1,078	1,865	5.1	57,899	104	5,944	271,727	1,095,083
Minnesota	125	13,901	551,113	3,331,744	8,659,036	9,125	23,717	6	573,242	1,173	62,602	2,028,615	13,597,025
Nonmetropolitan	73	3,768	73,165	762,275	3,085,504	2,087	8,451	10.4	128,741	305	11,871	585,728	5,048,696
Metropolitan	52	10,133	477,948	2,569,469	5,573,532	7,038	15,266	5.4	444,501	868	50,731	1,442,887	8,548,329
Duluth	11	1,175	40,202	263,083	822,618	720	2,254	6.5	44,759	74	2,855	147,988	1,749,866
Grand Forks	2	123	1,316	26,714	109,513	73	300	20.3	3,959	10	140	8,691	103,258
Mankato	2	187	10,621	43,237	111,319	119	305	4.1	9,215	16	1,401	38,703	306,517
Minneapolis-St. Paul-Bloomington	29	6,348	332,192	1,628,988	3,187,567	4,462	8,731	4.9	246,533	627	40,008	1,065,036	4,967,024
Rochester	4	1,583	63,498	418,190	849,125	1,145	2,325	6.6	120,565	109	3,281	109,122	815,850
St. Cloud	4	717	30,119	189,257	493,390	519	1,351	6.3	19,470	32	3,046	73,347	605,814
Missouri	120	18,455	769,249	4,184,603	10,059,966	11,463	27,635	5.4	590,743	1,170	70,183	2,927,912	25,702,949
Nonmetropolitan	49	2,693	87,210	411,888	1,705,226	1,129	4,727	4.7	82,681	237	9,491	595,770	5,440,797
Metropolitan	71	15,762	682,039	3,772,715	8,354,740	10,334	22,908	5.5	508,062	933	60,692	2,332,142	20,262,152
Cape Girardeau	3	506	18,086	90,561	213,869	249	587	5	16,666	40	1,760	73,245	1,290,840
Columbia	4	966	43,165	234,716	425,522	642	1,165	5.4	36,977	59	4,161	107,420	1,299,136
Jefferson City	3	243	12,686	51,163	155,688	139	427	4	10,804	28	1,464	70,378	705,416
Joplin	5	695	32,961	162,363	401,855	444	1,101	4.9	17,290	59	3,145	144,611	1,119,824
Kansas City	21	3,758	164,473	910,680	2,019,746	2,494	5,534	5.5	105,565	175	13,696	664,078	3,892,384
Springfield	5	1,514	76,254	401,199	1,018,543	1,100	2,792	5.3	72,568	84	7,166	216,432	3,008,040
St. Joseph	1	352	16,648	74,296	188,749	204	517	4.5	10,445	28	1,463	53,415	1,010,384
St. Louis	29	7,728	317,766	1,847,737	3,930,768	5,062	10,785	5.8	237,747	460	27,837	1,002,563	7,936,128
Nebraska	93	6,756	203,201	1,405,254	3,372,837	3,845	9,242	6.9	199,664	493	22,793	923,344	6,060,620
Nonmetropolitan	66	2,661	56,105	469,726	1,492,128	1,285	4,088	8.4	66,493	248	4,709	377,067	2,647,630
Metropolitan	27	4,095	147,096	935,528	1,880,709	2,560	5,154	6.4	133,171	245	18,084	546,277	3,412,990
Grand Island	4	264	7,207	61,028	198,333	166	544	8.5	4,927	34	847	28,195	141,428
Lincoln	8	1,498	44,586	349,214	566,945	957	1,552	7.8	25,372	60	4,628	138,926	528,016
Omaha-Council Bluffs	15	2,333	95,303	525,286	1,115,431	1,437	3,058	5.5	102,872	151	12,609	379,156	2,743,546
North Dakota	40	3,323	93,282	692,274	2,331,131	1,897	6,388	7.4	104,953	166	10,910	318,834	2,968,313
Nonmetropolitan	32	1,748	21,851	334,040	1,299,660	916	3,561	15.3	25,263	54	2,669	146,812	1,183,978
Metropolitan	8	1,575	71,431	358,234	1,031,471	981	2,827	5	79,690	112	8,241	172,022	1,784,335
Bismarck	3	505	23,436	111,339	293,747	305	805	4.8	20,621	39	2,488	48,128	344,937
Fargo	3	714	36,669	177,542	483,352	486	1,325	4.8	47,341	42	4,167	91,122	482,590
Grand Forks	2	356	11,326	69,353	254,372	190	697	6.1	11,728	31	1,586	32,772	956,808
South Dakota	57	4,222	109,069	927,445	2,695,682	2,538	7,387	8.5	92,303	189	12,352	359,830	3,133,765
Nonmetropolitan	43	2,351	31,025	494,745	1,649,765	1,353	4,521	15.9	38,862	126	5,050	197,640	1,564,498
Metropolitan	14	1,871	78,044	432,700	1,045,917	1,185	2,866	5.5	53,441	63	7,302	162,190	1,569,267
Rapid City	5	605	21,224	143,385	333,326	393	913	6.8	9,471	24	2,026	64,540	567,493
Sioux City	1	40	1,203	4,753	12,650	13	35	4	1,386	0	0	6,219	21,426
Sioux Falls	8	1,226	55,617	284,562	699,941	779	1,918	5.1	42,584	39	5,276	91,431	980,348

Note: These data represent hospital performance in the years 2015 – 2019 and do not reflect any impacts from the COVID-19 pandemic in 2020 and thereafter.

2019 Utilization, Personnel and Finances

CBSAs

FULL-TIME EQUIVALENT PERSONNEL					FULL-TIME EQUIV. TRAINEES			EXPENSES						
								LABOR				TOTAL		
Physicians and Dentists	Registered Nurses	Licensed Practical Nurses	Other Salaried Personnel	Total Personnel	Medical and Dental Residents	Other Trainees	Total Trainees	Payroll (in thousands)	Employee Benefits (in thousands)	Total (in thousands)	Percent of Total	Amount (in thousands)	Adjusted per Admission	Adjusted per Inpatient Day
144,792	1,586,860	75,060	3,431,822	5,238,534	117,619	9,172	126,791	$377,640,231	$97,798,365	$475,438,596	47.1	$1,010,271,112	$13,542.37	$2,517.38
16,857	155,492	20,586	431,056	623,991	2,007	425	2,432	37,990,709	9,848,267	47,838,976	50.0	95,730,556	9,130.95	1,417.32
127,935	1,431,368	54,474	3,000,766	4,614,543	115,612	8,747	124,359	339,649,522	87,950,099	427,599,621	46.8	914,540,556	14,263.72	2,739.99
15,875	125,137	9,477	300,614	451,103	4,769	605	5,374	31,814,853	7,819,652	39,634,504	48.8	81,141,173	13,416.76	2,098.41
3,612	26,491	4,292	75,088	109,483	127	48	175	6,982,762	1,770,217	8,752,979	50.9	17,210,613	10,219.6	1,154.59
12,263	98,646	5,185	225,526	341,620	4,642	557	5,199	24,832,091	6,049,435	30,881,526	48.3	63,930,560	14,650.65	2,690.48
1,358	16,635	1,000	40,579	59,572	848	106	954	3,883,647	1,067,884	4,951,531	48.8	10,143,104	10,703.13	1,606.19
689	5,535	613	14,990	21,827	37	0	37	1,324,370	358,905	1,683,275	51.5	3,270,483	9,393.84	1,052.98
669	11,100	387	25,589	37,745	811	106	917	2,559,277	708,979	3,268,256	47.6	6,872,621	11,463.46	2,141.62
23	461	9	1,185	1,678	0	0	0	98,800	32,474	131,274	50.3	260,881	9,722.4	1,242.94
50	1,197	45	3,030	4,322	0	3	3	321,283	74,200	395,483	51.8	764,100	8,451.59	1,392.22
1	713	8	1,155	1,877	0	0	0	125,522	23,591	149,113	33.3	447,650	8,728.33	2,429.42
247	3,272	53	7,123	10,695	231	9	240	730,447	175,769	906,216	49.8	1,819,788	11,679.23	2,202.86
8	586	18	1,186	1,798	0	0	0	113,734	23,161	136,895	46.6	293,477	9,974.75	1,884.79
101	2,792	47	6,546	9,486	574	94	668	625,175	251,638	876,812	45	1,949,047	20,380.49	2,997.27
10	391	11	800	1,212	0	0	0	80,231	22,084	102,315	46.4	220,426	7,123.83	1,762.21
72	871	32	1,831	2,806	0	0	0	170,289	42,582	212,871	51	417,791	1,111.	2,284.29
157	817	164	2,733	3,871	6	0	6	293,797	63,480	357,277	51.1	699,461	8,572.25	2,145.4
2,003	16,446	1,439	36,859	56,747	29	229	258	4,020,359	926,169	4,946,528	50.4	9,810,089	11,993.02	1,874.19
515	4,343	695	12,816	18,369	0	3	3	1,064,854	254,115	1,318,969	51.9	2,542,115	9,944.74	989.93
1,488	12,103	744	24,043	38,378	29	226	255	2,955,505	672,054	3,627,559	49.9	7,267,974	12,924.08	2,725.85
1,033	6,908	233	13,312	21,486	0	225	225	1,755,422	407,300	2,162,721	50.7	4,262,882	14,764.86	3,078.26
84	317	41	1,159	1,601	0	0	0	120,279	31,844	152,123	50.8	299,464	9,275.91	2,589.49
25	337	38	630	1,030	0	0	0	70,748	14,594	85,342	46.1	185,224	8,097.95	1,142.78
248	1,426	346	4,161	6,181	0	0	0	493,209	99,171	592,380	58.5	1,013,072	13,050.51	3,122.93
98	3,115	86	4,781	8,080	29	1	30	515,847	119,145	634,992	42.1	1,507,332	10,701.15	2,218.76
5,808	28,170	1,908	82,266	118,152	1,815	80	1,895	8,635,774	2,232,127	10,867,901	52.1	20,867,097	15,973.86	2,409.86
896	4,833	991	14,736	21,456	15	16	31	1,545,828	390,311	1,936,139	50.9	3,805,459	11,412.28	1,233.33
4,912	23,337	917	67,530	96,696	1,800	64	1,864	7,089,946	1,841,816	8,931,761	52.3	17,061,638	17,537.34	3,061.19
522	1,856	163	5,555	8,096	11	1	12	798,827	190,920	989,747	57.7	1,714,914	17,686.82	2,084.7
20	106	54	362	542	0	0	0	43,209	8,826	52,036	58.4	89,076	16,787.82	813.38
152	566	75	1,023	1,816	0	0	0	163,282	41,475	204,757	48.1	426,117	15,101.42	3,827.89
1,735	14,715	344	30,771	47,565	424	62	486	4,758,053	1,246,163	6,004,216	52.3	11,477,786	17,730.66	3,600.8
2,457	4,612	119	26,541	33,729	1,349	0	1,349	920,002	237,995	1,157,997	48.1	2,407,097	18,048.26	2,834.8
26	1,482	162	3,278	4,948	16	1	17	406,573	116,436	523,008	55.2	946,648	15,347.48	1,918.66
3,256	39,417	2,751	85,680	131,104	1,944	152	2,096	8,768,256	2,158,388	10,926,645	45	24,264,934	12,921.43	2,412.03
630	4,323	1,033	12,677	18,663	40	4	44	1,110,510	289,936	1,400,446	49.4	2,834,778	8,221.4	1,662.41
2,626	35,094	1,718	73,003	112,441	1,904	148	2,052	7,657,746	1,868,452	9,526,198	44.5	21,430,155	13,978.52	2,565.03
222	1,230	186	3,093	4,731	0	0	0	334,866	73,029	407,895	48.1	847,434	19,101.85	3,962.4
32	1,788	272	4,908	7,000	416	29	445	426,481	132,294	558,775	40.2	1,390,895	17,304.64	3,268.68
115	556	132	1,337	2,140	10	0	10	145,313	34,945	180,258	45.8	393,357	9,939.53	2,526.57
251	1,401	85	3,380	5,117	29	0	29	358,353	71,471	429,825	51.8	830,526	10,086.67	2,066.73
528	7,696	212	17,418	25,854	156	119	275	1,938,605	461,466	2,400,071	43.8	5,483,022	16,377.89	2,714.71
939	4,083	448	12,366	17,836	28	0	28	837,774	199,825	1,037,600	44.6	2,328,170	11,587.26	2,285.78
173	813	167	2,426	3,579	0	0	0	277,247	58,609	335,856	52.1	644,401	15,236.23	3,414.06
366	17,527	216	28,075	46,184	1,265	0	1,265	3,339,107	836,813	4,175,920	43.9	9,512,350	13,427.52	2,419.97
1,048	12,167	880	26,993	41,088	62	15	77	2,835,288	712,090	3,547,377	47.8	7,413,795	15,192.23	2,198.09
395	3,649	565	10,087	14,696	16	8	24	917,445	240,688	1,158,133	49.2	2,353,438	12,853.86	1,577.24
653	8,518	315	16,906	26,392	46	7	53	1,917,843	471,401	2,389,244	47.2	5,060,357	16,596.39	2,690.66
16	317	28	765	1,126	0	0	0	65,162	18,837	83,998	39.7	211,593	9,993.98	1,066.86
37	2,206	86	4,229	6,558	19	3	22	415,244	110,269	525,513	45.3	1,160,827	15,070.79	2,047.51
600	5,995	201	11,912	18,708	27	4	31	1,437,437	342,296	1,779,733	48.3	3,687,937	17,841.12	3,306.29
1,268	5,657	835	12,615	20,375	33	12	45	1,916,332	364,703	2,281,035	52.3	4,358,749	13,984.51	1,869.8
228	1,599	197	4,485	6,509	1	12	13	470,418	102,141	572,559	52.3	1,095,326	10,584.08	842.78
1,040	4,058	638	8,130	13,866	32	0	32	1,445,914	262,562	1,708,476	52.4	3,263,423	15,674.76	3,163.85
251	1,287	139	2,583	4,260	0	0	0	413,144	70,171	483,315	52.7	916,700	14,469.95	3,120.71
596	2,158	346	4,020	7,120	4	0	4	725,468	127,935	853,403	50.3	1,696,361	16,611.45	3,509.58
193	613	153	1,527	2,486	28	0	28	307,302	64,457	371,758	57.2	650,362	15,222.41	2,556.74
1,134	6,645	664	15,622	24,065	38	11	49	1,755,198	358,290	2,113,488	49.3	4,283,406	14,364.59	1,588.99
259	2,209	198	5,297	7,963	18	5	23	549,337	134,120	683,457	52.2	1,309,014	11,336.89	793.45
875	4,436	466	10,325	16,102	20	6	26	1,205,861	224,170	1,430,031	48.1	2,974,392	16,277.79	2,843.81
151	860	84	2,465	3,560	18	6	24	256,963	20,089	277,052	43.1	642,099	14,293.64	1,926.34
3	51	6	126	186	0	0	0	19,475	4,180	23,655	40.6	58,317	18,212.59	4,610.02
721	3,525	376	7,734	12,356	2	0	2	929,422	199,902	1,129,324	49.7	2,273,976	16,893.95	3,248.81

Note: These data represent hospital performance in the years 2015 – 2019 and do not reflect any impacts from the COVID-19 pandemic in 2020 and thereafter.

TABLE 8   **U.S. CENSUS DIVISION 7, WEST SOUTH CENTRAL**

U.S. Community Hospitals
(Nonfederal, short-term general and other special hospitals)

2019.Utilization, Personnel and Finances

CLASSIFICATION	Hospitals	Beds	Admissions	Inpatient Days	Adjusted Inpatient Days	Average Daily Census	Adjusted Average Daily Census	Average Stay (days)	Surgical Operations	NEWBORNS Bassinets	NEWBORNS Births	OUTPATIENT VISITS Emergency	OUTPATIENT VISITS Total
UNITED STATES	5,198	792,417	34,251,159	185,307,228	401,318,395	507,697	1,100,206	5.4	28,168,014	54,943	3,637,593	143,454,611	766,392,512
Nonmetropolitan	1,821	108,166	3,008,734	19,667,770	67,543,319	53,878	185,275	6.5	3,542,053	8,752	345,082	21,571,345	129,292,741
Metropolitan	3,377	684,251	31,242,425	165,639,458	333,775,076	453,819	914,931	5.3	24,625,961	46,191	3,292,511	121,883,266	637,099,771
CENSUS DIVISION 7, WEST SOUTH CENTRAL	880	100,863	4,159,278	21,792,893	45,109,543	59,713	123,848	5.2	3,417,851	7,335	517,514	18,544,338	75,084,536
Nonmetropolitan	283	12,611	361,827	1,676,994	5,853,606	4,599	16,082	4.6	331,456	1,054	46,377	2,843,591	12,209,572
Metropolitan	597	88,252	3,797,451	20,115,899	39,255,937	55,114	107,766	5.3	3,086,395	6,281	471,137	15,700,747	62,874,964
Arkansas	89	9,145	364,291	1,826,976	4,276,157	5,005	11,722	5	318,493	829	34,678	1,556,206	6,470,401
Nonmetropolitan	47	2,826	84,013	420,325	1,428,054	1,151	3,922	5	66,341	219	9,049	569,073	2,115,836
Metropolitan	42	6,319	280,278	1,406,651	2,848,103	3,854	7,800	5	252,152	610	25,629	987,133	4,354,565
Fayetteville-Springdale-Rogers	9	1,144	49,667	208,775	445,623	573	1,219	4.2	56,291	85	7,403	218,861	807,365
Fort Smith	7	798	33,410	168,690	369,948	462	1,014	5	44,765	45	2,907	138,092	535,867
Hot Springs	3	449	18,820	92,791	180,336	254	494	4.9	15,821	28	1,384	69,772	247,760
Jonesboro	4	725	33,367	162,735	391,118	447	1,072	4.9	16,390	46	2,450	97,749	482,182
Little Rock-North Little Rock-Conway	16	2,909	134,607	723,718	1,357,379	1,981	3,717	5.4	112,227	378	10,818	391,719	2,016,279
Memphis	1	11	499	1,076	6,605	3	18	2.2	402	0	3	22,271	25,667
Pine Bluff	1	258	9,812	48,533	93,813	133	257	4.9	6,256	28	664	45,043	227,347
Texarkana	1	25	96	333	3,281	1	9	3.5	0	0	0	3,626	12,098
Louisiana	155	15,226	566,912	3,138,996	7,231,473	8,599	19,844	5.5	494,745	933	60,330	2,806,279	13,522,911
Nonmetropolitan	42	1,985	58,020	288,846	852,489	791	2,337	5	58,683	112	6,427	371,740	1,551,286
Metropolitan	113	13,241	508,892	2,850,150	6,378,984	7,808	17,507	5.6	436,062	821	53,903	2,434,539	11,971,625
Alexandria	6	773	29,318	167,867	309,383	460	847	5.7	20,809	55	2,757	123,694	497,392
Baton Rouge	19	2,480	81,337	554,402	1,309,529	1,518	3,588	6.8	63,643	155	10,643	406,314	2,877,469
Hammond	8	422	14,200	85,741	187,790	235	515	6	17,627	26	1,130	100,890	656,115
Houma-Thibodaux	7	579	20,297	102,216	336,558	280	922	5	24,202	43	3,044	156,815	774,204
Lafayette	14	1,316	56,315	298,776	664,531	817	1,821	5.3	32,982	133	5,173	226,978	1,131,391
Lake Charles	7	761	28,473	146,042	359,073	400	983	5.1	29,080	54	3,606	148,447	607,056
Monroe	12	982	33,846	186,817	359,102	513	983	5.5	25,031	64	3,760	133,612	557,644
New Orleans-Metairie	30	4,367	160,809	935,213	2,127,150	2,562	5,860	5.8	167,752	206	16,877	824,943	3,330,703
Shreveport-Bossier City	10	1,561	84,297	373,076	725,868	1,023	1,988	4.4	54,936	85	6,913	312,846	1,539,651
Oklahoma	124	11,305	427,388	2,308,688	5,151,876	6,329	14,130	5.4	409,800	750	49,839	1,945,709	8,033,446
Nonmetropolitan	61	2,763	81,178	376,696	1,156,667	1,033	3,166	4.6	81,535	227	10,714	612,163	2,529,624
Metropolitan	63	8,542	346,210	1,931,992	3,995,209	5,296	10,964	5.6	328,265	523	39,125	1,333,546	5,503,822
Enid	2	256	8,491	44,893	106,763	123	293	5.3	8,175	16	1,161	36,523	152,587
Fort Smith	2	51	1,014	3,913	20,680	11	57	3.9	698	0	161	23,081	161,301
Lawton	2	530	15,930	127,550	316,738	350	868	8	14,491	43	1,961	73,902	246,154
Oklahoma City	31	4,541	175,206	1,007,634	2,048,705	2,760	5,613	5.8	191,825	299	21,111	761,311	3,259,734
Tulsa	26	3,164	145,569	748,002	1,502,323	2,052	4,133	5.1	113,076	165	14,731	438,729	1,684,046
Texas	512	65,187	2,800,687	14,518,233	28,450,037	39,780	78,152	5.2	2,194,813	4,823	372,667	12,236,144	47,057,778
Nonmetropolitan	133	5,037	138,616	591,127	2,416,396	1,624	6,657	4.3	124,897	496	20,187	1,290,615	6,012,826
Metropolitan	379	60,150	2,662,071	13,927,106	26,033,641	38,156	71,495	5.2	2,069,916	4,327	352,480	10,945,529	41,044,952
Abilene	6	731	25,165	141,312	273,353	387	748	5.6	19,923	27	2,719	103,495	430,296
Amarillo	5	907	43,730	203,826	343,081	559	940	4.7	28,190	54	4,187	131,381	378,842
Austin-Round Rock-Georgetown	30	3,694	169,854	880,941	1,502,031	2,415	4,125	5.2	122,162	330	26,667	763,922	2,150,768
Beaumont-Port Arthur	9	1,032	41,247	208,241	439,783	570	1,204	5	34,255	84	4,452	196,065	664,811
Brownsville-Harlingen	6	1,069	46,315	229,960	367,896	629	1,009	5	27,601	88	6,663	193,687	375,113
College Station-Bryan	7	572	25,803	110,235	258,912	302	721	4.3	24,852	62	3,616	121,985	804,268
Corpus Christi	6	1,172	56,445	313,364	507,711	860	1,391	5.6	45,100	73	6,507	243,124	636,678
Dallas-Fort Worth-Arlington	1	10	261	746	23,846	2	65	2.9	6,359	0	0	5,554	41,540
Dallas-Plano-Irving	77	10,632	444,683	2,440,595	4,433,664	6,683	12,149	5.5	346,192	761	64,539	1,943,995	5,885,692
El Paso	12	1,914	92,225	458,628	785,292	1,257	2,151	5	63,667	183	13,569	371,223	1,568,918
Fort Worth-Arlington-Grapevine	39	5,456	258,221	1,326,471	2,274,370	3,635	6,231	5.1	185,675	423	34,192	1,207,904	3,517,552
Houston-The Woodlands-Sugar Land	84	15,913	722,264	3,840,524	7,619,628	10,520	20,884	5.3	537,010	1,102	93,435	2,664,328	12,188,626
Killeen-Temple	6	1,012	49,231	229,533	564,903	629	1,548	4.7	43,611	66	4,603	219,895	2,161,974
Laredo	4	569	21,637	128,398	241,746	351	662	5.9	20,760	66	5,099	108,354	269,768
Longview	4	609	26,242	115,077	257,527	316	829	4.4	27,114	72	3,435	137,990	375,643
Lubbock	10	1,370	61,757	321,235	622,147	881	1,719	5.2	45,399	94	7,179	173,184	779,866
McAllen-Edinburg-Mission	8	2,181	96,298	463,860	869,886	1,270	2,383	4.8	109,810	185	15,293	371,852	984,352
Midland	3	342	12,578	72,199	148,703	197	408	5.7	9,049	30	2,612	73,893	172,710
Odessa	4	620	20,740	108,987	200,640	299	549	5.3	16,910	42	4,452	84,846	410,573
San Angelo	2	451	18,364	89,896	197,254	247	541	4.9	20,887	36	1,993	68,155	205,569
San Antonio-New Braunfels	24	5,865	254,772	1,327,042	2,346,914	3,637	6,430	5.2	197,016	359	30,674	1,067,566	4,131,349
Sherman-Denison	5	592	28,708	149,537	242,081	411	664	5.2	35,036	30	1,612	92,466	210,937
Texarkana	5	672	22,799	121,208	236,164	333	647	5.3	11,097	33	2,458	105,425	432,981
Tyler	8	1,207	55,216	299,386	556,016	819	1,523	5.4	46,522	37	3,800	154,778	1,111,924
Victoria	5	575	16,812	92,650	197,701	254	543	5.5	10,992	30	2,059	78,322	262,524
Waco	3	542	31,015	155,762	347,215	426	951	5	18,939	40	4,659	171,224	692,235
Wichita Falls	6	441	19,689	97,493	175,177	267	480	5	15,788	20	2,006	90,716	199,443

Note: These data represent hospital performance in the years 2015 – 2019 and do not reflect any impacts from the COVID-19 pandemic in 2020 and thereafter.

TABLE 8

U.S. CENSUS DIVISION 7, WEST SOUTH CENTRAL

U.S. Community Hospitals
(Nonfederal, short-term general and other special hospitals)

2019.Utilization, Personnel and Finances

Physicians and Dentists	Registered Nurses	Licensed Practical Nurses	Other Salaried Personnel	Total Personnel	Medical and Dental Residents	Other Trainees	Total Trainees	Payroll (in thousands)	Employee Benefits (in thousands)	Total (in thousands)	Percent of Total	Amount (in thousands)	Adjusted per Admission	Adjusted per Inpatient Day
144,792	1,586,860	75,060	3,431,822	5,238,534	117,619	9,172	126,791	$377,640,231	$97,798,365	$475,438,596	47.1	$1,010,271,112	$13,542.37	$2,517.38
16,857	155,492	20,586	431,056	623,991	2,007	425	2,432	37,990,709	9,848,267	47,838,976	50.0	95,730,556	9,130.95	1,417.32
127,935	1,431,368	54,474	3,000,766	4,614,543	115,612	8,747	124,359	339,649,522	87,950,099	427,599,621	46.8	914,540,556	14,263.72	2,739.99
8,032	186,306	14,026	359,107	567,471	5,745	1,485	7,230	38,230,418	9,029,029	47,259,447	43.4	108,791,173	11,923.18	2,411.71
1,044	16,410	3,952	43,210	64,616	180	23	203	3,640,387	849,682	4,490,069	47.8	9,388,473	7,418.97	1,603.88
6,988	169,896	10,074	315,897	502,855	5,565	1,462	7,027	34,590,031	8,179,347	42,769,378	43	99,402,699	12,648.46	2,532.17
1,248	16,052	1,524	31,349	50,173	184	17	201	3,040,326	653,169	3,693,495	45.9	8,049,928	9,242.58	1,882.51
329	3,869	746	9,315	14,259	104	4	108	758,182	172,882	931,064	51.2	1,817,044	6,607.46	1,272.39
919	12,183	778	22,034	35,914	80	13	93	2,282,144	480,287	2,762,431	44.3	6,232,884	10,458.53	2,188.43
196	2,236	167	3,805	6,404	1	1	2	345,088	72,830	417,917	43.2	967,547	8,768.54	2,171.22
76	977	119	1,985	3,157	0	0	0	210,342	42,338	252,679	41.3	611,969	7,608.24	1,654.2
20	646	35	972	1,673	0	0	0	104,602	24,649	129,252	43.5	297,126	7,870.68	1,647.62
53	1,190	41	2,144	3,428	44	3	47	204,962	49,583	254,545	42	605,993	7,371.02	1,549.39
556	6,636	335	12,140	19,667	35	7	42	1,322,727	272,704	1,595,431	45.3	3,521,975	13,430.09	2,594.69
3	24	3	65	95	0	0	0	6,615	1,664	8,279	46.7	17,740	5,791.55	2,685.77
14	442	69	839	1,364	0	2	2	82,025	15,894	97,920	48.8	200,713	10,582.76	2,139.5
1	32	9	84	126	0	0	0	5,784	624	6,408	65.2	9,822	10,382.68	2,993.61
2,441	26,447	3,673	59,003	91,564	618	48	666	5,186,280	1,119,205	6,305,485	41.8	15,069,875	11,148.67	2,083.93
209	2,674	560	7,255	10,698	14	4	18	559,286	125,824	685,110	48.7	1,405,618	7,607.23	1,648.84
2,232	23,773	3,113	51,748	80,866	604	44	648	4,626,994	993,381	5,620,375	41.1	13,664,257	11,709.43	2,142.07
9	1,194	131	1,971	3,305	0	0	0	192,968	43,502	236,471	41.1	575,667	10,375.55	1,860.69
484	4,117	572	9,748	14,921	106	0	106	741,465	157,924	899,389	38.1	2,363,350	11,904.43	1,804.73
103	836	112	1,876	2,927	0	0	0	225,085	51,635	276,720	57.1	484,534	14,728.83	2,580.19
90	968	146	3,004	4,208	0	3	3	228,893	46,603	275,496	42.8	643,752	8,992.58	1,912.75
166	2,199	264	4,732	7,361	71	4	75	426,500	111,503	538,003	44.9	1,197,959	9,623.09	1,802.71
122	1,201	253	3,108	4,684	3	15	18	232,984	53,247	286,231	42.2	678,191	9,501.8	1,888.73
85	1,286	155	2,956	4,482	17	1	18	264,731	62,882	327,613	44.1	743,083	10,996.42	2,069.28
743	9,072	1,088	17,536	28,439	329	18	347	1,816,178	331,561	2,147,739	38.3	5,613,332	14,892.44	2,638.9
430	2,900	392	6,817	10,539	78	3	81	498,189	134,525	632,713	46.4	1,364,389	8,117.11	1,879.67
858	17,338	1,643	37,264	57,103	240	154	394	3,682,479	821,140	4,503,619	41.9	10,758,964	10,602.96	2,088.36
251	3,391	695	9,207	13,544	53	12	65	811,628	178,605	990,234	48.1	2,056,791	7,762.3	1,778.2
607	13,947	948	28,057	43,559	187	142	329	2,870,851	642,535	3,513,385	40.4	8,702,173	11,606.91	2,178.15
6	305	20	568	899	0	6	6	63,603	13,843	77,446	42	184,387	9,427.71	1,727.07
5	54	43	233	335	0	0	0	16,291	5,138	21,429	61.1	35,050	6,467.93	1,694.86
103	397	163	1,282	1,945	24	0	24	150,714	26,797	177,512	50.3	352,776	8,911.86	1,113.78
416	7,920	470	15,761	24,567	151	136	287	1,621,228	366,734	1,987,963	38.6	5,143,507	13,385.56	2,510.61
77	5,271	252	10,213	15,813	12	0	12	1,019,014	230,021	1,249,036	41.8	2,986,453	9,924.37	1,987.89
3,485	126,469	7,186	231,491	368,631	4,703	1,266	5,969	26,321,333	6,435,515	32,756,849	43.7	74,912,406	12,725.16	2,633.12
255	6,476	1,951	17,433	26,115	9	3	12	1,511,291	372,371	1,883,661	45.8	4,109,021	7,599.11	1,700.47
3,230	119,993	5,235	214,058	342,516	4,694	1,263	5,957	24,810,042	6,063,145	30,873,187	43.6	70,803,385	13,243.61	2,719.69
1	1,232	147	2,537	3,917	0	71	71	201,269	44,967	246,236	45.4	542,501	10,603.59	1,984.62
0	1,520	65	2,716	4,301	0	4	4	261,409	61,725	323,134	45.3	712,834	9,259.63	2,077.74
285	7,815	225	11,771	20,096	336	11	347	1,342,462	288,030	1,630,493	37.9	4,305,929	13,958.04	2,866.74
3	1,642	200	2,841	4,686	0	0	0	283,677	60,630	344,307	40.5	850,232	9,050.61	1,933.3
10	1,381	116	2,196	3,703	17	2	19	257,611	51,928	309,539	45.7	678,043	8,711.4	1,843.03
0	1,015	77	1,894	2,986	0	0	0	184,941	45,559	230,500	40.4	570,122	8,854.76	2,201.99
86	2,291	103	3,722	6,202	91	3	94	403,240	106,324	509,564	38.6	1,320,913	14,135.58	2,601.7
0	30	6	136	172	0	0	0	6,910	2,065	8,976	26.4	34,038	4,079.79	1,427.39
234	22,556	475	36,644	59,909	1,606	115	1,721	4,864,137	1,108,699	5,972,836	43.8	13,639,754	15,871.7	3,076.41
68	3,346	101	5,914	9,429	48	1	49	609,446	152,439	761,885	41.5	1,837,275	11,388.8	2,339.61
11	12,250	447	18,749	31,457	327	126	453	2,314,622	585,963	2,900,585	43.6	6,657,274	1,424.	2,927.09
2,017	35,224	851	69,826	107,918	1,172	832	2,004	8,716,310	2,369,806	11,086,115	45.6	24,329,490	15,228.02	3193
0	2,100	298	4,549	6,947	459	13	472	399,329	92,447	491,776	38.3	1,284,581	10,001.25	2,273.98
0	725	26	1,213	1,964	0	0	0	123,729	24,325	148,054	44	336,232	7,829.92	1,390.85
0	1,156	57	1,873	3,086	0	0	0	172,007	37,135	209,142	40.2	520,628	8,449.43	2,021.65
0	2,935	209	5,012	8,156	0	0	0	500,930	80,270	581,200	40.8	1,423,635	11,161.83	2,288.26
138	3,065	225	6,735	10,163	0	0	0	544,312	121,874	666,186	46.3	1,437,407	7,823.73	1,652.41
3	493	44	1,529	2,069	0	44	44	135,560	29,306	164,866	48.8	338,115	11,718.55	2,273.76
0	666	89	1,712	2,467	0	6	6	160,185	40,015	200,200	41.2	485,968	12,411.06	2,422.09
0	675	54	1,549	2,278	0	0	0	131,152	27,811	158,963	39.5	402,076	9,894.57	2,038.37
111	10,716	674	16,610	28,111	495	11	506	1,863,712	430,799	2,294,511	42.5	5,398,943	11,358.95	2,300.44
68	943	62	1,886	2,959	23	0	23	172,736	46,643	219,379	50.3	436,552	8,851.25	1,803.33
0	928	119	1,300	2,347	0	0	0	148,839	36,052	184,891	42.1	438,823	9,054.25	1,858.13
99	2,612	365	5,609	8,685	74	23	97	484,667	107,749	592,415	42.7	1,388,335	12,398.73	2,496.93
29	765	87	1,484	2,365	22	0	22	137,416	31,917	169,333	47	359,943	9,391.87	1,820.64
66	1,186	53	2,224	3,529	24	1	25	217,417	51,948	269,365	41.5	648,942	9,213.22	1,868.99
1	726	60	1,827	2,614	0	0	0	172,018	26,719	198,736	46.8	424,796	10,850.74	2,424.95

Note: These data represent hospital performance in the years 2015 – 2019 and do not reflect any impacts from the COVID-19 pandemic in 2020 and thereafter.

CBSAs

TABLE **8**

U.S. CENSUS DIVISION 8, MOUNTAIN

U.S. Community Hospitals
(Nonfederal, short-term general and other special hospitals)

2019 Utilization, Personnel and Finances

CLASSIFICATION	Hospitals	Beds	Admissions	Inpatient Days	Adjusted Inpatient Days	Average Daily Census	Adjusted Average Daily Census	Average Stay (days)	Surgical Operations	NEWBORNS Bassinets	NEWBORNS Births	OUTPATIENT VISITS Emergency	OUTPATIENT VISITS Total
UNITED STATES	5,198	792,417	34,251,159	185,307,228	401,318,395	507,697	1,100,206	5.4	28,168,014	54,943	3,637,593	143,454,611	766,392,512
Nonmetropolitan	1,821	108,166	3,008,734	19,667,770	67,543,319	53,878	185,275	6.5	3,542,053	8,752	345,082	21,571,345	129,292,741
Metropolitan	3,377	684,251	31,242,425	165,639,458	333,775,076	453,819	914,931	5.3	24,625,961	46,191	3,292,511	121,883,266	637,099,771
CENSUS DIVISION 8, MOUNTAIN	439	49,513	2,112,291	10,799,364	24,057,237	29,584	65,919	5.1	1,733,446	4,289	258,112	8,569,341	44,047,399
Nonmetropolitan	199	8,279	194,937	1,417,525	5,353,081	3,885	14,660	7.3	305,396	854	33,590	1,612,111	9,152,570
Metropolitan	240	41,234	1,917,354	9,381,839	18,704,156	25,699	51,259	4.9	1,428,050	3,435	224,522	6,957,230	34,894,829
Arizona	80	14,038	655,961	3,152,127	6,059,583	8,634	16,604	4.8	476,761	968	73,933	2,403,474	9,238,375
Nonmetropolitan	9	307	12,803	37,907	169,818	104	466	3	18,859	48	2,579	97,926	413,396
Metropolitan	71	13,731	643,158	3,114,220	5,889,765	8,530	16,138	4.8	457,902	920	71,354	2,305,548	8,824,979
Flagstaff	3	342	14,043	71,117	141,608	194	388	5.1	14,395	33	1,546	41,087	184,348
Lake Havasu City-Kingman	4	512	21,642	95,544	213,056	262	585	4.4	20,558	31	1,555	153,042	628,098
Phoenix-Mesa-Chandler	43	9,076	447,051	2,209,182	4,105,514	6,052	11,248	4.9	299,580	627	53,558	1,451,838	5,978,585
Prescott Valley-Prescott	3	309	16,267	61,593	150,242	169	412	3.8	12,484	64	1,808	76,819	211,941
Sierra Vista-Douglas	4	160	6,401	22,967	101,604	63	279	3.6	6,195	10	741	74,778	231,995
Tucson	12	2,885	119,937	584,164	999,168	1,599	2,736	4.9	92,493	121	8,823	421,907	1,227,459
Yuma	2	447	17,817	69,653	178,573	191	490	3.9	12,197	34	3,323	86,077	362,553
Colorado	90	10,665	446,955	2,290,705	5,243,205	6,272	14,362	5.1	398,813	984	53,923	2,105,511	10,252,093
Nonmetropolitan	40	1,518	35,079	249,681	1,019,883	682	2,792	7.1	68,286	151	6,209	314,439	2,024,114
Metropolitan	50	9,147	411,876	2,041,024	4,223,322	5,590	11,570	5	330,527	833	47,714	1,791,072	8,227,979
Boulder	5	638	31,423	122,859	274,280	337	751	3.9	24,548	124	5,956	132,730	609,058
Colorado Springs	5	1,000	56,477	256,284	541,777	701	1,484	4.5	41,453	60	4,684	229,656	886,835
Denver-Aurora-Lakewood	26	5,574	247,115	1,284,544	2,504,006	3,518	6,860	5.2	195,198	503	27,099	1,029,553	4,905,576
Fort Collins	5	700	31,885	139,947	368,867	383	1,011	4.4	26,184	66	4,647	164,266	736,611
Grand Junction	3	378	14,598	83,144	189,869	228	520	5.7	11,547	46	1,934	69,219	368,407
Greeley	4	474	11,739	64,983	142,809	178	392	5.5	10,062	14	1,445	55,110	399,506
Pueblo	2	383	18,639	89,263	201,714	245	552	4.8	21,535	20	1,949	110,538	321,986
Idaho	46	3,468	138,405	639,152	1,599,552	1,751	4,385	4.6	141,985	336	19,277	688,976	6,433,916
Nonmetropolitan	24	739	17,231	116,078	457,377	318	1,254	6.7	36,297	92	3,849	175,468	1,143,521
Metropolitan	22	2,729	121,174	523,074	1,142,175	1,433	3,131	4.3	105,688	244	15,428	513,508	5,290,395
Boise City	9	1,399	63,464	283,827	581,580	777	1,595	4.5	58,731	134	8,519	263,382	3,282,485
Coeur d'Alene	4	426	19,379	81,719	195,102	224	534	4.2	16,932	14	1,941	54,193	669,463
Idaho Falls	3	345	12,404	58,791	122,505	162	336	4.7	6,732	35	1,183	85,927	240,203
Lewiston	1	123	5,669	16,807	39,358	46	108	3	3,015	22	565	29,410	151,642
Logan	1	20	511	2,904	16,918	8	46	5.7	1,216	4	95	1,044	7,330
Pocatello	2	185	8,195	35,300	89,621	96	246	4.3	8,348	15	1,208	35,783	292,442
Twin Falls	2	231	11,552	43,726	97,091	120	266	3.8	10,714	20	1,917	43,769	646,830
Montana	57	3,614	100,441	758,902	2,280,217	2,077	6,243	7.6	103,510	252	10,378	452,994	4,598,704
Nonmetropolitan	48	2,143	42,877	402,911	1,429,312	1,101	3,912	9.4	52,990	133	4,889	268,079	2,336,990
Metropolitan	9	1,471	57,564	355,991	850,905	976	2,331	6.2	50,520	119	5,489	184,915	2,261,714
Billings	5	614	28,817	143,156	312,444	393	856	5	25,030	57	2,650	93,475	1,132,514
Great Falls	2	522	12,958	142,379	378,677	390	1,037	11	12,716	24	1,350	40,204	654,552
Missoula	2	335	15,789	70,456	159,784	193	438	4.5	12,774	38	1,489	51,236	474,648
Nevada	43	6,309	282,453	1,539,908	2,829,490	4,221	7,766	5.5	140,690	327	29,049	956,217	3,342,671
Nonmetropolitan	11	403	8,560	58,125	239,465	160	656	6.8	14,193	31	1,432	97,100	408,620
Metropolitan	32	5,906	273,893	1,481,783	2,590,025	4,061	7,110	5.4	126,497	296	27,617	859,117	2,934,051
Carson City	2	240	12,497	60,340	131,449	166	360	4.8	9,929	12	1,011	40,694	375,347
Las Vegas-Henderson-Paradise	23	4,421	206,618	1,129,157	1,932,172	3,094	5,293	5.5	77,358	209	20,497	615,640	1,649,752
Reno	7	1,245	54,778	292,286	526,404	801	1,457	5.3	39,210	75	6,109	202,783	908,952
New Mexico	42	3,765	198,127	888,056	2,205,781	2,436	6,041	4.5	160,519	509	19,279	876,730	4,000,949
Nonmetropolitan	25	1,060	42,547	166,806	566,785	461	1,552	3.9	53,840	160	6,828	404,985	1,481,768
Metropolitan	17	2,705	155,580	721,250	1,638,996	1,975	4,489	4.6	106,679	349	12,451	471,745	2,519,181
Albuquerque	10	1,869	111,436	541,644	1,180,423	1,483	3,233	4.9	66,378	267	8,232	279,977	1,347,366
Farmington	1	198	9,467	36,685	92,119	101	252	3.9	5,348	22	1,026	65,426	712,385
Las Cruces	4	395	21,087	87,056	192,320	238	527	4.1	24,221	36	1,842	64,809	219,450
Santa Fe	2	243	13,590	55,865	174,134	153	477	4.1	10,732	24	1,351	61,533	239,980

Note: These data represent hospital performance in the years 2015 – 2019 and do not reflect any impacts from the COVID-19 pandemic in 2020 and thereafter.

CBSAs

TABLE 8

U.S. CENSUS DIVISION 8, MOUNTAIN

U.S. Community Hospitals
(Nonfederal, short-term general and other special hospitals)

2019 Utilization, Personnel and Finances

FULL-TIME EQUIVALENT PERSONNEL					FULL-TIME EQUIV. TRAINEES			EXPENSES						
								LABOR				TOTAL		
Physicians and Dentists	Registered Nurses	Licensed Practical Nurses	Other Salaried Personnel	Total Personnel	Medical and Dental Residents	Other Trainees	Total Trainees	Payroll (in thousands)	Employee Benefits (in thousands)	Total (in thousands)	Percent of Total	Amount (in thousands)	Adjusted per Admission	Adjusted per Inpatient Day
144,792	1,586,860	75,060	3,431,822	5,238,534	117,619	9,172	126,791	$377,640,231	$97,798,365	$475,438,596	47.1	$1,010,271,112	$13,542.37	$2,517.38
16,857	155,492	20,586	431,056	623,991	2,007	425	2,432	37,990,709	9,848,267	47,838,976	50.0	95,730,556	9,130.95	1,417.32
127,935	1,431,368	54,474	3,000,766	4,614,543	115,612	8,747	124,359	339,649,522	87,950,099	427,599,621	46.8	914,540,556	14,263.72	2,739.99
8,496	100,573	3,430	210,272	322,771	3,405	380	3,785	23,070,035	5,568,026	28,638,061	45.1	63,435,906	13,648.92	2,636.87
1,734	13,427	1,153	37,965	54,279	67	34	101	3,533,692	885,165	4,418,857	49.4	8,939,213	11,841.48	1,669.92
6,762	87,146	2,277	172,307	268,492	3,338	346	3,684	19,536,342	4,682,861	24,219,203	44.4	54,496,692	13,999.42	2,913.61
2,849	27,582	625	49,959	81,015	1,318	81	1,399	6,088,585	1,363,353	7,451,939	44.7	16,672,228	12,851.01	2,751.38
122	690	70	1,821	2,703	9	3	12	223,558	51,053	274,611	50.1	548,409	9,726.84	3,229.39
2,727	26,892	555	48,138	78,312	1,309	78	1,387	5,865,028	1,312,300	7,177,328	44.5	16,123,819	12,992.95	2,737.6
62	798	14	1,817	2,691	1	0	1	186,511	47,337	233,848	43.9	532,678	18,470.75	3,761.64
72	967	70	2,343	3,452	26	3	29	235,516	61,606	297,122	48.2	616,188	12,767.55	2,892.14
1,909	18,695	333	31,750	52,687	894	51	945	4,103,223	926,873	5,030,096	44.9	11,199,728	13,219.64	2,727.97
65	572	1	1,680	2,318	0	0	0	188,605	50,821	239,426	48	499,304	12,550.38	3,323.33
28	321	24	805	1,178	6	1	7	74,899	16,957	91,856	48.4	189,655	7,087.26	1,866.61
544	4,890	104	7,939	13,477	362	16	378	869,220	163,630	1,032,850	40.3	2,563,405	12,532.6	2,565.54
47	649	9	1,804	2,509	20	7	27	207,054	45,075	252,130	48.2	522,861	11,471.52	2,927.99
1,817	23,058	646	50,506	76,027	679	45	724	5,696,008	1,357,844	7,053,853	44.2	15,976,705	15,888.65	3,047.13
396	2,836	291	8,699	12,222	12	12	24	780,193	204,577	984,770	48.3	2,038,774	13,721.45	1,999.03
1,421	20,222	355	41,807	63,805	667	33	700	4,915,816	1,153,268	6,069,083	43.5	13,937,931	16,264.41	3,300.23
122	1,459	10	3,166	4,757	0	0	0	369,286	86,439	455,724	45.4	1,004,420	14,225.91	3,662.02
60	2,145	28	4,425	6,658	51	6	57	514,584	118,621	633,205	46.1	1,373,750	11,501.97	2,535.64
928	12,907	238	24,811	38,884	498	20	518	3,141,487	740,878	3,882,365	43.7	8,887,984	18,307.24	3,549.51
86	1,401	30	3,161	4,678	21	0	21	398,395	100,325	498,720	41.4	1,205,809	15,013.68	3,268.95
45	789	16	1,697	2,547	28	5	33	181,237	44,159	225,396	39.2	574,507	18,244.1	3,025.81
103	643	20	1,447	2,213	36	2	38	133,183	27,201	160,384	37.7	425,126	15,951.61	2,976.89
77	878	13	3,100	4,068	33	0	33	177,643	35,645	213,288	45.7	466,336	10,851.84	2,311.87
961	7,061	488	16,942	25,452	45	34	79	1,561,924	367,921	1,929,845	48	4,016,493	12,044.87	2,511.01
153	1,216	147	3,558	5,074	1	2	3	291,488	77,943	369,431	52.9	698,923	10,112.76	1,528.11
808	5,845	341	13,384	20,378	44	32	76	1,270,436	289,979	1,560,414	47	3,317,570	12,550.01	2,904.61
556	3,197	112	7,425	11,290	9	28	37	657,119	143,822	800,941	45.4	1,763,275	13,425.58	3,031.87
132	869	41	2,625	3,667	17	2	19	283,720	66,230	349,950	53.7	652,019	13,863.89	3,341.94
16	592	29	990	1,627	14	0	14	92,763	20,861	113,624	42.2	269,496	10,996.69	2,199.88
16	188	11	446	661	4	0	4	46,746	11,846	58,593	47.7	122,855	9,254.65	3,121.49
5	46	15	182	248	0	0	0	8,715	2,263	10,979	51.8	21,205	7,122.79	1,253.37
47	441	52	686	1,226	0	0	0	91,186	19,454	110,640	42.2	262,427	13,313.73	2,928.19
36	512	81	1,030	1,659	0	2	2	90,186	25,501	115,688	51.1	226,293	8,870.41	2,330.73
1,025	6,290	431	16,096	23,842	38	73	111	1,718,058	372,411	2,090,469	49.1	4,258,261	14,512.41	1,867.48
460	3,119	191	9,176	12,946	10	7	17	850,140	199,694	1,049,834	49.5	2,121,067	13,521.18	1,483.98
565	3,171	240	6,920	10,896	28	66	94	867,919	172,717	1,040,636	48.7	2,137,194	15,651.13	2,511.67
347	1,630	134	3,552	5,663	28	37	65	491,444	100,539	591,984	49.9	1,185,370	18,416.95	3,793.86
177	796	72	1,946	2,991	0	0	0	230,736	49,515	280,250	54	519,459	14,242.3	1,371.77
41	745	34	1,422	2,242	0	29	29	145,739	22,663	168,401	38.9	432,364	12,105.62	2,705.93
313	10,982	381	20,736	32,412	179	12	191	2,326,104	603,040	2,929,144	46.7	6,270,610	12,094.59	2,216.16
53	530	41	1,448	2,072	0	1	1	137,647	34,572	172,220	49.7	346,372	10,102.72	1,446.44
260	10,452	340	19,288	30,340	179	11	190	2,188,456	568,468	2,756,924	46.5	5,924,238	12,235.64	2,287.33
33	383	2	1,208	1,626	0	0	0	97,763	23,433	121,196	41.7	290,552	10,290.11	2,210.37
212	7,686	307	13,255	21,460	158	11	169	1,652,032	444,176	2,096,208	47.4	4,422,814	12,441.81	2,289.04
15	2,383	31	4,825	7,254	21	0	21	438,661	100,858	539,520	44.6	1,210,872	12,052.92	2,300.27
973	8,878	359	20,383	30,593	52	46	98	2,314,161	496,512	2,810,674	45.4	6,190,448	12,234.57	2,806.47
244	2,311	163	5,740	8,458	9	4	13	552,831	122,969	675,799	46.8	1,444,178	9,957.92	2,548.02
729	6,567	196	14,643	22,135	43	42	85	1,761,331	373,544	2,134,874	45	4,746,270	13,149.31	2,895.84
459	4,894	148	9,998	15,499	17	40	57	1,240,750	263,259	1,504,009	43.6	3,449,991	13,957.01	2,922.67
80	378	0	1,026	1,484	0	0	0	141,934	34,434	176,368	57.5	306,563	12,895.99	3,327.91
72	890	41	1,634	2,637	26	2	28	174,961	35,802	210,763	44.6	473,032	10,083.61	2,459.61
118	405	7	1,985	2,515	0	0	0	203,686	40,049	243,735	47.2	516,683	11,993.02	2,967.16

Table continues

CBSAs

Note: These data represent hospital performance in the years 2015 – 2019 and do not reflect any impacts from the COVID-19 pandemic in 2020 and thereafter.

TABLE 8

U.S. CENSUS DIVISION 8, MOUNTAIN CONTINUED

U.S. Community Hospitals
(Nonfederal, short-term general and other special hospitals)

2019 Utilization, Personnel and Finances

CLASSIFICATION	Hospitals	Beds	Admissions	Inpatient Days	Adjusted Inpatient Days	Average Daily Census	Adjusted Average Daily Census	Average Stay (days)	Surgical Operations	NEWBORNS Bassinets	NEWBORNS Births	OUTPATIENT VISITS Emergency	OUTPATIENT VISITS Total
Utah	53	5,664	248,428	1,151,548	2,597,017	3,153	7,115	4.6	269,936	737	46,849	862,136	4,889,471
Nonmetropolitan	18	647	14,281	98,484	422,987	270	1,159	6.9	31,817	104	4,552	107,367	342,521
Metropolitan	35	5,017	234,147	1,053,064	2,174,030	2,883	5,956	4.5	238,119	633	42,297	754,769	4,546,950
Logan	2	155	6,858	20,272	65,976	56	181	3	10,056	36	2,320	33,864	74,414
Ogden-Clearfield	9	1,090	42,301	206,891	387,304	567	1,060	4.9	38,660	138	7,713	140,385	481,903
Provo-Orem	7	771	38,164	151,080	312,131	413	854	4	42,696	133	10,310	119,110	378,593
Salt Lake City	16	2,717	128,635	608,232	1,266,764	1,665	3,472	4.7	129,943	310	19,530	404,096	3,389,983
St. George	1	284	18,189	66,589	141,855	182	389	3.7	16,764	16	2,424	57,314	222,057
Wyoming	28	1,990	41,521	378,966	1,242,392	1,040	3,403	9.1	41,232	176	5,424	223,303	1,291,220
Nonmetropolitan	24	1,462	21,559	287,533	1,047,454	789	2,869	13.3	29,114	135	3,252	146,747	1,001,640
Metropolitan	4	528	19,962	91,433	194,938	251	534	4.6	12,118	41	2,172	76,556	289,580
Casper	3	306	10,155	47,346	92,340	130	253	4.7	6,371	25	981	34,926	100,658
Cheyenne	1	222	9,807	44,087	102,598	121	281	4.5	5,747	16	1,191	41,630	188,922

Note: These data represent hospital performance in the years 2015 – 2019 and do not reflect any impacts from the COVID-19 pandemic in 2020 and thereafter.

TABLE 8

U.S. CENSUS DIVISION 8, MOUNTAIN CONTINUED

U.S. Community Hospitals
(Nonfederal, short-term general and other special hospitals)

2019 Utilization, Personnel and Finances

CBSAs

FULL-TIME EQUIVALENT PERSONNEL					FULL-TIME EQUIV. TRAINEES			EXPENSES						
								LABOR				TOTAL		
Physicians and Dentists	Registered Nurses	Licensed Practical Nurses	Other Salaried Personnel	Total Personnel	Medical and Dental Residents	Other Trainees	Total Trainees	Payroll (in thousands)	Employee Benefits (in thousands)	Total (in thousands)	Percent of Total	Amount (in thousands)	Adjusted per Admission	Adjusted per Inpatient Day
271	14,245	322	28,587	43,425	1,069	57	1,126	2,656,969	820,143	3,477,111	41.7	8,333,125	14,585.74	3,208.73
73	999	91	2,502	3,665	1	3	4	213,071	64,619	277,690	45.7	607,673	9,533.78	1,436.62
198	13,246	231	26,085	39,760	1,068	54	1,122	2,443,898	755,523	3,199,421	41.4	7,725,452	15,220.14	3,553.52
5	359	12	684	1,060	0	2	2	68,623	22,035	90,658	38	238,674	10,678.92	3,617.59
34	2,046	69	3,658	5,807	42	9	51	374,370	100,862	475,231	40.5	1,172,291	13,474.14	3,026.8
30	1,849	38	3,072	4,989	36	11	47	305,148	95,205	400,353	40.3	992,328	11,768.17	3,179.2
128	8,211	112	17,079	25,530	990	31	1,021	1,555,585	486,012	2,041,597	42.9	4,753,820	17,276.76	3,752.73
1	781	0	1,592	2,374	0	1	1	140,172	51,411	191,582	33.7	568,339	14,667.57	4,006.48
287	2,477	178	7,063	10,005	25	32	57	708,225	186,801	895,026	52.1	1,718,036	14,064.85	1,382.85
233	1,726	159	5,021	7,139	25	2	27	484,765	129,738	614,503	54.2	1,133,817	14,013.66	1,082.45
54	751	19	2,042	2,866	0	30	30	223,460	57,064	280,523	48	584,218	14,165.27	2,996.94
29	373	9	933	1,344	0	0	0	101,577	26,220	127,797	45.5	280,910	15,250.3	3,042.13
25	378	10	1,109	1,522	0	30	30	121,883	30,844	152,727	50.4	303,308	13,289.57	2,956.28

Note: These data represent hospital performance in the years 2015 – 2019 and do not reflect any impacts from the COVID-19 pandemic in 2020 and thereafter.

TABLE 8

U.S. CENSUS DIVISION 9, PACIFIC

U.S. Community Hospitals
(Nonfederal, short-term general and other special hospitals)

2019 Utilization, Personnel and Finances

CLASSIFICATION	Hospitals	Beds	Admissions	Inpatient Days	Adjusted Inpatient Days	Average Daily Census	Adjusted Average Daily Census	Average Stay (days)	Surgical Operations	NEWBORNS Bassinets	NEWBORNS Births	OUTPATIENT VISITS Emergency	OUTPATIENT VISITS Total
UNITED STATES............	5,198	792,417	34,251,159	185,307,228	401,318,395	507,697	1,100,206	5.4	28,168,014	54,943	3,637,593	143,454,611	766,392,512
Nonmetropolitan.............	1,821	108,166	3,008,734	19,667,770	67,543,319	53,878	185,275	6.5	3,542,053	8,752	345,082	21,571,345	129,292,741
Metropolitan..............	3,377	684,251	31,242,425	165,639,458	333,775,076	453,819	914,931	5.3	24,625,961	46,191	3,292,511	121,883,266	637,099,771
CENSUS DIVISION 9, PACIFIC	553	97,034	4,464,625	23,075,599	45,422,527	63,227	124,431	5.2	3,324,628	7,245	570,444	184,04,079	89,228,160
Nonmetropolitan.............	107	4,378	147,162	788,829	2,910,542	2,167	7,977	5.4	209,842	438	23,170	1,128,042	8,228,720
Metropolitan..............	446	92,656	4,317,463	22,286,770	42,511,985	61,060	116,454	5.2	3,114,786	6,807	547,274	172,76,037	80,999,440
Alaska............	20	1,606	49,888	382,686	907,761	1,050	2,488	7.7	63,536	179	7,831	329,868	1,839,981
Nonmetropolitan.............	14	553	10,768	118,735	417,769	326	1,145	11	21,248	45	1,921	88,262	547,300
Metropolitan..............	6	1,053	39,120	263,951	489,992	724	1,343	6.7	42,288	134	5,910	241,606	1,292,681
Anchorage.............	5	836	34,813	219,669	380,423	603	1,043	6.3	37,821	118	4,924	210,257	948,965
Fairbanks.............	1	217	4,307	44,282	109,569	121	300	10.3	4,467	16	986	31,349	343,716
California............	359	73,109	3,361,823	17,440,927	32,908,321	47,781	90,148	5.2	2,274,906	5,205	426,158	13,079,880	55,866,261
Nonmetropolitan.............	30	1,356	48,870	268,362	931,231	738	2,549	5.5	63,456	114	6,881	374,110	2,299,703
Metropolitan..............	329	71,753	3,312,953	17,172,565	31,977,090	47,043	87,599	5.2	2,211,450	5,091	419,277	12,705,770	53,566,558
Anaheim-Santa Ana-Irvine.............	27	5,888	277,781	1,273,878	2,302,157	3,489	6,308	4.6	192,162	365	38,746	959,897	4,601,390
Bakersfield.............	11	1,648	68,224	345,681	790,550	946	2,166	5.1	47,129	99	11,690	320,020	917,798
Chico.............	3	444	34,756	143,662	289,725	393	794	4.1	19,603	22	2,431	111,906	1,058,570
El Centro.............	2	268	10,901	43,033	120,388	118	330	3.9	9,139	33	3,018	91,197	383,570
Fresno.............	8	1,692	86,699	466,861	913,502	1,279	2,503	5.4	42,934	127	10,442	171,450	1,050,773
Hanford-Corcoran.............	2	248	18,040	48,546	115,509	133	317	2.7	10,723	20	811	113,606	526,071
Los Angeles-Long Beach-Glendale....	88	21,377	970,380	5,013,319	8,730,738	13,735	23,917	5.2	581,296	1,529	107,431	3,104,881	12,025,893
Madera.............	2	464	15,623	87,507	147,789	240	405	5.6	17,608	14	879	138,574	441,408
Merced.............	2	230	13,809	49,268	96,983	135	265	3.6	8,216	28	3,227	80,650	273,137
Modesto.............	6	1,098	54,543	286,702	522,755	786	1,431	5.3	33,368	87	7,152	199,205	515,487
Napa.............	2	289	11,025	57,712	145,552	158	399	5.2	10,868	10	830	41,315	207,316
Oakland-Berkeley-Livermore..........	20	4,511	197,707	1,122,297	2,159,343	3,076	5,915	5.7	143,791	339	28,629	959,702	3,667,062
Oxnard-Thousand Oaks-Ventura...	7	1,087	60,732	299,252	643,584	819	1,763	4.9	32,133	101	7,913	257,306	1,088,766
Redding.............	5	567	23,430	148,146	270,807	405	742	6.3	14,782	10	1,942	82,330	250,738
Riverside-San Bernardino-Ontario...	38	7,666	365,108	1,767,116	3,255,004	4,843	8,917	4.8	227,708	536	47,530	1,542,747	4,922,555
Sacramento-Roseville-Folsom........	17	3,907	202,742	997,287	1,824,327	2,731	4,997	4.9	152,778	316	26,367	857,349	3,409,433
Salinas.............	4	748	35,052	159,655	325,559	438	892	4.6	19,300	82	4,888	156,477	757,261
San Diego-Chula Vista-Carlsbad.....	19	6,121	288,923	1,513,162	2,562,481	4,145	7,020	5.2	204,786	453	37,330	931,564	3,883,835
San Francisco-San Mateo-Redwood City	17	4,761	164,531	1,277,377	2,522,233	3,498	6,910	7.8	125,249	183	16,833	671,630	4,405,950
San Jose-Sunnyvale-Santa Clara ...	11	3,361	162,159	858,485	1,643,863	2,352	4,504	5.3	130,106	292	24,737	556,552	3,710,215
San Luis Obispo-Paso Robles........	4	350	16,363	67,312	151,271	184	414	4.1	13,266	29	2,203	97,627	289,462
San Rafael.............	3	391	14,093	64,401	152,368	177	417	4.6	14,121	22	1,234	81,321	368,600
Santa Cruz-Watsonville.............	3	359	15,822	68,508	150,972	187	413	4.3	11,048	50	2,401	74,788	306,359
Santa Maria-Santa Barbara.............	5	887	38,440	220,495	421,638	603	1,154	5.7	23,980	53	4,631	144,955	519,944
Santa Rosa-Petaluma.............	8	826	36,450	177,908	417,911	487	1,145	4.9	45,204	60	4,554	151,960	561,238
Stockton.............	7	1,049	55,001	223,480	511,037	613	1,400	4.1	35,891	93	8,588	361,796	1,398,209
Vallejo.............	4	688	28,995	128,249	264,888	352	726	4.4	22,903	69	4,786	198,339	739,152
Visalia.............	2	595	33,901	208,388	408,612	571	1,119	6.1	15,084	39	6,362	193,425	1,029,335
Yuba City.............	2	233	11,723	54,878	115,544	150	316	4.7	6,274	30	1,692	53,201	257,031
Hawaii............	22	2,731	113,544	706,387	1,532,333	1,936	4,198	6.2	95,912	149	15,328	497,344	2,776,613
Nonmetropolitan.............	7	487	18,402	101,394	312,609	278	857	5.5	18,317	45	3,611	80,400	408,601
Metropolitan..............	15	2,244	95,142	604,993	1,219,724	1,658	3,341	6.4	77,595	104	11,717	416,944	2,368,012
Kahului-Wailuku-Lahaina.............	4	367	14,718	96,934	212,945	266	583	6.6	8,706	21	1,616	60,337	127,666
Urban Honolulu.............	11	1,877	80,424	508,059	1,006,779	1,392	2,758	6.3	68,889	83	10,101	356,607	2,240,346
Oregon............	61	6,975	348,059	1,602,392	3,588,356	4,394	9,831	4.6	361,731	647	41,043	1,571,368	12,816,471
Nonmetropolitan.............	26	962	40,771	148,409	599,264	410	1,643	3.6	49,846	130	5,707	320,080	2,881,197
Metropolitan..............	35	6,013	307,288	1,453,983	2,989,092	3,984	8,188	4.7	311,885	517	35,336	1,251,288	9,935,274
Albany-Lebanon.............	2	95	4,277	13,793	62,787	38	172	3.2	9,452	18	766	50,673	564,703
Bend.............	2	341	19,324	75,604	140,005	207	383	3.9	21,916	35	2,183	67,282	229,406
Corvallis.............	1	185	8,199	39,622	84,223	109	231	4.8	10,384	20	973	29,489	415,651
Eugene-Springfield.............	5	619	39,092	174,683	306,760	478	841	4.5	25,341	56	3,776	165,890	443,005
Grants Pass.............	1	122	6,928	26,290	62,900	72	172	3.8	6,530	12	738	41,099	309,195
Medford.............	3	519	23,110	122,604	248,706	335	681	5.3	23,628	34	2,273	91,518	916,822
Portland-Vancouver-Hillsboro........	17	3,564	174,886	865,915	1,821,973	2,374	4,991	5	195,328	297	19,846	645,252	6,216,998
Salem.............	4	568	31,472	135,472	261,738	371	717	4.3	19,306	45	4,781	160,085	839,494

Note: These data represent hospital performance in the years 2015 – 2019 and do not reflect any impacts from the COVID-19 pandemic in 2020 and thereafter.

TABLE 8

U.S. CENSUS DIVISION 9, PACIFIC

U.S. Community Hospitals
(Nonfederal, short-term general and other special hospitals)

2019 Utilization, Personnel and Finances

	FULL-TIME EQUIVALENT PERSONNEL				FULL-TIME EQUIV. TRAINEES			EXPENSES						
								LABOR				TOTAL		
Physicians and Dentists	Registered Nurses	Licensed Practical Nurses	Other Salaried Personnel	Total Personnel	Medical and Dental Residents	Other Trainees	Total Trainees	Payroll (in thousands)	Employee Benefits (in thousands)	Total (in thousands)	Percent of Total	Amount (in thousands)	Adjusted per Admission	Adjusted per Inpatient Day
144,792	1,586,860	75,060	3,431,822	5,238,534	117,619	9,172	126,791	$377,640,231	$97,798,365	$475,438,596	47.1	$1,010,271,112	$13,542.37	$2,517.38
16,857	155,492	20,586	431,056	623,991	2,007	425	2,432	37,990,709	9,848,267	47,838,976	50.0	95,730,556	9,130.95	1,417.32
127,935	1,431,368	54,474	3,000,766	4,614,543	115,612	8,747	124,359	339,649,522	87,950,099	427,599,621	46.8	914,540,556	14,263.72	2,739.99
14,739	213,943	8,392	428,039	665,113	12,397	1,094	13,491	62,090,364	18,853,168	80,943,532	48.7	166,107,584	18,754.58	3,656.94
1,011	8,844	669	25,827	36,351	20	58	78	2,876,970	798,890	3,675,859	51.3	7,164,481	12,990.83	2,461.56
13,728	205,099	7,723	402,212	628,762	12,377	1,036	13,413	59,213,394	18,054,279	77,267,673	48.6	158,943,103	19,137.31	3,738.78
283	2,925	182	7,030	10,420	95	10	105	916,791	206,876	1,123,666	51.6	2,175,918	19,374.73	2,397.02
102	807	85	2,507	3,501	0	3	3	309,928	95,704	405,632	56.3	720,286	1,844.	1,724.12
181	2,118	97	4,523	6,919	95	7	102	606,863	111,172	718,035	49.3	1,455,632	19,868.04	2,970.73
105	1,745	72	3,669	5,591	95	4	99	493,096	87,861	580,957	48.4	1,199,582	19,160.2	3,153.28
76	373	25	854	1,328	0	3	3	113,767	23,311	137,078	53.5	256,050	24,026.48	2,336.89
8,470	159,223	6,859	308,753	483,305	9,661	805	10,466	45,417,929	14,714,866	60,132,796	49	122,630,620	19,234.4	3,726.43
187	2,843	253	7,300	10,583	7	9	16	877,230	259,463	1,136,693	48.5	2,342,670	14,327.56	2,515.67
8,283	156,380	6,606	301,453	472,722	9,654	796	10,450	44,540,699	14,455,403	58,996,103	49	120,287,950	19,363.55	3,761.69
149	13,353	455	24,149	38,106	83	9	92	2,981,668	838,176	3,819,843	46	8,308,781	16,313.93	3,609.13
108	3,087	183	6,190	9,568	26	3	29	696,511	213,956	910,467	45.7	1,991,845	14,220.26	2,519.57
8	1,497	70	3,573	5,148	0	1	1	357,668	141,929	499,597	49.8	1,003,460	14,969.65	3,463.49
46	435	47	1,191	1,719	13	1	14	110,244	31,443	141,687	51	277,699	9,079.58	2,306.7
274	2,864	120	6,092	9,350	225	15	240	846,521	214,786	1,061,307	46.6	2,277,620	12,851.21	2,493.28
50	661	48	1,576	2,335	12	1	13	149,237	36,209	185,446	45.5	407,414	9,466.81	3,527.12
2,196	47,432	2,374	90,116	142,118	3,306	501	3,807	12,174,969	3,736,436	15,911,404	49.1	32,409,058	19,032.49	3,712.06
19	1,182	12	2,262	3,475	42	29	71	249,811	104,795	354,606	49.3	718,557	26,426.3	4,862.05
8	533	42	947	1,530	24	1	25	141,887	44,501	186,389	49.1	379,312	13,035.23	3,911.12
79	2,591	79	3,593	6,342	83	3	86	639,358	174,393	813,750	50.6	1,609,221	16,239.34	3,078.35
52	571	30	1,279	1,932	12	3	15	213,764	53,889	267,653	46.9	570,512	20,654.25	3,919.64
890	8,591	307	17,011	26,799	441	28	469	3,174,241	873,774	4,048,015	49.6	8,156,668	20,932.89	3,777.38
132	2,346	114	4,779	7,371	47	6	53	789,777	211,945	1,001,722	47.7	2,100,801	16,378.34	3,264.22
21	1,182	48	1,958	3,209	28	1	29	260,314	80,885	341,199	47.1	723,829	17,084.74	2,672.86
283	16,314	868	28,726	46,191	718	64	782	3,498,380	982,013	4,480,393	46.9	9,545,884	14,038.42	2,932.68
359	8,717	275	17,145	26,496	1,086	21	1,107	3,270,776	1,250,022	4,520,798	52.5	8,604,316	22,671.22	4,716.43
40	1,461	58	3,407	4,966	8	1	9	570,432	246,920	817,351	57	1,433,926	20,378.68	4,404.5
178	14,490	505	25,253	40,426	993	31	1,024	3,471,950	1,229,939	4,701,890	49.1	9,579,313	19,646.49	3,738.3
2,740	9,442	356	19,144	31,682	348	29	377	3,795,100	1,558,618	5,353,718	50.6	10,578,654	32,053.61	4,194.16
267	8,760	181	20,343	29,551	1,852	19	1,871	3,758,389	1,566,015	5,324,404	49	10,863,580	35,160.97	6,608.57
20	993	19	1,571	2,603	2	0	2	207,147	50,433	257,580	52.9	487,203	13,341.44	3,220.73
8	624	9	1,634	2,275	0	1	1	283,984	83,583	367,567	54.2	677,928	19,164.58	4,449.28
39	568	26	1,125	1,758	12	1	13	244,745	60,558	305,303	46.6	654,908	18,086.89	4,337.94
68	1,435	47	3,459	5,009	79	3	82	546,699	132,560	679,259	48.1	1,411,892	20,366.27	3,348.59
41	1,540	70	2,949	4,600	17	1	18	517,701	111,620	629,322	47.4	1,328,687	15,343.87	3,179.35
148	2,258	78	4,317	6,801	32	12	44	595,283	167,476	762,759	47	1,621,931	12,831.43	3,173.8
11	1,429	33	2,872	4,345	28	1	29	474,710	119,593	594,303	49.6	1,197,520	19,876.84	4,520.85
0	1,492	130	3,668	5,290	120	8	128	343,785	95,053	438,838	49.4	889,153	13,348.44	2,176.03
49	532	22	1,124	1,727	17	2	19	175,646	43,884	219,531	45.9	478,280	19,163.4	4,139.38
570	5,137	185	11,196	17,088	40	36	76	1,571,173	430,476	2,001,649	48.7	4,106,037	16,799.52	2,679.6
62	682	61	1,889	2,694	9	12	21	231,998	64,194	296,191	48	616,761	11,063.77	1,972.95
508	4,455	124	9,307	14,394	31	24	55	1,339,175	366,282	1,705,458	48.9	3,489,276	18,494.26	2,860.71
7	615	13	966	1,601	1	0	1	131,836	30,295	162,130	44.9	361,020	12,030.4	1,695.37
501	3,840	111	8,341	12,793	30	24	54	1,207,340	335,988	1,543,327	49.3	3,128,256	19,716.85	3,107.19
1,989	18,251	195	38,096	58,531	1,224	74	1,298	5,131,660	1,351,644	6,483,304	48.5	13,363,787	16,426.41	3,724.21
401	2,519	55	7,741	10,716	0	6	6	817,206	209,564	1,026,770	51.2	2,004,072	12,094.36	3,344.22
1,588	15,732	140	30,355	47,815	1,224	68	1,292	4,314,454	1,142,080	5,456,534	48	11,359,715	17,534.43	3,800.39
95	352	13	1,062	1,522	0	12	12	137,970	44,234	182,205	54.1	336,625	17,455.29	5,361.39
128	1,041	7	2,315	3,491	0	0	0	217,843	49,686	267,529	49.6	539,471	14,985.32	3,853.23
128	451	9	1,049	1,637	103	16	119	179,283	52,256	231,539	50.7	456,763	26,208.58	5,423.26
75	1,651	28	2,694	4,448	3	0	3	394,614	95,060	489,673	46.8	1,046,376	15,227.33	3,411.06
25	261	13	619	918	0	1	1	68,503	25,543	94,046	51.9	181,047	10,922.21	2,878.32
46	1,183	24	2,286	3,539	0	6	6	270,562	80,194	350,756	41.4	847,149	17,759.93	3,406.23
923	9,298	39	17,168	27,428	1,118	33	1,151	2,600,567	675,784	3,276,351	47.2	6,935,481	18,401.68	3,806.58
168	1,495	7	3,162	4,832	0	0	0	445,111	119,323	564,434	55.5	1,016,802	15,582.7	3,884.81

Table continues

CBSAs

Note: These data represent hospital performance in the years 2015 – 2019 and do not reflect any impacts from the COVID-19 pandemic in 2020 and thereafter.

TABLE **8**

**U.S. CENSUS DIVISION 9, PACIFIC
CONTINUED**

U.S. Community Hospitals
(Nonfederal, short-term general and other special hospitals)

2019 Utilization, Personnel and Finances

CLASSIFICATION	Hospitals	Beds	Admissions	Inpatient Days	Adjusted Inpatient Days	Average Daily Census	Adjusted Average Daily Census	Average Stay (days)	Surgical Operations	NEWBORNS		OUTPATIENT VISITS	
										Bassinets	Births	Emergency	Total
Washington............	91	12,613	591,311	2,943,207	6,485,756	8,066	17,766	5	528,543	1,065	80,084	2,925,619	15,928,834
Nonmetropolitan...............	30	1,020	28,351	151,929	649,669	415	1,783	5.4	56,975	104	5,050	265,190	2,091,919
Metropolitan..............	61	11,593	562,960	2,791,278	5,836,087	7,651	15,983	5	471,568	961	75,034	2,660,429	13,836,915
Bellingham.................	1	255	15,031	68,092	126,206	187	346	4.5	7,855	13	1,906	65,301	164,655
Bremerton-Silverdale-Port Orchard.	1	232	13,385	61,575	142,145	169	389	4.6	11,457	22	1,972	79,934	402,271
Kennewick-Richland..............	4	447	24,995	108,164	249,858	297	684	4.3	21,622	43	4,283	182,511	689,252
Lewiston.................	1	25	1,389	4,347	20,841	12	57	3.1	2,268	0	0	16,714	102,383
Longview.............	1	180	7,722	30,710	72,718	84	199	4	4,015	14	783	54,511	158,405
Mount Vernon-Anacortes..............	3	270	11,700	49,182	125,394	134	344	4.2	13,288	33	1,405	149,110	779,629
Olympia-Tumwater...............	2	401	24,607	28,245	55,796	78	152	1.1	30,024	49	2,767	82,724	473,054
Portland-Vancouver-Hillsboro.........	2	644	35,240	147,529	281,896	404	772	4.2	19,997	64	5,442	148,328	618,184
Seattle-Bellevue-Kent.............	22	5,272	250,883	1,388,374	2,867,222	3,807	7,854	5.5	199,569	374	33,524	1,006,449	6,911,477
Spokane-Spokane Valley.............	9	1,578	56,257	320,595	602,700	877	1,650	5.7	60,556	116	6,881	268,677	1,358,226
Tacoma-Lakewood................	6	1,465	77,306	398,793	782,440	1,093	2,143	5.2	55,805	118	9,509	360,245	922,552
Walla Walla.................	2	117	5,969	24,300	71,483	67	195	4.1	7,134	15	682	33,158	223,546
Wenatchee...............	4	408	23,544	103,297	235,401	283	645	4.4	16,146	45	2,629	94,253	482,596
Yakima.............	3	299	14,932	58,075	201,987	159	553	3.9	21,832	55	3,251	118,514	550,685

Note: These data represent hospital performance in the years 2015 – 2019 and do not reflect any impacts from the COVID-19 pandemic in 2020 and thereafter.

TABLE 8

U.S. CENSUS DIVISION 9, PACIFIC
CONTINUED

U.S. Community Hospitals
(Nonfederal, short-term general and other special hospitals)

2019 Utilization, Personnel and Finances

Physicians and Dentists	Registered Nurses	Licensed Practical Nurses	Other Salaried Personnel	Total Personnel	Medical and Dental Residents	Other Trainees	Total Trainees	Payroll (in thousands)	Employee Benefits (in thousands)	Total (in thousands)	Percent of Total	Amount (in thousands)	Adjusted per Admission	Adjusted per Inpatient Day
3,427	28,407	971	62,964	95,769	1,377	169	1,546	9,052,811	2,149,306	11,202,117	47	23,831,222	18,177.29	3,674.39
259	1,993	215	6,390	8,857	4	28	32	640,608	169,965	810,573	54.7	1,480,693	11,612.91	2,279.15
3,168	26,414	756	56,574	86,912	1,373	141	1,514	8,412,203	1,979,341	10,391,544	46.5	22,350,529	18,884.47	3,829.71
9	688	3	989	1,689	2	0	2	156,416	41,492	197,908	45.4	435,509	15,632.6	3,450.78
59	571	25	1,284	1,939	23	1	24	135,720	34,089	169,809	36.4	466,493	15,097.34	3,281.81
157	1,228	55	2,883	4,323	57	18	75	336,466	80,589	417,055	48.4	862,527	14,768.29	3,452.07
11	92	9	270	382	1	2	3	30,580	7,983	38,563	48.8	79,039	11,869.54	3,792.49
4	351	1	685	1,041	2	5	7	80,495	21,545	102,040	49.9	204,421	11,179.69	2,811.14
64	723	43	1,878	2,708	27	2	29	224,786	64,978	289,764	51.9	557,956	17,409.48	4,449.63
16	1,135	39	1,738	2,928	2	0	2	191,656	46,095	237,751	46.4	512,362	12,323.79	9,182.77
62	1,486	10	2,625	4,183	8	0	8	374,565	98,836	473,401	53.5	884,726	13,059.07	3,138.48
1,902	12,034	252	28,224	42,412	1,074	60	1,134	497,259	1,031,272	5,528,531	45.5	12,163,735	23,399.4	4,242.34
127	2,751	30	4,786	7,694	1	45	46	737,698	175,415	913,114	44.8	2,036,993	19,147.19	3,379.78
517	3,036	191	5,870	9,614	161	3	164	1,047,503	244,844	1,292,347	51.2	2,522,101	16,483.46	3,223.38
71	357	16	902	1,346	0	0	0	76,107	8,512	84,619	52.5	161,195	9,601.83	2,255.02
32	1,129	43	2,140	3,344	14	1	15	263,790	67,491	331,280	40.5	818,021	15,787.34	3,475.01
137	833	39	2,300	3,309	1	4	5	259,162	56,200	315,363	48.9	645,452	123,56.93	3,195.51

CBSAs

Note: These data represent hospital performance in the years 2015 – 2019 and do not reflect any impacts from the COVID-19 pandemic in 2020 and thereafter.

AHA Hospital Statistics © 2021 Health Forum LLC, an affiliate of the American Hospital Association **199**

Statistics for Health Care Systems and their Hospitals

The following tables describing health care systems refers to information in section B of the 2021 *AHA Guide*. Table 1 shows the number of health care systems by type of control. Table 2 provides a breakdown of the number of systems that own, lease, sponsor or contract manage hospitals within each control category. Table 3 gives the number of hospitals and beds in each control category as well as total hospitals and beds. Finally, Table 4 shows the percentage of hospitals and beds in each control category.

For more information on health care systems, please write to the Section for Health Care Systems, 155 N. Wacker Drive, Chicago, Illinois 60606 or call 312/422–3000.

Table 1. Multihospital Health Care Systems, by Type of Organizaton Control

Type of Control	Code	Number of Systems
Catholic (Roman) church–related	CC	26
Other church–related	CO	7
Subtotal, church–related		33
Other not–for–profit	NP	310
Subtotal, not–for–profit		343
Investor Owned	IO	80
Federal Government	FG	5
Total		428

Table 2. Multihospital Health Care Systems, by Type of Ownership and Control

Type of Ownership	Catholic Church–Related (CC)	Other Church–Related (CO)	Total Church–Related (CC + CO)	Other Not–for–Profit (NP)	Total Not–for–Profit (CC, CO, + NP)	Investor–Owned (IO)	Federal Govern–ment (FG)	All Systems
Systems that only own, lease or sponsor	18	6	24	185	209	17	4	230
Systems that only contract–manage	0	0	0	13	13	5	0	18
Systems that manage, own, lease, or sponsor	8	1	9	112	121	58	1	180
Total	26	7	33	310	343	80	5	428

Table 3. Hospitals and Beds in Multihospital Health Care Systems, by Type of Ownership and Control

Type of Ownership	Catholic Church–Related (CC)		Other Church–Related (CO)		Total Church–Related (CC + CO)		Other Not–for–Profit (NP)		Total Not–for–Profit (CC, CO, + NP)		Investor–Owned (IO)		Federal Govern–ment (FG)		All Systems	
	H	B	H	B	H	B	H	B	H	B	H	B	H	B	H	B
Owned, leased or sponsored	572	102,790	79	18,194	651	120,984	1,661	354,862	2,312	475,846	1,365	164,493	203	38,668	3,880	679,007
Contract–managed	43	2,442	3	485	46	2,927	128	9,283	174	12,210	104	5,712	0	0	278	17,922
Total	615	105,232	82	18,679	697	123,911	1,789	364,145	2,486	488,056	1,469	170,205	203	38,668	4,158	696,929

H = hospitals; B = beds.

Table 4. Hospitals and Beds in Multihospital Health Care Systems, by Type of Ownership and Control as a Percentage of All Systems

Type of Ownership	Catholic Church–Related (CC)		Other Church–Related (CO)		Total Church–Related (CC + CO)		Other Not–for–Profit (NP)		Total Not–for–Profit (CC, CO, + NP)		Investor–Owned (IO)		Federal Govern–ment (FG)		All Systems	
	H	B	H	B	H	B	H	B	H	B	H	B	H	B	H	B
Owned, leased or sponsored	14.7	15.1	2.0	2.7	16.8	17.8	42.8	52.3	59.6	70.1	35.2	24.2	5.2	5.7	99.9	100
Contract managed	15.5	13.6	1.1	2.7	16.6	16.3	46.0	52.3	62.6	68.1	37.4	24.2	0	5.7	100	98.5
Total	10.8	15.1	1.4	2.7	12.3	17.8	58.4	52.3	70.6	70.0	25.8	24.2	3.6	5.7	100	100

H = hospitals; B = beds.

*Please note that figures may not always equal the provided subtotal or total percentages due to rounding.

Note: These data represent hospital performance in the years 2015 – 2019 and do not reflect any impacts from the COVID-19 pandemic in 2020 and thereafter.

Glossary

This glossary explains specific terms as they are used in the tables and text of AHA Hospital Statistics

Ablation of Barrett's esophagus: Premalignant condition that can lead to adenocarcinoma of the esophagus. The non surgical ablation of the premalignant tissue in Barrett's esophagus by the application of thermal energy or light through an endoscope passed from the mouth into the esophagus.

Acute long term care: Provider specialized acute hospital care to medically complex patients who are critically ill, have multisystem complications and/or failure, and require hospitalization averaging 25 days, in a facility offering specialized treatment programs and therapeutic intervention on a 24 hour/7day a week basis.

Adjusted admission: An aggregate measure of workload reflecting the sum of admissions and equivalent admissions attributed to outpatient services. The number of equivalent admissions attributed to outpatient services is derived by multiplying admissions by the ratio of outpatient revenue to inpatient revenue.

$$\frac{\text{Adjusted}}{\text{admissions}} = \text{admissions} + [\text{admissions} * \left(\frac{\text{outpatient revenue}}{\text{inpatient revenue}}\right)]$$

Adjusted average daily census: An estimate of the average number of patients (both inpatients and outpatients) receiving care each day during the reporting period, which is usually 12 months. The figure is derived by dividing the number of inpatient day equivalents (also called adjusted inpatient days) by the number of days in the reporting period.

Adjusted inpatient days: An aggregate measure of workload reflecting the sum of inpatient days and equivalent patient days attributed to outpatient services. The number of equivalent patient days attributed to outpatient services is derived by multiplying inpatient days by the ratio of outpatient revenue to inpatient revenue.

$$\frac{\text{Adjusted}}{\text{inpatient days}} = \text{inpatient days} + [\text{inpatient days} * \left(\frac{\text{outpatient revenue}}{\text{inpatient revenue}}\right)]$$

Admissions: The number of patients, excluding newborns, accepted for inpatient service during the reporting period; the number includes patients who visit the emergency room and are later admitted for inpatient service.

Adult Cardiac Surgery: Includes minimally invasive procedures that include surgery done with only a small incision or no incision at all, such as through a laparoscope or an endoscope and more invasive major surgical procedures that include open chest and open heart surgery.

Adult Cardiology Services: An organized clinical service offering diagnostic and interventional procedures to manage the full range of adult heart conditions.

Adult day care program: Program providing supervision, medical and psychological care, and social activities for older adults who live at home or in another family setting, but cannot be alone or prefer to be with others during the day. May include intake assessment, health monitoring, occupational therapy, personal care, noon meal, and transportation services.

Adult Diagnostic/invasive catheterization: (also called coronary angiography or coronary arteriography) is used to assist in diagnosing complex heart conditions. Cardiac angiography involves the insertion of a tiny catheter into the artery in the groin then carefully threading the catheter up into the aorta where the coronary arteries originate. Once the catheter is in place, a dye is injected which allows the cardiologist to see the size, shape, and distribution of the coronary arteries. These images are used to diagnose heart disease and to determine, among other things, whether or not surgery is indicated.

Adult Interventional cardiac catheterization: Non surgical procedure that utilizes the same basic principles as diagnostic catheterization and then uses advanced techniques to improve the heart's function. It can be a less-invasive alternative to heart surgery.

Air ambulance services: Aircraft and especially a helicopter equipped for transporting the injured or sick. Most air ambulances carry critically ill or injured patients, whose condition could rapidlychange for the worse.

Airborne infection isolation room: A single-occupancy room for patient care where environmental factors are controlled in an effort to minimize the transmission of those infectious agents, usually spread person to person by droplet nuclei associated with coughing and inhalation. Such rooms typically have specific ventilation requirements for controlled ventilation, air pressure and filtration.

Alcoholism-chemical dependency partial hospitalization services: Organized hospital services providing intensive day/evening outpatient services of three hour or more duration, distinguished from other outpatient visits of one hour.

Alcoholism-chemical dependency pediatric services: Provides diagnosis and therapeutic services to pediatric patients with alcoholism or other drug dependencies. Includes care for inpatient/residential treatment for patients whose course of treatment involves more intensive care than provided in an outpatient setting or where patient requires supervised withdrawal.

Alcoholism-drug abuse or dependency inpatient care: Provides diagnosis and therapeutic services to patients with alcoholism or other drug dependencies. Includes care for inpatient/residential treatment for patients whose course of treatment involves more intensive care than provided in an outpatient setting or where patient requires supervised withdrawal.

Alcoholism-drug abuse or dependency outpatient services: Organized hospital services that provide medical care and/or rehabilitative treatment services to outpatients for whom the primary diagnosis is alcoholism or other chemical dependency.

Alzheimer Center: Facility that offers care to persons with Alzheimer's disease and their families through an integrated program of clinical services, research, and education.

Ambulance services: Provision of ambulance services to the ill and injured who require medical attention on a scheduled or unscheduled basis.

Ambulatory Surgery Center: Facility that provides care to patients requiring surgery who are admitted and discharged on the same day. Ambulatory surgery centers are distinct from same day surgical units within the hospital outpatient departments for purposes of Medicare payments.

Arthritis treatment center: Specifically equipped and staffed center for the diagnosis and treatment of arthritis and other joint disorders.

Assisted living: A special combination of housing, supportive services, personalized assistance and health care designed to respond to the individual needs of those who need help in activities of daily living and instrumental activities of daily living. Supportive services are available, 24 hours a day, to meet scheduled and unscheduled needs, in a way that promotes maximum independence and dignity for each resident and encourages the involvement of a resident's family, neighbor and friends.

Assistive Technology Center: A program providing access to specialized hardware and software with adaptations allowing individuals greater independence with mobility, dexterity, or increased communication options.

Auxiliary: A volunteer community organization formed to assist the hospital in carrying out its purpose and to serve as a link between the institution and the community.

Average daily census: The average number of people served on an inpatient basis on a single day during the reporting period; the figure is calculated by dividing the number of inpatient days by the number of days in the reporting period.

Bariatric/weight control services: Bariatrics is the medical practice of weight reduction.

Beds: Number of beds regularly maintained (set up and staffed for use) for inpatients as of the close of the reporting period. Excludes newborn bassinets.

Bed-size category: Hospitals are categorized by the number of beds set up and staffed for use at the end of the reporting period. The eight categories in Hospital Statistics are: 6 to 24 beds; 25 to 49; 50 to 99; 100 to 199; 200 to 299; 300 to 399; 400 to 499; and 500 or more.

Birthing room-LDR room-LDRP room: A single-room type of maternity care with a more homelike setting for families than the traditional three-room unit (labor/delivery/recovery) with a separate postpartum area. A birthing room combines labor and delivery in one room. An LDR room accommodates three stages in the birthing process—labor, delivery, and recovery. An LDRP room accommodates all four stages of the birth process—labor, delivery, recovery, and postpartum.

Births: Total number of infants born in the hospital during the reporting period. Births do not include infants transferred from other institutions, and are excluded from admission and discharge figures.

Blood Donor Center: A facility that performs, or is responsible for the collection, processing, testing or distribution of blood and components.

Bone marrow transplant: See definition for Transplant services on page 213.

Breast cancer screening/mammograms: Mammography screening – The use of breast x-ray to detect unsuspected breast cancer in asymptomatic women. Diagnostic mammography – The x-ray imaging of breast tissue in symptomatic women who are considered to have a substantial likelihood of having breast cancer already.

Burn care: Provides care to severely burned patients. Severely burned patients are those with any of the following: (1) second-degree burns of more than 25% total body surface area for adults or 20% total body surface area for children: (2) third-degree burns of more than 10% total body surface area; (3) any severe burns of the hands, face, eyes, ears, or feet; or (4) all inhalation injuries, electrical burns, complicated burn injuries involving fractures and other major traumas, and all other poor risk factors.

Cardiac electrophysiology: Evaluation and management of patients with complex rhythm or conduction abnormalities, including diagnostic testing, treatment of arrhythmias by catheter ablation or drug therapy, and pacemaker/defibrillator implantation and follow-up.

Cardiac intensive care: Provides patient care of a more specialized nature than the usual medical and surgical care, on the basis of physicians' orders and approved nursing care plans. The unit is staffed with specially trained nursing personnel and contains monitoring and specialized support or treatment equipment for patients who, because of heart seizure, open-heart surgery, or other life-threatening conditions, require intensified, comprehensive observation and care. May include myocardial infarction, pulmonary care, and heart transplant units.

Cardiac Rehabilitation: A medically supervised program to help heart patients recover quickly and improve their overall physical and mental functioning. The goal is to reduce risk of another cardiac event or to keep an already present heart condition from getting worse. Cardiac rehabilitation programs include: counseling to patients, an exercise program, helping patients modify risk factors such as smoking and high blood pressure, providing vocational guidance to enable the patient to return to work, supplying information on physical limitations and lending emotional support.

Case management: A system of assessment, treatment planning, referral and follow-up that ensures the provision of comprehensive and continuous services and the coordination of payment and reimbursement for care.

Chaplaincy/pastoral care services: A service ministering religious activities and providing pastoral counseling to patients, their families, and staff of a health care organization.

Chemotherapy: An organized program for the treatment of cancer by the use of drugs or chemicals.

Children's wellness program: A program that encourages improved health status and a healthful lifestyle of children through health education, exercise, nutrition and health promotion.

Chiropractic services: An organized clinical service including spinal manipulation or adjustment and related diagnostic and therapeutic services.

Closed physician-hospital organization (Closed PHO): A joint venture between the hospital and physicians who have been selected on the basis of cost-effectiveness and/or high quality. The PHO can act as a unified agent in managed care contracting, own a managed care plan, own and operate ambulatory care centers or ancillary services projects, or provide administrative services to physician members.

Community health education: Education that provides health information to individuals and populations, as well as support for personal, family and community health decisions with the objective of improving health status.

Community hospitals: All nonfederal, short-term general, and special hospitals whose facilities and services are available to the public. (Special hospitals include obstetrics and gynecology; eye, ear, nose, and throat; rehabilitation; orthopedic; and other individually described specialty services.) Short-term general and special childrens hospitals are also considered to be community hospitals.

A hospital may include a nursing-home-type unit and still be classified as short-term, provided that the majority of its patients are admitted to units where the average length of stay is less than 30 days. Therefore, statistics for community hospitals often include some data about such nursing-home-type units. An example is furnished by Montana, where in 1995 63.6 percent of all hospitals classified as community hospitals include nursing-home-type units. Expense, revenue, utilization, and personnel data for these hospitals include data about their nursing-home-type units. Thus, total admissions to Montana community hospitals in 1995 were 96,154; total inpatient days, 997,759; total expenses, $791,806,393; and total payroll expenses, $352,583,331. If nursing-home-type unit data were excluded, these same items would be 94,034; 457,340; 752,567,865; and $328,911841, respectively.

Note that before 1972, hospital units of institutions such as prison and college infirmaries were included in the category of community hospitals. Including these units made this category equivalent to the short-term general and other special hospitals category. Although these hospital units are few in number and small in size, this change in definition should be taken into consideration when comparing data.

Community outreach: A program that systematically interacts with the community to identify those in need of services, alerting persons and their families to the availability of services, locating needed services, and enabling persons to enter the service delivery system.

Complementary and alternative medicine services: Organized hospital services or formal arrangements to providers that provide care or treatment not based solely on traditional western allopathic medical teachings as instructed in most U.S. medical schools. Includes any of the following: acupuncture, chiropractic, homeopathy, osteopathy, diet and lifestyle changes, herbal medicine, message therapy, etc.

Computer assisted orthopedic surgery (CAOS): Orthopedic surgery using computer technology, enabling three-dimensional graphic models to visualize a patient's anatomy.

Control: The type of organization responsible for establishing policy concerning the overall operation of hospitals. The three major categories are government (including federal, state, and local); nongovernment (nonprofit); and investor-owned (for-profit).

Crisis prevention: Services provided in order to promote physical and mental well being and the early identification of disease and ill health prior to the onset and recognition of symptoms so as to permit early treatment.

CT scanner: Computed tomographic scanner for head or whole body scans.

Deduction from revenue: The difference between revenue at full established rates (gross) and the payment actually received from payers (net).

Dental Services: An organized dental service or dentists on staff, not necessarily involving special facilities, providing dental or oral services to inpatients or outpatients.

Diabetes prevention program: Program to prevent or delay the onset of type 2 diabetes by offering evidence-based lifestyle changes based on research studies, which showed modest behavior changes helped individuals with prediabetes reduce their risk of developing type 2 diabetes.

Diagnostic radioisotope facility: The use of radioactive isotopes (Radiopharmaceuticals) as tracers or indicators to detect an abnormal condition or disease.

Electrodiagnostic Services: Diagnostic testing services for nerve and muscle function including services such as nerve conduction studies and needle electromyography.

Electron beam computed tomography (EBCT): A high tech computed tomography scan used to detect coronary artery disease by measuring coronary calcifications. This imaging procedure uses electron beams which are magnetically steered to produce a visual of the coronary artery and the images are produced faster than conventional CT scans.

Emergency department: Hospital facilities for the provision of unscheduled outpatient services to patients whose conditions require immediate care.

Emergency room visits: The number of visits to the emergency unit. When emergency outpatients are admitted to the inpatient areas of the hospital, they are counted as emergency room visits and subsequently, as inpatient admissions.

Emergency services: Health services that are provided after the onset of a medical condition that manifests itself by symptoms of sufficient severity, including severe pain, that the absence of immediate medical attention could reasonably be expected by a prudent layperson, who possesses an average knowledge of health and medicine, to result in placing the patient's health in serious jeopardy.

Employment support services: Services designed to support individuals with significant disabilities to seek and maintain employment.

Enabling services: A program that is designed to help the patient access health care services by offering any of the following: transportation services and/or referrals to local social services agencies.

Endoscopic retrograde cholangiopancreatography (ERCP): A procedure in which a catheter is introduced through an endoscope into the bile ducts and pancreatic ducts. Injection of contrast materials permits detailed x-ray of these structures. The procedure is used diagnostically as well as therapeutically to relieve obstruction or remove stones.

Endoscopic ultrasound: Specially designed endoscope that incorporates an ultrasound transductor used to obtain detailed images of organs in the chest and abdomen. The endoscope can be passed through the mouth or the anus. When combined with needle biopsy the procedure can assist in diagnosis and staging of cancer.

Enrollment (insurance) assistance services: A program that provides enrollment assistance for patients who are potentially eligible for public health insurance programs such as Medicaid, State Children's Health Insurance, or local/state indigent care programs. The specific services offered could include explanation of benefits, assist applicants in completing the application and locating all relevant documents, conduct eligibility interviews, and/or forward applications and documentation to state/local social service or health agency.

Equity model: An arrangement that allows established practitioners to become shareholders in a professional corporation in exchange for tangible and intangible assets of their existing practices.

Esophageal impedance study: A test in which a catheter is placed through the nose into the esophagus to measure whether gas or liquids are passing from the stomach into the esophagus and causing symptoms.

Expenses: Includes all expenses for the reporting period including payroll, non-payroll, and all operating expenses. *Payroll expenses* include all salaries and wages. *Non-payroll expenses* are all professional fees and those salary expenditures excluded from payroll. *Labor related expenses* are defined as payroll expenses plus employee benefits. *Non-labor related expenses* are all other non-payroll expenses. Bad debt has been reclassified from an expense to a deduction from revenue in accordance with the revised AICPA Audit Guide. Note: Financial data may not add due to rounding.

Expenses per adjusted admission stay: Total expenses divided by adjusted admissions (see *adjusted admission*).

Expenses per adjusted inpatient days: Expenses divided by adjusted inpatient days (see *adjusted inpatient days*).

Extracorporeal shock wave lithotripter (ESWL): A medical device used for treating stones in the kidney or urethra. The device disintegrates kidney stones noninvasively through the transmission of acoustic shock waves directed at the stones.

Fertility Clinic: A specialized program set in an infertility center that provides counseling and education as well as advanced reproductive techniques such as: injectable therapy, reproductive surgeries, treatment for endometriosis, male factor infertility, tubal reversals, in vitro fertilization (IVF), donor eggs, and other such services to help patients achieve successful pregnancies.

Fitness center: Provides exercise, testing, or evaluation programs and fitness activities to the community and hospital employees.

Foundation: A corporation, organized as a hospital affiliate or subsidiary, that purchases both tangible and intangible assets of one or more medical group practices. Physicians remain in a separate corporate entity but sign a professional services agreement with the foundation.

Freestanding outpatient care center: A facility owned and operated by the hospital, that is physically separate from the hospital and provides various medical treatments and diagnostic services on an outpatient basis only. Laboratory and radiology services are usually available.

Full-field digital mammography (FFDM): Combines the x-ray generators and tubes used in analog screen-film mammography (SFM) with a detector plate that converts the x-rays into a digital signal.

Full time equivalent employees (FTE): Full time personnel on payroll plus one half of the part time personnel on payroll. For purposes of *AHA Hospital Statistics*, full time and part time medical and dental residents/interns and other trainees are excluded from the calculation.

General medical-surgical care: Provides acute care to patients in medical and surgical units on the basis of physicians' orders and approved nursing care plans.

Genetic testing/counseling: A service equipped with adequate laboratory facilities and directed by a qualified physician to advise parents and prospective parents on potential problems in cases of genetic defects. A genetic test is the analysis of human DNA, RNA, chromosomes, proteins, and certain metabolites in order to detect heritable disease-related genotypes, mutations, phenotypes, or karyotypes for clinical purposes. Genetic tests can have diverse purposes, including the diagnosis of genetic diseases in newborns, children, and adults; the identification of future health risks; the prediction of drug responses; and the assessment of risks to future children.

Geriatric services: The branch of medicine dealing with the physiology of aging and the diagnosis and treatment of disease affecting the aged. Services could include: Adult day care; Alzheimer's diagnostic-assessment services; Comprehensive geriatric assessment; Emergency response system; Geriatric acute care unit; and/or Geriatric clinics.

Government, nonfederal, state, local: Controlled by an agency of state, county, or city government.

Gross inpatient revenue: Revenue from services rendered to inpatients at full established rates (also known as "charges").

Gross outpatient revenue: Revenue from services rendered to outpatients at full established rates.

Group practice without walls: In this organization, the hospital sponsors the formation of a physician group or provides capital to physicians to establish one. The group shares administrative expenses, although the physicians remain independent practitioners.

Group Purchasing Organization: An organization whose primary function is to negotiate contracts for the purpose of purchasing for members of the group or has a central supply site for its members.

Health fair: Community health education events that focus on the prevention of disease and promotion of health through such activities as audiovisual exhibits and free diagnostic services.

Health Research: Organized hospital research program in any of the following areas: basic research, clinical research, community health research, and/or research on innovative health care delivery.

Health screening: A preliminary procedure such as a test or examination to detect the most characteristic sign or signs of a disorder that may require further investigation.

Heart transplant: See definition for Transplant services on page 213.

Hemodialysis: Provision of equipment and personnel for the treatment of renal insufficiency on an inpatient or outpatient basis.

HIV-AIDS services: (could include). *HIV-AIDS unit* – Special unit or team designated and equipped specifically for diagnosis, treatment, continuing care planning, and counseling services for HIV-AIDS patients and their families. *General inpatient care for HIV-AIDS* – Inpatient diagnosis and treatment for human immunodeficiency virus and acquired immunodeficiency syndrome patients, but dedicated unit is not available. *Specialized outpatient program for HIV-AIDS* – Special outpatient program providing diagnostic, treatment, continuing care planning, and counseling for HIV-AIDS patients and their families.

Home health services: Service providing nursing, therapy, and health-related homemaker or social services in the patient's home.

Hospice: A program providing palliative care, chiefly medical relief of pain and supportive services, addressing the emotional, social, financial, and legal needs of terminally ill patients and their families. Care can be provided in a variety of settings, both inpatient and at home.

Hospital unit: The hospital operation, excluding activity pertaining to nursing-home-type unit (as described below), for the following items: Admissions, Beds, FTEs (full-time, part-time, and total), Inpatient Days, Length of Stay, Net Revenue, and Total Expense.

Hospital unit of institutions: A hospital unit that is not open to the public and is contained within a nonhospital unit. An example is an infirmary that is contained within a college.

Hospitals in a network: Hospitals participating in a group that may include other hospitals, physicians, other providers, insurers, and/or community agencies that work together to coordinate and deliver a broad spectrum of services to the community.

Hospitals in a system: Hospitals belonging to a corporate body that owns and/or manages health provider facilities or health-related subsidiaries; the system may also own non-health-related facilities.

Image-guided radiation therapy (IGRT): Automated system for image-guided radiation therapy that enables clinicians to obtain high-resolution x-ray images to pinpoint tumor sites, adjust patient positioning when necessary, and complete a treatment, all within the standard treatment time slot, allowing for more effective cancer treatments.

Immunization program: Program that plans, coordinates and conducts immunization services in the community.

Indemnity fee for service: The traditional type of health insurance, in which the insured is reimbursed for covered expenses without regard to choice of provider. Payment up to a stated limit may be made either to the individual incurring and claiming the expense, or directly to providers.

Independent practice association (IPA): An IPA is a legal entity that holds managed care contracts and contracts with physicians, usually in solo practice, to provide care either on a fee-for-services or capitated basis. The purpose of an IPA is to assist solo physicians in obtaining managed care contracts.

Indigent care clinic: Health care services for uninsured and underinsured persons where care is free of charge or charged on a sliding scale. This would include "free clinics" staffed by volunteer practitioners, but could also be staffed by employees with sponsoring health care organizations subsidizing the cost of service.

Inpatient days: The number of adult and pediatric days of care, excluding newborn days of care, rendered during the entire reporting period.

Inpatient palliative care unit: An inpatient palliative care ward is a physically discreet, inpatient nursing unit where the focus is palliative care. The patient care focus is on symptom relief for complex patients who may be continuing to undergo primary treatment. Care is delivered by palliative medicine specialists.

Inpatient surgeries: Surgical services provided to patients who remain in the hospital overnight.

Integrated salary model: In this arrangement, physicians are salaried by the hospital or other entity of a health system to provide medical services for primary care and specialty care.

Intensity-Modulated Radiation Therapy (IMRT): A type of three-dimensional radiation therapy, which improves the targeting of treatment delivery in a way that is likely to decrease damage to normal tissues and allows varying intensities.

Intermediate nursing care: Provides health-related services (skilled nursing care and social services) to residents with a variety of physical conditions or functional disabilities. These residents do not require the care provided by a hospital or skilled nursing facility, but do need supervision and support services.

Intraoperative magnetic resonance imaging: An integrated surgery system which provides an MRI system in an operating room. The system allows for immediate evaluation of the degree to tumor resection while the patient is undergoing a surgical resection. Intraoperative MRI exists when a MRI (low-field or high-field) is placed in the operating theater and is used during surgical resection without moving the patient from the operating room to the diagnostic imaging suite.

Investor-owned, for-profit: Investor-owned, for-profit hospitals are those controlled on a for-profit basis by an individual, partnership, or profit-making corporation.

Kidney transplant: See definition for Transplant services on page 213.

Labor-related expenses: Payroll expenses plus employee benefits. *Non-labor-related expenses refers* to all other nonpayroll expenses, such as interest depreciation, supplies, purchased services, professional fees, and others.

Length of stay (LOS): LOS refers to the average number of days a patient stays at the facility. Short-term hospitals are those where the average LOS is less than 30 days. Long-term hospitals are those where the average LOS is 30 days or more. The figure is derived by dividing the number of inpatient days by the number of admissions.

Note that this publication carries two LOS variables: *total facility length of stay and hospital unit length of stay. Total facility* includes admissions and inpatient days from nursing-home-type units under control of the hospital. In *hospital unit length of stay*, nursing home utilization is subtracted.

Licensed practical nurse (LPN): A nurse who has graduated from an approved school of practical (vocational) nursing and works under the supervision of registered nurses and/or physicians.

Linguistic/Translation services: Services provided by the hospital designed to make health care more accessible to non-English speaking patients and their physicians.

Liver transplant: See definition for Transplant services on page 213.

Long-term: Hospitals are classified either short-term or long-term according to the average length of stay (LOS). A long-term hospital is one in which the average LOS is 30 days or more.

Lung transplant: See definition for Transplant services on page 213.

Magnetic resonance imaging (MRI): The use of a uniform magnetic field and radio frequencies to study tissue and structure of the body. This procedure enables the visualization of biochemical activity of the cell in vivo without the use of ionizing radiation, radio-isotopic substances, or high-frequency sound.

Magnetoencephalography: a noninvasive neurophysiological measurement tool used to study magnetic fields generated by neuronal activity of the brain. The primary uses of MEG include assisting surgeons in localizing the source of epilepsy, sensory mapping, and the study of brain function. When it is combined with structural imaging, it is known as magnetic source imaging (MSI).

Management services organization (MSO): A corporation owned by the hospital or a physician/hospital joint venture that provides management services to one or more medical group practices. As part of a full-service management agreement, the MSO purchases the tangible assets of the practices and leases them back, employs all non-physician staff, and provides all supplies/administrative systems for a fee.

Meals on wheels: A hospital sponsored program which delivers meals to people, usually the elderly, who are unable to prepare their own meals. Low cost, nutritional meals are delivered to individuals' homes on a regular basis.

Medical surgical intensive care: Provides patient care of a more intensive nature than the usual medical and surgical care, on the basis of physicians' orders and approved nursing care plans. These units are staffed with specially trained nursing personnel and contain monitoring and specialized support equipment for patients who, because of shock, trauma, or other life-threatening conditions, require intensified, comprehensive observation and care. Includes mixed intensive care units.

Mobile health services: Vans and other vehicles used to deliver primary care services.

Multi-slice spiral computed tomography (<64 slice CT): A specialized computed tomography procedure that provides three-dimensional processing and allows narrower and multiple slices with increased spatial resolution and faster scanning times as compared to a regular computed tomography scan.

Multi-slice spiral computed tomography (64+ slice CT): Involves the acquisition of volumetric tomographic x-ray absorption data expressed in Hounsfield units using multiple rows of detectors. 64+ systems reconstruct the equivalent of 64 or greater slices to cover the imaged volume.

Neonatal intensive care: A unit that must be separate from the newborn nursery providing intensive care to all sick infants including those with the very lowest birth weights (less than 1500 grams). NICU has potential for providing mechanical ventilation, neonatal surgery, and special care for the sickest infants born in the hospital or transferred from another institution. A full-time neonatologist serves as director of the NICU.

Neonatal intermediate care: A unit that must be separate from the normal newborn nursery and that provides intermediate and/or recovery care and some specialized services, including immediate resuscitation, intravenous therapy, and capacity for prolonged oxygen therapy and monitoring.

Net patient revenue: The estimated net realizable amounts from patients, third-party payers, and others for services rendered. The number includes estimated retroactive adjustments called for by agreements with third-party payers; retroactive adjustments are accrued on an estimated basis in the period the related services are rendered and then adjusted later as final settlements are determined.

Net total revenue: Net patient revenue plus all other revenue, including contributions, endowment revenue, governmental grants, and all other payments not made on behalf of individual patients.

Neurological services: Services provided by the hospital dealing with the operative and nonoperative management of disorders of the central, peripheral, and autonomic nervous system.

Nongovernment, nonprofit: Hospitals that are nongovernment, nonprofit are controlled by not-for-profit organizations, including religious organizations (Catholic hospitals, for example), fraternal societies, and others.

Nursing-home-type unit/facility: A unit/ facility that primarily offers the following type of services to a majority of all admissions:

- *Skilled nursing:* The provision of medical and nursing care services, health-related services, and social services under the supervision of a registered nurse on a 24-hour basis.

- *Intermediate care:* The provision, on a regular basis, of health-related care and services to individuals who do not require the degree of care or treatment that a skilled nursing unit is designed to provide.

- *Personal care:* The provision of general supervision and direct personal care services for residents who require assistance in activities of daily living but who do not need nursing services or inpatient care. Medical and nursing services are available as needed.

- *Sheltered/residential care:* The provision of general supervision and protective services for residents who do not need nursing services or continuous personal care services in the conduct of daily life. Medical and nursing services are available as needed.

Nutrition programs: Those services within a health care facility which are designed to provide inexpensive, nutritionally sound meals to patients.

Obstetrics: Levels should be designated: (1) unit provides services for uncomplicated maternity and newborn cases; (2) unit provides services for uncomplicated cases, the majority of complicated problems, and special neonatal services; and (3) unit provides services for all serious illnesses and abnormalities and is supervised by a full-time maternal/fetal specialist.

Occupational health services: Includes services designed to protect the safety of employees from hazards in the work environment.

Off-campus emergency department: A facility owned and operated by the hospital but physically separate from the hospital for the provision of unscheduled outpatient services to patients whose conditions require immediate care. A freestanding ED is not physically connected to a hospital but has all the necessary emergency staffing and equipment on site.

Oncology services: Inpatient and outpatient services for patients with cancer, including comprehensive care, support and guidance in addition to patient education and prevention, chemotherapy, counseling and other treatment methods.

Open physician hospital organization (Open PHO): A joint venture between the hospital and all members of the medical staff who wish to participate. The open PHO can act as a unified agent in managed care contracting, own a managed care plan, own and operate ambulatory care centers or ancillary services projects, or provide administrative services to physician members.

Optical colonoscopy: An examination of the interior of the colon using a long, flexible, lighted tube with a small built-in camera.

Orthopedic services: Services provided for the prevention or correction of injuries or disorders of the skeletal system and associated muscles, joints and ligaments.

Osteopathic hospitals: Osteopathic medicine is a medical practice based on a theory that diseases are due chiefly to a loss of structural integrity, which can be restored by manipulation of the neuro-muscular and skeletal systems, supplemented by therapeutic measures (such as medicine or surgery).

Other Intensive Care: A specially staffed, specialty equipped, separate section of a hospital dedicated to the observation, care, and treatment of patients with life threatening illnesses, injuries, or complications from which recovery is possible. It provides special expertise and facilities for the support of vital function and utilizes the skill of medical nursing and other staff experienced in the management of these problems.

Other long-term care: Provision of long-term care other than skilled nursing care or intermediate care for those who do not require daily medical or nursing services, but may require some assistance in the activities of daily living. This can include residential care, elderly care, or sheltered care facilities for developmentally disabled.

Other special care: Provides care to patients requiring care more intensive than that provided in the acute area, yet not sufficiently intensive to require admission to an intensive care unit. Patients admitted to this area are usually transferred here from an intensive care unit once their condition has improved. These units are sometimes referred to as definitive observation, step-down, or progressive care units.

Other transplant: See definition for Transplant services on page 213.

Outpatient care: Treatment provided to patients who do not remain in the hospital for overnight care. Hospitals may deliver outpatient care on site or through a facility owned and operated by the hospital, but physically separate from the hospital. In addition to treating minor illnesses or injuries, a free-standing center will stabilize seriously ill or injured patients before transporting them to a hospital. Laboratory and radiology services are usually available.

Outpatient care center (Freestanding): A facility owned and operated by the hospital, but physically separate from the hospital, that provides various medical treatments on an outpatient basis only. In addition to treating minor illnesses or injuries, the center will stabilize seriously ill or injured patients before transporting them to a hospital. Laboratory and radiology services are usually available.

Outpatient care center-services (Hospital-based): Organized hospital health care services offered by appointment on an ambulatory basis. Services may include outpatient surgery, examination, diagnosis, and treatment of a variety of medical conditions on a nonemergency basis, and laboratory and other diagnostic testing as ordered by staff or outside physician referral.

Outpatient surgery: Scheduled surgical services provided to patients who do not remain in the hospital overnight. The surgery may be performed in operating suites also used for inpatient surgery, specially designated surgical suites for outpatient surgery, or procedure rooms within an outpatient care facility.

Outpatient visit: A visit by a patient who is not lodged in the hospital while receiving medical, dental, or other services. Each visit an outpatient makes to a discrete unit constitutes one visit regardless of the number of diagnostic and/or therapeutic treatments that the patient receives. Total outpatient visits should include all clinic visits, referred visits, observation services, outpatient surgeries, and emergency room visits.

Pain Management Program: A recognized clinical service or program providing specialized medical care, drugs or therapies for the management of acute or chronic pain or other distressing symptom, administered by specially trained physicians and other clinicians, to patients suffering from acute illness of diverse causes.

Palliative Care Inpatient Unit: An inpatient palliative care ward is a physically discreet, inpatient nursing unit where the focus is palliative care. The patient care focus is on symptom relief for complex patients who may be continuing to undergo primary treatment. Care is delivered by palliative medicine specialists.

Palliative care program: An organized program providing specialized medical care, drugs or therapies for the management of acute or chronic pain and/or the control of symptoms administered by specially trained physicians and other clinicians; and supportive care services, such as counseling on advanced directives, spiritual care, and social services, to patients with advanced disease and their families.

Patient Controlled Analgesia (PCA): Patient-controlled Analgesia (PCA) is intravenously administered pain medicine under the patient's control. The patient has a button on the end of a cord than can be pushed at will, whenever more pain medicine is desired. This button will only deliver more pain medicine at pre-determined intervals, as programmed by the doctor's order.

Patient education center: Written goals and objectives for the patient and/or family related to therapeutic regimens, medical procedures, and self care.

Patient representative services: Organized hospital services providing personnel through whom patients and staff can seek solutions to institutional problems affecting the delivery of high-quality care and services.

Payroll expenses: Includes all salaries and wages. All professional fees and salary expenditures excluded from payroll, such as employee benefits, are defined as nonpayroll expenses and are included in total expenses.

Pediatric Cardiac Surgery: Includes minimally invasive procedures that include surgery done with only a small incision or no incision at all, such as through a laparoscope or an endoscope and more invasive major surgical procedures that include open chest and open heart surgery.

Pediatric Cardiology Services: An organized clinical service offering diagnostic and interventional procedures to manage the full range of pediatric heart conditions.

Pediatric Diagnostic/invasive catheterization: (also called coronary angiography or coronary arteriography) is used to assist in diagnosing complex heart conditions. Cardiac angiography involves the insertion of a tiny catheter into the artery in the groin then carefully threading the catheter up into the aorta where the coronary arteries originate. Once the catheter is in place, a dye is injected which allows the cardiologist to see the size, shape, and distribution of the coronary arteries. These images are used to diagnose heart disease and to determine, among other things, whether or not surgery is indicated.

Pediatric intensive care: Provides care to pediatric patients that is of a more intensive nature than that usually provided to pediatric patients. The unit is staffed with specially trained personnel and contains monitoring and specialized support equipment for treatment of patients who, because of shock, trauma, or other life-threatening conditions, require intensified, comprehensive observation and care.

Pediatric Interventional cardiac catheterization: Non surgical procedure that utilizes the same basic principles as diagnostic catheterization and then uses advanced techniques to improve the heart's function. It can be a less-invasive alternative to heart surgery.

Pediatric medical-surgical care: Provides acute care to pediatric patients on the basis of physicians' orders and approved nursing care plans.

Personnel: Number of persons on the hospital payroll at the end of the reporting period. Personnel are recorded in *Hospital Statistics* as full-time equivalents (FTEs), which are calculated by adding the number of full-time personnel to one-half the number of part-time personnel, excluding medical and dental residents, interns, and other trainees. *Per 100 adjusted census* indicates the ratio of personnel to adjusted average daily census, calculated on a per-100 basis.

Physical rehabilitation inpatient care: Provides care encompassing a comprehensive array of restoration services for the disabled and all support services necessary to help patients attain their maximum functional capacity.

Physical rehabilitation outpatient services: Outpatient program providing medical, health-related, therapy, social, and/or vocational services to help disabled persons attain or retain their maximum functional capacity.

Population: Population refers to the residential population of the United States. This includes both civilian and military personnel. Note that population is being used to calculate the values *for community health indicators per 1000 population.*

Positron emission tomography/CT (PET/CT): Provides metabolic functional information for the monitoring of chemotherapy, radiotherapy and surgical planning.

Positron emission tomography scanner (PET): A nuclear medicine imaging technology which uses radioactive (positron emitting) isotopes created in a cyclotron or generator and computers to produce composite pictures of the brain and heart at work. PET scanning produces sectional images depicting metabolic activity or blood flow rather than anatomy.

Primary care department: A unit or clinic within the hospital that provides primary care services (e.g. general pediatric care, general internal medicine, family practice, gynecology) through hospital-salaried medical and/or nursing staff, focusing on evaluating and diagnosing medical problems and providing medical treatment on an outpatient basis.

Prosthetic and Orthotic Services: Services providing comprehensive prosthetic and orthotic evaluation, fitting, and training.

Proton beam therapy: A form of radiation therapy which administers proton beams. While producing the same biologic effects as x-ray beams, the energy distribution of protons differs from conventional x-ray beams in that they can be more precisely focused in tissue volumes in a three-dimensional pattern resulting in less surrounding tissue damage than conventional radiation therapy permitting administration of higher doses.

Psychiatric pediatric care: The branch of medicine focused on the diagnosis, treatment and prevention of mental, emotional and behavioral disorders in pediatric patients.

Psychiatric consultation-liaison services: Provides organized psychiatric consultation/liaison services to nonpsychiatric hospital staff and/or departments on psychological aspects of medical care that may be generic or specific to individual patients.

Psychiatric education services: Provides psychiatric educational services to community agencies and workers such as schools, police, courts, public health nurses, welfare agencies, clergy, and so forth. The purpose is to expand the mental health knowledge and competence of personnel not working in the mental health field and to promote good mental health through improved understanding, attitudes, and behavioral patterns.

Psychiatric emergency services: Services of facilities available on a 24-hour basis to provide immediate unscheduled out-patient care, diagnosis, evaluation, crisis intervention, and assistance to persons suffering acute emotional or mental distress.

Psychiatric geriatric services: Provides care to emotionally disturbed elderly patients, including those admitted for diagnosis and those admitted for treatment.

Psychiatric inpatient care: Provides acute or long-term care to emotionally disturbed patients, including patients admitted for diagnosis and those admitted for treatment of psychiatric problems, on the basis of physicians' orders and approved nursing care plans. Long-term care may include intensive supervision to the chronically mentally ill, mentally disordered, or other mentally incompetent persons.

Psychiatric intensive outpatient services: A prescribed course of treatment in which the patient receives outpatient care no less than three times a week (which might include more than one service/day)

Psychiatric outpatient services: Provides medical care, including diagnosis and treatment, of psychiatric outpatients.

Psychiatric partial hospitalization program: Organized hospital services of intensive day/evening outpatient services of three hours of more duration, distinguished from other outpatient visits of one hour.

Psychiatric residential treatment: Overnight psychiatric care in conjunction with an intensive treatment program in a setting other than a hospital.

Radiology, diagnostic: The branch of radiology that deals with the utilization of all modalities of radiant energy in medical diagnoses and therapeutic procedures using radiologic guidance. This includes, but is not restricted to, imaging techniques and methodologies utilizing radiation emitted by x-ray tubes, radionnuclides, and ultrasonographic devices and the radiofrequency electromagnetic radiation emitted by atoms.

Radiology, therapeutic: The branch of medicine concerned with radioactive substances and using various techniques of visualization, with the diagnosis and treatment of disease using any of the various sources of radiant energy. Services could include: megavoltage radiation therapy; radioactive implants; stereotactic radiosurgery; therapeutic radioisotop facility; X-ray radiation therapy.

Registered nurse (RN): A nurse who has graduated from an approved school of nursing and who is currently registered by the state. RNs are responsible for the nature and quality of all nursing care that patients receive. In these tables, the number of RNs does not include those registered nurses more appropriately reported in other occupational categories, such as facility administrators, which are listed under *all other personnel* (Tables 1 and 2).

Rehabilitation services: A wide array of restoration services for disabled and recuperating patients, including all support services necessary to help them attain their maximum functional capacity.

Retirement housing: A facility which provides social activities to senior citizens, usually retired persons, who do not require health care but some short-term skilled nursing care may be provided. A retirement center may furnish housing and may also have acute hospital and long-term care facilities, or it may arrange for acute and long term care through affiliated institutions.

Robot-assisted walking therapy: A form of physical therapy that uses a robotic device to assist patients who are relearning how to walk.

Robotic surgery: The use of mechanical guidance devices to remotely manipulate surgical instrumentation.

Rural: A rural hospital is located outside a Metropolitan Statistical Area (MSA), as designated by the U.S. Office of Management and Budget (OMB) effective June 6, 2003. An urban area is a geographically defined, integrated social and economic unit with a large population nucleus. Micropolitan areas, which are new to the OMB June 6, 2003 definitions, continue to be classified as rural for purposes of this publication.

Rural Health Clinic: A clinic located in a rural, medically under-served area in the United States that has a separate reimbursement structure from the standard medical office under the Medicare and Medicaid programs.

Shaped beam radiation system: A precise, non-invasive treatment that involves targeting beams of radiation that mirrors the exact size and shape of a tumor at a specific area of a tumor to shrink or destroy cancerous cells. This procedure delivers a therapeutic dose of radiation that conforms precisely to the shape of the tumor, thus minimizing the risk to nearby tissues.

Simulated rehabilitation environment: Rehabilitation focused on retraining functional skills in a contextually appropriate environment (simulated home and

community settings) or in a traditional setting (gymnasium) using motor learning principles.

Single photon emission computerized tomography (SPECT): A nuclear medicine imaging technology that combines existing technology of gamma camera imaging with computed tomographic imaging technology to provide a more precise and clear image.

Skilled nursing care: Provides non-acute medical and skilled nursing care services, therapy, and social services under the supervision of a licensed registered nurse on a 24-hour basis.

Sleep Center: Specially equipped and staffed center for the diagnosis and treatment of sleep disorders.

Social work services (could include): Organized services that are properly directed and sufficiently staffed by qualified individuals who provide assistance and counseling to patients and their families in dealing with social, emotional, and environmental problems associated with illness or disability, often in the context of financial or discharge planning coordination.

Sports medicine: Provision of diagnostic screening and assessment and clinical and rehabilitation services for the prevention and treatment of sports-related injuries.

Stereotactic radiosurgery: Stereotactic radiosurgery (SRS) is a radiotherapy modality that delivers a high dosage of radiation to a discrete treatment area in as few as one treatment session. Includes gamma knife, cyberknife, etc.

Support groups: A hospital sponsored program that allows a group of individuals with the same or similar problems who meet periodically to share experiences, problems, and solutions in order to support each other.

Supportive housing services: A hospital program that provides decent, safe, affordable, community-based housing with flexible support services designed to help the individual or family stay housed and live a more productive life in the community.

Surgical operations: Those surgical operations, whether major or minor, performed in the operating room(s). A surgical operation involving more than one surgical procedure is still considered only one surgical operation.

Swing bed services: A hospital bed that can be used to provide either acute or long-term care depending on community or patient needs. To be eligible a hospital must have a Medicare provider agreement in place, have fewer than 100 beds, be located in a rural area, do not have a 24 hour nursing service waiver in effect, have not been terminated from the program in the prior two years, and meet various service conditions.

Teen outreach services: A program focusing on the teenager which encourages an improved health status and a healthful lifestyle including physical, emotional, mental, social, spiritual and economic health through education, exercise, nutrition and health promotion.

Telehealth: A broad variety of technologies and tactics to deliver virtual medical, public health, health education delivery and support services using telecommunications technologies. Telehealth is used more commonly as it describes the wide range of diagnosis and management, education, and other related fields of health care. This includes, but are not limited to: dentistry, counseling, physical and occupational therapy, home health, chronic disease monitoring and management, disaster management and consumer and professional education, and remote patient monitoring.

Tissue transplant: See definition for Transplant services below.

Tobacco treatment/cessation program: Organized hospital services with the purpose of ending tobacco-use habits of patients addicted to tobacco/nicotine.

Transplant services: The branch of medicine that transfers an organ or tissue from one person to another or from one body part to another to replace a diseased structure or to restore function or to change appearance. Services could include: bone marrow transplant program; heart, lung, kidney, intestine, or tissue transplant. The other transplant services include transplant services other than bone marrow, heart, kidney, liver, lung, tissue and heart/lung or other multi-transplant surgeries.

Transportation to health facilities: A long-term care support service designed to assist the mobility of the elderly. Some programs offer improved financial access by offering reduced rates and barrier-free buses or vans with ramps and lifts to assist the elderly or handicapped; others offer subsidies for public transport systems or operate mini-bus services exclusively for use by senior citizens.

Trauma center (certified): A facility to provide emergency and specialized intensive care to critically ill and injured patients. **Level 1:** A regional resource trauma center, which is capable of providing total care for every aspect of injury and plays a leadership role in trauma research and education. **Level 2:** A community trauma center, which is capable of providing trauma care to all but the most severely injured patients who require highly specialized care. **Level 3:** A rural trauma hospital, which is capable of providing care to a large number of injury victims and can resuscitate and stabilize more severely injured patients so that they can be transported to Level 1 or 2 facilities.

Ultrasound: The use of acoustic waves above the range of 20,000 cycles per second to visualize internal body structures.

Urban: An urban hospital is located inside a Metropolitan Statistical Area (MSA), designated by the U.S. Office of Management and Budget effective June 6, 2003. An urban areas is a geographically defined, integrated social and economic unit with a large population base. Micropolitan areas, which are new to the OMB June 6, 2003 definitions, are not considered to be urban for purposes of this publication.

Urgent care center: A facility that provides care and treatment for problems that are not life-threatening but require attention over the short term.

Violence prevention programs for the workplace: A violence prevention program with goals and objectives for preventing workplace violence against staff and patients.

Violence prevention programs for the community: An organized program that attempts to make a positive impact on the type(s) of violence a community is experiencing. For example, it can assist victims of violent crimes, e.g., rape, or incidents, e.g., bullying, to hospital or to community services to prevent further victimization or retaliation. A program that targets the underlying circumstances that contribute to violence such as poor housing, insufficient job training, and/or substance abuse through means such as direct involvement and support, education, mentoring, anger management, crisis intervention and training programs would also qualify.

Virtual colonoscopy: Noninvasive screening procedure used to visualize, analyze and detect cancerous or potentially cancerous polyps in the colon.

Volunteer services department: An organized hospital department responsible for coordinating the services of volunteers working within the institution.

Women's health center/services: An area set aside for coordinated education and treatment services specifically for and promoted to women as provided by this special unit. Services may or may not include obstetrics but include a range of services other than OB.

Wound Management Services: Services for patients with chronic wounds and nonhealing wounds often resulting from diabetes, poor circulation, improper seating and immunocompromising conditions. The goals are to progress chronic wounds through stages of healing, reduce and eliminate infections, increase physical function to minimize complications from current wounds and prevent future chronic wounds. Wound management services are provided on an inpatient or outpatient basis, depending on the intensity of service needed.

2019 AHA Annual Survey
American Hospital Association

HOSPITAL NAME: _____

CITY & STATE: _____

Please return to:
AHA Annual Survey
155 N Wacker Drive
Suite 400
Chicago IL 60606

A. REPORTING PERIOD (please refer to the instructions and definitions at the end of this questionnaire)

Report data for a full 12-month period, preferably your last completed fiscal year (365 days). Be consistent in using the same reporting period for responses throughout various sections of this survey.

1. Reporting Period used (beginning and ending date) ...... __ __ / __ __ / __ __ __ __ to __ __ / __ __ / __ __ __ __
   Month   Day   Year   Month   Day   Year

2. a. Were you in operation 12 full months
   at the end of your reporting period? .... YES ☐   NO ☐

   b. Number of days open
   during reporting period .... _____

3. Indicate the beginning of your current fiscal year .... __ __ / __ __ / __ __ __ __
   Month   Day   Year

B. ORGANIZATIONAL STRUCTURE

1. **CONTROL**
   Indicate the type of organization that is responsible for establishing policy for overall operation of your hospital. CHECK ONLY ONE:

   Government, nonfederal
   ☐ 12 State
   ☐ 13 County
   ☐ 14 City
   ☐ 15 City-County
   ☐ 16 Hospital district or authority

   Nongovernment, not-for-profit (NFP)
   ☐ 21 Church-operated
   ☐ 23 Other not-for-profit (including NFP Corporation)

   Investor-owned, for-profit
   ☐ 31 Individual
   ☐ 32 Partnership
   ☐ 33 Corporation

   Government, federal
   ☐ 40 Department of Defense
   ☐ 44 Public Health Service
   ☐ 45 Veterans' Affairs

   ☐ 46 Federal other than 40-45 or 47-48
   ☐ 47 PHS Indian Service
   ☐ 48 Department of Justice

2. **SERVICE**
   Indicate the ONE category that BEST describes your hospital or the type of service it provides to the MAJORITY of patients:

   ☐ 10 General medical and surgical
   ☐ 11 Hospital unit of an institution (prison hospital, college infirmary)
   ☐ 12 Hospital unit within a facility for persons with intellectual disabilities
   ☐ 13 Surgical
   ☐ 22 Psychiatric
   ☐ 33 Tuberculosis and other respiratory diseases
   ☐ 41 Cancer
   ☐ 42 Heart
   ☐ 44 Obstetrics and gynecology
   ☐ 45 Eye, ear, nose, and throat

   ☐ 46 Rehabilitation
   ☐ 47 Orthopedic
   ☐ 48 Chronic disease
   ☐ 62 Intellectual disabilities
   ☐ 80 Acute long-term care hospital
   ☐ 82 Alcoholism and other chemical dependency
   ☐ 49 Other - specify treatment area: _____

B. ORGANIZATIONAL STRUCTURE (continued)

3. OTHER

a. Does your hospital restrict admissions primarily to children? .... YES ☐ NO ☐

b. Does the hospital itself operate subsidiary corporations? .... YES ☐ NO ☐

c. Is the hospital contract managed? If yes, please provide the name, city, and state of the organization.... YES ☐ NO ☐

Name: _____ City: _____ State: _____

d. Is your hospital owned in whole or in part by physicians or a physician group?... YES ☐ NO ☐

e. If you checked 80 Acute long-term care hospital (LTCH) in Section B2 (Service), please indicate if you are a freestanding LTCH or a LTCH arranged within a general acute care hospital.

☐ Free standing LTCH   ☐ LTCH arranged in a general acute care hospital

If you are arranged in a general acute care hospital, what is your host hospital's name?

Name_____ City_____ State_____

f. Are any other types of hospitals co-located in your hospital?   YES ☐ NO ☐

g. If yes, what type of hospital is co-located? (Check all that apply)

1. ☐ Cancer
2. ☐ Cardiac
3. ☐ Orthopedic
4. ☐ Pediatric
5. ☐ Psychiatric
6. ☐ Surgical
7. ☐ Other _____

C. FACILITIES AND SERVICES

For each service or facility listed below, please check all the categories that describe how each item is provided **as of the last day of the reporting period**. Check all categories that apply for an item. If you check column (1) C1-19, please include the number of **staffed beds**.
**The sum of the beds reported in 1-19 should equal Section E(1b), beds set up and staffed on page 12.**

	(1) Owned or provided by my hospital or its subsidiary	(2) Provided by my Health System (in my local community)	(3) Provided through a formal contractual arrangement or joint venture with another provider that is not in my system (in my local community)	(4) Do Not Provide
1. General medical-surgical care ....(#Beds____)	☐	☐	☐	☐
2. Pediatric medical-surgical care ....(#Beds____)	☐	☐	☐	☐
3. Obstetrics............[Hospital level of unit (1-3):(____)] (#Beds____)	☐	☐	☐	☐
4. Medical-surgical intensive care..................(#Beds____)	☐	☐	☐	☐
5. Cardiac intensive care ....(#Beds____)	☐	☐	☐	☐
6. Neonatal intensive care ....(#Beds____)	☐	☐	☐	☐
7. Neonatal intermediate care.........................(#Beds____)	☐	☐	☐	☐
8. Pediatric intensive care...............................(#Beds____)	☐	☐	☐	☐
9. Burn care...(#Beds____)	☐	☐	☐	☐
10. Other special care _____ ....(#Beds____)	☐	☐	☐	☐
11. Other intensive care_____ ....(#Beds____)	☐	☐	☐	☐
12. Physical rehabilitation ....(#Beds____)	☐	☐	☐	☐
13. Alcoholism-chemical dependency care.......(#Beds____)	☐	☐	☐	☐
14. Psychiatric care ....(#Beds____)	☐	☐	☐	☐
15. Skilled nursing care ....(#Beds____)	☐	☐	☐	☐
16. Intermediate nursing care ....(#Beds____)	☐	☐	☐	☐
17. Acute long-term care ....(#Beds____)	☐	☐	☐	☐
18. Other long-term care ....(#Beds____)	☐	☐	☐	☐
19. Other care _____ ....(#Beds____)	☐	☐	☐	☐
20. Adult day care program	☐	☐	☐	☐
21. Airborne infection isolation room..............(#rooms____)	☐	☐	☐	☐
22. Alcoholism-chemical dependency care services				
a. Alcoholism-chemical dependency pediatric services .. (#Beds____)	☐	☐	☐	☐
b. Alcoholism-chemical dependency outpatient services....................	☐	☐	☐	☐
c. Alcoholism-chemical dependency partial hospitalization services	☐	☐	☐	☐
23. Alzheimer center..	☐	☐	☐	☐
24. Ambulance services	☐	☐	☐	☐
25. Air Ambulance services	☐	☐	☐	☐
26. Ambulatory surgery center..........................	☐	☐	☐	☐
27. Arthritis treatment center	☐	☐	☐	☐
28. Auxiliary..	☐	☐	☐	☐
29. Bariatric/weight control services.................	☐	☐	☐	☐
30. Birthing room/LDR room/LDRP room...........	☐	☐	☐	☐
31. Blood donor center	☐	☐	☐	☐
32. Breast cancer screening/mammograms........................	☐	☐	☐	☐

C. FACILITIES AND SERVICES (continued)

	(1) Owned or provided by my hospital or its subsidiary	(2) Provided by my Health System (in my local community)	(3) Provided through a formal contractual arrangement or joint venture with another provider that is not in my system (in my local community)	(4) Do Not Provide
33. Cardiology and cardiac surgery services				
a. Adult cardiology services	☐	☐	☐	☐
b. Pediatric cardiology services	☐	☐	☐	☐
c. Adult diagnostic catheterization	☐	☐	☐	☐
d. Pediatric diagnostic catheterization	☐	☐	☐	☐
e. Adult interventional cardiac catheterization	☐	☐	☐	☐
f. Pediatric interventional cardiac catheterization	☐	☐	☐	☐
g. Adult cardiac surgery	☐	☐	☐	☐
h. Pediatric cardiac surgery	☐	☐	☐	☐
i. Adult cardiac electrophysiology	☐	☐	☐	☐
j. Pediatric cardiac electrophysiology	☐	☐	☐	☐
k. Cardiac rehabilitation	☐	☐	☐	☐
34. Case management	☐	☐	☐	☐
35. Chaplaincy/pastoral care services	☐	☐	☐	☐
36. Chemotherapy	☐	☐	☐	☐
37. Children's wellness program	☐	☐	☐	☐
38. Chiropractic services	☐	☐	☐	☐
39. Community outreach	☐	☐	☐	☐
40. Complementary and alternative medicine services	☐	☐	☐	☐
41. Computer assisted orthopedic surgery (CAOS)	☐	☐	☐	☐
42. Crisis prevention	☐	☐	☐	☐
43. Dental services	☐	☐	☐	☐
44. Diabetes prevention program	☐	☐	☐	☐
45. Emergency services				
a. On-campus emergency department	☐	☐	☐	☐
b. Off-campus emergency department	☐	☐	☐	☐
c. Pediatric emergency department	☐	☐	☐	☐
d. Trauma center (certified) [Hospital level of unit (1-3) _____]	☐	☐	☐	☐
46. Enabling services	☐	☐	☐	☐
47. Endoscopic services				
a. Optical colonoscopy	☐	☐	☐	☐
b. Endoscopic ultrasound	☐	☐	☐	☐
c. Ablation of Barrett's esophagus	☐	☐	☐	☐
d. Esophageal impedance study	☐	☐	☐	☐
e. Endoscopic retrograde cholangiopancreatography (ERCP)	☐	☐	☐	☐
48. Enrollment (insurance) assistance services	☐	☐	☐	☐
49. Employment support services	☐	☐	☐	☐
50. Extracorporeal shock wave lithotripter (ESWL)	☐	☐	☐	☐
51. Fertility clinic	☐	☐	☐	☐
52. Fitness center	☐	☐	☐	☐
53. Freestanding outpatient care center	☐	☐	☐	☐
54. Geriatric services	☐	☐	☐	☐
55. Health fair	☐	☐	☐	☐
56. Community health education	☐	☐	☐	☐

C. FACILITIES AND SERVICES (continued)

	(1) Owned or provided by my hospital or its subsidiary	(2) Provided by my Health System (in my local community)	(3) Provided through a formal contractual arrangement or joint venture with another provider that is not in my system (in my local community)	(4) Do Not Provide
57. Genetic testing/counseling	☐	☐	☐	☐
58. Health screenings	☐	☐	☐	☐
59. Health research	☐	☐	☐	☐
60. Hemodialysis	☐	☐	☐	☐
61. HIV/AIDS services	☐	☐	☐	☐
62. Home health services	☐	☐	☐	☐
63. Hospice program	☐	☐	☐	☐
64. Hospital-based outpatient care center services	☐	☐	☐	☐
65. Housing services				
a. Assisted living	☐	☐	☐	☐
b. Retirement housing	☐	☐	☐	☐
c. Supportive housing services	☐	☐	☐	☐
66. Immunization program	☐	☐	☐	☐
67. Indigent care clinic	☐	☐	☐	☐
68. Linguistic/translation services	☐	☐	☐	☐
69. Meal delivery services	☐	☐	☐	☐
70. Mobile health services	☐	☐	☐	☐
71. Neurological services	☐	☐	☐	☐
72. Nutrition program	☐	☐	☐	☐
73. Occupational health services	☐	☐	☐	☐
74. Oncology services	☐	☐	☐	☐
75. Orthopedic services	☐	☐	☐	☐
76. Outpatient surgery	☐	☐	☐	☐
77. Pain management program	☐	☐	☐	☐
78. Palliative care program	☐	☐	☐	☐
79. Palliative care inpatient unit	☐	☐	☐	☐
80. Patient controlled analgesia (PCA)	☐	☐	☐	☐
81. Patient education center	☐	☐	☐	☐
82. Patient representative services	☐	☐	☐	☐
83. Physical rehabilitation services				
a. Assistive technology center	☐	☐	☐	☐
b. Electrodiagnostic services	☐	☐	☐	☐
c. Physical rehabilitation outpatient services	☐	☐	☐	☐
d. Prosthetic and orthotic services	☐	☐	☐	☐
e. Robot-assisted walking therapy	☐	☐	☐	☐
f. Simulated rehabilitation environment	☐	☐	☐	☐
84. Primary care department	☐	☐	☐	☐
85. Psychiatric services				
a. Psychiatric consultation-liaison services	☐	☐	☐	☐
b. Psychiatric pediatric care (#Beds_____)	☐	☐	☐	☐
c. Psychiatric geriatric care (#Beds_____)	☐	☐	☐	☐
d. Psychiatric education services	☐	☐	☐	☐
e. Psychiatric emergency services	☐	☐	☐	☐
f. Psychiatric outpatient services	☐	☐	☐	☐
g. Psychiatric intensive outpatient services	☐	☐	☐	☐

C. FACILITIES AND SERVICES (continued)

	(1) Owned or provided by my hospital or its subsidiary	(2) Provided by my Health System (in my local community)	(3) Provided through a formal contractual arrangement or joint venture with another provider that is not in my system (in my local community)	(4) Do Not Provide
85. Psychiatric services (continued)				
h. Psychiatric partial hospitalization services – adult	☐	☐	☐	☐
i. Psychiatric partial hospitalization services – pediatric	☐	☐	☐	☐
j. Psychiatric residential treatment – adult	☐	☐	☐	☐
k. Psychiatric residential treatment – pediatric	☐	☐	☐	☐
86. Radiology, diagnostic				
a. CT Scanner	☐	☐	☐	☐
b. Diagnostic radioisotope facility	☐	☐	☐	☐
c. Electron beam computed tomography (EBCT)	☐	☐	☐	☐
d. Full-field digital mammography (FFDM)	☐	☐	☐	☐
e. Magnetic resonance imaging (MRI)	☐	☐	☐	☐
f. Intraoperative magnetic resonance imaging	☐	☐	☐	☐
g. Magnetoencephalography (MEG)	☐	☐	☐	☐
h. Multi-slice spiral computed tomography (<64+ slice CT)	☐	☐	☐	☐
i. Multi-slice spiral computed tomography (64+ slice CT)	☐	☐	☐	☐
j. Positron emission tomography (PET)	☐	☐	☐	☐
k. Positron emission tomography/CT (PET/CT)	☐	☐	☐	☐
l. Single photon emission computerized tomography (SPECT)	☐	☐	☐	☐
m. Ultrasound	☐	☐	☐	☐
87. Radiology, therapeutic				
a. Image-guided radiation therapy (IGRT)	☐	☐	☐	☐
b. Intensity-modulated radiation therapy (IMRT)	☐	☐	☐	☐
c. Proton beam therapy	☐	☐	☐	☐
d. Shaped beam radiation system	☐	☐	☐	☐
e. Stereotactic radiosurgery	☐	☐	☐	☐
88. Robotic surgery	☐	☐	☐	☐
89. Rural health clinic	☐	☐	☐	☐
90. Sleep center	☐	☐	☐	☐
91. Social work services	☐	☐	☐	☐
92. Sports medicine	☐	☐	☐	☐
93. Support groups	☐	☐	☐	☐
94. Swing bed services	☐	☐	☐	☐
95. Teen outreach services	☐	☐	☐	☐
96. Tobacco treatment/cessation program	☐	☐	☐	☐
97. Telehealth				
a. Consultation and office visits	☐	☐	☐	☐
b. eICU	☐	☐	☐	☐
c. Stroke care	☐	☐	☐	☐
d. Psychiatric and addiction treatment	☐	☐	☐	☐
e. Remote patient monitoring				
1. Post-discharge	☐	☐	☐	☐
2. Ongoing chronic care management	☐	☐	☐	☐
3. Other remote patient monitoring	☐	☐	☐	☐
f. Other telehealth	☐	☐	☐	☐

C. FACILITIES AND SERVICES (continued)

	(1) Owned or provided by my hospital or its subsidiary	(2) Provided by my Health System (in my local community)	(3) Provided through a formal contractual arrangement or joint venture with another provider that is not in my system (in my local community)	(4) Do Not Provide
98. Transplant services				
a. Bone marrow	☐	☐	☐	☐
b. Heart	☐	☐	☐	☐
c. Kidney	☐	☐	☐	☐
d. Liver	☐	☐	☐	☐
e. Lung	☐	☐	☐	☐
f. Tissue	☐	☐	☐	☐
g. Other	☐	☐	☐	☐
99. Transportation to health services (non-emergency)	☐	☐	☐	☐
100. Urgent care center	☐	☐	☐	☐
101. Violence prevention programs				
a. For the workplace	☐	☐	☐	☐
b. For the community	☐	☐	☐	☐
102. Virtual colonoscopy	☐	☐	☐	☐
103. Volunteer services department	☐	☐	☐	☐
104. Women's health center/services	☐	☐	☐	☐
105. Wound management services	☐	☐	☐	☐

106. Does your organization routinely integrate behavioral health services in the following care areas?
Integration ranges from co-located physical and behavioral health providers, with some screening and treatment planning, to fully integrated care where behavioral and physical health providers function as a true team in a shared practice.

	Yes	No
a. Emergency services	☐	☐
b. Primary care services	☐	☐
c. Acute inpatient care	☐	☐
d. Extended care	☐	☐

107a. For each of the physician-organization arrangements, please report the number of physicians involved in these arrangements.

	Number of Involved Physicians	(1) My Hospital	(2) My Health System	(3) Do Not Provide
1. Independent Practice Association (IPA)	_____	☐	☐	☐
2. Group practice without walls	_____	☐	☐	☐
3. Open Physician-Hospital Organization (PHO)	_____	☐	☐	☐
4. Closed Physician-Hospital Organization (PHO)	_____	☐	☐	☐
5. Management Service Organization (MSO)	_____	☐	☐	☐
6. Integrated Salary Model	_____	☐	☐	☐
7. Equity Model	_____	☐	☐	☐
8. Foundation	_____	☐	☐	☐
9. Other, please specify _____	_____	☐	☐	☐

C. FACILITIES AND SERVICES (continued)

107b. For those arrangements reported in 1a, please report the approximate ownership share.

	Hospital ownership share	Physician ownership share	Parent corporation ownership share	Insurance ownership share
1. Independent Practice Association (IPA)..............	_____ %	_____ %	_____ %	_____ %
2. Group practice without walls................................	_____ %	_____ %	_____ %	_____ %
3. Open Physician-Hospital Organization (PHO)......	_____ %	_____ %	_____ %	_____ %
4. Closed Physician-Hospital Organization (PHO) ...	_____ %	_____ %	_____ %	_____ %
5. Management Service Organization (MSO)	_____ %	_____ %	_____ %	_____ %
6. Integrated Salary Model.......................................	_____ %	_____ %	_____ %	_____ %
7. Equity Model	_____ %	_____ %	_____ %	_____ %
8. Foundation	_____ %	_____ %	_____ %	_____ %
9. Other, please specify	_____ %	_____ %	_____ %	_____ %

107c. If the hospital owns physician practices, how are they organized?

	Percent	Number of physicians
1. Solo practice	_____ %	_____
2. Single specialty group	_____ %	_____
3. Multi-specialty group	_____ %	_____

107d. Of the physician practices owned by the hospital, what percentage are primary care? _____ %

107e. Of the physician practices owned by the hospital, what percentage are specialty care? _____ %

108. Looking across all the relationships identified in question 107a, what is the total number of physicians (count each physician only once) that are engaged in an arrangement with your hospital that allows for joint contracting with payers or shared responsibility for financial risk or clinical performance between the hospital and physician? (Arrangement may be any type of ownership.)

_____ Number of physicians

109a. Does your hospital participate in any joint venture arrangements with physicians or physician groups?   YES ☐   NO ☐

109b. if your hospital participates in any joint ventures with physicians or physician groups, please indicate which types of services are involved in those joint ventures. (Check all that apply)

1. ☐ Limited service hospital
2. ☐ Ambulatory surgical centers
3. ☐ Imaging centers
4. ☐ Other _____

109c. If you selected '1. Limited service hospital', above, please tell us what type(s) of services are provided. (Check all that apply)

1. ☐ Cardiac
2. ☐ Orthopedic
3. ☐ Surgical
4. ☐ Other _____

109d. Does your hospital participate in joint venture arrangements with organizations other than physician groups?   YES ☐   NO ☐

D. INSURANCE AND ALTERNATIVE PAYMENT MODELS

INSURANCE

1. Does your hospital own or jointly own a health plan? Yes ☐ No ☐

   a. If yes, in what states? States: _____

2. Does your system own or jointly own a health plan? Yes ☐ No ☐

   a. If yes, in what states? States: _____

3. Does your hospital/system have a significant partnership with an insurer or an insurance company/health plan? Yes ☐ No ☐

   a. If yes, in what states? States: _____

4. If yes to 1, 2 and/or 3, please indicate the insurance products and the total medical enrollment. (Check all that apply)

Insurance Products	Hospital	System	JV	Medical Enrollment	New Product	No	Do not know
a. Medicare Advantage	☐	☐	☐	_____	☐	☐	☐
b. Medicaid Managed Care	☐	☐	☐	_____	☐	☐	☐
c. Health Insurance Marketplace ("exchange")	☐	☐	☐	_____	☐	☐	☐
d. Other Individual Market	☐	☐	☐	_____	☐	☐	☐
e. Small Group	☐	☐	☐	_____	☐	☐	☐
f. Large Group	☐	☐	☐	_____	☐	☐	☐
g. Other _____	☐	☐	☐	_____	☐	☐	☐

If you have answered 'no' to all parts of questions 1, 2 and 3, please skip to question 8.

5. Does your **health plan** make capitated payments to physicians either within or outside of your network for specific groups or enrollees?

   a. Physicians within your network Yes ☐ No ☐ Do not know ☐

   b. Physicians outside your network Yes ☐ No ☐ Do not know ☐

6. Does your **health plan** make bundled payments to providers in your network or to outside providers?

   a. Providers within your network Yes ☐ No ☐ Do not know ☐

   b. Providers outside your network Yes ☐ No ☐ Do not know ☐

7. Does your **health plan** offer other shared risk contracts to either providers in your network or to outside providers? (i.e., other than capitation or bundled payment.)

   a. Providers within your network Yes ☐ No ☐ Do not know ☐

   b. Providers outside your network Yes ☐ No ☐ Do not know ☐

8. Does your hospital or system offer a self-administered health plan for your employees? Yes ☐ No ☐

D. INSURANCE AND ALTERNATIVE PAYMENT MODELS (continued)

ALTERNATIVE PAYMENT MODELS

9. What percentage of your **hospital's** patient revenue is paid on a capitated basis?   _____%

   a. In total, how many enrollees do you serve under capitated contracts?   Total enrollees: _____

10. Does your **hospital** participate in any bundled payment arrangements?   Yes ☐   Did previously but no longer doing so ☐   No ☐

If yes, please respond to 10a-10c:

   a. With which of the following types of payers does your **hospital** have a bundled payment arrangement? (Check all that apply)

      1. ☐ Traditional Medicare
      2. ☐ A Medicare Advantage plan
      3. ☐ A commercial insurance plan including ACA participants, individual, group or employer markets
      4. ☐ Medicaid

   b. For which of the following medical/surgical conditions does your **hospital** have a bundled payment arrangement? (Check all that apply)

      1. ☐ Cardiovascular
      2. ☐ Orthopedic
      3. ☐ Oncologic
      4. ☐ Neurology
      5. ☐ Hematology
      6. ☐ Gastrointestinal
      7. ☐ Pulmonary
      8. ☐ Infectious disease
      9. ☐ Other, please specify: _____

   c. What percentage of the **hospital's** patient revenue is paid through bundled payment arrangements?   _____%

11. Does your **hospital** participate in a bundled payment program involving care settings outside of the hospital (e.g., physician, outpatient, post-acute)?   Yes ☐   No ☐

   a. If yes, does your **hospital** share upside or downside risk for any of those outside providers?   Yes ☐   No ☐

12. What percentage of your **hospital's** patient revenue is paid on a shared risk basis (other than capitated or bundled payments)?   _____%

13. Does your **hospital** contract directly with employers or a coalition of employers to provide care on a capitated, predetermined, or shared risk basis?   Yes ☐   No ☐

14. Does your **hospital** have contracts with commercial payers where payment is tied to performance on quality/safety metrics?   Yes ☐   No ☐

15a. Has your **hospital** or **health care system** established an accountable care organization (ACO)?

   1. ☐ My hospital/system currently leads an ACO   **(Skip to 15b)**
   2. ☐ My hospital/system currently participates in an ACO (but is not its leader) **(Skip to 18)**
   3. ☐ My hospital/system previously led or participated in an ACO but is no longer doing so **(Skip to 16a)**
   4. ☐ My hospital/system has never participated or led an ACO **(Skip to 17)**

15b. With which of the following types of payers does your hospital/system have an accountable care contract? (Check all that apply)

   1. ☐ Traditional Medicare (MSSP and NextGen) **(Skip to 15c)**
   2. ☐ A Medicare Advantage plan **(Skip to 15d)**
   3. ☐ A commercial insurance plan (including ACO participants, individual, group, and employer markets) **(Skip to 15d)**
   4. ☐ Medicaid **(Skip to 15d)**

D. INSURANCE AND ALTERNATIVE PAYMENT MODELS (continued)

ALTERNATIVE PAYMENT MODELS

15c. If you selected Traditional Medicare, in which of the following Medicare programs is your hospital/system participating? (Check all that apply)

1. ☐ MSSP Track 1
2. ☐ MSSP Track 2
3. ☐ MSSP Track 3
4. ☐ MSSP Track 1+
5. ☐ NextGen
6. ☐ Comprehensive ESRD Care

15d. What percentage of your hospital's/system's patients are covered by accountable care contracts? _____%

15e. What percentage of your hospital's/system's patient revenue came from ACO contracts in 2019? _____% **(Skip to 18)**

16a. In what year did your hospital's/system's last ACO contract end? _____

16b. Which of the following types of payers did your hospital/system have an accountable care contract with? (Check all that apply)

1. ☐ Traditional Medicare (MSSP and NextGen) **(Skip to 16c)**
2. ☐ A Medicare Advantage plan **(Skip to 16d)**
3. ☐ A commercial insurance plan (including ACA participants, individual, group, and employer markets) **(Skip to 16d)**
4. ☐ Medicaid **(Skip to 18)**

16c. In which of the following Medicare programs did your hospital/system participate? (Check all that apply)

1. ☐ MSSP Track 1
2. ☐ MSSP Track 2
3. ☐ MSSP Track 3
4. ☐ MSSP Track 1+
5. ☐ NextGen
6. ☐ Pioneer
7. ☐ Comprehensive ESRD Care

16d. How many commercial accountable care contracts has your hospital/system previously been a part of? _____

17. Has your hospital/system ever considered participating in an ACO?

a. ☐ Yes, and we are planning to join one
b. ☐ Yes, but we are not planning to join one
c. ☐ No, we have not even considered it

18. Do any hospitals and/or physician groups with your system, or the system itself, plan to participate in any of the following risk arrangements in the next three years? (Check all that apply)

a. ☐ Shared savings/losses
b. ☐ Bundled payment
c. ☐ Capitation
d. ☐ ACO (ownership)
e. ☐ ACO (joint venture)
f. ☐ Health plan (ownership)
g. ☐ Health plan (joint venture)
h. ☐ Other, please specify: _____
i. ☐ None

19. Does your hospital/system have an established medical home program?

a. Hospital	Yes ☐	No ☐
b. System	Yes ☐	No ☐

20. Has your hospital/system established a clinically integrated network?

a. Hospital	Yes ☐	No ☐
b. System	Yes ☐	No ☐

E. TOTAL FACILITY BEDS, UTILIZATION, FINANCES, AND STAFFING

Please report beds, utilization, financial, and staffing data for the 12-month period that is consistent with the period reported on page 1. Report financial data for reporting period only. Include within your operations all activities that are wholly owned by the hospital, including subsidiary corporations regardless of where the activity is physically located. Please do not include within your operations distinct and separate divisions that may be owned by your hospital's parent corporation. If final figures are not available, please estimate. Round to the nearest dollar. Report all personnel who were on the payroll and whose payroll expenses are reported in E3f. (Please refer to specific definitions on pages 28-30.)

> **Fill out column (2) if hospital owns and operates a nursing home type unit/facility.**
> **Column (1) should be the combined total of hospital plus nursing home unit/facility.**

1. BEDS AND UTILIZATION

	(1) Total Facility	(2) Nursing Home Unit/Facility
a. Total licensed beds		
b. Beds set up and staffed for use at the end of the reporting period		
c. Bassinets set up and staffed for use at the end of the reporting period		
d. Births (exclude fetal deaths)		
e. Admissions (exclude newborns; include neonatal & swing admissions)		
f. Inpatient days (exclude newborns; include neonatal & swing days)		
g. Emergency department visits		
h. Total outpatient visits (include emergency department visits & outpatient surgeries)		
i. Inpatient surgical operations		
j. Number of operating rooms		
k. Outpatient surgical operations		

2. MEDICARE/MEDICAID UTILIZATION

	(1) Total Facility	(2) Nursing Home Unit/Facility
a1. Total Medicare (Title XVIII) inpatient discharges (including Medicare Managed Care)		
a2. How many Medicare inpatient discharges were Medicare Managed Care?		
b1. Total Medicare (Title XVIII) inpatient days (including Medicare Managed Care)		
b2. How many Medicare inpatient days were Medicare Managed Care?		
c1. Total Medicaid (Title XIX) inpatient discharges (including Medicaid Managed Care)		
c2. How many Medicaid inpatient discharges were Medicaid Managed Care?		
d1. Total Medicaid (Title XIX) inpatient days (including Medicaid Managed Care)		
d2. How many Medicaid inpatient days were Medicaid Managed Care?		

3. FINANCIAL

	(1) Total Facility	(2) Nursing Home Unit/Facility
*a. Net patient revenue (treat bad debt as a deduction from gross revenue)	.00	.00
*b. Tax appropriations	.00	
*c. Other operating revenue	.00	
*d. Nonoperating revenue	.00	
*e. TOTAL REVENUE (add 3a thru 3d)	.00	.00
f. Payroll expense (only)	.00	.00
g. Employee benefits	.00	.00
h. Depreciation expense (for reporting period only)	.00	
i. Interest expense	.00	
j. Pharmacy expense	.00	
k. Supply expense (other than pharmacy)	.00	
l. All other expenses	.00	
m. TOTAL EXPENSES (add 3f thru 3l. Exclude bad debt)	.00	.00
n. Do your total expenses (E3.m) reflect full allocation from your corporate office?	Yes ☐	No ☐

E. TOTAL FACILITY BEDS, UTILIZATION, FINANCES, AND STAFFING (continued)

4. REVENUE BY TYPE

*a. Total gross inpatient revenue.. _____.00

*b. Total gross outpatient revenue.. _____.00

*c. Total gross patient revenue .... _____.00

5. UNCOMPENSATED CARE & PROVIDER TAXES

*a. Bad debt (Revenue forgone at full established rates. Include in gross revenue.)............... _____.00

*b. Financial assistance (Includes charity care) (Revenue forgone at full-established rates. Include in gross revenue.).. _____.00

*c. Is your bad debt (5a) reported on the basis of full charges?   Yes ☐   No ☐

*d. Does your state have a provider Medicaid tax/assessment program?   Yes ☐   No ☐

*e. If yes, please report the total gross amount paid into the program. .... _____.00

*f. Due to differing accounting standards, please indicate whether the provider tax/assessment amount is included in:

    1. Total expenses   Yes ☐   No ☐

    2. Deductions from net patient revenue   Yes ☐   No ☐

6. REVENUE BY PAYER (report total facility gross & net figures)

	(1) Gross	(2) Net
*a. GOVERNMENT		
(1) Medicare:		
a) Fee for service patient revenue	_____.00	_____.00
b) Managed care revenue	_____.00	_____.00
c) Total (a + b)	_____.00	_____.00
(2) Medicaid:		
a) Fee for service patient revenue.................................	_____.00	_____.00
b) Managed care revenue	_____.00	_____.00
c) Medicaid Graduate Medical Education (GME) payments		_____.00
d) Medicaid Disproportionate Share Hospital Payments (DSH)......................		_____.00
e) Medicaid Supplemental Payments (not including Medicaid DSH Payments)		_____.00
f) Other Medicaid		_____.00
g) Total (a thru f)	_____.00	_____.00
(3) Other government	_____.00	_____.00
*b. NONGOVERNMENT		
(1) Self-pay	_____.00	_____.00
(2) Third-party payers:		
a) Managed care (includes HMO and PPO)........................	_____.00	_____.00
b) Other third-party payers...	_____.00	_____.00
c) Total third-party payers (a + b)	_____.00	_____.00
(3) All other nongovernment..	_____.00	_____.00
*c. TOTAL	_____.00	_____.00

(Total gross should equal 4c on page 13. Total net should equal 3a on page 12.)

	(1) Inpatient	(2) Outpatient
*d. If you report Medicaid Supplemental Payments on line 6.a(2)e, please break the payment total into inpatient and outpatient care.	_____.00	_____.00

*e. If you are a government owned facility (control codes 12-16), does your facility participate in the Medicaid intergovernmental transfer or certified public expenditures program?   Yes ☐   No ☐

	(1) Gross	(2) Net
*f. If yes, please report gross and net revenue.	_____.00	_____.00

Are the financial data on pages 12-14 from your audited financial statement?	Yes ☐	No ☐

E. TOTAL FACILITY BEDS, UTILIZATION, FINANCES, AND STAFFING (continued)

7. FINANCIAL PERFORMANCE – MARGIN

*a.   Total Margin _____ %

*b.   Operating Margin _____ %

*c.   EBITDA Margin _____ %

*d.   Medicare Margin _____ %

*e.   Medicaid Margin _____ %

8. FIXED ASSETS

a.   Property, plant and equipment at <u>cost</u>.. _____.00

b.   Accumulated <u>depreciation</u>... _____.00

c.   Net property, plant and equipment (a–b).. _____.00

d.   Total gross square feet of your physical plant used for or in support of your healthcare activities...................... _____

9. TOTAL CAPITAL EXPENSES

Include all expenses used to acquire assets, including buildings, remodeling projects, equipment, or property .... _____.00

10. INFORMATION TECHNOLOGY AND CYBERSECURITY

a.   IT operating expense.. _____.00

b.   IT capital expense.. _____.00

c.   Number of employed IT staff (in FTEs)... _____

d.   Number of outsourced IT staff (in FTEs)... _____

*e.   What percentage of your IT budget is spent on security?... _____ %

*f.   Which of the following cybersecurity measures does your hospital or health system currently deploy?
(check all that apply)

    1.   Annual risk assessment.. ☐
    2.   Incident response plan .... ☐
    3.   Intrusion detection systems .... ☐
    4.   Mobile device encryption .... ☐
    5.   Mobile device data wiping... ☐
    6.   Penetration testing to identify security vulnerabilities .... ☐
    7.   Strong password requirements.. ☐
    8.   Two-factor authentication .... ☐

*g.   Does your hospital or health system board oversight of risk management
and reduction specifically include consideration of cybersecurity risk?   Yes ☐   No ☐   Unsure ☐

*h.   Does your hospital or health system have cybersecurity insurance?   Yes ☐   No ☐   Unsure ☐

*i.   Is your hospital or health system participating in cybersecurity
information-sharing activities with an outside information sharing and   Yes ☐   No ☐   Unsure ☐
analysis organization to identify threats and vulnerabilities?

* These data will be treated as confidential and not released without written permission. AHA will however, share these data with your respective state hospital association and, if requested, with your appropriate metropolitan/regional association.

For members of the Catholic Health Association of the United States (CHA), AHA will also share these data with CHA unless there are objections expressed by checking this box ☐

The state/metropolitan/regional associations and CHA may not release these data without written permission from the hospital.

E. TOTAL FACILITY BEDS, UTILIZATION, FINANCES, AND STAFFING (continued)

11. STAFFING

Report full-time (35 hours or more) and part-time (less than 35 hours) personnel who were on the hospital/facility **payroll at the end of your reporting period.** Include members of religious orders for whom dollar equivalents were reported. Exclude private-duty nurses, volunteers, and all personnel whose salary is financed entirely by outside research grants. Exclude physicians and dentists who are paid on a fee basis. **FTE** is the total number of hours **worked** (excluding non-worked hours such as PTO, etc.) by all employees over the full (12 month) reporting period divided by the normal number of hours worked by a full-time employee for that same time period. For example, if your hospital considers a normal workweek for a full-time employee to be 40 hours, a total of 2,080 would be worked over a full year (52 weeks). If the total number of hours worked by all employees on the payroll is 208,000, then the number of Full-Time Equivalents (FTE) is 100 (employees). The FTE calculation for a specific occupational category such as registered nurses is exactly the same. The calculation for each occupational category should be based on the number of hours worked by staff employed in that specific category.

For each occupational category, please report the number of staff vacancies as of the last day of your reporting period. A vacancy is defined as a budgeted staff position which is unfilled as of the last day of the reporting period and for which the hospital is actively seeking either a full-time or part-time permanent replacement. Personnel who work in more than one area should be included only in the category of their primary responsibility and should be counted only once.

	(1) Full-Time (35 hr/wk or more) On Payroll (Headcount)	(2) Part-Time (Less than 35hr/wk) On Payroll (Headcount)	(3) FTE	(4) Vacancies (Headcount)
a. Physicians	_____	_____	_____	_____
b. Dentists	_____	_____	_____	_____
c. Medical residents/interns	_____	_____	_____	_____
d. Dental residents/interns	_____	_____	_____	_____
e. Other trainees	_____	_____	_____	_____
f. Registered nurses	_____	_____	_____	_____
g. Licensed practical (vocational) nurses	_____	_____	_____	_____
h. Nursing assistive personnel	_____	_____	_____	_____
i. Radiology technicians	_____	_____	_____	_____
j. Laboratory technicians	_____	_____	_____	_____
k. Pharmacists licensed	_____	_____	_____	_____
l. Pharmacy technicians	_____	_____	_____	_____
m. Respiratory therapists	_____	_____	_____	_____
n. All other personnel	_____	_____	_____	_____
o. Total facility personnel (add 11a through 11n)	_____	_____	_____	_____

(Total facility personnel (a-n) should include hospital and nursing home type unit/facility, if applicable.

Nursing home type unit/facility personnel should also be reported separately in 11p and 11q.)

p. Nursing home type unit/facility registered nurses	_____	_____	_____	_____
q. Total nursing home type unit/facility personnel	_____	_____	_____	_____

r. For your employed RN FTEs reported above (E.11.f, column 3) please report the number of full-time equivalents who are involved in direct patient care.   _____ Number of direct patient care FTEs

s. For your medical residents/interns reported above (E.11c. column 1) please indicate the number of full-time on payroll.by specialty.   **Full-Time (35 hr/wk or more) On Payroll**

    1. Primary care (general practitioner, general internal medicine, family practice, general pediatrics, geriatrics)   _____

    2. Other specialties   _____

E. TOTAL FACILITY BEDS, UTILIZATION, FINANCES, AND STAFFING (continued)

12. PRIVILEGED PHYSICIANS

Report the total number of physicians with privileges at your hospital by type of relationship with the hospital. <u>The sum of the physicians reported in 12a-12g should equal the total number of privileged physicians (12h) in the hospital.</u>

	(1) Total Employed	(2) Total Individual Contract	(3) Total Group Contract	(4) Not Employed or Under Contract	(5) Total Privileged (add columns 1-4)
a. Primary care (general practitioner, general internal medicine, family practice, general pediatrics).......	_____	_____	_____	_____	_____
b. Obstetrics/gynecology	_____	_____	_____	_____	_____
c. Emergency medicine	_____	_____	_____	_____	_____
d. Hospitalist..	_____	_____	_____	_____	_____
e. Intensivist	_____	_____	_____	_____	_____
f. Radiologist/pathologist/anesthesiologist	_____	_____	_____	_____	_____
g. Other specialist..	_____	_____	_____	_____	_____
h. Total (add 12a-12g)..	_____	_____	_____	_____	_____

13. HOSPITALISTS

a. Do hospitalists provide care for patients in your hospital? (if no, please skip to 14)................ Yes ☐ No ☐ (If yes, please report in E.12d)

b. If yes, please report the total number of full-time equivalent (FTE) hospitalists .... _____FTE

14. INTENSIVISTS

a. Do intensivists provide care for patients in your hospital? (if no, please skip to 15)................ Yes ☐ No ☐ (If yes, please report in E.12.e)

b. If yes, please report the total number of FTE intensivists and assign them to the following areas. Please indicate whether the intensive care area is closed to intensivists. (Meaning that only intensivists are authorized to care for ICU patients.)

		FTE	Closed to Intensivists
1.	Medical-surgical intensive care	_____	☐
2.	Cardiac intensive care	_____	☐
3.	Neonatal intensive care	_____	☐
4.	Pediatric intensive care	_____	☐
5.	Other intensive care	_____	☐
6.	Total	_____	

15. ADVANCED PRACTICE REGISTERED NURSES/PHYSICIAN ASSISTANTS

a. Do advanced practice nurses/physician assistants provide care for patients in your hospital? (If no, please skip to 16) YES ☐ NO ☐

b. If yes, please report the number of full time, part time and FTE advanced practice nurses and physician assistants who provide care for patients in your hospital.

Advanced Practice Registered Nurses _____ Full-time _____ Part-time _____ FTE

Physician Assistants _____ Full-time _____ Part-time _____ FTE

c. If yes, please indicate the type of service provided. (check all that apply)

1. ☐ Primary care   2. ☐ Anesthesia services (Certified registered nurse anesthetist)   3. ☐ Emergency department care

4. ☐ Other specialty care   5. ☐ Patient education   6. ☐ Case management   7. ☐ Other

16. FOREIGN EDUCATED NURSES

a. Did your facility hire more foreign-educated nurses (including contract or agency nurses) to help fill RN vacancies in 2019 vs. 2018?

More ☐   Less ☐   Same ☐   Did not hire foreign nurses ☐

b. From which countries/continents are you recruiting foreign-educated nurses? (check all that apply)

África ☐   South Korea ☐   Canada ☐   Philippines ☐   China ☐   India ☐   Other ☐

F. SUPPLEMENTAL INFORMATION

1a. Does your hospital provide services through satellite outpatient departments?   Yes ☐   No ☐

1b. Please indicate the clinical families of outpatient services offered along with the number of hospital outpatient sites by location.

		Number of on-campus sites	Number of off-campus sites
1. Airway endoscopy	☐	_____	_____
2. Ambulatory surgery	☐	_____	_____
3. Blood product exchange	☐	_____	_____
4. Cardiac/pulmonary rehabilitation	☐	_____	_____
5. Diagnostic/screening test and related procedures	☐	_____	_____
6. Drug administration and clinical oncology	☐	_____	_____
7. Ear, nose throat (ENT)	☐	_____	_____
8. General surgery and related procedures	☐	_____	_____
9. Gastrointestinal (GI)	☐	_____	_____
10. Gynecology	☐	_____	_____
11. Laboratory	☐	_____	_____
12. Major imaging	☐	_____	_____
13. Minor imaging	☐	_____	_____
14. Musculoskeletal surgery	☐	_____	_____
15. Nervous system procedures	☐	_____	_____
16. Ophthalmology	☐	_____	_____
17. Pathology	☐	_____	_____
18. Primary care	☐	_____	_____
19. Psychiatric care	☐	_____	_____
20. Radiation oncology	☐	_____	_____
21. Rehabilitation	☐	_____	_____
22. Skilled nursing	☐	_____	_____
23. Substance abuse/chemical dependency	☐	_____	_____
24. Urgent care	☐	_____	_____
25. Urology	☐	_____	_____
26. Vascular/endovascular/cardiovascular	☐	_____	_____
27. Visits and related services	☐	_____	_____
28. Other, please specify:_____	☐	_____	_____

2. Does the hospital participate in a group purchasing arrangement?   YES ☐   NO ☐
If yes, please provide the name, city, and state of the group purchasing organization(s).

Name: _____   City: _____   State: _____

Name: _____   City: _____   State: _____

Name: _____   City: _____   State: _____

3. Does the hospital purchase medical/surgical supplies directly through a distributor?   YES ☐   NO ☐
If yes, please provide the name of the distributor(s).

Name: _____

Name: _____

Name: _____

F. SUPPLEMENTAL INFORMATION (continued)

4. If your hospital hired RNs during the reporting period, how many were new graduates from nursing schools? _____

5. Describe the extent of your hospital's current partnerships with the following types of organizations for community or population health improvement initiatives.

	Not Involved	Collaboration	Formal Alliance
a. Health care providers outside your system	☐	☐	☐
b. Local or state public health organizations	☐	☐	☐
c. Local or state human/social service organizations	☐	☐	☐
d. Other local or state government	☐	☐	☐
e. Non-profit organizations	☐	☐	☐
f. Faith-based organizations	☐	☐	☐
g. Health insurance companies	☐	☐	☐
h. Schools	☐	☐	☐
i. Local businesses or chambers of commerce	☐	☐	☐
j. National businesses	☐	☐	☐
k. Other (list)_____	☐	☐	☐

6. Does your hospital have an established patient and family advisory council that meets regularly to actively engage the perspectives of patients and families?   Yes ☐   No ☐

7. Does your hospital have a policy or guidelines that facilitate unrestricted access, 24 hours a day, to hospitalized patients by family and other partners in care according to patient preference?

    a. ☐ Exists across all units

    b. ☐ Exists across some units

    c. ☐ Does not exist in any hospital unit

Use this space for comments or to elaborate on any information supplied on this survey. Refer to the response by page, section and item name.

_____

_____

_____

_____

_____

_____

_____

_____

_____

_____

_____

_____

As declared previously, hospital specific revenue data are treated as confidential. AHA's policy is not to release these data without written permission from your institution. The AHA will however, share these data with your respective state hospital association and if requested with your appropriate metropolitan/regional association.

On occasion, the AHA is asked to provide these data to external organizations, both public and private, for their use in analyzing crucial health care policy or research issues. The AHA is requesting your permission to allow us to release your confidential data to those requests that we consider legitimate and worthwhile. In every instance of disclosure, the receiving organization will be prohibited from releasing hospital specific information.

Please indicate below whether or not you agree to these types of disclosure:

[ ] I hereby grant AHA permission to release my hospital's revenue data to external users that the AHA determines have a legitimate and worthwhile need to gain access to these data subject to the user's agreement with the AHA not to release hospital specific information.

_____
Chief Executive Officer   Date

[ ] I do not grant AHA permission to release my confidential data.

_____
Chief Executive Officer   Date

With the exception of restrictions protecting certain confidential information, the results of this survey may be publically released.

Does your hospital or health system have an Internet or Homepage address?   Yes ☐ No ☐

If yes, please provide the address: http:// _____

Thank you for your cooperation in completing this survey. If there are any questions about your responses to this survey, who should be contacted?

_____   ( )_____
Name (please print)   Title   (Area Code) Telephone Number

___/___/___   _____   ( )_____
Date of Completion   Chief Executive Officer   Hospital's Main Fax Number

Contact Email address: _____

NOTE: PLEASE PHOTOCOPY THE INFORMATION FOR YOUR HOSPITAL FILE BEFORE RETURNING THE ORIGINAL FORM TO THE AMERICAN HOSPITAL ASSOCIATION. ALSO, PLEASE FORWARD A PHOTOCOPY OF THE COMPLETED QUESTIONNAIRE TO YOUR STATE HOSPITAL ASSOCIATION.

THANK YOU

INSTRUCTIONS AND DEFINITIONS FOR THE 2018 ANNUAL SURVEY OF HOSPITALS.
For purposes of this survey, a hospital is defined as the organization or corporate entity licensed or registered as a hospital by a state to provide diagnostic and therapeutic patient services for a variety of medical conditions, both surgical and nonsurgical.

1. **Reporting period used (beginning and ending date):** Record the beginning and ending dates of the reporting period in an eight-digit number: for example, January 1, 2019 should be shown as 01/01/2019. Number of days should equal the time span between the two dates that the hospital was open. If you are reporting for less than 365 days, utilization and finances should be presented for days reported only.
2. **Were you in operation 12 full months at the end of your reporting period?** If you are reporting for less than 365 days, utilization and finances should be presented for days reported only.
3. **Number of days open during reporting period:** Number of days should equal the time span between the two dates that the hospital was open.

SECTION B
ORGANIZATIONAL STRUCTURE
Instructions and Definitions

1. **CONTROL**
   Check the box to the left of the type of organization that is responsible for establishing policy for overall operation of the hospital.
   Government, nonfederal.
       State. Controlled by an agency of state government.
       County. Controlled by an agency of county government.
       City. Controlled by an agency of municipal government.
       City-County. Controlled jointly by agencies of municipal and county governments.
       Hospital district or authority. Controlled by a political subdivision of a state, county, or city created solely for the purpose of establishing and maintaining medical care or health-related care institutions.
   Nongovernment, not for profit. Controlled by not-for-profit organizations, including religious organizations (Catholic hospitals, for example), community hospitals, cooperative hospitals, hospitals operated by fraternal societies, and so forth.
   Investor owned, for profit. Controlled on a for profit basis by an individual, partnership, or a profit making corporation.
   Government, federal. Controlled by an agency or department of the federal government.
2. **SERVICE**
   Indicate the ONE category that best describes the type of service that your hospital provides to the majority of patients.
   General medical and surgical. Provides diagnostic and therapeutic services to patients for a variety of medical conditions, both surgical and nonsurgical.
   Hospital unit of an institution. Provides diagnostic and therapeutic services to patients in an institution.
   Hospital unit within a facility for persons with intellectual disabilities. Provides diagnostic and therapeutic services to persons with intellectual disabilities.
   Surgical. An acute care specialty hospital where 2/3 or more of its inpatient claims are for surgical/diagnosis related groups.
   Psychiatric. Provides diagnostic and therapeutic services to patients with mental or emotional disorders.
   Tuberculosis and other respiratory diseases. Provides medical care and rehabilitative services to patients for whom the primary diagnosis is tuberculosis or other respiratory diseases.
   Cancer. Provides medical care to patients for whom the primary diagnosis is cancer.
   Heart. Provides diagnosis and treatment of heart disease.
   Obstetrics and gynecology. Provides medical and surgical treatment to pregnant women and to mothers following delivery. Also provides diagnostic and therapeutic services to women with diseases or disorders of the reproductive organs.
   Eye, ear, nose, and throat. Provides diagnosis and treatment of diseases and injuries of the eyes, ears, nose, and throat.
   Rehabilitation. Provides a comprehensive array of restoration services for people with disabilities and all support services necessary to help them attain their maximum functional capacity.
   Orthopedic. Provides corrective treatment of deformities, diseases, and ailments of the locomotive apparatus, especially affecting the limbs, bones, muscles, and joints.
   Chronic disease. Provides medical and skilled nursing services to patients with long-term illnesses who are not in an acute phase, but who require an intensity of services not available in nursing homes.
   Intellectual disabilities. Provides health-related care on a regular basis to patients with developmental or intellectual disabilities who cannot be treated in a skilled nursing unit.
   Acute long-term care hospital. Provides high acuity interdisciplinary services to medically complex patients that require more intensive recuperation and care than can be provided in a typical nursing facility.
   Alcoholism and other chemical dependency. Provides diagnostic and therapeutic services to patients with alcoholism or other drug dependencies.
3. **OTHER**
   a. **Children admissions.** A hospital whose primary focus is the health and treatment of children and adolescents.
   b. **Subsidiary.** A company that is wholly controlled by another or one that is more than 50% owned by another organization.
   c. **Contract managed.** General day-to-day management of an entire organization by another organization under a formal contract. Managing organization reports directly to the board of trustees or owners of the managed organization; managed organization retains total legal responsibility and ownership of the facility's assets and liabilities.
   d. **Physician group.** Cooperative practice of medicine by a group of physicians, each of whom as a rule specializes in some particular field.
   f. **Co-located hospitals.** Co-location refers to two or more entities, with separate CMS Certification Numbers occupying the same building, or conjoined buildings.

SECTION C
FACILITIES AND SERVICES
Definitions

Owned/provided by the hospital or its subsidiary. All patient revenues, expenses and utilization related to the provision of the service are reflected in the hospital's statistics reported elsewhere in this survey.

Provided by my health system (in my local community). Another health care provider in the same system as your hospital provides the service and patient revenue, expenses, and utilization related to the provision of the service are recorded at the point where the service was provided and would not be reflected in your hospital's statistics reported elsewhere in this survey. (A system is a corporate body that owns, leases, religiously sponsors and/or manages health providers)

Provided through a partnership or joint venture with another provider that is not in my system. All patient revenues and utilization related to the provision of the service are recorded at the site where the service was provided and would not be reflected in your hospital statistics reported elsewhere in this survey. (A joint venture is a contractual arrangement between two or more parties forming an unincorporated business. The participants in the arrangement remain independent and separate outside of the venture's purpose.)

1. **General medical-surgical care.** Provides acute care to patients in medical and surgical units on the basis of physicians' orders and approved nursing care plans.
2. **Pediatric medical-surgical care.** Provides acute care to pediatric patients on the basis of physicians' orders and approved nursing care plans.
3. **Obstetrics.** For service owned or provided by the hospital, level should be designated: (1) unit provides services for uncomplicated maternity and newborn cases; (2) unit provides services for uncomplicated cases, the majority of complicated problems, and special neonatal services; and (3) unit provides services for all serious illnesses and abnormalities and is supervised by a full-time maternal/fetal specialist.
4. **Medical-surgical intensive care.** Provides patient care of a more intensive nature than the usual medical and surgical care, on the basis of physicians' orders and approved nursing care plans. These units are staffed with specially trained nursing personnel and contain monitoring and specialized support equipment for patients who because of shock, trauma or other life-threatening conditions require intensified comprehensive observation and care. Includes mixed intensive care units.
5. **Cardiac intensive care.** Provides patient care of a more specialized nature than the usual medical and surgical care, on the basis of physicians' orders and approved nursing care plans. The unit is staffed with specially trained nursing personnel and contains monitoring and specialized support or treatment equipment for patients who, because of heart seizure, open-heart surgery, or other life-threatening conditions, require intensified, comprehensive observation and care. May include myocardial infarction, pulmonary care, and heart transplant units.
6. **Neonatal intensive care.** A unit that must be separate from the newborn nursery providing intensive care to all sick infants including those with the very lowest birth weights (less than 1500 grams). NICU has potential for providing mechanical ventilation, neonatal surgery, and special care for the sickest infants born in the hospital or transferred from another institution. A full-time neonatologist serves as director of the NICU.
7. **Neonatal intermediate care.** A unit that must be separate from the normal newborn nursery and that provides intermediate and/or recovery care and some specialized services, including immediate resuscitation, intravenous therapy, and capacity for prolonged oxygen therapy and monitoring.
8. **Pediatric intensive care.** Provides care to pediatric patients that is of a more intensive nature than that usually provided to pediatric Patients. The unit is staffed with specially trained personnel and contains monitoring and specialized support equipment for treatment of patients who, because of shock, trauma, or other life-threatening conditions, require intensified, comprehensive observation and care.
9. **Burn care.** Provides care to severely burned patients. Severely burned patients are those with any of the following: (1) second-degree burns of more than 25% total body surface area for adults or 20% total body surface area for children: (2) third-degree burns of more than 10% total body surface area; (3) any severe burns of the hands, face, eyes, ears, or feet; or (4) all inhalation injuries, electrical burns, complicated burn injuries involving fractures and other major traumas, and all other poor risk factors.
10. **Other special care.** Provides care to patients requiring care more intensive than that provided in the acute area, yet not sufficiently intensive to require admission to an intensive care unit. Patients admitted to this area are usually transferred here from an intensive care unit once their condition has improved. These units are sometimes referred to as definitive observation, step-down or progressive care units.
11. **Other intensive care.** A specially staffed, specialty equipped, separate section of a hospital dedicated to the observation, care, and treatment of patients with life-threatening illnesses, injuries, or complications from which recovery is possible. It provides special expertise and facilities for the support of vital function and utilizes the skill of medical nursing and other staff experienced in the management of these problems.
12. **Physical rehabilitation.** Provides care encompassing a comprehensive array of restoration services for people with disabilities and all support services necessary to help patients attain their maximum functional capacity.
13. **Alcoholism-chemical dependency care.** Provides diagnosis and therapeutic services to patients with alcoholism or other drug dependencies. Includes care for inpatient/residential treatment for patients whose course of treatment involves more intensive care than provided in an outpatient setting or where patient requires supervised withdrawal.
14. **Psychiatric care.** Provides acute or long-term care to patients with mental or emotional disorders, including patients admitted for diagnosis and those admitted for treatment of psychiatric disorders, on the basis of physicians' orders and approved nursing care plans. Long-term care may include intensive supervision to persons with chronic/severe mental illness.
15. **Skilled nursing care.** Provides non-acute medical and skilled nursing care services, therapy, and social services under the supervision of a licensed registered nurse on a 24-hour basis.
16. **Intermediate nursing care.** Provides health-related services (skilled nursing care and social services) to residents with a variety of physical conditions or functional disabilities. These residents do not require the care provided by a hospital or skilled nursing facility, but do need supervision and support services.
17. **Acute long-term care.** Provides specialized acute hospital care to medically complex patients who are critically ill, have multisystem complications and/or failure, and require hospitalization averaging 25 days, in a facility offering specialized treatment programs and therapeutic intervention on a 24-hour/7 days a week basis.
18. **Other long-term care.** Provision of long-term care other than skilled nursing care or intermediate care for those who do not require daily medical or nursing services, but may requires some assistance in the activities of daily living. This can include residential care, elderly care, or care facilities for those with developmental or intellectual disabilities.
19. **Other care.** (specify) Any type of care other than those listed above.
    The sum of the beds reported in Section C 1-19 should equal what you have reported in Section E(1b) for beds set up and staffed.
20. **Adult day care program.** Program providing supervision, medical and psychological care, and social activities for older adults who live at home or in another family setting, but cannot be alone or prefer to be with others during the day. May include intake assessment, health monitoring, occupational therapy, personal care, noon meal, and transportation services.
21. **Airborne infection isolation room.** A single-occupancy room for patient care where environmental factors are controlled in an effort to minimize the transmission of those infectious agents, usually spread person to person by droplet nuclei associated with coughing and inhalation. Such rooms typically have specific ventilation requirements for controlled ventilation, air pressure and filtration.

22. **Alcoholism-chemical dependency care services.**
    a. **Alcoholism-chemical dependency pediatric care services.** Provides diagnosis and therapeutic services to pediatric patients with alcoholism or other drug dependencies. Includes care for inpatient/residential treatment for patients whose course of treatment involves more intensive care than provided in an outpatient setting or where patient requires supervised withdrawal. Please report staffed beds. <u>The beds reported here should also be reported under 13, alcoholism-chemical dependency care. This line item should be a breakout of the pediatric beds only.</u>
    b. **Alcoholism-chemical dependency outpatient services.** Organized hospital services that provide medical care and/or rehabilitative treatment services to outpatients for whom the primary diagnosis is alcoholism or other chemical dependency.
    c. **Alcoholism-chemical dependency partial hospitalization services.** Organized hospital services providing intensive day/evening outpatient services of three hour or more duration, distinguished from other outpatient visits of one hour.
23. **Alzheimer center.** Facility that offers care to persons with Alzheimer's disease and their families through an integrated program of clinical services, research, and education.
24. **Ambulance services.** Provision of ambulance service to the ill and injured who require medical attention on a scheduled and unscheduled basis.
25. **Air ambulance services.** Aircraft and especially a helicopter equipped for transporting the injured or sick. Most air ambulances carry critically ill or injured patients, whose condition could rapidly change for the worse.
26. **Ambulatory surgery center.** Facility that provides care to patients requiring surgery that are admitted and discharged on the same day. Ambulatory surgery centers are distinct from same day surgical units within the hospital outpatient departments for purposes of Medicare payment.
27. **Arthritis treatment center.** Specifically equipped and staffed center for the diagnosis and treatment of arthritis and other joint disorders.
28. **Auxiliary.** A volunteer community organization formed to assist the hospital in carrying out its purpose and to serve as a link between the institution and the community.
29. **Bariatric/weight control services.** The medical practice of weight reduction.
30. **Birthing room/LDR room/LDRP room.** A single-room type of maternity care with a more homelike setting for families than the traditional three-room unit (labor/delivery/recovery) with a separate postpartum area. A birthing room combines labor and delivery in one room. An LDR room accommodates three stages in the birthing process--labor, delivery, and recovery. An LDRP room accommodates all four stages of the birth process--labor, delivery, recovery, and postpartum.
31. **Blood donor center.** A facility that performs, or is responsible for the collection, processing, testing or distribution of blood and components.
32. **Breast cancer screening/mammograms.** Mammography screening - The use of breast x-ray to detect unsuspected breast cancer in asymptomatic women. Diagnostic mammography - The x-ray imaging of breast tissue in symptomatic women who are considered to have a substantial likelihood of having breast cancer already.
33. **Cardiology and cardiac surgery services.** Services which include the diagnosis and treatment of diseases and disorders involving the heart and circulatory system.
    a-b. **Cardiology services.** An organized clinical service offering diagnostic and interventional procedures to manage the full range of heart conditions.
    c-d. **Diagnostic catheterization.** (also called coronary angiography or coronary arteriography) is used to assist in diagnosing complex heart conditions. Cardiac angiography involves the insertion of a tiny catheter into the artery in the groin then carefully threading the catheter up into the aorta where the coronary arteries originate. Once the catheter is in place, a dye is injected which allows the cardiologist to see the size, shape, and distribution of the coronary arteries. These images are used to diagnose heart disease and to determine, among other things, whether or not surgery is indicated.
    e-f. **Interventional cardiac catheterization.** Nonsurgical procedure that utilizes the same basic principles as diagnostic catheterization and then uses advanced techniques to improve the heart's function. It can be a less invasive alternative to heart surgery.
    g-h. **Cardiac surgery.** Includes minimally invasive procedures that include surgery done with only a small incision or no incision at all, such as through a laparoscope or an endoscope and more invasive major surgical procedures that include open chest and open heart surgery.
    i-j. **Cardiac electrophysiology.** Evaluation and management of patients with complex rhythm or conduction abnormalities, including diagnostic testing, treatment of arrhythmias by catheter ablation or drug therapy, and pacemaker/defibrillator implantation and follow-up.
    k. **Cardiac rehabilitation.** A medically supervised program to help heart patients recover quickly and improve their overall physical and mental functioning. The goal is to reduce risk of another cardiac event or to keep an already present heart condition from getting worse. Cardiac rehabilitation programs include: counseling to patients, an exercise program, helping patients modify risk factors such as smoking and high blood pressure, providing vocational guidance to enable the patient to return to work, supplying information on physical limitations and lending emotional support.
34. **Case management.** A system of assessment, treatment planning, referral and follow-up that ensures the provision of comprehensive and continuous services and the coordination of payment and reimbursement for care.
35. **Chaplaincy/pastoral care services.** A service ministering religious activities and providing pastoral counseling to patients, their families, and staff of a health care organization.
36. **Chemotherapy.** An organized program for the treatment of cancer by the use of drugs or chemicals.
37. **Children's wellness program.** A program that encourages improved health status and a healthful lifestyle of children through health education, exercise, nutrition and health promotion.
38. **Chiropractic services.** An organized clinical service including spinal manipulation or adjustment and related diagnostic and therapeutic services.
39. **Community outreach.** A program that systematically interacts with the community to identify those in need of services, alerting persons and their families to the availability of services, locating needed services, and enabling persons to enter the service delivery system.
40. **Complementary and alternative medicine services.** Organized hospital services or formal arrangements to providers that provide care or treatment not based solely on traditional western allopathic medical teachings as instructed in most U.S. medical schools. Includes any of the following: acupuncture, chiropractic, homeopathy, osteopathy, diet and lifestyle changes, herbal medicine, massage therapy, etc.
41. **Computer assisted orthopedic surgery (CAOS).** Orthopedic surgery using computer technology, enabling three-dimensional graphic models to visualize a patient's anatomy.
42. **Crisis prevention.** Services provided in order to promote physical and mental wellbeing and the early identification of disease and ill health prior to the onset and recognition of symptoms so as to permit early treatment.
43. **Dental services.** An organized dental service or dentists on staff, not necessarily involving special facilities, providing dental or oral services to inpatients or outpatients.
44. **Diabetes prevention program.** Program to prevent or delay the onset of type 2 diabetes by offering evidence-based lifestyle changes based on research studies, which showed modest behavior changes helped individuals with prediabetes reduce their risk of developing type 2 diabetes.
45. **Emergency services.** Health services that are provided after the onset of a medical condition that manifests itself by symptoms of sufficient severity, including severe pain, that the absence of immediate medical attention could reasonably be expected by a prudent layperson, who possesses an average knowledge of health and medicine, to result in placing the patient's health in serious jeopardy.
    a. **On-campus emergency department.** Hospital facilities for the provision of unscheduled outpatient services to patients whose conditions require immediate care.
    b. **Off-campus emergency department.** A facility owned and operated by the hospital but physically separate from the hospital for the provision of unscheduled outpatient services to patients whose conditions require immediate care. A freestanding ED is not physically connected to a hospital but has all the necessary emergency staffing and equipment on site.

c. **Pediatric emergency department.** A recognized hospital emergency department capable of identifying those pediatric patients who are critically ill or injured, stabilizing pediatric patients, including the management of airway, breathing and circulation and providing an appropriate transfer to a definitive care facility.

d. **Trauma center (certified).** A facility to provide emergency and specialized intensive care to critically ill and injured patients. For service owned or provided by the hospital, please specify trauma level. Level 1: A regional resource trauma center, which is capable of providing total care for every aspect of injury and plays a leadership role in trauma research and education. Level 2: A community trauma center, which is capable of providing trauma care to all but the most severely injured patients who require highly specialized care. Level 3: A rural trauma hospital, which is capable of providing care to a large number of injury victims and can resuscitate and stabilize more severely injured patients so that they can be transported to level 1 or 2 facilities.

46. **Enabling services.** A program that is designed to help the patient access health care services by offering any of the following: transportation services and/or referrals to local social services agencies.

47. **Endoscopic services.**
   a. **Optical colonoscopy.** An examination of the interior of the colon using a long, flexible, lighted tube with a small built-in camera.
   b. **Endoscopic ultrasound.** Specially designed endoscope that incorporates an ultrasound transducer used to obtain detailed images of organs in the chest and abdomen. The endoscope can be passed through the mouth or the anus. When combined with needle biopsy the procedure can assist in diagnosis of disease and staging of cancer.
   c. **Ablation of Barrett's esophagus.** Premalignant condition that can lead to adenocarcinoma of the esophagus. The nonsurgical ablation of premalignant tissue in Barrett's esophagus by the application of thermal energy or light through an endoscope passed from the mouth into the esophagus.
   d. **Esophageal impedance study.** A test in which a catheter is placed through the nose into the esophagus to measure whether gas or liquids are passing from the stomach into the esophagus and causing symptoms.
   e. **Endoscopic retrograde cholangiopancreatography (ERCP).** A procedure in which a catheter is introduced through an endoscope into the bile ducts and pancreatic ducts. Injection of contrast material permits detailed x-ray of these structures. The procedure is used diagnostically as well as therapeutically to relieve obstruction or remove stones.

48. **Enrollment (insurance) assistance services.** A program that provides enrollment assistance for patients who are potentially eligible for public health insurance programs such as Medicaid, State Children's Health Insurance, or local/state indigent care programs. The specific services offered could include explanation of benefits, assist applicants in completing the application and locating all relevant documents, conduct eligibility interviews, and/or forward applications and documentation to state/local social service or health agency.

49. **Employment support services.** Services designed to support individuals with significant disabilities to seek and maintain employment.

50. **Extracorporeal shock wave lithotripter (ESWL).** A medical device used for treating stones in the kidney or urethra. The device disintegrates kidney stones noninvasively through the transmission of acoustic shock waves directed at the stones.

51. **Fertility clinic.** A specialized program set in an infertility center that provides counseling and education as well as advanced reproductive techniques such as: injectable therapy, reproductive surgeries, treatment for endometriosis, male factor infertility, tubal reversals, in vitro fertilization (IVF), donor eggs, and other such services to help patients achieve successful pregnancies.

52. **Fitness center.** Provides exercise, testing, or evaluation programs and fitness activities to the community and hospital employees.

53. **Freestanding outpatient care center.** A facility owned and operated by the hospital that is physically separate from the hospital and provides various medical treatments and diagnostic services on an outpatient basis only. Laboratory and radiology services are usually available.

54. **Geriatric services.** The branch of medicine dealing with the physiology of aging and the diagnosis and treatment of disease affecting the aged. Services could include: adult day care; Alzheimer's diagnostic-assessment services; comprehensive geriatric assessment; emergency response system; geriatric acute care unit; and/or geriatric clinics.

55. **Health fair.** Community health education events that focus on the prevention of disease and promotion of health through such activities as audiovisual exhibits and free diagnostic services.

56. **Community health education.** Education that provides health information to individuals and populations as well as support for personal, family and community health decisions with the objective of improving health status.

57. **Genetic testing/counseling.** A service equipped with adequate laboratory facilities and directed by a qualified physician to advise patients on potential genetic diagnosis of vulnerabilities to inherited diseases. A genetic test is the analysis of human DNA, RNA, chromosomes, proteins, and certain metabolites in order to detect heritable disease-related genotypes, mutations, phenotypes, or karyotypes for clinical purposes. Genetic tests can have diverse purposes, including the diagnosis of genetic diseases in newborns, children, and adults; the identification of future health risks; the prediction of drug responses; and the assessment of risks to future children.

58. **Health screening.** A preliminary procedure such as a test or examination to detect the most characteristic sign or signs of a disorder that may require further investigation.

59. **Health research.** Organized hospital research program in any of the following areas: basic research, clinical research, community health research, and/or research on innovative health care delivery.

60. **Hemodialysis.** Provision of equipment and personnel for the treatment of renal insufficiency on an inpatient or outpatient basis.

61. **HIV/AIDS services.** Diagnosis, treatment, continuing care planning, and counseling services for HIV/AIDS patients and their families. Could include: HIV/AIDS unit, special unit or designated team, general inpatient care, or specialized outpatient program.

62. **Home health services.** Service providing nursing, therapy, and health-related homemaker or social services in the patient's home.

63. **Hospice.** A program providing palliative care, chiefly medical relief of pain and supportive services, addressing the emotional, social, financial, and legal needs of terminally ill patients and their families. Care can be provided in a variety of settings, both inpatient and at home.

64. **Hospital-based outpatient care center-services.** Organized hospital health care services offered by appointment on an ambulatory basis. Services may include outpatient surgery, examination, diagnosis, and treatment of a variety of medical conditions on a nonemergency basis, and laboratory and other diagnostic testing as ordered by staff or outside physician referral.

65a. **Assisted living.** A special combination of housing, supportive services, personalized assistance and health care designed to respond to the individual needs of those who need help in activities of daily living and instrumental activities of daily living. Supportive services are available, 24 hours a day, to meet scheduled and unscheduled needs, in a way that promotes maximum independence and dignity for each resident and encourages the involvement of a resident's family, neighbor and friends.

65b. **Retirement housing.** A facility that provides social activities to senior citizens, usually retired persons, who do not require health care but some short-term skilled nursing care may be provided. A retirement center may furnish housing and may also have acute hospital and long-term care facilities, or it may arrange for acute and long-term care through affiliated institutions.

65c. **Supportive housing services.** A hospital program that provides decent, safe, affordable, community-based housing with flexible support services designed to help the individual or family stay housed and live a more productive life in the community.

66. **Immunization program.** Program that plans, coordinates and conducts immunization services in the community.

67. **Indigent care clinic.** Health care services for uninsured and underinsured persons where care is free of charge or charged on a sliding scale. This would include "free clinics" staffed by volunteer practitioners, but could also be staffed by employees with the sponsoring health care organization subsidizing the cost of service.

68. **Linguistic/translation services.** Services provided by the hospital designed to make health care more accessible to non-English speaking patients and their physicians.

69. **Meal delivery services.** A hospital sponsored program which delivers meals to people, usually the elderly, who are unable to prepare their own meals. Low cost, nutritional meals are delivered to individuals' homes on a regular basis.
70. **Mobile health services.** Vans and other vehicles used for delivery of primary care services.
71. **Neurological services.** Services provided by the hospital dealing with the operative and nonoperative management of disorders of the central, peripheral, and autonomic nervous systems.
72. **Nutrition programs.** Services within a health care facility which are designed to provide inexpensive, nutritionally sound meals to patients.
73. **Occupational health services.** Includes services designed to protect the safety of employees from hazards in the work environment.
74. **Oncology services.** Inpatient and outpatient services for patients with cancer, including comprehensive care, support and guidance in addition to patient education and prevention, chemotherapy, counseling and other treatment methods.
75. **Orthopedic services.** Services provided for the prevention or correction of injuries or disorders of the skeletal system and associated muscles, joints and ligaments.
76. **Outpatient surgery.** Scheduled surgical services provided to patients who do not remain in the hospital overnight. The surgery may be performed in operating suites also used for inpatient surgery, specially designated surgical suites for outpatient surgery, or procedure rooms within an outpatient care facility.
77. **Pain management program.** A recognized clinical service or program providing specialized medical care, drugs or therapies for the management of acute or chronic pain and other distressing symptoms, administered by specially trained physicians and other clinicians, to patients suffering from acute illnesses of diverse causes.
78. **Palliative care program.** An organized program providing specialized medical care, drugs or therapies for the management of acute or chronic pain and/or the control of symptoms administered by specially trained physicians and other clinicians; and supportive care services, such as counseling on advanced directives, spiritual care, and social services, to patients with advanced diseases and their families.
79. **Palliative care inpatient unit.** An inpatient palliative care ward is a physically discreet, inpatient nursing unit where the focus is palliative care. The patient care focus is on symptom relief for complex patients who may be continuing to undergo primary treatment. Care is delivered by palliative medicine specialists.
80. **Patient controlled analgesia (PCA).** Intravenously administered pain medicine under the patient's control. The patient has a button on the end of a cord than can be pushed at will, whenever more pain medicine is desired. This button will only deliver more pain medicine at predetermined intervals, as programmed by the doctor's order.
81. **Patient education center.** Written goals and objectives for the patient and/or family related to therapeutic regimens, medical procedures, and self-care.
82. **Patient representative services.** Organized hospital services providing personnel through whom patients and staff can seek solutions to institutional problems affecting the delivery of high quality care and services.
83. **Physical rehabilitation services.** Program providing medical, health-related, therapy, social, and/or vocational services to help people with disabilities attain or retain their maximum functional capacity.
   a. **Assistive technology center.** A program providing access to specialized hardware and software with adaptations allowing individuals greater independence with mobility, dexterity, or increased communication options.
   b. **Electrodiagnostic services.** Diagnostic testing services for nerve and muscle function such as nerve conduction studies and needle electromyography.
   c. **Physical rehabilitation outpatient services.** Outpatient program providing medical, health-related, therapy, social, and/or vocational services to help people with disabilities attain or retain their maximum functional capacity.
   d. **Prosthetic and orthotic services.** Services providing comprehensive prosthetic and orthotic evaluation, fitting, and training.
   e. **Robot-assisted walking therapy.** A form of physical therapy that uses a robotic device to assist patients who are relearning how to walk.
   f. **Simulated rehabilitation environment.** Rehabilitation focused on retraining functional skills in a contextually appropriate environment (simulated home and community settings) or in a traditional setting (gymnasium) using motor learning principles.
84. **Primary care department.** A unit or clinic within the hospital that provides primary care services (e.g., general pediatric care, general internal medicine, family practice, gynecology) through hospital-salaried medical and/or nursing staff, focusing on evaluating and diagnosing medical problems and providing medical treatment on an outpatient basis.
85. **Psychiatric services.** Services provided by the hospital that offer immediate initial evaluation and treatment to patients with mental or emotional disorders.
   a. **Psychiatric consultation-liaison services.** Provides organized psychiatric consultation/liaison services to nonpsychiatric hospital staff and/or departments on psychological aspects of medical care that may be generic or specific to individual patients.
   b. **Psychiatric pediatric services.** The branch of medicine focused on the diagnosis, treatment and prevention of mental, emotional and behavioral disorders in pediatric patients. Please report the number of staffed beds. <u>The beds reported here should be included in the staffed bed count for 14 psychiatric care.</u>
   c. **Psychiatric geriatric services.** Provides care to elderly patients with mental or emotional disorders, including those admitted for diagnosis and those admitted for treatment. Please report the number of staffed beds. <u>The beds reported here should be included in the staffed bed count for 14 psychiatric care.</u>
   d. **Psychiatric education services.** Provides psychiatric educational services to community agencies and workers such as schools, police, courts, public health nurses, welfare agencies, clergy, and so forth. The purpose is to expand the mental health knowledge and competence of personnel not working in the mental health field and to promote good mental health through improved understanding, attitudes, and behavioral patterns.
   e. **Psychiatric emergency services.** Services of facilities available on a 24-hour basis to provide immediate unscheduled outpatient care, diagnosis, evaluation, crisis intervention, and assistance to persons suffering acute emotional or mental distress.
   f. **Psychiatric outpatient services.** Provides medical care, including diagnosis and treatment, of psychiatric outpatients.
   g. **Psychiatric intensive outpatient services.** A prescribed course of treatment in which the patient receives outpatient care no less than three times a week (which might include more than one service/day).
   h-i. **Psychiatric partial hospitalization program – adult/pediatric.** Organized hospital services providing intensive day/evening outpatient services of three hours or more duration, distinguished from other outpatient visits of one hour.
   j-k. **Psychiatric residential treatment – adult/pediatric.** Overnight psychiatric care in conjunction with an intensive treatment program in a setting other than a hospital.
86. **Radiology, diagnostic.** The branch of radiology that deals with the utilization of all modalities of radiant energy in medical diagnoses and therapeutic procedures using radiologic guidance. This includes, but is not restricted to, imaging techniques and methodologies utilizing radiation emitted by x-ray tubes, radionuclides, and ultrasonographic devices and the radiofrequency electromagnetic radiation emitted by atoms.
   a. **CT Scanner.** Computed tomographic scanner for head or whole body scans.
   b. **Diagnostic radioisotope facility.** The use of radioactive isotopes (Radiopharmaceuticals) as tracers or indicators to detect an abnormal condition or disease.
   c. **Electron beam computed tomography (EBCT).** A high tech computed tomography scan used to detect coronary artery disease by measuring coronary calcifications. This imaging procedure uses electron beams which are magnetically steered to produce a visual of the coronary artery and the images are produced faster than conventional CT scans.

d. **Full-field digital mammography (FFDM).** Combines the x-ray generators and tubes used in analog screen-film mammography (SFM) with a detector plate that converts the x-rays into a digital signal.

e. **Magnetic resonance imaging (MRI).** The use of a uniform magnetic field and radio frequencies to study tissue and structure of the body. This procedure enables the visualization of biochemical activity of the cell in vivo without the use of ionizing radiation, radioisotopic substances or high-frequency sound.

f. **Intraoperative magnetic resonance imaging.** An integrated surgery system which provides an MRI system in an operating room. The system allows for immediate evaluation of the degree to tumor resection while the patient is undergoing a surgical resection. Intraoperative MRI exists when a MRI (low-field or high-field) is placed in the operating theater and is used during surgical resection without moving the patient from the operating room to the diagnostic imaging suite.

g. **Magnetoencephalography (MEG).** A noninvasive neurophysiological measurement tool used to study magnetic fields generated by neuronal activity of the brain. MEG provides direct information about the dynamics of evoked and spontaneous neural activity and its location in the brain. The primary uses of MEG include assisting surgeons in localizing the source of epilepsy, sensory mapping, and the study of brain function. When it is combined with structural imaging, it is known as *magnetic source imaging* (MSI).

h. **Multi-slice spiral computed tomography (<64+slice CT).** A specialized computed tomography procedure that provides three-dimensional processing and allows narrower and multiple slices with increased spatial resolution and faster scanning times as compared to a regular computed tomography scan.

i. **Multi-slice spiral computed tomography (64+ slice CT).** Involves the acquisition of volumetric tomographic x-ray absorption data expressed in Hounsfield units using multiple rows of detectors. 64+ systems reconstruct the equivalent of 64 or more slices to cover the imaged volume.

j. **Positron emission tomography (PET).** A nuclear medicine imaging technology which uses radioactive (positron emitting) isotopes created in a cyclotron or generator and computers to produce composite pictures of the brain and heart at work. PET scanning produces sectional images depicting metabolic activity or blood flow rather than anatomy.

k. **Positron emission tomography/CT (PET/CT).** Provides metabolic functional information for the monitoring of chemotherapy, radiotherapy and surgical planning.

l. **Single photon emission computerized tomography (SPECT).** A nuclear medicine imaging technology that combines existing technology of gamma camera imaging with computed tomographic imaging technology to provide a clearer and more precise image.

m. **Ultrasound.** The use of acoustic waves above the range of 20,000 cycles per second to visualize internal body structures.

87. **Radiology, therapeutic.** The branch of medicine concerned with radioactive substances and using various techniques of visualization, with the diagnosis and treatment of disease using any of the various sources of radiant energy. Services could include: megavoltage radiation therapy; radioactive implants; stereotactic radiosurgery; therapeutic radioisotope facility; X-ray radiation therapy.

a. **Image-guided radiation therapy (IGRT).** Automated system for image-guided radiation therapy that enables clinicians to obtain high-resolution x-ray images to pinpoint tumor sites, adjust patient positioning when necessary, and complete a treatment, all within the standard treatment time slot, allowing for more effective cancer treatments.

b. **Intensity-Modulated Radiation Therapy (IMRT).** A type of three-dimensional radiation therapy which improves treatment delivery by targeting a tumor in a way that is likely to decrease damage to normal tissues and allows for varying intensities.

c. **Proton beam therapy.** A form of radiation therapy which administers proton beams. While producing the same biologic effects as x-ray beams, the energy distribution of protons differs from conventional x-ray beams: proton beams can be more precisely focused in tissue volumes in a three-dimensional pattern, resulting in less surrounding tissue damage than conventional radiation therapy, permitting administration of higher doses.

d. **Shaped beam radiation system.** A precise, noninvasive treatment that involves targeted beams of radiation that mirror the exact size and shape of a tumor at a specific area to shrink or destroy cancerous cells. This procedure delivers a therapeutic dose of radiation that conforms precisely to the shape of the tumor, thus minimizing the risk to nearby tissues.

e. **Stereotactic radiosurgery.** A radiotherapy modality that delivers a high dosage of radiation to a discrete treatment area in as few as one treatment session. Includes Gamma Knife, Cyberknife, etc.

88. **Robotic surgery.** The use of mechanical guidance devices to remotely manipulate surgical instrumentation.

89. **Rural health clinic.** A clinic located in a rural, medically under-served area in the United States that has a separate reimbursement structure from the standard medical office under the Medicare and Medicaid programs.

90. **Sleep center.** Specially equipped and staffed center for the diagnosis and treatment of sleep disorders.

91. **Social work services.** Could include: organized services that are properly directed and sufficiently staffed by qualified individuals who provide assistance and counseling to patients and their families in dealing with social, emotional, and environmental problems associated with illness or disability, often in the context of financial or discharge planning coordination.

92. **Sports medicine.** Provision of diagnostic screening, assessment, clinical and rehabilitation services for the prevention and treatment of sports-related injuries.

93. **Support groups.** A hospital sponsored program that allows a group of individuals with common experiences or issues who meet periodically to share experiences, problems, and solutions in order to support each other.

94. **Swing bed services.** A hospital bed that can be used to provide either acute or long-term care depending on community or patient needs. To be eligible a hospital must have a Medicare provider agreement in place, have fewer than 100 beds, be located in a rural area, not have a 24-hour nursing service waiver in effect, have not been terminated from the program in the prior two years, and meet various service conditions.

95. **Teen outreach services.** A program focusing on the teenager which encourages an improved health status and a healthful lifestyle including physical, emotional, mental, social, spiritual and economic health through education, exercise, nutrition and health promotion.

96. **Tobacco treatment/cessation program.** Organized hospital services with the purpose of ending tobacco-use habits of patients addicted to tobacco/nicotine.

97. **Telehealth.** A broad variety of technologies and tactics to deliver virtual medical, public health, health education delivery and support services using telecommunications technologies. Telehealth is used more commonly as it describes the wide range of diagnosis and management, education, and other related fields of health care. This includes, but are not limited to: dentistry, counseling, physical and occupational therapy, home health, chronic disease monitoring and management, disaster management and consumer and professional education.

b. **eICU.** An electronic intensive care unit (eICU), also referred to as a tele-ICU, is a form of telemedicine that uses state of the art technology to provide an additional layer of critical care service. The goal of an eICU is to optimize clinical experience and facilitate 24-hour a day care by ICU caregivers.

c. **Stroke care.** Stroke telemedicine is a consultative modality that facilitates the care of patients with acute stroke by specialists at stroke centers.

d. **Psychiatric and addiction treatment.** Telepsychiatry can involve a range of services including psychiatric evaluations, therapy, patient education, and medication management.

e. **Remote patient monitoring.** The use of digital technologies to collect medical and other forms of health data from individuals in one location and electronically transmit the information securely to health care providers in a different location for assessment and recommendation.

98. **Transplant services.** The branch of medicine that transfers an organ or tissue from one person to another or from one body part to another, to replace a diseased structure or to restore function or to change appearance. Services could include: Bone marrow, heart, lung, kidney, intestine, or tissue transplant. Please include heart/lung or other multi-transplant surgeries in 'other'.

99. **Transportation to health facilities. (non-emergency)** A long-term care support service designed to assist the mobility of the elderly. Some programs offer improved financial access by offering reduced rates and barrier-free buses or vans with ramps and lifts to assist the elderly or people with disabilities; others offer subsidies for public transport systems or operate mini-bus services exclusively for use by senior citizens.

100. **Urgent care center.** A facility that provides care and treatment for problems that are not life threatening but require attention over the short term.

101. **Violence Prevention**
   a. **Workplace.** A violence prevention program with goals and objectives for preventing workplace violence against staff and patients.
   b. **Community**. An organized program that attempts to make a positive impact on the type(s) of violence a community is experiencing. For example, it can assist victims of violent crimes, e.g., rape, or incidents, e.g., bullying, to hospital or to community services to prevent further victimization or retaliation. A program that targets the underlying circumstances that contribute to violence such as poor housing, insufficient job training, and/or substance abuse through means such direct involvement and support, education, mentoring, anger management, crisis intervention and training programs would also qualify.

102. **Virtual colonoscopy.** Noninvasive screening procedure used to visualize, analyze and detect cancerous or potentially cancerous polyps in the colon.

103. **Volunteer services department.** An organized hospital department responsible for coordinating the services of volunteers working within the institution.

104. **Women's health center/services.** An area set aside for coordinated education and treatment services specifically for and promoted to women as provided by this special unit. Services may or may not include obstetrics but include a range of services other than OB.

105. **Wound management services.** Services for patients with chronic wounds and nonhealing wounds often resulting from diabetes, poor circulation, improper seating and immunocompromising conditions. The goals are to progress chronic wounds through stages of healing, reduce and eliminate infections, increase physical function to minimize complications from current wounds and prevent future chronic wounds. Wound management services are provided on an inpatient or outpatient basis, depending on the intensity of service needed.

106. Integration ranges from co-located physical and behavioral health providers, with some screening and treatment planning, to fully integrated care where behavioral and physical health providers function as a true team in a shared practice.

107a-b. **Physician arrangements.** An integrated healthcare delivery program implementing physician compensation and incentive systems for managed care services. Please report the number of physicians and ownership percentage for each arrangement.
   1. **Independent practice association (IPA).** A legal entity that holds managed care contracts. The IPA then contracts with physicians, usually in solo practice, to provide care either on a fee-for-service or capitated basis. The purpose of an IPA is to assist solo physicians in obtaining managed care contracts.
   2. **Group practice without walls.** Hospital sponsors the formation of, or provides capital to physicians to establish, a "quasi" group to share administrative expenses while remaining independent practitioners.
   3. **Open physician-hospital organization (PHO).** A joint venture between the hospital and all members of the medical staff who wish to participate. The PHO can act as a unified agent in managed care contracting, own a managed care plan, own and operate ambulatory care centers or ancillary services projects, or provide administrative services to physician members.
   4. **Closed physician-hospital organization (PHO).** A PHO that restricts physician membership to those practitioners who meet criteria for cost effectiveness and/or high quality.
   5. **Management services organization (MSO).** A corporation, owned by the hospital or a physician/hospital joint venture, that provides management services to one or more medical group practices. The MSO purchases the tangible assets of the practices and leases them back as part of a full-service management agreement, under which the MSO employs all non-physician staff and provides all supplies/administrative systems for a fee.
   6. **Integrated salary model.** Physicians are salaried by the hospital or another entity of a health system to provide medical services for primary care and specialty care.
   7. **Equity model.** Allows established practitioners to become shareholders in a professional corporation in exchange for tangible and intangible assets of their existing practices.
   8. **Foundation.** A corporation, organized either as a hospital affiliate or subsidiary, which purchases both the tangible and intangible assets of one or more medical group practices. Physicians remain in a separate corporate entity but sign a professional services agreement with the foundation.

107c-e. Report the number of physicians and specialty breakdown for physician practices wholly owned by the hospital.

108. Of all physician arrangements listed in question 107a. (1-9), indicate the total number of physicians (count each physician only once) that are engaged in an arrangement with your hospital that allows for joint contracting with payers or shared responsibility for financial risk or clinical performance between the hospital and physician (arrangement may be any type of ownership). *Joint contracting* does not include contracting between physicians participating in an independent practice.

109a-d. **Joint venture.** A contractual arrangement between two or more parties forming an unincorporated business. The participants in the arrangement remain independent and separate outside of the venture's purpose.

INSURANCE AND ALTERNATIVE PAYMENT MODELS
Definitions

4. Insurance Products

  a. Medicare Advantage. Health Insurance program within Part C of Medicare. Medicare Advantage plans provide a managed health care plan (typically a health maintenance organization (HMO) but also often a preferred provider organization (PPO) or another type of managed care arrangement) that is paid based on a monthly capitated fee. This Part of Medicare provides beneficiaries an alternative to "Original Medicare" Parts A and B Medicare, which provides insurance for the same medical services but pays providers a fee for service (FFS) directly rather than through managed care plans.

  b. Medicaid Managed Care. Services in through an arrangement between a state Medicaid agency and managed care organizations (MCOs) that accept a set payment – "capitation" – for these services.

  c. Health Insurance Marketplace. Also called health exchanges, are organizations set up to facilitate the purchase of health insurance in each state in accordance with Patient Protection and Affordable Care Act. Marketplaces provide a set of government-regulated and standardized health care plans from which individuals may purchase health insurance policies eligible for federal subsidies.

  d. Other Individual Market. Health insurance coverage offered to individuals other than in connection with a group health plan.

  e. Small Group. A group health plan that covers employees of an employer that has less than 50 employees.

  f. Large Group. A group health plan that covers employees of an employer that has 51 or more employees.

8. Self-administered health plan. A health plan in which the employer assumes the financial risk for providing health care benefits to its employees. The employer may or may not also be responsible for claims processing and the provider network.

9. Capitation. An at-risk payment arrangement in which an organization receives a fixed prearranged payment and in turn guarantees to deliver or arrange all medically necessary care required by enrollees in the capitated plan. The fixed amount is specified within contractual agreements between the payer and the involved organization. The fixed payment amount is based on an actuarial assessment of the services required by enrollees and the costs of providing these services, recognizing enrollees' adjustment factors such as age, sex, and family size.

10. Bundling. Bundling is a payment mechanism whereby a provider entity receives a single payment for services provided across one or parts of the care continuum. For example, an entity might receive a single payment for the hospital and physician services provided as part of an inpatient stay or might receive a single payment for the post-acute care services involved in a single episode of care. The entity then has responsibility for compensating each of the individual providers involved in the episode of care.

12. Shared risk payments. A payment arrangement in which a hospital and a managed care organization share the risk of adverse claims experience. Methods for sharing risk could include: capitation with partial refunds or supplements if billed hospital charges or costs differ from capitated payments, and service or discharge-based payments with withholds and bonus payouts that depend on expenditure targets

15. Accountable Care Organization (ACO) Contract. An ACO contract has two essential elements: (1) accountability for the total costs of care for the population of patients attributed to the primary care physicians in the organization; (2) financial incentives that link the magnitude of bonus payments to performance on quality measures (which could include technical quality, patient experience and/or health outcome measures) This will generally involve a contract where the payer establishes a target budget for one or more years for the total costs of care for the agreed-upon patient population, the payer tracks actual spending and performance on quality; and the provider receives bonus payments that could include a share of savings that are (or are not) contingent on meeting quality targets, with (or without) additional bonuses related to performance on those quality measures.

15c. Traditional Medicare ACO Programs

  MSSP. Medicare Shared Savings Program. For fee-for-service beneficiaries. The Shared Savings Program has different tracks that allow ACOs to select an arrangement that makes the most sense for their organization.

  NextGen. The Next Generation ACO Model is an initiative for ACOs that are experienced in coordinating care for populations of patients. It allows these provider groups to assume higher levels of financial risk and reward.

  Comprehensive ESRD Care. The model is designed to identify, test, and evaluate new ways to improve care for Medicare beneficiaries with End-Stage Renal Disease (ESRD.)

19. Patient-Centered Medical Home. The medical home concept refers to the provision of comprehensive primary care services that facilitates communication and shared decision-making between the patient, his/her primary care providers, other providers, and the patient's family.

20. Clinically integrated network. A clinically integrated network is a collection of healthcare providers, such as physicians, hospitals, and post-acute care treatment providers, that come together to improve patient care and reduce overall healthcare costs. Clinically integrated networks rely on evidence-based care guidelines to provide high-quality care across participating providers.

SECTION E
TOTAL FACILITY BEDS, UTILIZATION, FINANCES, AND STAFFING
Instructions and Definitions

For the purposes of this survey, a nursing home type unit/facility provides **long-term care for the elderly or other patients requiring chronic care** in a non-acute setting in any of the following categories: *Skilled nursing care *Intermediate care *Other long-term care (see page 21) The nursing home type unit/facility is to be owned and operated by the hospital. Only one legal entity may be vested with title to the physical property or operate under the authority of a duly executed lease of the physical property.

a. **Total licensed beds.** Report the total number of beds authorized by the state licensing (certifying) agency.

b. **Beds set up and staffed.** Report the number of beds regularly available (those set up and staffed for use) at the end of the reporting period. Report only operating beds, not constructed bed capacity. Include all bed facilities that are set up and staffed for use by inpatients that have no other bed facilities, such as pediatric bassinets, isolation units and quiet rooms. Exclude newborn bassinets and bed facilities for patients receiving special procedures for a portion of their stay and who have other bed facilities assigned to or reserved for them. Exclude, for example, labor room, post anesthesia, or postoperative recovery room beds, psychiatric holding beds, observation beds, and beds that are used only as holding facilities for patients prior to their transfer to another hospital.

c. **Bassinets set up and staffed.** Report the number of normal newborn bassinets. Do not include neonatal intensive care or intermediate care bassinets. These should be reported on page 3, C6 and C7 and included in E1b. beds set up and staffed.

d. **Births.** Total births should exclude fetal deaths.

e. **Admissions.** Include the number of adult and pediatric admissions (exclude births). This figure should include all patients admitted during the reporting period, including neonatal and swing admissions.

f. **Inpatient days.** Report the number of adult and pediatric days of care rendered during the entire reporting period. Do not include days of care rendered for normal infants born in the hospital, but do include those for their mothers. Include days of care for infants born in the hospital and transferred into a neonatal care unit. Also include swing bed inpatient days. An inpatient day of care (also commonly referred to as a patient day or a census day, or by some federal hospitals as an occupied bed day) is a period of service between the census-taking hours on two successive calendar days, the day of discharge being counted only when the patient was admitted the same day.

g. **Emergency department visits.** Should reflect the number of visits to the emergency unit. Emergency outpatients can be admitted to the inpatient areas of the hospital, but they are still counted as emergency visits and subsequently as inpatient admissions.

h. **Total outpatient visits.** A visit by a patient who is not lodged in the hospital while receiving medical, dental, or other services. Each appearance of an outpatient in each unit constitutes one visit regardless of the number of diagnostic and/or therapeutic treatments that the patient receives. Total outpatient visits should include all clinic visits, referred visits, observation services, outpatient surgeries (also reported on line E1k), home health service visits, and emergency department visits (also reported on line E1g).
Clinic visits should reflect total number of visits to each specialized medical unit that is responsible for the diagnosis and treatment of patients on an outpatient, nonemergency basis. (e.g., alcoholism, dental, gynecology.) Visits to the satellite clinics and primary group practices should be included if revenue is received by the hospital.
Referred visits should reflect total number of outpatient ancillary visits to each specialty unit of the hospital established for providing technical aid used in the diagnosis and treatment of patients. Examples of such units are diagnostic radiology, EKG, and pharmacy.
Observation services are those services furnished on a hospital's premises, including use of a bed and periodic monitoring by a hospital's nursing or other staff, which are reasonable and necessary to evaluate an outpatient's condition or determine the need for a possible admission to the hospital as an inpatient. Observation services usually do not exceed 24 hours; however, there is no hourly limit on the extent to which they may be used.
Home health service visits are visits by home health personnel to a patient's residence.

i. **Inpatient surgical operations.** Count each patient undergoing surgery as one surgical operation regardless of the number of surgical procedures that were performed while the patient was in the operating or procedure room.

j. **Operating room.** A unit/room of a hospital or other health care facility in which surgical procedures requiring anesthesia are performed.

k. **Outpatient surgical operations.** For outpatient surgical operations, please record operations performed on patients who do not remain in the hospital overnight. Include all operations whether performed in the inpatient operating rooms or in procedure rooms located in an outpatient facility. Include an endoscopy only when used as an operative tool and not when used for diagnosis alone. Count each patient undergoing surgery as one surgical operation regardless of the number of surgical procedures that were performed while the patient was in the operating or procedure room.

2a2. Managed Care Medicare Discharges. A discharge day where a Medicare Managed Care Plan is the source of payment.

2b2. Managed Care Medicare Inpatient Days. An inpatient day where a Medicare Managed Care Plan is the source of payment.

2c2. Managed Care Medicaid Discharges. A discharge day where a Medicaid Managed Care Plan is the source of payment.

2d2. Managed Care Medicaid Inpatient Days. An inpatient day where a Medicaid Managed Care Plan is the source of payment.

3a. Net patient revenue. Reported at the estimated net realizable amounts from patients, third-party payers, and others for services rendered, including estimated retroactive adjustments under reimbursement agreements with third-party payers. Retroactive adjustments are accrued on an estimated basis in the period the related services are rendered and adjusted in future periods, as final settlements are determined.

3b. Tax appropriations. A predetermined amount set aside by the government from its taxing authority to support the operation of the hospital.

3c. Other operating revenue. Revenue that arises from the normal day-to-day operations from services other than health care provided to patients. Includes sales and services to nonpatients, and revenue from miscellaneous sources (rental of hospital space, sale of cafeteria meals, gift shop sales). Also include operating gains in this category.

3d. Nonoperating revenue. Includes investment income, extraordinary gains and other nonoperating gains.

3e. Total revenue. Add net patient revenue, tax appropriations, other operating revenue and nonoperating revenue.

3f. Payroll expenses. Include payroll for all personnel including medical and dental residents/interns and trainees.

3g. Employee benefits. Includes social security, group insurance, retirement benefits, workman's compensation, unemployment insurance, etc.

3h. Depreciation expense (for reporting period only). Report only the depreciation expense applicable to the reporting period. The amount should also be included in accumulated depreciation (E8b).

3i. Interest expense. Report interest expense for the reporting period only.

3j. Pharmacy Expense. Includes the cost of drugs and pharmacy supplies requested to patient care departments and drugs charged to patients.

3k. Supply expense. The net cost of all tangible items that are expensed including freight, standard distribution cost, and sales and use tax minus rebates. This would exclude labor, labor-related expenses and services as well as some tangible items that are frequently provided as part of labor costs.

3l. All other expenses. Any total facility expenses not included in E3f-E3k.

3m. Total expenses. Add 3f-3l. Includes all payroll and non-payroll expenses as well as any nonoperating losses (including extraordinary losses). **Treat bad debt as a deduction from gross patient revenue and not as an expense.**

4a. Total gross inpatient revenue. The hospital's full-established rates (charges) for all services rendered to inpatients.

4b. Total gross outpatient revenue. The hospital's full-established rates (charges) for all services rendered to outpatients.

4c. Total gross patient revenue. Add total gross inpatient revenue and total gross outpatient revenue.

5. Uncompensated care. Care for which no payment is expected or no charge is made. It is the sum of bad debt and charity care absorbed by a hospital or other health care organization in providing medical care for patients who are uninsured or are unable to pay.

5a. Bad debt. The provision for actual or expected uncollectibles resulting from the extension of credit. Report as a deduction from gross revenue. <u>For Question 6 (Revenue by payer), if you cannot break out your bad debt by payer, deduct the amount from self-pay.</u>

5b. Financial Assistance (Includes charity care). Financial assistance and charity care refer to health services provided free of charge or at reduced rates to individuals who meet certain financial criteria. <u>For purposes of this survey, charity care is measured on the basis of revenue forgone, at full-established rates.</u>

5d. Medicaid Provider Tax, Fee or Assessment. Dollars paid as a result of a state law that authorizes collecting revenue from specified categories of providers. Federal matching funds may be received for the revenue collected from providers and some or all of the revenues may be returned directly or indirectly back to providers in the form of a Medicaid payment.

6. REVENUE BY PAYER

    6a1. Medicare. Should agree with the Medicare utilization reported in questions E2a1-E2b2.

    6a1a. Fee for service patient revenue. Include traditional Medicare fee-for-service.

    6a1c. Total. Medicare revenue (add Medicare fee for service patient revenue and Medicare managed care revenue).

    6a2. Medicaid. Should agree with Medicaid utilization reported in questions E2c1-E2d2.

    6a2a. Fee for service patient revenue. Do not include Medicaid disproportionate share payments (DSH) or other Medicaid supplemental payments.

    6a2c. Medicaid Graduate Medical Education (GME) payments. Payments for the cost of approved graduate medical education (GME) programs. <u>Report in 'net' column only.</u>

    6a2d. Medicaid disproportionate share payment (DSH). DSH minus associated provider taxes or assessments. <u>Report in 'Net' column only.</u>

    6a2e. Medicaid supplemental payments. Supplemental payments the Medicaid program pays the hospital that are NOT Medicaid DSH, minus associated provider taxes or assessments. <u>Report in 'Net' column only.</u>

    6a2f. Other Medicaid. Any Medicaid payments such as delivery system reform incentive program (DSRIP) payments that are not included in lines 6a2a-e. <u>Report in 'net' column only.</u>

    6e. Medicaid Intergovernmental Transfers (IGT) or certified public expenditure program. Exchange of public funds between different levels of government (e.g., county, city, or another state agency) to the state Medicaid agency.

7. FINANCIAL PERFORMANCE – MARGIN

    7a. Total Margin. Total income over total revenue. Nonoperating income is included in revenue in the total margin.

    7b. Operating Margin. Measure of profit per dollar of revenue calculated by dividing net operating income by operating revenues.

    7c. EBITDA Margin. Earnings before interest, tax depreciation and amortization (EBITDA) divided by total revenue.

    7d. Medicare margin. (Medicare revenue-Medicare expenses)/Medicare revenue.

    Medicare revenue = Patient revenue received from the Medicare program including traditional Medicare, Medicare Advantage, and any ACO, Bundled Payment, or other pilot program (net of disallowances)

    Medicare expenses = Cost of patient care for Medicare beneficiaries in traditional Medicare, Medicare Advantage and any ACO, Bundled Payment, or other pilot program. If actual costs cannot be obtained, use cost-to-charge ratios to estimate based on Medicare charges.

    7e. Medicaid margin. (Medicaid revenue-Medicaid expenses)/Medicaid revenue.

    Medicaid revenue = Patient revenue received from the Medicaid program including traditional Medicaid, Medicaid Managed Care, and any ACO, Bundled Payment, or other pilot program (net of disallowances)

    Medicaid expenses = Cost of patient care for Medicaid beneficiaries in traditional Medicaid, Medicaid Managed Care and any ACO, Bundled Payment, or other pilot program. If actual costs cannot be obtained, use cost-to-charge ratios to estimate based on Medicaid charges.

8. Fixed Assets. Represent land and physical properties that are consumed or used in the creation of economic activity by the health care entity. The historical or acquisition costs are used in recording fixed assets. Net plant, property, and equipment represent the original costs of these items less accumulated depreciation and amortization.

8d. Gross Square Footage. Include all inpatient, outpatient, office, and support space used for or in support of your health care activities. Exclude exterior, roof, and garage space in the figure.

9. Capital Expenses. Expenses used to acquire assets, including buildings, remodeling projects, equipment, or property.

10. Information Technology and Cybersecurity.

    a. IT Operating expense. Exclude department depreciation and operating dollars paid against capital leases.

    b. IT Capital expense. Include IT capital expense for the current year only. Any capital expense that is carried forward from the previous year should be excluded from this figure. Include IT related capital included in the budget of other departments. (e.g., lab, radiology) if known or can be reasonably estimated. Include the total value of capital leases to be signed in the current year.

    c. Number of Employed IT staff (in FTEs). Number of full-time equivalent (FTE) staff employed in the IT department/organization and on the hospital payroll.

    d. Total number of outsourced IT staff (in FTEs). i.e., contracted staff.

    e. Cybersecurity. Measures taken to protect against the criminal or unauthorized use of electronic data.

STAFFING

11. Full-Time Equivalent (FTE) is the total number of hours worked (excluding all non-worked hours such as PTO, etc.) by all employees over the full 12-month reporting period, divided by the normal number of hours worked by a full-time employee for that same time period. For example, if your hospital considers a normal workweek for a full-time employee to be 40 hours, a total of 2,080 would be worked over a full year (52 weeks). If the total number of hours worked by all employees on the payroll is 208,000, then the number of full-time equivalents (FTE) is 100 (employees). The FTE calculation for a specific occupational category such as registered nurses is exactly the same. The calculation for each occupational category should be based on the number of hours worked by staff employed in that specific category.

    a-b. Physicians and dentists. Include only those physicians and dentists engaged in clinical practice and on the payroll. Those who hold administrative positions should be reported in all other personnel. (11n)

    e. Other trainees. A trainee is a person who has not completed the necessary requirements for certification or met the qualifications required for full salary under a related occupational category. Exclude medical and dental residents/interns who should be reported on line 11c-d.

    f. Registered nurses. Nurses who have graduated from approved schools of nursing and who are currently registered by the state. They are responsible for the nature and quality of all nursing care that patients receive. Do not include any registered nurses more appropriately reported in other occupational categories, such as facility administrators, and therefore listed under all other personnel. (11n)

    g. Licensed practical (vocational) nurses. Nurses who have graduated from an approved school of practical (vocational) nursing who work under the supervision of registered nurses and/or physicians.

    h. Nursing assistive personnel. Certified nursing assistant or equivalent unlicensed staff who assist registered nurses in providing patient care related services as assigned by and under the supervision of a registered nurse.

    i. Radiology technicians. Technical positions in imaging fields, including, but not limited to, radiology, sonography, nuclear medicine, radiation therapy, CT, MRI.

j. **Laboratory technicians.** Professional and technical positions in all areas of the laboratory, including, but not limited to, histology, phlebotomy, microbiology, pathology, chemistry, etc.

k. **Pharmacists, licensed.** Persons licensed within the state who are concerned with the preparation and distribution of medicinal products.

l. **Pharmacy technicians.** Persons who assist the pharmacist with selected activities, including medication profile reviews for drug incompatibilities, typing labels and prescription packaging, handling of purchase records and inventory control.

m. **Respiratory Therapists.** An allied health professional who specializes in scientific knowledge and theory of clinical problems of respiratory care. Duties include the collection and evaluation of patient data to determine an appropriate care plan, selection and assembly of equipment, conduction of therapeutic procedures, and modification of prescribed plans to achieve one or more specific objectives.

n. **All other personnel.** This should include all other personnel not already accounted for in other categories.

o. **Total facility personnel.** Add 11a-11n. Includes the total facility personnel - hospital plus nursing home type unit/facility personnel (for those hospitals that own and operate a nursing home type unit/facility.)

p-q. **Nursing home type unit/facility personnel.** These lines should be filled out only by hospitals that own and operate a nursing home type unit/facility, where only one legal entity is vested with title to the physical property or operates under the authority of a duly executed lease of the physical property. If nursing home type unit/facility personnel are reported on the total facility personnel lines (11a-n), but cannot be broken out, please leave blank.

r. **Direct patient care RN.** Registered nurses providing care directly to patients. Direct patient care responsibilities are patient-centered nursing activities carried out in the presence of the patient (such as admission, transfer/discharge, patient teaching, patient communication, treatments, counseling, and administration of medication.)

12. **Privileged Physicians.** Report the total number of physicians (by type) on the medical staff with privileges except those with courtesy, honorary and provisional privileges. Do not include residents or interns. Physicians that provide only non-clinical services (administrative services, medical director services, etc.) should be excluded.

Employed by your hospital. Physicians that are either direct hospital employees or employees of a hospital subsidiary corporation.

Individual contract. An independent physician under a formal contract to provide services at your hospital including at outpatient facilities, clinics and offices

Group contract. A physician that is part of a group (group practice, faculty practice plan or medical foundation) under a formal contract to provide services at your hospital including at inpatient and outpatient facilities, clinics and offices.

Not employed or under contract. Other physicians with privileges that have no employment or contractual relationship with the hospital to provide services.

The sum of the physicians reported in 12a-12g should equal the total number of privileged physicians in the hospital.

a. **Primary care.** A physician that provides primary care services including general practice, general internal medicine, family practice, general pediatrics and geriatrics.

b. **Obstetrics/gynecology.** A physician who provides medical and surgical treatment to pregnant women and to mothers following delivery. Also provides diagnostic and therapeutic services to women with diseases or disorders of the reproductive organs.

c. **Emergency medicine.** Physicians who provide care in the emergency department.

d. **Hospitalist.** Physicians whose primary professional focus is the care of hospitalized medical patients (through clinical, education, administrative and research activity).

e. **Intensivist.** A physician with special training to work with critically ill patients. Intensivists generally provided medical-surgical, cardiac, neonatal, pediatric and other types of intensive care.

f. **Radiologist/pathologist/anesthesiologist. Radiologist.** A physician who has specialized training in imaging, including but not limited to radiology, sonography, nuclear medicine, radiation therapy, CT, MRI. **Pathologist.** A physician who examines samples of body tissues for diagnostic purposes. **Anesthesiologist.** A physician who specializes in administering medications or other agents that prevent or relieve pain, especially during surgery.

g. **Other specialist.** Other physicians not included in the above categories that specialize in a specific type of medical care.

15. **Advanced Practice Registered Nurses/Physician Assistants.** Registered nurses with advanced didactic and clinical education, knowledge, skills, and scope of practice. **Physician assistant.** A healthcare professional licensed to practice medicine with supervision of a licensed physician. Includes: **Nurse practitioner.** A registered nurse with at least a master's degree in nursing and advanced education in primary care, capable of independent practice in a variety of settings. **Clinical nurse specialist (CNS).** A registered nurse who, through a formal graduate degree (masters or doctorate) CNS education program, has expertise in a specialty area of nursing practice. CNSs are clinical experts in the diagnosis and treatment of illness, and the delivery of evidence-based nursing interventions.

15c. **Primary care.** Medical services including general practice, general internal medicine, family practice, general pediatrics, obstetrics/gynecology.

Emergency department care. The provision of unscheduled outpatient services to patients whose conditions require immediate care in the emergency department setting.

Other specialty care. A clinic that provides specialized medical care beyond the scope of primary care.

Patient education. Goals and objectives for the patient and/or family related to therapeutic regimens, medical procedures and self-care.

Case management. A system of assessment, treatment planning, referral and follow-up that ensures the provision of comprehensive and continuous services and the coordination of payment and reimbursement for care.

Other. Any type of care other than those listed above.

16. **Foreign-educated nurses.** Individuals who are foreign born and received basic nursing education in a foreign country. In general many of these nurses come to the US on employment-based visas which allow them to obtain a green card.

SECTION F. SUPPLEMENTAL INFORMATION
DEFINITIONS

1a. **Satellite facility.** Services are available at a facility geographically remote from the hospital campus.

1b. Report the number of sites for outpatient services on the hospital campus and off-campus (satellite) sites owned and operated by the hospital.

1. **Airway endoscopy.** Introduction of an instrument into the air passage while breathing spontaneously or under controlled ventilation. The airway is illuminated to look for any abnormalities under magnification and/or to perform a procedure in the upper or lower air passage.

2. **Ambulatory surgery.** Operations performed on patients who do not stay overnight at the facility (admitted and discharged on the same day.) Include endoscopy only when used as an operative tool and not when used for diagnosis alone.

3. **Blood product exchange.** Transfusion services or other blood product exchange procedures. Does not include general lab work.

4. **Cardiac/pulmonary rehabilitation.** A medically supervised program to help heart patients recover quickly and improve their overall physical and mental functioning. The goal is to reduce risk of another cardiac event or to keep an already present heart condition from getting worse. Cardiac rehabilitation programs include: counseling to patients, an exercise program, helping patients modify risk factors such as smoking and high blood pressure, providing vocational guidance to enable the patient to return to work, supplying information on physical limitations and lending emotional support.

5. **Diagnostic/screening test and related procedures.** A preliminary test or examination to detect the most characteristic signs of a disorder than may require further investigation. Examples include mammography, EKG, CBC, colonoscopy, bone density, diabetes, or cholesterol test.

6. **Drug administration and clinical oncology.** E.g., infusion therapies, chemotherapy.

7. **Ear, Nose, Throat (ENT).** Services for conditions of the ear, nose, throat, and related structures of the head and neck, such as sinus and nasal allergies, audiology, and speech/voice care.

8. **General surgery and related procedures.** Operations performed on patients who do not stay overnight at the facility (admitted and discharged on the same day.) Include endoscopy only when used as an operative tool and not when used for diagnosis alone.

9. **Gastrointestinal (GI).** Services for conditions of the GI tract, including both functional and structural gastrointestinal disorders.

10. **Gynecology.** Services and treatments dealing with the health of the female reproductive system. Services may or may not include obstetrics but include a range of services other than OB.

11. **Laboratory.** A medical or clinical laboratory where tests are usually done on clinical specimens in order to obtain information about the health of a patient as pertaining to diagnosis, treatment and prevention of disease.

12. **Major imaging.** Includes advanced breast imaging, MRI, PET, CT with contrast.

13. **Minor imaging.** Includes basic x-ray, nuclear medicine studies, CT without contrast.

14. **Musculoskeletal surgery.** Surgical procedures that aim to improve, manage or treat disorders, diseases, injuries or congenital conditions of the musculoskeletal system. The musculoskeletal system involves bones, joints, tendons, ligaments, and muscles, and is responsible for providing form and support, ensuring stability and allowing movement to the human body.

15. **Nervous system procedures.** Services dealing with the operative and nonoperative management of disorders to the central, peripheral and autonomic nervous systems.

16. **Ophthalmology.** Consulting, diagnostic and treatment services for all conditions affecting the eyes.

17. **Pathology.** The medical practice dedicated to the general study of disease and its processes as well as the specific diagnosis of disease. Pathology procedures are performed by a physician clinical pathologist. Services may be performed after outpatient surgical procedures.

18. **Primary care.** Provision of primary care services (e.g., general pediatric care, general internal medicine, family practice, gynecology) focusing on evaluating and diagnosing medical problems and providing medical treatment on an outpatient basis.

19. **Psychiatric care.** Medical care, including diagnosis and treatment, of psychiatric outpatients.

20. **Radiation oncology.** The controlled use of radiation to treat cancer either to cure, or to reduce pain and other symptoms caused by cancer.

21. **Rehabilitation.** Services providing medical, health-related, therapy, social, and/or vocational services to help people attain or retain maximum functional capacity.

22. **Skilled nursing.** Provision of non-acute medical and skilled nursing care services, therapy, and social services under the supervision of a registered nurse.

23. **Substance abuse/chemical dependency.** Provision of medical care and/or rehabilitation treatment services to outpatients for whom the primary diagnosis is alcoholism or other chemical dependency.

24. **Urgent care.** Provision of care and treatment for illnesses or injuries that require prompt attention but are typically not of such seriousness as to require the services of a traditional emergency room.

25. **Urology.** Services that focus on surgical and medical diseases of the urinary tract system.

26. **Vascular/endovascular/cardiovascular.** Medical services for preventing, diagnosing and managing arterial, venous and lymphatic disorders.

27. **Visits and related services.** An outpatient clinic visit. Includes both new and established patients; visits of all intensity.

2. **Group Purchasing Organization.** An organization whose primary function is to negotiate contracts for the purpose of purchasing for members of the group or has a central supply site for its members.

3. **Distributor.** An entity that typically does not manufacture most of its own products but purchases and re-sells these products. Such a business usually maintains an inventory of products for sales to hospitals and physician offices and others.

5. **Types of Partnerships:**
   a. Health care providers outside your system (Include other hospitals health care systems, FQHCs, community clinics)
   b. Local or state public health organizations (Include public health departments, institutes, etc.)
   c. Local or state human/social service organizations (Include food, housing/rental assistance, energy assistance, transportation assistance)
   d. Other local or state government (Include municipal, city or county government, including public safety and policy/legislative initiatives at a local level)
   e. Non-profit organizations (Include National health associations, United Way, YMCA, Service leagues, healthy communities coalitions)
   f. Faith-based organizations
   g. Health insurance companies
   h. Schools (Include childhood, primary and secondary schools and colleges/universities)
   i. Local businesses or chambers of commerce
   j. National businesses or chambers of commerce
   k. Other (list)·

   Scale of partnerships:
   Not involved. No current partnerships with this type of organization
   Collaboration. Exchange information and share resources for a similar mission to enhance the capacity of the other partner
   Formal Alliance. Formalized partnership (binding agreement) among multiple organizations with merged initiatives, common goals and metrics

6. **Patient and family advisory council.** Advisory council dedicated to the improvement of quality in patient and family care. The advisory council is comprised of past/present patients, family members, and hospital staff.